"SWELL SUFFERING"

"SWELL SUFFERING"
A BIOGRAPHY OF MAURINE WHIPPLE

by
Veda Tebbs Hale

Greg Kofford Books
Salt Lake City, Utah
2011

Copyright © 2011, Veda Tebbs Hale
Cover design copyright © 2011 by Greg Kofford Books, Inc.

All rights reserved. No part of this book may be reproduced in any form or by any means without permission in writing from the publisher, Greg Kofford Books. The views expressed herein are the responsibility of the authors and do not necessarily represent the position of Greg Kofford Books, Inc.

2015 14 13 12 11 10   5 4 3 2 1

www.koffordbooks.com

Library of Congress Cataloging-in-Publication Data

Hale, Veda, 1936-
  Swell suffering : a biography of Maurine Whipple / by Veda Tebbs Hale.
      p. cm.
  Includes index.
  ISBN 978-1-58958-122-7 -- ISBN 978-1-58958-124-1 (pbk.)
  1. Whipple, Maurine, 1903-1992. 2. Mormon authors--20th century--Biography. 3. Novelists, American--20th century--Biography. 4. Mormons--Utah--Biography. I. Title.
  PS3545.H425Z68 2009
  813'.52--dc22
  [B]
                            2009039780

Contents

Foreword by Douglas D. Alder — vii

Prologue and Acknowledgments — ix

Chapter

1	Cinderella, Ashes and All	1
2	St. George Childhood	13
3	The University of Utah, 1922–26	37
4	In and Out of the Classroom, 1926–32	53
5	The Devastating Romances of 1932–37	73
6	The Pivotal Moment, 1937	103
7	Winning the Fellowship	109
8	Achievement and Complications at Yaddo	129
9	The Push to Finish	159
10	Publication: A Flash of Fame	175
11	"A Heart Turned Inside Out": 1941	191
12	Doing Her Bit for the War: 1942–43	225
13	Another Long Shot at Love, 1943	235
14	*This Is the Place: Utah*	245
15	Two Suffering Souls	263
16	The Failed Sequel, 1946–47	275
17	Utah Centennial, 1947	293
18	Detour into Magazine Writing, 1948	303
19	"Anybody's Gold Mine": 1949	317
20	Flirting with *Collier's*, 1951–52	327

21	"Grand Ideas": 1954–60	349
22	Charlie Steen: 1962–66	357
23	Easter Pageant, 1963–75	365
24	Maurine Versus St. George, 1967–75	373
25	The 1970s: Flickerings of Potential Flames	379
26	A Small Hold on Hope	395
27	An Unraveling Life	403

Postscript	427
Index	431
About the Author	457

Foreword

DOUGLAS D. ALDER

From my desk in the Archive of the Val A. Browning Library at Dixie State College in St. George, I have the unusual delight of reflecting on Maurine Whipple. Behind me is the door to the collection where Veda Tebbs Hale has deposited a large number of Maurine's manuscripts and letters and her own research notes. Directly in front of my working space is an unusual handmade desk. Maurine's father, Charlie Whipple, built it for her writing.

In a nearby conference room are three portraits—Juanita Brooks, Andrew Karl Larson, and Maurine Whipple. I am humbled by their stature as writers. It is especially impressive to realize that they were doing their work when St. George's population numbered about six thousand people and Dixie College had fewer than five hundred students. The library then contained some ten thousand volumes. How could three such achievers come out of this isolated place?

Maurine is the most curious. She was not a faculty member. She thought of herself as a writer of national stature and hoped to find a patron to underwrite her career. But her life was a complicated confusion of unfulfilled dreams. She never found a great lover to enable her aspirations of husband and family. She never landed a teaching position that lasted longer than a year. She never located a pot of gold to underwrite her possibility of being the West's great writer. This plight fits many would-be writers, yet Maurine Whipple actually made it once—big.

Veda Hale tells three stories in her biography of Maurine Whipple. The first is the success saga of an obscure, aspiring writer who overcame isolation to reach national prominence, thanks at least in part to an amazing editor, Ferris Greenslet, who saw her manuscript as "literature and not dogmatism." He enabled the project and allowed Maurine to hope that the resulting success would replace the many voids in her life.

The second story is how Maurine captured the essence of pioneer Mormonism in Utah's remote southwestern desert. Readers cannot but be amazed at how Whipple's characters in the novel entice them into the soul of the Mormon attempt at utopia. Obviously Whipple is absorbed into the dream. And "dream" is the word she uses.

The third is the long postlude, the failure to produce a sequel and the consideration of its causes. Here the reader is tempted to consider unmet human needs and how they spiral into Maurine's family disasters, depression, and poverty.

There are many moments of compassion and hope, both on the part of Maurine and of her several would-be rescuers. The reader is called upon to search himself or herself, to ask if he or she could respond creatively to the needs of this complex figure. As Veda Hale says, "Thus, the novel ends by speaking reassurance and strength to the victim in all of us. Even though negative circumstances and death win, they do not triumph. The ultimate victory goes to something else—to the serene and beneficent forces of love that Maurine termed the 'Great Smile.'" (Chapter 9, p. 21)

Eugene England once said that *The Giant Joshua* is still the best Mormon novel. I read it fifty years ago. Then I examined it more closely when I moved to St. George in 1986. As an aspiring novelist, I was impressed with the well-crafted sentences on almost every page. I knew from my own attempts at fiction that such an achievement was not only a creative gift but a well-honed craft.

As soon as I arrived, I visited Maurine at the Meadows Retirement Center. I soon discovered that she could consume a lot of my time, a pattern that many people before me had discovered. Little did I realize that she was doing exactly the same thing with Veda Hale, who was helping her bring order to her personal papers. But Veda had an extra dimension of sympathy and determination to tell Maurine's story. It has been a delight to read Veda Hale's artful biography of Maurine Whipple and live it all again.

⋄ Prologue ⋄

Where better to start to understand a life than to hold the hands that lived it? And so I did. Eighty-seven-year-old hands. They were small, soft, with skin so finely textured I doubted fingerprinting would even be possible. The hands trembled. I wondered, *Thin-skinned? Does she feel more acutely than most?* Yet there was strength in Maurine Whipple's square-chinned face, the fine skin still relatively smooth and wrinkle free. Strange. There were no laugh lines on the outside of her eyes—no crow's feet.

It was in her eyes, not on her skin, where I saw the effects of suffering. Light gray, they could shine with an easy softness one moment and flicker with static the next. They could also hold a gaze easily, convincing you she understood more about you than you cared for her to know—perhaps even more than you knew about yourself.

This was how I observed Maurine Whipple at our first meeting in November 1990. She was in the St. George Care and Rehabilitation Center where she had been since 16 May 1989. My husband, Glen, and I had moved to St. George in January of 1990. My own family roots are there. My people were like the people Maurine wrote about.

Maurine is the author of *The Giant Joshua* (New York: Houghton Mifflin, 1941), perhaps the best Mormon novel of the twentieth century, certainly one acclaimed highly by a maturing church starting to appreciate its own literature. Its richness of narrative texture, the vividness of its characters, and its forthright treatment of the rigors of both pioneering and polygamy have ensured that it has never lacked for enthusiastic admirers.

Maurine was too old and infirm to sort her papers when her legal guardian, Carol Jean Jensen, with her permission, turned them over to Dennis Rowley, archivist at the Harold B. Lee Library at Brigham Young University, in September 1983. She undoubtedly would have removed some personal papers if she had been well enough to screen them, because some present a darker, more chaotic portrait than the picture of the struggling and misunderstood artist that she carefully tried to present to the world. But I believe that, despite her fear-honed instinct for preserving her image, a deeper voice within her called out for full expression and trusted that her life, thus left open, would be understood and respected, even loved, by a future generation to whom she had contributed her hopes and dreams.

Relatives and others associated with her in the kind of everyday living that knits lives together became exasperated with her "constant whining" to be understood. Her siblings have good reason to feel hurt by the bleakness of her childhood memories. Maurine's sensitivity and giftedness gave her the capability for creating a fine piece of literature, but accompanying those gifts were character traits that frequently made her so demanding, irritating, and aggravating that even her closest kin had to protect themselves from her with boundaries against which she bruised herself. It is small consolation, either for them or for Maurine, to realize that she was the primary victim of her prickly neediness.

This biography is an effort to recreate both the facts of Maurine's life and also Maurine's perception and interpretation of those facts. Any biography is partially a creative construction, and Maurine's perceptions were more creative than most. I attempt to chart, accurately but sympathetically, the areas in which Maurine's interpretations seem exaggerated and unreasonable. I have provided a pseudonym for two men whose path crossed hers so briefly and (for her) calamitously. These individuals appear in the text as Rob Riley and Nick Spencer. Maurine requested that I not embarrass their families, and I have honored that request.

The Whipple Papers

My own materials collected from Maurine are of three types. Since I never knew from day to day whether she was going to be sufficiently alert and interested to engage in a formal interview, I went prepared for anything; and as our relationship developed into an increasingly easy intimacy, many of the best sessions were informal conversations as I drove her around town or as we ate lunch. I usually went prepared with a list of questions or topics. Usually she would respond to them, but sometimes she would turn the conversation to another topic altogether. I jotted down notes as we talked in a series of stenographers' spiral notebooks, often after our meetings so as not to interrupt the flow of reminiscences. These notebooks will not, unfortunately, be very useful for other researchers, since it did not occur to me to date the entries and the notes themselves are in a half-homemade shorthand. I followed the same note-taking procedure when I interviewed Maurine's associates and others who knew her. I audio- or videotaped several, but not all, of the many interviews with Maurine I conducted. These I donated to the Whipple Collection at Dixie College. Unless otherwise noted, quotations from Maurine herself are from my interviews with her.

Second only to Maurine's own memories are her papers, now at the Archives and Manuscripts Division (now L. Tom Perry Special Collections), Harold B. Lee Library, Brigham Young University, Provo, Utah, and other documents once in the possession of her friend and legal guardian Carol Jean Jensen (now deceased), in St. George. Although it is impossible to know what was destroyed or lost, the papers that have survived are voluminous. Maurine wrote her drafts in longhand. For *The Giant Joshua*, she obtained the ends of newsprint rolls and cut them into large sheets. Many pages from the original draft exist in her hand in the Whipple Papers, Perry Special Collections, Harold B. Lee Library, thus scotching persistent rumors that Juanita Brooks was the real author.

After Brigham Young University collected her papers, other papers that had been overlooked in odd boxes emerged; they, along with much that I collected, are now housed, along with photocopies of some of the most important originals, in the Maurine Whipple Collection, Archive of the Val A. Browning Library, Dixie College, St. George, Utah. Maurine also apparently inherited much of the Whipple family photograph collection, but unfortunately most of them are unidentified. A majority of these photographs are at Brigham Young University, with some at Dixie College.

Acknowledgments

I am indebted to many who helped with this project. I never would have begun without Marilyn Brown's enthusiastic insistence. Eugene England, Levi S. Peterson, Richard H. Cracroft, Bruce W. Jorgensen, Curtis Taylor, Lavina Fielding Anderson, and Michael Austin all encouraged me, telling me I was the one in a position to capture Maurine's life and should get started before Maurine died. I was skeptical about their faith in me but stirred by their passionate conviction that Maurine was an important figure in Mormon cultural life whose history was worth preserving. Marilyn helped edit the manuscript in certain beginning stages, and Lavina carried on from there. Her expertise and desire to be involved in this project kept me going through many discouraging years.

Curtis Taylor, then co-owner of Aspen Books, also took a personal interest in the project. David J. Whittaker and Dennis Rowley welcomed me to BYU's archives, willingly trusted me with the papers despite my lack of professional training, and helped me understand how best to tackle the project.

"SWELL SUFFERING"

Camie Carter Sullivan Higgins of St. George, who had been Maurine's occasional typist and friend, was interested and helped me in many ways, particularly in finding residents of southern Utah who shared memories of Maurine: Douglas D. Alder, Bart Anderson, Vira Blake, Mary Nielson Campbell, Russell Clark, Ludie Lytle Cox, Fern and Jasper Crawford, Donald A. Dolowitz, Judy Gubler Farnsworth, Evelyn Harris, Montrue Larkin, Merrill Lee, Betty Macferson, Glen Nielsen, Mary Morris Phoenix, Faun Pickett, Arlo Prisbrey, and Loraine (husband) and Anna (wife) Cox are a few of the many people who knew Maurine and helped me find information.

Although Maurine's relatives must have had many ambiguous feelings about this project, they were courteous and helpful. I'm particularly indebted to Maurine's nephew and nieces: the late Larry Jolley of Washington, Utah; Colleen Jolley Haycock of Las Vegas, Nevada; and Carol Ann Whipple Anderson of Calgary, Alberta, Canada. Loa Moss Brown, Maurine's cousin, shared some of the McAllister family stories. Maurine's sister-in-law Alice Titus Whipple, now deceased, cordially shared her memories with me in 1991–92.

Other helpful people were Julia Vandegrift of Salt Lake City and her sister and brother in law, Shirley and Dale Westwood. My brother Daniel Tebbs and his wife, Karen, listened to me tell Whipple stories on our walks around our home ranch near Panguitch. My best supporters were closest to home: my husband, Glen B Hale, was endlessly supportive and cheerful, even when he was regularly perplexed because it was never quite "finished." My sons and daughters-in-law—Glen Tebbs and Sarah Bradford; Brent Jonathan and Kris Dalton; and Jason Daniel and Erin Parker—though not particularly fans of Maurine Whipple, were as resolved as I that this project must be seen through to its completion.

Many readers familiar with *The Giant Joshua* contributed opinions, criticism, and insights when Maurine's name surfaced on the Association for Mormon Letters email list.

Carol Jensen merits special recognition. Toward the end of Maurine's life when she felt truly abandoned, Carol came to her rescue. A plural wife whose husband had died and whose children had married, Carol became Maurine's legal guardian and loyal friend in 1982 and served faithfully until Maurine's death. She never received any monetary payment for the hours she spent assuring that Maurine could keep her dignity. Carol immediately became a wonderful liaison between Maurine and me. More, she also became my friend.

PROLOGUE

Despite the material and emotional aid from these many sources, I am, of course, responsible for the accuracy of this portrait of Maurine Whipple and my interpretation of her.

1

CINDERELLA—ASHES AND ALL

One summer night in August 1937, Maurine Whipple, a thirty-four-year-old schoolteacher from St. George, Utah, perched on the hard, cold steps of a fraternity house in Boulder, Colorado. With what must have been great passion, she poured the ashes and cinders of her failed life into the sympathetic ears of forty-five-year-old John Peale Bishop, a nationally known poet, novelist, teacher, and talent scout from the East. He was in Boulder to teach at the annual Rocky Mountain Writers' Conference, and Maurine was one of his students. The gritty realism of her novella, "Beaver Dam Wash," and her autobiographical "Confessions of a She Devil" had caught his artistic attention, and now she was using a further construction of her autobiography to continue to appeal to his personal sympathy.

Maurine wanted to be rescued. And she wanted that rescuer to be a fascinating man. She wanted to be rescued from the social limitations of her life. Rescued from the poverty of her past and foreseeable future. Rescued from her spinsterhood. So far, no man of the desired quality had been willing to take on her neediness, but she never gave up hoping that the next man in her life would solve her problems. More than any man Maurine met before or after, Bishop did change Maurine's life, but not in any way Maurine dreamed.

After listening to her towering tale of woe, he exclaimed: "My God! What swell suffering! Great literature is born from suffering like that!"[1]

John Peale Bishop brought Maurine's talent to the attention of Houghton Mifflin Publishing. She was asked to add a chapter or two to a novella, "Beaver Dam Wash," making it the conventional size for a novel. Boldly, she countered with an idea for a book about her country and her people. Her writing and description of what became *The Giant Joshua* interested Ferris Greenslet, Houghton Mifflin's literary editor and vice president.

Thus came into her life another "prince" of a different kind, and *The Giant Joshua*, Maurine's only published novel, came into being.

The Giant Joshua appeared in January 1941, a mammoth 637-page work that has been compared in regional depiction and celebration to Margaret Mitchell's 1936 best-seller *Gone with the Wind*.[2] The comparison is not strained. Both authors were women at a time when most "serious" writing was still done by men. Both skillfully poured variations of their own and their family's lives into their books, and both used their people's historical participation in a national movement between 1860 and 1890—the Civil War in Georgia in Margaret Mitchell's case, the Mormon exodus to the West and settlement of southern Utah in Maurine's—to bring history alive. Both were almost the same age. Mitchell had been born in 1902, Maurine in 1903. Both produced only a single enormous novel, each with an exceptionally appealing heroine whose romantic anticipations were thwarted by circumstances.

One difference, however, is in their heroines. When Scarlet O'Hara's privileges and wealth are swept away by the war, she reshapes circumstances to her advantage by sexiness, bitchiness, and ambition. Maurine's Clory is also deprived early of her privileges and wealth, not by war, but by a religious ideal that swept her father and his young children to a future of deprivation and suffering. Like Scarlet, Clory is spunky. She does not knuckle under to life. A victim of circumstances, she wins the reader's heart through her courage, cheerfulness, hard work, and innate refinement. Where Scarlet is salty, Clory is sweet. Her life is one of pathos, rather than tragedy. Where Scarlet is left with "tomorrow is another day," Clory is left on her deathbed with "the Great Smile," a symbol, Maurine told me, of the "peace that passeth understanding" that everyone can hope to find someday.

Another important difference between the two authors is that the men in Margaret Mitchell's life shielded her from food-and-shelter worries. Maurine, yearning for marriage and a family, struggled mostly alone for material security, and what male help she had was not of the intimate kind. Then, too, Mitchell's novel catapulted her into lasting fame, became perhaps the most successful publishing venture of her day next to the Bible, and was made into a classic and remunerative movie.[3] Maurine's book brought her fame of a difficult sort, no money to speak of, and much heartache, as she struggled to write something else as worthy.

Slavery and polygamy: both the renowned remnants of barbarism that the Republican Party of mid-nineteenth-century America used as its moral and political agenda. Margaret Mitchell wrote on slavery, Maurine on polygamy. Mitchell's parents were children of slave owners and Maurine's parents were themselves the children of polygamists.

Maurine's grandparents, John Daniel Thomas McAllister
and his third wife, Cornelia Lenzi.

A photograph of Maurine's maternal grandmother, Cornelia Lenzi McAllister, shows a kindly looking, attractive woman, her waved, gray hair parted in the middle. She is wearing a cameo brooch, a gift from her own mother, pinned to her bodice. She gave it to her daughter Annie; and when Annie died, Charlie, Maurine's father, had it made into a locket for Maurine. She treasured it and called it her "link" to the past. Maurine said this locket was stolen in the 1970s when her St. George home was burglarized. She grieved its loss for the rest of her life.

A portrait of John Daniel Thomas McAllister, her paternal grandfather (he usually went by his initials) hangs in the St. George Temple where he presided. It shows strong, handsome features, bold eyes, thick, wavy hair, and a full beard.[4] Maurine borrowed not only his features for Abijah ("Handsome Mac") MacIntyre in *The Giant Joshua* but also his commanding and sensuous presence, an impression she had gathered from listening to some of his nine wives talk.

J. D. T. McAllister had married his eighth wife, Ann Eliza Wells, when she was twenty-one and he was fifty-three, 23 December 1880, in the St. George Temple. That same day, temple workers commemorated Joseph Smith's birthday with a service in the temple and a public social that lasted until midnight. John's journal notes only, "A glorious time," without mentioning which wife or wives accompanied him to the party.[5] Cornelia likely didn't go, as her fourth baby was born three days later. It is tantalizing to speculate that Matilda, the seventh wife, the one he had married and brought with him when he was sent to St. George, had her third and last child, Amy, two days less than nine months later, while Ann Eliza's first child was not born for two years.[6] Did J.D.T. try to comfort Matilda and stay with her after the party? Did she know that he had married Ann Eliza that same day? One can only look at the dates on a genealogy sheet and speculate.

Maurine, knowing much more, often speculated about how it was for these people. She knew that thirteen years later, on 4 May 1893, obeying Church President Wilford Woodruff's call, J.D.T. succeeded Anthon H. Lund as second president of the Manti Temple when Lund left to preside over the European Mission.[7] He was to take only one wife with him to this new assignment, and he designated the youngest, Ann Eliza Wells, his eighth wife and one most likely to bear him more children, as the one to go.[8] This fact is especially interesting since six of the other wives seem to have adjusted to this eighth marriage; however, Matilda was so deeply hurt and unhappy, feeling herself displaced, that she returned to Salt Lake City and divorced J.D.T. on 12 January 1886. Daughter Amy died two years later at age seven. Maurine said she knew of these women's feelings, because the sickly Matilda spent much time in Cornelia's home when Annie was young, "and naturally women talk." Then strangely, despite the divorce, Matilda spent her final illness in Manti in John's and Ann Eliza's home. When she died 29 July 1897 at age forty-two, after a three-month illness during which Ann Eliza cared for her, John had her resealed to him a week later on 5 August 1897, with their twenty-year-old daughter, Tempie, acting as her mother's proxy.[9] This incident indicates that J.D.T. had some success in handling a delicate situation and keeping his "kingdom" intact. It also speaks well of Ann Eliza, who cared for this unhappy seventh wife.

At the time of the move to Manti, Ann Eliza had given birth to five children, ranging in age from eleven to two. Her sixth and last child was born in Manti in 1902, when John was seventy-five. Thirty-eight years after Matilda's death, Ann Eliza was buried beside Matilda in the Manti City Cemetery—two women ever linked to each other through one husband.

Although Maurine's mother, Annie, no doubt missed closer contact with her father after he moved to Manti the year she turned fourteen, she was not estranged from him. In early 1899 she visited Manti, stayed with J.D.T. and Ann Eliza, and did temple work. He was seventy-two and Annie was twenty-two. This pleasant and faith-affirming time for Annie probably contributed to her distress when her own husband, Charlie, stopped wearing temple garments and going to church.

J.D.T. McAllister died on 18 January 1910 just a month before his eighty-third birthday. He took sick suddenly on a rare visit to St. George and died in Cornelia's home. Maurine, then seven, said she remembered Cornelia standing next to another wife at the deathbed, both women weeping and embracing each other. It is patient, uncomplaining Cornelia who lies in death beside J.D.T. in the St. George Cemetery. A tall stone marks the family burial spot, listing the names of John, Cornelia, and four children.

Annie remained physically and emotionally close to her mother and siblings, including many of the half-brothers and -sisters. After marriage, she and Charlie lived an easy walk from Cornelia. Cornelia's youngest daughter, Grace, and Grace's husband, Charles Richard Sullivan, moved in with Cornelia after she grew older, then bought the home.

Cornelia's room was a private space. No one was allowed in without an invitation.[10] Maurine described for me the walls, covered with photographs, cards, and other memorabilia. "Every available inch of space harbored a treasured knickknack. Every article in that room, no matter how insignificant, had its tender memories." She further remembered, "I was often in her house. She let me look at her things and told me stories. She couldn't hear. But she still loved music."

Cornelia, deaf after a childhood illness, was skilled at lip-reading, so the grandchildren learned that whispering was perfectly adequate. However, Cornelia preferred monologues to conversations and visibly blossomed as she told and retold the stories of her life to an attentive audience, probably most often young Maurine.

Maurine gave her heroine, Clory, her grandmother's dignity. "I felt proud of my grandmother," Maurine often told me. She described how "most every day she dressed carefully in her one good dress, put on earrings, and walked to visit a friend. It seemed she was special, not like so many other women in town. She carried herself with poise. There was something of quality about her that couldn't be covered over by a lifetime of hardship. She was a little figure in a black silk dress, her lovely white hair nicely waved, her fine aristocratic nose powdered."[11]

Cornelia's death on 3 December 1920 had a powerful impact on seventeen-year-old Maurine. In the biographical essay she wrote about Cornelia, Maurine recreated Cornelia's final moment, echoes of which appear in Clory's deathbed scene in *The Giant Joshua*: "Suddenly, in place of the misery, a smile of utter sweetness flooded her countenance. She needed no word to tell them that someone had come out of the dim past to help her begin the long journey. Her passing seemed to be symbolic of her whole life—a soul that could smile in the face of death, itself."[12]

That final smile became the conclusion of *The Giant Joshua*, a moment of affirmation even in the face of bodily dissolution.

Cornelia's contribution to *The Giant Joshua* is direct, unambiguous, and almost completely positive. But Maurine also drew from her father's side of the family, and those borrowings are more problematic.

Eli Whipple, Charlie's father, was born 17 October 1820 in Luzern, Warren County, New York, just over the Poultney River that runs between Vermont and New York. On 7 January 1842 at age twenty-one, he married twenty-six-year-old Patience Foster, the daughter of Allen Foster and Patience Earl Foster, born 5 May 1815 at Marcellus, Onondago County, New York. When news of the California gold rush reached the East, soon after the birth of the third child, the family took passage to Panama. They crossed the isthmus overland, and then sailed up to San Francisco.

Eli found it more profitable to establish a sawmill in San Mateo County at what is now Redwood City in northern California. How he learned about Mormonism and from whom is not clear. According to one account, at least, he was baptized before leaving Pennsylvania.

John R. Young, a Mormon missionary on his way home from Hawaii in 1857, visited the family in Redwood City and found Patience "bitter against Mormons."[13] But it is clear from his account that Eli was a Mormon and that missionaries knew they could find hospitality and earn some money at his sawmill. Young later baptized Patience.

In December 1857 with Johnston's Army stalled at Fort Bridger, Brigham Young summoned the far-flung colonists to retreat to Utah. John Young helped Eli prepare to make the thirteen-hundred-mile trip to Utah. In October conference of 1861, the forty-one-year-old Eli was among those called to go to St. George. In 1862, Erastus Snow, who headed the Church in southern Utah, asked him to set up a sawmill in Pine Valley. For the next twenty-five years, Eli operated his sawmill in different locations in that alpine area.[14]

On 19 December 1868, Eli married as his second wife Caroline Lytle Peters, a twenty-eight-year-old divorcée twenty years his junior. Born 18 April 1840 in Nauvoo, the daughter of John Lytle and Christena Diana Whitner/Wittner Lytle, Caroline had married Lyman Peters in Salt Lake City the month before she turned fifteen and had given birth to two children. Caroline bore Eli seven children between 1869 and 1882. Charlie was the fifth.

Before the most intense phase of the federal raids against polygamy, sixty-seven-year-old Eli Whipple went to St. George for the Fourth of July in 1877 and came back two days later married to eighteen-year-old Mary Jane Legg. Since he had not consulted Patience or Caroline, this sudden addition of a youthful wife caused quite a stir in the family. Mary

Jane and her sister, Sarah, had been living in Pine Valley for over a year, so the family probably knew her.

Eli had built Patience a substantial frame house in Pine Valley, while Caroline spent most of her time in the mountains running a dairy at a place still called "Cabin Creek." According to Maurine, bears and Indians were not uncommon visitors. Caroline's reputation for fortitude and resolution is well deserved. During the cruelly cold winters when the dairy herds were returned to lower elevations, Caroline spent at least a few seasons in a cellar on the lot on 100 South between Main Street and First South in St. George, a lot that had been assigned to Eli when he first came to St. George. Eventually Eli constructed a house over the cellar. After Caroline's death in 1912, Charlie and Annie bought this home, in which Maurine grew up.

Maurine believed that each grandfather in his own way was a zealous Mormon. Each was also strongly motivated by the preaching from Church leaders to increase their heavenly kingdom.

When the serious crack-down on polygamy came after the passage of the Edmunds-Tucker Act in 1887 gave new teeth to federal officers, Eli, like scores of other Mormons in the same situation, decided to move Mary Jane and her children to Mexico. He established her first in Colonia Juarez and later in Colonia Dublan, both in the northern province of Chihuahua. Mary Jane eventually gave birth to four more children, the last when Eli was seventy-six. He had thus fathered twenty-one children, ten sons and eleven daughters, in addition to helping raise Caroline's son and daughter by her first husband.

When Eli left, Caroline's seven children by him ranged from eighteen to five. Caroline had a very difficult time scratching together enough financial resources for the family's needs, and they suffered chronic privation that sometimes became acute. Before Eli's dream of uniting his large family came to pass, he died 11 May 1904 at age eighty-four on his farm in Colonia Dublan. Patience had died 17 January 1890 at Pine Valley, thirteen years before Maurine was born; but Maurine remembers her reputation in the family as that of a good, kind woman, one of the little valley's midwives. Caroline died 6 December 1912, and Maurine, age nine, heard her say to her daughter during her final illness, "Don't hold me, Leah. I've got to go."

Eli's son Charlie, as an adult, can be forgiven for not being enthusiastic about the Church. His father's belief in the glorious future of the Church only seemed to have caused him to make decisions that deprived his children of present necessities.

Maurine's feelings about polygamy were complex and ambiguous. Although she grew up hearing stories from her grandmother, mother, aunts, and other women about the difficulties of polygamy, she was astute enough to realize that it could benefit some women by providing a unit of feminine solidarity with another woman or women who understood, more than any other woman could, what it meant to be married to a particular man. *The Giant Joshua*, however, is perhaps best known for the intimate bitterness of female jealousy and the male's struggle against favoritism that it portrays. However, to see only these negative traits does *The Giant Joshua* a disservice. Maurine also saw a man's effort to communicate impartial commitment to more than one woman. If he were awkward, autocratic, or both, the struggle could leave him emotionally isolated, without a close relationship to anyone.

So it was that neither of Maurine's parents was a stranger to poverty and suffering. Both were preschoolers when the Edmunds Act (1882) declared war on Mormonism, and had not reached adolescence before the Edmunds-Tucker Act added greater federal ferocity to the combat.[15] Charlie was born 22 January 1878 in St. George. Annie, a half year older, was born 25 May 1877 in Salt Lake City. Charlie's mother was a second wife, Annie's a third. Both mothers lived mostly alone and sometimes in hiding during the "Raid" of the 1880s when federal marshals stalked polygamist husbands and wives. It was a time of confusion and fear. Children learned to deny knowing their fathers and to conceal their own names.

Though much was the same for Charlie and Annie, especially during those childhood years, their home lives differed markedly. Charlie grew up thirty miles north of St. George in Pine Valley, a beautiful but rough world of sawmills and mountains. He shouldered man-sized responsibilities early, helping his mother during summers to milk cows and make butter and cheese to sell to miners and lumbermen. In winters when the family moved to St. George, he did whatever chores an absent father didn't. His father and mother were committed Mormons, but Pine Valley of Charlie's youth had "the name of being one of the roughest towns in this section of country. Peddlers from Santa Clara brought up loads of Dixie wine when they came for lumber. As a result there was a great deal of drinking and gambling."[16]

Charlie and Annie, second-generation Mormons, missed the excitement and commitment entailed in the conversion experience; they and their peers were mostly caught in the struggle for survival, Charlie much more than Annie. In contrast, Annie could look out the south window of her mother's St. George home at the temple across the street.[17] Until she was sixteen, her father, John Daniel Thompson McAllister, the temple president, returned home each evening (when it was her mother's turn to have him), formal and dignified in clean broadcloth and linen, telling holy anecdotes. Furthermore, he presided over the St. George Stake, which then included all of Washington County and stretched as far south as Panaca and Las Vegas, Nevada. Perhaps most tellingly, he also had the security of a salary paid by the Church.

This social and economic security contrasted sharply to the status of Charlie's father. Eli Whipple come home (when it was Charlie's mother's turn to have him), sweaty, dirty, wearing jeans and flannel, and exhausted from the sawmill. The stories he told were of rough loggers and natural violence. He could not count on his next dollar coming into his hands except from his own ingenuity and labor.

Eli, a committed Mormon, was a counselor to Pine Valley's bishop, William Snow, but that was no match for the prestige of Annie's father. Eli Whipple seldom saw Church dignitaries, and his contribution to the kingdom was to provide lumber for its buildings. He was known for the impressive amount of strenuous physical labor he could do and for the work he could get out of other people, especially his family. J.D.T. McAllister was known for his loyal dependability in carrying out important ecclesiastical assignments and how he could inspire others, including his family, to stay strong in the faith.[18]

Another difference between the two families was the attitude toward women. Eli married physically strong women. Most of his daughters were also robust and did a great deal of physical labor. He expected all of them to pull their own weight.[19] Eli reportedly thought there were only two ways to do things, "his way or the wrong way, and he was for seeing that the world did things his way."[20] He expected his second wife, Caroline Lytle Whipple, Maurine's grandmother, to tough it out with little husbandly support even when Eli was in Pine Valley. After he left for Mexico with a young third wife, she and her children were basically on their own, often facing bears and Indians in the mountains, as she kept the dairy going.

J.D.T.'s third wife and Maurine's other grandmother, Cornelia Lenzi McAllister, had a dependable share of her husband's salary—fifteen dollars a month.[21] Although not lavish, she could count on it. She had an adequate home in a safe, peaceful, religious setting.

Maurine, for the first seventeen years of her life, observed her dignified, serene McAllister grandmother and longed for a life of security, too. "Oh, to have someone take care of me!" "Oh, to have the name of a good, important man!" She was still voicing variations of these laments to me and others at the end of her life.

Maurine, at five foot four, was built more like her mother and Grandmother McAllister and prided herself on her small hands and feet. Part of her feeling may have come from what she thought was appropriately feminine, but her vanity may have also contained a kernel of rejection of her Whipple heritage. Eli had exceptionally large hands, and later generations of cousins used to jokingly demand, "Let me see your hands."[22] Large hands and the work they could do, they agreed, meant that they, for sure, were Eli Whipple's grandchildren. Maurine was not lazy, but she was seldom able to do strenuous labor without triggering an accident or illness.

Yet she failed to fit smoothly into the McAllister side either. McAllisters were noted for their musical ability. J.D.T.'s rich baritone was legendary. Maurine's mother had a beautiful alto voice and played both the piano and organ.[23] Her brothers played guitar and banjo and sang, while her sister, Florence, played the piano and sang. In entertainment-starved St. George, these talents were genuinely appreciated. As a child, Maurine thought she could not sing parts or play an instrument well. She wryly told me that St. George's beloved music teacher, her cousin Joseph McAllister, was convinced that she should be able to sing and insisted she try for him. "Terrified of making a fool of myself, I was unable to utter a note," Maurine told me.

Coincidentally, both grandfathers wrote poetry. Eli's surviving verses are probably best described as entertaining doggerel. J.D.T., while probably not of much higher grade, had broader circulation. Some of his texts were made into songs, and his "The Handcart Song" still appears in the contemporary songbook for Primary children.[24]

Maurine revered her grandparents and thrilled to stories of their devotion and faith. She saw them as torchbearers for a stirring ideal. Ironically, her efforts to recreate the reality of their lives in *The Giant Joshua* brought chiding from those who felt she was "exposing" these pioneers to criticism. She also loved her parents—but not together. "Together" just didn't work for them or for her. But there was little she could do about it—except choose to suffer.

Notes

[1] In conversations with me during 1990–92, Maurine often told of this occasion and how it affected her. She told basically the same story to many people.

[2] Bruce W. Jorgensen, "Retrospection: Giant Joshua," *Sunstone* 3, no. 6 (September–October 1978): 7.

[3] The gushy publisher's preface to the "Illustrated Motion Picture Edition" of *Gone with the Wind*, published December 1939, announced that more than 2 million copies

CINDERELLA—ASHES AND ALL

of the first edition had been sold and that it had been read by an estimated 10 million. It did not attempt to estimate the millions who had seen the movie (or the millions more who have seen it in video). Vivian Leigh starred in the movie, produced by David O. Selznick, adapted for the screen by Pulitzer Prize winner Sidney Howard, and directed by Victor Fleming.

4 Lucile McAllister Weenig, *Biography of J. D. T. McAllister: Utah Pioneer, and Related Families* (Orem, Utah: Impressive Printing, 1980), 160.

5 Quoted in ibid., 200.

6 Ibid. Cornelia's sixth and last child, Wilford Woodruff Lenzi, was born 1 July 1882. John's other wives were past childbearing.

7 Janice Force DeMille, *The St. George Temple: The First 100 Years* (Hurricane, Utah: Homestead Publishers, 1977), 212.

8 A. K. Hafen, *Devoted Empire Builders: Pioneers of St. George* (St. George, Utah: Dixie Mission Chapter, Sons of Utah Pioneers, 1969), 85.

9 Weenig, *Biography of John Daniel Thomas McAllister,* 197–200.

10 Lenzi McAllister Sullivan (grandson), St. George, Utah, notes written January 1980, quoted in ibid., 185.

11 Maurine Whipple, "Biography," 1; Maurine Whipple Collection, L. Tom Perry Special Collections, Harold B. Lee Library, Brigham Young University, Provo, Utah, with photocopy in Maurine Whipple Collection, Archive, Val A. Browning Library, Dixie College, St. George, Utah. Documents in both collections hereafter cited as BYU, photocopy Dixie College.

12 Ibid., 9.

13 John R. Young, *Memoirs* (Salt Lake City: Deseret News, 1920), 106. The nephew of Brigham Young, he was the son of Lorenzo Dow Young and Persis Goodell Young.

14 Ibid., 119.

15 Polygamy had been illegal since the Morrill Act (1862), which was basically couched as an anti-bigamy act. The Edmunds Act (1882) and Edmunds-Tucker Act (1887) together made it very difficult for polygamists and almost destroyed the Church. James B. Allen and Glen Leonard, *The Story of the Latter-day Saints,* 2d ed. (Salt Lake City: Deseret Book, 1992), 402–3, 413–14.

16 Bessie Snow and Elizabeth Snow Beckstrom, "A History of Pine Valley," in *Under Dixie Sun: A History of Washington County by Those Who Loved Their Forebears,* edited by Hazel Bradshaw (Panguitch, Utah: Printed by Garfield County News for Washington County Daughters of Utah Pioneers, 1950), 190.

17 Cornelia's first home in St. George was a cottage on the southeast corner of the temple lot. Annie M. Sullivan Hall, "History of Cornelia Agatha Lenzi McAllister," typescript, 3, Daughters of Utah Pioneers Museum, St. George, Utah; photocopy Dixie College Archives. The temple's north parking lot now occupies the house site.

18 Ervin L. Herbert, *The Whipples: A History of the Whipple Family. 350 Years from Captain John Whipple to the Children of Eli Whipple* (n.p., 1983), 23, 67. Herbert is the son of Elvira Whipple Herbert, the first child of Eli Whipple and his third wife, Mary Jane Legg Whipple. He compiled and wrote this book in 1973. Copy at the St. George Family History Center.

[19] Ibid., 92.

[20] Ibid., 67.

[21] Annie M. Sullivan Hall, "History of Cornelia Agatha Lenzi McAllister," 4; typescript, Daughters of Utah Pioneers Museum, St. George, Utah; photocopy Dixie College.

[22] Herbert, *The Whipples*, 92.

[23] According to Hall, "History of Cornelia Agatha Lenzi McAllister," 4: "Annie and Grace were the most popular duo in Southern Utah. They were included in every program and every party ever held. Their older sister, Jane, was the accompanist. The younger son, Wilford, went to Salt Lake to school, then studied music for two years at Boston Conservatory of Music. He settled in Salt Lake and taught music the rest of his life."

[24] John Daniel Thompson McAllister (1827–1910), "The Handcart Song," *Children's Songbook* (Salt Lake City: Corporation of the President, Church of Jesus Christ of Latter-day Saints, 1989), 220. This version includes a verse written for an earlier edition by Lucile Cardon Reading (1909–82), former editor of the Primary's publication, *Children's Friend* (renamed *The Friend* in 1971).

2

ST. GEORGE CHILDHOOD

    Charlie Whipple and Annie McAllister married on 5 September 1901 in the Manti Temple, Annie's father officiating. Charlie had turned twenty-three in January; Annie was eight months older. In the next sixteen years, they had six children, all born in St. George. Maurine (nicknamed "Rene" by the family) was born on 20 January 1903, followed by Ralph two and a half years later on 23 August 1905 and Charles Ray three years later on 26 July 1908. When Maurine was nine, Florence was born on 12 May 1912, followed by George Wayne on 7 January 1915, just two weeks before Maurine turned twelve. The last child, Grace, was born 17 March 1917 and died four days later. Strangely enough, Maurine did not mention this child to me, although she would have been fourteen when the baby was born and must have been affected by her death.

    Maurine described Charlie as "a tall, good looking, strong-silent man who was often cast in the role of the villain in the community's dramatic events. He liked doing drama and performed a great deal in his early day. He had dark eyes and hair and came by a brooding look easily." No doubt his good looks had appealed to Annie while they were courting, but he had, no doubt, also deliberately softened his rough ways and tried to appear religious to win her. He had some money, too, which came from an interest in a silver mine that he and his brother John had found near Lund, Nevada. According to Maurine, the two had been the first white men to explore the area.

    John Whipple's biography, written by his wife, does not mention Charlie at all. But John actively prospected for silver exploration and his biography told about several claims he had found. One, the Silver Horn Mine, four miles north of Bristol, Nevada, he had sold to "an English Company" in 1906 for $10,000. With the money, he paid off the mortgage on Sunnyside, his ranch lying across the Nevada state line in White Pine, County.[1] He was able to build his herd to a thousand cows and branch out into purebred Herefords. It seems likely, therefore, that John and Charlie had jointly found and sold an earlier silver claim.

Almost immediately after the wedding, Charlie and Annie moved to Logan where they attended the Utah Agricultural College (now Utah State University). Although Charlie was bright and enjoyed science, he made carpentry his emphasis while Annie took cooking and sewing classes. Maurine cynically thought that Charlie had decided what Annie would study. "Papa was thinking of himself and how Mama could serve him better," was her opinion. As the school year drew to a close, Annie became pregnant in April with Maurine. They finished the school year but then moved back to St. George, not only because Charlie needed a job to support Annie and the baby but because he also felt responsible to help his mother and two younger sisters, Leah, who turned twenty-two that year, and Effie, two years younger.

Charlie started an ice business at 600 Diagonal Street on the northwest side of town, near the house where Maurine later lived under the red Sugarloaf sandstone hills. In a blazing desert, ice was a popular commodity. Maurine remembered the glory of tasting something cold in the hot summers and how little children would walk to the ice plant with their pennies to buy a piece of ice.

Annie's brief personal history notes that the couple made their first St. George home "in the old Atkin house."[2] Maurine retained one memory: "It had a nice bay window."

Just before Maurine turned nine, Charlie's mother, Caroline Lytle Whipple, died in December 1912. Charlie and Annie moved into her home at 186 South 200 East with Maurine, seven-year-old Ralph, four-year-old Ray, and seven-month-old Florence. This house must have started out as a respectable dwelling, and Charlie certainly had the skills to remodel and maintain it, but it became an intensifying embarrassment to Maurine, as it grew increasingly outdated and run down. Although Maurine claimed that Charlie always had good automobiles and kept them in good repair, shiny, and neat, apparently he neglected his house. It was one of the many things Maurine resented about him. She recalled that she and Annie often complained of the cold in the winter. The house was drafty and had no central heating nor, for many years, indoor plumbing. At one time, she remembered that she and Ralph tore a hole in the wall so that Charlie would have to fix a modern bathroom "or live with an opening for the neighbors to look in." Curiously, although Charlie was negligent about furnishing and maintaining the house, he lavished pains on a large bookcase to house his collection of books, mostly on scientific subjects. He also built a secret compartment in it.

ST. GEORGE CHILDHOOD

In addition to the house's other deficiencies, it became increasingly crowded by the lumber business that Charlie started on the same lot and expanded as the family's chief means of support. "How Mama hated the sound of those saws!" Maurine recalled.³

Maurine felt that her parents, during their early years of marriage, were "two young people in love." However, in the 120 months between Maurine's conception and Florence's delivery, Annie was pregnant for fifty-four of them. The physical demands of repeated pregnancies, plus caring for young, closely spaced children must have been exhausting, even if she and Charlie had been more compatible than they were. The relationship wavered into an unhealthy combination of duty, guilt, and acrimony about the time Maurine was in grade school—perhaps as early as 1909. According to Loa Moss Brown, Maurine's first cousin once removed, her grandmother Jane McAllister Moss, Annie's sister, described Charlie as "very attentive to Annie early in the marriage. Whenever he came back from a trip, he brought her something nice—dishes, or jewelry, or something for the house. Such thoughtfulness was unusual in that day when most people were very poor." But something went wrong, and rumors began circulating that Charlie had relationships with other women. Well-known in the community was a long-term friendship with Artemissia ("Misha") Seegmiller, herself descended from an old pioneer family.⁴ Maurine usually maintained that this relationship was just a friendship, that Misha "could talk his language" and "liked to play cards," which Annie did not. Loa saw it differently. "Everyone in town knew of Charlie's alternative," she commented. "He didn't bother to conceal it, and his car could be found in front of the other woman's house almost every day."⁵

Mary Morris Phoenix, about thirteen years younger than Maurine and a columnist for the St. George *Spectrum*,⁶ confirmed that Charlie's other women were no secret in the community. In addition to Misha, Charlie also squired Florence ("Flo") Foremaster around. Flo, who was eleven years older than Maurine, also taught in the public school system. A third well-recognized girlfriend was Tillie Winsor (born 11 March 1889, died 1955), eleven years Charlie's junior. Mary, a professional colleague of both Flo and Tillie, commented: "Charlie used to drive those three and other women to places they needed to go. Other men drove women places too. It wasn't that unusual for St. George." She recalls Charlie driving the car when a group of women teachers, including herself, went to a teachers' convention. Charlie said hardly anything on the trip and neither Misha nor Flo treated him with any kind of special attention. Loraine Cox, the husband of Anna Cox, Maurine's lifelong friend, confessed that he could never figure Charlie out.

He had assumed that Charlie would marry "Mishie" after Annie died—"but he didn't."

As a result of Charlie's affairs, Annie was left struggling with the emotional burden and embarrassment of an unfaithful husband, which meant for her the perception that she had little social support. Furthermore, there was an element of emotional cruelty in Charlie's deliberate public humiliations of Annie. Charlie bought one of the first cars in St. George in about 1917 or 1918 when Maurine was in her early teens. He often took the family for drives, especially on Sundays; but through Maurine's high school years, he insisted that one—sometimes both—of his lady friends accompany the family. Maurine bitterly remembered Annie, hunched down in the corner of the back seat while Charlie and his current woman, installed on the front seat, laughed and talked. Maurine writhed with shame and hated it when her friends told her that Annie looked "beaten, little, and weak."

"Poor Mama," Maurine told me in 1992. "She had such a hard time feeling any self-worth around Papa."[7] There was also more than a suggestion of sexual incompatibility in Charlie's and Annie's relationship. Loa remembered that someone once commented on "poor Annie" in her grandmother's presence. Jane responded crisply, "Don't pity her. She brought it on herself. I used to tell her, 'Annie, if you don't take care of your husband, you'll rue the day you didn't.'" Loa described both Jane and Annie as equally devoted to the Mormon Church but felt that Annie was excessively Victorian in sexual matters while Jane was more down to earth.

Maurine recognized that Annie didn't know how to keep Charlie happy. Annie didn't share his interests, and she wanted her family life to be genteel and revolve around the Church, as it had in her mother's home. Despite Charlie's flagrant infidelity, they never separated, much less divorced; and Annie continued to bear children despite his affairs, showing that she continued her sexual relationship with him. He was finally excommunicated about 1928 after an affair with, as Maurine remembered, a Swiss girl from fruit-growing Santa Clara, about ten miles west along the Virgin River. Maurine described the girl's parents as poor, not far removed from thinking that polygamy was all right, and flattered that an established man like Charlie would pay attention to their daughter.

Even after World War I, the Latter-day Saints in St. George still lived with the heritage of polygamy all around them. Those who had entered the practice before the 1890 Manifesto were accepted with little or no stigma. Still others married polygamously after 1890 but before 1904 when Joseph F. Smith issued the sterner Second Manifesto, threatening excommunication for those participating, a penalty that was still not implemented until about 1911. During that time, some Church leaders, including Joseph F.

Smith, publicly condemned the practice in the United States, while quietly encouraging and authorizing it in Mexico and other locales. Those involved in that period were largely forgiven. But after 1904, Senator-Apostle Reed Smoot insisted that the Church take strenuous steps to divorce itself from polygamy. Although there were hold-outs, the tide had turned in the Church. Within a generation, polygamists had gone from being heroes of the faith to being shamed and shunned. Some families made the transition more completely and more gracefully than others.

Charlie, married in 1901, had seen his own father take a much younger wife and, for all practical purposes, abandon his own mother. Was Charlie skeptical about the purity of Eli's motives? If polygamy existed, in part, to give men sexual access to women under the guise of religious obedience, why wasn't taking a mistress publicly simply a less deceptive variation of the same practice? And technically, it would have been a possibility, though a remote one, for Charlie to have entered into such an arrangement with the covert blessing of an accommodating Church leader. He probably knew men who had done just that. What he himself thought about his sexual accommodations, however, must remain speculation.

Although Maurine was sympathetic with her mother's plight, she also sympathized with her father's need for compatible companionship. She mused, "Mama probably never was taught anything about sex or how to be interesting to a man. If my father had been able to have had another wife, it might have been one of those times when polygamy could have worked. Certainly it would have been better than the way things were." She also felt that her parents' religious differences severely complicated the marriage. She felt that her father was never devout even as a young man, and that, after five or six years of marriage, he simply dropped the facade of orthodoxy. He stopped going to church and doffed his temple garments. According to Maurine, Annie "tried bitterly not to sleep with him after he took off his 'garments,'"[8] because she feared she would be living in sin.

Although Maurine says she noticed discord between her parents by the time she was five or six, it seems more likely that Charlie maintained a nominal appearance of orthodoxy out of respect for Annie's father until McAllister's death in January 1910 and his own mother's death two years later. However, a sensitive oldest child like Maurine would have felt the tensions much earlier. Maurine hated her father for hurting her mother but was simultaneously irritated with Annie for not standing up to him. In one telling document she wrote:

> I have had contemporaries tell me since we've grown up that they used to hate passing our lot—there was a sort of dread about the place.

"SWELL SUFFERING"

My father was terrifying to children. All the years were a constant bickering between my parents, with my mother quite unconsciously teaching me to so hate my father that I vowed at an early age to save her from him. He was a fairy-tale ogre to me, she the good princess.... She was more afraid of him than we were. When I think of the meekness with which she submitted to his insults, I long to rise up and tear down the universe! All those years when her mother and beloved sisters didn't dare enter her home for fear he would insult them! The time she asked him for money for butter, and I stood there on the door-step and watched him throw it at her, contemptuously, as if she were a dog!

My father never used round, mouth-filling oaths to us, but I think his inhuman satire and the venom he could put into "you damn little devil" were harder to bear. He was completely unable to see any viewpoint but his own, and he had a conviction that once having spoken, his word became like God's, omnipotent and irrevocable.[9]

Yet despite Maurine's contempt, in her very next paragraph she wrote about seeing Charlie much differently through their correspondence while she was at college. She found him "generous, stimulating, affectionate. ... It was pathetic how eagerly he responded to my slight overture of affection. I think he probably wanted to live vicariously in his children, and we just didn't come up to his expectations."[10]

Maurine maintained that the household revolved around Charlie. "Papa had to have his food just right," Maurine told me. "Every day Mama would plan what to have and then ask Papa for the money to go around the corner to Mathis Market to buy what she needed, and every day one of us children went to Brooke's to get a quart of milk. We didn't often eat together. Usually Mama would fix something and then leave the kitchen while Papa ate." Pies were Annie's specialty, and Maurine took pride in sending friends samples of her mother's cookies or fruit cakes. But for herself, cooking was another area in which, subconsciously, she seemed determined to distance herself as far as possible from her mother.

In contrast to Maurine's unhappy memories, her younger sister Florence nostalgically describes delicious meals—better than those of most of her friends because Charlie was such a "good provider." She would come home from school to Annie's still-warm bread, served with "Mother's good grape or plum jelly on it, or spread with delicious pear preserves!"[11] Perhaps significantly, Florence's memories do not include her own labor in the kitchen as Maurine's do.

Maurine's memories of Annie during those years are also punctuated by the regular appearance of new babies. Maurine pictured her mother as an angel, loathing the carnality represented by the pregnancies: "She was almost always an invalid, my father didn't believe in doctors and thought she should bear her children with all the equanimity of an Indian squaw.... Oh God, how I used to long for a man's two fists!"[12]

Annie was physically fragile. Her talents and interests lay in homemaking, sewing, and especially music. Maurine remembered Annie playing Grandmother Cornelia's organ in the dark: "She had a lovely low alto voice and could play with such tenderness that our eyes would fill with tears. She didn't read a note, but she was a goddess in music."[13]

Maurine loved her mother—yet hated her weakness; hated her father—yet loved his strength. Maurine's own passionate and intense nature left her tortured by the perpetual swinging of this love-hate pendulum. In contrast, in Florence's childhood memories, her parents were simply there, but their personal relationship apparently never registered on her consciousness. Instead, she affectionately and nostalgically describes "many happy hours spent in family 'get togethers.' I remember particularly the huge dinner table in my Aunt Jane Moss's large kitchen (she was my mother's oldest sister)[.] The table would be loaded with baked beans, salads, pickles, vegetables and cakes and pies."[14] These lavish feasts would be followed by songfests at Aunt Jane's piano, a legacy from J.D.T. McAllister, who always gathered as many family members as he could for evening singing, usually on the front porch, weather permitting.

Another of Annie's legacies to her elder daughter was the usefulness of illness as a retreat. Maurine remembered coming home from grade school one day "with a frightened beating in my chest. The doctor, kind but blundering, told me I had leakage of the heart!" Apparently no one explained to the child that it was a benign condition and that she would grow out of it. She said she went to sleep for years "with my finger on my pulse. Until years later the specter of the fear of death haunted my footsteps." She was genuinely prone to chronic respiratory infections; but almost certainly, some of her many ailments as an adult were psychosomatic.

Although Maurine, like her frail mother and Grandmother Cornelia, had no tomboy tendencies, she admired her father's physical prowess. He rode his "wheel" (bicycle) to and from the ice plant and once rode it 160 miles to Sunnyside Ranch in company with his brother John, who was on horseback. John had to lope to keep up and had to change horses to keep going. Another time Charlie went alone, camped overnight, and started out so early that he arrived at the ranch at dawn, surprising everyone there. Charlie claimed, probably without boasting, that he could beat any horse, if he had good roads.[15] Maurine did not talk as if she was ever very interested in her father's hobbies or businesses, but she mentioned with respect his habit of setting daily goals on long cycling journeys and his coolness in dealing with dangerous situations.

Charlie Whipple was undoubtedly intelligent and hungry for learning, a hunger which went largely unsatisfied in St. George. He sustained a love of astronomy through the years, a popular hobby among his peers as well, possibly because of the enticing, velvety nights of St. George's summers when many people slept outside. When he was an old man, he wrote with satisfaction that he had been asked to instruct a Boy Scout troop about astronomy and how much he liked doing so.[16]

Maurine blamed her father for not understanding her and for not being the right kind of father to nurture her creative spirit. She repeatedly told of overhearing St. George resident Wally Mathis say to her father, "If I had a girl like that, I would build her a house and say, 'Go to it, kid.'" Maurine would sigh wistfully: "If I'd been a daughter of Wally Mathis's, I'd be climbing golden stairs." However, Maurine's sister-in-law Alice thought that Maurine was actually Charlie's favorite.[17]

In 1906 when Maurine was three, Charlie launched a third business besides the ice house and lumber yard. Charlie, Shem Hardy, and Shem's stepson, Johnny Pymm,[18] leased the Opera House, installed an electric generator in the wine cellar because there was no electricity in town, and brought the first moving picture show to town. Later they used a portable generator mounted on Brigham Jarvis's wagon. After eighteen successful months, Charlie, Shem, Will Nielson, and Wally Mathis built the Electric Theater on Tabernacle Street.

Maurine loved the atmosphere of the theater and was likely exposed to it often. During the day, Charlie would work at his lumber and carpentry trade, then during the evening run the theater. Arlo Prisbrey, one of Maurine's students when she taught a few classes in St. George in the first semester of 1929–30, also remembered Charlie as both "a good businessman" but "a cold fish," substantiating both of Maurine's opinions about her father.[19]

At first the Electric Theater showed silent films without music. Ralph and Ray, when they were old enough, were put to work "running the moving picture projectors, doing the janitor work, and keeping the old heating stoves stoked with firewood in the winter time." Florence recalled "two huge wood-burning heaters on the stage of the building, one on each side, as well as one up in the inside up front, and these heaters took a lot of wood and coal." She recalls minor interruptions to the movie as the boys swung "the big doors of the stoves open" and shoved in more logs. Florence also recalled some vivid details about early movie technology and her role in the family business:

In those days the length of a movie was very short, about an hour, and the price was only 10 cents. Then, as they increased in length, the price went up to 10 cents for children and 25 cents for adults. The local businesses used to advertise between reels, as for many years they would run one reel, rewind it, and run the next reel. During this period of waiting, they would flash slides on the screen with printed advertising. The slides were glass and Father always printed the advertising on them in red and green ink.

It was my job when I was smaller to wash the slides clean each day. My pay for this was 10 cents. When I became older, after talking pictures were introduced, the theater was remodeled and modernized with carpets in the foyer and aisles and real plush seats! Then I was advanced to the job of selling popcorn and running the electric popcorn machine. My pay for this was the grand sum of 50 cents for a night's work.[20]

Florence, although she doesn't say so, was following in Maurine's footsteps as janitor and popcorn girl. Until the Great Depression when the theater was lost, the children worked at the theater every night it was open. As a result, Maurine saw all of the silent films and early talkies that came to town, usually more than once. Almost inevitably she absorbed much dramatic technique at an early age. Perhaps more importantly, she also absorbed the melodramatic plots of westerns, romances, and epics.

Maurine's memories of the theater are very affectionate. She remembered how the elderly Uncle Johnny and Aunt Eva Pymm (courtesy titles), were the theater's characters. Uncle Johnny had been a cowboy on the Arizona Strip, the rough and isolated land lying between the Utah state line and the north rim of the Grand Canyon. He and Eva sat in "Pymm's pew," the same place on the balcony for every movie. When the action became tense, Aunt Eva would invariably scream, "You damn fool! Look behind you!" Maurine claimed that no one minded—it just added to the fun. The time needed to change reels was "a good sociable time." While the magic lantern slides and advertisements were cast on the screen, children used the time to run around, stretching their legs, "and everyone would visit."[21]

During the years that Maurine was the popcorn girl, she did some of her writing behind the popcorn machine and forever after said that the fragrance of freshly buttered popcorn brought back the urge to write. Summers were pleasant, but winter nights were sheer misery for her, as the lobby was drafty and she always loathed being cold.

She remembered her father's ingenuity in trying to attract customers and keep the theater solvent during the Great Depression. One promotion was arranging for patrons to collect points to be applied toward dishes. Another was giving each paying customer a small sack of pine nuts. Maurine remembered the "click, click" of the cracking nuts, the crunch of the shells underfoot, and the task of sweeping them up the next day.

In contrast to Maurine's generally happy memories about the theater, Florence described it in essentially negative terms, the only time in her autobiography when she admits problems in their family life: "I can see now why my mother never liked the moving picture business because it took our whole family away from home every night. We didn't have the warm, happy association with each other in the evenings as a family unit that we should have had. Consequently, our family was never a very close-knit family."[22]

As a child and teenager, Maurine's neighborhood was her world. The Whipple home, located at 186 South between Main Street and Second East, was close to the high school and the Tabernacle. The drug store, Mathis Market, and the Electric Theater were on Tabernacle Street, the next block north.[23]

Most St. George families drew on their rural pasts enough to keep a garden, chickens, and a cow. Annie wanted both a garden and a cow, recalled Maurine, but "no one would take care of the garden, so it was given up. The cow was always deemed unwise. The men were too involved in the lumber business and neither Mama nor I were the kind of girls who could handle such things. Mama just wanted flowers." Annie used to send Maurine flowers by travelers when Maurine was teaching away from home; but for the most part, they came from other people's gardens.

When George was born in January 1915, thirty-eight-year-old Annie had what the family then called a nervous breakdown, most likely severe postpartum depression. Maurine, who turned twelve that same month, stayed out of school for most of the spring to take care of George, Annie, and the house. She made up the school work during the next year, 1915–16. George, a "blue baby," had eczema, was irritable, and needed almost constant tending. Maurine was a protective and loving older sister, conscientiously following the treatment prescribed for his irritated skin. According to Maurine, who remained extremely defensive and loyal about him during his adult years, he became a confirmed alcoholic after a terrible experience in World War II. She kept trying to help him, even when everyone else gave up on him. In the late 1950s, she launched an in-depth study of alcoholism, in part because of her intense desire to find some way to reclaim his wasted life.

What influence did this time of being a caregiver have on twelve-year-old Maurine? She probably had to deal with several intensely conflicting emotions. On the one hand, she adored her baby brother, knew that she was essential to the survival of the family and the care of her mother, and could feel noble for her sacrifice, as she rose to her parents' expectations. But no twelve-year-old could have been completely competent in doing all the cooking and housekeeping, let alone caring for a bedfast, depressed mother, and tending four younger siblings, one of whom was a constantly crying baby. This burden would overwhelm many adult women. At an age when most girls were making close school friends, it was a dangerous time to miss a normal girlhood. She was afraid for her mother's life, racked with worry about her own health, and perhaps subconsciously resentful of all that she was asked do and the fun she missed. Ruth Foremaster Truman, a girl about Maurine's age in St. George, recorded a nostalgic picture of the easy camaraderie from which Maurine was likely excluded: "[We had] a big crowd, or gang, of boys and girls and when things were quiet enough, all we had to do was go out on the Sidewalk and 'thrill' and the kids would come from all directions. We called our end of town 'tin can alley'. The northwest end of town was 'sand town' and the southwest was 'mineral park.'"[24] The gang played street games, made candy at someone's house, or just hung around on someone's porch and talked.

As a child and teenager, Maurine enjoyed the few visits she paid her cousins at Sunnyside Ranch.[25] It is doubtful that she enjoyed the tasks of a working ranch, but she liked the closeness that distance imposed on the cluster of human beings. Ranch people had to work together and depend on each other for much of their entertainment. Visits were social events. Round-ups were staggered so that one ranch could help the other. She was enamored with the romance of cowboy life. Her six cousins were from three years her senior to ten years younger than Maurine. They exchanged letters through at least the elementary school years, some of which Maurine kept. She also kept several photos showing a pond with a small rowboat, apparently kept for the children's entertainment.

Relationships with Uncle John's family were less comfortable after Maurine graduated from college. When she visited the ranch, she got the feeling the family thought she considered herself better than they were. They didn't understand the romantic idealism with which she viewed ranching, nor could they understand why she would want to write about it.

Conspicuously but, ironically, almost absent from Maurine's memories of her childhood and teenage years is the Mormon Church. Although it dominated the landscape, the cityscape, the region's history, and her family's history, Maurine did not talk about the easy integration of religious and social life that we would expect from a woman who grew up in a small Mormon town. It is true that she grew up before the intense focus on training and retaining Mormon heritage that young people now get. Even regular attendance at sacrament meeting, let alone the panoply of other meetings that proliferated during the 1950s, was not a cultural expectation for her generation. Nor, as a grown women, would she have fit comfortably into the Relief Society, then a dues-paying self-selected organization. (Membership in it became automatic for all Mormon women over age eighteen in the early 1980s.) She did not tell me stories about her baptism, about singing hymns, attending Primary as a subteen, or enjoying Young Ladies' Mutual Improvement Association parties. She had no tales of teachers in Church auxiliaries who influenced her life, either for good or for ill. I found no indication that any leader ever took a personal interest in her or helped her advance in spiritual understanding even though she shared with me experiences with God and believed in miracles. She claimed that she taught Sunday School as a teenager.

Possibly Maurine absorbed Mormon culture into the very marrow of her bones without ever becoming conscious of it as a religion. However, her sister Florence's autobiographical sketch chats happily about her baptism in the font with bronze oxen that stood in the basement of the St. George Temple and meetings at the Dixie College Academy, while the entire town gathered at the tabernacle for sacrament meetings. Almost certainly, Maurine experienced these events too; but for her they must have meant something different. Virtually her only Church-related comment was that she and the children of Abner B. Harris and May Brooks Harris were good friends because their home life was somewhat similar: Both had mothers who had to scheme to get them to Church meetings so their inactive fathers wouldn't find out.[26]

Unquestionably Maurine had a prickly relationship with authority of most kinds, and that included ecclesiastical authority. Before writing *The Giant Joshua*, she accepted Church callings to plan and lead dramatic or dancing programs and apparently got tired of it. Nellie McArthur Gubler remembered that, when she and Maurine were teaching school in Virgin, Utah, in 1929–30, Maurine said she wouldn't teach another Church class "unless she got paid for it," which was not, of course, something the Church did.[27] I speculate, however, that if she had had a loving and mutually respectful Mormon marriage to a traditional man who was attached to the institutional church and provided religious leadership in the home, she likely would have lived her Mormonism in a traditional way.

From earliest childhood, Maurine felt things with painful intensity. That passion for transmuting sordid realities into romantic ideals was no doubt a defense, but it was also a handicap. Once when I found a page in her papers describing a sensuous early memory, Maurine listened intently when I read to her. Then she said: "If that didn't really happen, it could have. It would be about how I would feel. You can use it." I raised my eyebrows and reminded her, "This is a biography, Maurine. It should be as near the truth

ST. GEORGE CHILDHOOD

This damaged photograph of Maurine about age two is the only one of her as a child. She remembers her mother giving her a flower to hold and telling her, "I'm proud of you" for behaving well and looking pretty. Lee Library Photographic Archives, Brigham Young University.

as we can make it." She waved her hand dismissively: "It doesn't matter. It's true enough." While this "true enough" standard imposes special problems on a biographer, it goes far toward explaining Maurine's own attitude toward both her life and toward writing.

Another autobiographical fragment, "When I Get Big," portrays her as a child with a flare for fantasy. She, her brothers, and her cousins would make a play area out of an old plum tree with an irrigation ditch at its root, shrouded by a tangled grapevine that made a sort of canopy from the branches. She described how "our impersonation craze always found me a majestic Lady Macbeth in distress and a sweeping train, or a pillow-stuffed Black Mammy. I was going to be an actress. . . . My ambition began away back in the day when fairy princesses and wicked witches were the chief edibles of mental consumption."[28]

She wrote summer plays, "charging a pin for gallery admission and a safety-pin for the rocking-chair loges." And she wrote, "Once when I had thoughtfully provided the cast with a climactic repast of real home-made ice cream and chocolate cake during the last scene, the audience arose as one man and mobbed us."[29]

"SWELL SUFFERING"

She characterized herself to me as like most little girls, "except perhaps," she once added reflectively, "—except maybe I wanted things more. I remember wanting to be important in the first grade, and desiring the main part in a program, not getting it and how terribly bad I felt." In the photograph of her first-grade class, Maurine is very serious. She described herself as "so funny—so intense, white-faced, hair pulled back showing off a big forehead. I looked like a horse with the heaves." Maurine used this self-deprecatory humor all her life, delighting lecture audiences with it but also protecting herself—laughing first before others could laugh at her. "I just wanted to grow up like other girls," she often said, "have a husband to take care of me and have nice babies. But I never could be like the other kids. I tried. Oh how I tried!"

Just before starting *The Giant Joshua*, she wrote a reminiscence about discovering the "release of words" that came when she discovered how to "[put] my ache on paper."

> Somehow writing began to be a religion with me. Of course the fact that I carried notebook and pencil around with me only made me more queer to my fellows. I got to feel the habit was shameful, and used to suffer sitting up in bed on cold winter nights after every one else was asleep in order to be alone to practice it....
>
> My ever-recurring dream must have started during those early years. Now I know it must have been [born] of desperation—a craving for beauty and escape from the ugliness of reality—but whatever its source I have never been able to get rid of it. Even now I sometime dream of this lady (who somehow thinks like me) poised, miraculously shorn of homeliness and awkwardness and self-consciousness, charmingly descending a stair-way in a house eloquent of serenity and hospitality. There is always a rose garden in front and a cow in the back yard—I suppose because all my life I have suffered vicariously [from] my mother's longing for a flower garden, and because when I was little I used to cry for milk. Not always in my dream is there money in that house, but always there is peace.[30]

Because this elegant dream-woman played the piano, Maurine was frantic to take lessons, especially when she realized that she lacked the McAllister talent for singing. She was crushed when her father refused permission, but she never expressed jealousy when Charlie later allowed Florence to learn piano. To be fair, Charlie's decision may have been based more on Florence's obvious talent (she was picking out tunes by ear on an old organ at age five and six), on Annie's fervent support (Florence says, "My mother became determined to have me take lessons"), on their obvious parental desire to encourage a compensatory talent (Florence had a crippled foot), and on the more stable family finances that a younger child frequently benefits from.³¹

Maurine compensated by concentrating on academic honors, where she set an impressive record. That would have been enough for some young women, but America was two generations away from admitting that a woman could be both smart and popular. As a result, Maurine's aggressive competitiveness in pursuit of her secondary goal undercut her chances to achieve her first goal—popularity with her peers. She wrote bitterly: "My four years of high school were marked by mental victories but lacerated with heartaches for the kind of lemonade-and-cake good times other girls were having on the easy hospitable porches of their homes. Our house didn't have a porch."³² Once again, she was blaming her family home for its lack, rather than finding another locale for serving her lemonade.

Although feeling like a miserable outcast is something of a tradition for American adolescents, Maurine's claim to be an outsider during her teen years deserves some examination. Certainly the family was not affluent, but there is no indication that the Whipples suffered from greater poverty than many in St. George at the time. In fact, they were probably considered better situated than most. Maurine felt very self-conscious about the inferiority of her clothes. She blamed her father's stinginess rather than her mother's reluctance to sew at a time when many Mormon mothers made all of their daughter's clothes, even formal gowns. In fact, Annie did sew, though perhaps she lacked the knack of making clothes as stylish as Maurine wanted.

Photographs of Maurine show her as attractive enough, with reddish (hennaed) brown hair, a high, smooth brow, and even features in a rectangular face. In most photographs, her expression is serious. She was of medium height—five foot four—with small, well-shaped hands and feet. Until her mid-thirties, she was slender, even thin, at approximately 100 pounds. (In 1927 in her first year of teaching she wrote, "Oh, if I could only get fat and beautiful!"³³) Her legs were shapely, and she enjoyed wearing shorts when they became fashionable after World War II.

Ray and Florence do not seem to have suffered from Maurine's shattering sense of inferiority. In fact, if George's yearbook, with numerous positive comments from classmates, is any evidence, he was considered quite popular.³⁴ However, Ralph's and George's alcohol abuse suggests that something may have been awry in their self-images. Maurine was very proud of Ray, wished she were more like him, but also lamented, "If only he had had my burning drive to be somebody!" Ray's daughter, Carol Ann Whipple Anderson, said that Maurine encouraged Ray "to go to the University of Utah to get a teacher's certificate in drama. He was very good at the drama part, stayed three and a half years, but decided the teaching part was not for him. But he enriched the St. George community with his acting all his life. I feel he was a much more fulfilled person for the experience."[35] Ray's and George's contemporaries remember them as popular, smart, and talented.

Florence was pretty, learned to play the piano well, and was accepted into a group of popular girls. She had been lame from birth, when the midwife, coping badly with a breech delivery, pulled Florence through the birth canal by her foot, causing, according to Florence's autobiography, "a partial paralysis, a . . . bad limp all my life and . . . much heartache." She always had to wear custom-made orthopedic oxfords, never pretty shoes. Maurine blamed both the midwife for the initial problem and Charlie for not getting a doctor and for not trying harder to get the damage repaired. Once again, she seems to be blaming her father unfairly. According to Florence, "When I was about eight years old, our family doctor, Dr. D. A. McGregor, had a specialist come down from Salt Lake City, a Dr. McFarland. He performed surgery on my leg, but the operation wasn't successful."[36] Significantly, although Florence confessed to "heartache" over this handicap, which left her walking with a limp, she did not make it the source of a tragedy-blighted life but instead cheerfully wrote in her autobiography: "I think my parents were extra good to me because of my problem foot."[37]

Perhaps Ralph, the oldest son, shared Maurine's sense of social exclusion. Maurine loved him very much. At times, she told me that Charlie didn't respect Ralph because he was too much like their "angel mother." At other times, she told me that Ralph was Charlie's favorite—even though she again blamed Charlie for bad parenting where Ralph was concerned. He worked hard as his father's assistant in the lumber business and as the theater projectionist, but Charlie seldom gave him any praise or open appreciation. Ralph stammered, and Maurine thought there was a connection between this emotional starvation and his speech defect. However, as evidence that Charlie loved Ralph, Maurine said that, when Ralph was seriously ill, Charlie not only called for the elders to administer to Ralph by the laying on of hands but also prayed himself. "He really loved Ralph very much. But the sad thing was that Ralph never knew."

When Ralph completed the sixth grade, the teacher held him back a year, thinking it would "break" him of stammering. Maurine was furious with the teacher and even more furious with Charlie for not defending Ralph. Luckily, Ruby Bryner, a later teacher, involved Ralph in plays, coached him in music and drama, and helped him conquer his stammer. He was always shy, but his musical talent helped him socially. He and Ray played banjo and guitar and sang, performing often at gatherings. They also played in the Earl J. Bleak orchestra that provided the music for many dances during the 1930s and 1940s. Ralph had been the only brother who tried to fill

Maurine's social needs. Mary Phoenix remembers that he would take Maurine to the town dances and dance with her as she tried out new steps, "fantasizing that she was making a pretty picture."[38]

At age thirty-two, Ralph married a divorcée, Ida Johnson Beatty, of nearby La Verkin on 3 May 1937.[39] Perhaps because of the divorce, the Whipples did not receive Ida warmly, Maurine told me. Ida had a daughter, Jeannie, by her first marriage, but she and Ralph had no children together.

Juanita Leavitt Pulsipher (later Brooks), then a young widow with a son,[40] was teaching at the Washington Normal School the same year Maurine was a high school senior. Juanita remembered Maurine as a "precocious senior, editor of the school paper and year book."[41] Maurine may have longed to trade these positions for the easy, gossipy camaraderie of the "popular" girls and fellows she watched from the margins; but Brooks's comment shows that Maurine did have an accepted place in the social structure, one that allowed her to participate in significant ways. Certainly, if she had really felt deeply alienated from St. George life, it seems likely that she would have moved away and stayed away instead of returning persistently all of her life.

When I asked Maurine to name a teacher who had helped and encouraged her writing, she couldn't remember any: "They assigned themes—that's about all—but there just wasn't much encouragement for ambitious writing. Attention went to sports and music." Issues of the *Dixie Owl*, the St. George Normal School's paper, show that Maurine was on the staff for the entire four years. She is listed as "contributor" in several issues. As a freshman in 1918–19 she was given credit for the "Fun and Philosophy" section. In May 1921 she wrote "Toastin' the Seniors," a humorous poem that also expressed ambitious sentiments.

Maurine's literary rival during those years was Violet Roundy, whose name appears oftener than Maurine's in the school publication. Violet won the honor pin, which Maurine remembered desperately wanting and felt she deserved. This award, given at graduation to the best scholar, included both the pin and the right to give a commencement speech. Maurine's explanation to me of why this honor went to another reveals her deep-seated sense of anxious inferiority: "The senior class had gone on an outing to Pine Mountain. On the way back, we stopped at the volcano. All the kids hiked to the top. I came down early." When the principal, Joseph K. Nicholes,[42] asked Maurine why she had come down alone, she said "there was a large flat rock up there and the kids were laying out on it. Who knew what they were doing! He was offended and thought I thought I was too good for the other kids—insinuating they were doing bad things." Maurine lacked a boyfriend and probably felt too self-conscious to be around the youthful couples. When I suggested that she pretended she didn't care, Maurine agreed but added that the school secretary told her she overheard Nicholes' comment about the outing as evidence that Maurine thought she was "too good" for the other students. Maurine also felt that she was not given the award because of her father's reputation in the community for moral looseness, although no one ever suggested that this was part of the reason.

She bore up stoically during graduation but then retreated with her humiliation to the only place where she could cry with some privacy—the outhouse. She concluded the story with a gesture of defiance and determination by pulling herself together and, as she tells it, writing the following poem on the spot. This scenario seems unlikely, if the graduation occurred in the evening, since most outhouses were not equipped with light. In any case, it represents both her disappointment and her gallant resolution to rise above it:

> Dreams
> Dreams that branch and bloom
> On the stalk of a dear desire
> Dreams that live and linger
> With hope a funeral pyre—
>
> For thus is the wisdom of ages
> Summed in a single phrase:
> Dream—and your soul in ashes
> Kindles anew its blaze.[43]

Maurine remembered Nicholes unpleasantly as rigid and unkind, even though he wrote her a very complimentary and positive letter of recommendation in May 1934 when she was applying for a recreation position in Las Vegas. Mary Nielson (later Campbell), seven years younger than Maurine and also school paper editor and yearbook aide, had different memories. When Nicholes joined the faculty at BYU, he encouraged Mary to take some writing classes there, predicting she would be the Edna Ferber of southern Utah. I asked Maurine why she thought he failed to predict that she would become a writer. Maurine sighed: "You just don't know how it was. Mary was from the in-circle. I just wasn't."

It was never totally clear to me what Maurine meant by this. Mary herself was puzzled that anyone would think her family was elite.[44] But to Maurine it was obvious. Although the Nielsons were poor with eleven children, they were emotionally stable, active Mormons, with the children respecting and learning from both parents. The father had a respectable reputation in the community. To Maurine, this family difference was enormous; her parents had, she felt, been dysfunctional because they were raised in poverty-stricken polygamous households with largely absent fathers, and Charlie's rejection of the Church exacerbated their dysfunction. Probably Maurine read back into her adolescence the feelings of deeper adult exclusion that steadily intensified as her dreams of romance repeatedly flamed up, only to flicker out. She often told me about watching from the sidelines as Wyatt Walker Miles,[45] a handsome and popular student and future doctor, danced with the more favored girls, particularly Louie Harris, a year older than Maurine. The fact that he was five years Maurine's senior—a significant difference at that age—did not seem to help Maurine view the situation more realistically. Although crushes on unreachable men are typical of most adolescent girls, for Maurine the pattern lasted her entire life. "Girls like me couldn't have beaux or dates," she asserted. I could hardly believe this statement and questioned it. "Well, sometimes the boys would walk us home from the dance or whatever, and they would stand by the gate and talk," she admitted. Broodingly, she tormented herself with "ifs." "I guess I could have been popular enough, if I had tried harder to be like other girls."

Florence seemed happily oblivious to these differences that were all-important to Maurine. She married early and also enjoyed a lifelong attachment to and engagement in Mormonism, the only one of Charlie and Annie's children who did.

Part of Maurine's standard presentation of her unhappy adolescence was that she never had even a single date in high school and only one invitation. A boy from Santa Clara walked some ten miles to her home in St. George to ask her to a dance. She accepted, thrilled; but before the next weekend, she said, he died in an accident. Another time, she told me he was murdered. I have found no substantiation for either story; but the fact that she told it over and over suggests that it represented being cruelly deprived of the security that having a husband, home, and children represented. More functionally, this story also represents the pattern that she would use again and again to explain her singleness to herself and others—that she didn't have a man because of some tragic event: the war, an industrial accident, malice and misunderstanding, or just cruel fate. It was a way of dealing with the losses in a way that made it impossible to blame either her or the men. Furthermore, it also meant that she never had to accept responsibility for the termination of a relationship.

Maurine's approach/avoidance tactics in relationships with men were curious. She certainly had enough physical attractiveness to appeal to a man. She consoled herself by thinking that the men who avoided a relationship with her were, as she said, "afraid of a woman who was so honest. A direct, no-games approach to romance"—that's how she explained her social difficulties and terrible emotional neediness. In fact, one of the most painful facts about her relationships, apparent throughout her adult life, is that her own approach was anything but "no-games." Another reason I think she felt unpopular is because she would not settle for a boy or man she felt was inferior. He had to be the caliber of a Wyatt Walker Miles or she wanted nothing to do with him.

She envied other girls' casual friendliness and especially their flirtatious wiles. The few times she tried to copy these techniques, she confessed, she performed clumsily, felt foolish, and repelled the men she tried to attract. She seems to have had no comprehension that her earnest, even dogmatic, attempts to make men "understand women"—especially her—were monumentally counterproductive. Perhaps on some level she was acting out her mother's refusal to "take care" of Charlie—to pamper, coax, and admire, to coddle his male ego and make his home a cozy, comfortable nest. Annie was a wonderful woman, even, it was said, a saint. Why did Charlie have to be tricked into valuing her? Why did any good woman have to "trick" a man?

One of Maurine's role models—one she could have followed more closely—was a cheerful, contented single woman. Julia Foster managed the co-op store and also ran the community's social center, "The Hub."[46] Maurine, who clerked for her for at least one summer, described her as a marvelous person, a successful businesswoman with a sense of humor and "chin that had continued to grow after the rest of her stopped." She also suffered from goiter, a frequent malady in St. George due to the lack of iodine. Maurine used Julia as a prototype for the witty and folk-wise "Sarah Jane" of her lectures during war time and later. Sarah Jane, for instance, gave young women good advice about saving their earnings for college instead of spending them on the pretty glass earrings in the store. Maurine also put in this character's mouth humorous quips like: "A man would have to tie me up to kiss me. That's why I keep a rope on the porch."

Even though Julia Foster deflected malicious jokes at her expense by making them first, Maurine remembers her as the butt of many jokes circulating in St. George. "There was no party in town but what someone had a new Julia Foster joke, and you made social points by adding to the trove," Maurine said. Did Maurine add to those jokes in a desperate attempt to increase her own popularity? Perhaps, but she also compensated for this youthful cruelty by using Julia's self-deprecatory technique, though never, I believe, in such a healthy way.

ST. GEORGE CHILDHOOD

Notes

1 Mrs. J. L. [Fammie (sic) Nelson] Whipple, "The Life of John Lytle Whipple, 1874–1966," 1961, typescript, Archives, Val A. Browning Library, Dixie College, St. George, Utah; hereafter Dixie College. Fammie was John's second wife. John and Rose Ellen married 3 July 1893 and had ten children.

2 "History of Annie McAllister Whipple," holograph, 4 pp., n.d., Whipple Collection, Perry Special Collections, Lee Library, Brigham Young University, Provo, Utah; hereafter BYU.

3 Annie M. Whipple, Letter to Maurine, n.d., holograph, Whipple Collection, BYU; photocopy Dixie College.

4 Artemissia Seegmiller and her twin Emma was born 24 March 1894 to Charles Seegmiller and Ida Maria Morris Seegmiller. Misha taught grade school in St. George but her reputation never seemed to be affected by this extramarital liaison. She never married and had no children.

5 Loa Moss Brown, interviewed by Veda Tebbs Hale, 7 May 1992 at her home, 31 West 200 South in St. George, Utah; holograph notes in my possession. Though J.D.T. McAllister was a respected churchman, he was poor, and Loa acknowledged that she empathized with Maurine's persistent feelings of never being as good as the families at the pinnacle of St. George society.

6 Mary Morris Phoenix was born 2 June 1916 and died 22 December 1998. I interviewed her between 1991 and 1995, returning often for clarification on otherwise puzzling information.

7 Annie McAllister, Letter to Maurine Whipple, 24 April 1927; inserted in Maurine Whipple, "My First Diary," January 1927–October 1928, Whipple Collection, BYU; photocopy Dixie College.

8 Maurine Whipple, "Confessions of a She Devil," ca. 1937, 4, 5; 34 pp. holograph and 18 pp. typescript, Whipple Collection, BYU; photocopies of both at Dixie College. Both holograph and typescript are virtually identical except for one paragraph in the holograph describing a disagreement in 1937 with Grant Redford of Cedar City, Utah. Maurine confirmed most of the material in our conversations.

9 Ibid., 5–6. Carol Ann Whipple Anderson, Ray's daughter, and Colleen Jolley Haycock, Florence's daughter, and Larry Jolley, Florence's son, interviewed for this biography, all remember Charlie as a warmly affectionate grandfather. None of the three expressed fear of him or a desire to avoid him.

10 Ibid., 7.

11 Florence Whipple Jolley, "History of Florence Whipple Jolley," January 1976, holograph, 15 pp., 2.

12 Maurine Whipple, "Diary of a She Devil," 6.

13 Ibid., 5–6.

14 Jolley, "History," 3.

15 Maurine Whipple, untitled notes about Charlie Whipple, n.d., Whipple Collection, BYU; photocopy Dixie College. I read these notes to Maurine and, prompted

33

by them, she added additional information about Charlie and expressed pride in his accomplishments.

16 Charlie Whipple, Letter to Maurine Whipple, n.d. but apparently after Annie's death (1956); Whipple Collection, BYU; photocopy Dixie College.

17 Mary Phoenix, for one, said, "Charlie Whipple was all right. He was an honest businessman, paid his bills and dealt friendly with people. You can't blame ol' Charlie. So he wasn't a church goer and practically lived with that woman. Still he was a good father." Mary Phoenix, Interviewed by Veda Hale, 1993.

18 Sherman Capner Hardy, son of A. P. and Elizabeth Hardy, was born 21 June 1865, in Grafton, Utah, and moved to St. George with his parents. He married Agnes Donald Pymm on 12 October 1887 and, after her death, Isabella M. Grundy, in 1921. He was a mail carrier, game warden, superintendent of Apex Mining Company, and city marshall (1918–19). He had no children and died 15 February 1959. A. K. Hafen, *Devoted Empire Builders: Pioneers of St. George* (St. George, Utah: Dixie Mission Chapter, Sons of Utah Pioneers, 1969), 56, 108.

19 Arlo Prisbrey, Interviewed by Veda Tebbs Hale, 25 May 1992; notes in my possession.

20 Jolley, "History," 5.

21 The theater was restored in 1992; the same projector, now an antique was part of the restoration.

22 Jolley, "History," 5.

23 Eventually Ray and Alice Whipple bought the house and lumber business in the 1960s, remodeled the house, and ran the business. They sold it in the 1980s. An office building now stands on the property.

24 www.softcom.net/users/paulandsteph/ahtsr/bertsfamilyi.html (accessed June 2008).

25 John Lytle Whipple (born 7 April 1874, died 22 December 1966) married Rose Ellen (Eleanor) Warren on 3 July 1893. After her death, he married Fammie Nelson, but Rose Ellen was the mother of his ten children, three of whom died young.

26 Seamstress May Brooks Harris, the daughter of George Brooks Sr. and Emily C. B. Brooks, was born 7 February 1877, and married Abner B. Harris, a laborer at the Apex Mine, on 3 June 1901. She died 30 October 1966. Some of their five children—Louie, Grant B., Edith, Goldie, Helene, and Evelyn—played a role in Maurine's adult life.

27 Nellie McArthur Gubler, Letter to Veda Hale, 2001.

28 Maurine Whipple, "When I Get Big," n.d., holograph, Whipple Collection, BYU; photocopy Dixie College.

29 Whipple, "Confessions of a She Devil," 3.

30 Ibid.

31 Jolley, "History," 4. Charlie ordered the piano in Salt Lake City, had it shipped by train to the railhead at Modena, and freighted it the last sixty-four miles to St. George.

32 Whipple, "Confessions of a She Devil," 8–9.

33 Maurine Whipple, "My First Diary," 8 January 1927.

34 George Whipple, in [St. George High School] *Yearbook, 1933*, Whipple Collection, BYU.

ST. GEORGE CHILDHOOD

35 Carol Ann Whipple Anderson, Letter to Veda T. Hale, Calgary, Alberta, 6 August 1992, Whipple Collection, Dixie College.

36 Jolley, "History," 3. "Dr. McFarland" should not be confused with the Macfarlane family of St. George. Florence also spells the family's name as "Macfarline."

37 Ibid.

38 Mary Morris Phoenix, Interviewed by Veda Hale, April 1994; notes in my possession.

39 Ida Johnson Beatty, was born 30 July 1904, and died 13 June 1944. Her parents were Abraham Owen Johnson and Louisa Elizabeth Belliston Johnson.

40 Juanita Leone Leavitt Pulsipher Brooks was born 15 January 1898 to Dudley Henry Leavitt and Mary Hafen Leavitt in the tiny Mormon community of Bunkerville, Nevada. An outstanding historian, she published fifteen books and thirty-six articles and is best known for *The Mountain Meadows Massacre* (Stanford, Calif.: Stanford University Press, 1950; 2d ed., Norman: University of Oklahoma Press, 1962), and *John Doyle Lee: Zealot, Pioneer Builder, Scapegoat* (Glendale, Calif.: Arthur H. Clark, 1961; 2d ed. rev. Salt Lake City: Howe Brothers, 1984). Both books were landmarks in the scholarly treatment of Utah's most painful historical episode, and her high standards and scholarly professionalism changed how Mormon history was written. A member of the Utah Beehive Hall of Fame, she received honorary doctorates from the University of Utah, Utah State University, and Southern Utah University. With occasional time off to raise her family, she taught at Dixie College from 1925 to 1965 and purchased the campus's first set of carillon bells. Levi S. Peterson, *Juanita Brooks: Mormon Woman Historian* (Salt Lake City: University of Utah Press, 1988), 147.

41 Ibid., 117.

42 Joseph K. Nicholes, born 10 October 1887, died 4 October 1964.

43 Maurine Whipple, "Dreams," ca. 1922, holograph, Whipple Collection, BYU.

44 Mary Nelson Campbell, interviewed April 1944, Mary became an outstanding teacher in California and had a good relationship with Nicholes all her life.

45 Wyatt Walker Miles was born 6 December 1897 to Arthur Fredrick Miles and Ida Walker Miles. Katharine Miles's brother, he taught school in Panguitch in the 1920s, then became a doctor.

46 Julia Putnam Foster was born 9 August 1879 to Charles Franklin Foster Sr. and Pamelia Asenall D. Foster in Pine Valley. She successfully owned and managed a general mercantile store on the southwest corner of Main and First North streets that also housed "The Hub," a community social center. Maurine Whipple, "A Characterization of Julia Foster," May 1926, English 107, Lesson 1, Extension Division, University of Utah, holograph, Whipple Collection, BYU; photocopy Dixie College.

※ 3 ❦

THE UNIVERSITY OF UTAH, 1922-26

Maurine wrote that she hitchhiked to college at University of Utah in the fall of 1922.[1] Maurine's friend, Warren Cox,[2] owner of the local Arrowhead Hotel, had a non-Mormon guest going to Salt Lake City.[3] So it was that Maurine quickly put "two middy blouses, one skirt, a coat made from a hand-me-down, and twenty-five dollars in cash in a cardboard suitcase and, with shining eyes headed for the big city."[4] She was nineteen.

When she got to Salt Lake City, she asked to be let out downtown so she could buy a dress, shoes, and stockings. She wanted to present herself in the best possible light at the door of her mother's half-sister, Julia May McAllister Nielson Silver. Aunt May's husband had died the year before. Nine months later on 8 September 1922, her son had died of blood poisoning while serving in the Southern States Mission. This would have been shortly before Maurine got there. The other five children ranged in age from twenty-four to seven. Maurine stayed there a few days, but it was uncomfortable under the grieving circumstances.

One advantage of Maurine's large polygamous family was that she did not lack for relatives. The next morning, she went to visit Aunt Annie and Uncle Hyrum Folsom. Maurine's mother was named for Aunt Annie, the half-sister of her grandmother Cornelia. Annie and Hyrum lived in a small apartment at 155 North Main #45. Although quarters were cramped, they were very kind and insisted they could "make do" until she could find better accommodations.[5]

Maurine loved them, their cat, their jolliness, and their player piano. Helpfully, they contacted an acquaintance, who had some connection to the university. Uncle Hyrum took Maurine the next day to the campus where he helped her get a job at the cafeteria. When she let everyone know that she really wanted to work in the library, she was encouraged to sign up for a class in library science, although it doesn't appear that she did. Although grades are not available except to close relatives, Maurine's transcript shows that she signed up for a heavy load of classes in 1922–23: English, physical education, zoology, public speaking, Spanish, education, psychology, and business.[6]

When school was out in the spring of 1923, she returned to St. George. Ralph's appendix ruptured, but his ailment was not diagnosed until peritonitis had set in. Ralph's convalescence was long and complicated. The hospital was closed for the summer so the operation was performed at home with Maurine acting as doctor's assistant and then as Ralph's devoted nurse. She carefully followed the doctor's instructions, even when nursing required her to perform such difficult and unpleasant tasks as cleaning the draining incision. Maurine felt that Ralph, whom she called "the sweetest boy that ever lived," would have died without the doctor's care and her nursing—that neither her mother nor anyone else in the family would have been able to handle the difficult situation.

The twenty-eight-year-old attending physician, Clare Woodbury,[7] was in St. George because his father, also a doctor, had died 2 July 1923. Clare had come to attend the funeral and stayed to take over his father's practice. Maurine felt that his marriage was not a happy one, but perhaps she was groping for a way to justify her one-sided romantic feelings. She grew very close to him during the heady experience of working side by side to save her beloved brother's life and soon was deeply infatuated. Even after Ralph's recovery, Maurine seized every opportunity to continue seeing Woodbury, using her own real or imagined ills as excuses. Once she had visited his office so late in the evening that Annie came to retrieve her and lectured her all the way home about her inappropriate behavior. Maurine, shaken, pled, "Don't tell Papa." Annie, used to keeping things from Charlie, agreed.[8] Maurine's obsession with this educated, cultured doctor lasted for years, perhaps deflecting her attention from less glamorous but more attainable young men. For the rest of her life, she was fascinated with doctors, easily finding them objects upon which to pin her romantic hopes.

Maurine claimed that her relationship with this doctor never involved any physical intimacies—that Woodbury was always professional, kind, and "decent"; but she also admitted that she would have considered marrying him as his plural wife, had polygamy been legal, probably even if it weren't. After all, wasn't there another doctor in town who had a second wife and the community tolerated it? She also admitted recasting him in her fictional memoir, "Confessions of a She Devil," written about ten years later, as an experienced seducer of young girls, before whose experienced charms she was well-nigh helpless. But she insisted to me that Woodbury was an honorable man.[9]

Maurine apparently made an effort to turn her experience with Woodbury into fiction. The last page of a short story in holograph (all that has survived of the manuscript) tells about the protagonist going for the doctor late at night when her brother takes a turn for the worse. She meets a girl on the stairs coming from the doctor's room.[10] Another hand, probably one of Maurine's college English teachers, has penciled at the bottom of the page: "Bringing in the girl helps as a story; but it clouds the problem. Make clear-cut solutions of your problems." There never seemed to be a "clear-cut" conclusion to her infatuation with doctors.

Maurine's recycling of different versions of this summer's experience shows the depth of her fascination with Woodbury, the liveliness of her imagination, and her deep sexual vulnerability. This kind of heartache would eventually become part of the creative ferment that produced *The Giant Joshua*.

Maurine's places of residence during her four years in college had blurred by 1990–91. However, she stayed at least part of her sophomore year with George McCallister Moss, her first cousin, and his wife, Thelma.[11] They kindly offered her a room rent-free since George had a good job with the railroad.[12] George's brother, Gilbert, was also living with them.

Also apparently during her sophomore year, she stayed with her father's sister, Effie Whipple Burraston, and her husband, Alma Powelson Burraston. Here she shared a bedroom with another boarder, Florence Foremaster,[13] an older woman working on her master's degree. "Flo," almost exactly eleven years Maurine's senior, taught in St. George, and her name was later linked to Charlie's as one of "his lady friends." No one I talked to, including Maurine, seemed to know just exactly what that meant. "Only in St. George," Maurine would say and just shrug. Maurine claimed that she and Flo got along fine at this time, often taking walks together and even racing around the block sometimes.

Maurine again registered for a heavy course load in 1923–24: business, public speaking, anatomy, Spanish, education, hygiene, sociology, physiology, philosophy, and English.

During the summer of 1924, between Maurine's sophomore and junior years, her sister Florence recalls that the family visited Charlie's sister, Leah Whipple Rance, in Bakersfield, California. "What a trip that was!" recalls Florence, who was twelve at the time. They visited Los Angeles and took a boat trip to Catalina Island. Florence remembered the large desert turtle they found and took home for a pet.[14] Florence also recalls visits to Yosemite and Sequoia, both national parks in California. Another family trip

"SWELL SUFFERING"

Maurine's family during one of her summers home from college in 1924 or 1925, posed around Charlie Whipple's car. Left: Maurine, Ray, Florence and George on the running board, Charlie at the wheel, Annie, and Ralph. Lee Library Photographic Archives, Brigham Young University.

was to Yellowstone Park in Wyoming: "On all these trips we camped out—cooking our meals over campfires and sleeping on folding camp cots or on beds made up in the car."[15]

Maurine's photograph collection documents some of these family trips, including her presence during these college summers; but she never mentioned them to me or wrote about them. Once again, she seemed to have edited out of her past experiences that which could have been pleasant and supportive family memories.

Maurine could not afford to attend summer school, so she dutifully returned to St. George during her college years. She said she "helped in the movie theater, clerked for Julia Foster, helped Jet Snow[16] with her spastic daughter, Pauline, bottled fruit with my mother, and had fun." An undated clipping from an unidentified newspaper in her scrapbook after *The Giant Joshua*'s publication in January 1941 says: "She also coached dramatics; and since she also knew physio-therapy she has been able to help support herself by giving treatments to a young victim of infantile paralysis," possibly a reference to Pauline. Maurine said she always had a predisposition to help the disadvantaged and found working with Pauline rewarding. She thought that, given more time, she could have helped the child acquire many more skills.

THE UNIVERSITY OF UTAH, 1922–26

She also claims that she wrote "To My Child" for Pauline. It may be true that she wrote the poem first for Pauline, but she used it in many situations where she wanted to make a child feel special, saying she wrote it just for him or her.

> To My Child
> If I could bridge the gap between our generations,
> If I could view the world with your young eye,
> If I could fathom all your expectations
> And know the meaning of each smile or sigh.
>
> If I could rid your heart of every sorrow,
> If I could make your troubles mine,
> If I could promise joy for each tomorrow
> I would not lift a finger, Child of mine.
>
> Instead, I'd pray for strength to let you blunder.
> I'd pray for patience to withhold advice—
> I'd pray for wisdom to let you grope and wonder,
> So trust experience as the one sure price.
>
> But, child of mine, so little I'm permitted—
> These two cupped palms encompass all my pelf:
> A love that's God-like in that it's committed:
> To give you freedom to become yourself.[17]

"Fun" didn't involve many boys, but Maurine reconnected easily with her "club" of girls. They had all taken cooking and home economics in high school and continued the association by getting together at different girls' homes and cooking a meal. Nights in St. George, after the day's blistering heat, were especially pleasant. "The thing to do was for your group of girls to go for walks, and the place to walk was around the temple. The roses were beautiful," she said nostalgically. "Moonlight, roses, and the white temple were just about all a young girl could stand of beauty, peace, and promise. We would laugh, sing, tell hopes and dreams, and draw out of any romance any lucky girl might be having all we could." Maurine claimed to have an extrasensory ability to predict the future of romances and often did so correctly. Perhaps, given her writer's ability to observe detail, she could.

Maurine loved to swim and often went to Dodge Pond west of town with her first cousin, Lenzi M. Sullivan, the son of Annie's full sister Grace McAllister Sullivan. They often tried different kinds of stunts, and Maurine became good at standing on her head in the pool. In future years when she was troubled by recurring sinus infections, a doctor told her she had probably done too much of that kind of thing and damaged her sinuses.

Maurine's transcript for her junior year, 1924–25, shows her registering for only three classes—English, psychology, and public speaking.[18] Either the transcript is incomplete, Maurine dropped out for one or more quarters, or she was barely a part-time student for the entire year.

At one point—and it was possibly during this junior year—Maurine roomed with Katharine Miles from St. George in a boarding-house.[19] Maurine could not recall the surname of their landlady, whom they called Aunt Flora, although she was not related to either. Maurine enjoyed Katharine and liked the boardinghouse but remembered that Katharine disliked Aunt Flora's standard dessert: heated bread and preserves. Maurine didn't mind, because she was "usually too tired to care." She and Katharine would save their money and go to the plays put on by two brothers, Ralph and Charles W. Cloniger, at the Salt Lake Theater.[20] Katharine alluded to these evenings when she wrote in 1927 to answer Maurine's invitation to visit her in Salt Lake City:[21] Maurine said that neither she nor Katharine had a special beau, but they both had a crush on the usher ("the divine Ralph"), which made for more girlish fun.

During at least part of Maurine's junior or senior year, she said she lived in a cheap one-room apartment with another girl, whose name she couldn't remember, eating her meals nearby at an inexpensive cafeteria. What stood out for her about this year were some of the other young people in the same building. One couple had a story-book romance, the kind Maurine dreamed of. Possibly mixing this story with another account—or even a short story or movie—Maurine told a muddled melodrama about the girl's pregnancy turning toxic. When she died, Maurine tried to comfort the dead girl's lover, assuring him that a relationship as unique as theirs would surely continue into the next life, even without a Mormon temple wedding. She told another melodramatic tale from this apartment building—a fellow who committed suicide when his girlfriend left him. Maurine once again cast herself as the consoling big sister; but her version of this story seemed confused and somewhat improbable.

Maurine also remembered double dating with two couples from this Salt Lake City apartment house. They went dancing at Saltair, the popular resort on the shores of the Great Salt Lake. Maurine's date may have been Russell Clark, since he told me about a blind date with Maurine—dancing at Saltair with some other friends. He recalled enjoying the evening and would have liked to go out with Maurine again, but he was too poor—struggling to hold a job and go to school. This could have been Maurine's chance to marry a doctor, because Clark did become a successful physician, but the relationship didn't go further.

Also during this year, Maurine met Floyd and Myrtle Carnaby, with whom she remained in contact for most of her life. Floyd taught school in Huntington Beach, California, and Myrtle was a high school counselor. Maurine occasionally visited them, and her papers contain letters and holiday cards from them. Betty McPherson, a friend of Maurine's during the 1960s and 1970s, taught school in Newport Beach and remembered Maurine's frequent visits to the Carnabys. Betty felt strongly there was "something" between Maurine and Floyd and that Myrtle was jealous of the attraction. Floyd reportedly visited St. George without Myrtle on occasion. "On one of these occasions," said Betty, "we decided impulsively to have a party. So Floyd goes to the college, finds some young people who have a band, brings them and the food to Maurine's house, and my mother, Floyd and I had a wonderful time."[22]

In Maurine's senior year, she said she at first had trouble finding housing that met her liking and budget. She was invited to board at Maude May Babcock's,[23] then the fifty-eight-year-old dramatics teacher at University of Utah. For Maurine, enthralled with theater, this arrangement should have been a dream come true; but her first night's stay was ruined because one of Babcock's beloved dogs had just whelped on the bed assigned to Maurine. Maurine didn't know what to do and supposed she was expected to share the bed. Although Maurine saw the humor, her sense of being made to feel second-best came through. Furthermore, the next morning, Miss Babcock found her too slow in helping wash the breakfast dishes and snapped, "Well, I don't know about you, but I've got classes to attend to." Maurine felt humiliated and said she stayed only three days.

It may have been at this point that she moved to the Beehive House, formerly Brigham Young's residence but at that point managed by the LDS Church as a sort of YWCA for single Mormon girls from out of town. A matron supervised the girls and conducted classes in basic etiquette and culture. Maurine enjoyed the dormitory-style arrangement, with several girls in a large room. Part of their view, she says, was the missionary home straight through the block on the north side of North Temple Street where missionaries stayed for a week of training before departing for their assignments. The girls enjoyed watching the building and waving to the young men. One missionary climbed down out of his window and scrambled up through theirs for a clandestine visit. "It was all innocent fun," she insisted. At the Beehive House, Bernice Waddoups became her best friend.

The most unfortunate thing to happen this year was a fall in the street where she bumped her front teeth on the streetcar track. This injury caused persistent problems for the next fourteen years, until after finishing *The Giant Joshua*, she had the teeth pulled and a denture plate fitted.

After Maurine's graduation in the summer of 1926, Bernice visited St. George and was surprised to find Maurine's family still with an outdoor privy. "My mother kept it scrupulously clean, but I was still ashamed at not having a more modern home," Maurine said.[24] Only one of Bernice's letters survived, tucked inside Maurine's 1927 diary.

Academically, Maurine remembered her junior and senior years as the high point of college. Her transcript, however, shows that she took only two more classes as a senior than she did during her academically skimpy junior year: geology, education, English, hygiene, and physics. Despite her bitter memories, she was apparently fitting well into the English Department program, writing with greater skill and confidence. Her photograph does not appear in the yearbooks for her freshman or sophomore years (1922–23, 1923–24), but her junior and senior photographs show an attractive girl, her thick hair waved in the style of the day. In the fall of 1924, the yearbook indicates that she pledged Chi Delta Phi, a national honorary literary sorority organized in Utah in 1924–25, and in the 1925–26 yearbook she was listed as a full member. Her story, "The Christmas Dress" appeared in the 1925 Christmas issue of the *Pen*, the school's literary magazine.[25] Both her membership and her publication document successes in which she could take pride.

When asked about teachers, it was an English professor, George Perham, who stood out most vividly in Maurine's memory. He required his students to write numerous themes and often praised hers. Maurine's most successful one was "One, Two, Three, Keek," a description of swimming at the university's pool. This title came from the chant of the swimming instructor, a man with a European accent. She contrasted these pleasant swimming facilities with the irrigation ditches running through St. George in which she had splashed and waded as a child. Unfortunately, she said, Perham took this essay with him when he moved back east, and no finished copies appear in her papers.

Maurine kept other examples of her college themes. In some of the more creative projects is evidence that *The Giant Joshua* was starting to take shape in her mind. A red sunbonnet (Clory's trademark) and a woman dying in childbirth (as third wife Willie did) because the afterbirth was not successfully delivered appear in one short story, "Mormon Saga."[26] In another sketch, "The Story of a Man's Life," she describes a man dying by inches but determined to stay alive so that his pension from the Spanish-American War could continue to support his children until they graduate from high school. This character reappears as Clory's son Jimmy, in "Cleave the Wood," one of her titles for the unfinished sequel to *The Giant Joshua*.[27] Maurine said she based this character on Jim Oakason of Sand Town, a neighborhood in northwest St. George, whose daughter was her friend. (No family by that name appears in the 1900 census or St. George ward records; but a likely candidate in the correct locale is Phillip Ostenson, who had a daughter, Alva, of Maurine's age.) Maurine told me several times about visiting this home and witnessing the father's tenacious dedication to his children's welfare. The detail she lingered on was that this brave man was grateful for enough elbow left after amputation that he could hold a fly swatter in its crook.

Another significant essay from this time, "The Divine Artist," describes an admirable father who encourages his children to reach the highest artistic goals possible.[28] Although this father is obviously Maurine's fantasy of the way she wished Charlie had been, the drive of the musician-daughter for supreme excellence may represent Maurine's own passion to make good in college and later to produce something of excellence.

One teacher, who signed herself "Love, Carmen!", wrote an extended comment on Maurine's character sketch of Julia Foster. She commented on "the great danger of letting a marked characteristic become caricature" and warned Maurine that "she had a tendency to fall into that trap.... Also you showed a distinct tendency toward cleverness. It plays the devil with young people who naturally love approbation and 'smartness,' as you do."[29]

An insight into Maurine's view of her creative process at this stage appears on a page she handed in with an English assignment: "The danger I undergo of wholly ruining this second exercise is the danger of becoming mechanical and artificial. If I write my character sketch with the detailed methods of characterization on the table before me, my sketch could hardly help but be mechanical—formulated, as it were, like an arithmetic problem. On the other hand, if I absorb the rules into my subconscious mind and forget about them when I write, my sketch will be easy and natural." She received a B+ on that assignment.[30]

Two additional compositions show Maurine trying to handle her inferiority complex with satire. In "Literary Club," which is incompletely preserved, a group of snobbish clubwomen try to appear learned. "A Compromise," which Maurine has labeled "University Shorts" and "Early Writing," is a heavy-handed criticism of private schools, perhaps an attempt to feel better about not having had a pampered upbringing.[31]

Her writing ability nearly got her in serious trouble when she befriended a girl who was on the verge of failing English. This student, whose name Maurine didn't remember, asked Maurine for help in writing her English assignments. Maurine took one of the assignment ideas and outlined it, showing the girl how to write it. The student handed it in just as Maurine had written it. Their teacher recognized it as Maurine's work, and the university's ethics committee called them both in. The girl cleared Maurine of any intentional wrongdoing but was expelled for cheating. Mary Phoenix remembered a vague rumor that Maurine had been expelled from the University of Utah for selling papers. The rumor may have been an exaggeration of this particular incident, for there is no record that Maurine's record was otherwise jeopardized.[32]

Also, during her senior year, Maurine did the student teaching required for her teaching degree, probably at Stewart Junior High, because she kept a copy of its undated eighth-grade paper that mentions her in an article. Because of her desire to rise above her own background, she felt determined to help her own students achieve more than they thought they could. She said she initiated a creative writing contest, felt that she had succeeded, and was proud of the good grade she received.

Two of her claims can be balanced with more objective information: being poor and being a social misfit. She certainly was not in affluent circumstances, but neither was she suffering actual privation. She consistently had part-time jobs as an undergraduate—which was neither unusual for a college student nor an unrealistic expectation from her parents. She sometimes added a second job at the university bookstore. Living with relatives doubtless was a significant savings. Furthermore, Charlie regularly sent her twenty dollars a month, a fact that she often omitted in presenting herself as a struggling student. She also formally borrowed money from him as well as taking out a student loan from the university. On 14 February 1927, the dean of women congratulated her on repaying her loan so rapidly, and Maurine recorded with obvious relief: "I have paid back all my debts except Papa's."[33]

She remembers how she just couldn't do enough in college. "It was all there, all available to me. It was hard not to sign up to do more than was possible." As a result, she would register for over-full, hectic schedules, fail to get enough sleep, and then fall ill with sinus and bronchitis infections.

A few hints suggest that her portrayal of her restricted social life was also exaggerated. Among her papers was a letter signed "George," apparently from a fellow employee at the bookstore. "They certainly love you and personally I am afraid I'll be soon in the same boat with them. Who knows?"[34]

Maurine blamed part of her social ineptitude on an almost pathological constraint in sexual matters, a trait that she sometimes lamented and sometimes flaunted. To one of her lovers, she wrote defiantly: "Most of the fellows I know think I'm queer when I won't be necked and seduced. I've been made fun of all my life because I wouldn't be pawed—in college they used to call me 'Old Frigidaire.'"[35] This restraint, she claimed, chilled a promising romance with "Jerry." He is probably the Gerald Irvine who is listed in the *Polk Directory*, 1925, as a lawyer in Salt Lake City and who wrote her a congratulatory letter after the publication of *The Giant Joshua*: "I have always had faith in you since our college days."

Maurine still speculated fifty years later, whether Jerry would have married her if she had been "smarter." She describes herself as "so naive and pure" that she would not allow Jerry to kiss her. Her own awkwardness was exacerbated by the protectiveness and Victorian prudery of Aunt Effie and Uncle Alma, with whom she said she was then living. "They kept the pressure on to so avoid the very semblance of being a bad girl that I was always very self-conscious when a young man brought me home." Maurine lamented more than once about how she had arranged matters so that Jerry agreed to take her to a fraternity party—a big occasion—which she called a date. (She made arrangements of this kind frequently, she confessed.) Afterwards, when he lingered in saying goodnight, she fended off a kiss. So instead, he gave her his fraternity handshake, a gesture with strong romantic implications. But that was the climactic moment of their relationship. Several years afterward she met him on the street, now married and a successful lawyer. He told her that, if she had let him kiss her instead of shaking hands, "that's all it would have taken."[36] Whatever the truth, he went down in her memory as another missed opportunity for marriage.

One college crush was so painful that Maurine refused to talk about it or identify the man involved. (I have assigned him the pseudonym of Rob Riley.) He was a pre-medical student. She admired him greatly but could only dream of a romance with him. He later became a doctor and lived in California. When I asked for more details about this individual, she shied sharply away and said she "could not remember." Pressured, she became agitated and said she "would not remember." And except for saying that she went to see him while in California and that he had been very unfriendly, she would not discuss him. Such an emphatic refusal to remember was a distinct signal that the episode was too painful to talk about. Russell Clark, who, as mentioned, had dated Maurine once at college, remembered this individual as a popular campus personality, handsome and talented. From a prominent Mormon family, he had a successful medical career, reared a fine family, and served in many Church positions. Clark also refused to disclose his surname.[37] This infatuation was emotionally devastating for Maurine. (See chap. 5.)

Maurine's social life, according to her recollections, continued to be a wasteland during her senior year. She went to the Junior Prom with "the homeliest boy who ever lived." Predictably, she wished she "had been nicer to him. He had wonderful manners and was probably a fine person—probably would have made a good husband. But I just wasn't too smart."

She never tried to pledge a social sorority (she belonged to the national honorary literary sorority) and explained with unalloyed bitterness that she was never rushed. "Oh my, no! You never tried to get *in*. They came after you. They took in only the top girls. They didn't ask other types like me. Once when I went to visit Aunt May Silver she said 'Oh, if my boy had lived, he was so popular on campus. He'd have helped you!' Maybe he would have helped, I don't know. I never had anyone to help me." Maurine keenly felt the lack of these kinds of connections.

When Maurine graduated from the University of Utah in June 1926, with honors[38] and a secondary teaching certificate, her father and mother came to Salt Lake City, bringing along one of Charlie's lady friends. Maurine was still annoyed about it at age eighty-seven, because this woman didn't want to stay for the graduation exercises. As a result, her only relative present was her mother's brother, Wilford Woodruff McAllister,[39] who taught private vocal and instrumental music lessons. He gave her a compact, the only graduation gift she remembered receiving.

On balance, Maurine's college years were probably generally positive. However, she remembered them as negative or, at best, as ambiguous. She never got over feeling like a naive, poverty-stricken country girl, ill prepared and poorly dressed. Bright enough to keep up with her peers academically, she concealed her uneasiness under a facade of self-assurance. As in high school, she was not contented with her academic success, and envied the privileged sorority girls. She relentlessly tormented herself with "what if's." Could she have fit in had she been born in their circumstances? What would life have been like had her grandfathers not gone to southern Utah? Not been polygamous? Would her father have been different? And if he had been affluent and had influential connections, wouldn't her life have been much better? She genuinely felt that she really was an aristocrat—a sensitive, creative artist trapped in hideously wrong circumstances.

Notes

[1] Maurine Whipple, "Confessions of a She Devil," ca. 1937, 34 pp. holograph, and 18 pp. typescript; Maurine Whipple Collection, L. Tom Perry Special Collections, Harold B. Lee Library, Brigham Young University, Provo, Utah, with photocopy in Maurine Whipple Collection, Archive, Val A. Browning Library, Dixie College, St. George, Utah. Documents in both collections hereafter cited as BYU, photocopy Dixie College. In this chapter, I quote consistently from the typescript.

[2] Warren Cox was born 4 July 1872 to Isaiah Cox and Elizabeth Ann Stout Cox and married Mary Etta Lee on 5 September 1894. He died 3 July 1954.

[3] Maurine later published an account, written with hyperbolic naiveté, of this trip with Mrs. Hartog, Maurine's first "close-up Gentile." Maurine's "innocents abroad" narrator calls her "Mrs. Warthog." Maurine Whipple, *This Is the Place, Utah* (New York: Alfred A. Knopf, 1945), 20–24.

[4] Whipple, "Confessions of a She Devil," 8.

[5] Annie Eliza Lutz Lenzi (born January 1879) was Hyrum's plural wife and bore him eight children. At that point, she was Hyrum's only legal wife; the first wife, Nancy Broadbent (married 29 December 1866, bore nine children) had died 11 January 1889 in Salt Lake City.

[6] Office of Transcripts and Verification, University of Utah, email message, 26 August 2002.

[7] Clare Watson Woodbury was born 19 March 1895, Parowan, Iron County, Utah, to Franklin Jeremiah Woodbury and Melissa Vivian Watson. He married Lola Andrus 24 June 1914. He took over his father's practice in St. George in 1923, then moved to Salt Lake City in 1930 where he had offices in the Medical Arts Building on Stratford Avenue. He went to Las Vegas in 1933 or 1934 and lived there for the rest of his life. Maurine saw him professionally in Salt Lake City and perhaps in Las Vegas as well.

[8] Interview with Maurine Whipple by Veda Hale, 1991.

[9] Ibid.

[10] Last page, not paginated, not titled, not dated, holograph: Whipple Collection, BYU; photocopy Dixie College.

[11] George was born 14 June 1898 and died 19 November 1966 at Provo. His wife, Thelma Lou Ruston, five years his junior, survived him and married Mitch Villanueva.

[12] Thelma Moss Villanueva, interviewed in St. George, 13 September 1993. Although Thelma was ninety, she remembered Maurine. When I asked if Maurine helped with the children or housework as compensation for the rent-free arrangement, Thelma laughed and said "No, Maurine was good at being too busy with other things." George and Gilbert were the sons of Annie's oldest sister, Jane McAllister Moss. Maurine also occasionally stayed with George when she was passing through Salt Lake City in future years. He lived at 67 South 1300 East, near the University of Utah.

[13] Florence Foremaster was born 21 January 1892 and died 23 August 1987 in St. George.

[14] Florence Whipple Jolley, "History of Florence Whipple Jolley," 5, January 1976, holograph, 15 pp.

[15] Ibid., 6.

[16] Jetta Snow ran a beauty shop, and was married to Delworth Snow. Pauline was still alive in 2001 and living in the St. George Care Center.

[17] At least three copies are included in Whipple Collection, BYU, with another holograph at Dixie College.

[18] Office of Transcripts and Verification, 26 August 2002.

[19] Katharine was born 25 February 1901 to Arthur F. Miles and Zaidee Walker Miles in St. George. She married A. Karl Larson, a noted historian from nearby Hurricane, and with him edited the diaries of her grandfather, Charles Lowell Walker. She died 3 July 1975.

[20] Ralph was an actor and Charles the manager. According to the 1925 and 1926 *Polk Directory*, they lived at the Hotel Utah.

[21] Katharine Miles, Letter to Maurine Whipple, [no date] 1927, Whipple Collection, BYU.

[22] Betty McPherson, interviewed in St. George, 1994 by Veda Hale. Betty's mother, who had retired to St. George, was LaVern Durfey.

[23] Maude May Babcock (1867–1954) was Utah's first lady of the theater and of physical education. She founded the University of Utah Departments of Speech and of Physical Education and personally produced more than 300 plays. She died 31 December 1954 after a long illness. *Utah History Encyclopedia*, http://www.media.utah.edu/uhe/b/Babcock,Maude.html (accessed September 2006).

[24] Maurine Whipple, Interviewed by Veda Hale, 1991.

[25] This story tells of an elderly woman who befriended a mentally retarded teenage girl. The old lady's anticipation at her son's Christmas gift turned to disappointment when it arrived—a dress totally unsuited to a woman of her age and obviously selected by her "modern" daughter-in-law. Sensing the woman's disappointment, the girl made a harrowing trip to the hospital to tell the doctor son what she thought and was killed in a traffic accident. A twenty-page typescript with all top left corners missing, retitled "Thou Shalt Love Thy Neighbor," is in the Whipple Collection, Perry Special Collections, BYU. Maurine made revisions on the *University Pen* published copy and offered it unsuccessfully to the *Improvement Era* in 1939. It was printed with these 1939 revisions and others she wished to make in *Sunstone*, December 1991.

[26] Maurine Whipple, "Mormon Saga," 26 pp. typescript; Whipple Collection, BYU; photocopy Dixie College. The red sunbonnet also appears in her "The Story of a Man's Life," 21 December 1924, written for English 111 (Expository Biography). The final draft is in a notebook labeled "University Composition Book for English lec. A. M. at 944 Lake Street," Whipple Collection, BYU; photocopy Dixie College. In "The Story of a Man's Life," the mother arrives with the original settlers in 1861. Though disappointed with the bleakness of the desert, she enthusiastically waves her red sunbonnet and leads the way triumphantly into the hot, dry valley.

[27] Whipple, "The Story of a Man's Life."

THE UNIVERSITY OF UTAH, 1922-26

28 Maurine Whipple, "The Divine Artist," ca. 1922–24, 8 pp., holograph; Whipple Collection, BYU; photocopy Dixie College. The top left corners of this manuscript are missing down about three inches. Maurine and I collaborated on a probable reconstruction.

29 Maurine Whipple, "A Characterization of Julia Foster," May 1926, English 107, Lesson I, Extension Division, University of Utah, holograph, Whipple Collection, BYU; photocopy Dixie College.

30 Untitled one-page holograph, Whipple Collection, BYU; photocopy at Dixie College.

31 Maurine Whipple, "Literary Club," and "A Compromise," both holograph, both in Whipple Collection, BYU; photocopies Dixie College.

32 Interview with Mary Phoenix by Veda Hale, 1992.

33 Lucy M. VanCott, Dean of Women, University of Utah, Letter to Maurine Whipple, 14 February 1927, inserted in Whipple, "My First Diary," Whipple Collection, BYU; photocopy Dixie College. Maurine was teaching high school English in Monroe, Utah. (See Chap. 4.) The notation about her debt to Charlie appears in her diary on 5 February 1927.

34 Maurine Whipple, Interviewed by Veda Hale, 1991.

35 Maurine Whipple, Letter to Rob Riley, n.d., ca. summer or fall 1936; holograph, Whipple Collection, BYU Library.

36 Maurine Whipple, Interviewed by Veda Hale 1991.

37 Russell Clark, Interviewed by Veda Hale, 1993.

38 Whipple, "Confessions of a She Devil," 11. Her diploma is not among her papers.

39 Wilford Woodruff McAllister was born 1 July 1882 and married Lucile Young about 1910.

❧ 4 ❧

IN AND OUT OF THE CLASSROOM, 1926–32

Fresh out of college and full of romantic dreams, Maurine desired to do great things but hoped her career would be combined with a husband, home, and children. She was hired in Monroe, Sevier County, in central Utah to teach high school English. She wanted to teach in St. George, in the high school division of Dixie Junior College.[1] She told me she thought she could have taught in St. George—that Juanita Brooks was leaving to work on a master's degree at Columbia and that she could have had her position teaching high school English and journalism.

In fact, this version of a possible past is a good example of Maurine's unreliability when fact meets memory. The widowed Juanita and her young son were living with Leland and Elsie Hafen in the corner house west of the Whipple home. Instead of leaving St. George, Juanita was actually returning. She had graduated from Brigham Young University in the spring of 1925 with a B.S. in food and nutrition. However, the mix of classes she took gave her enough English, speech, and debate to be hired to teach these subjects,[2] and she had accepted an offer from E. M. Jenson, president of LDS Church-owned Dixie College, to teach English and debate in its high school division. She would not leave for Columbia until September 1928.

Juanita thus had three advantages over Maurine, who graduated from the University of Utah a year later. Juanita was the widow of a man with an impeccable Mormon standing, she was struggling to raise her child, so aiding her was an act of charity, and she had a degree from a Church-owned institution, seemingly guaranteeing her orthodoxy. Maurine believed that the Mormon elites of St. George viewed the University of Utah as the

53

place where "good Mormon children lost their testimony." Had she lost hers? When I asked her, she shrugged and said she never thought about it much. "I guess I thought the Church was true. It was all I knew of religion. But when I finished college, I knew I was different. I knew, too, that I never was the kind of Mormon that people like Juanita were. Sometimes I resented that fact, resented my father for not helping me be that kind of Mormon. But, you know, you just have to be what you were born and raised to be, and I struggled long and hard trying to figure what that was." In any case, she saw another coveted prize (a teaching job in St. George) go to someone else and, being Maurine, took it personally instead of seeing it as a simple function of bad timing.

Another opportunity opened late in the hiring season. She didn't hear about it because E. M. Jenson, the Dixie College president, talked to Charlie instead of to her. Without consulting Maurine, Charlie decided that she should go to Monroe, where she had already accepted a teaching contract. He quickly made arrangements for her to leave with someone traveling to Monroe. When she found out what had happened, she was terribly upset, feeling that she could have been honorably released from the Monroe contract. Speculating on her father's motives many years later, Maurine thought he resented the community's disapproval of him and felt no inclination to accommodate local officials, although she grudgingly admitted that he might have also thought it would be good for her to be away from the family. Whatever the case, she was still voicing her anger at him in 1990–92.

For Maurine, Monroe was the unfortunate start of six bumpy years as a teacher. "If only I could have taught in St. George where people knew me," she lamented, "I would have been all right." Her regret and resentment festered for the rest of her life.

Three other things spoiled that first year of teaching. First, she was assigned to teach a rowdy class of junior boys whom she described as near delinquents and whom she allowed to establish an over-familiar relationship with her. Second, she bitterly resented how one of the young women teachers, Bernice Hughes, flirted with the principal and, she thought, got special favors. But perhaps most significantly, she had an intense, mostly one-sided, and very unhappy romance, a relationship that provided the model for a string of doomed love affairs for the next forty years.

The documentation for these events comes from her diary, the only one she ever kept. It began on 8 January 1927, five months into her first year of teaching, and ended 6 October 1927 at Georgetown, Idaho, a few weeks after the beginning of her second year of teaching. There are no entries for the summer. She used a "Poor Richard School Series" composition book. She titled it "Diary," adding a subtitle in parentheses: "My First Romance."

The diary is frank, hopeful, and dream spangled. From it emerges an image of Maurine as socially immature, trying hard to understand herself, struggling to get her professional feet under her, embroiled in social interactions she didn't understand, and frightened, at age twenty-three, of possible spinsterhood. Unintentionally, it also reveals her unselfishness, her compassion, her great vulnerability, and her courage in acknowledging her faults. The handwriting is neat and very legible, her spelling and punctuation good. She also pasted or inserted letters, cards, and notes from correspondents. Those before 8 January help set the stage for the times covered by the diary. A small photograph (2x2") of Maurine and Hyrum Lee, the object of her ardent dreams, is glued on the top left corner of the first page.

The first of the inserted letters, dated 31 August 1926, is from Utah's Superintendent of Public Instruction. It acknowledged that she had conscientiously called to his attention that she had not yet finished a university correspondence course, even though the University of Utah had issued her the diploma. The writer commended her honesty and explained that the department was satisfied with her credentials because the university had issued her diploma.[3]

As this preserved correspondence shows, Maurine heard fairly regularly from her mother, Annie, and sister Florence. Hints about Maurine's difficulties gleam in their sympathetic mentions. On 4 September 1926, when Maurine was in Salt Lake City (reason unknown, probably something to do with her health), Annie encouraged: "I believe now after you get those wisdom teeth out and get rid of the infection you are going to be all right." She also passed on the news that brother Ray and some friends had formed a theater troupe, which they took to Mesquite, hoping to make money. Ray "was going to the U next winter. Papa said he will help. Ralph says he won't go to school anymore."[4]

Although Annie does not mention a visit home from Maurine, her next letter, dated 3 October 1926, came after Maurine had been to St. George, gone on to Monroe, and begun teaching. Annie was "glad that Maurine's last letter was a little more encouraging." On 29 October 1926, Annie again wrote, reporting how happy Maurine's letter had made the family and how they all "vied with each other to read it." Maurine's experiences as a novice teacher had apparently lost no color in her recital of them, for Annie sympathized with how hard she was working and added that Katharine Miles, who was teaching English in St. George, had loyally said she thought Maurine should be paid more for all the extra work. Annie may not have suspected that Maurine made a point of complaining regularly about her teaching, for she added supportively on 19 January 1927 that Maurine "should tell them that she had too much to do and *demand* an assistant."

A little family news also pops up in the letters. Fourteen-year-old sister Florence, writing on 1 December 1926, attributed her good grades from a Miss Musser to being Maurine's sister and enthused, "I'm sure lucky to be your sister!" She also mentions a family ride in Charlie's "new car" to nearby Bloomington after "a splendiferous Thanksgiving." Touchingly, she also assures Maurine that Maurine's friend Ruby Bryner had been doing Florence's crippled foot a "world of good" with her physical therapy.[5]

A second letter from Florence, written 18 January 1927, describes an oil well that had just been drilled near St. George. "It lacks 6 feet of being as high as the tabernacle." The next year, Maurine would use oil speculation as an element in "Beaver Dam Wash," the novella that launched her literary career.

Ironically, only two letters from Hyrum Lee,[6] the object of Maurine's adoration, have survived; but she records with quivering intensity many encounters with him in this brief diary. Hy clerked at the Monroe Drug Store, owned by his stepfather, Harry Shepard Bell. The drugstore was a popular gathering place for the town's young people; and twenty-one-year-old Hy, popular and easy-mannered, was well integrated into the life of the community. He had been Monroe High School's student body president and a football star. It was well-known that his high school sweetheart was Flaral Josephine Christensen, a year his junior, who was bussed fifteen miles with the other students from her home town of Elsinore to high school in Monroe. She had served as high school vice president during Hy's term of office.

Maurine's one-sided, well-documented romance with Hy Lee is significant for two reasons. First, it is documented as it occurred, instead of being reconstructed in romantic but not-always-accurate anguish after the fact. Second, it shows a pattern of dealing with men that Maurine employed for her whole life despite its uniform lack of success. When a man she found attractive showed interest in her, all of her romantic sensibilities flared into blazing life. She became obsessed, unleashed her hopes, dreamed unchecked of a future of rosy domesticity, lavished unstinting adoration upon the object of her affection, willingly remade herself in the image she thought he desired, and was, in short, willing to do anything but allow the relationship space in which to develop naturally and slowly. The man in question, however much he may have initially been attracted by (and taken advantage of) Maurine's reasonably good looks, flattering adoration, and eager willingness, rapidly reconsidered. His second reactions obviously include feeling smothered by her worship, fearful of her relentless haunting, manipulated by her attempts to fascinate him, and ultimately bored by her attempts to engage his pity with her suffering. Since Maurine usually did not abandon a relationship unless the man either rebuffed her with direct brutality or literally fled from her, most of these men probably ended up feeling angry and guilty that they had been obliged to behave in an ungentlemanly way, thereby slamming the door on the possibility of a cooler, slower-paced, and more satisfactory friendship. In short, Maurine in love recklessly flung gasoline on the flames, then nursed the resulting scars and ashes from the explosion until another relationship tempted her to try her luck again. This pattern or portions of it were apparent in at least five relationships between 1926 and 1950.

Maurine's diary shows that Hy did, in fact, flirt with her and make the first declarations of affection; but her heedless, headlong response forced him into a retreat. Flaral was the ultimate benefactor of Maurine's aggressiveness, showing up to smooth Hy's pillow while he recuperated from an operation for appendicitis. They were married 20 June 1928 in the Manti Temple. Hy gave up his plans for college and settled down with Flaral as a well-respected businessman. He managed the ZCMI in Glenwood, some thirty miles from Monroe, for a year. It closed because of the Great Depression, as did his next store, the St. George ZCMI, which he managed until 1930. He opened a women's ready-to-wear, "Lee's Style Shop," on Main Street in St. George less than two blocks from the Whipple home. Maurine had to pass it often. It must have been a painful reminder of her lost love. In 1935 Hy moved to Beaver and operated a pharmacy. For a time he managed both stores, plus another he established in Milford; but the Depression forced the closure of all but the Beaver store. The gregarious Hyrum was active in politics and community affairs. In this he took after his relative, Utah's popular governor, J. Bracken Lee. He served on the city council, as county commissioner, and twice as state representative (1944, 1971). Hy and Flaral had three sons.[7]

Maurine talked readily to me about most of the "swell suffering" she had experienced, but she would not talk about Hyrum Lee. When I unearthed the diary in 1991, she refused to read it, claiming simultaneously that it was the most difficult time of her life up to that time and also that Hyrum Lee wasn't very important. Her diary belies this dismissiveness. The romantic losses that Maurine regretted with undiluted bitterness were the two or three men who occupied the social and intellectual sphere she longed for but never could move into comfortably; and despite Hy's "roughness," he was a solid citizen who could have given her a secure and respectable position.

During spring break the first week in March, Maurine retreated to St. George's sunshine where the apricots were just blooming and where she had the appreciation of her family. It restored her vivacity and good spirits. She returned to Monroe in an all-night snowstorm, resolved to endure to the end of the school year and seek another position. Whatever lingering hopes she may have entertained for her relationship with Hy were dashed when he kissed Bernice Hughes in front of her and then refused Maurine's invitation to attend the Senior Banquet. Drearily she wrote on 5 April: "Five more weeks and then I'll never, never see him again. I wish it was here now so that I could start to forget."

The steadily souring relationship with fellow teacher, Bernice Hughes, had also worn on her nerves, but the real discouragement was being fired. "Mr. White glibly explained that they are going to put a man in head of the department," she recorded. The principal may have justifiably felt that the boys needed stronger discipline than Maurine was providing; and the convention of giving preference to men, as the heads of families, had been strongly reinforced by Depression rates of unemployment. "I have failed as a teacher, I guess," she wrote unhappily on 1 May 1927. White refused to give her a letter of recommendation, thus making it impossible for her to teach in Utah.

As an inexperienced teacher, she was no doubt trying to find a personal style that felt comfortable but unfortunately opted for a "one of the gang" approach that did nothing to discourage over-familiarity. For instance, she recorded in her diary that she bet three of these students five pounds of chocolates apiece that they wouldn't be able to earn B's or better. One of the three won, and Maurine distributed the candy to the class. The students gave her a "peanut bust" (a bag of peanuts was shared in honor of a chosen person) to celebrate her birthday in January. In February she recorded that four of these boys had started coming into her study period and teasing her. She "fought off" one boy who was trying to kiss her. "I have bawled them out properly, though," she wrote in her diary, "and I believe they'll behave now. I can't afford to lose my professional reputation over a few boys." The situation apparently got no better. Without explanation, in early April she recorded: "I have given up the sophomore boys definitely to Mr. White, in English." Since she has mentioned difficulty only with the junior boys, the dimensions of this particular problem are not clear; but almost certainly her principal would not have been pleased with her lack of conventional discipline.

Apparently she received only one observation visit. In January, her diary tells about Superintendent Ashman and Principal White attending her sophomore English class. The students, whom she characterized as the "dullest, deadest bunch," were not very interested in her exposition of *Enoch Arden* by Alfred, Lord Tennyson. It is a poem of unconditional and unrequited love, separation, isolation, and eternal longing. Maurine would almost certainly have been fascinated by such a tale, but it would, for that very reason, have held no charms for a crowd of teenage boys. Maurine came out of the experience feeling inconsolable. Ashman and White "listened very patiently and then spent about half an hour criticizing me unfavorably. There wasn't one redeeming feature, evidently, to my work."

One thing Maurine did not mention in her diary was teaching some dance classes. A woman who attended junior high in Elsinore recalled that Maurine came there to teach dancing in the school gym. Apparently Maurine here began what was to become a pattern of organizing dance classes to earn a little extra money in whatever community she lived.[8]

The undated rough draft of a play also shows that Maurine tried to turn some of her Monroe experience into literature. The protagonist, a young teacher, struggles against the principal's favoritism for another young flirtatious teacher; the play ends with the protagonist being vindicated and understood. While writing this draft may have been therapeutic for Maurine in dealing with her feelings about Bernice Hughes, it contains no hint of a romance with a Hy Lee figure.[9]

Bruised from this bad experience in Monroe, Maurine must have looked forward to the summer in St. George. Instead, it turned out to be full of drama, embroiling her in the heartaches of her family. Matters were in crisis because of her father's flagrant affair with Hilda (Maurine requested that I withhold her surname), the daughter of a Swiss family in a nearby village. Annie was so depressed that her McAllister relatives arranged for her to visit her half-sister Julia May Nielson McAllister Silver in Salt Lake City. Despite the difference in their ages, the two half-sisters had been close as youngsters according to Maurine. May was the daughter of Matilda Nielson, J.D.T. McAllister's seventh wife, and had lived with Cornelia, Annie's mother, when she was young.

Maurine and Ralph, who turned twenty-one that summer, were very concerned about the family dysfunction and determined to talk to Hilda. Maurine wrote that Charlie's sister (unnamed) "found out about my father's latest affair with a woman and shamelessly convinced me it was my duty to stop it. I was scared to death and woefully young, but it never occurred to me to shirk a duty. So I traced down the girl, got hold of an incriminating letter, faced my father with it—and went out and vomited for two hours. I've always carried other people's burdens. My parents always seemed like my children to me."[10]

A third version from her "Confessions of a She Devil" includes this allusion: "The next summer I went to the University of California at Los Angeles. There I was offered a marvelous opportunity but had to go home again." What was that "marvelous opportunity"? "Confessions" has no details, and she couldn't remember when I asked her in 1991. "Confessions" continues: "I found my mother in a mental collapse, my father the self-confessed parent of his latest girl-friend's child recently born in the town hospital and a town posse on its way to lynch him." (When I read this story to Maurine in 1991, asking what part was factual, she said to cross out "a town posse on its way to lynch him" and substitute "was gossiping.")

Possibly during this crisis, Charlie did pack his things and leave. But Maurine told me that "he drove around the block and then came back, saying he wasn't going to take the coward's way out, that he was going to stay and fight the talk."[11] She regretted that family counseling hadn't been available in the 1920s, believing that her father might have accepted it at that moment.

Maurine made only one entry in her diary about that summer, writing on the last page of her diary, 6 October 1927:

> I have prospects of being able to help my mother to happiness (which, I am afraid, will never be complete again) and my two brothers to college. Only a bit of money would make them all so happy, but all my education has not made me a financial wizard—yet.
>
> If I could only patch our family troubles up. Papa's affair with Hilda in all its sordid tragedy and the nightmare weeks last summer when I feared for mamma's sanity have left me rather moody. Even if mamma would forgive his sin . . . they could never be happy because he cannot see religion as she can, and he has hurt her too many times for her to take him back unless he puts on his garments and joins in family prayers and all the rest of it. At first I was too dazed to think but now I am becoming reconciled to even that.

Despite Maurine's sympathies with her betrayed and humiliated mother, she did not accept uncritically traditional standards of sexual morality, including Mormonism's strict rules. Perhaps because the Mormon script of female chastity had not produced the desired results for Annie (and Maurine may have begun to suspect that it would not work for her either), she was appraising alternatives in men's and women's roles. Although she despised Bernice Hughes, the fact remained that Bernice got favors from her boss, kisses from Hyrum Lee, and marriage to a respected man while Maurine got a stony dismissal without a recommendation, a humiliatingly public rejection from Hy, and no marriage. Yes, Charlie was unfaithful and unfair to Annie; but if Annie had failed to meet his needs for sex and affection by not being a "real" woman, didn't that help explain his transgressions—perhaps even excuse them? What she seemed to resent so deeply was the shattering discord in her home. And for that, she blamed Annie as much as Charlie.

Psychologically, on at least some level, Maurine seems to have transferred her resentment to the Church, perhaps in a superhuman effort to retain love for her father. She felt bitter about Mormon teachings that simultaneously contributed to Annie's puritanical attitudes and, probably, to Charlie's acceptance of psychological polygamy to justify his thinking that he needed more than one woman. This reaction manifests itself most clearly in 1967 when Charlie was a tottering eighty-nine years old and decided he wanted to be rebaptized and have his priesthood and temple sealing restored. Maurine wrote an eloquent and perhaps not strictly accurate letter to the Church's First Presidency, then consisting of David O. McKay, Stephen L Richards and J. Reuben Clark. This letter may have remained a draft, never finished and never mailed, even though it reads like a complete document. I have not found any documentary evidence that Charlie had been reinstated.[12] She wrote, defending her father: "Sometimes leaders of the church make mistakes, since they, also, are human beings. The thing that happened to my father was done hastily, without investigation and was in some respects an outgrowth of personal malice. . . . The fact that my father lived out his life honestly, and with good-heartedness all these years and without bitterness against those who had served him so badly, is something of which I am proud. But this kind of life comes about not because of the community, but in spite of it." It was her opinion that "my father doesn't need forgiving by this community—But the community needs forgiving by him! If you would judge—first understand."[13]

Undoubtedly Maurine wished she had been more understanding and forgiving as a young woman, but her feelings about her father were continually conflicted. Although she often expressed disgust, disappointment, and even outright dislike for him, she would instantly fly to his defense if she felt he was being attacked. "That's just the way men are," she'd say in justification. "And my father had been raised with the idea that women should be out to please him. He was a good man. He just didn't know how to express himself." It is true that Charlie was a good man in many ways. He was an honest, conscientious businessman, kind and helpful to many people and dearly beloved by his grandchildren. For all his unhappiness in marriage, he did not abandon his wife and children.

It also seems reasonable that some of Maurine's tolerance for Charlie's indiscretions came from her own infatuation with Dr. Clare Woodbury. Although Maurine may have persistently told others that she was interested only in a diagnosis and cure and had fended off advances from Woodbury, it seems reasonable to ascribe the restraint to Woodbury, not Maurine

Complicating Annie's and Charlie's problems during that tension-fraught summer, Maurine needed to make a career decision. Smarting from her rejection in Monroe, she cast about for something to do besides teach school, but Charlie would have none of it. He saw teaching as a suitable profession for an unmarried woman. Furthermore, her college education had been expensive and she had not taught long enough to get any kind of return for it.

Unable to teach in Utah because of White's refusal to give her a letter of recommendation, she obtained a contract to teach high school English and drama in Georgetown, Idaho, just across the Utah border in Bear Lake County. But despite her high hopes, working in Georgetown, a community of about 500, halfway between Soda Springs and Montpelier, produced a second bad teaching experience.

In recalling that year Maurine complained about the citizens' hygiene: "50 degrees below in the winter, a place where children were sewed into their winter underwear, no sanitary understanding, many living in a half-human way." Maurine's scorn probably reflects her level of maturity more than actual conditions. It is doubtful if Georgetown was any more "backward" than St. George.

In a disastrous continuation of her teaching experience in Monroe, Maurine immediately got off on the wrong foot with Walter E. Clark. She claimed that Clark did not have a college degree and was suspicious of anyone who did, fearing for his job. In this, she was mistaken. Lewis Munk, who became an English teacher at Montpelier High School with a legendary reputation for teaching excellent writing to his students, explained that Walter Clark was the first man from Georgetown to be college-educated, a rare achievement for a teacher then. He had also assumed a man's job in supporting his family when he was only a boy. Where Maurine saw pomposity, Lewis Munk saw "self-confidence." He conceded, however, that, despite willing and effective service on community tasks that no one else wanted, coupled with great generosity with his means, Clark and his family had never "learned how to get along with other people" and "were never very popular with other members of the village."[14] Thus, Maurine's opinion of Clark as being stern and cold might have been justified from her viewpoint.

Maurine claimed, with unabated bitterness in 1991: "He never had, or long ago gave up, any idealistic dreams of bettering those poor people. It was lack-luster teaching he preferred." (Munk termed this characterization "ridiculous.") It is easy to see Maurine as role-playing the victim—once again casting herself as the idealistic teacher throwing herself futilely against a harsh and repressive status quo. The reality is probably that her terrible thirst to make a difference, exacerbated by her lack of tact and experience, put her on a collision course with Walter E. Clark as it had with C. A. White.

Lewis Munk, a student at Brigham Young University at the time, remembers from visits home that Maurine was a lively and entertaining teacher. When he and his date rode to a winter basketball game in the same

IN AND OUT OF THE CLASSROOM, 1926–32

Maurine strikes a puckish pose, her arms akimbo framing the faces of two students, Mildred Munk (Jensen), Lewis's younger sister, on the left, and Lucille Bacon. Maurine was their drama teacher. Photo courtesy of Karen Jensen.

sleigh as Maurine, Maurine vivaciously and wittily monopolized the conversation "to the point that my date was pretty upset." Munk admired Maurine's writing and called her "brilliant."[15]

Maurine boarded with Agnes and Jess McCammon,[16] a couple she called "just plain good." They obviously reciprocated her affection. She shared a bed with the children, which kept her physically warm during the subzero Idaho nights and which probably also consoled her for the absence of her own brothers and sister. She remembered with relish eating hot cereal in the mornings with real cream—a luxury unknown in her own family. Maurine stayed in touch with this family for years, letting them know whenever she published something and receiving news from Agnes or Jess about the family and town. It might have been her first close experience with a healthy family, and she never tired of telling how much she enjoyed living with them.

Roland Bee of Escalante, Utah, another of Maurine's students in Georgetown, liked her very much, enough to attend her funeral in St. George in 1992, where I interviewed him. He recalled: "She had red hair, was lively, and danced well. She took our class on a sleigh to an open house the railroad was having. We got to ride on the turn table." He was impressed when a traveler showed up with a bouquet of roses from Maurine's mother in March when there was still three feet of snow in Georgetown. He agreed that Maurine "pushed hard to get things done." Once when Maurine needed lights for a pageant, the school authorities "said they didn't know how to get them, so Maurine hitchhiked to Montpelier, Idaho, and borrowed them from J.C. Penney's." He also remembered how Maurine hated the cold. "And it was cold! Sometimes 20 below in daytime, 44 below night—so cold a new gun wouldn't fire."

Maurine always claimed that she and youngsters "clicked" if she were allowed to be herself. From the evidence, it sounds as if she was right.

Despite Maurine's heavy teaching schedule, she found time to write at least one short story of unrelieved pathos, "The Lord Giveth," and a slightly longer version with the same title and plot.[17] The first-person narrator, a teacher, is enchanted with one of her students, Zelda, apparently about age eight or nine. This child's love for learning and winning personality make her "a ray of sunlight in the otherwise gloomy circumstances of the primitive school." When she becomes ill, the family is too poor to provide any treatment except prayer. The teacher swoops in, insisting, "My money will pay for a doctor." But it is too late; the doctor she brings is unable to do anything except watch with the rest of them as Zelda dies.

In the only fall entry in her diary, on 6 October 1927, she wrote: "My appendicitis operation—still a surprise to me—must come off soon by the 'feel' of my side." Obviously Ralph's summer appendectomy had alerted her to the symptoms.[18] In January 1928, she turned twenty-five; and in early February 1928, the operation was performed at the Pocatello hospital. Arrangements to recuperate with a local family, whom she did not know, made her uncomfortable and she moved to a local hotel where she wrote much of her novella, "Beaver Dam Wash." It is an expansion of a short story, "Quicksand," published by the University of Utah's literary magazine, *Pen*, in June 1926.

Although the final typescript has not survived, various synopses generally resemble each other. Probably influenced by the unrelentingly naturalistic school of Theodore Dreiser and Frank Norris, this tale with its heavy-handed symbol of the quicksand has as its protagonist Bill Graham, a good-natured fat man, who is easily kept happy by his dream of bringing in an oil well that will make him rich and turn Beaver Dam into a boom town, friends who admire his dream, and hard-boiled eggs for breakfast. Because of his honesty and good will, the locals respect him and cooperate with him. But his wife, who had married him hoping for affluence, holds herself aloof and tries to shield her teenage son and daughter from contact with the local people.

Although Maurine describes herself as having friends in Georgetown, there was little possibility for romance, at least not with the kind of man she wanted. In her sole diary entry that fall, she speculates frankly about the candidates. Rulon Beach Lindsay (1903–64), "a medic," is the most appealing: "I imagine I could like Rulon. But everything in the winter is still in the budding stage." The second, Ray Reeves, was apparently not local, for he "suddenly appeared on the scene last spring but, although I like him and he would mean legitimate escape, I could not marry him. I will never get married I fear. But I am quite content." This last sentence is best described as gallant self-deception, but the sentence preceding it turned out to be an accurate prediction—except for a four-month marriage that she never referred to again after divorcing her husband. (See chap. 5.) Elaborating on her "contentment," she mused philosophically: "Do I think of Hy? Every day of my life. But 'parting is such sweet sorrow'[19]—and I am at peace, comparatively. As long as there is no wild joy of loving and being loved there can be no sorrow of parting. I would like the experience of wifehood and motherhood, but I believe I'd rather forego it than accept it in a half-hearted fashion. I'm afraid there will never be any more Hy's for me."

Again, Maurine's school year ended on a discouraging note. Clark did not offer a contract for another year and, like White, refused to give her a letter of recommendation.[20] Maurine thought he was threatened by her abilities and personality. More likely their personalities were simply incompatible. Several teachers, she said, tried to convince her to stay in Idaho, and a superintendent from a neighboring county offered to hire her to teach eighth grade. However, Maurine had had enough of Idaho.

Despite her two negative experiences, Maurine believed things would go well if she could teach where people knew her. Hoping to work into a position at Dixie High School, she spent the first few months of the 1928–29 school year working part-time there for thirty dollars a month. She seems to have been a teacher's aide, helping with an English class and supervising a typing class. For her personal pleasure, she took vocal and piano lessons and entered heartily into the social life of the town's young people, perhaps because she found them less judgmental than the adults, perhaps because she was trying to hang on to her youth. A glimpse of her year comes from an enthusiastic letter to her twenty-four-year-old brother Ray, who was in Bakersfield, California, staying with their father's sister, Aunt Leah Whipple Rance, and searching for work. She encouraged Ray to come home and participate in a sort of unnamed work-study program, details unknown. Then she teased: "Everything's so *darned* much fun this year. Come on home.... Wish I could enclose a check." Maurine also describes the creation of a locally made movie: "A regular story with local actors: Evelyn Harris, Nita Seegmiller, Lollie Orton, Alton Fordham, Myles Judd, Milt Walker, and many others. Myles and I did the heavy work. The fellow shot the final fadeout in front of Foster's, with an audience that wasn't at all tactful. Maybe you don't think it wasn't hot!"[21]

The cameraman/director of this silent movie had a straightforward economic interest, which was to get paid to promote Charlie's Electric

Theater. Maurine said he promised the town would love it, and they did. Maurine, with her dramatic flair, did not need to be coaxed to participate.

Also during the summer of 1928, Charlie let Maurine stage plays in the Electric Theater. "She was talented and had something special about her," remembered Arlo Prisbrey, who attended some of these productions. "There wasn't money to be made. She just did it to help provide some fun for the community."[22] Maurine's good friend Evelyn Harris was the lead in a three-act play that Maurine wrote. The script has not survived, and Evelyn remembered the plot only vaguely "as a melodrama with heroines and villains. Maurine went the extra mile and borrowed an authentic old dress for me to wear."[23] She also remembered that Maurine asked local singers to perform between acts.

Restlessly Maurine wanted to find something besides teaching, but again Charlie insisted that she stick with education. She persuaded A. J. Ashman, the Sevier County superintendent of schools, to investigate her situation in Monroe and provide her with a recommendation so that she could be hired to teach full-time in Utah. In "Confessions of a She Devil," she admitted her fear: "What if I might never attain to the 'higher life?' I clutched frantically at youth and fun forever passing me by. My college years had been like a long, dark tunnel with a light at the end. Now there wasn't even a light."[24]

After Thanksgiving 1928, the school at Virgin, Utah, in Washington County had enough students to qualify for another teacher; so for the rest of the 1928–29 school year, Maurine lived thirty-one miles north and east, near Zion National Park, and taught a combined fourth-fifth grade, a departure from her training in junior high or high school. Nellie McArthur (later Gubler) taught the first three grades while Carl Fenton Workman, also the principal, taught sixth grade. Workman (1907–32) was four years Maurine's junior. Conditions were primitive. There was no electricity or indoor plumbing. Nellie remembered that "one of the steps leading to the school's second floor had a big hole in it that we were always afraid some student would fall through."[25]

Nellie was engaged to Emil Gubler in her hometown of Santa Clara and usually went home every weekend. She described the working relationship among the three teachers as pleasant and cordial. "We all boarded at the Cornelius Hotel ($25 a month) across the street from the school, usually spent our evenings together, and often gathered around to enjoy Carl's phonograph records or to sing, accompanied by Maurine on the banjo and Carl on the guitar or chording on the piano. We all three worked energetically on the programs and plays and not only engaged the students but supplied a large share of the community's entertainment."[26]

IN AND OUT OF THE CLASSROOM, 1926–32

During these months, Maurine told me, she often felt "melancholy, . . . buried in obscurity with my dreams slipping through my grasp." She also spent much time sitting by the Virgin River, "brooding about life." Perhaps it was also the time when the river assumed the character that she assigned it in *The Giant Joshua*—remorseless and indifferent to human needs and struggles.

Still, in retrospect, this year was her best—and only positive—teaching experience. Maurine was free to do what she liked and probably could have stayed on for the 1928–29 school year. Nellie was offered a contract (she declined because of her forthcoming marriage) and thought Maurine must have received a similar offer. "I didn't remember any reason that she wouldn't have been and certainly the students liked her." Young Carl Workman didn't come back either, but she didn't know why.[27]

Discouraged about teaching, Maurine struck out that summer in a new direction. She told me that she went to California to study dramatics, tap dancing, and directing recreational projects, which were beginning to be funded under federal relief programs. It is not clear how long she was in Los Angeles, living with a Mrs. Pike, who was a friend of her Grandmother McAllister. Maurine made the acquaintance of a congenial sister and a brother (she could not remember their names) with whom she spent some "wonderful days at the beach," one of the few times, she claimed, that she "relaxed and had fun." She felt, perhaps optimistically, that the brother, who was in dental school, would have asked her to marry him; but "Mother would lie on the bed and repeat my name over and over. 'Come home, Maurine. I need you.' I would hear it in my head until I couldn't stand it anymore and finally packed up and went back to St. George." She discovered that Annie had, in fact, been mentally calling her home, but things were about the same as when she left—not good but hardly a crisis either.

Maurine did not record the Great Depression's impact on her family; but Florence, who turned seventeen five months before the stock market crashed in October 1929, recorded in her autobiography: "It was a terrible time all over the nation—many banks closed and an untold number of people lost thousands of dollars. I remember my father and my brother Ralph had money in a savings and loan company in Salt Lake and they lost all or most of it." She also told how broken-hearted she felt when she didn't think her parents could afford the money to pay the tuition her senior year (1929–30). Then when it was almost too late to register, her father gave her six $5.00 gold pieces he had saved as "collector pieces."[28]

During the summer of 1930, Maurine ventured further into community recreation. Among her papers is a professionally printed program on expensive paper announcing "The Dance as Interpreted by Students of Maurine Whipple, Richfield, Utah" on 17–19 August 1930. Maurine claimed not to remember any details about this summer, commenting only, "I guess if you have that program I was there in Richfield. I was always going from pillar to post in those days."

In 1930, twenty-five-year-old Ralph, also not married, was still working with Charlie in the lumber business. He had a motorcycle and, Maurine said, drove very recklessly. Despite her sympathy, she does not seem to have had much insight into his private torments. He had begun to drink excessively.

Twenty-two-year-old Ray was attending the University of Utah that fall with encouragement and some financial help from Maurine, who yearned to see him capitalize on his dramatic and musical abilities. She considered him the most talented member of the family. As a sophomore, he had the lead in an important play; but "it just never meant as much to him as it did to me." Ray left the university after three and a half years, perhaps because of financial difficulties. According to his daughter, he was just three months short of graduation, lacking only his student teaching to obtain a teaching certificate. He used his drama talent in St. George productions of various kinds, played in several dance bands, and taught himself to play the electric guitar, to the delight of his children. His "long and happy musical career" ended when he lost a finger in an accident at the lumberyard where he first worked for Charlie in the family business but eventually bought Charlie out.[29]

In August 1930, twenty-seven-year-old Maurine, with what must have been great relief during depression times, signed a contract to teach English, dramatics, and physical education in Heber City, Wasatch County, about thirty miles east of Salt Lake City. Her salary was $1,300.[30] Among her genuine achievements, noted in the yearbook, she directed two plays, one of which took second place and another third place in county competition. But once again, Maurine alienated her principal. She described proposing some recreational and cultural activities for the girls, only to be told that school did not have adequate facilities. So on her own she identified a storage room that could be used, found other places for the stored items, and planned a play to raise money for equipment. The principal, J. William Bond, as she said, "resented it and made things miserable for me." She disregarded him and pushed ahead with the play, taking the female lead while the men's coach, whom she didn't like because she claimed he "was lazy," took the male lead. She felt that he tried to develop a romance between them but, rather uncharacteristically, she flatly rejected his advances and refused to spend any time with him after the play was finished. This coach wrote candidly in her yearbook at the end of school: "I hope in the years to come you will look back at your experience in Heber as pleasurable and educational. I can't yet understand why things have been like they have this year. Maybe we'll never know. I am surely glad I have had the chance to meet you and I do hope we will always be friends even though we may not be in the same locality. Yours for a good time, a happy life and a great big brutal boyfriend. Coach Fred Frosty Richards B.S. BYU 1927 Biology, Phys Ed. Athletics."

The play was successful in raising the money to start the P.E. program she wanted. The students appreciated it, but the principal did not. Maurine must have hoped that, despite the problems, she would be offered a teaching contract for the next year (1931–32). She felt immense pressure to aid her family financially and not add to its burdens; but once again, the same scenario played itself out: no contract and no letter of recommendation.

Virtually every margin of her copy of the yearbook was filled with messages from the students. Many of them lamented that she would not return the next year. A repeated theme was that she was a "good sport." Others apologized for not "dressing" for gym, said they "had learned a lot," thanked her for help with personal problems, and even said "she had been the best teacher they'd ever had."

Maurine admitted to me that she often "chummed" with the students, finding it easier to make friends with them than with the other teachers. This inability to establish close relationships with her age and professional peers reveals that her personal insecurities had not diminished with the years nor had her social skills improved.

Maurine did not return to St. George for the summer of 1931. Instead, she was in Salt Lake City, working as a summer playground recreation director. She asked Florence to come "play the piano for the dancing classes," and the two sisters boarded at the Beehive House, sleeping on the large open-air porch on the second story and entertaining visitors "in the big front parlor" where they gathered around the piano for singing. They also attended some of the plays presented at the Salt Lake Theatre.[31] After a couple of months, Florence returned to St. George, where she married Ben Jolley at the Whipple home on 8 August 1931.[32]

Maurine returned to the University of Utah in the fall of 1931 with Ray, took some physical education, speech, and education classes, and continued working with the city's recreation department where she could use her drama and dance talents. She was twenty-eight, still self-conscious about her appearance and clothes. Her photograph in the Heber High yearbook (1930–31) shows her as slim with medium-length thick hair, which she said she hennaed to an attractive shade of red, and clear-skinned. Petite and graceful, she was a good dancer and outgoing, but something about her discouraged close relationships with the kind of young men she would tolerate, and prevented her from fitting in smoothly with the principals and faculties of the schools where she taught. Even she could tell that her career as a teacher was going nowhere.

Notes

[1] In 1923, the LDS Church, which owned the former Dixie Academy (by now called Dixie High School), changed its name to Dixie Junior College and dropped the first two years of high school.

[2] Levi S. Peterson, *Juanita Brooks: Mormon Woman Historian* (Salt Lake City: University of Utah Press, 1988), 68.

[3] A. E. Matheson, Assistant Superintendent, Utah Department of Public Instruction, Letter to Maurine Whipple; Maurine Whipple Collection, L. Tom Perry Special Collections, Harold B. Lee Library, Brigham Young University, Provo, Utah, with photocopy in Maurine Whipple Collection, Archive, Val A. Browning Library, Dixie College, St. George, Utah. Documents in both collections hereafter cited as BYU, photocopy Dixie College.

[4] Annie McAllister Whipple, Letter to Maurine Whipple, inserted in Maurine Whipple, "My First Diary," 4 September 1926.

[5] Ruby Bryner was born 21 July 1900. She married Bliss Lamayne Finlayson, 3 June 1931. Ruby taught dramatic arts, physical education, and English in St. George.

[6] Hyrum Levi Lee was born 3 March 1905, the second of the seven children of Arthur Edwin Lee (born 20 December 1887, Marysville, Piute County, Utah), and Bertha Josephine Anderson Lee (born 8 May 1886, Monroe, Utah). Hy's father died 16 March 1818 when Hy was thirteen. When Hy was seventeen, his mother married Harry Shepard Bell. Hyrum graduated from high school in 1925 at age twenty, possibly because Utah's public schools were closed for much of 1918 because of the influenza pandemic.

[7] Merrill Christensen Lee, interviewed by Veda Hale 25 October 2000 at Merrill's home 360 North 100 East, Beaver, Utah. Notes in my possession.

[8] Maurine R. Gould, interviewed by Hyrum Ipson, 7 August 2000, Monroe, Utah, letter reporting his findings in my possession. Maurine always claimed that she taught herself to dance, learning some of the steps through a correspondence course.

[9] Maurine Whipple, "The Humanizing of Mona," n.d., 4 pp., holograph Dixie College.

[10] Maurine Whipple, undated draft of letter to Tom Spies, ca. 1941–42, Whipple Collection, BYU; photocopy Dixie College.

IN AND OUT OF THE CLASSROOM, 1926–32

11. Maurine Whipple, "Confessions of a She Devil," ca. 1937, 34 pp. holograph and 18 pp. typescript, Whipple Collection, BYU; photocopies of both at Dixie College. The quotations are from the typescript, pp. 11–12.

12. The only baptismal date on his genealogical record is that of his first baptism as a child.

13. Maurine Whipple, Letter to First Presidency David O. McKay, Stephen L Richards, and J. Reuben Clark, 2 March 1967; Whipple Collection, BYU; photocopy Dixie College.

14. Lewis Munk disagreed with Maurine's view of Clark as "dominating." On the contrary, "he was a good teacher, willing to do what was asked of him. Our school library was a shambles, and he made it one of the best in the state." Lewis Munk, Letter to Lavina Fielding Anderson, n.d. [ca. April 2001], used by Munk's permission.

15. Ibid.

16. As a widow, Agnes temporarily moved to St. George where she became a practical nurse-companion to elderly individuals but soon moved back to Idaho with one of her charges. Maurine told me "that any elderly person who had Agnes as his or her companion was lucky."

17. Maurine Whipple, "The Lord Giveth," ca. 1926, 16 pp. typescript, Whipple Collection, BYU; another 18 pp. typescript is at Dixie College.

18. The operation can be dated by a letter from Florence, written on 5 February 1928, in which Florence teases: "How do you write to people who are laid up in hospital with appendicitis?" Whipple Collection, BYU.

19. Shakespeare, *Romeo and Juliet*, II.11.

20. Maurine had written in her diary on 6 October 1928: "Lucille Hart came just when I needed her, too. I think I would have died if all the winter had been as lonely as that first week. But Lucille materialized (partly because I made friends with her worried aunt on the train) and she is very sweet. We'll probably never be very dear friends, but she'll help me to at least pretend to be young again, and we'll help each other live through this winter."

21. Even though Maurine's letter to Ray is undated, the episode can be dated with some confidence to this time period since Myles Judd, eight years Maurine's junior, was, according to his tombstone, born in 1911 and died in 1936. Maurine's letter is at BYU Library, photocopy Dixie College.

22. Arlo Prisbrey, interviewed 25 May 1992, by Veda Hale, St. George; notes in my possession.

23. Evelyn Harris Lipton, interviewed in St. George, by Veda Hale, in 1994 and June 1995.

24. Maurine Whipple, "Confessions of a She Devil," 13.

25. Nellie McArthur Gubler, Letter to Veda Hale, 13 April 2001.

26. Ibid.

27. Ibid.

28. Florence Whipple Jolley, "History of Florence Whipple Jolley," January 1976, 11; 23 pp. holograph, photocopy in my possession, courtesy of Florence's daughter, Colleen Jolley Haycock, of Las Vegas, who has the original.

[29] Carol Ann Jolley Anderson, Letters to Veda Tebbs Hale, 7 July 1992 and 11 November 2002.

[30] Contract with Wasatch County Schools, [no date] August 1930; Whipple Collection, BYU.

[31] Jolley, "History," 13.

[32] Ibid.

⚜ 5 ⚜

THE DEVASTATING ROMANCES
OF 1932-37

Maurine turned twenty-nine in January 1932. She was stranded as an old maid, without prospects and without a career. The sequence of events in Maurine's life during the early 1930s is hazy. She found a job working for the Salt Lake City Recreation Department in a federally funded program to provide recreation for disadvantaged youngsters and create jobs. Maurine's contact was Charlotte S. Stewart, a friend who was supervisor for municipal recreation and who had been a member of the Church's Young Women's Mutual Improvement Association general board since 1914. She was a sterling role model of a single Mormon woman, active and respected in the community, professionally and educationally secure, surrounded by supportive siblings whose educations she had helped finance, and clearly a valuable member of the Church. Maurine could have learned from her but instead saw only the discrepancies. Still, although they did not become close, Maurine could always count on a good reference letter from Charlotte when she needed one.[1]

Maurine had the same job during the summer of 1931. Ray was attending the University of Utah during 1931–34. In 1931, Maurine's transcript shows that she also took classes in physical education, speech, and education.

Maurine described her job at the Neighborhood House, a recreation project in a poor neighborhood. "My job took me to the west side of town when nobody else, not even trained police-women, could handle the gang warfare, racial conflicts, reform-school alumni, and drug victims, one of whom committed an axe-murder just before I arrived. I got my share of abuse, too, but I stood it." Maurine took satisfaction from her work and later wrote, with unconscious patronage, "Eventually those poor starved misfits became my friends."[2]

The job did not pay well—fifty dollars a month, she told me—but it provided Maurine with an opportunity to test her idealism and to see if she could make a difference in the lives of young people. She organized and supervised tap and interpretative dance classes, ball games, and dramas. With determination, persistence, and creativity, she enticed the neighborhood youth to participate. She often told the story of how, one night as she started to step onto the streetcar, the drowsy driver started away, causing her to fall and break her ankle. He claimed that it wasn't his fault; but one of Maurine's students, who had witnessed the accident, confirmed that the car had indeed started too soon. As a result, Maurine received some compensation for her medical bills.

Maurine concluded the summer of 1931 with a program that she told me had impressed the directors and made the youngsters and their parents proud and grateful. Her sense of satisfaction endured into her old age—a decided contrast to her bitter and ambiguous feelings about teaching in the public schools.

She still defined her goal in life as a husband and family, relegating writing to a hobby, until she happened to bump into Lillian Maude McQuarrie on a Salt Lake streetcar in 1931 or 1932. It was a turning point, and writing acquired a new seriousness.

Lillian, born in St. George in 1904, was one year Maurine's junior. She also came from an old St. George pioneer family, but her immediate family had moved away from St. George when she was in high school—seventh grade, Maurine recalled. After two years of business school (1924–25), Lillian had married Henry Noelte and given birth to a daughter, Marian, who was five or six when Lillian and Maurine met again. Apparently Lillian divorced Noelte in 1930 or 1931, since she was using McQuarrie as her surname in 1931 and supporting herself as a stenographer/secretary.[3] Lillian was one generation further removed from plural marriage than Maurine since her great-grandparents, not her grandparents, were St. George polygamists.[4]

Lillian became a loyal friend, a trusted confidant, and an enthusiastic fan of Maurine's talent. Maurine, in turn, provided staunch emotional support as Lillian engaged in a series of romantic relationships. Their quick bonding occurred not only because of their shared past in St. George, but also because of a shared interest in writing and the loneliness of women facing the world without the economic and emotional security of a good husband. Like Maurine, Lillian also had a negative relationship with her father who had no use for the Church. Unlike Charlie, he drank to excess. Both had a feeling of being marginalized in Mormon society.

Lillian differed from Maurine in her driving ambition to succeed as a writer. She had already sold her first story to *Liberty* magazine[5] and was, at the time of their meeting in the summer of 1932, gathering notes for a historical novel about Utah life in the 1860s. Maurine found Lillian's company stimulating. The two quickly started swapping ideas for short stories, plays, and novels in addition to sharing personal experiences. The first two or three years of their renewed relationship are hazy. Their letters began in 1935 when Lillian, by then married to Emerson Evans, was in San Francisco, and Maurine was in Rawlins, Wyoming, where she had organized dancing classes. Lillian filled in one detail in her first letter, dated 3 July 1935, by reminding Maurine: "Los Angeles did a lot for both of us that year we were there. You'll remember that I had hit a new low. There's something in the combination of the two of us that is constructive. I don't know what it is."

In this same letter, Lillian reported that she was diligently reading through back issues of the *Salt Lake Tribune* and *Deseret News*; and in a 1935 letter, she excitedly told Maurine about a book, *The History and Crimes of Mormonism*, that she had discovered and read "avidly" in the summer of 1933. In Los Angeles, she read 1861 issues of the *Los Angeles Star* to get a broader picture of the times and concluded: "All the western states were as barbarous as Utah, but not under the guise of religion."[6]

Maurine couldn't (or wouldn't) remember many details about their time in Los Angeles—just that they "explored life." Lillian no doubt was more employable than Maurine, thanks to her skills as a stenographer. An undated clipping after the publication of *The Giant Joshua* says that Maurine "taught literature and acted as a movie extra." Maurine confirmed to me she "did get a few chances to be in the background of some movies" and that she "tried a lot of things to make money without much success."

Maurine's friendship with Lillian came at a time when she was reevaluating her connection to Mormonism. Neither woman found much of a spiritual or social home in Mormonism. "I can never intend to write anything that will be even faintly controversial," mused Lillian in 1938. "I don't think it's worth that much. I've thought about it until it's gradually faded out to a dull pink like the stitch marks of an appendectomy." She queried: "You had hardly been conscious of Mormons before, had you? I mean, I didn't think you had."[7]

It seems like a strange way to characterize Maurine. Although she had not yet positioned herself as a writer vis-à-vis Mormonism as material, Maurine felt strongly that the truth was worth writing about, never wanted to deliberately hurt the Church or her people, and had a genuine affection for and grounding in pioneer stories. But perhaps Lillian was consciously aware of Mormonism in a way that Maurine was not. Were Mormonism's truth claims important to Maurine? Probably not. When I asked her directly if she had had a conversion experience—a "testimony"—she reflected: "Well, I just always thought it was true. But, no, probably not like you mean." Their voracious reading had expanded their vision of the world, and they found it intellectually stimulating to understand Mormonism against this broader backdrop.

Lillian summarized her own position: "The Church was simply responsible for our background but did not constitute any powerful, earth-moving force in our lives. We could love it, cherish it as our particular folkway, but at the same time treat it as one would a beloved, but eccentric relative—tolerated in context, and certainly not attacked."[8] Although Maurine may have admired and perhaps even envied Lillian's brisk casualness, I feel that she did not completely share this perspective. She sensed something greater in Mormonism. She recognized and wanted to celebrate "the Grand Idea" of brotherhood that early St. George so bravely tried.

Maurine considered herself active, in the sense that she attended Sunday meetings, at least until the early 1930s. Included in her papers is a program from Los Angeles's Wiltshire Ward sacrament meeting on which she had doodled, indicating that she attended meetings at least sometimes, even when she was out of town. She told me she had read the Book of Mormon, Bible, and the Church magazines, that she had always gone to church and usually held a position (often MIA dance director), so she would have gleaned some doctrine, but she was "more a reflector of how that doctrine affected people." Living at the Beehive House came with the strong expectation, if not the obligation, to attend Church meetings and keep Church standards. Among her papers is a program from 25 January (no year) announcing a dance review by eighty-one children sponsored by Wilford Ward in Salt Lake Valley to which a ward member's budget card would admit them.[9] Maurine and Floyd Carnaby are listed as the teachers. She later gave the bishop's name as a job reference. On another occasion, her dance students in St. George presented a festival as a fundraiser for the Primary.[10]

Maurine seemed oddly reticent in 1991 and 1992 to speak of Lillian, even though the evidence is clear that Lillian was very important in Maurine's life and maturation as a writer. She apparently wanted to disassociate herself from what she felt was Lillian's negative reputation. Lillian lived her life with a certain sexual casual looseness of which Maurine disapproved. With a kind of endearing primness, Maurine told me: "She smoked, too. She could never teach me to do it." But perhaps the biggest difference between them was Lillian's hard-headed, even cynical, realism contrasted with Maurine's soft-hearted, even sentimental, romanticism: "She tried hard to make me see I was silly in my ideas about love and men."

Maurine probably did seem naive and unsophisticated to Lillian when they met. In a rambling letter of abject self-explanation to a later lover, Maurine bitterly said: "I was raised to believe that intimacy with a man bound you to him forever and ever. I wanted to be able to face men squarely, honestly. But I learned most men didn't appreciate my thinking."[11] It also seemed clear that she hoped sexual intimacy—even short of intercourse—with a man would bind him to her, despite repeated experiences to the contrary. She was ready to listen to an expert, and she considered Lillian one. Maurine said she was both scandalized and fascinated by the rumors that Lillian had had at least two affairs, one with a man in Cedar City and a married man from Las Vegas. More to the point, Lillian had no trouble attracting the men she wanted, while Maurine, despite her most strenuous efforts, repeatedly failed.

Humbly, Maurine was willing to accept Lillian as a guide into the mysteries of relationships, even if it meant jettisoning her St. George attitudes. When I asked her about those attitudes, Maurine's feelings were clear, but she found it difficult to articulate what she meant. It had something to do with the combination of rigid sexual morality combined with under-the-surface acceptance of unorthodox relationships. St. George's isolation, its difficult past, its extreme loyalty to its dead, plus the way polygamy had woven its way through the entire community, setting the tone, flavoring the interactions, whether any particular individual was a polygamist or not, not to mention the strikingly high percentage of actual polygamous involvement[12]—all contributed to St. George's distinctive attitudes. Maurine also fumbled to articulate to me another idea she had absorbed growing up: A superior man, like J.D.T. McAllister, "was worth sharing." A man like that could successfully love more than one woman—in fact, needed to love more than one woman—while women "should strive to be attached to righteous, superior men, not settling for inadequate husbands."

Juanita Brooks's biographer captured one manifestation of this attitude. Attending graduate school at Columbia in 1928, Juanita became acquainted with a woman who had been having an affair with a married man for ten years. Unlike others, Juanita found the situation understandable and mused to a correspondent: "Because the two were committed to each other," the woman was less an adulteress than "really living in polygamy. . . . I guess it does amount to about the same thing."[13] Juanita was expressing a kind of conceptual confusion that also baffled Maurine. The behavior was blameworthy even for Mormons by standards of Christian morality, but this

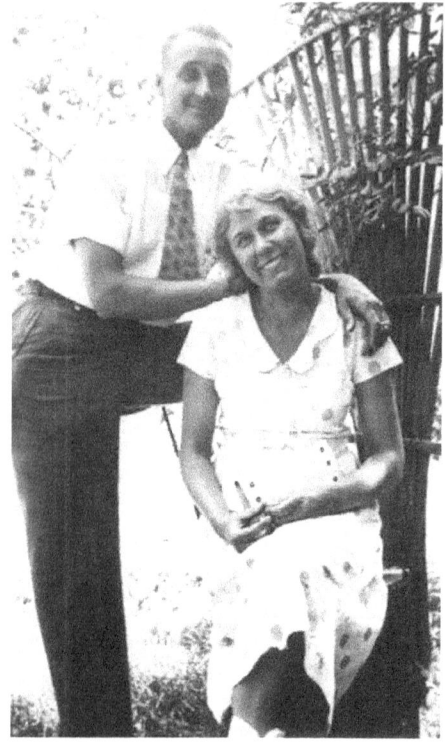

Maurine with Emil de Neuf, whom she married in about 1932. The union was unhappy and very brief—only four months. Despite her dreams, she never remarried. Lee Library Photographic Archives, Brigham Young University.

same behavior had been praiseworthy one or two generations earlier for Mormons. Did believing a thing really make it right?

Maurine often told me how confusing it was for her generation, struggling to cope with rules that had changed since their mothers and grandmothers were young. Many girls, finding themselves marginalized socially because of their polygamous ancestry and unable to attract a high-caliber husband, were susceptible to "affairs with attractive, capable, married men." She felt that such women could end up either "rationalizing their conscience" when having an affair, or "resenting the social restrictions" that kept them single or unable to have a superior man. A third reaction was to "get rid of social rules" about sexual morality altogether. This was, she felt, "what Lillian had done." Lillian recorded her own hard-boiled philosophy in a 1935 letter to Maurine: "I would not stand another period of loneliness and drifting. . . . I would pick up with a tramp first. That's my philosophy," she said. "Take a second or third rate person rather than have an empty life."[14]

Maurine put herself in Lillian's hands, followed her instructions to the letter, and finally said those magic words, "I do," probably in the fall of 1932.[15] Maurine did not mention this marriage until I had found a letter from "Emil" in her papers. When I interviewed Maurine, age eighty-eight, holding the letter in my hand, she refused to tell me Emil's last name or anything about him. "It just doesn't matter—the marriage was a mistake, a big mistake, one not worth talking about," she insisted. "I got into it because I felt desperate for security, half sick most of the time, and I hoped that marriage would give me time and peace to write." Her only other comment was that the marriage was an unmitigated disaster—over in four months. When I pressed, she became furious with me and threatened never to talk to me again. It was apparent that she still suffered great guilt and remorse over the relationship. She knew she hadn't been fair to Emil, and she cared for him enough that she regretted adding more pain to his life. She had tried to follow Lillian's ruthless philosophy but could not sustain the consequences.

From her few grudging comments, additional research, and some clues I could piece together in her papers, a sketchy picture emerged. Emil ("Buzz") de Neuf was certainly not the hobo that Lillian had cynically advised Maurine to take up with. He was more like a traveling salesman, working in the installation and services division of RCA Photophone, Inc. (Photophone equipment was needed in producing sound for movies. Emil worked as a trouble-shooter on this equipment.) Born perhaps in Seattle or San Francisco, he was not a Mormon. His job had brought him to Salt Lake City, and his mother was sometimes with him. At least some of the time, his mother went with him into the field, cooking his meals and making a home for him. He had been married once and his wife had left him for a man with a wooden leg, taking the two children with her.

At the time he and Maurine met, he was living in the same boarding-house. Thus, he was a handy target when Maurine begged for Lillian's help in finding a man. "Bleach your hair and buy a red suit," was Lillian's first advice. "Feeling like a fool," Maurine said she did. Then Lillian helped arrange for Maurine to have opportunities to talk to Emil. When he happened to mention his upcoming birthday, Lillian pounced. She had Maurine buy a man's handkerchief, embroider Emil's initial in a corner, and lay it beside his dinner plate on his birthday. He was impressed and proposed a short time later. "He was good-looking and nice," Maurine conceded.

They were married by a Salt Lake City justice of the peace who asked, "Are you sure you're marrying for the right reasons?" Maurine told me that she felt sick at the question, knowing that she wasn't. She said she tried hard. She desperately wanted it to work. Certainly growing up in Charlie's and Annie's house, she had no reason for believing that marriages ended when things got tough. But Emil was still on the rebound from his divorce. "He just couldn't get over it," Maurine commented with considerable sympathy, and the depth of the wound to his self-image was reflected in his continual, incredulous lament: "And to think she left me and married a man with a wooden leg!" She was deeply touched when he wept at Christmas over a tie from his children.

Still, desperate for affection, Maurine felt rebuffed by his obsession with his ex-wife's departure and recognized almost at once that "he really didn't love me. He had no sympathy for my personal interests, refused to let me send home for my books or continue my graduate classes at the university. He didn't like books or women who tried to write." Further, because he was a non-Mormon and not from Utah, "he didn't understand my people." Maurine, who loved to dance, was further discouraged because "he couldn't even dance."

But worst of all, Emil couldn't break away from his mother's emotional bondage, even though, in Maurine's opinion, it had destroyed his first marriage. In about 1931, Maurine had achieved a coveted goal by winning the leading role in a University of Utah production of *The Silver Cord* by Sydney Howard. She played a young wife whose husband could not detach himself from the emotional domination of his mother, and the obvious parallels between Maurine's marriage and *The Silver Cord* seemed to seal their doom. These parallels, naturally, also mean that Maurine could have overlaid the fictional plot with its popular Oedipus complex on her marriage and that Emil's mother played no role in the break-up of her marriage. Without more evidence one way or another, it is impossible to say; but my personal feeling is that Maurine was not fabricating that element. Maurine told me, "He expected his wife to wait on him and cater to his whims as his mother did." She resented his expectation that she would have a "hot, tasty meal" ready on no or little notice "whenever he returned." Cooking never was one of Maurine's strengths, and their kitchen seems to have been ill equipped.

Except for accompanying Emil on a few business trips, she spent the winter of 1932–33 in their cold apartment, 47 South 300 East No. 16, confused, frustrated, and mostly alone. "I can't recall all the nightmare of that winter," she wrote in "Confessions of a She Devil." "Suffice it to say that my clinic doctor convinced me that my husband had an Oedipus complex too severe for him to enter into any kind of successful matrimonial relationship. I was wrecked mentally and physically. My doctor explained to me that my only hope of health lay in speedy divorce, and, failing remarriage, intimacy with some man, deliberately but of course as decently as possible. I believed him unreservedly and I still think he's right from a purely scientific point of view. I know now that the only flaw in his theory lies in the fact that I am a woman with a heart and not a cow."[16]

To me during a moment of rare candor, she mused: "Maybe with someone else, he [Emil] could have worked out his difficulties, but the relationship just wasn't for me. He was gone a lot, so we weren't together very much. But the reason I left him was because we didn't think alike on hardly anything, and I just didn't love him." She said she left without demanding anything. In 1992, she wanted Emil to be remembered as "a good man."

Perhaps it was about this time—in the late spring or early summer of 1933 with the marriage's termination—that Lillian and Maurine had their spree of "exploring life" in Los Angeles.

If I am interpreting Maurine's tangled feelings correctly, then another element must be considered. She was still infatuated with Clare Woodbury, the doctor who had saved Ralph's life and to whom she had acted as nurse. According to Maurine's mostly autobiographical sketch, after her divorce: "I went south with incipient tuberculosis. I flew straight to Clare in Las Vegas. By then I was willing to be content with crumbs. I offered to live on the back streets of his life all my days. But when I gave him the thing he had been trying for a decade to get, and the end of the chase was in sight, he was no longer interested."[17]

She may well have sought treatment from him. Although stressing to me that his behavior had been impeccably professional, never crossing the line into intimacy, she frequently reminisced with still-fresh yearning about how he had scolded her for neglecting her health, prescribed some medication, and put her under a heat lamp to help loosen the congestion in her chest. When she got up to go, she fainted. Sixty years later, she still cherished the memory of his response—worry and kindliness.

The summer of 1933 brought Maurine to another low point in her life. She was thirty, on her own, unwell, not proud of herself, aware that her training as a teacher in public schools was not going to get her a job, and unsure of just how she would make a living.

Maurine bounced back from the divorce, possibly from relief that she was out of an emotionally damaging situation, possibly under the bracingly cynical influence of Lillian. She was certainly prompted by economic necessity. In 1933, Utah's unemployment rate hovered at 35 percent, the fourth highest in the nation. Annual income per capita had dropped 50 percent by 1932, and even on the eve of World War II it had risen to only 82 percent of pre-Depression levels. By the spring of 1933, 32 percent of the people were getting "all or part of their food, clothing, shelter, and other necessities from government relief funds." A third of Utah's banks failed; and most Utahns would have been in a desperate plight without government assistance.[18]

The Works Progress Administration would have seemed like a good niche for Maurine, but it did not begin until 1936. Maurine's family was going through hard times with the lumberyard and the movie theater on the skids.

Maurine decided to create her own job in recreation. Among her papers at BYU are six letters of recommendation written in May 1934, which she solicited in her campaign to create a job in Las Vegas much like the work she had done in Salt Lake City.[19] That job had apparently lost its funding, but she hoped to create one that would be funded by a combination of charitable institutions which she herself would mobilize. Nevada had been as hard hit by the Great Depression as Utah, but some of the effects were mitigated by 1931 legislation legalizing gaming while the on-going Hoover Dam project continued to provide steady jobs and hope. According to Maurine, Charlotte Stewart had heard about the job possibility in Las Vegas and encouraged her to check it out. At Maurine's request, Stewart even sent a telegram recommending Maurine to help prepare the way.[20]

Maurine's enthusiastic campaign succeeded, but not for her. After she showed how it could be done, a local woman got the job. Maurine used this disappointment as the basis of an embittered autobiographical essay, "Big Dog Eats Little Dog."[21] It is not clear what audience she had in mind or when she wrote it (it is undated and was never published), but it is an ax-grinding piece, designed to show the unfairness and stupidity of government relief. When I asked her about it in 1992, she acknowledged that it was written at the depth of the country's Depression and certainly at the depth of her personal depression. She insisted that the facts were "not far from the truth."

When the other woman was hired, one who had connections to a man in city government, Maurine caught a ride back to Utah and spent the rest of the summer in St. George licking her wounds. She may have taught some dance classes as well. In the fall—the "mellow Indian summer"—she hitched a ride to Salt Lake City with a truck driver and learned from Charlotte Stewart about "a branch of government relief set up for just such people as you, school teachers out of jobs. It's the new Adult Education program of the F.E.R.A" (Federal Education Reclamation Agency).

In her letter of application, Maurine explained her dream: "To help the people back to normal living, to everyman's belief in his star again" by teaching dancing and wholesome recreation. She wrote in "Big Dog Eats Little Dog" that she was hired on October 10, 1934, for fifty dollars a month "and was happy I could give joyfully to an inspiring movement for our troubled times." She provides no details about what the job entailed but describes it as "a meaty job full of ideals and service to humanity. It had so renewed my self-respect that I was actually taking time to cream my face every night. It had come after long years of hopeless wanderings; because I so liked being a part of a plan to help lift people out of despair, I had given up an offer (gained after a year's constant hammering) to work in the Los Angeles City recreation department. . . . I . . . hugged my job to my breast. I loved it. It meant to me what a husband and children meant to other women."[22]

Then in what may be a fictionalized episode, Maurine describes receiving a telephone call on New Year's morning informing her that funding for the program had ceased. Maurine's sense of personal betrayal was real—but there was no one but big government to blame. The essay ends with an expression of real fear, bitterness, and resentment: "So the long years of wandering were to begin again. And the forced cheerfulness. And the hunger—and worst of all, the thought of the final frantic cringing for Relief. I wonder about the New Deal. It is all so confusing."[23]

In this essay, she is the victim of larger economic forces, even though those forces are translated through the sexually immoral, the politically corrupt, and the financially dishonest. Furthermore, although Maurine had no demonstrable interest in politics, this essay almost amounts to a political statement. Her fear and bitterness were real. The fact that she shared them with millions of fellow Americans did not lessen her misery.

Furthermore, Maurine had spontaneously complicated her life again by rebounding from her divorce and from Clare Woodbury's final repudiation of her offer to become his mistress. She admits in her "Confessions" that she "went a little crazy. But I solemnly began an intimacy with a chap named Burke."[24] He was the "therapy" that she says her doctor prescribed to overcome the physiological effects of Emil's Oedipus complex. Maurine was obviously all too willing to give it a try. If it had succeeded, she may have launched herself on a course more closely paralleling Lillian's; but because it failed, she attributed it to her inherent nobility.

Unfortunately, she plunged immediately into another ruinous relationship in a new locale: this time with Nick Spencer[25] at the brand-new town of Boulder City, Nevada. In the process, she demolished a satisfying career that seemed to promise economic security—at least until the dam was finished. This situation also set in train a series of events that resulted in the high point of Maurine's creative life: the writing of *The Giant Joshua*.

The construction of Boulder Dam is a dramatic story in the history of the American Southwest. In 1928 President Calvin Coolidge signed the Boulder Canyon Project Act. The following June, with the endorsement of the new president, Herbert Hoover, it passed. It authorized the construction of a massive concrete dam, seven hundred feet high, at Black Canyon on the Arizona-Nevada border that would create a reservoir 120 miles long and enough water that every person on earth could have 5,000 gallons of it. It would supply water for a quarter of a million acres in California's fertile Imperial Valley and cost $48,890,995.

It was a project that had glamour and the sizzling energy of a whole people united for a great cause. The fact that its construction coincided with the Great Depression offered Americans an opportunity to concentrate on the thrilling optimism taking visible shape in the western desert instead of the bad economic news.

In the fall of 1934, when Maurine got to Boulder City, the project was roaring toward completion, the exquisite arch of the dam face rising higher with each pour under the sun that burned all day and the lights that burned all night. It seems almost inevitable that Maurine would have been drawn to the energy of this united national effort. She responded by developing her own usual, high-energy, high-quality recreational program. This was probably the time when Maurine claimed that Lillian McQuarrie, then a stenographer in Salt Lake City for Firestone Company, grub-staked her by working overtime and earning fifty dollars which she gave to Maurine. Maurine never forgot Lillian's generosity and reciprocated after *The Giant Joshua* was published, sending Lillian money just when Lillian was in a financial crisis. These two friends claimed they could communicate telepathically.

Among Maurine's papers is a printed program describing an impressive and ambitious song-and-dance revue for ninety-six children held 19 December 1934, suggesting that she had been in Boulder City for at least three months. Interestingly enough, she had adopted a new personality: "Rene de Neuf," a combination of her family's nickname and the name of the man she had just divorced.[26]

By any measure, Maurine had entered Boulder City and made herself a success. She had created a place for herself she could control—not based on ephemeral government funding and not subject to authorities who could be swayed by "sex appeal." She said she bought books of games and dramas. She liked to claim that she learned dancing by correspondence. The harsh desert, which shocked and drained many immigrants from greener lands, revitalized Maurine. People were part of America's biggest project until World War II. Pride was in the air. They also had money and little to spend it on. Soon Maurine had mothers and children learning marches, tap-dancing, and participating in programs of popular and patriotic songs. They eagerly acted in plays she wrote or adapted. It was fun and—since she could charge modest fees—financially rewarding.

If Maurine had focused on professional success, her life might have turned out differently. Instead, she sabotaged herself with another romance gone wrong. In this instant city whose population cut across regions and social classes, old structures had dissolved. Friendships and romances sprang up with the speed of desert plants germinating after a brief rainstorm. Availability, rather than suitability, was the dominant criterion in this situation of social anonymity.

In this setting, Nick Spencer and Maurine found each other. I gleaned from a draft of a letter that they spent Christmas 1934 together, so they had met very soon after Maurine reached Boulder City. She described him as "good-looking, fun, and, an excellent dancer—not like Emil." She did not say what his job was. He was a Mormon, too, a recently returned missionary. "My mother would have been so happy if I could end up with a man like that!" She said. Soon she was head over heels in love and, without waiting for the wedding, threw herself sexually into what she sincerely thought was the relationship of her life with her longed-for "eternal" mate, complete with a temple-marriage commitment—after they "repented," of course.

According to Maurine, Nick had left a serious girlfriend in his hometown. He may have felt torn between two commitments or he may have realized quite soon that the affair with Maurine was a flash in the pan. Maurine, always given to trying to control things, may have decided to precipitate a decision by moving the repentance process along. LDS Church policy mandated the confession of sexual sins as part of the repentance process; and probably during the spring of 1935, she decided to confess their transgression to the one Mormon bishop in Boulder City. Such confessions were supposed to guarantee her a fresh start. She also may have wanted to confess other indiscretions she had not told Nick about. However, in going first and going alone, she made a shattering tactical mistake.

She did not tell me everything she told the bishop, but the bishop apparently put together a picture of Maurine as a scheming woman, older than Nick—possibly by seven or eight years, briefly married, and one who had been involved with other men. She decided later that this bishop was the kind who blamed the woman if an otherwise worthy priesthood holder commits a sexual transgression and who felt that he, as bishop, should intervene immediately to save the priesthood holder from a bad woman. Maurine later learned, or deduced, that the bishop quickly called Nick in, quoted scriptures, brought the full weight of his office to bear upon him, and ordered him to confess his transgression in fast meeting or be excommunicated. Nick obeyed. Naturally, breaking things off completely with Maurine was also part of his "repentance." If her version of this episode in "Confessions of a She Devil" is accurate, Nick blackened her reputation among other decent men: "Nick hated and abhorred me so openly as his temptress, that in that town of men I became sort of a female pariah."[27]

Maurine was bewildered, humiliated, and devastated. In addition to the destruction of her romantic dreams, she felt personally condemned. What about her? What about the intent of her heart? What about her soul?

"SWELL SUFFERING"

Why didn't the bishop care to help her through the steps of repentance? She felt that she, like her father, had been railroaded by the callous and the malicious, then ignored by the priesthood leaders. Then she found out that the bishop had a local woman with a questionable reputation deliver the day's takings from his job—what that was, she didn't say—to the bank. Maurine told me that the woman had, in fact, during the first months of Maurine's residency in Boulder City, encouraged Maurine not to be so concerned about conventions but to find a man and enjoy a casual relationship. Maurine juxtaposed the bishop's regular association with this woman against his horrified concern for Nick's "purity." The resulting picture spelled hypocrisy to her. She tried to shrug it off, characterizing the incident in "Confessions of a She Devil," as "just another case of discovering the infantile nature of another bishop and daring him to do his infantile worst."[28]

But her letters to Nick tell another heart-breaking story. In anguish, she poured out her hopes for a reconciliation on paper. Two pages of a draft or drafts have survived; but there must have been many more, since she bitterly comments that in one of her letters was "something you could use against me if you chose."[29] In the one surviving fragment that provides a hint of the timing, she begged Nick that they might at least end their relationship without rancor.

Maurine had made a friend, Dorothy Kreutzer, in Boulder, who was sympathetic during this time of heartbreak. Dorothy was a widow whose husband, George, had recently died of a heart attack, leaving Dorothy with two children. Maurine told me that Dorothy had traveled widely and, at one time, lived in New York City. Maurine admired her sophistication and appreciated her friendship and support during the failed affair with Nick.

What made this bruising repetition of rejection all the more painful was that Maurine was seeing a living experiment in the "Grand Idea" being lived out before her eyes. To her, the vision of Boulder Dam and Boulder City paralleled the vision of the Mormon pioneers in building St. George and its temple. Why couldn't it parallel her own life, too?

Maurine tried to capture both feelings in a short story called "Hell, It's Worth It!"[30] Speaking through an unnamed female protagonist (a telephone operator) in first person, she describes the affair with Ken, a popular, fun-loving man, who was on the cement-pouring crew and was a good dancer. This short story is an excellent piece of writing. The climactic scene of construction describes the "milling confusion of twenty thousand people come to see President Roosevelt dedicate Boulder Dam," then the emptying streets as the workers and their families depart, and the closing down of the telephone exchange.

THE DEVASTATING ROMANCES OF 1932–37

In one version, Ken falls into the last pour and is buried in tons of concrete.[31] The dam thus becomes his monument, a testimony to human beings cooperating to construct something much bigger than the individual. This theme is important in showing that Maurine was groping toward the concept she would explore to much better effect later in *The Giant Joshua*. But psychologically, of course, Maurine was burying the dead relationship in a medium that only the resurrection could change.

More significant for Maurine's artistic development is that protagonist finds comfort in seeing her broken heart in relation to the whole. In *The Giant Joshua*, Maurine would use the same technique—foregrounding an individual life with its frustrations and brokenness—against a grandly sweeping background that gives purpose and meaning to small lives and makes the defeat of one individual less dreadful.

Maurine knew she had to leave Boulder City and its heartaches. She apparently told Lillian that she planned to pay a prolonged visit to her Uncle John and Aunt Rose Ellen at their ranch, Sunnyside, near Lund, Nevada. Lillian seized on this suggestion, advising her "to try to find a nice cowboy to be interested in."[32] She followed up on this encouragement: "Then this summer's end when you are incorporated over at Sunnyside, I'll pay you a visit, and we'll talk it over. Maybe someone interesting will be there by then."[33] Maurine told me that she had once (probably not this summer) tried to "bury" herself in the ranch's solitude, only to find out that she didn't fit there either. "They couldn't just treat me as one of them," she said.

At this point, Lillian dangled another lure in front of Maurine. Writing. She was going to the Rocky Mountain Writers' Conference in Boulder, Colorado, in August and had almost finished her novel based on a St. George character whose polygamy was an open secret. In a 3 July 1935 letter, she had exclaimed exasperatedly, "The Southern Utah book I'm working on is sending me nuts," and she asked for Maurine's help in identifying the "little things" that "make St. George the only place in the world that would accept Franklin for his worth, without throwing him out for his morals." She circled around the strange Mormon-style triangle that, she felt, could exist only in the historical context of polygamy.[34]

Lillian had put her finger on the very problem that Maurine would confront, and solve magnificently, in *The Giant Joshua*—capturing the spirit of a people, the temper of a town, the "atmospherics" that recreated a culture. Maurine almost certainly would have responded to this request to the best of her ability, but neither her letter nor Lillian's manuscript has survived.[35]

As the contrast between Maurine and Lillian makes plain, Lillian was pragmatic, an unblinking realist, while Maurine was much more of a romantic idealist, further hampered by her perfectionism that seldom let her push a project to completion despite seasons of intensive labor. Maurine's life pattern shows that she grasped eagerly at intimate relationships, always convinced that she was acting for the "right" reason—true and overwhelming love. Maurine claimed that this difference between her and Lillian eventually led to the cooling of their friendship; but even from a friendly perspective, there are times when Maurine's "idealism" is virtually indistinguishable from denial. Nor did she seem to learn from experience, as the next four (possibly five) relationships within the next two years show— and there may have been more.

The extent to which these relationships were platonic may have depended more on the man than on Maurine. Her "Confessions of a She Devil" contains this revealing passage: "Having to fight my own body's insidious, dark, secret craving as well as that of the hunting male, to whom I seem inevitably to be his natural prey, I have learned that I, my essential self, cannot always win the battle."[36] Certainly, she seems to have hurled herself from one devastating relationship to another with desperate haste, not giving herself time to heal or reflect on and learn from her experience.

In a conversation with me, Maurine said she left Boulder City in May or June 1935 with Dorothy Kreutzer, who had taken a job in Salt Lake City as a secretary. Maurine probably stayed with Dorothy while she looked unsuccessfully for work. Lillian was also living in Salt Lake City. After Maurine exhausted the possibilities in Salt Lake City, she went to Rawlins, Wyoming, to teach dancing. Her obvious and repeated success with children's dance and recreation is something she liked to talk about. Maurine had lamented: "It's the wasted years that get me." Lillian's sympathy met this grief unstintingly: "I do know what you mean . . . . And yet, what are you going to spend them on? You'd have spent that time just the same."[37]

A couple of weeks later on 18 July, Lillian again wrote to Maurine in Rawlins, this time calling Nick a "dirty rat." Lillian argued that it would not have been a good match anyway—that Nick, like Emil, had no appreciation for books or tolerance for Maurine's writing. Sympathetically, Lillian said she had cried over Maurine's confession that "she felt tarnished and motheaten." She encouraged Maurine to pull herself together, advising: "Anybody who reaches your age and mine without the benefit of so-called 'tarnishing' experiences, is still a child and should never have been weaned." She quoted a recent motion picture, *The Flame Within,* in which the heroine, Ann Harding, bravely encourages her lover to disregard social pressure: "All the waters of the Seven Seas can't sink a ship unless the water gets inside." Lillian encouraged Maurine in the same way and further advised: "You've got to love people into dismissing their prejudices against you. Do it silently and never say a word to them. They'll know it. Picture them being friendly.

See yourself talking and laughing with them." Lillian herself was trying to do that and also anticipated a long conversation with Maurine focused on "that futile driving that ends in distraction, and is driven by the creative urge, which is only sex in the last analysis."[38]

She had little patience with Maurine's attempt to achieve Mormon orthodoxy by "repenting." What Maurine needed instead, she counseled frankly, was

> a time of playing around. Of course you were cheated out of it, and you've got to have it. That carefree stage of life when everything is delicious and silly and priceless. And you don't mean marriage. Really. You mean fooling around, and talking about Popeye, and dance steps, and popular songs, and getting the best looking boy in the crowd from the others, and winning little popularity contests (not staged). Isn't this what you mean? Of course you need this. I know it. I didn't have it until after I was married and divorced and had a child and broke away.[39]

Lillian's unvarnished prescription for "fooling around," whatever its amorality for women in their thirties, does sound like the innocent fun Maurine missed as a young girl when she carried instead much responsibility for her younger siblings and for her mother. Instead of toying with "Popeye, and dance steps, and popular songs," she had brooded over her father's infidelity and the ever-present threat of death—her own, her mother's, her younger brother's, and baby Grace's.

But Maurine couldn't take Lillian's ruthlessly realistic approach. In Rawlins, she seems to have had her third romance within a year: Burke, Nick, and Jerry Richardson. Mercifully, it was a doomed but dignified short relationship, which she, for a change, terminated. She confirmed to me that she used this experience in writing an untitled short story about a beautiful dance instructor in a small Wyoming town who becomes the target of a local masher. She spurns his advances in favor of a young doctor from the South who is just passing through. She sees in him something "superior" and decides she would "rather have a few hours of something wonderful than nothing at all." In his cabin, they engage in passionate kissing but, like a gentleman, he does not violate his "southern tradition of Rotten-Logging"—or sharing the same bed but without sex. During that night, she pretends that it will last forever and conceals her broken heart the next morning as they part. He takes his leave from her with regret, and she consoles herself by thinking that he really did find her attractive and liked her, even though this night of virginal passion would inevitably damage her reputation.[40]

Maurine's whereabouts for the rest of the summer are not clear; but in the fall, she succeeded in finding a job not far from the bottom of the education ladder at Latuda, Utah. This coal-mining town had seen its best days and would be a ghost town by 1966.[41] In Maurine's application, she dropped her age from thirty-two to twenty-seven and claimed a double minor in dancing and Spanish. (She had taken a Spanish class as a freshman in college, and obviously hoped it would enhance her chances of being hired.) Her contract specified that she would teach English and physical education in junior high for $120 a month.[42]

This school experience in the fall of 1935 was even more traumatic than any of her other devastating five years of teaching. In her "Confessions" she wrote: "That maniac of a principal went insane and I had to protect the kids. I was so terrified of him, but somebody had to stand by the kids."[43] To me she explained that the principal had punished one of the students so ferociously that Maurine intervened to stop him.

But even worse than having to deal with yet another principal with whom she was at odds, she was raped. She told me she lived in a hotel-boarding house, where all the boarders ate in a dining room and shared the living room. One afternoon, she arrived from school tired and sat down in the living room to read the paper. She was alone until a "big, mean-looking man" came in, struck up a conversation, and then, deciding she was a "certain kind of girl," made a crude pass. When Maurine rebuffed him, he became angry, pushed her onto the couch, and raped her.

Stunned, in pain, and terrified, Maurine said she made her way to her room and tried to decide what to do. Because of the nature of the town and times, she knew it would have done her no good to report it. She could not handle the stress, and so quit her teaching job. The record at the Carbon County School District indicates she had taught for only six weeks—meaning that the rape probably occurred in early October. Not surprisingly, it also notes that the school would not give her a letter of recommendation. Latuda was the end of her public school teaching experiences. She wouldn't try again.

She probably made her way to Salt Lake City, fearing she was pregnant, and she probably turned to Lillian for support. As it turned out, she *was* pregnant. Mercifully, she found a doctor who believed her story, understood the situation, and referred her to a doctor who would perform abortions. Although she loved children and longed for a family, she did not express any regrets to me about her decision. Given her circumstances, the times, her lack of resources, and the trauma of the rape, abortion seemed the only solution. An unwed pregnancy "would have killed Mama," she told me repeatedly, and she never told her family about the abortion. In old age, she still thought she had made the right decision.

She does not remember too clearly what she did for the next few months. She probably stayed in Salt Lake City after the abortion and may have found odd jobs that let her get by. She was deeply depressed and was probably suffering from what we would now call post-traumatic stress syndrome. In Maurine's day, there was no counseling or support for a raped woman—only blame and shaming.

She longed for the desert but did not dare return home in her hour of need: "I was always the one who had to be strong," she told me. "I could never go to them with my needs. There was too much unhappiness at home most of the time anyway." In one letter, Lillian commented on how much she admired Maurine's "healing yourself from the urge to commit suicide after what happened in Helper [sic]."[44]

Maurine couldn't remember where she went next. A letter from Lillian on April 16, 1938, alludes to her going after a teaching position in Los Angeles, so she apparently spent several weeks there applying for one. Still recovering from the rape, she was staying with her Aunt Vira Herbert, Charlie's half-sister.[45] A kind, strong woman, Vira allowed Maurine to work for her board and room after Maurine failed to find a job, either as a teacher or perhaps as a clerk in a department store.

According to Alice Titus, who married Ray in 1936, "Maurine was Charlie's favorite. He would do anything for her and often gave her money.[46] No doubt such ready rescues, though humiliating to Maurine, also meant that she did not have to face the discipline of an absolute choice: work or starve.

During this time in Los Angeles, which, as nearly as I can reconstruct, was the summer of 1936, she suffered her most devastating romantic reversal to that date. She would not divulge her lover's surname, a decision I have respected in assigning him the pseudonym of Rob Riley. (Rob was not his first name.) She had probably met Rob, then a pre-med student at the University of Utah, when she was taking classes and working for the city recreation department. She encountered him again when he was doing his internship in the Los Angeles area. Among Maurine's papers at BYU is a typewriter-paper box of approximately twenty-five partial drafts of letters to Rob, all holograph, all undated. There is no way to know whether she reworked all—or any—of them to a final stage and sent any of them.

When I innocently brought some photocopies of these letters to Maurine in 1992, asking her what it was all about, she became extremely agitated and angry. She wanted to be taken to Brigham Young University to retrieve the letters and became enraged when told that was not possible. It was Maurine's most intense emotional reaction to any part of her past. Although she was often lonely and miserable and although she also contemplated suicide after the rape, it is only in conjunction with this affair that she seriously took steps to end her life. Discussing that relationship comes very close to violating her privacy; but *The Giant Joshua* has its roots in this period of her most extreme anguish. Any account of Maurine's life would be incomplete without it.

The letters contain few concrete details, but this much becomes clear: Rob and Maurine had a brief sexual affair while Maurine, now thirty-three, was living with Aunt Vira. Both had been very vulnerable. Rob was lonely and unwell and Maurine was rebounding from Nick's rejection of her in Boulder City. She saw herself as a Cinderella finally to be rescued. Always she felt herself born to some grand destiny. This had to be it, her hero, her soul mate, the socially superior intellectual and doctor she had longed for all her life. The affair in its euphoria lasted only a short time—a few weeks at most. She talked about meeting him "in the spring" and falling "in love with you on the spot. . . . I'd never met anybody like you in all my life. You were perfect." She unabashedly saw Rob as "the knight of whom I used to dream, come to straighten the tangle of my days." She recalls "being so visibly joyous that first Saturday that people stared at me on the street. . . . No wonder I didn't sleep! I didn't want to. I didn't want to lose one precious minute of staying awake to be happy in!"

In one passage, she gives what appears to be a more honest picture of how the affair had begun: "I thought we had agreed to love each other and then part . . . at the end of the summer." She might have agreed to such an arrangement but without seriously believing that they would carry it out. She apparently returned to St. George at some point during that summer, probably after Rob told her that he wanted to end the affair completely. She responded violently, accused him of ruining her life, and plunged into despair, hating herself for thinking there was some fairy-tale ending for her.

She did not return to Los Angeles but went to Cedar City, sixty miles north of St. George and a college town with some interesting drama activities. Here she again organized and taught her own dance and recreation program. She lived in a hotel—the El Escalanti, which she described to me as "a respectable place with modern conveniences." (It is no longer standing.) She was desperate to change her life and made at least one attempt to go overseas, since on September 11, 1936, she drafted a letter to the president of the Lions' Clubs in Garland, Utah, in Cache County, asking for information about a scholarship "to study recreation in the Chile University."[47] It is not known if she ever sent this letter; there is no answer among her papers.

Among the people she met in Cedar City in the fall of 1936 was Dr. Arnold LaMar Graff, whom she consulted for some of her many physical ailments. He must have liked her, for he asked her to help his wife, Delores Jensen Graff, who was overwhelmed with their young children. Sixteen years younger than her husband, by the end of 1936 Delores had given birth to three sons eighteen months apart. As Maurine tells the story, she quickly won over the children, becoming a much-appreciated friend of the family.[48]

With pressure from her family to find a permanent job, Maurine looked hopefully toward a faculty position for 1937–38 at Cedar City's Branch Agricultural College (now Southern Utah University), then a junior college. With a regular salary, at least that part of life would be better. Hoping to impress influential people in Cedar City who might influence the job decision, she tried to seize what she thought could be her big opportunity. During 1935 and 1936, the administration of Zion National Park service encouraged an interdenominational Easter service in the spectacular redrock park which, thanks to its lower elevation, usually has blooming plants as much as a month before Cedar City. Some of the townspeople, including faculty from the drama department at the college, were planning an even bigger and better Easter pageant for the spring of 1937. With her creative ideas, dramatic training, and dance experience, Maurine could see herself making a major contribution. She took steps to make her name and capabilities known to those in positions to help her.

The director was Grant Hubbard Redford. Maurine did not have a romantic relationship with him, but it must still be counted as her fifth disastrous but mercifully brief relationship in five years. Redford was born 25 December 1908 in Seattle, Washington, to Thomas L. Redford and Gwen Hubbard Redford and had graduated from Utah State Agricultural College (now Utah State University). He had been hired in 1936 as an instructor of speech and drama at the College of Southern Utah and was made head of the English Department that same year, a position he held until 1943. He would marry Ione Higbee of Cedar City on June 27, 1938;[49] but when Maurine met him, he was a handsome, capable, single man, age twenty-eight, who also lived at El Escalanti. He enjoyed talking about books, writing, and many of the philosophical and psychological topics that Maurine and Lillian liked to explore. It was natural for them to strike up a friendship. Given Maurine's intense desire to be loved by an important man, she probably wanted a deeper involvement; but Redford, five years her junior, seems to have avoided such an entanglement from the first, insisting on only a casual friendship.

A few letters between them have survived; and their content makes it clear that Maurine was still so starved for understanding and acceptance that she told him much of her pitiable life story. She always claimed that she wanted only friendship with Redford. But it is more likely that she still wanted rescue. She wanted to be cared for. She wanted someone to solve her problems for her and to love her. Predictably, Redford not only declined this proffered role but also did not accept her offer to help him produce the pageant.

The pageant was very important locally. As a student, Redford had toured the United States for two years with the European Passion players of Freiburg, Germany. He wrote the script and took the role of Christ for the Cedar City's pageant. Workmen from the federally funded Civilian Conservation Corps built an amphitheater near the Altar of Sacrifice in Zion National Park, and the staging took advantage of natural outcroppings.[50] In 1937, approximately five hundred participated in the orchestra, chorus, and other roles. Attendance was five thousand that year and ten thousand in 1938. By 1940, it was attracting national attention; but the next year, J. Reuben Clark and David O. McKay, counselor in the LDS First Presidency, asked the pageant committee to discontinue it, which they did.[51]

To Maurine, Redford's refusal of her help was another severe blow to her self-worth. She felt he blocked her, not only from participating in the pageant, but also from any respectable job with the college or community. She does not come out of the next few months with much dignity or maturity, but the importance of this time period is again crucial in preparing the ground for *The Giant Joshua*. If Maurine had been hired at the college, it seems likely that she would never have written her masterwork.

Maurine wrote Redford a scorching letter,[52] which he answered on 18 January, presumably just a few days later, being brutally frank about how her self-pity sabotaged any success she might expect. However, he also said some nice things about her and admitted "there was wheat among the chaff," by which he referred to her talent. He praised her short story (probably "Hell, It's Worth It") saying that it "thrilled him."[53] Maurine, in an emotional reversal which must have been as disconcerting as her original attack, sent Redford an undated, remorseful follow-up letter, but that was the end of it. Redford did not respond. Redford's frankness to Maurine dampened, though it did not quench, her self-pity. But it did give her some experience with objectivity that would stand her in good stead when she began *The Giant Joshua*.

A better indication of her emotional fragility, however, was that she left off writing her intimate disclosures to Grant Redford only, in a manner of speaking, to hurl herself aboard a train bound for San Francisco to attempt reconciliation with Rob Riley. Once again, this effort was a dreadful episode that left her in even deeper despair. According to the undated letter drafts which seem to refer to it, she caught the train on impulse and arrived virtually penniless, probably staying with Lillian. "I was so broken-hearted and grief stricken over things here at home," she wrote Rob, "I had to laugh once more! It was like flying to an oasis of happiness in a sea of misery. I felt that if I could just be with you once more, then I could face all the days and months of suffering ahead of me." But Rob was outraged and felt she was trying to manipulate him into taking care of her. Maurine wrote that she was particularly hurt when he suggested "that they involve an attorney in effecting the separation so that there would be no strings." Maurine denied that she wanted money. "I don't mind being broke at all." Instead, seeing him was "a glorious gamble . . . the most important thing in my life just then, . . . and laughing and getting things straightened out so that we could be friends again."

She insists that she could have parted from him as agreed "with never a regret" (a statement whose accuracy must be doubted), but only with the understanding that they loved each other. What shattered her was "to find out you'd really hated me for ever so long! It was such a blow. Nothing in all my life has ever hurt like that! Something snapped inside of me. I went completely crazy for a little while." She begs: "Understand I never did blame you for not loving me. I know I'm not worth loving much. But I was so humiliated! You must have thought I was so forward and bold. If only you'd told me just that way last June." Suffering and anxious, she tries to explain herself and salvage something from their relationship. The letters make agonizing reading. What man alive could understand a woman like this? One has to remember (and even hope) that she never mailed any of the letters, and their form—stream-of-consciousness outpourings—suggests that she never finished them.

Heroically, she releases him from any responsibility for her and promises: "I'll make a gay old spinster. I'll raise cats and dogs and cookies for other people's children. I tell you, honey, I'll build me a fine life, really. . . . Being able to love you with a clear conscience even if I'm in Africa means more to me than being married to any other man. . . . You won't even need to ever see me again or think of me if you don't want to—but I'll be somewhere believing in you, forever and ever." As a ploy for sympathy (if anything like this letter was actually sent), it certainly failed; but in terms of revealing Maurine's own most passionate desires and longing, the message is heart-wrenchingly clear.

In these letters, she depicts herself as an old-fashioned girl, heart-hungry and loyal—an image that she would recreate later with other men. Tellingly, this passage, like many similar efforts with other men, begins with "You see . . ." I read these passages as Maurine's effort to literally "see" herself and her life differently. These "you see's" signal her effort to remake herself and to reconstruct a version of her life that she can live with emotionally and spiritually:

> You see, Rob, most of the girls I knew either wanted careers or a rich man. I didn't want either. I wanted an old-fashioned chance at life with a man I could love, a chance to force from the world the sort of liv-

ing pattern I wanted—to lose myself in helping some man get to the top of the heap, to raise fine children, to put down roots somewhere and make life a lovely and gracious thing. I'd love the kind of hardship involved in that because it would be building something. . . .

I've wanted so desperately to belong some place in the world, to have a niche of my own, to know that somebody cared, even a little. I've never had a home. I've always longed for a home. You can't blame me for dreaming of even a furnished room, poor if you like, but rich because you would come sometimes and I could call it "home."

She obsessively evokes this dream: Rob as her hero, a modest but gracious home, her hunger for love. She implores him to understand, not to laugh at her. She comforts herself by repeatedly pledging to love him always from afar and repeats her resolve: "I will always be able henceforth to stand on my own feet, it served its purpose. You see, you really did me a favor: you taught me that there is nothing that can ever happen again that I can't take."

However, her resolve to "stand on my own feet" was a brave masquerade. When she finally faced Rob's second rejection and fully realized her humiliation, she became suicidal. In "Confessions of a She Devil," without mentioning Rob, she describes the crisis in terms that echoes the dog imagery she had used with Grant Redford: "I suppose when a dog is kicked often enough it stays down. Anyway, last spring I went to San Francisco to kill myself. I could make suicide look more like an accident that far away. I got all ready to swallow the dozen sodium amytal capsules when the humor of the situation struck me. I was so damned sorry for myself. And then Lillian had a baby; how could I kill myself when she was having a baby? So I had to put it off."[54]

In 1992 as Maurine and I discussed "Confessions of a She Devil," she added more details. Lillian, her daughter Marion, and Emerson were under considerable financial strain because Emerson had lost his job in July 1937 and was ill. A persistent problem with communication was exacerbating the already strained relationship; Lillian would not learn until 1940 that Emerson was actually in love with Marion, Lillian's teenage daughter.[55] In a letter to Maurine in the spring of 1938, Lillian shuddered at the memory of the winter of 1936–37." The worst thing that has ever happened to me is living through winter before last." Emerson had never liked Maurine because he saw her as a reminder of Lillian's "checkered" past; and for most of their marriage, Lillian tried to maintain domestic peace by sneaking opportunities to write Maurine.[56] Having the emotionally overwrought Maurine in the house must have increased the tensions all around. When Lillian went into labor, her relationship with her husband had deteriorated so much that it was Maurine who sat by her bedside in the hospital, holding her hand. Between contractions, they talked about how disastrous life seemed for both of them.[57]

Just before Lillian was wheeled into the delivery room, she made Maurine promise that, before she killed herself she would give her writing a big try. Money or no money, job or no job, Maurine would get to the Rocky Mountain Writers Conference in Boulder, Colorado, later that month. Lillian had attended at least once, in 1935, and felt it might wake Maurine up to a talent she, Lillian, knew she had. Maurine promised.

In "Confessions," Maurine summarized: "Writing was literally all I had left for which to go on living, and I had to find out how much hope lay in that" (18). It seems ironic that Lillian, who wanted to write a great Mormon novel gave birth to a flesh and blood child on July 7, 1937, while Maurine, who thought she desperately wanted a man and his flesh-and-blood child, would, on this same day, begin giving birth to a great Mormon novel.

The four years between 1933 and 1937 were crammed with the worst of the "swell suffering" that John Peale Bishop would admire only a few months later. She had lost at least two jobs, created and lost two more, been married divorced, suffered rape and an abortion, and plunged into six romantic relationships—counting the revival of interest in Clare Woodbury, and Grant Redford's prudent holding her at arm's length. In her sexual affairs with Nick Spencer and Rob Riley, she had, not just unsuccessful romances, but spectacularly and devastatingly disastrous relationships. She would never stop yearning for a protective knight, for true love, and for her myth of domestic bliss; but after acting on her promise to Lillian in the summer of 1937, she would finally have something to build her life on besides men who didn't want her. Joshua would be the only knight she could ever count as her own.

Notes

[1] I was unable to locate an office in the state, county, or city government that had records of the Recreation Department or other employment records for Maurine.

2 Maurine Whipple, Letter to Penn Smith, ca. early 1950s; Maurine Whipple Collection, L. Tom Perry Special Collections, Harold B. Lee Library, Brigham Young University, Provo, Utah, with photocopy in Maurine Whipple Collection, Archive, Val A. Browning Library, Dixie College, St. George, Utah. Documents in both collections hereafter cited as BYU, photocopy Dixie College. 1950s, holograph BYU; photocopy Dixie College.

3 1931 *Polk Directory* for Salt Lake City.

4 Ironically, Lillian's ancestry is much clearer than her personal history. Her paternal great-grandfather, Hector McQuarrie, was born in 1834 in Scotland, became a Mormon, immigrated to Salt Lake City in 1855, married Agnes Gray in 1857, moved to St. George in 1861, and also married his wife's niece, Janet Gray. He died in 1920. His son, Lillian's grandfather, was Robert Gary McQuarrie, born in Salt Lake City in 1858.

5 Lillian McQuarrie, Letter to Maurine Whipple, 16 April 1938; holograph BYU; photocopy Dixie College.

6 Lillian McQuarrie, Letter to Maurine Whipple, 3 July 19385; BYU; photocopy Dixie College. The book was probably *Life in Utah or the Mysteries and Crimes of Mormonism, being an Exposé of the Secret Rites and Ceremonies of the Latter-Day Saints with a Full and Authentic Account of Polygamy and the Mormon Sect from Its Origin to the Present Time* (1870) by J. H. Beadle of dime-novel fame, 576 pp.

7 McQuarrie to Whipple, 16 April 1938.

8 Lillian McQuarrie, Letter to Maurine Whipple, 16 April 1935; holograph BYU; photocopy Dixie College.

9 Although this program is not dated, Maurine has jotted on it, "All the waters of the seven seas," a line from a movie that Lillian quotes in a letter written 18 July (no year, but from internal evidence, I date it to 1936).

10 Maurine told me she taught Sunday School when she was in high school. Perhaps she was assisting the regular teacher or taught as a substitute, but ward records in St. George do not mention her in any capacity. The St. George dance program is dated 25 May (no year), and I have deduced its location because the students listed were St. George girls, including Ruby Seegmiller, Jane Pace, and Willaneta Brooks.

11 Maurine Whipple, Letter to Rob Riley, n.d., ca. summer or fall 1936; holograph BYU; photocopy Dixie College.

12 According to Larry M. Logue, *A Sermon in the Desert: Belief and Behavior in Early St. George, Utah* (Urbana: University of Illinois Press, 1988), 51: "Plural marriage in St. George deeply affected family life. Almost two-thirds of all wives' experience in the town was in plural marriages, as were half of all child-years."

13 Quoted in Levi S. Peterson, *Juanita Brooks: Mormon Woman Historian* (Salt Lake City: University of Utah Press, 1988,) 78 note 67.

14 McQuarrie to Whipple, 3 July 1935.

15 The exact date is not known. Maurine did not keep her marriage certificate and only relatives are allowed access to vital records within this period.

16 Maurine Whipple, "Confessions of a She Devil," typescript, 15.

17 Ibid., 4.

THE DEVASTATING ROMANCES OF 1932-37

18 John S. McCormick, "The Great Depression," *Utah History Encyclopedia*, http//www.media.utah.edu/UHE/d/Depression,Great.html (accessed July 2003).

19 Recommendation letters were from Anne D. Kilsey, Superintendent of Public Instruction, Bear Lake County, Idaho; Herbert B. Maw, Dean of Men, University of Utah and later Utah's governor; Parnell Black, Assistant District Attorney in Salt Lake City, Judge A. E. Ellet, Salt Lake City; C. R. Cummings, bishop of Wilford Ward, Salt Lake City; and even one from Joseph K. Nicholes, principal of Dixie High School during her years there as a student, BYU.

20 Charlotte S. Stewart, Telegram to "Judy," date illegible except for year 1934; BYU.

21 Maurine Whipple, "Big Dog Eats Little Dog," n.d., 20 pp. holograph; Whipple Collection, BYU; photocopy Dixie College. The manuscript is damaged and incomplete. Because it was never published, some of the sheets are apparently unintegrated scenes.

22 Ibid., 20. There is no documentary evidence that she was offered this job, although it seems likely that she would have applied for such a position.

23 Ibid.

24 Ibid., 16.

25 Nick Spencer is a pseudonym. He is identified only by his first name (which is not "Nick") in her papers. Maurine would not tell me his surname because she felt that he had returned to the conventional Mormon mainstream and that discussing the episode might embarrass him or his children.

26 Anna Cox saved this program and some sheet music of popular tunes of the 1930s arranged for piano from Maurine's home before it was torn down in the late 1980s. Dixie College.

27 Whipple, "Confessions of a She Devil," 16.

28 Ibid., 18. If her phrasing is not mere rhetoric, it suggests that she had had other negative encounters with other bishops, although I have no other details.

29 Maurine Whipple, Letter (incomplete draft) to Nick Spencer, n.d., holograph; Whipple Collection, BYU; photocopy Dixie College.

30 Maurine Whipple, "Hell, It's Worth It!", 1936, exists in three versions: (1) A thirteen-page holograph, "We Built the Dam"; (2) A fourteen-page typescript, "Hell, It's Worth It," the carbon copy of a typescript on onion skin with corrections in Maurine's hand, and (3) a sixteen-page typescript, also titled "Hell, It's Worth It." All three are in the Whipple Collection, BYU, with photocopies of the first and third at Dixie College.

31 The tour guide at the dam site maintained, in the tour I took, that, although workers died on the job, no bodies were left in the concrete.

32 McQuarrie to Whipple, 3 July 1935.

33 Lillian McQuarrie, 933 E. 300 South, Salt Lake City, Letter to Maurine Whipple, 18 July 1935; BYU, photocopy Dixie College.

34 McQuarrie to Whipple, 3 July 1935.

35 The St. George polygamist and his family found out about Lillian's book and reacted angrily to both Lillian and Maurine, in no uncertain terms. Lillian had gathered information under the guise of getting it for Maurine, because she thought Maurine had the better connections with people in town. Maurine was upset by this deviousness, went

to the parties involved, and set the record straight, which cooled her relationship with Lillian. For her part, Lillian never wanted to hurt anyone. When she found out how much antagonism her project had aroused, she said she destroyed the manuscript. Lillian McQuarrie, Letter to Maurine Whipple, 17 January [no year; presumably 1936], holograph BYU; photocopy Dixie College.

36 Whipple, "Confessions of a She Devil," 16.

37 McQuarrie to Whipple, 3 July 1935.

38 McQuarrie to Whipple, 18 July 1935.

39 Ibid.

40 Maurine Whipple, "Rotten-Logging," ca. 1936, 16 pp.; holograph BYU; my typescript from this holograph at Dixie College.

41 *Deseret News*, August 2, 1966.

42 Maurine Whipple, contract, Carbon County School District, photocopy in my possession.

43 Whipple, "Confessions of a She Devil," 17.

44 Lillian McQuarrie, Letter to Maurine Whipple, October 5, 1950; typescript Whipple Collection, BYU; photocopy Dixie College. Latuda was six miles from Helper, a larger town.

45 Elvira Whipple Herbert was born in Pine Valley, Utah, on October 6, 1878, to Eli Whipple and Mary Jane Legg Whipple, Eli's third wife. She managed a boarding house in Los Angeles at 1681 West 25th Street, and died 29 October 1954 in Tulare, California.

46 Alice Titus Whipple, Interviewed by Veda Hale, 12 June 1991.

47 Maurine Whipple, holograph rough draft of letter to J. D. Denton, Lions' Club President of Garland, Utah, 11 July 1936; Dixie College.

48 Maurine includes this family in the acknowledgments of *The Giant Joshua* but misspells their name as "Graf." Johanna Graff Brown, interviewed by Veda Hale, 29 December 2000.

49 Clipping from unidentified newspaper, n.d., in "Grant Redford" file, Special Collections, Library, Southern Utah University, Cedar City, Utah. Photocopy Dixie College.

50 D. C. Dix, "Pageant Resurrection to Be Featured Again at Beautiful Zion Park," *Salt Lake Tribune*, April 10, 1938, n.p., clipping, Archives, Southern Utah University.

51 D. C. Dix, "The Passion Play of the West," *Utah Magazine*, April 1939, 6–7, 23–24. According to "Zion Pageant Stopped at Church Request," *The Bucian* (College of Southern Utah student newspaper), March 11, 1941, in "Easter Pageant" file, Special Collections, College of Southern Utah, their reasons were: "The mass exodus from southern Utah communities breaks the Sabbath and detracts from church services in those communities; impersonation of the Savior in the pageant, with spectators and perhaps participants of various faiths and degrees of faith would almost inevitably produce an impersonation that could not receive church approval."

52 Maurine Whipple, Letter to Grant Redford, n.d. (before 18 January 1937), typescript. Maurine could type, though not well. Whipple Collection, BYU; photocopy Dixie College.

53 Grant Redford, Letter to Maurine Whipple, 18 January 1937, holograph; Whipple Collection, BYU; photocopy Dixie College.

54 Whipple, "Confessions of a She Devil," 17–18.

55 In 1992 Maurine didn't (or wouldn't) remember about this episode in Lillian's life. By coincidence, during one of my visits with Maurine, her friend, Evelyn Harris, also came to visit, heard our conversation, reminded Maurine of this episode, and helped her fill in the details.

56 McQuarrie to Whipple, 3 July 1935.

57 Whipple, "Confessions of a She Devil," 18.

6

THE PIVOTAL MOMENT, 1937

Through all the turmoil of Maurine's personal life, her troubled relationship with her family, and her repeated failures to find economic security, her love for Utah's Dixie was perhaps the one constant of her life. She said she called it "whispers from the red dust. I always knew I had to catch those whispers. And as a life of my own became more and more hopeless, the louder those whispers became. But I just didn't have enough confidence to think I could really write the book I envisioned, even after all the pounding Lillian did on me. Had I succeeded in being a part of the Easter pageant and if that had led to my getting a permanent teaching position, I doubt I would have ever gotten around to it."

It is still unclear whether Maurine entered her 30,000-word novella "Beaver Dam Wash" in the first-novel category of the Rocky Mountain Writers' conference in Boulder City, Colorado, or whether Lillian forced Maurine's hand by doing it for her. Maurine told me that Lillian did it. Whatever the case, Maurine said she rallied, borrowed the money from the St. George bank, and went to the conference, which opened 28 July 1937 and apparently closed on 4 August. There she found praise and enthusiastic encouragement from visiting critics John Peale Bishop[1] and Ford Maddox Ford,[2] and from Whit Burnett,[3] English professor at Columbia and editor of *Story Magazine*.

No complete manuscript of "Beaver Dam Wash" has been found. It apparently had its genesis in "Quicksand," a short story published in the June 1926 issue of *Pen*, the University of Utah's literary magazine, when Maurine was a senior and which she expanded while recuperating from appendicitis during her teaching year in Idaho.[4] (See chap. 4.) Maurine's papers also include a detailed synopsis in three versions.[5]

Maurine described Bishop's critique of "Beaver Dam Wash" in a 1971 interview with Maryruth Bracy and Linda Lambert: "He told me that, out of all the first novels he'd ever read, mine was the only one that was funny. And it was unforced humor. I hadn't tried to be funny. He also said there was no breast-beating in it. Most autobiographical novels, first novels, are just full of how tough the world's been and you beat your breast and cry aloud to the stars and all that. Most beginning writers are pretty melodramatic. Well, this wasn't about me at all. It had nothing of me in it except the country, and he couldn't get over that. He told me that I had this innate gift in handling material in this unforced way." Burnett commented: "It was simple, moving, tender and beautiful. . . . I was moved, but not by humor."[6]

The writers' conference was a heady experience. Maurine had come from an environment where she was considered not only a failure, but a rather pathetic one. Here, she was praised and sought after as someone with worthwhile talent and "swell suffering"[7] that could make great literature. What's more, she was awarded the novel scholarship for the 1938 conference.[8]

Clippings from the *Boulder Daily Camera* describe the schedule Maurine would have followed for the three-week conference.[9] No doubt days were filled with workshops, master classes, individual conferences, and a certain amount of free time for personal interactions and "retreat" time for working writers. Maurine apparently wrote "Confessions of a She Devil" at the conference, possibly as part of a workshop assignment.

If there was a fly in Maurine's ointment, it was the shock of finding Grant Redford at the conference. The holograph of "Confessions of a She Devil" contains a paragraph about Redford's presence: "Last winter I lost the business I had built up in Cedar City because a certain very influential Mr. G., claiming that I antagonized his artistic temperament, eased me out of my job. I mention this because whom should I run into here at the conference but this same Mr. G, still both artistic and influential!"[10] She marked through this paragraph and it does not appear in the typescript. Apparently Maurine, wisely paying attention to her common sense, decided it would not enhance her own reputation as a serious writer to air personal enmities to strangers who would also be meeting Redford, especially since Redford's credentials were so much more impressive than her own. She ignored him. However, as this passage makes plain, despite the groveling camaraderie she pressed on Redford in her last letter in January 1937, she never really forgave him and in 1992 still had no good words for him.

Some measure of Redford's status is that he was singled out for a journalistic profile. According to an article at the time, "Among the Writers," Redford was working on a second novel and also soliciting articles for the *Intermountain Review*, a periodical he had started with two friends in 1936 "with the idea of providing a place to publish and crystallize the growing consciousness of the West as a social and literary entity."[11]

Maurine's own recollections of this all-important three-week conference were obviously shaped by the experiences that led directly to *The Giant Joshua*. Unquestionably, those experiences were Ford Maddox Ford's appreciation of "Beaver Dam Wash," since he influenced Ferris Greenslet, at Houghton Mifflin, to read it. John Peale Bishop seems to have paid the most attention to her personally. She told and retold her "Cinderella" story about sitting on the back steps of the dormitory (or sometimes fraternity house) talking to Bishop until four o'clock (sometimes two). Even though Bishop was not her romantic Prince Charming, he was the next best thing—an intellectual who, as she said, "spoke my language and liked me." In describing this enchanted night to Maryruth Bracy and Linda Lambert in 1971, Maurine says that Bishop went beyond a writing critique to personal encouragement that was "rain to my thirsty soul. "He also told me that I could be one of the greatest women writers of my time, if I had a little help and a decent environment and some encouragement. I had to have people. In other words, I couldn't be beaten down all the time. He said that if I could have peace of mind, food, and a place to live . . . but, of course, that's been my trouble."[12]

To do her justice, Maurine tried other, more admirable ways of meeting her emotional needs, but without much success. Perhaps after living through many more heartaches, her well-rehearsed victim's pose was all she had left. Years of her humiliating and constant pleas for understanding lay ahead and they are, unquestionably, fatiguing for a reader; but it helped me to remember that those pleas were a desperate survival tactic, exacerbated by poor health and loneliness. But anyone exposed to this exhibition of self-pitying inferiority can also understand why those to whom she presented herself in this way reacted eventually with dismay and, almost always, dismissal.

I had my own paradoxical experience with Maurine's self-pity contrasted with her ability to capture hard-edged narrative reality. In October 2000, I was in the BYU Special Collections wading through the box of thirty-three pages that Maurine had written to Rob Riley, reproaching him for betraying and abandoning her. They were repetitious, groveling, pleading, and self-pitying. I felt embarrassed for Maurine, irritated by her tone, and exhausted by reading them. Then I noticed that a few were written on the backs of a typescript. I turned the pages over and began reading a draft of "Hell, It's Worth It," her short story about Boulder Dam,[13] which Maurine bitterly told Redford she had destroyed. Redford had praised this story, telling Maurine that it had "thrilled" him.[14] After a few minutes of reading, I thought I knew what Redford had experienced. There I was holding pages, one side filled with a desperate scrawl that I could hardly make myself read because of the extravagant, painful rambling, while on the other side, written by the same person, appeared tight, wonderful prose capturing the spirit of human accomplishment and transforming pain. This experience was all the more poignant because I had also read Maurine's anguished draft letters to Nick Spencer and knew how heartbreaking the reality had been which she had transformed so powerfully into fiction. She had done exactly what John Peale Bishop had suggested—turned her "swell suffering" into great literature. I understood why these literary critics recognized genuine talent in her. It was this same talent, I might add, which kept me plugging through document after discouraging document, interview after disheartening interview, trying to understand how the two sides of Maurine Whipple could coexist.

It was hard then and is still hard now to accommodate the two Maurines. She returned to St. George after the writers' conference, her mind whirling with possibilities and hopes. She felt renewed and new, but she was returning to people who saw her as the same old Maurine.

Notes

[1] John Peale Bishop (1892–1944) published four books of poetry, a volume of short stories, a novel, and many critical essays. He also served on the staff of Paramount Pictures, as managing editor of *Vanity Fair*, and as poetry reviewer for the *Nation*. See Alexander Leitch, *A Princeton Companion* (Princeton, N.J.: Princeton University Press, 1978); on Compton's Home Library, *The Complete 1998 Edition Reference Collection, 1998*, CD–ROM, Version 101.

[2] Ford Maddox Ford (1873–1939) an English novelist, poet, and critic, edited the *Transatlantic Review* and *English Review*. Among the best-known of his forty-five books are *The Good Soldier* and *Parade's End*. Maryruth Bracy and Linda Lambert, "Maurine Whipple's Story of *the Giant Joshua*," *Dialogue: A Journal of Mormon Thought* 5 (Autumn/Winter 1971): 55–61. He was one of Ernest Hemingway's first publishers.

[3] Whit Burnett was born 14 August 1899 in Salt Lake City where he attended Granite High School with Emerson Evans, Lillian's husband. Lillian McQuarrie, Letter to

Maurine Whipple, 4 May 1938; BYU; photocopy Dixie College. He and his wife, Hallie Southgate (1908–91), wrote numerous how-to-write books and articles and co-edited *Story Magazine*. He spent most of his career at Columbia University (J. D. Salinger was one of his students) and died in 1973.

4 Maurine Whipple, "Quicksand," *Pen*, June 1926, 8–9, and reprinted ibid., 1947, 26, 74, in a special issue commemorating the centennial of the Mormon pioneers' arrival in the Salt Lake Valley.

5 These three versions, none dated and all titled "Quicksand," are: (1) a twelve-page holograph synopsis, its upper left corner torn away, that Carol Jensen found in a deteriorating cupboard on Maurine's porch after most of her papers had been taken to BYU; Maurine Whipple Collection, L. Tom Perry Special Collections, Harold B. Lee Library, Brigham Young University, Provo, Utah, with photocopy in Maurine Whipple Collection, Archive, Val A. Browning Library, Dixie College, St. George, Utah. Documents in both collections hereafter cited as BYU, photocopy Dixie College. (2) a two-page typescript synopsis, also damaged; (3) a five-page typescript synopsis, also damaged. The last two versions are at BYU, photocopies at Dixie College.

6 Whit Burnett, Letter to Maurine Whipple, 18 August 1937; BYU; photocopy Dixie College.

7 "Swell" was a common slang expression meaning "wonderful" or "great."

8 Lillian McQuarrie, Letter to Maurine Whipple, 21 March 1938, BYU, photocopy Dixie College.

9 Photocopies of newspaper clippings courtesy of the Carnegie Branch Library for Local History, Boulder, Colorado. Official conference literature described its history: "From a regional undertaking in 1930, the conference has grown to a truly national institution, bringing students from 30 states," the director pointed out. Even famous New England conferences lacked its diversity of talent and "cosmopolitan" air. "Sherwood Anderson and Other 'Top' Authors to Lead Writers' Conference," *Boulder Daily Camera*, April 17, 1937.

10 Maurine Whipple, "Confessions of a She Devil," holograph, 33.

11 Jeane LaGrone Smith, "Among the Writers," *Boulder Daily Camera*, 4 August 1937, courtesy Carnegie Branch Library.

12 Bracy and Lambert, "Maurine Whipple's Story," 56.

13 The version that Maurine had recycled in her draft letters to Rob Riley was missing pp. 2 and 7 and had two page 12's. Four additional versions, all with the same title, are in the Dixie College Library archive: (1) A yellowed typescript with corrections in Maurine's hand. Its first page is missing, and it ends in mid-sentence on p. 14; (2) A yellowed typed copy that includes Maurine's handwritten corrections on #1, some additions, and some repositioned paragraphs; (3) A carbon copy of #2 with additional penciled corrections in Maurine's hand; (4) A clean typescript containing the corrections from #3.

14 Grant Redford, Letter to Maurine Whipple, 18 January 1937, typescript, photocopy Dixie College.

❧ 7 ❧

WINNING THE FELLOWSHIP

When Ferris Greenslet of Houghton Mifflin saw "Beaver Dam Wash," he liked it and offered her a contract, but said she had to make it "'a little bit longer.' . . .because it is better to launch a young writer on a longer book—it's better for your career."[1]

This initial message was the beginning of a relationship chronicled in eighty letters and ten telegrams preserved in Maurine's papers. The first is dated February 1, 1938, and the last to be preserved is dated October 3, 1942. At the height of their correspondence during the intensive work on *The Giant Joshua*, Greenslet was writing sometimes every three or four days and seldom less than once a week. Apparently, most of Maurine's letters to Greenslet have not survived.

By the time the contract was arranged, Maurine had had several weeks to reflect on her experience in Boulder. Some measure of her self-confidence was that she had not spent those weeks paralyzed by "why me?" fears. Instead, she was laying the foundation of an even more elaborate project.

> So I wrote back and told him I'd had this idea for *The Giant Joshua* as long as I could remember. He asked me if I could write a synopsis of it, so I did. I've still got it. It's the synopsis of the three generations. What I was interested in was the evolution of the Mormon idea, and I'd had that in mind, including the plot, ever since I was in grade school. So I sent it to him. He said, "Will you write us a chapter?"
> Some of the old people were alive then—Uncle Charlie Seegmiller was 95, Aunt Jane [Thompson Bleak] was 90 something—and I just went and talked to them. I got so immersed in that era—reading everything and wandering the hills and sitting upon the red hills and visualizing everything—that it was almost as if I had lived through it myself.

Anyway, I wrote the first chapter almost the way it exists today. In fact, I remember I started the first sentence by saying something about Clory moving on the black lava rock and finding it still warm although it was the first of December. I sent this back to him and he wired back. He said, "There's such a tremendous difference between what you've done in 'Beaver Dam Wash' and what you've done in this that we'd rather start with *The Giant Joshua*." He said "Beaver Dam Wash" was infantile compared to this other.[2]

Greenslet also told her that her synopsis and two sample chapters would let her apply for the thousand-dollar fellowship that Houghton Mifflin offered yearly to new authors working on a first novel. These materials, upon which Maurine's destiny hung, would be due in January 1938, four months away, accompanied by a photograph, application, and some letters of reference.

So it was that sixty-one-year-old Ferris Greenslet entered Maurine's life. It is very doubtful that *The Giant Joshua* would have been written without him. He was Houghton Mifflin's literary editor for fifty-two years and, from that position, introduced Laura Krey, Stuart Cloete, Willa Cather, and Henry Adams to the reading public.[3]

Greenslet had become the company's vice president two years before his association with Maurine began in 1936 and was at the height of his mature powers when he worked with her on *The Giant Joshua*. Warm, scholarly, and gentlemanly, Greenslet became a father figure, mentor, and gentle but relentless taskmaster for the talented but erratic thirty-four-year-old Maurine. Maurine, for her part, worshipped him and claimed anyone could write a book with Greenslet behind her. Even after he firmly used his retirement to distance himself from Maurine's personal and professional woes and even when she was raging against what she considered her exploitation by Houghton Mifflin, she had only great fondness and gratitude for "F. G.," as she sometimes called him. "Best editor in the United States at the time. And I guess he'd be one of the best in the world," she said in a 1971 interview.[4]

Even though "he just never understood how it was to be poor" and, in her mind, therefore permitted Houghton Mifflin to negotiate an unfair contract with her, she explained it away by saying that he thought she was young, that the first book would get her name known, and that financial rewards would come with later books. She added: "An editor is worth his weight in gold. It isn't everybody who can read the first two or three chapters of a work and even the first draft and see the potential; in other words, see what can be created as a whole from a very small part. It takes a very special kind of imaginative empathy to do it.[5]

WINNING THE FELLOWSHIP

Ferris Greenslet did for Maurine what Lillian McQuarrie couldn't do. Along with consistent emotional support, he offered professional mentoring with the easy authority of a cultured and well-educated male. He was undoubtedly accustomed to the tremulousness and insecurities of young writers; but in Maurine's case, his encouragement and unwavering insistence that she concentrate only on writing were absolutely crucial to the production of *The Giant Joshua*. He provided strength for Maurine to face down those who minimized and dismissed her talent while also helping to provide the physical climate so the writing could proceed.

To write the synopsis and two chapters that Ferris Greenslet requested, the cash-strapped Maurine (her only income was from a few dance students) had no choice but to continue her residence in the uncomfortable north bedroom of Charlie's and Annie's house under the disapproving look of people who thought she should be out looking for a steady job as a schoolteacher. She said Charlie was one of them, but he let her stay in the house rent free. Annie cooked for Maurine, did her laundry, and perhaps babied her too much. Maurine said, "Mother didn't like being around Father and his criticisms, so she often came in to be with me. She'd say, 'I won't bother you. I just want to sit by you.'" Maurine was clearly a privileged character in the household, taking little part in the chores.

This period was not particularly easy for Charlie and Annie, either. They had a house full. In addition to Maurine and George, Ray and his new wife, Alice, were living with them. Alice Titus was a nurse working at the Grand Canyon when Ray, just back from playing in a band on a cruise ship, joined another band at the Grand Canyon lodge. Alice was, according to Maurine, "not a Mormon, but from a prominent Masonic family in Salt Lake City, and when she married Ray, we all wanted to look good in her eyes. I really liked her." It was clear that Maurine felt this union was a step up for the Whipples. Ray and Alice had married the autumn before on 26 September 1936, and Alice had become pregnant in May 1937 with their first child.

Ray had tried to find work in California, then returned to St. George at Charlie's request where he worked in the family lumber business and began building a home. Ray was the strongest of the brothers, the one best able to withstand his father's dominance. He was also good at steering clear of entanglement in Maurine's problems. Alice's friendship and concern may, in fact, have overcompensated for Ray's distance, and she was Maurine's best ally during these early months of writing, providing sympathy and encouragement. She would often bring Maurine a hot drink made of liquid Jell-O to keep her going during the cold winter days and nights.[6] Of all the members of her family, Maurine gave most credit to Alice for her help. In a 1980 interview, Maurine commented, "If it hadn't been for Alice, I couldn't have written Joshua."[7]

George was twenty-three but also still living at home, showing distressing signs of drinking, and breaking loose in wild ways. But Maurine's heart particularly ached for thirty-one-year-old Ralph, feeling that he was fated to die young. He was still driving his motorcycle recklessly over the red hills, had discovered that drinking relieved his stuttering, and was keeping company with equally reckless friends. He had married Ida Johnson Beatty, a divorcée with a daughter named Jeannie, just a few months earlier on 3 May 1937; but the six-month-old marriage had not settled him down.[8]

Florence and Ben, though contented as a couple, were struggling financially and had two children, Colleen, born January 22, 1932, and Charles Larry, born February 23, 1937. They were living in Pioche, Nevada, where Ben was a miner. Despite the distance, Maurine remained anxiously involved in their lives, as Florence's record of a family emergency shows. In about January 1938 when Maurine was finishing up the synopsis and two chapters to send to Ferris Greenslet, eleven-month-old Larry crawled under the washing machine after his ball. An exposed gear "bored a hole in his head, contaminating the wound with dirt and grease. His face became red and swollen and he was critically ill—the doctor said if the erysiphis got in to his eyes, it would go to his brain and kill him." Florence brought the baby to St. George and Maurine helped her keep the hot boric acid packs on his head day and night. Then the town doctor, Dr. McGregor, suggested trying a new medicine called Sulfanilamide—the very first of the wonderful sulfa drugs. Maurine misunderstood the dosage and gave the baby twice as much as the doctor ordered, but in only a few days he was healed. Florence always claimed "it was that mistake that saved the baby's life."[9]

Maurine told me this same story more than once when she wanted to make the point that she could not simply concentrate on her writing—that she had to "take care of the family."

In actuality everyone in the family seemed willing to give Maurine a chance to make good on her golden opportunity. Simultaneously terrified and energized, Maurine worked hard in writing the synopsis and sample chapters to accompany her application for the fellowship.

She explained in a 1971 interview:

> I went through an awful lot just for a chance to apply for the fellowship. I used to teach tap-dancing after school was out and I'd do my research in the morning and then I'd work at night and lots of times I'd work all night long. I discovered that the best stuff came to me when I was so exhausted I could no longer think logically and I'd go to bed. And right when I was dozing off, then the words would start coming. I never

analyzed it, but I know now that it's the subconscious that writes for you. I didn't know what it was; I just knew that the real creative stuff that I didn't have to dig for, that I knew was right, came to me when I was half-asleep, when my conscious mind no longer functioned.[10]

For Christmas 1937, a big box of chocolates arrived from Houghton Mifflin. It was visible proof to Maurine's relatives, friends, and detractors that important people in Boston believed in her. On 24 January 1938, Maurine mailed off a brief synopsis and the first two chapters. A lengthy rough draft of the holograph letter she sent Greenslet with these chapters has survived, confessing that her detailed synopsis and character studies were not quite ready yet.

Greenslet must have asked Maurine for more details about the plot, because she explained: "I have been interested in the evolution of the Mormon idea and the plot for a book ever since I was in grade school." She volunteered to borrow more money to come East so they could "talk over my plans for the book." She then expressed her own confidence that it was a good plot and said that the "few people with whom I have shared it agreed." But she was worried because she had read that "generation" novels were no longer fashionable. She thought hers would have to be one, because "it would take three generations to tell the story of a Mormon town, which would be the one main character." She thought the first section must show "the unusual influences which made the town and the people as they were." Then the present—apparently dealing with Cowboy Jim (Clory's son), and his talented daughter Lenzi, who "has to choose between international fame as a vocal artist and finding happiness at home"—could be handled "with the unusual results arising from the welter."[11]

Maurine's intuition that St. George itself was the main character of her novel was remarkably accurate, accounting for the power of the first half of the novel during the settlement period but also the sense that the plot was fraying away during the last part into a cycle of generalizations and repeated hardships with fewer of those brilliant and vivid individual scenes that makes the first part of the novel so engrossing. However, as this letter reveals, Maurine had not fully conceptualized the plot. The synopsis, as Greenslet later helped Maurine realize, was too much for one book, thus generating her plans for a never-realized trilogy. Maurine's plan was to take Mormonism's "Grand Idea" full circle, concluding with its triumph a century after settlement. Had Maurine actually finished this trilogy, its positive third volume may have reduced the negative reactions she received from her family and friends from the challenging and bitter-sweet chronicle of Clorinda MacIntyre's gallant coping with the hardships of polygamy, frontier life, poverty, bereavement, and eventual abandonment. They would have found "right" and validating granddaughter Lenzi's choosing to give up "worldly" success and fame for the peace and fulfillment of St. George and Mormondom.

An intriguing passage in this rough-draft letter that has been crossed out may show Maurine experimenting with how to present her identity as a writer: "It's as if in the beginning there was a pleasant little stream which dared to go adventuring into unknown lands; but there it met obstacles, boulders, cataclysms which changed and re-made its very soul; so that today it is a mad torrent flowing in a precipitous canyon capable of doing great damage, and hard to control." Was she likening herself to the little stream? And did her crossing out of the passage indicate her hope that she could control the mad torrent, turning it into a fertile stream?

She concluded her long letter with considerable and not quite accurate optimism: "I have complete dates worked out and complete details of all these situations; I can assure you there is no doubt of 'literary honesty' throughout the tale and every incident is typical of the locality."[11]

On 31 February 1938, Greenslet enthusiastically wired: GREATLY LIKE AND ADMIRE THE WRITING AND FIRST CHAPTERS OF GIANT JOSHUA. YOU UNDOUBTEDLY HAVE SOMETHING. NOT ENTIRELY SOLD ON PLANS FOR COMPLETION BUT WILL WRITE AT LENGTH ABOUT THIS IN A DAY OR TWO. COMPLIMENTS AND CONGRATULATIONS.[12]

The next day, 1 February, he wrote the promised critique. He agreed to put "Beaver Dam Wash" on hold and have Maurine plunge into *The Giant Joshua*: "I judge from reading the synopsis and the emotional effect of its ending on me (yes, even in synopsis the ending was very moving) that your imagination is decidedly 'het up' over the material of the concluding chapters."

He pointed out that she had made a historically inaccurate statement: "You say 'President Buchanan signs the anti-polygamy bill in 1874.'" James Buchanan had been president during the Utah War of 1857–58, but the president in 1874 who signed the Poland Bill was Ulysses S. Grant. Greenslet gently used this example to stress that Maurine needed to get the historical background "copper-fastened, both because of the hen-minded readers . . . and because [a] solid foundation of this sort makes for better architecture in the superstructure." He told her he was sending her a biography of Joseph Smith, saying, "It may put an idea or two into your head."[13]

For Greenslet, the question of Mormonism's truth claims would have been irrelevant; but the fact that he saw Maurine's synopsis as emotionally moving validated it as literature, not dogmatism. I doubt that Maurine had orthodox views on Mormonism's exclusive claims to the truth;

but I know that she powerfully believed that her people had a cultural tradition of mythic proportions, one that bound them together and gave them amazing endurance, and one that made them as successful as any who have tried to live the Golden Rule of brotherhood. That is what the ending of the synopsis implies.

In mid-February, Greenslet gave her further advice about how to apply for the fellowship, telling her to have those writing letters of reference to send them to the committee. He also focused on the book's theme, putting his finger unerringly on the projected parts about which Maurine was least knowledgeable—the cowboy life of Clory's son Jim and the choice Clory's granddaughter must make between the glamour of "the world" and affiliation with her hometown: "I think the town, not Jim, is the story: that and, as you say, Brotherly Love, always, of course, as displayed in the lives of your characters." He expressed some concern whether she could "give the Hollywood, New York, and Paris chapters the same accent of reality that I find in the beginning."[14]

What happened between the end of January when Maurine sent off the chapters and May 25, when she got a telegram announcing the results, is a blank in Maurine's documentary record. She may have simply withdrawn into exhaustion for a few weeks or maintained her writing schedule, grimly determined to press on regardless of the outcome with Greenslet. She apparently stayed in town as winter thawed into St. George's early, lovely spring. The first document to survive during this hiatus is a letter from Lillian, written on 21 March 1938. She had not heard from Maurine nor written to her since the night of Lloyd's birth in July 1937—which means that she had waited in vain for a report from Maurine about what had happened at the Boulder conference. Now she wrote because a mutual friend, Fern Dalby, had written that she had won the scholarship to the 1938 conference for poetry and that Maurine had won the same award in the novel category. Lillian expressed her confidence that Maurine had "arrived" and said: "There'll be no stopping you, because you have the genius if anyone ever did. I've always maintained that, and I always will."[15]

The hints in this letter in the spring of 1938 do not explain Maurine's silence during the summer of 1937, especially when she must have known that Lillian would be anxious to know how the writers' conference had gone. However, there is a possibility that, given Maurine's past and an inconclusive but provocative letter in Maurine's papers, that Maurine and Emerson knew they would like each other only too well. Maurine, with her powers of observations, would have sensed that there was trouble ahead for Lillian and Emerson and didn't know how to warn Lillian and so chose to distance herself.[16] Whatever the case, it seems petty of Maurine not to have shared the news of her success. It is a tribute to Lillian that in none of her thirty letters and one telegram preserved in Maurine's papers did she express any hint of jealousy. Her letters are always full of happiness for any success Maurine achieved.

Maurine, prodded by guilt, must have written back promptly, filling in the details of the conference and the fellowship competition, for Lillian's next letter came on 16 April, barely three weeks later, "So bloomin' thrilled . . . I had to sit right down and answer. . . . Rene, think of what it's all going to mean to you? I mean, maybe it won't be the thrill it might to someone like me who really can't expect much, but it is going to pave the way for you to get to where you'll be more comfortable, more secure, and healthier." She also added hopes for Maurine's personal happiness: "Someone, somewhere, who sees eye to eye with you, and we can have back yards that meet, and morning glory vines, and a whole hell of a lot of hours to talk in, over back fences."

She then continued with news of her own. Lloyd had proved to be a difficult baby, and Lillian wrote with some exasperation: "I have given up about a year and half to Lloyd, now, and I'm not willing to give up any more time in bum health and nervous fits for anybody. . . . I can hardly raise my heels two inches from the floor. But it's only in spells, and I get over it. And my hair, meanwhile, is going white. It's almost 'salt and pepper' grey, now. I part it so it isn't quite that bad, but you'd be surprised. I don't care, you understand, but it's the first blow, I guess, that ever comes." Lillian's gallant realism should have set a good example for Maurine, who was still hennaing her hair, not only to brighten its color but also to strengthen her pose that she was much younger than she was.

Another hint that the relationship between Maurine and Lillian's husband was not an easy one comes in this letter: "I wish you two could like each other and understand each other. You are very much alike, as I probably said before, and there's not much hope of your ever being really friendly, but I'd rather have that than almost anything I know. You probably know exactly how I feel about this."

Lillian concluded her letter with redoubled congratulations: "Please remember that I'm thrilling with you. . . . I get so . . . lonesome sometimes I could go on a little voyage, myself, and leap off when the ship got under way. I do have everything, as you say, and I said the other day that if I couldn't be happy now, I ought to have my head bashed against a brick building. But there's always the magic behind the moon that I'm crying for, and I don't know what it looks like."[17] Maurine liked that phrase, "the magic behind the moon," and underlined it on the letter.

Again Maurine responded quickly, this time sending Lillian a copy of "Confessions of a She Devil," which she had most probably written at the writers' conference. Lillian responded promptly on 1 May 1938, saying that its hard-knocks narrative was a great deal "in purpose and meaning" like a short story Lillian herself had written for the conference, most likely the one she attended in 1935. But rather than brooding over the rejection of her story or feeling jealous of Maurine, Lillian generously praised "Confessions" and encouraged Maurine to think about several other story topics.

She added more family news. Emerson had just lost another job and had succeeded in making Lillian "plough . . . under" her "mystic drivel" although Lillian was recalcitrant enough to insist, "I don't know that I like it." Teenage daughter Marian had also moved home again after living with her father's parents, requiring Lillian to make more adjustments.[18]

Then, events happened hastily. Utah's telegraph line ran only as far south as Cedar City, and messages to St. George had to be telephoned on. On May 25, 1938, Charlie Whipple's telephone rang, and the telegrapher read the telegram with its earth-shattering news: "BOARD OF DIRECTORS VOTED THIS MORNING TO AWARD YOU THIS YEARS FICTION FELLOWSHIP KEEP IT QUIET UNTIL JUNE SIXTH WHEN FORMAL ANNOUNCEMENT WILL BE MADE. FIRST PAYMENT FIVE HUNDRED DOLLARS DUE JULY FIRST. TWO SCHOOLS OF THOUGHT HERE IN REGARD TO COMPLETION PERSONAL CONFERENCE THEREFORE HIGHLY DESIRABLE. AM TIED UP WITH MEETINGS AND FISHING TRIPS UNTIL JUNE TWENTY SECOND WOULD BE DELITED [sic] TO SEE YOU HERE ANY TIME AFTER THAT. COMPLIMENTS AND CONGRATULATIONS. FERRIS GREENSLET."[19]

It is doubtful that Maurine concealed the news from her family until June, but there is no record of their reaction. She conscientiously kept the news from the local paper until 9 June. Then the weekly *Washington County News* headlined: "Maurine Whipple Awarded Fellowship and Prize of $1,000 for Novel." It said she had "won out against 1500 fiction writers, both amateurs and professionals who this year submitted novels in this contest."[20] The article reported that the novel was "nearly completed," that she would receive the first $500 payment on July 1 and the second on January 1, "shortly after which the book will be completed and published by Houghton Mifflin Company." For herself, Maurine was stunned by her good fortune. To the end of her days, she occasionally said in wonderment that she could not understand how any of her creations could be "worth more than four bits." When she made that kind of remark to Lillian before hearing the news, Lillian wrote back, "You've heard me spout about writing so much you must have been sickened on the whole subject long ago. I had to learn the whole thing from outside, while you already had it."[21]

"SWELL SUFFERING"

Ferris Greenslet's request for a personal conference coincided with Maurine's desire to go to Boston to participate in the publicity that awarding the fellowships was supposed to generate. Whether the winner's presence was expected is not clear—probably not immediately, since the public announcement was 6 June and Greenslet made it clear that he was on vacation until 22 June. Still, Greenslet encouraged Maurine to come and invited her to stay with him and Ella at their country home in Ipswich, Massachusetts.

Terrified of appearing dowdy, Maurine confided her worries to Alice, who helped Maurine persuade Charlie to pay for some new clothes. The women's store in town, just a block and a half from Maurine's home was owned and operated by Hyrum Lee, her first great love from Monroe. It seems unlikely that, even in this moment of triumph, Maurine could bear to enter. Alice helped solve the dilemma and persuaded Charlie to drive both women to Bakersfield, California, where they stayed with his sister, Leah Rance. After more than fifty years, Maurine could still remember those new clothes and lovingly described them to me down to the last detail. At the largest women's apparel store in town, Alice and Maurine found a dark green, three-piece suit made of "an unusual fabric" (she never knew its name) that was on sale because the woman who had ordered it had changed her mind. Maurine loved it, and the color flattered her hennaed hair. They bought a felt hat with a turned-down brim on one side and a curling pheasant feather on the other. Other purchases included a yellow sweater, a few blouses, beads, brown shoes, and a purse. Added to a dotted-Swiss dress Maurine had purchased at ZCMI, these items made an adequate wardrobe. She apparently did not ask Annie to sew her an outfit as she had done in the past for special occasions.

Furthermore, it was toward Alice that Maurine felt grateful, not to Charlie. However, when Maurine showed that she was serious about writing, Charlie expressed his fatherly pride by making a desk for her, now part of the furnishings in the Heritage Room of the Dixie College Library. The top has inlaid wood arranged in a geometrical pattern. Maurine often demanded that this desk be shipped to wherever she was living. Arlo Prisbrey, who told me about the desk, did the shipping through his trucking company and commented. "It must have meant a great deal to Maurine, as it wasn't cheap to ship and she never seemed to have much money."[22] The same article in the St. George weekly paper that announced her award also announced her trip east. She would be returning by way of the Rocky Mountain Writers' Conference at Boulder, Colorado, and that "in view of this Houghton-Mifflin fellowship, she is advised by the conference director, Edward Davidson, that this scholarship has advanced to a teaching fellowship."[23]

WINNING THE FELLOWSHIP

This first trip east was a big event in Maurine's life, and she wrote a highly colored account about it, stressing the comforts of the trip. She said she was hoping the Union Pacific Bus lines, a sightseeing subsidiary of the Union Pacific Railroad, would use the article in its advertising, but it was never published. She lengthened the trip (and increased the expense) by taking overnight stops—riding in style.[24]

Maurine's luggage was packed with dreams. She saw herself as heading for the elite and cultured world where people lived the life she felt she should have inherited. But she was paying for this trip by a loan from Charlie, who must be repaid from her fellowship money. And underneath her attractive new suit was the same vulnerable little girl with a new batch of dreams headed for fame—and also more heartache.

When she reached Boston, "I went to the YWCA, then I informed those at Houghton Mifflin I was there. The president of the company, Hardwick Moseley, said he was coming to take me to dinner. I didn't know how soon, but I thought I would have time to take a bath. But I was wrong. I was in the bathtub when he got there. He had to wait and when I was finally ready to go, he let me know he lived in the suburbs and now would miss the last train home. So my first step in with the Boston people started off on a bad note."

When Greenslet found she was at the YWCA, he informed her that the company had reserved a room at a hotel for her, so she transferred her things, and, as she enjoyed telling me, "It was a grand place, indeed!" The next morning, by her account, Greenslet, an avid early-morning fisherman, shocked her by phoning at 4:00 A.M. to invite her to spend two weeks with him and his wife at their summer place—essentially joining them during his two weeks of annual vacation.

A few years later, she published in *Quote* a self-deprecating story that portrayed her as naive and gauche to the amused sophisticates in Boston.[25] Greenslet had commented that a Whipple had signed the Declaration of Independence and Maurine had quickly claimed him as an ancestor only to be told that this Whipple had died childless.[26]

Ipswich itself was wonderful and so was the Greenslet home: "It was like stepping into my dream world—that gracious mode of living I knew was out there. I remember the place in detail. It was exactly what New England aristocracy should be like—the lovely, old fashioned garden, the bergamot growing near the door, the maid, the wonderful, elegant entry, the library and formal dining room, and then the guest room—my room, for a few nights. It was just the most wonderful room you can imagine. You walked up two steps to this darling bed with dotted Swiss curtains around it. There was a beautiful little desk, a comfortable chair just meant to sit in to read. It was all just so glorious I hardly could sleep for fear I'd miss the joy of being there."

The maid served dinner. Another Houghton Mifflin dignitary was a dinner guest, and Maurine found the talk congenial and interesting, joining in without any awkwardness that she remembered. The topic of the war threatening in Europe came up. Greenslet told Maurine if the war didn't come, he would take her to Tahiti. He thought she would like it, because the people lived a simple life resembling the neighborliness of early St. George. Apparently Greenslet was much taken with Maurine, perhaps thinking he had discovered another Willa Cather.

Maurine wanted more from the relationship with Greenslet than a professional one. She wanted to be "adopted" by him and his world. He represented the kind of father she thought she should have had—a cultivated gentleman from a moneyed family, with interesting, influential friends and intellectual interests.

Maurine told the dinner guests a series of St. George stories. She may have unconsciously shaded them to add local color and make the local characters more eccentric than real life because Greenslet "just couldn't get over why people would ever put up with things the way I was describing how it was in early St. George and even now. And he seemed to be probing me to see what made me tick. I know I looked all right in my new clothes. I think I held my own, and he never did figure me out. He didn't give up easily, though, and took me deep sea fishing to put me in a situation that might break my composure. I did get seasick, but not enough that I couldn't hide it. We didn't catch any fish though, and Greenslet laughed about that, saying I didn't bring him luck. I didn't tell him I had a jinx." After leaving the boat, they stopped to wipe their muddy shoes on some green plants. An old-timer came along and said, "You folks know you're standing in a bed of poison ivy?" They often laughed about that. Maurine felt that she had triumphed by resisting Greenslet's curiosity, remaining inscrutable, and concealing her physical discomfort.

Despite her wariness, Maurine yearned to yield to Ferris Greenslet's management. When I asked whether his many services and accommodations were just routine because of the author/editor relationship, Maurine said, "I don't know. At the time, I felt that I was of special interest to him and that he became my good friend, because he liked me." Maurine couldn't have known what the normal author/editor relationship was; and, oh, how she needed to feel that someone special liked her! For a time, he spread healing balm on her heart, perennially bruised from relationships with men—beginning with Charlie Whipple and coming right down to Grant Redford and Rob Riley.

Maurine's papers include a loose sheet with this undated note, not apparently part of a manuscript: "It was precisely because he did value good taste, good breeding, human values, that his opinion of the Whipple family meant so much to me. The first time I visited his office, I found him pouring over that monumental tome, *The Massachusetts Book*; and it was he who first made me aware . . . 'that a man isn't just a man—he's the summation of all those uncounted generations of men whose blood flows in his veins, and when it's blood with character, he has the right to be proud.'"[27] She told me that she hoped she made him see that the pioneers of St. George "had blood with character and deserved admiration and respect, regardless of what one thought of their religion."[27]

Maurine never once mentioned Ella Greenslet, Ferris's wife, in her memories of those two weeks; and I unfortunately didn't think to focus the conversation in that direction. It appears, however, that Greenslet took the responsibility for hosting Maurine and filling her days—usually with fishing, since that was the passion of his life. According to his biographical sketch, he was "proudest of his angling prowess . . . and his visits to London received more notice in *Fishing Gazette* than in the *Bookseller*. No year passed between 1910 and 1955 without several of his articles about fishing, particularly salmon and trout fishing, appearing in fishermen's magazines throughout the world."[28] Fishing is not always a sport for the gregarious; and whether Greenslet might genuinely have preferred to spend his vacation without the company of an aggressively conversational, inexperienced, and insecure writer seems never to have crossed Maurine's mind. It is a measure of Greenslet's own culture and breeding that it did not. On the contrary, he seemed to have used this time to convince Maurine that she was capable of writing, not just a good book, but "a *great* book." She explained: "Having dedicated his life to good writing, any example of it could set him on fire."

Greenslet and Maurine did not, apparently, spend all of their time fishing, since Greenslet's secretary, Margaret Moody, a kindly and tactful woman, told Maurine what to expect on the publicity trip, gave her some grooming tips, and "taught me how to curl my eyelashes."

Maurine remembered only a single sentence of Greenslet's advice as he put her on the train to New York. He told her "not to let all the publicity get to me, that if I stayed sane, it would be a wonder." He may not have known that the publicity angle to be played up was the exoticism of her Mormonism. In an exquisite irony, Maurine, who had felt marginalized from Mormon society all her life, was now to be made a spokeswoman for the Mormon people. She rose loyally to the occasion. A clipping from a Boston paper reporting an interview quotes her as saying: "Miss Whipple doesn't think that the remarkable personality of Brigham Young was half appreciated. He was a great leader and business executive, because he knew how to handle people.... He encouraged music and fun on the march, and if his followers seemed weary or downcast he would call for a fiddler and lead a cotillion himself. The Mormons were the happiest people that ever lived. They sang their way across the continent and they idolized Brother Brigham."

The article continued by reporting Maurine's claim:

> Not all Mormon women were unhappy in polygamy but that her grandmother, Cornelia Lenzi, was. Cornelia became the wife of the fifty-year-old missionary who had led her and her father across the plains. His other wives were older and resented her youth and fragility. Later, she understood their feelings when her husband, on being transferred to a different responsibility, discarded her for another young wife. From her mother, Miss Whipple has heard of the "polygamy raids" by United States marshals, and how she and others were made to give evidence against their parents. Her mother has often told of hiding in the sage brush on freezing [nights].[30]

In New York, LeBaron ("Lee") Barker, Houghton Mifflin's East Coast representative, and a Mr. Barron of the Associated Press, made the arrangements; but the New York phase lacked the magic of her two weeks in Boston. "There was no one half as good as Greenslet," she said. She told me that she didn't "click" with Barker, finding him distant, egotistical, and rude to his wife, Leslie, a cultured woman dying of cancer who had already had one arm amputated. Maurine spent the Fourth of July weekend at their country home and saw echoes of how Charlie Whipple treated Annie in the Barkers' relationship.

She evidently concealed her feelings well, since Barker wrote to Greenslet: "She is certainly one of the nicest authors I have met in a long, long time, and I hope that she will never lose her genuineness. She has so much warmth and vitality that it is bound to creep into her work."[31] As a publicist, she could hardly fault him, since there were many articles in the papers and radio interviews. She even said a stranger came up to her on the street; he'd recognized her as the fellowship winner from her photograph in the papers.

She said she spent time walking up and down Broadway, "gawking at the sights. I visited a Jewish man I'd met at the writer's conference, heard his family expound the good of communism and the fear of war." Considering the resemblances between philosophical communism and her vision of "the grand idea of brotherhood," I asked whether she found it appealing. She never had, although she could not say why exactly. "I could just feel the difference," she said.

She also made some Mormon connections. She became homesick, cried when she heard the Mormon Tabernacle Choir broadcast, and was a house guest of Mormons in the wealthy suburb of Scarsdale. She could recall only a few names: Mr. and Mrs. T. S. Vanderford and a stake president whose wife, Evelyn, (she could not recall more) was a lovely woman who helped Maurine in many ways. They put her in contact with a radio station owner, which resulted in another interview in an unusual venue.[32]

People were interested in her, as she told me, "because I was a curiosity from an unfathomable Mormon west, but most weren't as endearing in their approach as Greenslet. One insensitive man asked me if I ever wrote poetry. Like a damn fool I said not very often but shared with him my poem 'Dreams.' He laughed, wrote it down and announced to the group: 'Hear this, Miss Whipple also writes poetry.' Then in a falsetto voice [he] recited my poem. I went along with it, acting like I knew it was no good. But no one knew how it hurt, nor the real reason it was written at all."

The main event of the publicity was a press conference where the fellowship winners were introduced. Maurine could remember nothing about the other awardees, what she said, or even if she said anything. She was just relieved, she told me, that she had been able to walk up on the platform without doing something idiotic.

Maurine was something of a celebrity when the Rocky Mountain Writers' Conference opened on about July 10. According to the letters she preserved, she met people at this conference who influenced her career and personal life; however, she remembered virtually none of them when I asked her about them. For instance, a man who signed his letter only "Paul," thanked her for the loan of her dictionary, complimented her "great perspective" in her writing, and also thanked her for helping in some other way not specified.[33]

A letter from John Peale Bishop, which she received after she returned to St. George, comments mystifyingly: "You may be sure that having known you, I listened to no tales against you. I cannot even remember the incident in the dormitory to which you refer. I dare say I was there, but whatever it was immediately left my mind."[34] Maurine was unable—or unwilling—to give any further details about this episode which had, at the time distressed her. Throughout her life, she combined what seemed to be abandoned recklessness in her private relationships with an old-maidish prissiness where her public reputation was concerned. She often told me that "a single woman can't be too careful. Someone's always watching her."

Lillian's letter of 13 July reached Maurine in Boulder. She marveled, "I can't understand any such figure as $50,000. I can't picture it, nor realize it, so it doesn't mean a thing to me. Your $1,000 prize sounds a great deal more. How does it feel to be successful and rich and famous and beautiful and etc.? Be sure and let me know, before I start your biography."[35] Maurine had obviously shared this detail about her hopes for an affluent future with what seemed like a fabulous amount of money with Lillian, along with Charlie Whipple's skepticism. As matters turned out, Charlie was right.

Three short articles followed her progress in the *Washington County News*. On August 25, an article reported that she had been gone a total of ten weeks, five of them at the Rocky Mountain Writers' Conference in Boulder, to which she had gone directly from the East. The article quoted her as saying, with mingled satisfaction and defensiveness, that the trip had just been "one round of meetings, conferences and interviews, but had all been very wonderful. However, I have been exploited for statements I never made and my hair is no more red than when I left Dixie. These stories are merely a part of permitted publicity, and must be so accepted."[36]

Back in St. George, her season of being the glamorous center of attention was over. From what she told me, friends and relatives soon tired of hearing about how wonderful Greenslet was, how fantastic his home was, and how many important people had wanted to meet her. It had been hard enough for her to believe. Sober St. Georgians, who had little in their background to help them imagine what it was like, listened to the stories and agreed that it "sounded wonderful," but in front of them was the same impractical Maurine they had known all their life—still jobless, still husbandless. What had she done to deserve all that fuss? And had, in fact, all that fuss really been made over her?

Fortunately, Ferris Greenslet gently but firmly tugged Maurine back to the reality of the hard work that awaited her. While she was at the writers' conference, he wrote genially on 19 July 1938: "I suppose you will be settling down to work, at least when you have finished instructing the young idea at Boulder. Do not rush yourself, and do your work by day rather than by night; just send the product along to me a chapter or two at a time as you feel like it, spilling yourself on paper to this address whenever occasion arises. We shall be eager to hear how we all look to you in perspective after you get back to St. George, of which I consider myself now the second foremost living authority."[37]

Significantly, when I read Maurine this letter, she said she remembered thinking, when she received it: "Yes, he might know more facts about St. George than anyone in the East. But facts don't make an understanding, and the moods and the subtle reasons for certain actions, he would never know." She was already carving out a role for herself which she would occupy for the rest of her life: that of the true interpreter of her people. This was a role that had both advantages and disadvantages. On the one hand, she unquestionably did know St. George's history and people with an insider's intuitive keenness that amounted to a sixth sense. That knowledge gave her the strength to resist attempts to impose another interpretation on it. On the other hand, her position was a lonely and isolated one. She owned, rather than shared, that interpretation, keeping genuine outsiders at a distance rather than allowing them to become participants. And she could hardly assume this same attitude toward St. Georgians, when she had defined her identity up to that point as being marginalized and excluded from true belonging.

After the conference and for the rest of 1938, it was back to the routine of the "old, north bedroom." Maurine realized more than ever that she was locked into a frightening commitment. She had to produce something to match all the glory.

Notes

[1] Maryruth Bracy and Linda Lambert, "Maurine Whipple's Story of the *Giant Joshua*," *Dialogue: A Journal of Mormon Thought* 5 (Autumn/Winter 1971): 56.

[2] Ibid., 56–57; Maurine Whipple Collection, L. Tom Perry Special Collections, Harold B. Lee Library, Brigham Young University, Provo, Utah, with photocopy in Maurine Whipple Collection, Archive, Val A. Browning Library, Dixie College, St. George, Utah. Documents in both collections hereafter cited as BYU, photocopy Dixie College. However, I have not been able to find the telegram Maurine refers to.

[3] Ferris Greenslet was born 30 June 1875 in Glens Falls, New York, to George Bernard Greenslet, a merchant, and Josephine Ferris Greenslet. He graduated Phi Beta Kappa from Wesleyan University (1897) and earned his M.S. (1898) and Ph.D. (1900) from Columbia. After graduation, he became a researcher at the Boston Public Library (1901), then worked for the *Boston Advertiser* before becoming associate editor of the *Atlantic Monthly* in 1902. He married Ella S. Hulst of Cambridge on 25 April 1905 and they had two children. He loved Boston and refused to become editor of the prestigious *Dictionary of American Biography* because it would have required moving to New York. W. J. Burke and Will D. Howe, *American Authors: 1640 to the Present Day*, 3rd ed. rev. by Irving Weiss and Anne Weiss (New York: Crown Publishers, 1972), 250–52.

[4] Bracy and Lambert, "Maurine Whipple's Story," 56.

[5] Ibid.

6 Maurine always expressed respect and love for Alice to me; but as Maurine became more erratic and demanding in later years, their relationship deteriorated. In 1990, Alice, after having a portion of her stomach removed surgically, limited their contacts stringently as a way of protecting herself from the upsetting stress.

7 Maurine Whipple, Interviewed by Jon Green, 22 July 1980, transcript BYU; photocopy Dixie College.

8 Ida was born 30 July 1904 to Abraham Owen Johnson and Louisa Elizabeth Belliston Johnson of La Verkin, Utah. She and Ralph had no children. Ralph's death was in December 1943. Ida herself died the next year on June 13, 1944.

9 Florence Whipple Jolley, "History of Florence Whipple Jolley," January 1976, 17–18; 23 pp. holograph, photocopy in my possession, courtesy of Florence's daughter, Colleen Jolley Haycock, of Las Vegas, who has the original.

10 Bracy and Lambert, "Maurine Whipple's Story," 58.

11 Maurine Whipple, Letter to Ferris Greenslet, n.d. 1938; BYU, photocopy Dixie College.

12 Ferris Greenslet, telegram to Maurine Whipple, 31 January 1838; BYU, photocopy Dixie College.

13 Ferris Greenslet, letter to Maurine Whipple, 1 February 1938, BYU, photocopy Dixie College. Greenslet nearly always typed his letters. In 1931, Houghton Mifflin published *Joseph Smith and His Mormon Empire* by Harry M. Beardsley.

14 Ferris Greenslet, Letter to Maurine Whipple, February 1938; BYU, photocopy Dixie College. Her papers do not identify those who wrote letters of reference for her. "Chloe" was an early name for the character of Clory in *The Giant Joshua*.

15 Lillian McQuarrie, Letter to Maurine Whipple, 21 March 1938; BYU, photocopy Dixie College. At this point, Lillian and Emerson were living at 500 Oak Street, Apt. 20, San Francisco, and Lloyd was eight months old.

16 An undated holograph draft of a letter from Maurine to "Darling" is an emotional farewell letter to someone's husband, regretting a relationship that had gotten out of hand. She mentions the wife's name—"Lillian"—and warns the husband that his constant criticism of the little boy (whom she calls "Johnny"—not "Lloyd") will damage the boy, just as Charlie had damaged her. Whipple Collection, BYU. Although this letter is not dated, Lillian's divorce from Emerson was final by September 24, 1940, and she had married George Benedict by 1949.

17 Lillian McQuarrie, Letter to Maurine Whipple, 16 April 1938; typescript BYU, photocopy Dixie College.

18 Lillian McQuarrie, Letter to Maurine Whipple, 1 May 1938; BYU, photocopy Dixie College.

19 Ferris Greenslet, Telegram to Maurine Whipple, May 25, 1938; BYU; photocopy Dixie College.

20 "Maurine Whipple Awarded Fellowship and Prize of $1,000 for Novel," *Washington County News*, June 9, 1938, unpaginated clipping, Whipple Collection, BYU.

21 Lillian McQuarrie, Letter to Maurine Whipple, 16 April 1938; BYU, photocopy Dixie College.

22 Arlo Prisbrey, interviewed 25 May 1992, St. George.

23 "Maurine Whipple Awarded," 1.

24 Maurine Whipple, "From St. George to Boston by Bus," 6 pp. holograph; BYU, photocopy Dixie College.

25 Maurine Whipple, "I Laughed at This One," 28 September 1942, *Quote*, 8; BYU.

26 Two John Whipples, one accompanied by a brother, arrived in America during the early 1630s. One, who landed in 1632 in Dorchester (now part of Boston), Massachusetts, settled in Providence, Rhode Island. The second John Whipple and his brother, Matthew, settled in Ipswich about the same time. No known connection has been found between the two Johns. It was probably the John Whipple House on South Main Street in Ipswich, Massachusetts, that Greenslet sent Maurine to view with his secretary, since it was owned and maintained by the Ipswich Historical Society. It was demolished before 1999 to make way for a road. www.Whipple.org/docs/fags.html (accessed July 1999). General William Whipple signed the Declaration of Independence but had no children who survived infancy.

27 Maurine Whipple, untitled note beginning "It was precisely," n.d., holograph, 1938 file; BYU.

28 Burke and Howe, *American Authors*, 251.

29 Whipple, untitled note beginning "It was precisely," n.d.

30 "Maurine Whipple Arrives for Visit," undated clipping from unidentified newspaper, continued from p. 1. The article ended in mid-sentence. Maurine Whipple scrapbook; BYU, photocopy Dixie College. Although some wives were forced to testify against their husbands, Maurine is mistaken in saying that Cornelia or her children were.

31 Quoted in Ferris Greenslet, Letter to Maurine Whipple, July 19, 1938; BYU, photocopy Dixie College. Greenslet pointed out the coincidence of the similar LeBaron/Barron names in this letter.

32 Two-page transcript of a radio broadcast, "Energine Newsreel," with Bob Barrie, on Sunday, 10 July 1938; BYU, photocopy Dixie College. It is brief with only a few comments from Maurine about *The Giant Joshua* and Mormonism.

33 Paul [no surname], Letter to Maurine Whipple, n.d.; BYU, photocopy Dixie College. Other correspondents named Paul who appear in her papers are Paul Engle, author of *Always the Land*, who sent her a copy of this book in 1941, and Paul de Kruif, the science writer, whose *Reader's Digest* articles on Tom Spies drew Maurine's romantic attention to him. I have no information, however, indicating that either attended the 1938 conference. More likely candidates seem to be Paul Horgan or another conference participant.

34 John Peale Bishop, Letter to Maurine Whipple, n.d.; BYU, photocopy Dixie College.

35 Lillian McQuarrie, Letter to Maurine Whipple, 13 July 1938; BYU, photocopy Dixie College. Lillian's reference is the only mention of this sum—apparently representing Maurine's expectations.

36 "Maurine Whipple Reports on Trip to East," *Washington County News*, 25 August 1938, n.p., Maurine Whipple scrapbook, BYU, photocopy Dixie College. The same page of the scrapbook includes two other unpaginated clippings from the *Washington County News*: "Miss Maurine Whipple Receives Considerable Publicity," 4 August 1939; and "Los Angeles Times Features Maurine Whipple," 11 August 1938.

"SWELL SUFFERING"

[37] Ferris Greenslet, Letter to Maurine Whipple, July 19, 1938; BYU, photocopy Dixie College.

8

ACHIEVEMENT AND COMPLICATIONS AT YADDO

The Giant Joshua would be a monkey-wrench in the Houghton Mifflin machine for the next two years. Of course, Maurine's book was to be longer than most fellowship winner books. But had Houghton Mifflin known just what effort would be required to make their advertising ploy pay off, it seems doubtful they would have taken the challenge. Without the talented and gallant Ferris Greenslet, Maurine's book likely would not ever have reached publication. Rather than the twelve months Greenslet had outlined as the schedule, the actual production of *The Giant Joshua* lasted three and a half years.

Maurine described her writing process to me. She said she needed to work herself into a state where she could "let go and move into a different consciousness." Then she could weave incidents from her life and those of her ancestors and other St. George pioneers into true but new patterns. Caught in this process, she could not hurry it.

The published novel, set in St. George between the first settlement in 1861 and about 1894, follows Clorinda Agatha Lenzi MacIntyre, the sixteen-year-old third wife of community leader Abijah MacIntire, through the arduous process of settling the new community, enduring repeated dam wash-outs on the Virgin River, heat, thirst, exhaustion, starvation, disease, poverty, isolation, ill health, childbirth and the deaths of all but one of those children, triumphal visits from Brigham Young—but especially the complicated emotional and economic dynamics of polygamy. The silver question that shines through the entire novel is whether these Mormons' faith is strong enough for its members to withstand each and every knee-buckling blow of fate. And unquestionably, *The Giant Joshua* wears well as historical fiction. One indication is that it is still in print and is presently on a list named "Our Favorite Novels written in English."[1]

Perhaps importantly where Maurine herself was concerned, writing gave her a new tool for dealing with her own life. In creating Clory, she wrote the woman she wanted to be—a woman who did not deserve what she got either, but who, unlike herself, was popular and whose inner nobility could not be broken. Clory is charming, vivid, intelligent, and spunky in ways Maurine Whipple wished she were. That she could create such a popular, likeable fictional character is interesting and begs the question: Do all of us have this better inner character buried within us?

Maurine later exaggerated the discomforts of the north bedroom, in which she did much of her writing, but it is true that the room had three doors, a real recipe for draftiness. It was too cold in the winter, too hot in the summer.

Maurine's method of working was to hang large pieces of paper from newspaper roll-ends around the room, "In front of my desk, I had each character. Like Abijah. I'd have what he looked like when the book started, everything about him. If he had ingrown toe nails, I put it down. I put down what he must have been thinking about, what he was like in his youth, where he came from, did he have any brothers and sisters, what made him tick. And then, as the story went on, I would put how he changed, why he turned into what he was."[2] She also recorded each character's speech patterns, jotting down snippets of conversation and idiosyncratic expressions. She also festooned the walls with bits and pieces of history, lists, character sketches, and sample paragraphs. The Maurine Whipple Collection at Brigham Young University contains cards and photographs from her Grandmother McAllister's day. Punctured with pin holes, they could have been some of the very items that hung in Cornelia's room; and perhaps many reappeared on Maurine's walls.

She composed her drafts in pencil on oversized scissored sheets of newsprint about two feet square, making relatively few revisions and corrections as she went along. When evening came, her right arm would be aching with fatigue, her brain numb. As long as the weather was warm enough, she would end her evening's work with a walk to the Sugarloaf where, in a rock hollow still warm from the sun, she would watch the sunset and let the day's writing and the next day's plans rise up and mingle unconsciously. Her characters would be with her, she said, sometimes whispering their next-day's exploits to be added to the growing pile of newsprint back in the north bedroom.

As darkness settled over St. George, Maurine would climb down by the north end of the red rocks where vines and flowers grew in the shade and dampness, then head west across the hill. She would follow rough steps

ACHIEVEMENT AND COMPLICATIONS AT YADDO

Maurine frequently hiked up on Sugarloaf, the red sandstone formation overlooking St. George, where she would watch the sun go down. BYU Library Photograph Collection.

down to the road leading into town and drift back home, already mapping out the next day's work.

The "research" that Maurine described herself as doing was largely drinking in the old stories directly from those who had lived through pioneer times. She said many times that, even as a child, she had "paid attention to the old stories" and she credited twenty-four old-timers in *The Giant Joshua*'s acknowledgments. She knew that "those of the pioneer generation often felt neglected and overlooked" but wanted it understood, in no uncertain terms, that St. George "would not have existed without people like them." Although they may not have been able to articulate the concept, Maurine thought they sensed that their pioneering effort had "represented the powerful spirit, not only of the Mormon exodus to the West, but also of a heroic try by humans to live a higher vision of life."

Despite her compulsion to position herself as unappreciated in St. George, she also admits that most St. George residents encouraged her writing. She let those who might object to a novel, like her mother's eldest sister, Jane McAllister Moss, think she was writing nonfiction. Jane did not forgive Maurine for the deception. Loa Moss Brown, Jane's oldest grandchild remembered. "When the book came out, Grandma was upset. She thought the stories in the book didn't reflect well on the family."[3]

But most of St. George's elderly residents willingly shared their memories. "Aunt" Jane Bleak[4] was ninety-two in 1937, but Maurine said she still had sharp memories of the old days. Charlie Seegmiller,[5] who turned ninety-five in 1937 and was mostly bedfast, also told Maurine vivid stories about the past. She had listened raptly to Brigham ("Briggy") Jarvis,[6] the father of her friend Mabel, as he related the pioneers' agonizing struggles to dam the Virgin River. Briggy died in 1933, but daughter Mabel loved history and had preserved her father's memories.

Maurine also owed some of her local color to the people of Pine Valley. She told me about girlhood visits to the Pine Valley summer home of Peter Ephraim Beckstrom and Emma Marian Bracken Beckstrom, who lived in St. George near Maurine during the winters. Maurine remembered on those visits lying in bed, straining to overhear the stories the adults were telling "because I knew all those stories were so important! I could just see my grandmother and the others as they talked!"

Zaidee Walker Miles, the daughter of Abigail Middlemass Walker and Charles Lowell Walker, had become the guardian of many pioneer relics and records and let Maurine comb them for information. Maurine quoted some of Charlie Walker's homespun poetry in *The Giant Joshua*.

In a 1941 letter to a friend, she said that "Annie [Atkin] gave me some of the best details."[7] Annie had grown up in St. George, then married Vasco Tanner, a zoologist at BYU who supplied Maurine with information about Indians. Much of what she wrote about Indians in the area, unfortunately, had to be cut to shorten the book.

Another St. George resident who helped Maurine was Juanita Brooks, unquestionably its best-known native daughter. She responded generously to Maurine's requests for help, much to her credit, but she was somewhat dismayed at the results. "I read every line of [Maurine's] book before it went in the first time," Juanita told Dale Morgan "and then again went over the printer's dummy with her. I knew of some historical discrepancies, which I could not get her to change. I found many things which she did modify or cut, and I gave her an abundance of local items and folk-lore."[8] Maurine listed Juanita first in *The Giant Joshua*'s acknowledgments: "Mrs. Juanita Brooks, who from the very beginning has been an inspiration, and without whose constant encouragement I would never have attempted the book in the first place."

Maurine received unsolicited suggestions and historical anecdotes from other people. One helpful insight was from a local friend, Donald P. Seegmiller, who sometimes took Maurine horseback riding. He wrote of a recent Sunday afternoon visit to the cemetery when "those long shadows that seem longer in Dixie than anywhere else, were lending rich enchantment to the whole valley and the hills surrounding. . . . It was breath taking. What a cause that could bring people from such wide-flung points as these to Dixie land!—a God forsaken waste of rock and desert! Can we afford to let it die in the minds and hearts of this generation? Can such a force ever die completely? Give one of your characters a 'spiritual rebirth' amid such surroundings."9

Perhaps the most important resource upon which Maurine drew in weaving the story of *The Giant Joshua* was her own family, going two generations back to the settlement of St. George by her grandparents: the Whipples and the McAllisters, the Lytles and Lenzis. Maurine's writing was not just a fictionalizing of their historical experience, nor was it a historicizing of her fictional characters. Rather, the process was a subtle, complex, and almost organic growth. As she searched her experience for characters, her own ancestors were among the most vivid; but in creating them, she freed them from the limitations of biography to act for themselves—but only within the limits of what was both possible and probable, given the pioneer setting between 1861 and about 1887.

By far the most important ancestral pair that Maurine summoned into her fictional world were her mother's parents: the charismatic John Daniel Thomas McAllister and Cornelia Agatha Lenzi McAllister, his deaf third wife. Cornelia became the inspiration for Clory—Clorinda Agatha Lenzi MacIntyre, while J.D.T. McAllister took on new life as her exasperating, endearing husband, Abijah MacIntyre.

Although a full exploration of how Maurine made use of her family history in *The Giant Joshua* lies beyond the scope of this biography, that relationship is intricate and complicated. Her creative use of the family background for its emotional impact is probably one of the reasons that some of her relatives were unhappy with the novel. The novel spoke with such emotional conviction that they could not readily remember that it was a work of fiction.

Events of the three years it took to complete *The Giant Joshua* are mostly documented from Ferris Greenslet's and Lillian McQuarrie's letters to Maurine, which supplement her memories of that grueling but exhilarating period. Lillian's letters are sparse but more personal. Greenslet's are warmly supportive as Maurine reports her personal calamities but focus pressingly on moving the novel forward. Maurine, for her part, struggled with her perpetual discontent and physical infirmities, complained about her working situation and her health, managed with Greenslet's help to spend three months in a writers' colony in 1939, and darted about restlessly on distracting and expensive trips. Luckily she was not involved in a difficult romantic relationship, but she was desperately lonely. She needed masculine support. In every way but the erotic, Ferris Greenslet became "the man in her life." Courtly and teasing by turns, he kept an impressive balance between the professional and the personal, providing a kind of emotional centering that Maurine with her desperate neediness had never had. His unwavering expectation that she not only could but would produce a great novel kept her steadied and on task despite what amounted to much turbulence in her personal life.

We know little about Maurine's experience at the second writers' conference in Boulder, Colorado. It would appear from small clues in her later correspondence that she had made many friends. Soon after she returned she received a friendly message on 11 August 1938 from Hardwick Moseley, president of the Houghton Mifflin's Chicago office, expressing regret that he and his wife didn't get to see her on her way home and proffering a stately compliment that if she participated in the 1939 writers' conference, she would be "the brightest star who has attended . . . if *The Giant Joshua* has been published."[10]

In late October, Ferris challenged her to keep surprising him, since "curiosity is gnawing at my vitals sharper than a serpent's tooth,"[11] a statement Maurine must have made a witty comment about, for he responded in November: "The serpent is just coming out on the other side, but all right!"[12]

Maurine must have mentioned that she had heard that Bernard DeVoto, an Ogden-born novelist-historian then occupying an influential position as columnist for *Harper's Bazaar*,[13] had announced in his "The Easy Chair," that no one would ever write a good Mormon novel, for Greenslet reassured her in late November: "I should never dream of reading Bernard DeVoto's Easy Chair meditations, and I didn't read his remarks on Mormon novelists until this minute. We will show him that he is a lousy prophet."[14]

Evidently Maurine consulted Greenslet about a nonfiction article, "Mormon Saga,"[15] which seems to be early work on a character who would become Clory in *The Giant Joshua*. The heroine was high spirited and had a red sunbonnet, like Clory, but died in childbirth. This death was the result of not seeking medical care when the placenta failed to deliver and her husband, obeying Brigham Young's admonition, depended instead on prayer and faith. At September's end, Greenslet advised her that it would be a mistake to "take Mr. Lee's offer at the present."[16] Lawrence Lee, editor of *Virginia Quarterly Review*, was offering five dollars per printed page "for that portion of your work which runs in the manuscript from pages 39 through 60." Greenslet offered to show the manuscript to Ted Weeks at the *Atlantic Monthly* where he felt she could sell it at "a more satisfactory figure."[17] The *Atlantic* turned it down and there is no evidence that it was ever printed in the *Virginia Quarterly Review*.

ACHIEVEMENT AND COMPLICATIONS AT YADDO

For Christmas, Maurine sent Greenslet a box of the local pine nuts, with an elaborate description of the best "method of gorging." She also asked him to look at a manuscript by Lillian. Lillian's correspondence does not describe this manuscript, and Greenslet sent Lillian a firm rejection. Dejectedly, Lillian reported: "I got my book back from H. M. with quite an unexpected comment. The main characters are not attractive enough to make it anything but dubious merchandise. That was the *last* comment I would have thought of. But they know their oats, so that's that. I'm glad it's put in it's [sic] place at last. Sigh! Sigh!"[18]

Maurine had failed to settle down to consistent production but had promised, in Greenslet's words, "to start vigorous writing the first of the year." He wrote that this was "good news," and temptingly added that "the second shipment of gold will fly to you through the air."[19] By this he referred to the second installment of five hundred dollars that would complete the fellowship payment.

The rest of the letter spells out his and Houghton Mifflin's expectations, probably in greater detail than had existed up to this point. He wanted to publish the book for the 1939 fall list, which meant having material "for the dummy" (preliminary design) by the end of March or early April. This meant, he wrote, "the first chapter in more or less finally revised form, an approximate estimate of the complete length of the whole, which may be changed later if necessary, and a list of chapter titles, if any." The complete manuscript could take as long as June or July, if necessary. Then to relieve the pressure from these deadlines, he added, "All of the above, however, is wishful thinking, and you mustn't rush your writing beyond its natural pace."[20] It was a loophole that he probably did not expect Maurine to seize so quickly.

Lillian also wrote at Christmas time. Maurine had written her a "swell" letter, evidently suggesting that she might visit her, a comment Lillian welcomed with enthusiasm even though, because of her asthma, she and baby Lloyd were living, not with Emerson in San Francisco, but with her sister at 4535 W. 11th Place in Los Angeles.[21]

Maurine had evidently sensed a note of discouragement and had encouraged Lillian by quoting to her a line from Ann Harding's movie role in *The Flame Within*: "All the waters of the Seven Seas can't sink a ship unless the water gets inside." Lillian had earlier quoted this statement to Maurine at a low moment in Maurine's life in the summer of 1935 and now wrote ruefully: "Thanks for the tip about the waters of the seven seas. I remember, now. I *did* feel that way once, didn't I? Just jog my memory occasionally. I need it. Lots of love to you, Rene, my very dearest friend."[22]

Lillian wrote again, immediately after New Year's, with the decision that she and Emerson had both decided that San Francisco's climate was making their asthma worse and that they were moving back to Utah. "Emerson is leaving S.F. for Salt Lake tomorrow, taking Marian with him. She will stay with mama and he will be with his family. He is going into business with his sister in her studio. Then I will go there as soon as he gets things straightened around and a place rented." This chatty paragraph of family business does not even hint at the domestic catastrophe developing under Lillian's nose. (See chap. 11.) Anticipating loneliness before Emerson sent for her, Lillian renewed her invitation to Maurine to visit, pluckily announced that "for the first time in many moons" she was "getting a little umph back," and that Lloyd, whom she was trying to toilet-train, "will reach the age of reason pretty soon, and all will be well."[23]

On 3 January 1939, Ferris Greenslet sent the rest of the fellowship money and encouraged: "I hope it finds you hard at it, and in the best of health and spirits."

Maurine, who had acquired a much-unneeded distraction, a puppy named Spotty, promptly cashed the check, paid many bills, and went off to Lillian, probably leaving the puppy with her family. It is not known how long she stayed or what she did. Sometime before February, she was back in St. George, sick in bed where Annie could nurse her. She may have begged an advance and an escort from Harrison Leussler, Houghton Mifflin's West Coast representative, since a letter from her agent in May 1941 refers to traveling expenses "incurred a year ago, when you were sick with Pneumonia, and Leussler had to come down and cart you off somewhere or other."[24] She apparently wrote an apologetic letter of explanation to Greenslet, who responded warmly on 9 February: "Don't siphon any energy into worrying when you can't work. I am terribly sorry but not in the least 'mad.' Please don't let me ever see that word again in our correspondence. I have absolute confidence in Joshua and you. Forget the deadline and just do the best you can, when you can."[25]

Maurine wrote again before she received this letter, asking for an advance against royalties for her doctor's bill. On 16 February, Greenslet responded: "Your letter of February 9, with Sunday coda, will send me back to Florida next week in top spirits." This wording suggests that she had mailed off something, just what is unclear. However, Greenslet refused her plea for more money: "I don't think we better chisel anything out of the chapter payments for doctors' bills, etc. I'm sure that in the long run Joshua will very amply support you in the style to which you have been accustomed."[26] This lighthearted allusion was probably no comfort to Maurine, who had become "accustomed" primarily to poverty.

Even during his absence, Greenslet saw to it that Maurine received a regular stream of compliments and encouragement from Betty Leighton, his typist, and Robert N. Linscott, Houghton Mifflin's editor in charge of novels. It shows not only his sensitivity to her needs, but perhaps also his awareness of the importance in a small town of the regular arrival of envelopes with that prestigious Boston return address.

Maurine then stuck out the next three months at home but sent Greenslet nothing. In other words, after writing the synopsis and two chapters that she had sent off in January 1938, and whatever it was she sent east in February, Maurine had not finished another new chapter—and a full year had passed. Alice described Maurine as "preferring research to writing, putting off the actual writing itself at the littlest excuse, lingering interminably over breakfast. I tried to hurry her along, promising to go for a walk with her about 4:00 P.M., if she would stay in her room and work the rest of the day."[27] This strategy was usually successful.

After Alice's baby, Carol Ann, was born in February 1939, Maurine and Alice on their walks pushed her, well-bundled up, in the baby buggy; but Carol Ann herself rapidly became a distraction to Maurine's writing. Maurine loved children, and this niece was a beautiful and adorable baby. Carol Ann always held a special place in her heart, and Carol Ann remained fond of Maurine as an adult, sending Christmas cards from her home in Canada and writing occasionally between times with news of her children.[28]

Greenslet concealed his apprehension about Maurine's productivity with a quip in mid-February: "From now on, I hope it will be like the situation in the Good Book, where it was not Joshua but the sun which stood still."[29] Greenslet further sympathetically advised her 14 March 1938, after Maurine complained again of illness: "Don't overwork yourself during your convalescence, and eat freely of yeast or other vitamin producing agents for several weeks."[30] Significant vitamin research was in its infancy at this period; and Maurine, ever alert for solutions to her many health problems, had already started to collect information as it appeared in magazines or books.

Still, Greenslet must have seen that only a miracle could have produced the desired first draft by the end of March. Maurine's family and neighbors, tied to jobs with regular hours or demanding farming schedules, must have wondered how she could dart off to California in the middle of a project. Still, it is possible to argue that Maurine was listening to her own intuition and her way of becoming saturated in her subject may have needed a long visit with someone like Lillian.

Maurine must have excused her lack of productivity to Greenslet by claiming that her working conditions were impossible. Greenslet took the complaint seriously and investigated the possibility of Maurine's admission to an artists' colony like Yaddo near Saratoga, New York. It would be free,

Maurine Whipple was very fond of her niece, Carol Ann, daughter of Ray and Alice Whipple, and the family dog Jacky. BYU Library Photograph Collection.

she would be surrounded by congenial people, and the only demand on her would be to work.

    Despite Maurine's bouts of poor health, she had been revising the first two chapters, which describe the 1861 arrival of the Mormon pioneers in the St. George area.[31] Chapter 1 introduces the reader to a small group led by Abijah MacIntyre accompanied by his three wives. The youngest, Clory, quickly endears herself to the reader because of her positive, playful spirit. The second chapter describes the settlers' camp routine and their arrival at John D. Lee's two-story rock home in New Harmony, where Clory is dismayed at the pitiful state of the earlier settlers. She resolves not to let herself become like them. The camp prepares for another hard day, with the volcanic black hills to traverse before they can reach St. George. When the ox of a fellow traveler collapses, Clory watches Abijah exercise priesthood authority, blessing the ox with consecrated oil and the laying on of hands. She reflects how Abijah was "in many ways a great man. He was ruthless, fanatical, bigoted—a man more capable of winning respect than affection—but a man to be depended on when you needed him, a man who got things done" (47). The group is also delayed by the birth of a baby, but they push on and reach the main body of the pioneers after dark. As they walk the last weary way, the women think of renewing relationships with friends, and the men dream of the city they will build in the wilderness.

The campfires grew closer. Faint noises drifted to the tired travelers. Under the friendly starlight, advancing to meet them beyond the flare of the flames and the protecting white-topped circle, marched a group of shouting, singing people.

Clory felt as if her heart would break with joy. Song spontaneously burst forth from all the weary caravan.

Come, come, ye Saints — no toil nor labor fear,
But with joy—wend your way!
Though hard to you — this journey may appear,
Grace shall be—as your day!
Gird up your loins, fresh courage take;
Our God will ne-ever us forsake . . .[32]

In this passage, Maurine strikes the novel's key theme: the power of a great, unifying cause to lift the individual human soul.

On 18 March 1939, Greenslet let her know that he had received these "two perfected chapters" and proofs of the long-delayed promotional photos, which Houghton Mifflin paid for.[33] It is not clear which photograph Greenslet was talking about. No author's photo appeared on the dust jacket of the published book.

A few days later, Greenslet wrote again. He and two other editors had read the revisions "with admiration and pleasure." In comparison with the first draft, he assured her "you have done good, creative revisions." He approved "Clory" as a nickname for "Clorinda," finding it "light and romantic." Looking ahead toward the finished book, he queried whether a frontispiece consisting only of a giant Joshua and its botanical name might not be "a little bleak" but asked her to send along a good photograph of one. He also asked her to consider epigraphs for each chapter, even suggesting they be taken from the Book of Mormon or the sermons of Brigham Young. He also offered epigraph suggestions for the three volumes in the trilogy: "This is the place" for Book 1; "We believe all things, we hope all things, we have endured many things, and hope to be able to endure all things" for Book 2; and "To love one another and to serve one another," for Book 3.[34]

Maurine, meanwhile, had gone off to Los Angeles again and wrote Greenslet, apparently approving his suggestions and wondered if they should continue the quotation in the second epigraph with "if there be anything virtuous, lovely, or of good report or praiseworthy. . ." Greenslet responded on 6 April that "there ought to be no difficulty in finding a suitable place to slip [it] in."[35] (As published, *The Giant Joshua* used no epigraphs.) She had sent along a list of corrections for the first two chapters, and he promised they would be "duly made in the manuscript." Maurine had asked Elden Beck, a botanist at Dixie College,[36] to provide some information about Joshua trees to Greenslet, and Greenslet returned the manuscript in this letter with thanks "to have been so fully instructed." She had obviously been half-defiant and half-apologetic about this second trip to California, for Greenslet responded soothingly: "Of course I am neither shocked nor ashamed of you in Los Angeles. If it is doing you good, that is the best place for you to be."[37]

Under the circumstances, it seems that Maurine was not exercising much thrift. Most of the first installment of five hundred dollars had paid for her first trip east. Now the second installment was likewise apparently gone. And what Maurine was actually doing in California is a mystery.

Greenslet's connections opened the door for six weeks at Yaddo beginning June 2.[38] He sent congratulations on her acceptance 21 April: "I have known people who have stayed there four or five months. I gather that the six weeks stipulated is a sort of purgatorial period, during which one shows whether or not he is taking advantage of his opportunities and not raising too much hell of any kind."[39]

Elizabeth Ames, Yaddo's executive director, followed up with a letter of confirmation and explanation on 24 May. Maurine was expected to arrive 20 June and leave on Friday, 4 August. Someone would meet her train, if Maurine sent word about when she would be arriving. The only employee tip expected from her was a one-time three dollar fee. She should be prepared for rain, "since your studio may be at some distance from the house." Visitors should not call before 4:00 P.M. "The one rule to which there must be no exception and the observance of which we ask unconditionally . . . is this: Please do not go to another person's studio at any time unless you are invited to do so, and when you do go, please remember that someone may be at work in an adjoining studio."[40]

Maurine was ecstatic and accepted without hesitation. Almost certainly she saw herself as launched on a lucrative and glamorous writing career. Yaddo was her chance to exchange the day-long whine of saws, her mother's incomprehension of what she was doing, her father's criticism, the continuing marital tension, and particularly St. George's summer inferno for peaceful, cultured surroundings, association with promising and established writers, and the opportunity to have her physical needs met in elegance. It must have seemed like a passport to heaven.

Even though 20 June was almost a month away and Greenslet obviously expected her to make good use of the intervening time, she apparently spent most of her time engaged in research, for Greenslet's letter on 18 May refers to "20 large pasteboard envelopes" filled with her research.[41] Greenslet explained encouragingly: "If you are industrious like the busy bee, and Mrs. Ames sees the manuscript piling up an inch a month, I am willing to bet good money that she will keep you until it is finished, which, naturally, would be all right with us."[42] (In fact, Maurine received a six-week extension until 20 September.)

Approximately two weeks before her scheduled arrival date, Greenslet wrote to her on 5 June 1939 in care of Hardwick Moseley at Houghton Mifflin's Chicago office. Genially concealing his misgivings, if he had them, about the lagging schedule, he reported on his fishing and promised "a conference," either in Boston "or at the [Yaddo] studio some afternoon after 4:00."[43]

On 19 June 1939, Greenslet solicitously wrote again, addressing the letter to Maurine at Yaddo where she was to check in the next day. Perhaps already suspecting from her spotty production record that self-discipline was difficult for her, he gave her tactful but excellent advice about settling down and establishing a work routine:

> I am a great disbeliever in telling anyone else how to do it, but I should think if you get yourself at once into the habit of doing from 1,000 to 1,500 words of rough draft, no matter how rough, every morning, and perhaps either revising it or thinking about the next morning's work every afternoon, you will be pleased and surprised at the progress you will make. Fifteen hundred words would, I figure, only be five or six pages of your manuscript, which ought not to be too heavy a job for a forenoon. I gather from literary biography as well as from conversation with hundreds of authors that it is about the standard conservative stint for a working half-day. I don't think it matters in the least how rough it is, or how much it has to be revised later. The great thing now, I am sure, is to get the basic book out of your system.[44]

Yaddo was a mansion on a four-hundred acre estate located about half a mile from the Hudson River, within walking distance of the Saratoga horse-racing complex. Eleven years before Maurine's arrival, Eudora Welty and Katherine Ann Porter had been guests there.[45] The owner, Spencer Trask died in 1909, followed by his wife, Katrina, in 1922. By 1926, their wishes to see it remodeled into an artists' colony had been fulfilled. George Foster Peabody, a lifelong family friend, philanthropist, and Katrina's second husband, hired Elizabeth Ames as executive director.[46] Ames almost certainly set the schedule and tone of the place; and Maurine, in a heart-wrenching replay of all of the problems she had had with school principals, did not get along with her.

Maurine was assigned "a semi-detached studio about half a mile," she said, "from the main house equipped with a little stove, desk, and two rooms, one for sleeping, one for working." The studio through the wall was occupied by a woman whom, she told me, she suspected of being no better than a prostitute —"she was gone most the night and didn't seem to be working on anything creative."

In 1946 when Yaddo asked former guests to fill out a questionnaire evaluating their stay, Maurine did so in considerable detail and not quite coherently. She must have regretted her emotional intensity, because the original is still in her papers. When asked what she least liked about the place, she particularly protested against some of the "silly restrictions."

> It was like we were not supposed to say good morning to people even when they're servants and the impossibility of conversing with the director [Mrs. Ames] or persuading her to entertain any viewpoint other than her own. I think as a whole the business of diminishing returns depends upon the individual. For instance if you are a mature and serious worker sufficiently engrossed in your job, you are willing to put up with the infantilism of some of Yaddo's rules. Now that I am more mature and more dedicated to my work, I could do good writing at Yaddo indefinitely, regardless of the distractions of rules or the play-boys and girls who were guests that summer.[47]

She expanded harshly on this last point, terming her fellow guests "artists" in name only—"play-boys and girls who used Yaddo as a free vacation resort immune from all restrictions of decent human conduct and where one could spend his time in a drunken stupor or sexual excess without hindrance." She conceded that some were "serious craftsmen" (she doesn't identify any) and admitted that some exchanges had stimulated her work but complained that these individuals "fled" soon after she arrived. The "crowd at Yaddo," she wrote contemptuously, were "pseudo. Simply pseudos." She decried the "compulsory happiness" and "false cheerfulness" laid on for "breakfast and dinner," possibly suggesting that her own desire for emotionally intense confidences was colliding with the civilized facade of good manners and general light conversation that the other guests would have considered socially acceptable. Maurine continued: "What you miss in them is the 'gemulhict' [sic: *gemütlichkeit*] that's the only German word I know, and it means friendliness."

In response to the question about whether there was enough opportunity for social interaction, she responded that "more social life should have been encouraged and more exchanges with the intellectual and artists in nearby Saratoga." She also expressed her life-long craving for "someone on my level to talk with and help clarify my own work." And she thought that "more of a normal atmosphere would be a good thing . . . and less of the self-conscious 'ivory tower' attitude. Yaddo should be considered a workshop, realistic, matter-of-fact. After all, if an artist thinks of himself as an 'artist,' he certainly isn't one!" This rather odd statement may reflect the romantic belief that true art is natural and spontaneous, flowing virtually unconsciously from the artist, so that anyone who defines himself as an artist has automatically become artificial.

She also candidly accused the Yaddo administration of sexism. She was one of four women in residence, compared to twenty men, and she felt that "Elizabeth Ames disliked women and excluded them as much as possible." Maurine obviously had a personality difference with Elizabeth Ames, possibly because she had tried to make her into a confidant and was rebuffed. This scenario is suggested in a stiff rebuke from Ames:

> I should before now have acknowledged your note telling me that you are happy at Yaddo. I should be sorry if this were not true; for that would mean a waste both of your time and of Yaddo's resources which are after all so rare and so desired by many. I think the best return you can make for what you say you are enjoying and profiting by, is to try more and more to keep your own troubles and problems to yourself. For doing this, you increase the enjoyment that Yaddo can afford others. After all, who hasn't a grave problem, and yet how little discussion we hear of those problems, which, of course, is what one expects in a gathering of adults.[48]

In an undated character sketch, Maurine drew a prickly portrait of Mrs. Ames: "Fixed opinions of people she never altered. When once made, usually erroneous. . . . idea that art is dreaming, communion with nature . . . instead of the pain and sweat it actually is. So no noise. No loud laughter. Hushed footsteps. Whispers. Awe and reverence."[49]

One of the rules Maurine violated was to converse with the servants. She actually felt more comfortable with some of them than with most of the guests and told me of going on an outing to a beautiful lake with a young woman employee. She found the men, for the most part, simultaneously immature and over-sexed. One guest, identified only as Nathan, "speaks with a . . . little-boy lisp." Freddie, a painter, was "overly influenced by Salvador Dali" and had "shocking sexual obsessions."

Maurine does not suggest that she found any of these guests romantically appealing, although casual affairs obviously flourished, In turn, her fellow artists apparently did not find her either physically attractive or intellectually stimulating, and once again, Maurine felt marginalized. The conversation was like "having the talk flow right over you, stamping you out, denying your right to live." What could Maurine offer to make herself sound interesting? John Peale Bishop had been impressed by her "swell suffering," and Ferris Greenslet had been fascinated by her difficult life in St. George, as if she had been from a foreign country. So it was largely her own problems and background, as Elizabeth Ames's rebuke makes plain, that Maurine at Yaddo had used to constructed her personal story, and this tactic had backfired, leaving her socially stranded.

Nor was that the only dissatisfaction. Maurine followed her St. George schedule by working until mid-afternoon, then taking a walk. After St. George, Maurine found her studio too chilly even in the middle of summer—she probably also found it too isolated—and Elizabeth Ames accommodatingly gave her permission to write in the ballroom. Still Maurine couldn't settle down. She told me: "I felt something as I worked in that big room. Didn't see anything but felt it. I think the place was haunted. I can't explain why I felt something was not quite right."

Rather luridly, she began to see occult influences all over Yaddo. A male guest who suffered sinus infections attracted her sympathy, and she tried to relieve his symptoms with hot packs. Although she insisted to me that there was no romance, she also used the phrase, "When we broke up"—possibly meaning ending a close relationship—"he gave me something for a keepsake. It was shaped like a human more than anything else and was supposed to have extraordinary powers. But I couldn't see magic in it." In 1991, she no longer had whatever it was he gave her, nor would she come up with any more details than this.

She also had the impression that two of the guests had "escaped from Hitler's Germany and that they had been involved in his black magic in some way." Maurine also told me that "Mrs. Ames didn't want me to talk to them, saying 'they were too different.'" She had the impression that one of them wasn't there to work and asked him if her impression was true. He replied, "No, I'm here to get away from something." Then she claimed that soon after, mysteriously, one of these men dropped dead.[50] On another loose sheet, she described Yaddo as "a cross between a concentration camp and a girls' boarding school."

She described the dining arrangements: "The 'guests' or 'inmates' had one good meal together at dinner and a light lunch, both served on priceless china, with gold dipped utensils so heavy they were hard to hold. I was always afraid I would commit some breach of etiquette. And there was a servant like a guard standing around to make sure no one walked away with anything."

A brand-new experience for her was attending an evangelical Christian tent revival. She wrote a colorful and detailed essay about this experience, which survives as eight pages of holograph notes.

ACHIEVEMENT AND COMPLICATIONS AT YADDO

Despite Maurine's willingness to be distracted, she was, at last writing, and finished Chapter 3, which provides a frame within which to tell the inspiring epic of Mormon suffering and sacrifice. About a month after reaching Yaddo, she sent it off in longhand to Greenslet, who arranged to have it typed for her.

On 28 July 1939, a month and eight days after Maurine entered Yaddo, she received a pleased telegram from Greenslet: PAUL AND I ALL STEAMED UP OVER CHAPTER THREE. A LITTLE OVER WRITING HERE AND THERE BUT NOTHING TO WORRY ABOUT NOW. YOU HAVE RIPENED DURING FALLOW YEAR. FLASH BACK OF MORMON HISTORY BEST EVER WRITING."[51] He followed it up with a letter repeating his praise from the telegram and adding, "This is sincere as hell. . . . The imagistic resume of Mormon history is such hot stuff as it stands that there would be no earthly reason to break it up and spread it through other chapters. I have nothing particularly [sic] to criticize in this chapter except perhaps an occasional heaping up of adjectives or high-erected phrase."[52]

Chapter 3, covering pp. 57–91 in publication, shows seventeen-year-old Clory, married but still a virgin, fussing and frolicking as the serious work of getting the wagons over Black Ridge is going on. Maurine wrote an extensive scene of Clory's absorption with her clothes and hair, about which Greenslet opined: "What might be called the boudoir episode, dealing with underwear, hair-dos, etc., is all right once, but I think once is enough." Clory's forty-one-year-old bridegroom, Abijah, who is waiting till their arrival at St. George to consummate the marriage, chastises her for her light-mindedness and confines her to the wagon. She pouts, falls asleep, then awakens as Erastus Snow leads the people in a collective and personalized remembering of Church's history meant to bind the many nationalities together in their common cause. This storying provides flashbacks showing the people's reverence for Joseph Smith, their sufferings at Haun's Mill and Nauvoo, and the sorrowful but resolute trek west. Clory, thrilled by the call to nobility, grasps the grandeur of the future, which is called in the next to last chapter of the book by "another Clory" the "Land-of-the-Unlocked-Door." Impish, imperfect, and immature, Clory still emerges from this chapter with depth of soul. Her resolve clears and focuses, answering the reader's inevitable questions: "Why did they do it? How *could* they do it?"

No wonder Greenslet was pleased, reassured that his instincts were still good and that the story his dilatory, exasperating Maurine was telling was important. He encouraged her mightily: "I honestly think that the writing is better and the imagination shown more powerful and convincing than in Chapter One and Two." Maurine had obviously complained of loneliness, for he hastily added a postscript: "I am still troubled by your loneliness."[53]

Maurine also continued her research, asking reference librarians at the Utah State Historical Society for the sego lily's Indian name (it meant "butterfly"), requesting a copy of Assistant Church Historian Andrew Jenson's *Church Chronology,* and asking for such standard histories as Leland H. Creer's *Utah and the Nation* (Seattle: University of Washington Press, 1929), and some works by Levi Edgar Young, a General Authority and professor of history at the University of Utah. Marguerite S. Sinclair, a librarian with the Utah Historical Society, whom Maurine lists in the acknowledgments of *The Giant Joshua,* generously volunteered additional information that Maurine did not have enough background to request: items of St. George history from the unpublished journals of Jacob Hamblin and James Godson Bleak. She also shared Maurine's letters with Claire Wilcox Noall, then researching Mormon women doctors.[54] Claire, according to Marguerite, had heard of Maurine, was interested in her work, and wanted to meet her. It was a flattering connection.

Apparently Maurine was again broke, for she begged a fifty-dollar grant in mid-August from Elizabeth Ames from an emergency fund administered by Yaddo.[55] Maurine continued to complain to Greenslet about her isolation and loneliness, coaxing him to visit her. On 15 August 1939, he responded sympathetically but firmly: "I am distressed by your loneliness, but I have always heard, and should judge by my own experience, that that pain is very favorable to successful literary composition. I don't personally know anyone at Yaddo, or in Saratoga, and I can't think of anyone in Glens Falls, the place of my birth, that would be of any help to you." One of his acquaintances, however, had asked Max Ascolli, who was en route to Yaddo, "to look you up when he got there. Max, it seems told Dale that he could always work better when he had a pretty lady to walk out with on Sunday afternoons. Did he fail to charm you, or what?"[56]

Maurine told me that she and Ascolli had, in fact, "had many conversations and shared some of the same views of the world but that the great differences in background kept the relationship formal." Maurine was still unhappy. Greenslet hypothesized that he guessed she "got in with the wrong side," that he knew Yaddo had a "reputation that sometimes went to the bizarre." But unhappy or not, Maurine did write.

Only a couple of weeks after completing Chapter 3, Maurine sent off Chapter 4. Greenslet enthusiastically wired on 14 August: "MORE THAN PLEASED. . . ." Maurine had also confided her financial worries to him—this would have been the same week that she had wangled fifty dollars from the Yaddo emergency fund—and he responded with a combination of generosity, tact, and firmness. Though he couldn't allow the company to send her money, he personally sent fifty dollars as a loan. He also had another possible placement for "Mormon Saga" and wrote that he would send it on "with a seductive word." Equally helpfully, he promised to tell Elizabeth Ames "how pleased we all are here at the progress you are making with JOSHUA at Yaddo, and expressing the honest hope that she will keep you there as long as possible."[57]

Chapter 4, describing Clory's sexual initiation, is twenty-two pages long (pp. 90-112). Abijah invites Clory to investigate with him a piece of land he would like to claim. Merry at the outing and delighted with the day, Clory is irresistibly, innocently seductive. Abijah, unable to contain himself, startles and affronts her with his abrupt consummation of the marriage. A disappointed Clory discovers what is meant by wifely "obedience" and climbs silently back into the wagon: "Well, there's one thing he won't have to worry about any more, she said fiercely to herself; I'll never think of him as an uncle again!" (97) Unable to resist her youthful freshness, Abijah spends every night for the next few weeks in Clory's tent, causing considerable gossip. His son, Freeborn, who is closer in age to Clory, is becoming aware of incipient feelings for her. Bethsheba, the first wife, has to stand night guard alone to keep the coyotes away and bitterly tells the other women: "Men's men, . . . just like piss-ants is piss-ants. And if any man of mine wants to wet his pants over a pair of lily-white hands that shrink from a cow teat . . ." (p. 100).

It likely would have been difficult for Maurine to write this chapter in her north bedroom, while Charlie and Annie wrangled or Charlie angrily stormed out of the house to take one of his lady friends driving. Besides, it would have been difficult to write this chapter and then walk down the streets of St. George past the descendants of men and women who had been produced by such polygamous acts as were so recently sanctioned by the Church but who never talked about it. Especially when Clory, instead of continuing to be disgusted with sex, actually finds she could enjoy it "if only he'd play a little" (102) and teases Abijah in bed. This is probably the chapter LDS Apostle John A. Widtsoe was thinking of when he labeled *The Giant Joshua* "lurid."[58] And what, in fact, did Annie and Charlie think? Maurine shrugged when I asked her. She told me: "I never had an in-depth conversation with either of them about anything in the book."

In this same chapter, Maurine does another thing that lifts her narrative out of melodrama into art. She shows Bathsheba's positive qualities in describing the Christmas flood of 1861. Sheba, strong and almost six feet tall, works courageously beside the men to rescue the people from the ravening Santa Clara Creek. This episode reminds the reader that, in colonizing a harsh frontier, Sheba, not Clory, is the best kind of wife to have.

Greenslet apparently planned to visit Maurine, but on 17 August, he sent a telegram: "Inextricably lashed to mast by business and family complications."[59] She may have also tried to extract an invitation to come visit him, for in the letter which followed the telegram, he regretfully explained that he was very busy, their house was "full," "and the matter of transportation is complicated." He suggested an alternative: "To get the things that are chiefly troubling you off your chest, how about setting them down concisely on paper and let your psychoanalyst friend here at Park Street [he meant himself] see what he can make of them? At any rate, I would like to try."[60]

Maurine probably did not need to be invited twice to explain herself on paper and must have fired off the results by return mail. Only four days later on 22 August, Greenslet tried to get her to "pull up your socks." He reminded her of the crisis building in the world. "Your fellow Houghton Mifflin author, Adolf Hitler, has just started things I have got to deal with this morning, so no more now.[61]

The war in Europe was escalating. On September 1, 1939, Germany invaded Poland. The peace negotiations of England's Prime Minister Neville Chamberlain were breaking down. Maurine, steeped in nineteenth-century St. George, seems to have been virtually oblivious to the international crisis. Certainly, nothing in Greenslet's letters to her between June and the U.S. entry into the war in December 1940 suggest that they discussed the war news in any detail. In fact, on 5 September 1939 Greenslet reminded her again, with a possible note of exasperation, that her personal crisis was occurring against the backdrop of a major international crisis.[62]

Maurine must have fired off a snappish letter to Greenslet. Greenslet responded patiently with unfailing courtesy on 8 September: LETTER RECEIVED. CAN YOU COME OVER HERE FOR A DAY OR TWO NEXT WEDNESDAY? WE'LL REIMBURSE YOU FOR TRAVELLING EXPENSES AND TAKE CARE OF YOU WHILE IN BOSTON, HAVE A GOOD TALK AND START YOU WEST FULL OF CODFISH AND COURAGE. CHEERIO.[63]

Did Maurine pay the visit as requested? And if so, with what results? This two-week blank is made more mysterious by Greenslet's next letter, dated 20 September 1939. With some asperity, he wrote: "Nothing could possibly be more cockeyed than your idea that we are trying to strong-arm you into some remote spot for the sake of getting you off our hands, or that anybody would be 'angry' with you if you didn't stay put."[64] With some hesitation, he agreed that finding a place in the East at off-season rates might work for her. Obviously, Maurine was desperate to find some alternative to Charlie's north bedroom, but her options were severely constrained by her lack of money. Greenslet praised her "production of three excellent chapters," meaning that she had finished Chapter 5 by the time her extended stay at Yaddo was over. He also praises her for "constantly improving chapters during the period in question," indicating that she was simultaneously making revisions.

Chapter 5 (pp. 113–34) begins with the forty-day rainstorm, a dramatic scene of how a personal crisis is resolved by requiring individuals to sacrifice for the good of the community. Clory, frightened by an Indian, reacts, not like rock-ribbed Bathsheba, but like a panicky girl. Free finds her, and Maurine paints an irresistible picture of the childhood playmates, standing on the very verge of deeper possibilities as a man and woman. When Abijah on his way to council meeting met them at the edge of the clearing, "she could almost see the mood spurt apart like a dissolving soap bubble" (126–27). Abijah berated them in front of the family. Bethsheba blamed Clory and belittled Abijah, who overreacted further with threats of blood atonement for adultery and the inner conviction that his wives were eluding his control. Heatedly, he dragged them before Erastus Snow and the high council. Snow had been dealing with Orson Pratt Jr., an apostle's son who had expressed disbelief in the Prophet Joseph.[65] He was reluctant to sit in judgment, but he knew "you couldn't whip the desert without togetherness. The Group Faith—the ability to live outside oneself, for something greater than oneself, to sacrifice oneself for the Common Good. Some day they would be strong enough to afford dissenters—now salvation lay only in complete and disciplined togetherness" (132). He acknowledged reasons for doubts, including Brigham Young's ruthlessness, but "you had to be ruthless to colonize" (132). Orson Jr. sadly acknowledged that, even on his mission, he knew he did not have a "testimony that Mormonism is true," that he did not want to be expelled from the community, but that he could not lie to remain a member (132). Erastus noticed Abijah, Clory, and Free, and thinks, sighing, that the not-yet-formed relationship "must go down, even as Orson, before the Vision. There was no other way" (133). He announces that they have not committed sin but ladles out rebukes for all. Clory must "beware of giddiness." Freeborn "needs to find a wife of his own," and Abijah is "like the butterfly who passed all the flowers in the garden to light on the manure in the barnyard" (133–34).

Maurine had pled for a second extension at Yaddo, which was refused. She must have left with very mixed feelings. On the one hand, she had produced three chapters in three months, whereas she had finished no new chapters in the previous eighteen. But her hoped-for integration into cultured eastern living had not occurred. Worse, she felt not only marginalized but attacked. One officer of the Houghton Mifflin Company in New York, LeBaron ("Lee") Barker, whom she had met on her first trip east and, very possibly, again before entering Yaddo was now reacting negatively to Maurine and she to him. A nasty rumor had reached Greenslet, which she maintained came from Barker. The only written documentary description of it is a lengthy letter she wrote seven years later to Don Congdon, an editor at Simon and Schuster, because she was sure he had heard the rumor from one of the publishing partners who, she thought, lived next door to the Barkers in 1939. As she understood it, Barker, for reasons that may never be clear, had told Ferris Greenslet that Maurine had either had an abortion or had given birth by caesarian section the spring before entering Yaddo and soon before visiting the Barkers. Of course, there had been an abortion, but it was both secret and not recent; the caesarian operation is completely improbable. But pieces of Maurine's version of this story are not internally consistent, and the 1946 letter is obviously shaped to explain why she felt she could no longer remain associated with Houghton Mifflin:

> Just before I was to join Lee and go out to his house for the weekend, I got sick and went to see a doctor recommended by my friend Martha MacGregor who works on the Daily News as reviewer. The doctor is well known in NY and had a fine practice, but I can't remember his name just now, although I can find out if necessary. There was nothing wrong with me, but I was late for my appointment with Lee, then excused myself by saying, "I've had a brush with a doctor," and thought no more about it. That fall, just before I came home to finish Joshua, Greenslet insisted that a friend of his, Dr. Charles Lund, one of the medical deans of Harvard, give me a physical check-up. (I used to feel like a horse being groomed for a race.) Lund threw the bomb-shell. He told me that Greenslet had told him I'd had a Caesarian operation in the spring! Naturally outraged and horrified and mystified, I dashed back to FG and confronted him with the story. He claimed that Lee had written him the information just after my visit in the spring [1939]. Of course the whole business was insane—you don't have an operation like that and go to a cocktail party. But when I insisted that Max Lieber [her agent] ask Lee about the letter—when I was trying to make peace with HM. Co. after *Joshua* was published—Lee denied having written it. Thus Greenslet or Lee lied to me—and with no provocation and in the one sure way of hurting a woman. I've never known which one lied to this day, but it was the knowledge that such stuff could go on in the halls of HM Co that turned me against them completely. It broke my heart. I love that firm and was so childishly proud to belong! I could have forgotten the money but I couldn't forget *that*.[66]

Greenslet appended a noncommittal postscript to his 20 September letter: "I am returning Dr. Magovern's certificate 'To Whom It May Concern,' which is obviously addressed to me more than anyone else. I am glad to have seen it, and consider the production of three excellent and constantly improving chapters during the period in question little short of a mental marvel." He does not mention Barker, acknowledge a rumor, say he believed it, nor apologize, which he almost certainly would have done had he committed a social transgression. Was Magovern the doctor whose name Maurine couldn't remember? Did the certificate state that Maurine's abdomen, while marked with an appendectomy scar, did not have a C-section scar? (It would have been impossible to certify an abortion one way or another after the passage of more than a year.) His mention of "the period in question" seems to mean her three months at Yaddo, not when she came east to accept the fellowship. Perhaps he remembered sending a letter to her in care of a doctor when she was in Salt Lake City before coming east to enter Yaddo. This was Dr. Maud Callison. But if Maurine had something to hide, why would she leave this clue around?

On 13 November, approximately three weeks after Greenslet wrote about the rumor the first time, he made what could have been an oblique reference to it again: "I haven't seen him [Barker] since I saw you, but when I do I certainly shan't tell him more than that he was decidedly wet in his knowledge of feminine anatomy."[67] Greenslet, in the same letter, expresses pleasure that her health is better—which would be a meaningless statement if he was referring to a surgery more than a year old (especially if it had not taken place). However, Maurine was so often ill and so frequently told people about it that he could have been referring to the fact that her usual respiratory congestion was better. It also seems uncharacteristic of Greenslet's impeccable courtesy to have made such a coarse joke if he was referring to an abortion.

And even given the generally prudish social mores of 1939, why would either Greenslet or Barker have cared about Maurine's sex life? Were they trying to account for her lack of productivity and dramatic mood swings by hypothesizing the hormonal changes of pregnancy? Were they afraid that loose morals would create a public relations scandal? Although not enough is known about Barker, nothing in Greenslet's life or his relations with Maurine suggests the kind of almost unusual interest that Maurine's letter implies. Had she told some version of her rape and subsequent abortion in a bid for sympathy that had been misunderstood and misrepresented? I didn't know enough about it to have quizzed her while she was alive. However, she did tell me how hurt she had been when she had to realize that Greenslet didn't really care about her, just about the book, and she did confide her dislike for Barker. Whatever her reason for seeing a doctor, either an abortion or a C-section seems ludicrously unlikely compared to the probability that it was one of her usual ailments: painful menstruation, infected teeth, and respiratory illness.

Greenslet was probably taking pains not to get more entangled in any aspects of Maurine's life than necessary to keep *The Giant Joshua* moving. The book had to be finished or the company's goals for the fellowships would be thwarted. So he continued to express concern and encouragement, and Maurine continued to cling to the belief that she was special in his eyes.

There is some direct evidence that Lee Barker was capable of maliciousness and that an irresponsible or even vindictive rumor might not have been impossible from him. After the publication of *The Giant Joshua*, Maurine wrote to Samuel G. Houghton, president of Houghton Mifflin. The letter has not survived, but she apparently asked about Lee Barker, for Houghton candidly told her that Lee's wife's death from cancer had knocked "the props out from under" Lee. Houghton opined that "some people became peevish when their basis of life was destroyed." He then paid Maurine a generous compliment by saying she was "different," that she "must have a kind of unsinkable quality to survive." This last comment suggests that he may have known she had suffered an injustice and admired her for going on.

The most poignant sentence in Maurine's carefully constructed version of herself is her heartbreaking confession that she was "so childishly proud to belong." To belong to a praiseworthy family, to a popular group in high school, to a recognized sorority in college, to an admiring husband—she had been denied those relationships. And now, she had also been exiled from the bright, cultured company that, thanks to Ferris Greenslet's kindness, she had enjoyed so briefly.

When Maurine left Yaddo in September 1939, she may have hoped that Greenslet would relent and invite her to his home. He did not, and his letter of 20 September lacks her address, which he invariably put in the lower left-hand corner. Thus, right up until the Yaddo staff drove her to the train or bus station, she had not informed him about her final decision—just that she would be looking for a place in Provincetown, Rhode Island.

In this letter, he kindly and skillfully soothes her hurt (she was "cockeyed" to think Houghton Mifflin was trying to get her "off our hands") and refocuses her on the main goal—continuing the excellent progress she had made on *The Giant Joshua*. He also confirms an arrangement they worked out when she called at his office. Houghton Mifflin would pay her fifty dollars for each completed chapter, the sum to be deducted from her royalties. Was it a kind of penance for having believed Lee Barker's rumor about her—if, in fact, he had? Was it his keen editorial eye, seeing that Maurine was so shaky emotionally because of her even shakier finances that more frequent rewards would keep her working when she might otherwise sink into depression? It certainly seems a generous and flexible move on his part, which she later translated to mean more of Houghton Mifflin's exploitation of her.

Maurine told me that she boarded with a woman who lived "across the Hudson River." When I pressed for names or details, she shrugged my questions away. Excavating such minutiae obviously bored and irritated her. What she did remember was the atmosphere in the house, which dated to colonial times. It was alive with essences from the past, and she had three separate and vivid ghostly encounters. In the first, she was standing on the riverbank one evening watching the houseboats. Suddenly she felt so strong a "presence" that, frightened, she turned to go into the house. Then she noticed footprints appearing where she had felt someone had been standing—moccasin prints. She rushed into the house and walked up the staircase toward her room. As she did, she felt what she assumed was this same presence. This experience recurred so frequently that she decided the person was friendly and began thanking it at the door of her room. She believed it was an Indian woman whom she described as "charming."

She told me of her second experience with past time in this house this way: "From my window I could see a grove of very old trees. Under these trees, I once saw a group of men in colonial garb in some kind of conference." In the third experience, she was at the head of the stairs when she felt a pulling so strong that she had to grab the stairwell post. She looked into the room below and saw a dignified-looking man sitting by the fire, flanked by friends, all wearing clothes from the colonial period. They seemed to be having an enjoyable conversation, she said. Maurine was uncannily sensitive to the past. It was one of the influences that made *The Giant Joshua* so vivid.

But for Maurine, visitations from colonial America were another distraction she could ill afford. Clory's voice was calling her from the Sugarloaf.

Notes

[1] *Counter Punch Summer Reading List: Our Favorite Novels Written in English, America's Best Political Newsletter*, edited by Alexander Cockburn and Jeffrey St. Clair (Petrolia, Calif.) www.counterpunch.org/novels062122003.html-101 K (accessed July 2006).

[2] Maryruth Bracy and Linda Lambert, "Maurine Whipple's Story of *The Giant Joshua*," *Dialogue: Journal of Mormon Thought* 5 (Autumn/Winter 1971): 57.

[3] Jane McAllister Moss died on 2 July 1961 at age ninety-three, still upset at Maurine.

[4] Jane Thompson Bleak (1845–1942), in A. K. Hafen, *Devoted Empire Builders: Pioneers of St. George* (St. George, Utah: Dixie Mission Chapter, Sons of Utah Pioneers, 1969), 18.

[5] Charles William Seegmiller Sr. was born January 2, 1842, at Manheim, Ontario, Canada, to Johann Adam Seegmiller and Anna Eve Knechtle Seegmiller. He reached Utah in 1866, married Marianne Forsyth on 1 February 1868, came to St. George that fall, moved to the Muddy Mission in Nevada, then to Sevier County, and returned to St. George in 1877. A farmer and a tanner, he served in the Sunday School, in a bishopric, and as an ordinance worker. He died May 4, 1946. Hafen, *Devoted Empire Builders*, 117.

[6] Brigham Jarvis (1850–1933) in Hafen, *Devoted Empire Builders*, 63.

[7] Maurine Whipple, Letter to Elden and Florence Beck, 10 May 1941; Maurine Whipple Collection, L. Tom Perry Special Collections, Harold B. Lee Library, Brigham Young University, Provo, Utah, with photocopy in Maurine Whipple Collection, Archive, Val A. Browning Library, Dixie College, St. George, Utah. Documents in both collections hereafter cited as BYU, photocopy Dixie College.

[8] Levi S. Peterson, *Juanita Brooks: Mormon Woman Historian* (Salt Lake City: University of Utah Press, 1988), 117.

[9] Donald P. Seegmiller, Letter to Maurine Whipple, 30 October 1939; BYU, photocopy Dixie College.

[10] Hardwick Moseley, Letter to Maurine Whipple, 11 August 1938; BYU, photocopy Dixie College.

[11] Ferris Greenslet, Letter to Maurine Whipple, 28 October 1938; BYU, photocopy Dixie College.

[12] Ferris Greenslet, Letter to Maurine Whipple, 21 November 1938; BYU, photocopy Dixie College.

[13] Bernard DeVoto (1897–1955). In addition to his five novels, he is best known for essays and articles in *Harper's* (especially his column, "The Easy Chair"), the *Atlantic Monthly*, *Saturday Review*, and others.

[14] Greenslet to Whipple, 21 November 1938.

[15] "Mormon Saga," 23 pp., 1926, typescript of story written for a correspondence course from University of Utah; BYU, photocopy Dixie College. Another version has been edited to make it shorter. Also in Maurine's papers are various loose pages from copies or other versions. According to Greenslet, Letter to Whipple, 28 April 1939, Allen did not consider "Mormon Saga" because he never printed historical fiction. Greenslet proposed either Whit Burnett's *Short Story*, which paid "perhaps $50.00" or Robert Penn

ACHIEVEMENT AND COMPLICATIONS AT YADDO

Warren's *Southern Quarterly*, a very distinguished organ, for slightly more, maybe $75.00." Neither of these editors accepted it.

16 Lawrence Lee, editor of *Virginia Quarterly Review*, 19 September 1938; BYU, photocopy Dixie College.

17 Ferris Greenslet, Letter to Maurine Whipple, 28 September 1938; BYU, photocopy Dixie College.

18 Lillian McQuarrie, Letter to Maurine Whipple, 2 January 1939; BYU, photocopy Dixie College. There are no other clues about this novel's plot, but it is presumably a second novel set in St. George, not the one about the St. George polygamist, which she destroyed because of the family's angry response.

19 Ferris Greenslet, Letter to Maurine Whipple, 21 December 1938; BYU, photocopy Dixie College.

20 Ibid.

21 This information about Lillian's location comes from a letter to Maurine, 7 December 1938; BYU, photocopy Dixie College.

22 Lillian's sister was Thelma Maude McQuarrie Bennett. Born 18 April 1902, she was a year older than Maurine and two years older than Lillian. She married William Porter Bennett on 22 November 1922 and died 20 March 1979.

23 McQuarrie to Whipple, 2 January 1939.

24 Maxim Lieber, Letter to Maurine Whipple, 16 May 1941; BYU. Maurine had hired Lieber as her literary agent in January 1941. He said he was answering Maurine's question of 10 May about expenses being deducted from her royalties.

25 Ferris Greenslet, Letter to Maurine Whipple, 9 February 1939; BYU, photocopy Dixie College.

26 Ferris Greenslet, Letter to Maurine Whipple, 16 February 1939; BYU, photocopy Dixie College.

27 Alice Titus Whipple, Interviewed by Veda T. Hale, September 1991, notes in Veda Hale Collection, Dixie College Archive.

28 Maurine's nieces and nephews in southern Utah, confronted by Maurine's overwhelming neediness, learned to keep busy with their own lives and preserve their psychological distance. Carol Ann's geographical distance provided the equivalent buffer.

29 Greenslet, Letter to Whipple, 16 February 1939; BYU, photocopy Dixie College.

30 Ferris Greenslet, Letter to Maurine Whipple, 14 March 1939; BYU, photocopy Dixie College.

31 The summary that follows comes from the published version, not from the various draft versions.

32 Maurine Whipple, *The Giant Joshua* (Boston: Houghton Mifflin, 1941), 56; hereafter cited parenthetically in the text.

33 Greenslet to Whipple, 14 March 1939.

34 Ferris Greenslet, Letter to Maurine Whipple, 18 March 1939; BYU, photocopy Dixie College.

35 Ferris Greenslet, Letter to Maurine Whipple, 22 March 1939; BYU, photocopy Dixie College.

[36] Beck later taught at Brigham Young University in Provo, where a scholarship for botany students was established in his name.

[37] Ferris Greenslet, Letter to Maurine Whipple, 6 April 1939; BYU, photocopy Dixie College.

[38] Margaret Moody, Telegram to Maurine Whipple, 18 April 1939; Margaret Moody, Letter to Maurine Whipple, n.d.; BYU, photocopy Dixie College.

[39] Ferris Greenslet, Letter to Maurine Whipple, 21 April 1939; BYU, photocopy Dixie College.

[40] Elizabeth Ames, Executive Director of Yaddo, 24 May 1939; BYU, photocopy Dixie College.

[41] Ferris Greenslet, Letter to Maurine Whipple, 18 May 1939; BYU, photocopy Dixie College. Greenslet sent that letter to Maurine in Salt Lake City, in care of Dr. Maud Callison, Suite 516, Templeton Building, Salt Lake City. Maud Pace Callison, born 5 July 1880, [New] Harmony, Washington County, Utah, married Valentine Byrd Callison 2 July 1902, died 17 September 1968. AncestralSearch record from FamilySearch website. According to the 1930 U.S. Census, for Salt Lake City, ED #21 Sheet #16A Page#16, Entry #170, Line #39–40, both Callisons were "osteopathic physicians" by profession. It is not clear what ailment Maurine was receiving treatment for, but once again, ill health was hampering her work.

[42] Ferris Greenslet, Letter to Maurine Whipple, 18 May 1939; BYU, photocopy Dixie College.

[43] Ferris Greenslet, Letter to Maurine Whipple, 5 June 1937; BYU, photocopy Dixie College.

[44] Ferris Greenslet, Letter to Maurine Whipple, 19 June 1937; BYU, photocopy Dixie College.

[45] This detail was included in a PBS series that aired 29 December 1991, on writers that featured Katherine Ann Porter. http://www.spa.net/yaddo/yaddo/history.htm (accessed September 2006).

[46] Maurine Whipple, untitled and undated notes, holograph, BYU.

[47] Maurine Whipple, one-page untitled questionnaire, dated 1948; BYU, photocopy Dixie College.

[48] Elizabeth Ames, Letter to Maurine Whipple, 17 August 1939; BYU, photocopy Dixie College.

[49] Maurine Whipple, "Mrs. Aims", n.d., 1 p. holograph; BYU, photocopy Dixie College.

[50] Maurine's papers includes an undated clipping from an unidentified newspaper about Dr. R. A. Bermann, an author, who died at age fifty-six at Yaddo. Subheadings in the article are: "Noted Austrian Newspaper Man," "Refugee from the Nazis," "Saved by Friends in Vienna—Wrote 'The Mahdi of Allah' in 1932 and 'Bimini.' He was arrested when the Nazis occupied Austria in May 1838; but thanks to the intervention of friends, he came to the United States in August 1938 and was working on his autobiography at his death.

[51] Ferris Greenslet, Telegram, 28 July 1939; BYU, photocopy Dixie College. "Paul," though obviously on the editorial staff at Houghton Mifflin, is not identified by full

name in the correspondence, but was in the "back room" with "the girls." Ferris Greenslet, Letter to Maurine Whipple, 24 November 1939; BYU, photocopy Dixie College.

52 Ferris Greenslet, Letter to Maurine Whipple, n.d. but, from the content, was written close to his telegram of July 28, 1939. BYU, photocopy Dixie College.

53 Ibid.

54 Noall's major work is a fictionalized history: *Intimate Disciple: A Portrait of Willard Richards, Apostle to Joseph Smith—Cousin of Brigham Young* (Salt Lake City: University of Utah Press, 1957). She published a five-part series, "Utah's Pioneer Women Doctors," in the *Improvement Era* 42 (January–August 1939) and followed it up with a lengthy article, "Mormon Midwives," for the *Utah Historical Quarterly* 10 (1942): 84–144.

55 Ames to Whipple, 17 August 1939.

56 Ferris Greenslet, Letter to Maurine Whipple, 25 July 1939; BYU, photocopy Dixie College. Max Ascolli (Greenslet spelled the name "Ascoli") (1898–1978), the Italian-born editor of the leftist *Reporter Magazine* was known as an educator, scholar, intellectual, anti-fascist activist, and a sociologist. http://www.dantealightevi.net/cambridge/events.html (accessed August 2006).

57 Ferris Greenslet, Letter to Maurine Whipple, 15 August 1939; BYU, photocopy Dixie College. On 18 August, he had changed his mind about trying to place the story without giving a reason and sent it back.

58 "On the Book Rack," *Improvement Era* 44 (February 1941): 93.

59 Ferris Greenslet, Telegram to Maurine Whipple, 17 August 1937; BYU, photocopy Dixie College.

60 Ferris Greenslet, Letter to Maurine Whipple, 17 August 1939; BYU, photocopy Dixie College.

61 Ferris Greenslet, Letter to Maurine Whipple, 22 August 1939; BYU, Dixie College. Houghton Mifflin was publishing the English translation of *Mein Kampf*.

62 Ferris Greenslet, Letter to Maurine Whipple, 5 September 1939; BYU, photocopy Dixie College.

63 Ferris Greenslet, Telegram to Maurine Whipple, 6 September 1939; BYU, photocopy Dixie College.

64 Ferris Greenslet, Letter to Maurine Whipple, 20 September 1939; BYU, photocopy Dixie College.

65 Apostle Orson Pratt and his family arrived in St. George in March 1862. Orson Jr. was excommunicated 13 September 1864 after he and three other men started a newspaper in which they featured articles asking questions about the Church and the leaders. Karl Larson, *"I Was Called to Dixie:"The Virgin River Basin: Unique Experiences in Mormon Pioneering* (1961; Salt Lake City: Deseret News, 1979 printing), 424 note, suggests that perhaps "the key to Orson Pratt, Jr's, problem with the local church" was that some of these articles reexamine the truthfulness of some Mormon beliefs.

66 Maurine Whipple, Letter to Don Congdon, 14 November 1946; BYU, photocopy Dixie College. There is no other evidence that Maurine visited Barker before entering Yaddo.

67 Ferris Greenslet, Letter to Maurine Whipple, 13 November 1939; BYU, photocopy Dixie College.

9

THE PUSH TO FINISH

After Maurine left Yaddo and Cape Cod, she was sad and depressed. She felt mostly dissatisfied with Yaddo, bruised by her marginalization, and shaken by Lee Barker's malicious gossip (and the possibility that Greenslet had believed him) which she interpreted as a spiteful attack on her morals and reputation. But balanced against these negatives was a record of solid production. Could she keep the momentum?

By September, St. George was cooling down slightly from its furnace summer. Alice and Ray were building their new house and enjoying their baby daughter. But Florence's family was experiencing a crisis. Her husband, Ben, had been caught in a mine cave-in at Pioche on 15 July, while Maurine was at Yaddo, and the company had sent him to Los Angeles by train, accompanied by the company doctor and Florence. Charlie and Annie drove to Pioche to retrieve seven-year-old Colleen and two-year-old Larry, who had been left with friends.

At the Good Samaritan Hospital in Los Angeles, Ben "underwent surgery on his back," wrote Florence. "The doctors told me at the time that his back was broken and his spine was injured so severely that there wasn't much hope that he would ever walk again, as he was paralyzed from the waist down. He was hospitalized in that hospital for ten months. This was a very hard and trying time for all of us."[1]

Maurine undoubtedly worried about the situation but pressed forward with the book. On 13 November, Greenslet enthusiastically acknowledged the receipt of Chapter 6: "Hooray! Oh boy! Or, as you Mormons probably say, selah! And also Hallelujah!"[2] She had evidently told him that her health was better, and he confidently predicted that her new energy was "sure to make JOSHUA go even better, and the better it goes the fitter you will feel, thus establishing a benevolent circle in place of the vicious circle that you were caught in at Yaddo last summer."³

Chapter 6, thirty-nine pages long (135–74), contains a crucial scene of reconciliation to the harsh landscape. Clory, pregnant, is determined to have her own house and struggles to lay up the sods herself. Her friend, Palmyra, also hating the wilderness, conspires with Clory to leave. They agree to stay if Palmyra's husband, David, can show them "one pretty thing." An Indian guides them to a natural bowl in the desert, brimming with blooming sego lilies. It is a transformative moment and the two girls decide to stay.

Apparently Maurine was still worried that Vardis Fisher's novel, *The Children of God*, had damaged the market for *The Giant Joshua*. Greenslet reassured her: "I am more and more convinced that in the eyes of posterity it will be but as a pup tent beside the great tabernacle of JOSHUA."⁴ Then he added temptingly, "There is another $50.00 here raring to go as soon as we get that chapter seven."⁵

Maurine sent Greenslet some local chrysanthemums by express, which, he wrote just before Thanksgiving, had arrived in "first class condition . . . and we are all thinking thankfully of you."⁶ That Maurine would go to the bother and expense of shipping fresh flowers to Boston shows how desperately she wanted Greenslet and his staff to like her, but it also reveals her emotional fragility and her financial impracticality, which, as a strategy, likely worked against her the next time she begged Greenslet for more money.

Greenlet also encouraged her: "The badge of the reception committee is on my chest for Chapter Seven. Don't trouble to get it typewritten if not convenient. We will be glad to do it here, returning copy to you." This comment suggests that Maurine had found a local typist but probably had complained about both the time and the expense. Greenslet's Miss Moody was "retiring to domestic life" but his new secretary, Betty Leighton, took over Maurine's typing.⁷

Maurine completed Chapter 7 within the next month, for Greenslet wrote on 20 December 1939: "I guess you got your $50 for Chapter Seven." The typescript was en route to her for corrections. The chapter was lengthy, sixty-five pages in the published book (175–240). It describes a killing St. George summer of drought, followed by torrential rain that washed away ditches and dams. Clory gives birth to her first child, Calistra Agatha MacIntyre ("Kissy"). The chapter concludes with Brigham Young's rousing sermon, challenging the people to build the tabernacle and establish better schools (175–240).

THE PUSH TO FINISH

Greenslet was proofing another copy of the typescript, "interrupting myself from time to time to read choice bits in the back room."[8] Maurine liked knowing that her "team" at Houghton Mifflin appreciated her work.

Maurine, perhaps presuming on Greenslet's obvious pleasure, must have tried to wheedle another advance from him, for he wrote back a lengthy letter after Christmas, never departing from a cordial tone, but making it clear that she had extracted her last concession that was not tied to production.[9]

On 28 December 1939, the same day as Greenslet's letter, Robert N. Linscott, Houghton Mifflin's editor in charge of the novels, wrote to tell Maurine that he had read the new material with "the greatest delight. Good as you were before, Maurine, I think you're getting even better as you go along. It lives and moves."[10]

Lillian's next surviving letter came 14 December 1939 (the previous one in the collection had been written 2 January 1939). She enthused: "Gee, I'm glad the book is getting done by 100 page lots. That's swell." She comments about Maurine's tired eyes and encourages her by saying she believes they will get better when they can rest.[11]

Maurine did not resist the temptation—or the duty—she felt to help Florence and spent about two weeks with her, from just before Christmas until about mid-January 1940.[12] Florence was leaving her two children alone in the afternoons while she visited Ben in the hospital.

Maurine was still visiting Florence when she made another attempt to engage Greenslet in solving her problems. He broke his own rule and the company's by advancing her fifty dollars himself, even though she had not yet completed Chapter 8.[13] Responding to his trust, Maurine sent that chapter off to him by 10 January. It is also lengthy, covering fifty pages in its published form (241–91). It moves the plot forward describing settlement conditions as becoming somewhat more stable in the 1860s. Brigham Young visits again and is honored with a "homespun dress" ball. A child is missing, supposedly stolen by Indians. Free now knows he loves Clory but struggles to find happiness without her. A poor harvest brings the threat of starvation. The Mountain Meadows Massacre, committed in September 1857, receives increased federal attention; and John D. Lee, soon to become the official scapegoat, is shunned by his neighbors.

A spur of a different sort to Maurine's productivity came from Reva Holdaway Scott of Hayward, California, whom Maurine had met when she was living in the Beehive House in 1926. Reva had also written a Mormon historical novel, but Houghton Mifflin had turned it down, because "Whipple's covered the same subject." Reva complimented Maurine in January 1940 for having "made the biggest hurdle by being accepted by a

N.Y publisher."[14] Despite the sincerity of Reva's congratulations, it served notice to Maurine that someone else might write a historical novel about her people if she didn't.

Just at this moment when Maurine was gradually accepting that she was never really going to be "adopted" by the wealthy literary eastern establishment and just when she must have strained her long-suffering family's resources and patience to the maximum, a second "prince" came to her rescue. He was a St. George native: Joseph Walker. He was the brother of Zaidee Walker Miles and the uncle of Maurine's first high school crush, Wyatt Walker Miles. Dr. Walker, like Greenslet, was sixty-two. He was practicing medicine in Hollywood specializing in urology.[15] Florence and Ben probably turned to him for help, and Maurine undoubtedly consulted him about her medical problems. But when Dr. Walker and his wife, Tina, read some of the work Maurine was doing, they were very impressed and went further with her, initiating a friendship that remained interested and supportive for about five years.

Walker willingly treated Maurine's ailments: recurrent sinus infections, painful menstrual periods, and intensifying dental problems from college days. He seems to have not expected payment, but Maurine always tried to contribute something meaningful to a relationship. In this case, she made and gave him a copy of some poems by his father, Charles Lowell Walker, which she had obtained from Zaidee. She quoted some of them in *The Giant Joshua* as having been written by her character, David Wright. Joseph thanked her warmly: "It is interesting thru their lines to peep into the minds of those hardgutted, stubborn, determined old rascals who made whoopee and committed all sorts of deviltry in the wastelands of their vast desolation."[16]

Born on Joseph Smith's birthday and probably named for him (he signed his letters to Maurine "St. Josif"), Walker was a strong cultural Mormon, but not a believer. He took the position that Mormonism had been, if not a mistake from its outset, then certainly corrupted and detrimental to many by the time it reached the generation of the pioneers' children. Still he had great affection for his people, southern Utah, and his culture. Striking a good-humored, self-deprecatory pose, he satirized anything in his environment, past or present, that took itself too seriously. In addition to supplying medical assistance and emotional support, he was a gold mine of anecdotes, historical tidbits, and human insights, which he passed along in well-written letters, many of which could stand alone as personal essays. Maurine's papers include sixteen of these letters, the first dated 15 January 1940, the last 22 December 1945. There were very likely others that have not survived. She included insights from some in *The Giant Joshua* and later opinions and a quotation in *This Is the Place: Utah*.

The Walkers' unstinting affection, their unreserved admiration of her writing ability, and their open pride in her achievement was balm to the bruises of indifference that Maurine said—probably with exaggeration—characterized the reactions of people in St. George. Walker habitually opened his letters to her with endearments: "Lovely," "Wonderful," "Honey," "Our Dear Maurie," "Wayward Sister." Maurine shared with them a copy of her manuscript. Walker's encouragement included such compliments as singling out a sentence, for instance: "All desert plants are emphatic—they have to lead with their chins" and praised her: "In those dozen words, you did more for the desert than Van Dyke did in his large Vol. in which in Tux and with glass in hand knee-high boots and African hat on head he wandered for years thru the desert and . . . no more saw or felt the desert than an anatomist sees or feels the human body as he works in the dissecting room. . . . The word 'emphatic' would never come to Van Dyke, and never, never would he think of going to the sports pages to find the one perfect action synonym with oomph."[17]

He also passed on Tina's unreserved admiration and joy in Maurine's achievement: "Tina is so thrilled with the book. . . . [I] hear coming from her room peals of laughter and when I go to see what it is all about, her eyes are wet and she continues to exclaim, 'You Maurine, you Maurine, you have done it, you have done it. At last the story is told as it should be and how on earth did you ever do it? . . . I pinch myself to think that one of our St. George girls did it.'"[18] To know from these representatives of her own people that she had "got it right" must have been as sweet to Maurine as praise from the outside audience represented by Ferris Greenslet and his colleagues at Houghton Mifflin. Now the team was definitely in place that could coax the book out of what might seem like a misplaced genius.

Dr. Walker also spoke directly to Maurine's fears that she would be outclassed by Vardis Fisher and Bernard DeVoto: "There is a something in your pages not found in Vard's, that could never be thot of by De Voto, that defies the art of the historian and would confuse and confound the orthodox teller of tales. I can't find a word for it . . . but it seems to me that you have written the idioms of a people's life."[19]

Although Greenslet's combination of coaxing, cajolery, financial flexibility, and seemly genuine affection never flagged during the production of *The Giant Joshua*, he was focused on extracting the book from her, one painful chapter at a time. Maurine, looking back later, commented bitterly: "Joshua was my introduction to the business world; what I had thought was friendship turned out to be all too often merely a bedside manner."[20]

Joseph and Tina Walker, however, had no business motive in their sincere and enthusiastic support. They provided another kind of belonging needed for the creation of *The Giant Joshua*—sympathetic and sophisticated awareness from people who were not only her own people but also at home in the broader world she longed to enter. Walker's educated, good-humored encouragement, his willingness to share his own experiences and observations, his open admiration of Maurine's writing ability, and his concern for her health, combined with Greenslet's editorial skills and enthusiasm, created a delicately balanced environment. Together they gave Maurine the kind of support that had not existed earlier and which never existed again.

In Walker's first surviving letter, dated 15 January 1940, Maurine was living on a date ranch he owned in the Coachilla Valley, near Cathedral City, California. The warmer, dryer climate of the California desert soothed Maurine's tortured sinuses, but she apparently stayed for only a few weeks.

On the same day as Walker's letter, 15 January 1940, the typist Betty Leighton wrote in behalf of Greenslet who was in Florida. She added a personal comment: "I'm delighted to find Free still alive—I thought you were going to kill him off in the flood. Is there a prayer of your letting him live until the end of the book, or are you going to shoot him dead in the war? He keeps getting more and more appealing and I hate to think of life in the cotton fields without him."[21] Betty also forwarded the holograph, the ribbon copy,[22] and a carbon copy to Maurine which is how Maurine had an extra copy to let Joseph and Tina read.

Maurine was working on Chapter 9, but it is not clear how much she was able to do while in California. This chapter, which covers forty-seven pages in the published *The Giant Joshua* (292–339), ends with Free's being killed by Indians. He had started to be careless, both with his personal safety and his reputation. Clory is so heartsick and guilt-ridden that she has a miscarriage in the next chapter.

Betty Leighton wrote two letters to Maurine in March. On the 19th, she reported that Greenslet had bronchial pneumonia but that the retyping was going well. In her March 28 letter she wrote: "Mother reads the sheets as they fall out of the typewriter."[23] "After two weeks in the hospital and three weeks of depressed and irritable convalescence," Greenslet wrote on 1 April 1940: "I am now pretty much myself again. If you keep on at that pace, I don't see why you shouldn't be the Pulitzer winner, yourself, of 1940."[24]

Writing Chapter 10 took almost two months. Greenslet received it on 2 April 1940 and sent Maurine her fifty dollars. On 18 April, having read the last three chapters, he praised her: "With each new chapter I think afresh how much better this is than Vardis Fisher."[25]

In Chapter 10 (340–406 in the published volume), Clory suffers a miscarriage and Free is buried. Heartbroken, Clory climbs the red hill where she encounters Erastus Snow, also in a reflective mood. He wonders: "Was a man a fool, then, to reach for the stars?" (352) Clory whispers, "'Trying is all that counts.'" Chapter 10 presents a defense of polygamy by showing how women can live in love and harmony, as Palmyra's mother and sister-wife had done and as Palmyra herself and her sister-wife, Lucy, were doing. And in a strong scene, the family wagon tips over and Kissy is thrown out and knocked unconscious. Abijah, far from being hard-hearted, reacts with seldom-seen love for his little daughter, gives her an immediate blessing, and reveals to Clory, five months pregnant, a faith and nobility of character that make her respect and even love him.

Time passes. Clory has two more children. Abijah leaves on a mission to England, while the three wives get along as best they can. The grasshopper plague and "fly time" help produce what was called black canker,[26] that carries away all three of Clory's children and one of 'Sheba's. Clory's grief, as she wraps Kissy's little body in her mother's paisley shawl, was so convincing that at least one reader could not believe that Maurine had not also suffered through the death of a child.[27]

Maurine was in a productive phase. Chapter 11 (406–53) took only three weeks to write, generating "the statutory fifty smackers" when it arrived in Boston on 23 April 1940. The long fallow period of immersion and absorption was paying off in a sustained outpouring of creativity that Maurine would never match again in her life. Greenslet, in his acknowledgment letter, ran over Maurine's summer plans: finish the manuscript by 1 July—attend the Rocky Mountain Writers' Conference, and have her teeth fixed. He also added judiciously: "As the thing has progressed, adjective pruning seems less and less necessary. I think it could be confined to the first few chapters only, and I'll try to get at those between now and the time you finish the book." He anticipated publication in November.[28]

Chapter 11, forty-six published pages (406–53) begins with Erastus Snow challenging would-be quitters: "No one has actually starved yet, has he? The thing that makes you quit is the *fear* that you'll starve! It's like a forced march, putting one foot in front of the other. . . . The past is dead. Don't worry about the future. All you have to do is live one day to the next. And I *promise* you in the name of the Lord, things'll get better" (410).

From the mission field, Abijah blamed Clory for the deaths of her children: "It was God's judgment on you, Clorinda Agatha" (436). Instead of being either angry or depressed, Clory resolved to be a better wife and learned to tan buckskin so she could earn money by making gloves. Woven into Clory's tapestry of personal chastening and resolve are the government's beginning efforts to suppress polygamy and break the political and economic hold the Church has on the Utah Territory.

"SWELL SUFFERING"

While working on the next chapter, Maurine apparently asked for Greenslet's help in being accepted at the MacDowell artists' colony for the next summer. Greenslet assured her on 30 April: "I have written this morning to Mrs. MacDowell, telling her again what a good girl you are and asking her what about her colony this year."29 In answer to her query about applying for the Guggenheim Fellowship, awarded annually for research and creative work, he responded less encouragingly: "Successful publication carries great weight with them, although if *The Giant Joshua* should be as successful as we hope, you might be too rich to be considered by them as a needy applicant."30 He also alluded to her well-rehearsed despair that Vardis Fisher's *Children of God* would be the only Mormon novel readers would read by writing "Your story of Mormonism is FROM THE INSIDE. . . . We are referring to GIANT JOSHUA as a story of Mormon life from the woman's point of view, which ought to hold Vardis Fisher."31

After writing Chapter 11 in only three weeks, Maurine now followed it up with Chapter 12, sent only another three weeks later. Greenslet responded on 13 May with her fifty-dollar check.32 Linscott, responding to Chapter 11 the same day, concluded his complimentary note: "Bless you, my child, for the pleasure you are giving me."33 He couldn't have said a nicer thing. Maurine frequently said how she loved making people feel that she was enhancing their enjoyment, understanding, or enlightenment. It was her mode of paying her way in the world.

In the forty-five-page Chapter 12 (454–99), Abijah returns from his mission and judges Clory to be at last "a wife worthy of a High Priest and Seventy" (464). He had seen her mother in Philadelphia and brought Clory a silver castor and bottle of perfume. They find a brief interlude of marital bliss. Clory gets a real house instead of the dugout and bears, after a long, dangerous labor, a son she names Jim. Even more rewarding is another of her rare spiritual experiences: "Hardly daring to breathe, denying the flesh and the material walls about her, invoking the Spirit thing, there came one of those rare instances that had sustained her all her life. Horizons parted—laughter lived" (490).

In contrast, Willie, Abijah's meek and silent second wife, gives birth to a daughter, Templena ("Tempie"), and dies in lingering agony when the afterbirth is not delivered. Abijah, sure that his priesthood blessing will be efficacious, follows Brigham Young's counsel and refuses to send for the doctor. Clory promises to raise Tempie and finally learns the secret of Willie's calm and unshakable faith. A survivor of a handcart company that left too late in the season, Willie had witnessed the deaths by starvation and cold of her husband and two children but had refused to yield, dragging herself forward when she had to crawl on her hands and knees—even on her elbows. Willie said that what sustained her was "'a voice, not a whisper, but still and low said to me: 'If you will leave your 'ome, father and mother, you shall have Eternal Life.' I 'ave heard the same voice since, not in dreams but in daylight, when in trouble and uncertain which way to go; and I *know God lives* and guides this people called Mormons.'" Her eyes filled with the mystery of "the last long trek," Willie's dying words to Clory were: "'Don't never knuckle under to life, Clory. Don't never knuckle under, if you 'ave to crawl—all—the—way!'" (498–99) The power of this passage convinced me that Maurine, on some level, knew about this "voice" from personal experience. She, on more than one occasion, confirmed it to me but usually shied away from divulging specifics.

In another three weeks, Chapter 13 was also finished—the fourth time in a row Maurine had done a three-week sprint. Greenslet, in his complimentary letter on 3 June, said about the fifty dollars he was sending, "Better bury the last-mentioned so that the Germans won't get it until after you've got your new teeth."[34] It is doubtful if Maurine, living and breathing the nineteenth century, was more than remotely aware of the greatest military struggle of the twentieth century. In fact, Joseph Walker commented after a visit from Maurine about how he and his wife had welcomed her "detachment from this world about us with which you came from your world."[35]

Chapter 13, forty-five published pages long (500–534), is full of wonderful historical information. Two of Brigham's wives, Amelia Folsom and Lucy Bigelow, share his winter in St. George. Clory takes organ lessons from Lucy, who also introduces silkworm-raising to the women. Maurine here puts into Clory's mind another characterization of polygamy: "They said polygamy was a principle for refining the spirit. If you could live in it gracefully you had conquered the flesh and your own soul, and one who had conquered his own soul had just about conquered life!" (519) This chapter also asserts an expression of triumph that many readers miss, seeing Clory's life only as one of failure and defeat: Clory realizes that she has done her own soul-conquering, learning how to live with 'Sheba and how to find contentment with Abijah: "Even if your breasts do sag from too much nursing and you've got a little tummy so that no amount of corseting can bring your figure back, you're happy! You've licked the thing that tried to lick you!" (519).

In contrast to this peace is the news of John D. Lee's trial and execution for the Mountain Meadows Massacre. Federal prosecutions for polygamy intensify. An aging Brigham Young arrives to dedicate the temple and dies within the year. The chapter ends with the words, "Truly, an epoch had passed" (534).

Maurine's depiction of Brigham Young has generally won critical acclaim. Eugene England, a biographer of Young, wrote about Maurine's

Brigham: "I find her not only intuitively dead center on his qualities but able to give them marvelous imaginative life."³⁶

Chapter 14 was shorter, twenty pages (535–55). It reached Boston on June 10. The discovery of silver at nearby Leeds tides the community over after another flood (in Chapter 13) wipes out its agricultural foundations again, but the prosperity that comes from selling produce and other items to the miners brings its own challenges. Abijah struggles between his religious zeal and his love for Clory and his children, which he defines as a human weakness. In another moment of clear-sighted maturity, Clory realizes she can choose her attitude.

Maurine had been keeping up this night-and-day pace since March and was wearing out. Then came another strand in the delicate web of support that made it possible for the book to be finished. She told me that a friend, the "angelic" La Ree Milne,³⁷ had seen her working away in the oven-hot north room, "perspiration running down my forehead and looking very bedraggled. She then briskly announced that she was going to fix that." La Ree persuaded her fiancé, Bud Lamoreaux, to take Maurine to a hunting cabin on Beaver Mountain owned by his friends.³⁸

The coolness of Beaver Mountain rejuvenated Maurine, and the alpine beauty refreshed her spirit. Instead of being a distraction, it was a spur. She worked almost nonstop, determined to have the novel finished before she left for the Rocky Mountain Writers' Conference in late July. She told me about this period: "When I became too groggy to focus, I would go outside and sit in the ditch. After a few days, my mother joined me, both to look after me and to get away from Papa. Mama fixed the meals, used cheese cloth to improvise a screen against insects, and swatted flies. But I couldn't share much of the manuscript. And then Papa came. . . . I can remember how she looked when she saw him across the clearing and said she feared she'd have to go back with him. It was such a sad resignation, Oh, how I wished she would stand up to him!" Maurine gave a long sigh and was quiet for a few minutes, looking very sad. She lay back down on her bed in the care center, turned her face to the window, and murmured several times: "Poor Mama. Poor Mama."

Greenslet's surviving letters do not mention when Chapter 15 (556–92) reached him, but it must have been between June 10 and 19. This chapter describes Brigham Young's funeral in Salt Lake City in 1877, the publication of St. George's first paper, *The Vepricula*, the mounting pressures against polygamy, and the arrests of David Wright and Erastus Snow. Clory's son, Jim, now fourteen, assumes a more defined character as a boy who likes the outdoors and cowboy life. He was a disappointment to Abijah, who wanted a scholarly and pious son. Clory, at age forty-two, is weakened from repeated miscarriages and fears of the future. Her hands are covered with bleeding lesions from working the buckskins and from the alkali in the water. She keeps them bandaged.

The date Maurine finished *The Giant Joshua* can be narrowed down from her correspondence with Joseph Walker. On 13 July, Walker wrote that he and Tina retrieved a manuscript copy of "the poor, dear lovable 'Pup'" from Warren Cox. "Poor little devil, he surely looked as if he had a hard trip over the desert."[39] Tina became "desperately ill," spiking a fever so high that she was delirious. Beside himself with anxiety while awaiting the arrival of a specialist, Joseph reported to Maurine: "In her delerium [sic] she repeatedly called out her heartfelt praises of your book and of you. Perhaps this is the most sincere and generous praise that could be offered. For all unguarded, her subconscious self poured out its pent-up emotions and reactions."[40]

Despite his concern about Tina, Walker remembered to send Maurine progesterone to ease her "painful menstrual periods" and also sleeping pills, warning her to use them sparingly and to "try for natural sleep now the book was finished." He also encouraged her to stop drinking tea and coffee and thereby achieve more restful sleep.[41]

On 19 July Greenslet wrote triumphantly: "The last two chapters are here, and here's our check for $100."[42] Chapter 16, thirty-two pages long (592–624), contains another crucial conversation on the red hill between Clory and Erastus Snow: Snow muses: "The way I look at it, the thing we've got that's immortal is an Idea. And maybe that's why we've been persecuted. . . . Maybe, human nature being what it is, the world will always stamp upon that Idea. . . . But you can't kill it, Clorinda Agatha—it's older than the world. . . . " (620)

In jarring contrast to this moment of transcendent insight, Abijah is called as president of the newly constructed Logan Temple. Clory, urgently wanting to be in the more cultured north, pleads: "'You are going to take me with you, aren't you, Abijah?' She tried to keep the desperation out of her voice. 'Sheba's too old and I can work, I'—She remembered her bandaged hands white against the black of his coat and hastily thrust them behind her—'I can keep a big house, preside at socials. You used to say all I was good at was parties. Well, now . . . I can have more babies . . .'"(602)

Instead, Abijah marries a young wife, vulgar and sensual but presumably fertile, while Clory is left behind, because Abijah thinks she will not add to his impressive posterity. Clory does not tell Abijah she is pregnant, fearing it will just be another miscarriage. In Maurine's own family history, her Grandfather J.D.T. McAllister, called from the St. George Temple to preside over the Manti Temple, made essentially the same choice, taking with him a new wife who was most likely to provide him with more children. Maurine had grown up knowing at least three of the left-behind wives, including her own grandmother. She knew the family stories from the women's point of view. She knew that the eighth wife, Matilda, had died at age forty-two, after being so brokenhearted she had divorced J.D.T. (See Chapter 9.) This grounding makes the situation in the novel more substantive than just a sentimental scene.

The chapter ends with Erastus's dream of how to solve the annual floods, not with the perennially unsuccessful dams, but with a spillway. The spillway is a good example of how Maurine used historical records to verify and gain information about certain dramatic events, but still took her deep inspiration from the place itself or from an insignificant detail that made a historical event come alive for her. In addition to telling the story of the spillway as part of Erastus Snow's story (621–24), she also wrote about it in an unpublished essay, "The Miracle of the Spillway," claiming it was a dramatic technological breakthrough.[43]

Chapter 17, only eight pages long (625–33), begins with a lengthy scene of nostalgia, as Clory's granddaughter, about seventy years in the future, comes upon the cherished relics from the past: the cane, the rosewood desk, and other gifts from Clory's mother. The narrator, also named Clory, feels that she has discovered "the Land of the Unlocked Door." This mood changes dramatically when the nineteenth-century story resumes. Clory, pregnant and abandoned by Abijah, is frightened by a neighbor's dog. "Then it jumped. A wrenching and tearing. The smell of blood. Clory stooped and picked the dead baby up in her apron and turned and walked back home" (629–30).

I talked to Maurine about this scene, telling her that it bothered me because it seemed artificial, a way to make Clory even more of a victim, alone with no one to help her. Maurine almost agreed with me, but then said. "But it could have been like that. My grandmother had had a terrible scare with dogs and was terrified of them. So was my mother." She never did explain why her grandmother's scare made her mother afraid, too, or whether either experience had brought on a miscarriage. During the period of sharpest surveillance by federal marshals, "there were more dogs than usual in the community because they could give an early warning of strangers. For a while, loose dogs roaming the community became a menace."

"Did you mean that the dog didn't actually attack?" I queried. "It seems that it would have smelled the blood as Clory miscarried and really hurt her."

"Oh, you know how a dog is, even a friendly one. It will come up too fast and sometimes jump up on you. I meant it like that. But even though it was friendly, it scared Clory."

"And the baby came?"

THE PUSH TO FINISH

"Yes, like that. Quick. But the dog was tame. It didn't hurt her."

The novel concludes with Clory's deathbed epiphany. Again, Maurine reached into her past when, at age seventeen, she saw the agony on her dying grandmother's face turn into peace and radiance: "Already the radiance is trembling on the horizon, the flushed light leans down from the west, the Great Smile beckons. And suddenly, with the shock of a thousand exploding light-balls, she recognizes the Great Smile at last. That which she had searched for all her life had been right there in her heart all the time. She, Clorinda MacIntyre, had a testimony!" (633)

Thus, the novel ends by speaking reassurance and strength to the victim in all of us. Even though negative circumstances and death win, they do not triumph. The ultimate victory goes to something else—to the serene and beneficent forces of love that Maurine termed the "Great Smile." An anonymous reviewer for *Time* magazine, although not commenting on Clory's epiphany, praised the last thirty pages as "a strong groundswell [reaching] almost to the edge of grandeur."[44] As Maurine wrote this final passage, Mormonism holds up as an ideal, providing the strength and faithfulness to "endure to the end." Clory did endure. She didn't give up. She didn't abandon Mormonism. She didn't withdraw herself from her people. Nor did she abandon her own staunch and quiet dignity.

In Maurine's eyes, the triumph of that self-knowledge is a certitude freighted with joy fully comparable to the more conventional "testimony" of a truth as that affirmed by many orthodox Mormons. Certainly, knowing Maurine's own struggles and relentless challenges, it is fair to assume that she was also saying something about her own life.

There is some evidence that Maurine struggled to find the right way to end the novel. Her papers contain two typed pages of an alternate conclusion, written later than the original synopsis, because it is different than the ending described there. In it, Julia, Abijah's new wife in the published version, is a "pert minx with her bold, rib-boned bustle" (598) while in this synopsis, she is "shy, pale, scared to death." Clory builds Julia's confidence and also shows her own generosity of spirit by giving Julia her own prized red dress.[45]

When I talked with Maurine about this alternate ending, she agreed that she had written it early, perhaps when she was working on the first full synopsis in January 1938. She thought she had described this second ending to Greenslet in a letter, but her letters have not survived and his do not mention it. Perhaps they discussed it in person in the spring of 1938. It ends when Abijah and his new wife are waving good-bye. "Clory and Bathsheba were shoulder to shoulder in the open doorway, waving, too. In utter astonishment Clory turned to the gray-headed wizened unexpectedly pitiful older

"SWELL SUFFERING"

woman she had hated so long: 'I never understood before how you must have felt about me!' she . . . ." [page ends][46]

Notes

[1] Florence Whipple Jolley, "History of Florence Whipple Jolley," January 1976, 18; 23 pp. holograph, in possession of Colleen Jolley Haycock, of Las Vegas; photocopy in my possession, courtesy of Colleen Haycock.

[2] Ferris Greenslet, Letter to Maurine Whipple, 13 November 1939; Maurine Whipple Collection, L. Tom Perry Special Collections, Harold B. Lee Library, Brigham Young University, Provo, Utah, with photocopy in Maurine Whipple Collection, Archive, Val A. Browning Library, Dixie College, St. George, Utah. Documents in both collections hereafter cited as BYU, photocopy Dixie College.

[3] Ibid.

[4] Ibid. Greenslet did not read Fisher's novel until the following September, so most of his dismissal of Fisher seems to have been designed to keep up Maurine's spirits. Greenslet, Letter to Maurine Whipple, 1 September 1940; BYU, photocopy Dixie College.

[5] Greenslet, Letter to Whipple, 13 November 1939; BYU, photocopy Dixie College.

[6] Ferris Greenslet, Letter to Maurine Whipple, 24 November 1939; BYU, photocopy Dixie College.

[7] Ibid.

[8] Ferris Greenslet, Letter to Maurine, 20 December 1939; BYU, photocopy Dixie College.

[9] Ferris Greenslet, Letter to Maurine Whipple, 28 December 1939; BYU, photocopy Dixie College.

[10] Robert N. Linscott, Letter to Maurine Whipple, 28 December 1939; BYU, photocopy Dixie College.

[11] Ibid.

[12] Greenslet sent letters to Maurine at Florence's address 4 and 10 January 1940; BYU, photocopy Dixie College.

[13] Greenslet to Whipple, 4 January 1940.

[14] Reva Holdaway Scott, Letter to Maurine Whipple, 6 January 1940; BYU; photocopy Dixie College. She was the author, under the name of Reva Holdaway Stanley,

THE PUSH TO FINISH

of *A Biography of Parley P. Pratt: The Archer of Paradise* (Caldwell, Ida.: Caxton Printers, 1937) and achieved her goal of finding a national publisher under the name Reva Lucile Scott for *Samuel Brannan and the Golden Fleece* (New York: Macmillan, 1944).

15 Joseph Walker was born 23 December 1878 to Charles Lowell Walker and Abigail Middlemass Walker. On 19 November 1908, he married Christina ("Tina") Woodbury, born in 1881 to George J. Woodbury and Rowena Romney Woodbury. Walker graduated from Jefferson Medical College, Philadelphia (June 1908), practiced briefly in Rexburg, Idaho, Oregon, and Washington, and then set up his practice in Hollywood. In 1914 he studied in Vienna, Austria, and restricted his practice to urology after 1917. He and Tina reared a niece, Rowena Woodbury Backer. Walker died 18 June 1964 in Glendale, California.

16 Joseph Walker, Letter to Maurine Whipple, 15 January 1940; BYU, photocopy Dixie College.

17 Joseph Walker, Hollywood, Letter to Maurine Whipple, 16 July 1940; BYU, photocopy Dixie College. Maurine's description of the desert plants appears in *The Giant Joshua*, 189–90.

18 Joseph Walker, Hollywood, Letter to Maurine Whipple, 13 July 1940; BYU, photocopy Dixie College.

19 Joseph Walker, Letter to Maurine Whipple, 13 July 1940; BYU, photocopy Dixie College.

20 Maurine Whipple, Letter to Don Congdon, Simon and Schuster, 14 November 1946; BYU, photocopy Dixie College.

21 Betty Leighton, Letter to Maurine Whipple, 15 January 1940; BYU, photocopy Dixie College. This letter was addressed to General Delivery at Cathedral City.

22 The ribbon copy takes its impression from the ribbon, not from the carbon paper.

23 Betty Leighton, Letter to Maurine Whipple, 10 and 28 March 1940; BYU, photocopy Dixie College.

24 Ferris Greenslet, Letter to Maurine Whipple, 1 April 1940; BYU, photocopy Dixie College.

25 Ferris Greenslet, Letters to Maurine Whipple, 2 and 18 April 1940; BYU, photocopies Dixie College. Fisher's *Children of God* won the Harper Prize in 1939, but Maurine kept mentioning it because people were reading and talking about it in Utah.

26 Pioneer doctor, Stiddy Weeks (a barely disguised name for herbalist pioneer doctor Priddy Meeks) identifies it as the "the plague of Winter Quarters about which people still spoke in hushed whispers." *The Giant Joshua*, 399.

27 Hughie Call, (1890–1969) a bereaved mother and aspiring author from Montana, was so moved by Maurine's book that she came to St. George to visit Maurine and was startled that Kissy's death was not autobiographical. Houghton Mifflin published Call's book, *Golden Fleece*, in 1942 (reprinted 1961 and 1981) and her *The Little Kingdom* in 1964, which described her daughter's death. Call also wrote *Rising Arrow* (1955) and *Shorn Lamb* (1969).

28 Ferris Greenslet, Letter to Maurine Whipple, 23 April 1940; BYU, photocopy Dixie College.

[29] Ferris Greenslet, Letter to Maurine Whipple, 30 April 1940; BYU, photocopy Dixie College.

[30] Ibid.

[31] Ferris Greenslet, Letter to Maurine Whipple, 10 May 1940; BYU, photocopy Dixie College.

[32] Ferris Greenslet, Letter to Maurine Whipple, 13 May 1940; BYU, photocopy Dixie College.

[33] Ibid.

[34] Ferris Greenslet, Letter to Maurine Whipple, 3 June 1940; BYU, photocopy Dixie College.

[35] Joseph Walker, Hollywood, Letter to Maurine Whipple, 5 September 1940; BYU, photocopy Dixie College; punctuation standardized.

[36] Eugene England, "Whipple's *The Giant Joshua*: A Literary History of Mormonism's Best Historical Fiction," posted to Association of Mormon Letters email list, 18 March 1997, 20. His biography is *Brother Brigham* (Salt Lake City: Bookcraft, 1980).

[37] La Ree Milne Lamoreaux was born 10 November 1910 and died 1 June 1971.

[38] Ferris Greenslet, Letter to Maurine Whipple, 3 July 1940; BYU, photocopy Dixie College.

[39] Joseph Walker, Letter to Maurine Whipple, 13 July 1940; BYU.

[40] Walker to Whipple, 13 July and 16 July 1940.

[41] Joseph Walker, Letter to Maurine Whipple, 17 July 1940; BYU, photocopy Dixie College.

[42] Ferris Greenslet, Letter to Maurine Whipple, 19 July 1940; BYU, photocopy Dixie College.

[43] Maurine Whipple, "Miracle of the Spillway," n.d., ca. 1970s when she was collecting material for her *The Unpromised Land*. Each chapter was to be able to stand on its own. 18 pp., typescript, Dixie College. See also an audio tape of this document, titled "Taming of the Virgin River" read by Gene Pack, at Dixie College. Andrew Karl Larson, *"I Was Called to Dixie": The Virgin River Basin: Unique Experiences in Mormon Pioneering* (1961, Salt Lake City: Deseret News, 1979 printing), 373, gives basically the same story, attributed to Charles W. Seegmiller.

[44] "Mormon Wife," *Time*, 6 January 1941, unpaginated clipping; BYU, photocopy Dixie College.

[45] Maurine Whipple, no title, n.d. but ca. 1938, 2 pp., typescript; BYU, photocopy Dixie College. The first page or pages of this synopsis are missing.

[46] Maurine Whipple, loose sheet, holograph; BYU, photocopy Dixie College.

≫ 10 ≪

PUBLICATION: A FLASH OF FAME

Maurine must have been stunned with fatigue when she went off to Boulder, Colorado, and her fourth year at the Rocky Mountain Writers' Conference. In Boston, Greenslet rolled up his sleeves to go to work cutting the manuscript of *The Giant Joshua* and editing it for publication. He wrote genially on 19 July 1940, a letter she received at the conference: "I think we may be going to propose to you rather more drastic cutting than I had originally expected. . . not forgetting the well-known aphorism I have quoted to you before, 'that the more the marble wastes, the more the statue grows.'"[1] He sent her a contract to act as the publisher's talent scout, an arrangement she had probably initiated, hoping to pick up a little extra money. If she found a publishable manuscript she would receive $100.[2] There is no evidence that she ever found such a prize.

She badly needed dental work done[3] and must have asked Greenlet's advice about getting an office job or arranging a loan to pay for the work. He responded with his usual warmth and said about the office-job idea: "I don't really think you are that kind of animal" but thought Houghton could probably arrange to advance her some money.[4]

Maurine spoke at the writer's conference on "The Materials of Fiction,"[5] but probably her best contribution was as a living example of how her earlier attendance at this conference had made her success possible. Her papers include a letter from Albert Maltz, a soon-to-be-successful Hollywood screenwriter, whom Maurine met there. His letter suggests that Maurine had spilled out her woes to him and that he had not responded with the kindness she desired. However, he does not figure significantly in her life, even if he might have been a good contact when she was trying to sell the movie rights to *The Giant Joshua*.

A warm letter from an otherwise unidentified Mrs. Josiah H. Chase, who had also attended the conference, adds some details about Maurine's participation: "I don't have to tell you that I know you are going to be a success. I knew that the night I heard you read your last chapter. I knew it the day I heard you talk at the panel." She added that she didn't think Maurine would be happy until she "got started on Joshua's brother (if you haven't started on it all ready). And when you get into that you won't rest until it is finished. And that is the price you pay for genius, my dear. You are slave and not master to your talents and you wouldn't have it otherwise."[6] Though this friend appears to want to be involved in Maurine's life, I found no further evidence in Maurine's papers of more correspondence.

Also attending the conference was Dorothy Nyswander, then working in New York City. Maurine spent the next Christmas with her in New York. In 1934, Dorothy had launched Juanita Brooks on her Works Progress Administration (WPA) project of collecting and transcribing pioneer diaries.[7] Although the program had been created to help women like Maurine, Maurine told me she hadn't even heard of it. "You just don't know how it was. My family just weren't the kind who got helped by that kind of thing. Papa just dominated. We just weren't of the inside families." Maurine then recalled, "I felt sorry for Dorothy because she had big dreams to write a great book and had little money or talent." Ironically, it was Dorothy who built a stable and productive career in the public health field, while Maurine's situation remained precarious, always scrambling.[8]

Maurine must have written Greenslet soon after she returned to St. George, saying she was ill but volunteering to come to Boston for in-person consultation on cutting the manuscript when she felt better. Greenslet responded by return mail that she must return the manuscript immediately, with or without her input. She wasn't happy about doing it, but apparently did.

She had obviously fired off a protesting letter to Houghton Mifflin, for on 20 August, Bob Linscott wrote her soothingly that they would try to incorporate her suggestions and changes: "Now that I have read the whole book, I want to tell you—and more emphatically than before—what a magnificent job you have done. I have always been confident it would be a great novel but I had no idea how great it would be until I read it over all at one time instead of isolated chapter by chapter. It will be a real pleasure to give the book the kind of promotion and (I hope) the sale it deserves."[9]

Greenslet finished reading *The Children of God* on vacation in Maine. He reported on 1 September 1940 that he had "slogged" through Fisher's "so-called" epic and "it is really hard dull reading, devoid to my taste, of the smack of life that makes Joshua. The reader doesn't give a damn about any of the characters. You have it all over him like a tabernacle."[10] He added a gloomy note about the international situation: "Like all the world I'm very low in mind this morning. I saw quite a lot of the last war, and the idea of another in my life time is almost more than I can stand. But war does not hurt the sale of really honest books like Joshua." On that date, the newspapers would have been describing the awful ordeal of "the blitz," launched against Britain by Germany. This was the pessimistic environment *The Giant Joshua* would encounter in its debut. However, this very fact added to the impact it would make, for here was a book telling the story of a tough, determined people with high ideals worth fighting for, people with the same commitment to cooperation in a cause that would be needed to save the world from the Nazi threat.

What exactly Maurine negotiated on the edited manuscript is not known. After spending at least a few days in St. George in August, she went to California to visit the Walkers.[11] She could count on their unstinting admiration for her writing and, probably, their sympathy, knowing that many good parts would have to be cut from the book. Unlike some people in St. George, Dr. Walker and Tina Walker thoroughly approved of her interpretation of pioneer days. On 5 September, after she returned to St. George, Joseph's note passed on Tina's evaluation that "every page of the book [manuscript] rings as true as the flapping of a Monday washing in a Dixie sandstorm." He continued, affirming the special intellectual understanding they had: "We, too, are a couple of lonely kids hunting around for something we will never find, but we are enjoying the hunt. And to think that right out of our old village came one who had lived the same life, known and felt the same things and had been stung to the extent that she too knew what attack after attack of intellectual hives was, was, in deed a treat. . . ."[12] Walker, too, lamented the state of the world facing another war. Then he commiserated with Maurine for an injury to her foot, referring lightly to "the jinx that hoodoos your days." Walker's casual mention sounds as if "the jinx" was already a familiar joke between them.

Maurine pled again with Greenslet to let her come east, but he told her on 12 September to wait until she received the galley proofs. "The proofs will go to you, not chapter by chapter, but in big batches, probably only two or three batches altogether. We will send them by air mail, and if you return them by the same conveyance, very little time will be lost." He assured her she could "smooth the joints" and even "make reinstatements of small matters that may have been inadvertently and unwisely omitted."[13] He also mentioned the Twentieth-Century Fox production of *Brigham Young,* soon to be released, starring Tyrone Power, Linda Darnell, and Dean Jagger in the title role.[14] He felt it would "open the pores of the public to Mormon literature."

"SWELL SUFFERING"

On 27 September, Greenslet's secretary, Betty Leighton, sent a quick note, since Greenslet and Linscott were on vacation. She complimented Maurine for spelling that was "invariably perfect." Maurine had evidently mentioned her plans to make a pack trip into the Arizona Strip to observe a fall round-up to collect material for the sequel. Since Betty knew Maurine should have been busy reviewing the proofs, she added: "I do hope this doesn't mean your pack trip will have to be given up, as branding calves is my idea of a noble accomplishment. What about bulldogging steers?"[15]

Don Seegmiller, a young friend, sometimes loaned Maurine a little black horse and frequently took her riding near St. George. Among Maurine's papers is an unfinished and untitled rough draft about a horse caught in quicksand.[16] Seegmiller claimed that the horse episode had actually happened, almost as she had used it.[17] But the trip to the ranch, which would have been the Seegmillers' mentioned by Betty, was postponed and Don also stayed in St. George and was present when Maurine read her galley proofs to Juanita Brooks. Maurine said, "It was so terribly difficult to take some of those parts and tell them they couldn't be in the book. I promised I wouldn't forget them and would find a way to use them in something later."[18] One big cut was a section on the local Indians.

After the cutting of the manuscript, Joseph Walker arranged for Maurine to see a dentist, so she returned to California for two weeks in late October and early November.[19]

Maurine had proposed a book cover in May 1940—a desert landscape "with a parade of Mormons coming over the horizon rim."[20] Greenslet had liked it and must have commissioned an artist to create a picture. Advance copies went out, probably in mid-December to a long list of key people in Maurine's life; and congratulations started pouring in before the year's end.

Joseph Walker sent his St. George relatives and friends a flat of "Star Choice" dates from his farm in Coachilla Valley. He must have given Maurine a quantity for she recalled distributing them as gifts for friends. He had written an enthusiastic letter to his sister, Zaidee Walker Miles, a summary of which appeared in the *Washington County News*. It lauded Maurine as "one of the greatest friends this section has ever had: The girl has re-created the life of the [eighteen] Sixties with a truthfulness and sympathy and understanding as never has been done before by anyone in Utah."[21]

On 21 December 1940, Lillian wrote from Salt Lake City about some sad news: "Someday when I can tell it without turning the knife in my back, I'll let you in on the dirt. It's the most tragic thing I can imagine." Lillian was not exaggerating. Her shock at discovering that her daughter and her husband were in love, and her subsequent divorce from Emerson, final in September 1940, must have been numbing. She generously invited Maurine to come visit for a week, since "I have an apartment alone, and there's no one to get jealous because I'm talking to a pal. That's always been my trouble: too many possessive people around me."

She then passed on from her own trouble to rejoice with Maurine: "And dough-trouble is over for you, too. Gee, I'm glad about it all, kid. You've deserved this break more than anyone I know."[22] This is just one of the indications that Maurine and everyone else expected her to make a lot of money.

Maurine headed east a few days before Christmas, since a letter Greenslet sent to her in St. George on 20 December had to be forwarded to her in New York City. It has not survived, but it apparently contained disappointing information about the financial expectations. Angry, Maurine drafted a hasty and threatening telegram to Greenslet:

> Yours of the twentieth just caught up with me. Cannot come Boston unless you pay all expenses, including transportation, hotel, and meals. Present trip taken on basis of old three thousand to fifteen thousand dollar estimate. Under new estimate, after I have subtracted honorable debts which I have listed to you as I incurred them during past three years, I will have just two hundred dollars with which to take medically imperative vacation, get back out West via Pullman, find a place to settle since Utah temporarily closed to me, and live until next November royalty. Will not cash current fifty until further word. Checking out hotel Tuesday. Please reply via Western Union soon possible.[23]

There is no record of a reply, if any, but on 27 December 1940 Greenslet wrote to Maurine at the Prince George Hotel in New York City. "I am enclosing our check for fifty smackers, to speed your approach." He cautioned Maurine not to expect too much attention from him, as far as the holiday festivities went. However, "Bob Linscott would be available to wassail you to your heart's contents." Maurine may have hinted for another invitation to Greenslet's home, but he told her that he recommended the Lincolnshire Hotel where she could have a bedroom with attached bathroom for about $3.50 a day.[24]

As far as promotion went, Henry Houghton, the company's president of Houghton Mifflin, was planning to spend Thursday morning, 3 January, taking her "around the principal Boston bookstores to meet the chief clerks, and get you to autograph a few copies in each store. . . . There is no point in trying to pull any regular 'autograph party,' until after the book has been widely and favorably reviewed, and actually got going." Friday afternoon at her hotel would be "a cocktail party of some size, inviting key persons from the book trade, literary critics, and radio book commentators, some Boston authors, and selected members of the office staff."25

The Giant Joshua was officially released on 1 January 1941. Maurine was in New York by at least 9 January, because, in a wave of confidence about the future, she hired Max Lieber as her literary agent. Her anxieties about money must have vanished in the glow of success, for most of the reviews were warmly complimentary.

Avis M. DeVoto, wife of Bernard DeVoto, wrote in the *Book-of-the-Month-Club Bulletin* that the heroine of *The Giant Joshua* was "one of the most appealing women in modern fiction." Then she added: "But perhaps Miss Whipple's greatest achievement is in getting on paper the social history which brings the period into focus. Here are the engrossing details of living—the clothes, the food, the remedies, the deaths and births, the preparing of bodies for burial. These people appear in the round—a tough, hardy lot, rough of tongue, bursting with vitality."26

Bernard DeVoto's complimentary review appeared on 4 January 1941: "*The Giant Joshua* is excellent reading and it catches a previously neglected side of the Mormon story and that is the tenderness and sympathy which existed among a people dogged by persecution and hardships, forced to battle an inclement nature for every morsel of food they ate and to struggle for every moment of genuine happiness."27

Omnibook Magazine condensed the book for its March 1941 issue.28 *Time* magazine, the first week in January in one of the earliest reviews, devoted three columns with a portrait of Maurine: "It is not merely a good fictional history of a special group and period; it is also a good novel about human beings in general."29

A letter from John Peale Bishop, then holding Harvard's endowed chair in the novel, rejoiced: "I am happy for you, but happier still for the sake of American literature."30

Maurine gave away many autographed copies, especially to people who had helped her, and she wrote numerous letters of thanks to appreciative fans. One of Maurine's first gift copies went to Agnes and Jess McCammon, the affectionate family in Georgetown, Idaho, who had made her school-year there bearable. Agnes wrote excitedly: "Oh Rene we were so thrilled for you so happy after so much hard work you have accomplished so much. Old Walter Clark has got to a place where he has to at last look up to you. You always did say you would show him. . . . Your School kids are all so proud you are the subject here in Geo. Town. We are shouting about the book."31

It is true that a significant number of hometown people were not pleased by the novel. One of the most painful evaluations—the anecdote Maurine invariably repeated—was her father's. When Greenslet mailed her the first advance copy, Charlie Whipple talked the postmaster into giving it to him, read it, told Maurine that it was a "vulgar" book, and refused to talk about it.

Another deeply wounding comment she repeated came from her sister-in-law, Alice, whom Maurine said she overheard saying, "Maurine will never get praise from the family. We know her too well."

Annie read it but there is no record of her opinion. My observation was that Maurine, like Charlie, felt that Annie was too naive to be taken seriously. Annie's reactions were certainly contradictory: proud when the letters of praise came but ashamed whenever there was criticism from local quarters. Maurine remembered that most of the ladies from Annie's Relief Society and her friends in Daughters of Utah Pioneers were offended, thinking that Maurine had portrayed St. George pioneers negatively. "George's [her younger brother] opinion was the only one I didn't have to worry about, as he was the only one in the family satisfied with the book." At this point, he was out of the country, serving with his unit in the Philippines and obviously had things on his mind other than a tempest in the St. George teapot.

Maurine said many St. Georgians paid her the backhanded compliment of assuming (sometimes correctly) that she had modeled her "characters" on their own relatives. Others, who could not see their people in the novel, were insulted, thinking that their ancestors' stories were "more important" than those which were included. Some lobbied her to include their family's stories in the next book. As late as 1991, some local people had still not brought themselves to read *The Giant Joshua* because they remembered how much pain it had caused their parents.[32]

On the more positive side in St. George, *The Giant Joshua* sold at the Big Hand Cafe for $2.75, where Maurine also did at least one signing.[33] The Big Hand was frequented by cowboys, and this advertisement suggests that the book was finding a ready audience among St. George's more unorthodox citizens. Maurine always enjoyed the cowboys and had an easy, bantering relationship with them, something like her friendship with Joseph Walker.

The local paper reported that Glen Snow gave a book review to an "overflow crowd at the library" in late January, rating *The Giant Joshua* "far ahead of" either Vardis Fisher's *Children of God* or Paul Bailey's *For This My Glory*.[34]

On 30 April 1941, the Dixie Reviewers, a St. George book club, named Maurine an honorary member and sent her a letter expressing their appreciation "for your fine achievement."[35] On 31 May 1941, the *Washington County News* reported that Mrs. Roxy Romney hosted an openhouse for Maurine in St. George's library attended by perhaps fifty people.[36] Lou Harris, a pretty St. George friend whose popularity Maurine had envied in high school, sent her a warmly congratulatory card: "Because we have known each other's personal problems for years I feel I can detect the personality progress you have made. So—may I say you are one celebrity who knows how to take success exuberantly gracefully? Just carry on in the same ol' spirit."37 All of these friendly gestures must have warmed Maurine's lonely heart and helped push back the hurt from the unfriendly ones.

Another letter came from Gerald Irvine, a boyfriend from her student days at the University of Utah. Now a successful lawyer and assistant to the city attorney in Salt Lake City, he passed on congratulations from other quarters: "My friends are all proud that they knew you when you were in school and are boasting of the fact. Jake Trapp told me it was a powerful book and well done. Herb Maw, gov. told me you had 'written the real story about the Mormons.' Large window displays were showing prominently in New York and Washington."38

Her high school principal, Joseph K. Nicholes, said: "You have written beautifully the achievements of a superior people through their purposes and emotions. The background of your great study is true, therefore, your book will live." He closed by repeating, "I am grateful to you."39 This appreciation must have been particularly gratifying since Maurine felt that he had disliked her in high school and had mentored a younger girl, Mary Nielson Campbell, in hopes that she would become southern Utah's Edna Ferber.

Dorothy Kreutzer enthused: "Everyone I know who has read it, or is reading it, is pleased with it. Was very interested to learn through ZCMI that it was in its second edition already!!" She offered Maurine her guest room whenever Maurine visited Salt Lake City.40

Samuel G. Houghton wrote from Reno, Nevada, praising the book for "its historical accuracy," then added perceptively: "I suspect F.G., 'who is on the side of the angels' [Maurine had dedicated the book to Greenslet with this quotation], had much to do with your persistence and being constantly on your side as well, he possibly made you feel yourself a member of the glorious company. Of such feelings come the great doings in any art form. One has to be convinced he is a member of a great company, a special world of people, with an almost apostolic job."41 This comment identified Maurine's deep hunger, never fully satisfied, to "belong." Such a truism coming from the president of Houghton Mifflin, who had hired Greenslet to do just what he had so skillfully done, should have made Maurine reevaluate her slowly festering attitude toward Greenslet.

Albert Maltz, the Hollywood screenwriter she had met at the Rocky Mountain Writers' Conference the summer before, praised her technique: "You write awfully well, you feel people and their relationships—in short you've got a Grade A pasteurized flow as a writer and if you keep growing and keep grasping important themes the sky is the limit." Her achievement, as he put it, "struck terror into me since I must try to do the same thing for my own historical work and it doesn't seem to me as though I can ever succeed so well." Maurine did appreciate his comment that "there must be many thousands of people who, like me, can now feel that they understand something of Mormons and Mormonism."[42]

The publication of *The Giant Joshua* also brought Maurine genuine fan letters—readers who had such strong responses to the book that they wanted to reach out to its author, whom they had never met. Over the years they accumulated into a folder two or three inches thick. For the most part they are positive, some life-changing.

A woman from British Columbia, after reading *The Giant Joshua*, invited in "two eager bright-eyed young things"—Mormon missionaries—who came to her door.[43] It was not unusual for Maurine's readers to feel such a bond with her that they would take the time to learn more about Mormonism. Maurine hadn't been shy about announcing her Mormonism and defending it when needed.

But against this generally positive background, one review weighed heavier than all the rest. In Mormonism's tight-knit and hierarchical world, the question active Mormons asked was: "What does the Church think of it?" By "the Church," they meant "the General Authorities," whose opinion, by extension, represented God's evaluation. That answer came from Apostle John A. Widtsoe. He wrote a short review in the regular book column in the February 1941 issue of the Church magazine *Improvement Era*. He did not suggest banning the book, but his few negative sentences affected Maurine's life more than any other words written about the book:

> The example selected, a life defeated because of polygamy, leaves a bitter, angry distaste for the system. That is unfair. Emotional upsets in human relationships and mistakes in life are not peculiar to polygamy. Proportionately, there were fewer unhappy marriages under "Mormon" polygamy than under monogamy. The evident straining for the lurid obscures the true spirit of Mormonism, and misleads the reader.
>
> The story follows in method modern "literary realism." This detracts from its beauty, and adds no strength.
>
> In the dissection of human emotions, however, one feels that he is treading water rather than touching bottom. Perhaps the author is beyond her own depth. . . . J.A.W.[44]

Widtsoe offered no detailed analysis or evidence to support his generalization that polygamous marriages were proportionally happier than monogamous marriages. Why realism detracted from "beauty" or what he considered to be historical "mistakes" are not known. Maurine brooded over this review, feeling painfully criticized and rejected. She wondered, without much hope, if Widtsoe would have accused her of "straining for the lurid" if he or his people had been sent to St. George to colonize. "I just wrote about what I knew—and that was the good and the bad," she told me. "I knew I wasn't absolutely accurate historically. But for the sake of the space, I had to capture what I could of history. Sometimes I just pulled things together and had them happening in a cluster."

Maurine didn't have much knowledge of or sympathy with any of the larger literary philosophies. She thought Widtsoe objected to the details in *The Giant Joshua* because they departed from the idealized and heroic portrayal of the superhuman pioneer that had already become the Mormon myth. "Men do not like to recognize any unholy mixture in themselves—nor do women," she said.

Time has proved that the novel is bigger than even valid criticisms. The most unfortunate result was that Maurine—desperately desiring to belong, urgently trying to win a hearing for the "Grand Idea," and hypersensitive to every critical breath—internalized Widtsoe's review as "the Church's" judgment upon her. It is impossible to say how much influence this review had on the many strategies of sabotage that she inflicted on herself and her writing for the next five decades, but it played a definite role. For one thing, whether correctly or incorrectly, it became part of the pattern of persecution that Maurine felt she suffered under, a Mormon counterpart to the exploitation and neglect that she felt Houghton Mifflin had dealt her. She lamented: If only she could have finished the trilogy, then Mormons *en masse* and Mormon leaders would see that she was really sustaining the faith, not tearing it down. *The Giant Joshua* told only part of the story—the story of terrible suffering on the part of that first generation. Carrying the story through to the third volume would show the power and beauty of the culture erected on that foundation of pioneer sacrifice. It would have made plain, she felt, that the results would be the best the world had to offer. Yet at the same time, despite many starts, she never followed through and the last two volumes of the trilogy remained unwritten.

Maurine was remarkably consistent in her vision of the book. As early as 1938, she had told an interviewer that she was writing about people "who wanted to see if the Sermon on the Mount would work. They had bigotry and intolerance, but that was part of the times. But they did have one essential idea of brotherly love, and it was very beautiful."[45] Or as she stated in another interview, one when she thought she could tell the whole story in a single volume: "I wanted to tell the story of three Mormon generations in Utah, a story culminating with my own generation; and I wanted the reader left with a positive answer to the question: 'Humans being such as they are, CAN brotherhood succeed as a way of life?'"[46]

Maurine simply could not bring herself to shrug off the negative reactions, hold to her inner light, and go on as historian Juanita Brooks was able to do despite decades of mild ostracism in St. George, and as novelist Virginia Sorensen was able to do—largely by leaving Utah permanently. Maurine felt that Houghton Mifflin slacked off on its advertising, partly because they felt that the book would sell itself and, more sinisterly, because she suspected that "the Church" asked the publisher to stop promoting it.

Eugene England reported a few corroborating details:

> Someone, apparently Elder Levi Edgar Young, who was then president of the New England States Mission, was asked to review the book for the publisher. He convinced Houghton Mifflin to reduce the press run because it was anti-Mormon and would not sell in Utah. (According to Whipple, Houghton Mifflin originally planned on a big Utah sale—and even thought *Joshua* might be made required reading for all Mormons because it was so sympathetic!)
>
> I qualify all of this because, having yet found no independent verification, I have only Whipple's word for this scenario, although Clinton Larson [England's colleague in BYU's English Department] told me he was present as a young missionary in the mission office in the fall of 1940 when Elder Young was reading the page proofs and pronounced the book a damned lie.[47]

Even if this ominous scenario is true and Houghton Mifflin accommodated dire warnings from the Mormon hierarchy, it is also likely that Maurine simply did not understand that no advertising campaign is likely to continue beyond a few crucial weeks. A more balanced view comes from looking at the printing history. I have no information on the number of copies in the initial print run; but Greenslet told Maurine that it sold 5,500 copies in its first thirty days.[48] *The Giant Joshua* placed fifth in *Harper's* Poll of the Critics on the top ten books for the first quarter of 1941.[49] On 26 January 1941, the New York *Herald Tribune* rated *The Giant Joshua* ninth in its list of "What America Is Reading."[50]

In August 1841, Juanita was on a panel for a Writers' Round-up in Salt Lake City discussing "whether the great Mormon novel would ever be written."[51] There is no indication of whether *The Giant Joshua* figured in the discussion, but Maurine was apparently one of the "dozen writers" who participated "in a round table discussion of the modern novel and especially the recent 'Mormon novels.'" (Interestingly, Lillian McQuarrie was "chairman of the banquet" for this event, and Maurine probably stayed with her on this trip to Salt Lake City.)[52]

Obviously, insider and outsider opinions differed on *The Giant Joshua*. The book has always had a following and has gone through cycles of receiving critical attention and being ignored. Its place in the history of Mormon literature, however, is clear.

And just what is the message of the book? Maurine responded to one interviewer by reading Clory's words from the last chapter of *The Giant Joshua*: "The torch was lit, even if it were only a tallow slut. Life would go on. . . . She felt a detached pity for the generations yet to come who couldn't plan and build a world. Each generation with its desert to cross . . . but . . . there were always the Joshua trees, if poor stumbling humans will but lift up their eyes . . . always the Joshua trees, pointing toward the Promised Land" (632; ellipses hers).[53]

Understanding the context of Maurine's life makes it clear that the novel emerged from a psyche that had experienced deep suffering, one with a desperate need to communicate its own exaltation of an ideal. Maurine's work also poses profound questions about the meaning of human existence. Even though the book, like her life, contains flaws and failures, it succeeds in communicating her need to express an ideal and the possibility of transcendent knowing, which overrides the stark fact of death. It introduces truthfully the people of St. George, their bitter struggles in a harsh environment, the suffering that brought them wisdom, and their persistent adherence to an ideal that transcended the limitations of their lives. Most readers, when finishing the book, feel that an honest portrayal of a historic era has reached beyond the limitations of history to shine a light on human universals. If "masterpiece" means that a work of art has enlightened human understanding of those universals, then *The Giant Joshua* is worthy of the name.

Holly Miller Jones, while reading this biography in manuscript, wrote on the last page of this chapter: "I wonder, after reading this chapter, about my own reaction to *Joshua* when I read it for the first time as a college freshman. I couldn't put the book down, yet when it was over I was devastated, thinking 'How can the Church be true when such events happen because of the Church? How could God really have asked "His people" to practice polygamy?' So my response, initially, was that it portrayed the Church in a horrible way, even though I liked the book enough that I read it in almost one sitting. So interesting that so many non-members thought the book helped them see Mormons in a better light. I don't understand exactly what would cause these differing reactions. Very interesting to me."

My personal observation is that Holly's reaction is typical of younger readers who know very little of early Mormonism. Many are angry

PUBLICATION: A FLASH OF FAME

at Maurine for making them see into a past that they don't want to be there. Rather they want to keep the wonderful feelings they have had attending the many Church-sponsored programs. If they allow themselves to mature spiritually, as Holly has done, they can still fully embrace their religion, "warts and all." The book will probably always cause differing reactions, and probably none of them will be mild. That, too, is the mark of a masterpiece..

Notes

[1] Ferris Greenslet to Maurine Whipple, 19 July 1940; original in Maurine Whipple Collection, L. Tom Perry Special Collections and Manuscripts Division, Harold B. Lee Library, Brigham Young University, Provo, Utah; photocopy in Maurine Whipple Collection, Archive, Val A. Browning Library, Dixie College, St. George, Utah. Documents in both collections hereafter cited as BYU, photocopy Dixie College.

[2] Ferris Greenslet, Letter to Maurine Whipple, 5 August 1940; BYU.

[3] Maurine had false teeth when I knew her in 1990–92. Whether she had false teeth made this early, I don't know. Perhaps she simply found a dentist to repair the damage from falling in a Salt Lake City street when she was in college and hitting her mouth on street-car tracks. Joseph Walker arranged for a dentist named Anderson to do major repairs during a two-week period in early November 1945.

[4] Ferris Greenslet, Letter to Maurine Whipple, 5 August 1940; BYU, photocopy Dixie College.

[5] Information taken from an undated clipping torn from an unidentified newspaper, loose sheet, Whipple Scrapbook; BYU, photocopy Dixie College.

[6] Mrs. Josiah H. Chase, Minneapolis, Minnesota, Letter to Maurine Whipple, 11 November [1940]; BYU, photocopy Dixie College. Nothing more is known about her.

[7] Levi S. Peterson, *Juanita Brooks: Mormon Woman Historian* (Salt Lake City: University of Utah Press, 1988), 100.

[8] Dorothy Bird Nyswander (1894–1998), after many successes in the public health field, returned to Berkeley (1946) as a full professor and created an internationally recognized School of Public Health, coupled with much international consulting throughout the 1950s and 1960s.

[9] Robert N. Linscott, Letter to Maurine Whipple, St. George, Utah, 20 August 1940; BYU, photocopy Dixie College.

[10] Ferris Greenslet, Letter to Maurine Whipple, 1 September 1940; BYU, photocopy Dixie College.

[11] Joseph Walker, Letter to Maurine Whipple, 5 September 1940; BYU, photocopy Dixie College.

[12] Ibid.

[13] Ferris Greenslet, Letter to Maurine Whipple, 12 September 1941; BYU, photocopy Dixie College.

[14] *Brigham Young* was released 20 September 1940 by Twentieth-Century-Fox, eight days after Greenslet wrote his comments about it. "Exhibit Features Materials from 1940s Film 'Brigham,'" *Daily Herald*, 6 July 2001, C-3.

[15] Betty Leighton, Letter to Maurine Whipple, 27 September 1940; BYU, photocopy Dixie College.

[16] See "Horse in Quicksand," n.d., ca. October 1940, 12 pp. holograph, with the opening and conclusion missing; BYU, photocopy Dixie College.

[17] Donald Seegmiller, Letter to Veda Hale, 29 December 1992; Dixie College.

[18] Donald Seegmiller, Letter to Maurine Whipple, 7 January 1945; BYU, photocopy Dixie College.

[19] Joseph Walker, Letter to Maurine Whipple, 10 October 1940; BYU, photocopy Dixie College.

[20] Ferris Greenslet, Letter to Maurine Whipple, 10 May 1940; BYU, photocopy Dixie College.

[21] Joseph Walker, "Dr. Joseph Walker Sends Dates and Letter Giving Interesting Information about Their History," *Washington County News*, 30 January 1940, Whipple Scrapbook; BYU, photocopy Dixie College.

[22] Lillian McQuarrie Evans, Letter to Maurine Whipple, 21 December 1940; BYU, photocopy Dixie College.

[23] Maurine Whipple, Telegram to Ferris Greenslet, n.d., two holograph pages; BYU, photocopy Dixie College.

[24] Ferris Greenslet to Maurine Whipple, 27 December 1940; BYU, photocopy Dixie College. The letter was sent to Maurine at the Prince George Hotel in New York City.

[25] Ibid.

[26] Avis M. DeVoto, *Book-of-the-Month Club News*, edited by Harry Scherman, January 1941, unpaginated clipping in Whipple Scrapbook; BYU, photocopy Dixie College.

[27] Bernard DeVoto, *Saturday Review of Literature*, 4 January 1941, loose sheet at Dixie College, page not noted. Maurine frequently told me that DeVoto came to a book-signing in Boston, watched how she handled the crowd, and was impressed. When the crowd thinned, he introduced himself, took her to lunch, and was polite and interested in her from then on. In her mind, he remained always a "fine gentleman."

[28] M. M. Gefion, publisher of *Omnibook*, Letter to Maurine Whipple, 13 March 1941; BYU, photocopy Dixie College.

[29] "Mormon Wife: *The Giant Joshua*, Maurine Whipple, Houghton Mifflin ($2.75)," *Time Magazine*, 6 January 1941, unpaginated clipping, Whipple Scrapbook; BYU, photocopy Dixie College.

PUBLICATION: A FLASH OF FAME

30 John Peale Bishop, Letter to Maurine Whipple, n.d., holograph; BYU, photocopy Dixie College.

31 Maurine Whipple, Letter from Agnes McCammon, February 1941; BYU, photocopy Dixie College. Punctuation as per original.

32 Nedra Henrie Tebbs, conversation with an unnamed temple worker in St. George, September 1991.

33 Advertisement, *Washington County News*, Thursday, 30 January 1941, not paginated. It identifies the Big Hand as "Distributor for this District" and announces a signing on Sunday, 2 February 1941.

34 Paul Dayton Bailey (1906–87) was the author of works in several genres: horror thrillers, history, newspaper publicity, magazine serials, short stories, and poetry.

35 Roxy Romney, Letter to Maurine Whipple, 31 April 1941; BYU, photocopy Dixie College. Roxy Maria Stowell Romney was born 13 April 1889 and died 8 December 1963.

36 *Washington County News*, ca. January 1940, Whipple Scrapbook; BYU, photocopy Dixie College.

37 Lou Harris, postcard to Maurine Whipple, n.d.; BYU, photocopy Dixie College. Lou Harris Miller Smith was born 15 April 1902, married Penn Smith, and died 28 November 1955.

38 Gerald Irvine, Letter to Maurine Whipple, n.d., holograph; BYU, photocopy Dixie College.

39 Joseph K. Nicholes, Provo, Utah, Letter to Maurine Whipple, 6 December 1941, holograph; BYU, photocopy Dixie College.

40 Dorothy Kreutzer, Letter to Maurine Whipple, 7 February 1941; BYU, photocopy Dixie College. She meant the second printing, which came out in early 1942.

41 Samuel G. Houghton, Reno, Nevada, Letter to Maurine Whipple, 21 March 1941; BYU, photocopy Dixie College. He signed his letter "Sam," another way of including Maurine as part of the writing fraternity.

42 Albert Maltz, Letter to Maurine Whipple, n.d.; BYU, photocopy Dixie College.

43 Jennie Elliot (?), Victoria B.C., Letter to Maurine Whipple, 29 November 1950; BYU, photocopy Dixie College.

44 [John A. Widtsoe], "On the Book Rack," *Improvement Era* 44 (February 1941): 93.

45 Peter Kihss, "Girl Writer, Born to Be Angel, Likes Sin That Has Glamour," *New York World-Telegram*, 8 July 1938, Whipple Scrapbook; BYU, photocopy Dixie College. The interview is accompanied by a photograph of Maurine in a polka-dot dress and wearing a hat.

46 The clipping had the heading torn off, nor are the date and name of publication identified. It is accompanied by a photograph of Maurine leaning her head on her hand. Whipple Scrapbook; BYU, photocopy Dixie College.

47 Eugene England, "Whipple's *The Giant Joshua*: The Greatest But Not the Great Mormon Novel," *Annual of the Association for Mormon Letters, 2001* (Provo, Utah: AML, 2001), 61.

"SWELL SUFFERING"

[48] Ferris Greenslet, Letter to Maurine Whipple, 3 February 1941; BYU, photocopy Dixie College.

[49] "Harper's Poll of the Critics: Twenty Reviewers Vote on the Best Fiction and Non-Fiction Books Published during January, February, March 1941," clipping in Whipple Scrapbook; BYU, photocopy Dixie College.

[50] "What America Is Reading," New York *Herald Tribune*, 26 January 1941, Sec. IX, p. 23, Whipple Scrapbook; BYU, photocopy Dixie College.

[51] Levi S. Peterson, *Juanita Brooks: Mormon Woman Historian* (Salt Lake City: University of Utah Press, 1988), 119.

[52] An accompanying photograph shows Maurine and Ernest Lawrence examining the schedule. "Writers: Utah Authors Gather for Annual Round-up," *Deseret News*, 8 August 1941; BYU, photocopy Dixie College.

[53] Maurine Whipple, "Transcript of January 21, 1941—Maurine Whipple," Interviewed by Warren Bower, WNYC Radio, 21 January 1941, 3, 4 pp. typescript, Whipple Scrapbook; BYU, photocopy Dixie College. Warren Bower edited a publication called *Reader's Almanac*, was on the English faculty at New York University, and did a spin-off program of fifteen-minute radio interviews. This particular program, his seventieth, was broadcast Tuesday afternoon, 21 January 1941, from Washington Square College at New York University.

⇨ 11 ⇦

"A HEART TURNED INSIDE OUT," 1941

The publicity for *The Giant Joshua* focused on "the woman's perspective," and, therefore, questions of feminism came up frequently in interviews with Maurine. Many of the questions focused on Maurine's own status as a single woman with what looked like a glamorous writing career. But Maurine still had her heart set relentlessly on a husband and children. She announced that women were never "career women at heart."[1] To many, her attitude seemed like fuzzy romanticism. But Maurine kept dreaming, and those dreams were now ticking to a faster tempo. She would be thirty-nine January 20, 1942, and the double-front war was scything down many worthy men. However, 1941 seemed to offer another chance to have her dream come true, and this possibility promised to be nearly perfect. In the dazzling light of her new celebrity status after *The Giant Joshua*'s publication, she flew to the flickering and ultimately fickle flame of true love and the man she desperately wanted to make into the great love of her life.

He was Tom Douglas Spies (1902–60), then something of a scientific celebrity for his important vitamin research, including the role of the B-12 complex in preventing and curing pellagra. Paul de Kruif, a medical reporter, had published two articles in the *Reader's Digest*, one in December 1940, before Maurine's relationship with Tom started, and the next in May 1941. Both reported that Spies, in residence at Hillman Hospital, Birmingham, Alabama, was the man who had discovered that "some people suffer from a chronic chemical famine which could be corrected by vitamin doses."[2] Tom also had a teaching appointment and clinic at the University of Cincinnati College of Medicine, Department of Internal Medicine, at the Cincinnati General Hospital. He never married, reportedly "never accepted a fee from his patients," and "could only call home any hotel room where he was engaged in medical research."[3] Maurine gave me some information about his background. "He had grown up on a southern plantation and had observed how different diets had affected people in the social strata of his community. Those on the low economic end seemed to have the same specific symptoms, which suggested a widely shared disease. Thus he had narrowed it down until he discovered which vitamin they lacked."

Vitamin research had received a sudden impetus at the beginning of World War II because reports from Europe indicated that German soldiers were being dosed with vitamins, supposedly making them superhuman. U.S. doctors and scientists were under considerable pressure to match these new nutritional technologies. Thus, Tom Spies was not only well-educated, warm-hearted, and bright, but he was also a hero needed in the home-front fight against the Nazi peril.

Maurine could not always remember the timetable of this affair; but even after fifty years, she linked their relationship to the heady days immediately after her novel's release. She was in New York 27 December 1940. It is not clear when she first got there, but she evidently divided her time between Boston and New York according to the schedule of the Houghton Mifflin's publicist. On 9 January, she was in New York again and still seems to have been there on Friday, 17 January, when she is listed as seated at the speakers' table at a prestigious "Town Hall" luncheon—the equivalent of a major television talk show today—at Hotel Astor.[4] The topic was "The Importance of Humor in the Arts."

But that was not likely where she met Tom Spies. As Maurine told me the story in 1991–92, Florence Doubleday, wife of Frank N. Doubleday, who owned the well-known publishing firm, enjoyed meeting Maurine, perhaps at the Town Hall luncheon, and invited her to a party in a large New York hotel. It was not a typical cocktail party, for Florence had an unusual way of bringing interesting people together. She would install her special guests in separate rooms from the actual party where they waited until summoned separately. As Maurine related this cherished story to me:

> A knock came on my door. When I answered, standing there was a handsome and mysterious stranger, a man with a haunting unexplainable aura, great compassion blazing in his wonderful eyes—tired eyes, but eyes that, when smiling, took you up onto a higher level with him, and you wanted to stay forever in his sight. He spoke. Something about his mistake, about knocking on the wrong door, then the quick realization that he was invited to the same party as I was. "Oh, then we'll walk down together."

This was a story no one dared interrupt with questions. When she got started, it was as if she had to speak every magical word before she could stop. She says she "recognized Spies's name from the *Reader's Digest* article." Her own background in vitamin therapy made her a knowledgeable listener—that plus the fact that she said she fell in love on the spot. Her story continued:

> Tom didn't care about the party. He wanted to talk. He rented a buggy, and we went for a ride in Central Park and then for a walk. It was snowing. I had no gloves. He took my hand, warming it, holding it in his own pocket. The snow flakes—big and perfect—slowly added their own tiny glitter to our two kindred spirits finally finding each other. Eternal mates. I felt like two halves of a whole were coming together at last—the past serving only as the terrible price paid for such happiness. He stopped. Looking deep into the great awe in my eyes, he said: "There will never be any quarreling in our home, will there." It wasn't a question, it was a simple statement of fact, implying a wonderful thing.

Usually, this winter walk was the only version of their first meeting that she would relate. Unlike her refusal to discuss Rob Riley or Nick Spencer, and her rage when asked to, she was not reluctant to focus on Tom Spies. She would relax into a reverie that recreated the powerful romantic and erotic emotion she associated with his name. No doubt the relationship had been worked and reworked in her mind for fifty years.

If pressed, what she would add compromised and confused that story. She admitted reading an article about Tom that mentioned Tom's mother as a Salt Lake City resident. She said: "I looked her up and visited her. She liked me. I was interested in his work, was about Tom's age, unmarried, a woman who had done something in life, and she wanted me to see Tom when I went east. In fact, she thought Tom needed someone like me and that I should go back there and marry him." This meeting had to be after 1938 when Maurine won the Houghton Mifflin fellowship, since it is difficult to see Maurine before that point as "a woman who had done something in life." The first *Reader's Digest* article by de Kruif came out only the month before the publication of *Joshua* but does not mention his mother.

Nor was Florence Doubleday's party the first contact between Maurine and Tom. Among Maurine's papers are five letters that Tom wrote before they met. Nearly all of Tom's correspondence with Maurine was short notes, dictated to his secretaries. The first pre-1940 or 1941 letter, written 15 July 1938, congratulates Maurine for winning the fellowship—probably because his mother had mentioned knowing Maurine and encouraged him to write. A gap of more than two years follows, but Maurine then initiated or reinitiated the correspondence, for he responded on 20 September 1940: "You were very thoughtful to write me." He had been in Salt Lake, he said, "visiting and lecturing." He gives no hint about whom he was visiting, but it seems logical that it was his family. He promised: "I expect to buy a copy of your book and sometime I shall obtain your autograph." Again Maurine must have responded and again he thanked her, on 3 November 1940, "for your cordial letter. I shall be in New York next week. I think you should come back through here. It is a little out of the way if you are going to be in the east, and plan to return home by way of Chicago."[5] There is nothing to prove they hadn't met soon after that. Tom wasn't writing a personal letter, which probably annoyed Maurine. It had been dictated to a secretary.

On 10 January 1941, Tom wrote: "Glad to get your note. I do hope you can come to Cincinnati; it would be grand to see you." On 18 January 1941, Tom sent another brief dictated note: "I have your book with undeserved inscription and I shall cherish it."[6] In short, their encounter at the Doubleday party may very well have been magical, but it was magic with considerable groundwork.

Curtis Taylor, then a partner in Aspen Books, befriended Maurine late in life after he had read *The Giant Joshua*. When he interviewed her on 3 January 1989, Maurine told the fairytale romance of the walk in the snow and said she knew something about Spies's vitamin research going on at the time, but added the dramatic touch that "our romance was doomed because Tom died within the year of cancer."[7] Spies actually lived for nineteen years, dying of cancer in February 1960.[8] To Maurine, it was apparently easier to mourn a tragic death within months of their meeting than to face the bitter truth that, once again, a man to whom she had given her heart turned away from her. In one of her undated rough-draft letters to Tom, she talked about a consistent pattern in her life—"the conviction of being doomed."[9] But even "doom" was a sort of answer. The reality is that Maurine never understood why love always eluded her.

Maurine's whereabouts are not easy to trace after the release of her book. A friend, Dorothy Nyswander, wrote on 20 January 1941, to Maurine in New York: "I am so very happy you are having such a whirl, and was infinitely rejoiced about the easing up of the financial situation with the lecture date." (Maurine later claimed she had to give a lecture to college students to earn enough money to get back to St. George.) Interestingly, Dorothy also wished her "best of luck on the movie end," suggesting that Maurine was already hoping to sell movie rights to *The Giant Joshua*.[10]

Maurine almost missed out on the opportunity to give the lecture at Columbia University, because Lee Barker couldn't be bothered to put the class professor in touch with her. Many times she bitterly told me that it was "because of his egotistical rich-man's contempt for someone like me."

"A HEART TURNED INSIDE OUT," 1941

On 21 January 1941, Maurine made the disastrous decision of hiring a literary agent, Maxim ("Max") Lieber.[11] The contract allowed the agent "to collect and receive the proceeds of all sales, checks being made payable to the said Agent. In other words, all royalties went first to Lieber, who took his percentage off the top, and he started doing it with any money due Maurine, even though he had had no part in placing *The Giant Joshua*. Although the situation is certainly more complex than Maurine's view, it is hard not to interpret what happened as an unscrupulous willingness to take advantage of her inexperience and naivete.

On 23 January 1941, Robert Linscott sent Maurine a short note through her newly hired agent responding to what must have been an expression of dissatisfaction with the publicity or a demand for reassurance of some sort: "Bless you Maurine, for all your activities! Of course you're a success. How could you help but be. Here's the shiny print [photograph] you want, together with our blessing. F.G. gets back February 1st and will be looking forward to hearing from you."[12] The letter contains no hint of whether Maurine had returned to St. George at that point, but her papers include a letter from Tom dated 30 January 1941.[13] He said he had dictated two letters, one to Mrs. Doubleday and one to Mrs. Grace Goddard, and had instructed that a notation be put on the Doubleday letter that "a copy of each letter was being sent to Maurine Whipple."[14]

Obviously Maurine knew both women. Why else would he make it clear that Maurine was receiving copies of his notes to them? Had they been playing matchmaker to get Maurine and Tom together? Maurine's and Tom's "magical" evening must have taken place at least by this point.

Although an advertisement in the *Washington County News* on Thursday, 30 January 1941, said Maurine would be doing a book signing at the Big Hand Cafe three days later on 2 February, she obviously didn't make it. On 31 January 1941 she was in the Georgetown Hospital near Washington, D.C., where Tom Spies sent her a telegram: "SO SORRY THE BUG HAS CAUGHT UP WITH YOU IT IS A DIRTY SHAME HAVE ASKED A CLOSE FRIEND OF MINE DR. CHINN TO PAY YOU A SOCIAL CALL."[15] Maurine told me that this "Dr. Chinn" had indeed come to see her and had asked her to leave Tom alone—that Tom had important work to do." She was annoyed, she told me. "Couldn't he see how much I could contribute to Tom's life and work?"

Greenslet mailed a letter to Maurine on 3 February at Washington, D.C., where she was the houseguest of Douglas Bement, an acquaintance from one of the three Rocky Mountain Writers' Conferences she had attended.[16] Greenslet wrote: "Desolated to hear that you are prostrated with flu in Washington. I am interested and, on the whole, glad, to hear that you have tied up with Max Lieber, a most dependable fellow, as your general agent. If it had been simply a question of serial rights, I think perhaps Brandt and Brandt would have done as well for you, but as a total agent, Lieber is undoubtedly the best that you could have selected." Furthermore, because Maurine had hired Lieber, Greenslet explains, "etiquette forbids that we should have any further correspondence on any matters of business, although we can still correspond as before on literary and personal matters; but perhaps it is no breach of etiquette to tell you that the check that will go to Lieber for you the first of next week, represents 75% of the royalties earned by the January sales, about 5500 copies, ought to run to somewhere around $1,500, I am asking Lieber to ask you for a formal signed authorization for future payments to him."[17]

Despite Greenslet's impeccable courtesy, it must have been a relief to him to set some more distant boundaries in their relationship. One would hope that Greenslet didn't realize that Lieber would take his commission from this money due her at that point. Maurine certainly didn't.

Maurine's answering letter on 8 February, to which Greenslet refers in his letter of 11 February, obviously contained a complaint that "members of the firm" didn't like her and that her book wasn't receiving adequate publicity. Greenslet answered patiently, again in care of Bement: "I deeply appreciate and respond to your preliminary expressions. Honestly, I think you exaggerate somewhat in what you say about 'members of the firm' not liking you, and, again honestly, I believe that we are, all of us, pushing JOSHUA with all our might. Of course the only actual 'members of the firm' whom you have met here are our Mr. Laughlin, Mr. Ticknor, Mr. Thompson, and myself." These individuals do not appear elsewhere in the correspondence, and it is not clear what branch of the firm they belonged to—possibly the publicity office. Maurine had also complained about the quotations from the book used in advertisements for the *New York Times* and *Herald Tribune* and wanted others used.[18] The patient Greenslet said he "would see what he could do."

On 7 February she received a letter from Tom addressed to her at Bement's residence, asking her to meet him at the airport in Washington, D.C. He was flying in to deliver a lecture on nutrition. Her papers include the rough notes she took on that lecture. She eagerly jotted down examples of people she knew who manifested the deficiency symptoms he talked about.[19] For instance, Tom mentioned that "crack-pots" are deficient in one of the acids (there is a question mark by the word) and Maurine had written "Mrs. Doubletalk [Florence Doubleday] needs some to assuage her craving for adventure?" When he mentioned that riboflavin deficiency produces red eyes, she scribbled: "Saw a lot of eyes like that. I'm wondering if not back of those curious epidemics of 'pink eye' that affected my childhood, although I never had it." She wrote "good, excellent" next to his story that a friend's wife "became loving again after being given thiamin chloride."

Tom must have planned his schedule to allow a few days in Washington, D.C., for very soon thereafter—perhaps the very night of his lecture, it appears they stayed together in a hotel room. Maurine later, in an undated rough-draft letter—possibly never finished—wrote that she had expressed fear that he would think she was cheap, but Tom had said just the right thing. "You'll apologize to me for that someday. There's nothing cheap about either of us." She also recalled that he said, "I do not care what happens just so you don't stop loving me."

Like her painfully personal outpourings to Rob Riley and Nick Spencer, reading this correspondence invades Maurine's privacy. The fact that she kept it in its own file for the rest of her life suggests that Tom Spies was an anguished episode in the past upon which she could not close the book and walk away. Yet this episode and the intense suffering it engendered both confirm and help explain her hypersensitivity, her almost pathological longing for love, her forever unrequited yearning for acceptance; and it is a clue to help us understand why it was so difficult for her to find the emotional strength to again write in an inspired way. Without understanding these most intimate wounds, we cannot hope to explain her life, the single great achievement of *The Giant Joshua*, or the crippling that forever after hampered her work. Perhaps there is no way that flesh and blood human beings could reach and heal Maurine's damaged psyche, because it might be that her infinite neediness exceeded the capacity of any human being. But she certainly thought Tom could have done it. It is interesting to speculate about the great writing that she might have done under the umbrella of Tom's love, protection, and the feeling of belonging that being his wife could have brought. I think Maurine, herself, never quit wondering. I think she resented to her dying day the fact that the other great books never got out of her head and heart and mostly blamed Tom.

An effort to understand such thinking places real demands on the reader. It is easy to react with embarrassment, impatience, and a kind of horrified pity to Maurine's anguished outpourings—not only to Tom, but to other men whom she tried to make over into her rescuer, her prince. But such a reaction focuses the reader's attention in the wrong place: on himself or herself, rather than on understanding Maurine and the forces that produced her. I believe that Eugene England gave her this kind of honest, respectful attention when he said: "Whipple developed, as a result of something that happened to her, a crippling paranoia, a persistent bitterness about her experience. She did not complete her trilogy or write many more Mormon stories.

And some kind of attention must be paid to that . . . by anyone who cares about Mormon literature. At least I can't help feeling a haunting, unfocused guilt—a sense of responsibility which I try to discharge by trying, as I am now, to pay honest, appreciative attention to her achievement."[20]

England thought that the crippling blow was the rejection by her own people and "the Church" of *The Giant Joshua*. Based on these letters and others like them that England did not see, it seems more likely that the blow was Maurine's desperate, deadly heartbreak caused by a lack of the love she craved. However, there is seldom just one cause of tragedy. In Maurine's case, she never healed from the deep wounds of her childhood, a childhood that never felt complete. Her need to try to complete that childhood could also be part of the reason her life seems largely dysfunctional and her attempts at love so disastrous.

The affair with Tom—at least its fully physical component—probably did not last longer than a few days or, at most, a couple of weeks. Tom and Maurine were likely being cheered on by Mrs. Doubleday.

The next document in her correspondence of the time is a letter from Tom to "Miss Whipple" dated 25 February 1941 and mailed to Maurine in Los Angeles.[21] From the letter, dictated as usual, it seems that Maurine had bronchitis and had gone "back on the desert." Tom was on a business trip to "the canal Zone" and would be gone three weeks. He wrote "I am enclosing a carbon copy of a letter to Mrs. 'Doubletrouble,'" and jotted beside this word: "better name?" Perhaps he and Maurine had a private joke about the bothersome contact with Mrs. Doubleday. He signed the letter himself, instead of, as frequently happened, having it signed by his secretary. Maurine must still have been crushed at its impersonal sound.

He included a carbon copy of a letter he had dictated the same day to Florence Doubleday, hinting at a joint project Maurine was trying to set up with Florence. Their plan was to publicize Tom's work, become involved in fund-raising for it, and even to write a biography of Tom. Courteously but very clearly, Tom refused their assistance.[22] It was the first indication in the correspondence that Maurine was handling this wonderful relationship wrong.

Disconcertingly, for the rest of April, Maurine received only short letters from Tom. She must have been imploring him to let her come visit, offering to write an article on his clinic, and trying to entice him with other schemes to support his work. He dictated short notes to Margaret Higgins, his secretary at the Hillman Hospital in Birmingham, putting Maurine off with excuses that he is "too busy," or "ill," or "out of town," or that this is simply "not a good time to come." Rather formally, he assured her on 28 April 1941, when she was in St. George, that "my friendship and interest in you and your work, however, have not altered in the least." He encouraged her to keep on writing to him, saying that her letters were "most interesting."[23]

It is not clear when she returned to St. George. Life with her family remained strained, the marital disharmony between her parents still unresolved. Maurine was generous, giving Annie money to buy some of the things she dreaded asking Charlie for.[24] Maurine also gave eight hundred dollars to Florence, since Ben was permanently paralyzed from the waist down, and she claimed Colleen and Larry, their children, as partial dependents on her 1941 income tax.[25] Maurine liked to claim that she solicited help from local people to build a home for Ben and Florence in Washington, ten miles northeast of St. George, and proudly credited her "badgering" for getting action, especially from her father. After their eighteen months of hospital insurance was up, Ben and Florence had come back to make the best life they could on Ben's pension of ninety dollars a month. Ben, four years Florence's senior, became a cabinet maker and outlived both Florence and Maurine, dying on 19 April 1996 at age eighty-seven.[26] Maurine considered the family "the happiest people I know."[27] Her concern and generosity were real, but she was apparently somewhat tactless and invasive as well, and Ben set firm boundaries to safeguard his own space.

Furthermore, Maurine's generosity and desire to make her family more comfortable financially collided with her lack of understanding about money management. She really didn't have much money left by the spring of 1941, and she felt that people were cheating her. She may have been right in thinking that most people in her environment thought that writing a national best-seller meant she was rich.

There was much to worry about in her life. But overshadowing all was her dread at Tom Spies's odd silences and distance and the looming presence of the second volume of the trilogy that everyone was expecting her to write. Her incessant traveling may have been an effort to distract herself from both concerns. By 31 March[28] she was in Salt Lake City being honored at an open house hosted by Dean R. Brimhall, a businessman and federal Depression projects appointee who had a Ph.D. in psychology from Columbia.[29] His wife, Lila Eccles Brimhall, was an actress and a professor of speech and theater at the University of Utah. The Brimhalls were somewhat disaffected from Mormonism and likely thought they recognized a kindred spirit in Maurine. Dean was Fawn McKay Brodie's maternal uncle and actively encouraged her to write the naturalistic biography of Joseph Smith published in 1945 for which she was excommunicated shortly after its publication.[30] Attending the open house were many of Maurine's former teachers, classmates, and former Dixieites, including Dr. and Mrs. Angus M. Woodbury, Dr. and Mrs. Walter C. Cottam, and LeRoy Cowles, president of the University of Utah, who arranged for Maurine to deliver a lecture in support of the war effort at the university on 20 May.[31]

On 4 March 1941, Tom sent Maurine another brief note to the general delivery office at Indio, California. Indio is near the San Bernardino Mountains approximately fifteen miles east of Cathedral City. Here Joseph Walker grew dates. Tom was returning some unspecific "enclosures"—photographs, perhaps—and announced that he was leaving within "a few minutes" for another business trip. He concluded: "Do hope that you will take care of yourself. Always with all good wishes."[32]

Maurine was still getting her mail in Indio when he wrote again on 5 April 1941. Although he had taken ship to the Panama Canal by way of giving himself a vacation, he had flown back to his clinic at Birmingham, then had gone "to Chicago for a Council meeting of the American Medical Association." He again signed it: "Always with all good wishes." Maurine must have written to him in the meantime, but he does not comment on any news from her.[33]

By 17 April, the date of Tom's next communication, Maurine was in Los Angeles staying with Maud Pace Callison, an osteopath, who was originally from St. George. Maurine was likely receiving treatment since an accident in September or October 1942 had apparently damaged her spine, made sitting painful, and, humiliatingly, caused urinary incontinence. Maurine refused to tell me any details about the accident. Also emotionally painful was the fact that Tom was sending only impersonal dictated notes in which he rebuffed as "not the right time" her increasingly pressing offers to visit his clinic.

Maurine was apparently living with or near a woman named "Genie" in Los Angeles, since Genie wrote on 28 April assuring Maurine that she (Maurine) had left the apartment clean and that Genie had taken care of Maurine's electrical bill. Maurine in 1991 could not remember this woman, but she had apparently confided her love-hopes to her since Genie said: "I take it that little Tomisino is going to wait until next year to put in her appearance," a reference to Maurine's anticipation that she and Tom would marry and have children.[34]

Maurine had returned to St. George by late April, for Tom dictated a warm but disjointed letter on the 28th, complaining of his "hectic" schedule. He mixed both negative and positive information in a way that must have confused Maurine:

> Many things have changed completely since I last saw you. My friendship and interest in you and your work, however, have not altered in the least, and it was most difficult for me to tell Miss Higgins to write you that I didn't think it would be wise for you to come this year. I have thought over the whole matter a great deal, and I still am of that opin-

ion. The world has changed so much that I am afraid it would be completely a waste of time. I should like to discuss the whole matter with you in detail when you come east again.

Do let me hear from you from time to time, for you write most interesting letters and I love to hear from you. I am looking forward to seeing you as soon as you are traveling eastward.

How are the bronchi? I trust all goes well with you. I loved the desert flowers and wish I might come out and get a bit of rest myself.

He signed it: "With kindest regards, Sincerely yours . . ."[35]

On 3 May 1941, Tom dictated another note to Maurine, still in St. George, calling her attention to the quotations from *The Giant Joshua* in the *Reader's Digest*. "They are very striking, and I was terribly pleased to see them. Do take care of yourself and let me hear from you. Sincerely yours . . ." He did not mention an article by Paul de Kruif on a medical topic in the same issue that referred to him.

On 10 May, Maurine was back in St. George, since she wrote a thank-you note from there to Elden and Florence Beck in Provo, warmly thanking them for being so "darned sweet" during her recent visit. She would have stayed longer, she explained, but "she had to get home and answer her big pile of letters." She also reported wonderful news: "The U.S. Navy has ordered 150 Joshuas for its private library!" These copies would go into libraries on ships and bases around the world.[36]

Then she returned to California, where Harrison Leussler, Houghton Mifflin's West Coast representative in Palm Springs, apparently escorted her to various bookstores and perhaps to some speaking engagements.[37] Maxim Lieber wrote on 16 May 1941 that "she wasn't being charged for the expenses of a 'present' tour with Leussler." Lieber also discouraged her from writing a "series of articles dealing with historical background. As a compromise, he suggested picking one she could do "without too much trouble" and letting him "explore the market" with it."[38] This feedback suggests that Maurine was exploring many options besides settling down to capitalize on *The Giant Joshua*'s success by writing the second volume of the trilogy.

Maurine now was given a new direction, something she could do to help the war effort. She gave a successful speech (date unknown) in behalf of Writers for the War Board at the invitation of a regent of the University of Redlands, L. E. Nelson. This appearance launched her wartime lecturing career to help sell war bonds. She invariably recalled her success with that first experience as a lecturer with great satisfaction.

A longer, dictated letter came from a frazzled Tom Spies, dated 12 May 1941 and addressed to Maurine in St. George. "These few hectic remarks I make because your letters always stimulate me very much indeed.

I am sure that the greatest work which you could do for posterity would be to write up a real thing on Brigham Young. By all means, convince the eldest living grandson. Please tell him you know how sacred the subject is and that without his help it could never be done."

He then hypothesized that her "stomach trouble" was caused by overwork. He was leaving the next morning for meetings with the Medical Committee of the National Foundation for Infantile Paralysis in New York, the Committee on Nutrition of the National Research Council in Washington, D.C., and a presidential National Conference, followed by AMA meetings, again, in Cleveland during the first week in June.

Rather mysteriously and abruptly, Tom apparently rebuffed another attempt to get an invitation: "As to the Hillman [Hospital], I am sure I will not be here enough to be of use to anyone this year." But he also commented, with apparently genuine enthusiasm: "I can't tell you how pleased I am to know that you met my sister, Mary. She is a darling, and I know must have loved you very much. Do see her as often as you will be in Salt Lake City. As she probably told you, I sent her a copy of your book."[39] Maurine told me, as part of her comforting Spies story, that Mary had assured her that she, Maurine, "was the only girl Tom had ever written home about, the only girl his mother wanted to have go back there and marry her son."

In Tom's 12 May 1941 letter, the last dictated paragraph hints: "There are many things I should like to talk to you about but they don't seem subjects for writing."[40] Maurine was superbly ignoring the one message he was trying to get across: Keep your distance.

On 20 May 1941, Maurine was back in Salt Lake City, delivering what had now developed into her war-support lecture. This time it was to the University of Utah Alumni Class, to the School of Education, and to a thousand freshmen.[41] On this visit, she was the guest of honor at two teas, one given by Chi Delta Phi and the other by the "Thi Delta Phi Association of Woman Students of the University of Utah," the national literary sorority she had pledged as a junior in college.

A gap of about a month follows in the correspondence with Tom. It is easy to imagine Maurine, tense and yearning to be with him, unable to settle down to write, yet involved and busy in important activities, as he was. She apparently decided to move matters forward on her own. A dictated return letter from Tom on 15 June to Maurine at St. George said, rather formally, that he was "delighted" she planned "to spend a few days here with us." In a businesslike way, he told her he would not be available during 18–22 and 27–29 June because he and de Kruif were giving "a coast-to-coast broadcast on nutrition."[42]

It is easy to suspect that Maurine was racking her brains to keep Tom's interest engaged and asking his advice on financial matters was one way, but she should have realized he would see only too well how time-costly she could become. He advised her, in the same 15 June letter: "I know very little about publishing, writing, or business."[43]

An airmail letter from Tom to Maurine in St. George followed on 20 June, encouraging her not to come before "the middle of the first week in July" and warning, "Many things may come up, but I am sure you would understand."[44]

Tom telegraphed to Maurine at the Newhouse Hotel in Salt Lake City on 30 June: "DELIGHTED YOU ARE COMING SHALL MEET YOU AIRPORT 1:45 PM. Maurine must have flown east on 1 July, her heart in her throat—and on her sleeve—her eyes filled with dreams about the future that she wanted with Tom. The actual visit was a shattering, desolating disappointment. From the inconsistent stories she told me, plus the few clues in her despairing draft letters to Tom later, here's what happened.

Tom insisted she fly to his clinic in Birmingham. It is not clear when he communicated this message to her, since he was sending her letters and telegrams every few days and these instructions appear nowhere. Maurine, construing his suggestion as a sign that he was very anxious to see her, borrowed money to make the trip. When she landed, somewhat nauseated from the bumpy flight, she was sure he was in mystical communion with her, since he brought a thermos of some alcoholic beverage that he said would settle her stomach. Accompanying him was a member of his research staff—not his secretary, Margaret Higgins, but a woman, probably Jean Grant, who was manifestly devoted to him. (She had received one of the five copies of Maurine's book that Tom had ordered from Houghton Mifflin in the spring.) In a motherly way, she took Maurine to a hotel and saw that she was comfortably settled.

The next day, Tom gave her a tour of the clinic. Maurine was impressed with the scope of Tom's responsibilities, the dedication of his fellow workers, and the palpable sense of "mission" radiated by everyone there, especially by Tom. She also claimed that the women at the laboratory were visibly in love with Tom and instantly jealous of her as the "chosen one." Tom came to her room the next morning, greeting her with a rose and a lingering kiss. He took her for a drive down a street of Southern-style mansions, many owned by other doctors. "Which one would you like?" he asked. Maurine read the question as a proposal. She was overcome with wonder and love. It was too perfect!

Then came the reaction of those around him. She sensed that some of Tom's coworkers feared that she might somehow distract Tom from

"SWELL SUFFERING"

making his great contribution to the world. Perhaps he had been involved romantically with some of the staff. In one of Maurine's draft letters written to Tom, she related a grueling afternoon with one sweet-talking woman:

> I know Nellwyn expected to marry you for ten years and so she intended to "break us up." She even intimated that you knew all this. She laughed and said, rather bitterly, "When I asked Tom if I could take you with me he stiffened, but I told him I wouldn't hurt his precious Maurine any!" And then she concluded, "Besides, all Tom really cares about is his stomach!" Then, to cap the climax, she refused to bring me back to town, and when we finally did get back she stopped to shop and drink cokes. I was simply wild. And then, of course, when we did get to the country club she clung to me like a leech for fear you and I would have a minute alone.
>
> When you bawled me out that night at dinner she was radiant. And the next morning when you made me face all those women in the clinic, you should have seen her gloat! Her plan to estrange us had succeeded beyond her wildest dreams. But she disappeared when I went to go. She didn't quite have the nerve to tell me goodbye. Now I hope you won't blame me because I've told you this. It is the absolute truth. I've even tried to remember her exact words. Of course, it's the sort of thing that should never, never be told in a letter. And it goes terribly against my grain to say anything mean about a person. But I would not be worthy of your affection or even friendship if I allowed you to go on misjudging me.
>
> Frankly and from a purely feminine view point, I wouldn't trust Nellwyn nor her so-called friendship. Whether it was me or any other woman you cared for, she'd try to make trouble. She can't help it. But Frances and Jean and Margaret! Ah! There you have honest women. I'd trust and love those three under any and all circumstances. . . .
>
> That last morning when I was crying after you left, Frances came in and understood the situation without a word. She scolded me for grieving. "You don't know how Tom has counted on your visit!" she said. And of course, I didn't know. That was the trouble. . . .
>
> Every writer's curse is loneliness, because his work, itself, is the loneliest, cruelest job in the world. That's why I work so hard—because I have no choice. And to have Frances and Jean and Margaret to turn to after the day's work would be heaven, indeed.

After Maurine's careful construction of these paragraphs to show that, despite her accurate appraisal of the catty Nellwyn, she valued and respected feminine friends of the caliber of Frances, Jean, and Margaret, she moved on to her next point—that she had seen Tom only in a crowd. Although she mentioned "long visits up in Miss Bomer's sitting room," she also noticed that they never had dinner or even lunch alone and reproached him: "You saw them every day and you only saw me once in a lifetime, and it seemed to me if I meant anything to you, you would want to concentrate on me for the time being." She denied on "my word of honor" that she was trying to pressure him to take more time "off from . . . work."[45]

Apparently sex had lost its magic, too. She said in one page of outpourings that Tom had called himself "a cardboard lover" but rushed to defend him: "I could tell you were dead on your feet and . . . I was heartsick inside because in spite of your weariness you made the effort to be gay and have parties for me. . . . There are times when nobody can rise to a single added demand, let alone make love!" There may also have been an open quarrel. She describes herself as "hurt and bewildered" and quotes Tom as exclaiming bitterly, "You are just another damned woman, after all." She wrote: "If you didn't say 'damned,' you meant it."[46]

Maurine was apparently planning to stay indefinitely and was shocked when Tom came to her room one morning when she was barely out of bed. "Get dressed," he ordered. "I'm putting you on a plane home." He offered no explanation and gave her no chance to ask questions. Apparently Jean Grant was with them when he took her to the train station, for Maurine remembered her parting words, spoken in a private moment: "Remember, Maurine, out of all the girls in the world, you were the one chosen by Tom. The one that could have been his, had it not been for his calling in the world. You were the only one he considered."

Maurine left Birmingham for Washington, D.C., probably about 5 July, numb with shock. The affair was over and she knew it, but she just couldn't accept it. She stayed briefly with Dean and Lila Brimhall, confiding her heartbreak to them. They were patient and sympathetic listeners. Maurine told me that Lila, a gracious, cultured woman, "helped me with my wardrobe and in other matters of grooming and social behavior." They must also have given her bracing advice based on their view of her wonderful future as a writer, never realizing how little Maurine valued it compared to love and marriage.

As she continued on to New York City, she invented the hopeful myth that a letter of explanation from Tom would be waiting at her hotel. Among her papers is an undated draft of a letter to Tom that she had begun in Washington, D.C.: "My instinct is to drop you an impersonal little thank-you note and run like hell, like any animal hunting cover to lick its wounds." Instead, she agonizes for pages, going back over the visit, analyzing what went wrong. In this and other letters, she begs, "What is it you want of me, Tom? I was willing to walk out of your life, if you wanted that. Do you want my love? Or do you want my friendship? I am yours. Whatever you desire of me you shall have."

In another page of a rough draft letter, she confesses, "Even when I got to New York I was too beaten down to do anything but cry." She should have been conducting business, making decisions about what to write that would make money. She tried placing a movie script, "I, Janet," with the Mitchell J. Hamilbing Agency. Unfortunately, the script has not survived. It was her first try at a script; the agency representative who wrote to her said: "The dialogue—that is, the 'things said,' not the thoughts—seemed very natural and effective to me." But this correspondent was troubled by how Maurine communicated her characters' mental processes.[47]

A disappointment like this did not help Maurine's sagging spirits. It seems obvious that part of her wanted to show Tom she didn't need him, while another part wanted him to see that he had ruined her life and had to be responsible for her. She also says in the loose pages of a letter draft that she went to Boston and talked to someone at Houghton Mifflin, presumably Ferris Greenslet, offering the company first option on a travel book about Utah that she had already outlined. The company declined. What I think Houghton Mifflin wanted—and what she told me she was obligated to provide—was the sequel. What she meant by "obligated," I don't know. Angry with Houghton Mifflin over the disappointing financial returns of *The Giant Joshua*, she didn't want to give it the sequel and preferred to satisfy the obligation either with "Beaver Dam Wash" or perhaps the travel book.

She had not heard from Tom when, on 14 July, still in New York, she drafted a begging letter to Paul de Kruif, asking for help in finding a job. She claimed that her agent "had absconded with about eight hundred dollars." De Kruif apparently did not respond.[48]

She also wrote despairingly to Dean Brimhall, also on 14 July: "You were right. There is no letter. I guess that's a form of evasion. I can't get over the conviction that there's something terribly wrong with me. I wish I knew a good psychoanalyst." A measure of her irrationality is that she told Dean Brimhall she had consulted a psychic in New York who assured her that a letter would be waiting for her in St. George.[49]

Then the passionately desired letter from Tom, written on 12 July, arrived at her hotel. But when she ripped it open, it was another dictated note that said noncommittally: "Your letter came, and I am glad you enjoyed visiting the clinic. We are terribly hectic this time of year. I shall write you later in St. George. Regards and good wishes."[50] In her 1998 interview with Curtis Taylor, Maurine still remembered the tone: "It didn't say anything about us. Tom just said that he was glad that we had this time together. He wanted me to know that there was so much going on." What had she said in her letter to him? Had she summoned up the discipline and dignity to send him an "impersonal little thank-you note" or had she committed to paper instead the tortured howls of the wounded animal? In either case, he had outdone her in "impersonality."

Maurine reported to one interviewer that she had gone east again in 1942 (she didn't say what month) to see her brother George off for military service in the Pacific. Tom came to her hotel—she didn't say in what city, but George's troop train left from Chicago—bringing a little girl. Maurine had the impression that the child may have been his niece. In any case, the child was a kind of chaperone "to help him stick with his resolve." He and Maurine talked "a little," but only "in the hotel lobby." Maurine also offered Taylor another improbable explanation: "I finally came to see and understand that he had to make a choice, you see. He was too much in love. I think if he had married a woman that he didn't love very much it might have worked out, but I doubt it. I don't think he could have done that."[51]

When she headed west again, probably a day or two after receiving the 12 July letter, she said she felt that she was literally leaving her heart behind her. She dreaded the return to a world she felt she could no longer face. She lengthened her itinerary, deliberately going through the long, lonely spaces of Texas to southern California where she could count on sympathy and support from Joseph and Tina Walker. She claimed she wept her way across the nation, tears that came in a flood of pure despair. The worst of it was that she simply did not understand what had gone wrong. Why? Why? Why? When she told me this part, she murmured that the train wheels were chanting the question.

Maurine was apparently in Salt Lake City about the end of July, for a letter reached her from Jean Grant. Written on 24 July from Hillman Hospital, it had taken a circuitous route: via Houghton Mifflin who forwarded it to St. George, where Annie forwarded it to 333 Federal Building in Salt Lake City. Perhaps Maurine was traveling at random, trying to run away from her grief.

Maurine had evidently tried to make a confidante of Jean, spilling her sorrow, for Jean wrote sympathetically: "Although all the nice things you said about me in your letter pleased me very much, what you said about yourself made me very sad." Like the Brimhalls, Jean encouraged Maurine to look on the bright side: "How I wish I were in your shoes. Although I do not wish you in mine, for you would not be half so well off as you are. You see, you have so much that is entirely yours. A real gift that few have and you do not have to depend on others." Jean tried to explain that "things were too hectic" during Maurine's visit and "are still in a turmoil." Tom "does look exhausted" but "has the exceptional gift of apparently throwing aside all his cares and making it very gay for his friends." Jean asked for news "about the book and short story"—it is not clear which "short story" this would be—

"SWELL SUFFERING"

and encouraged the despondent Maurine: "Please do not give up writing. The sun will shine again for you I feel sure."⁵²

Also from Salt Lake City, Maurine sent Dean Brimhall some handkerchiefs—possibly because she had wept into his—and an undated thank you letter. She bravely said, referring to herself in third person, that she wanted him to remember "that Maurine has stopped bumping her head against stone walls, that Maurine is at work on The Book, trying to make it the best Book she is capable of writing, and that a great deal of her endeavor stems from your belief in her, and your encouragement."⁵³ Although Maurine's despair and desperation were real, so was her pluck. She wanted to be "hard-gutted" like her pioneers, to get up after her orgy of grief and stagger the next mile. If that "next mile" had been another rocky stretch pulling a handcart, I doubt that it would have been as hard as the load of heartache she now pulled.

On 9 August, she was in Salt Lake City, attending the League of Utah Writers' annual round-up and, as a "celebrity, . . . let[ting] them in on her experiences, her secrets of writing and selling."⁵⁴ No letters from Lillian, if there were any, have survived from 1941, but she chaired the round-up banquet and almost certainly the two women talked about the jagged direction their lives had taken—Lillian's divorce from Emerson, and Maurine's shattered heart that could not be consoled by her successful novel.

Ironically, on the same day as the round-up, 9 August, Tom's secretary, Margaret Higgins, at the Hillman Hospital, was writing Maurine that Tom had had an infected toe and then an abdominal abscess "almost the size of a grapefruit, which had required surgery. He stood the operation very well, and is getting along fine." Maurine's panic can only be imagined, and she wrote at once. Again, it was Margaret who answered soothingly: "Thank you so much for your letter. Dr. Spies also enjoyed hearing from you." She reported that as soon as Tom could travel, probably in a week or ten days, he planned to finish his convalescence on a cruise under medical attention "and it really will be the wisest thing he could do at this time."⁵⁵ Maurine undoubtedly would have dropped everything and flown to Tom's side at the slightest word from him. Instead, she was being warned off again.

Tom himself dictated a polite note on 29 August from the hospital, "I cannot tell you how very beautiful I think the [photograph of the] Joshua tree is . . . even lovelier than you describe it. Nor can I tell you how much I appreciate your sending it to me. I shall always cherish it." It was the second time he had told her he would "always cherish" something she had given him, and by now the phrase had a conventional, not a personal, ring. His note informed her he was leaving immediately on "a twelve day cruise to Venezuela" to recuperate. It was a comfort to think that his reason for his treatment of her was because he was ill and wanted to save her. But Maurine was hurt that he didn't want her help.

When Maurine finally dragged herself back to St. George at the end of August, she tried to avoid people as much as she could, "for it was difficult to predict when I would start crying again." It was probably during this time of depression in the latter half of 1941 that her reputation for being curt and eccentric began to grow. Her only consolation—and it wasn't much—was spending hours alone on the St. George hills: "Oh, the miles and miles I walked back and forth on the Sugarloaf, begging for comfort, understanding!" she moaned. But the beloved landscape held no peace for her. Also gone was her easy rapport with the past. She could not resurrect it, either for her own comfort or to create the altered state of consciousness which held the delicate equilibrium that had been vital in producing *The Giant Joshua*.

She poured out her agony in letters, keeping the drafts among her papers. They were abject. In 1991–92, she wanted to believe that she had never sent them. Perhaps she didn't.

"I've turned my heart inside out for you," she wrote. "All these months I have been dreaming and praying for just one thing. That you would let me live in the city where you were. It would be a consolation; it would give me such a sense of belonging to know that you were there. . . . Or, if it bothered you to know I was near you, I could live in a nearby city. Just so we could be together maybe once a year."

She promised to change, to become anything he wanted her to be, to act any way he wanted her to act. "For you I would live on the back streets all my days. Don't you see, I'd rather have a minute of life with you than the whole of life with any other man? I'm willing to share your life on any terms. I'd be there when you wanted me," she promised. "I'd be there to cook for you, and entertain your friends, help you, and rub your back, put hot compresses on your eyes, and most of all, to love you. Wouldn't you like to know there was always someone loving you come rain or shine?" She swore that he'd be proud of her, that she had made herself "pretty and charming," that she had even bought a becoming "bright green" frock, that she could have a baby, and that she would be "a darned good mother."

In perhaps the most nakedly revealing sentence in this entire correspondence, she cried, "Married to you, I'd turn into the gracious lady of my childhood dream." She flattered him extravagantly: "When I think what you are trying to do I break out in gooseflesh. There's something Godly about it. You are wholeheartedly selfish just as genius must forever be, but your selfishness is Homeric and all of humanity must bow in humble gratitude before it."

She talked directly about their sexual relationship in terms that revealed her idealism: "You made me feel that the thing between us was something sacred and still. Are you going to be like other men who plead and cheat and lie in order to get a woman and then when they are sated, turn on her with contempt because she was generous? . . . Oh, Tom, you don't know what it's like to be considered prey. Nothing but a . . . a hunk of flesh. Until you despise all men and your soul within you shrivels with contempt." In a passage that combines agony and artfulness, she lamented: "Do you remember just before . . . the first time, I said I was afraid. And you in your foolishness thought I was afraid of the usual thing? Well, now I am telling you what I was really afraid of—I have always known that when I gave the key it would be for keeps. That I could never live inside my fortress alone again. That if the man did not value the key, all the winds of hell would forever howl inside my fortress with me." At the same time, she offered him a non-monogamous relationship if that was what he wanted: "I'd be pleased right now if I thought you were having love with Frances or Jean. They're fine women, and it would be good for you." She promised to leave him alone: "I could arrange to be away each summer while the blitz was on," she said, referring to intensive research periods. "I don't even want what most women want. . . . I want just what you can afford to have. . . . I have love enough to stretch over the periods when women as such cease to exist for you. I don't even want the usual married life, Tom"(ellipses hers).

With faultless good manners and charming little dictated notes, Tom refused everything.

Maurine should have been working full speed on her sequel to capitalize on the interest in *The Giant Joshua*, but she was too distracted, unable to give up the dream of becoming Tom Spies's wife, of living genteelly in a southern mansion, entertaining interesting people, writing more nationally acclaimed books, and bearing his wonderful little namesake Tom.

She had enough energy to fire Max Lieber in an angry and self-pitying letter written 30 August, demanding that he return "*Beaver Dam Wash*" and some photographs "that are priceless to my family" that he was handling for an unspecified contact with *Who* magazine. (There is no evidence that he did either.) She also gave him a version of Houghton Mifflin's dealings with her that is important since it predates the version she later told Don Congdon in 1946. (See Chapter 16.) She apologized for her "appalling" ignorance of business matters, but continued in an explosion of accusations: "Every author with whom I have talked has been shocked to learn an agent would capitalize on a book already published." She claimed that, when she came east, she thought she would have "from three to fifteen thousand dollars advance sales," but then found "I'd made only two thousand dollars which equaled the exact amount of my debts and left me flat broke; I repeat, you knew all this and yet you were willing to take me over the skids too. . . . The final blow is the letter I just received from Mr. Alber that he hasn't made a single booking on my 'five thousand dollar' lecture contract. Nor will he."[56]

Maurine was not being completely fair to Lieber. He had written some quite constructive criticism on 27 June 1941 about her short story, "The Time Will Come."[57] This story, written a full five months before Pearl Harbor, is a tour de force of imagination for a childless woman in a country still at peace. Maurine told me that the story originated in a poignant glimpse of her neighbor, forty-one-year-old Elsie Frei Hafen, standing at her gate and watching her twenty-year-old son, Keith Leland Hafen, who was in the Air Force, walk down the street toward the bus station to report for duty.[58] Maurine sensed that he would never come back up that street alive, and he didn't, even though she couldn't have known that at the time she wrote the story. It is a story of strong mood and opinions, but not much plot. It does make one identify with a woman's view of war. However, it sharply contradicted the national mood of patriotism. The country's mothers needed to be convinced of the necessity of sacrificing their sons, not withholding them.

Lieber had advised that "the piece is out of step with the country's mood."[59] He meant that a war was on and stories reminding one how ridiculous war is wouldn't be popular.

And there was always Tom. During his cruise, she had constructed a more hopeful scenario—the one she later told Curtis Taylor. Tom really did love her. He just knew he was sick—probably had cancer—and was trying to spare her. Cautiously, that fall, she continued the correspondence from St. George where she stayed, apparently until sometime in November.

On 18 September 1941, Tom dictated a note to Maurine thanking her for photographs and "the rattles," possibly from a rattlesnake. He was still weak. "I am cutting everything to the very bone so my friends and family suffer from short, blunt letters." Two weeks later on 1 October, another dictated note arrived, thanking Maurine for her note and claiming, somewhat improbably, "It is always grand to hear from you." He complained of trouble with his teeth and passed on Paul de Kruif's address in Michigan for some scheme Maurine had in mind—although "I imagine he will tell you as I think he did the Sunday we had lunch with him in New York that he preferred not to have an agent."[60] Maurine's papers include no letters from de Kruif.

An encouraging sign that Maurine was trying to get a grip on her slipping career again came on 6 October 1941 when she invited Elden Beck (the salutation did not include Florence) to go onto the Arizona Strip with her, the Dunbars (whom she called "writers from Indiana and grand folks"), and "the government man guide" (unnamed). Maurine wanted Elden to take colored photographs to accompany an article that she was planning to submit to a national magazine. She didn't think she could sell the article for more than a hundred dollars, but she offered to divide the fee evenly with him and felt that having their names in print would be good advertising. Elden couldn't go and she later consoled him by saying it had rained. She also excitedly reported that Ray and Alice had just had their second child, a son named John David.61

On 17 October 1941, Tom again dictated a polite note, once again keeping Maurine at arm's length. He vaguely said that her desert country was "wonderful, and sometime when I have a bit more free time, if such should be my lot, I do want to get out there and see it." But he also suggested strongly: "I hope your work is coming well and that you are keeping busy. If you are like some of the rest of us, you are most happy when you are most occupied." Then he added briskly that he was having "a very hectic period" and would be in Cincinnati and Youngstown, Ohio, from 24 to 28 October. Maurine underlined these cities' names, possibly mulling over plausible excuses for turning up in one of them.62

On 23 October 1941, she dictated a cheerful letter to Tom, giving him a colorful version of her expedition to the Arizona Strip. Perhaps she "dictated" the letter as a snide way of pointing out that most of his letters had been similarly dictated. She had accompanied a party of government people to the Arizona Strip so that she could amass more local details for a possible movie script. A rock had rolled on her left foot, cutting and bruising three toes, and the wound had become infected. She announced but downplayed the injury, instead reporting defiantly how busy she was. She had spent much time in Hollywood that fall (an exaggeration at best) because "the movies were considering Joshua very seriously," and she might "decide to work in one of the studios and move down." Was she trying to make him jealous when she said she had so many friends among film people that a visit to Hollywood was always "a gala time"? She undercut this ploy by admitting that she wasn't much for night-clubbing, even with "the most charming of escorts."63 The typist's initials were "JB"—possibly Juanita Brooks? If so, this elaborately glamorous picture of Maurine's life, created in the presence of another St. George woman, would not play well in the local culture.

And perhaps it didn't sit well with Tom either. Maurine, in a letter to Dean Brimhall in early December, said that she hadn't heard from Tom. She said, "I dictated the last letter, and now he's dropped me flat. I've promised Lila never to start up again. So—it's Hollywood and work and a career, and all those things I've fought against. And it's also learning to like the things I've fought against! And I guess I'm lucky at that!"64

This letter was written the day Pearl Harbor was attacked. I never asked Maurine where she was or what she was doing when she heard the news. Perhaps this letter was written and mailed before she heard news of the attack. But that tragedy would have been small in comparison to how she felt about losing Tom's love.

Although the article she wrote on the Arizona Strip was not published until an updated version appeared in *Collier's* on 24 May 1952—a six-page article with five photographs—*Look* commissioned her in October to do a serious story on the LDS Church, illustrated by Earl Thiesen, one of the staff photographers. This was indeed an important assignment and a boost to her self worth. In a letter to J. Reuben Clark, first counselor in the First Presidency, on 25 October, when the war must have looked inevitable to many, J. C. Herrick, the West Coast editor, explained that the magazine wanted "a story that would prove inspirational to many of its fifteen million readers. If the American republic were to survive World War II, its citizens must display fortitude and character. In seeking these qualities to showcase, we were tremendously impressed by the strength of the Mormon pioneers against hardship and near disaster as related in Miss Maurine Whipple's novel, *The Giant Joshua*."65

Maurine included an article dated 31 October 1941 from an unidentified paper in her scrapbook reporting that she had already sent in a preliminary draft and that Thiesen had begun photographing "ceremonies such as the christening of babies, MIA and Children's Primary activities, Relief Society work, LDS welfare activity, dramatics and dancing."66

Naturally, Maurine was, as she wrote to Dean Brimhall on 13 November, "thrilled about this *Look* assignment.... The magazine wants to please the Mormon people (without propaganda, of course, and without pulling facts) and I'm slanting the writing that way."67 She must have embarked on the project with high hopes, not only for the boost to her career that national exposure would bring but also for this heaven-sent opportunity to showcase her publicity-hungry, missionary-conscious church with a positive piece in a high-circulation publication. Surely this article would erase Elder Widtsoe's disapproving review and cause a reappraisal of *The Giant Joshua*?

She was wrong. Perhaps it was at this time that the "ilk" event occurred. This incident was part of her personal repertoire of explanatory stories that she told repeatedly, often with inconsistencies in setting and time. Sometimes she thought it happened when she was gathering information for a magazine article, or sometimes it was for her travel book about Utah; at other times, she remembered it in conjunction with delivering her wartime lecture in Salt Lake City. What didn't change was the hurt—still there in every retelling, as raw as when it had first happened. She was visiting some welfare project with various dignitaries, one of whom was Harold B.

Lee (sometimes Clark, in her retelling). Lee, as president of Pioneer Stake in Salt Lake Valley, had headed up the Church's Welfare Program in the 1930s and was ordained an apostle in April 1941. The group encountered another General Authority in the hall or on the street. Sometimes she said that it was Heber J. Grant himself, then Church president (which seems unlikely), and sometimes (and more probably) it was Apostle John A. Widtsoe. This man shook his finger at her and said: "I'll have you know, young lady, we want nothing to do with you or those of your ilk." This event, real, imagined, or exaggerated, went into Maurine's already well-seasoned feelings of rejection, exacerbating her heartbreak and loneliness. She usually ended this recollection by saying that the General Authorities "tried very hard to persuade *Look* to let the Church provide the writer for the article. But *Look* declined."

Contemporary documentation of a genuinely negative encounter with Widtsoe exists in a letter Maurine wrote to Dean Brimhall on 13 November 1941. Although not using "ilk," she told Brimhall that she, Thiesen, "and [Harold B.] Lee (whom Clark sent to 'help' us) met Widtsoe on the street and he informed us he prided himself on his 'frankness', wasn't in sympathy with me nor my motives nor my book. In fact, he considered all three 'vulgar.'" He could not have picked a more stinging adjective—the very condemnation that Charlie had used against Maurine's novel. She concluded the comment to Brimhall wryly but accurately: "I don't suppose the authorities will like me any better when I finish than before!"68

Regardless of this reiterated disapproval, Maurine resonated to the "Grand Idea" of the original concept of the Church and threw herself into the job. As I read her enthusiastic letters to Elden Beck, it seems to me that she characteristically overdid what was wanted, involving so many individuals and organizations that they got in each other's way.69 By 10 November, the photographer had come up with a different focus for the article and Maurine told Elden Beck she was "tired of trying to please everyone."70 The article, "Meet the Mormons," appeared on 10 March 1942.

Elbert R. Curtis, president of the Western States Mission, who had advance information about it, instructed his missionaries to use it as a door opener: "This article gives some of the finest publicity to us as a religious people that has ever been presented to a reading audience the size of the one that this magazine has.... National polls taken in the past have proved that public opinion and beliefs are influenced a great deal by the material printed in magazines and papers, and we as wide awake ambassadors of the Gospel can capitalize on such favorable publicity in gaining friends for ourselves and the church."71

This gesture of official approval was sweet but rare, and it did not take away the sting of the official rejection she had already suffered. Possibly in reaction, Maurine found herself broadening her relationships with more liberal Mormons. Although she didn't necessarily want to join the ranks of the disaffected, other marginalized Mormons, like Dean Brimhall, saw Maurine as one of their own, while the few active Mormons who saw the greatness of the whole as keenly as she did, did not actively mentor her. She told me that she was doing a kind of research in this association with the disaffected, developing the character of Clory's son Jimmy, who was becoming a dissenter. But the real reason was probably that she yearned so desperately for a place to belong.

Apparently through Brimhall, she met Nels Anderson, and Maurice Howe, who were skeptics and mildly critical of the Church.[72] (Maurine told me she called Brimhall, Anderson, and Howe the "three Nephites.") Brimhall was the most influential. He wrote judiciously to Maurine on 26 June 1941 after sending her some research material: "I don't want you to think I did very much in the way of spending time because I have kept for a number of years a rather elaborate file on the culture patterns of the Mormons." Brimhall did give her good advice: "My own impression is that you ought to write your novel in accordance with your own ideas because if you put too much confidence in people like me and Anderson you won't write with the same fervor as you would if you wrote things that originated in your own heart."[73]

This letter was both wise and mature; but when Maurine admired a man, it was hard not to listen and reflect his attitudes. She had met Dean's niece, Fawn McKay Brodie, some time this year. In November Fawn answered a request from Maurine for information about her uncle, David O. McKay, then a counselor in the First Presidency. Fawn described him much as a novelist would a character: "He wears the mantle of authority well. There is something in his bearing that suggests the law and the gospel. When he walks into a room he dominates it at once; no matter how few or many are gathered there they all listen to him, friend and scoffer alike. He expects this. He has always received a kind of worshipful deference from his wife and family that is partly the reason I think. If he had married a shrew instead of a shadow he might have been different."[74]

In a postscript, Fawn added: "Sometimes I think Mormonism is a curse. No matter how emancipated you pride yourself on being, you never can sever quite all the cords that bind you to it. And life is so much too complicated as a result." Maurine wrote on the envelope of Fawn's letter: "Later Lenzi." In the sequel, Lenzi would have been Clory's granddaughter.

Doing the *Look* article and having it accepted gave Maurine some confidence in the realm of nonfiction. The material she had collected for the sequel, plus material about contemporary Mormonism compiled as background for the *Look* article later helped her to write a book on Utah. She told me that "Earl Thiesen encouraged me and even wanted to collaborate." She also said that the manager of Deseret Book, whose name she did not remember, had approached her, explaining that "a good guide to the state was desperately needed." Both the armed forces and defense industries were generating massive mobility among America's citizens. People who had never traveled far from their home towns suddenly became travelers across the continent. Maurine said she hadn't been sure such a book would make much money, but, as she told me, she wanted to "do something for the war effort and also something to celebrate her people, possessors of the 'Grand Idea.'"

She sent Tom pine nuts as a Christmas present in an attempt to revitalize their dead relationship. He responded on 19 December with thanks and the comment that he had received the 1941 Scientific Award of the American Pharmaceutical Manufacturers' Association for his work in synthesizing vitamins. Maurine's passionate desire to applaud, sustain, and share his achievements must have exploded—and backfired—for Tom replied austerely on 29 December: "I have read your long letter and received your Christmas presents. They have disturbed me considerably, in view of the fact that I realize that I cannot divide myself so that I can be a true friend to the people who wish to be friends with me. I personally prefer for my life to be uncomplicated so that I can give all of myself to my work."[75]

Inside, where her reality lived, Maurine knew it was over. Something crucial died. But in about November 1942, she wrote yet another agonized appeal to Tom:

> It isn't that I'm afraid for myself. The terror haunting me is that something will happen to you, or that for some reason I will not ever see you again. . . . You know, in less than a month it will be a year since we met. And every single night since then I've lain in bed and called up your image just before going to sleep. It's such a habit now that if I forget, I automatically wake up in the night and summon you. If I can trace your features until I feel your presence there beside me, it's as if you were kissing me, and then I feel safe and warm and tucked in, and I can go back to sleep again.

Maurine could not always tell when she stepped over the line from drama to melodrama. Furthermore, she could not always tell when her most insistent claims of "naked honesty" became themselves a mask. She turned thirty-nine the month after she wrote this letter (20 January 1942) and she kept trying to pump life into this dead relationship for another year. She made one of her more desperate attempts in 1942, consulting a Dr. Thomas A. Kopiloff (Maurine spelled it several ways). He was possibly a psychiatrist, in Cincinnati, where Tom maintained a research laboratory at its university. Katileff replied on 2 December "Confirmed case you presented me. Diagnosis I made definitely confirmed serious. Treatment can't be forced. Patient won't accept treatment. If treatment, much accomplished."[76]

Maurine apparently ignored his warning that "treatment can't be forced" and concentrated on his diagnosis of "serious condition," following up her face-to-face visit with an even more urgent appeal on paper, since an undated draft is preserved in her papers. She began by describing her own symptoms. It has been "such an obsession" for three years that she couldn't work. Even with sleeping pills, "I would start awake, tears streaming down my cheeks. I actually thought I was losing my mind." She describes, not quite truthfully, that the "most dreadful feature" of this nightmare experience was being "denied the ordinary outlet of talk." With considerable drama, she announced: "I am not exaggerating when I say that both our lives and our welfare depend on whether or not he'll take treatments." Twice she offered to send Tom's letters on to Kopiloff, saying she hoped he could "find some clue that would help you get inside his [Tom's] reserve."

She next wrote an overwrought autobiographical section ("I am quite desperate.... I haven't any more will nor courage") and described taking over the care of her family "since I was six years old," dealt with a "mother crushed with the persecution of a tyrannical, unfaithful husband," and assuming the responsibility for rearing, educating, and financing the medical care and marriages of her five siblings. She lamented that she is now "nearly forty years old and life has passed me by." After complaining about being overworked as a child, in the same paragraph she somewhat illogically volunteers: "I wouldn't even care if he didn't make a living. I'd be so happy to support him and the children, too."

The tone slipped abruptly in the next paragraph to accusation. Tom misjudges women as "spoiled, frothy creatures," jumping to conclusions in his personal life in a way that he would never do "in a scientific way and yet that's just what he's done in a personal way. He refused to find out about the real me. And then, of course, he had the attitude that since he is a messiah the end justifies the means, no matter how many lives he ruins to reach that end. He thinks he is exempt from any personal responsibility toward society for his acts."

From this shrill point, she became threatening: Either Kopiloff has to "get him to take treatment" or Maurine will "write him what I think about him. . . . I have a right to tell him. He should be made to face reality." In addition to this motivation, Maurine says, she has to "face him with his misdeeds, for the sake of some other woman. He is so used to sycophants that it might pierce his self-satisfaction to hear the truth for once. Unless that happens, he'll go on being a menace to society."77

Maurine may have sent this letter, or something very like it, since Kopiloff answered brusquely in early January 1943, with his diagnosis of Maurine herself: "Sorry you continue to be disturbed. Suggest you consult a psychiatrist. I recommend Dr. David A. Young, Salt Lake City. Nothing you can do here at present. Strongly advise you drop the whole matter."78 There are no more letters from Tom. It is some measure of her emotional imbalance that she did not realize Tom would have been furious, and rightly so, with such an attempt to get another professional to intervene in his private life.

Maurine brooded over Tom Spies until she lost her sense of perspective, if only briefly, and decided in 1947 that he was guilty of breach of promise and, at the least, owed her enough money to live on while she finished the sequel to *The Giant Joshua*. She had a private detective find his address and wrote one more letter, a six-page, single-space typed letter—a missive that drips with self-pity and reprises the major themes of every "you see" letter that she ever wrote, but soft-pedaling the anguished outpourings of accusations she had earlier flooded him with and, fortunately, not bringing up the breach of promise matter. It wavers between patronage (she presents herself as understanding him perfectly while "you knew less about what makes people tick than any person, layman or physician, I've ever contacted"), arrogance (her "contribution to the world"), and blame ("loneliness and heartbreak and the babies" plus making her lose "the *Look* Mgz. job"). She asked him for $500 and, if he won't give her the money, asked him to ask Paul de Kruif to present her as a victim of the lack of socialized medicine. Then she offered to dedicate the sequel to him.

This dreadful letter is dated 31 January 1947 from Salt Lake City. There is no indication of who typed it for her; she probably did it herself. Surely Lillian, a skilled typist, would have talked Maurine into toning it down or scrapping it altogether. Indeed, there is some reason to hope that Maurine did not send it since her papers includes both the ribbon copy and the carbon copy. In any case, he did not answer it.79

Maurine would fall in love with other men. She would wheedle and posture, presenting herself sometimes as a devil-may-care comrade-in-arms and sometimes as a vulnerable maiden in need of rescue. She never stopped longing for love, hoping for it, angling for it. But something broke in her with the end of her brief and disastrous affair with Tom Spies, and she was never the same again.

"A HEART TURNED INSIDE OUT," 1941

Notes

1 "Book Notes," undated clipping from unidentified publication; Maurine Whipple Collection, L. Tom Perry Special Collections, Harold B. Lee Library, Brigham Young University, Provo, Utah, with photocopy in Maurine Whipple Collection, Archive, Val A. Browning Library, Dixie College, St. George, Utah. Documents in both collections hereafter cited as BYU, photocopy Dixie College.

2 Paul de Kruif, "Vitamins for Everybody," *Reader's Digest*, May 1941, 61. Paul de Kruif, one of the earliest science popularizers, made his name as a medical reporter with *Microbe Hunters* (New York: Harvest Books, 1926). He also wrote *Men against Death*; *Germ Killers*; *The Sweeping Wind: A Memoir*, and with Sidney Howard, *Yellow Jack: A History*.

3 Tom Spies, Obituary, *New York Times*, 29 February 1960, page not identified; BYU, photocopy Dixie College.

4 "Books—Authors," *New York Times*, 9 January 1941, page not identified; and "The Importance of Humor in the Arts," program, Town Hall luncheon, 17 January 1941, both in Whipple Scrapbook; BYU, photocopy Dixie College.

5 Tom Spies, Letters to Maurine Whipple, 15 July 1938, 20 September and 3 November 1940, dictated and typed; BYU, photocopy Dixie College.

6 Tom Spies, Letters to Maurine Whipple, 10 and 18 January 1941; BYU, photocopy Dixie College.

7 Maurine Whipple, Interviewed by Curtis Taylor, 3 January 1989, transcript, 78; audio recording and typescript in Charles Redd Center, Brigham Young University; photocopy Perry Special Collections.

8 Spies, Obituary.

9 Maurine's papers include several rough-draft letters, written in longhand on large sheets of newsprint. It is difficult to determine how many of these kinds of letters there were, because none is seemingly complete (salutation to signature), and it is hard to decide where one ended and another began. None is dated; but from internal evidence, they were all written between June and late December 1941. These rough-draft letters are in a folder labeled "Tom Spies," BYU, photocopy at Dixie College. I quote from them in this chapter without further citations.

10 Dorothy B. Nyswander, Letter to Maurine Whipple, 20 January 1941; BYU, photocopy Dixie College.

11 Contract, 21 January 1941, photocopy of original, Dixie College. In addition to being a literary agent, Lieber was involved in an organization called the American Features Writers Syndicate which was suspected during the McCarthy years of being involved in Communist espionage. He spent 1950–68, first in Mexico, then in Poland, "a

refugee from the domestic cold war," http://homepages.nyu.edu/~this/navasky.html (accessed June 2002). Maurine had no association with him after 30 August 1941.

[12] R. N. Linscott, Letter to Maurine Whipple, 23 January 1941; BYU, photocopy Dixie College.

[13] Tom dictated four known letters on 30 January 1941: one each to Mrs. Doubleday, Mrs. Goddard, Houghton Mifflin, and Maurine. In the one to Houghton Mifflin, he asked the publisher to mail copies of *The Giant Joshua* to Miss Ann Spies, Dr. Genevieve Delfs, Miss Jean Grant, Miss Frances Bomer, and Mrs. Joseph Allen.

[14] Tom Spies, Letters to Grace Goddard and Florence Doubleday, both dated 30 January 1941; typescript on onion skin, with "TDS:mrs, cc: Miss Maurine Whipple" at the bottom. BYU, photocopy Dixie College. These two women do not appear again in the correspondence. Mrs. Goddard may have been the widow of Henry W. Goddard, president of Spencer Wire Company, who became president after his death in 1927 and served until the company dissolved in 1933.

[15] Tom Spies, Telegram to Maurine Whipple, 31 January [1941]; BYU, photocopy Dixie College. The year is missing from the telegram, but Greenslet's reference to the flu she had in Washington, D.C., in the next paragraph dates the telegram, too.

[16] Bement was an English professor at George Washington University. Ferris Greenslet, Letter to Maurine Whipple, C/o Douglas Bement, 632 Ridge Drive, N.W., Washington D.C., 3 February 1941; BYU, photocopy Dixie College. Maurine's papers contain no letters from Bement. Perhaps the correspondence did not survive or, equally probably, the friendship did not survive a week of Maurine, suffering from the flu and complaining that her publisher was victimizing her.

[17] Ferris Greenslet, Letter to Maurine Whipple, 3 February 1941; BYU, photocopy Dixie College. The next day, Robert N. Linscott, Letter to Whipple, 4 February 1941, sent her a brief note accompanying "follow-up advertisements of '*The Giant Joshua*.'" He added: "It is a pleasure to see the reorders coming in. I do hope we will be able to find for it as large a sale as it deserves." This statement is a polite but noncommittal acknowledgment of Maurine's dissatisfaction.

[18] Ferris Greenslet, Letter to Maurine Whipple, 11 February 1941; BYU, photocopy Dixie College.

[19] Maurine Whipple, untitled notes on Tom Spies lecture, February 1941; BYU.

[20] Eugene England, "Whipple's *The Giant Joshua*: The Greatest But Not the Great Mormon Novel," *Annual of the Association for Mormon Letters, 2001* (Provo, Utah: AML, 2001), 61–62.

[21] Tom Spies, Letter to Maurine Whipple, 25 February 1941, mailed C/o Preston, 1267 So. Dunsmuir Avenue, Los Angeles. No one surnamed Preston appears in Maurine's correspondence.

[22] Tom Spies, Letter to Maurine Whipple, 25 February 1941, and carbon copy of Tom Spies, Letter to Florence Doubleday, 25 February 1941; both in BYU, photocopy Dixie College. Tom had received a letter from Mrs. Doubleday on 4 February 1941, which he answered on 25 February 1941; BYU, photocopy, Dixie College.

[23] Tom Spies to Maurine Whipple, 28 April 1941; BYU, photocopy Dixie College.

"A HEART TURNED INSIDE OUT," 1941

24 Maurine's 1941 checkbook stubs show three checks to Annie, two for "washing" for $5.00 and one for $30 with no memo entry. The only checkbooks surviving are in the Dixie College Archives. Maurine told me how much she enjoyed giving her mother money to buy just anything she wanted. There was also at this same time a check written to Ralph for $50, no indication for what, and one to "Papa" for $2, for "phone call."

25 Maurine paid $61.80 in income tax for 1941, the tax on $4,599.25, which was the amount reported by Houghton Mifflin. She tried to persuade the Internal Revenue Service to average her income over 1937, 1938, 1939, and 1940—an arrangement which is allowed now but not then. An appeal failed, and she had to pay the full amount. 1941 tax statement, BYU.

26 Benjamin E. Jolley, Obituary, *St. George Spectrum*, 28 April 1996; Dixie College.

27 Maurine Whipple, "Florence and Ben's Story," 1, 10; ca. 1952, 10 pp., holograph; Dixie College.

28 "Maurine Whipple Returns from Salt Lake City," *Washington County News*, 8 April 1941.

29 Dean R. Brimhall (1881–1972)'s biography is archived with his papers at Special Collections, Marriott Library, University of Utah, Salt Lake City (hereafter Brimhall Papers).

30 Fawn Brodie, *No Man Knows My History: The Life of Joseph Smith* (New York: Alfred A. Knopf, 1945); see also Newell G. Bringhurst, *Fawn McKay Brodie: A Biographer's Life* (Norman: University of Oklahoma Press, 1999).

31 "Maurine Whipple Returns from Salt Lake City," *Washington County News*, 8 April 1941, prints the guest list from the Brimhalls' openhouse. Angus M. Woodbury, born 11 July 1886 in St. George, married Grace Atkin, another St. George native, on 15 January 1909. The two died in an automobile accident 1 August 1994. Walter P. Cottam (March 1894–28 August 1964) married Effie Cot (27 September 1888–28 August 1964). This article adds that on "May 20 Maurine is to return to lecture before school of education, which will give her an audience of 1,000 freshman students."

32 Tom Spies to Maurine Whipple; 4 March 1941; BYU, photocopy Dixie College.

33 Tom Spies, Letter to Maurine Whipple, 5 April 1941; BYU.

34 Genie [no surname given], Letter to Maurine Whipple, 28 April 1941; BYU, photocopy Dixie College. Genie also told Maurine that a quotation from *The Giant Joshua* had appeared in the May 1941 *Reader's Digest* in the "Toward More Picturesque Speech" column: "There were whispers of color still left in the evening sky . . . mountains eating away at the horizons" (80).

35 Tom Spies, Letter to Maurine Whipple, 28 April 1941; BYU, photocopy Dixie College.

36 Maurine Whipple, Letter to Elden Beck, 7 May 1941; BYU, photocopy Dixie College. Beck, a zoologist at BYU with a specialty in little-known spiders, had taught at Dixie College during the late 1930s when Maurine was writing *The Giant Joshua* and had, at her request, sent Ferris Greenslet some information about Joshua trees. He had also given her help in getting the flora and animals right in her book. Amazingly, some of Maurine's letters to Beck have survived since he gave his papers to BYU, which included them. Like Maurine's, his papers remain uncatalogued as of 2003.

"SWELL SUFFERING"

37 *Desert Sun* (Palm Springs, Calif.), no reporter's name, headline, date or page number on clipping, Whipple Scrapbook, BYU, photocopy at Dixie College.

38 Maxim Lieber, Letter to Maurine Whipple, 16 May 1941; BYU, photocopy Dixie College.

39 When Tom ordered his five books from Houghton Mifflin on 30 January 1941, he had asked them to send one copy to Mrs. Joseph Allen, 4132 South 23rd St. East, Salt Lake City, and another to Ann Spies, 2501 Avenue J., Galveston, Texas. He had not earlier mentioned "Mary."

40 Tom Spies, Hillman Hospital, Birmingham, Alabama, Letter to Maurine Whipple, St George, 12 May 1941; BYU, photocopy, Dixie College.

41 "Maurine Whipple Returns from Salt Lake City," *Washington County News*, 8 April 1941, announced this forthcoming lecture.

42 Tom Spies, Letter to Maurine Whipple, 15 June 1941; BYU, photocopy Dixie College. A follow-up note on 24 June told her the broadcast was scheduled for the "LISTEN AMERICA program over the NBC red network" on Friday, 27 June, at 10:30 p.m. (Eastern Daylight Time)"; BYU, photocopy Dixie College.

43 Ibid.

44 Tom Spies to Maurine Whipple; 20 June 1941; BYU, photocopy Dixie College.

45 Ibid.

46 Ibid.

47 Erik (no surname), Letter to Maurine Whipple, New York City, 14 October [1941]; BYU, photocopy at Dixie College Archive.

48 Maurine Whipple, draft of letter to Paul de Kruif, 14 July 1941; BYU, photocopy Dixie College.

49 Maurine Whipple, draft letter to Dean Brimhall, 14 July 1941; BYU, photocopy, Dixie College.

50 Tom Spies, Hillman Hospital, Birmingham, Alabama, Letter to Maurine Whipple, unnamed hotel, 432 Fourth Ave, New York, 12 July 1941; BYU, photocopy, Dixie College.

51 Whipple, Interviewed by Curtis Taylor, 3 January 1989, transcript, 78; audio recording and typescript in Charles Red Center, Brigham Young University; photocopy in Whipple Collection, BYU.

52 Jean Grant, Letter to Maurine Whipple, 24 July 1941; BYU, photocopy Dixie College.

53 Maurine Whipple, Letter to Dean Brimhall, n.d., but ca. later summer or fall 1941; Brimhall Papers.

54 Ernest A. Lawrence, president of Salt Lake Chapter League of Utah Writers, Letter to Maurine Whipple, 14 March 1941; BYU, photocopy Dixie College. This letter sets a tentative date of 13–14 July, but an article headlined "Writers: Utah Authors Gather for Annual Round-Up," *Deseret News*, 8 August 1941, Whipple Scrapbook; BYU, photocopy Dixie College, identifies the round-up as happening "tomorrow."

55 Margaret Higgins, Letters to Maurine Whipple, 9 and 21 August 1941; BYU, photocopy Dixie College. The second letter reached Maurine at University Apartments, No. 5, 212 South 13th East, Salt Lake City.

"A HEART TURNED INSIDE OUT," 1941

56 Maurine Whipple, Letter to Max Lieber, 30 August 1941; BYU, photocopy Dixie College.

57 Four versions of this story exist: (1) a twenty-three-page holograph in first-person with a schoolteacher as narrator; (2) a twenty-four-page typescript with the same narrator; (3) a twenty-five-page typescript with a bank clerk as third-person narrator; (4) a twenty-page typescript in third person with the bank clerk as narrator. The first three versions are at BYU, the fourth version at Dixie College. In 1991, Maurine and I revised this story, experimenting with making the mother identify with the Native American past of the locale and the beauty of the desert. In the original, the mother hates the desert and the Indian ruins near the town. Thus, the fifth version is Maurine's last piece of creative fiction.

58 Elsie Frei Hafen was born 4 August 1897, married Leland Hafen on 12 December 1917, gave birth to Keith Leland Hafen on 26 August 1921, and died 26 March 1966. Keith, a lieutenant in the 358th Bomber Squadron, the 303 Bomber Group ("Hell's Angels"), was killed in action over Rotterdam, The Netherlands, on 31 March 1943. Engraved on his tombstone in the St. George cemetery is the B-17, "Two Beauts," of which he was copilot.

59 Max Lieber, Letter to Maurine Whipple, 27 June 1941; BYU, photocopy Dixie College.

60 Tom Spies, Letters to Maurine Whipple, 18 September and 1 October 1941; BYU, photocopy Dixie College.

61 Maurine Whipple, Letter to Elden Beck, 24 October 1941; Elden Beck Papers, L. Tom Perry Special Collections, Harold B. Lee Library, Brigham Young University, Provo, Utah (hereafter cited as Beck Papers).

62 Tom Spies, Letter to Maurine Whipple, 17 October 1941; BYU, photocopy Dixie College.

63 Maurine Whipple, Letter to Tom Spies, 17 October 1941, carbon copy; BYU, photocopy, Dixie College.

64 Maurine Whipple, Letter to Dean R. Brimhall, 7 December 1945, Brimhall Papers.

65 J. C. Herrick, West Coast editor of *Look* magazine, Letter to First Presidency, Attn: Mr. J. Reuben Clark, 25 October 1941; BYU, photocopy Dixie College. On the bottom of the page, Maurine has written: "Please return, Dean. This is a copy of the letter that hired the gun!"

66 Tribune Intermountain Wire Service, "Book on Utah's Dixie Leads to Magazine Article: *Look* Editors Engaged 'Giant Joshua' Author to Help Prepare Pictorial Study of Life, Customs," 31 October 1941, paper not identified, p. 8. This clipping was not in Maurine's scrapbook, but in a box of loose papers that Carol Jensen found and turned over to me, now at Dixie College.

67 Maurine Whipple, Letter to Dean Brimhall, 13 November 1941, Brimhall Papers.

68 Ibid.

69 Maurine Whipple, Letter to Elden Beck, 24 October 1941; Beck Papers.

70 Maurine Whipple, Letter to Elden Beck, 10 November 1941; Beck Papers.

71 Elbert R. Curtis, Letter to Missionaries, 25 February 1942; BYU, photocopy Dixie College.

72 Nels Anderson, a Mormon sociologist, was director of the Works Progress Administration's Section on Labor Relations. Maurice L. Howe, Letter to Maurine Whipple, 4 June 1941; BYU, photocopy Dixie College. Maurine wrote "Frank" on the letter, suggesting that she meant to use some of the information for a character in her sequel to *The Giant Joshua*.

73 Dean R. Brimhall, Letter to Maurine Whipple, 26 June 1941; BYU, photocopy Dixie College. The memo appears: "Enclosure, pages from *Deseret News*, Nov. 24, 1938." These pages show President Heber J. Grant receiving a box containing a thousand pieces of silver from Kennecott Copper Company.

74 Fawn Brodie, Letter from Hanover, New Hampshire, to Maurine Whipple, 12 November 1941; BYU, photocopy Dixie College.

75 Tom Spies to Maurine Whipple, 29 December 1942; BYU, photocopy Dixie College.

76 Dr. Thomas A. Kopiloff, M.D., Cincinnati, Letter to Maurine Whipple, 2 December 1942; BYU, photocopy Dixie College.

77 Maurine Whipple, Letter to Dr. Kopiloff, n.d., holograph on double-wide paper, much damaged; BYU, photocopy Dixie College.

78 Dr. Thomas A. Kopiloff, Cincinnati, Ohio, Letter to Maurine Whipple, 7 January 1943; BYU, photocopy, Dixie College.

79 Maurine Whipple, Letter to Tom Spies, ca. summer 1948; ribbon and carbon copy; Dixie College. The original has been folded, as if it has been in an envelope.

12

DOING HER BIT FOR THE WAR: 1942-43

Wanting to appear independent and successful to the unfailingly courteous but increasingly remote Tom Spies, Maurine rented an apartment in Hollywood, hoping to enlarge her career by also becoming a scriptwriter. Even though the advice she had received from Max Lieber and his cronies had been that *The Giant Joshua* would not make a good movie, she didn't believe them. But her "jinx" struck again. On 27 January 1942, she wrote Elden Beck from Tucson, Arizona: "The gas stove had exploded, burning my face, hands, arms, and singeing my hair." She was in Tucson recuperating with "friends"—probably the Don Seegmiller family.[1] The accident ended this attempt to "storm" Hollywood and added to the bitterness she felt for the place ever after.

To add to her misery, during February 1942, Maurine suffered from bladder infections. She consulted an urologist specialist, Elmer Belt.[2] When she wanted someone to see her as special, she frequently gave him or her a gift copy of *The Giant Joshua*. She did this for Dr. Belt. She also, later, sent him much information on pioneer medicine, including a copy of the diary of Priddy Meeks, an early doctor in southern Utah. For her part, Maurine was an appreciative audience for his hobby—collecting books and especially Leonardo da Vinci items. Belt had become interested in da Vinci's anatomical drawings and investigations during medical school and, at this point, had established a library-museum on Wilshire Boulevard in Los Angeles, which displayed his collection and served as a reference library for the study of the Italian Renaissance.[3]

After Elmer and his wife, Maryruth, read *The Giant Joshua*, they were impressed enough to invite Maurine to visit them, probably in late February 1942. An undated thank-you note conveys not only Maurine's sincere gratitude, but her unsubtle attempt to enlist the Belts as her new sponsors. "As you know, I've been monstrously peevish because I was cheated of so much of the income from Joshua. But lately I've been thinking (having so much time in which to think!) that maybe if events hadn't conspired just as they did, I might never have gotten to know you and Maryruth." She ended her note with a Navajo phrase she had taken to using, "Hojohni Na-shada: Travel the trail of beauty, my friend."[4]

Belt wrote back 5 March 1942, a letter sparkling with allusions to his practice and to his glittering circle of acquaintances and political liberals. Opinions of men like Belt had a powerful influence on Maurine's strong but unsophisticated political thinking. At this time, England was still enduring the Nazi blitz, the British fortress of Singapore had fallen in February with 25,000 prisoners taken, and the Japanese continued their expansion into Borneo, Java, and Sumatra.

The local paper in Palm Springs, California, reported on its society page on 3 March 1942 that "Miss Maurine Whipple had taken a hacienda in Palm Springs for the remainder of the season."[5] She admitted to me that "hacienda" was hardly an accurate term but said she had settled down to enjoy a small cottage for March and April. She apparently made at least one trip to Hollywood during early March because she wrote a highly colored letter to Elden Beck, announcing dramatically: "I have severed my ties with Hollywood, I can't stand the cheap, insincere people there." Racked by real loneliness but unable to resist melodramatic hyperbole, she confessed: "I would give ten years of my life to feel that I belonged somewhere, was needed and wanted somewhere. Isn't it silly to long so desperately to raise chickens and flowers and babies! I can't stand this kind of life much longer. . . . Are there any unmarried men in Provo, Elden? Any widowers who would take on a gal who's lost her faith and her courage? . . . I am so desperately tired and so sick of loneliness. I never wanted fame. I hate it. . . . Surely there must be some old man who'd be willing to take me on. Huh? I meet plenty of men who want me! want me to have affairs! I think Brigham was right, even unto polygamy."[6]

On 24 March 1942, her youngest brother George, age twenty-seven, married Flora Linderberger, a girl from a fine family from Redlands, California. Flora's father, a teacher, sometimes wrote to Maurine, sharing with her his desire to write.[7] Maurine's "hacienda" was in the same housing court as the young couple's honeymoon home. Now the comfort of having George near was tinged with anxiety that he would soon be sent overseas.

A change was in store for Maurine as well. Soon after her despairing letter to Elden Beck, she received a letter from L. E. Nelson, a regent of the University of Redlands in California, who had been impressed by her speaking ability the year before. Now, he wrote that he was "definitely interested" in booking her "for a lecture tour to encourage the war effort." He told her that, to give her experience, he had booked her with the California Writer's Club, the Writer's Round Table at Hollywood, and at three locations in Redlands: the California Writers' Guild, the Contemporary Club, and the University of Redlands.[8] She borrowed money to visit him in Los Angeles where they met at a hotel.

She recalled with relish that, in their lengthy conversation, Nelson assured her she had the ability to make a major contribution to the war effort. "Ordinary people have the right and obligation to help," he said. So she went back again to St. George and worked on her lecture, seeing it as a parallel contribution to Tom Spies's scientific work, something she could do to match his selfless sacrifice. She described how she would climb the red hill called the Sugarloaf and, in the "light cave," named such because there was an opening in the top through which light streamed, would practice out loud, training herself to project her voice to the back of the room.

Simultaneously, in early April 1942 she received word that Doubleday's Dollar Book Club had bought rights to condense *The Giant Joshua* and that she could anticipate about $1,800 in revenue. With that good news, she wrote an upbeat letter to Dean Brimhall, asking for suggestions about breaking into news reporting. She wanted to do more human interest stories, like the article that had just come out in *Look*.[9] But one might suspect that her real purpose was to have an excuse to be in the East closer to Tom—just in case.

Even if Brimhall had responded encouragingly, Maurine's opportunities were actually on the West Coast. On 24 April, after she had delivered the lectures Nelson arranged, she had the pleasure of reading a positive report about her lectures in the *Los Angeles Times*, that quoted her stirring advice: "Take advantage of all your opportunities here. They are God-given. What will count is what you make of them. You are the soil for a better world after the war[;] you have a hard job ahead of you, as hard as that of the pioneers of the past, you are the pioneers of the future. The hope of the world is with you. If you fail, the world after the war as we know it will be gone."[10]

Maurine was apparently also working on both fiction and nonfiction, although there is no way of knowing how seriously. A partial letter from a Palm Springs correspondent named Ruth (no surname given) commented, "By the way, I search every list that comes out and no Arizona Strip by Maurine Whipple."[11] However, Maurine was definitely launched as a lecturer for the duration of the war.

"The Arizona Strip," a novel which would never be finished, was a conventional Western romance without much Mormon content, a love triangle between an outlaw, an indomitable sheriff (in one version he was described as a Mormon), and a girl who doesn't quite know her own mind. The sheriff was at least partly based on Lewis Fife, sheriff of Iron County, and his tracking down a cattle-rustler and bank-robber, John N. ("Jack") Weston, and his girl friend, Daisy Butler.[12]

It was probably during these weeks in Palm Springs that Maurine also worked on a piece called "The War from the Standpoint of Your Favorite Old Maid." It was apparently designed as an article or perhaps part of a lecture: "I've decided the best thing America's old maids can do for their country is to observe. Every army has to have observers, doesn't it?"[13] In this fragment's hearty and healthily self-deprecating humor, Maurine is obviously trying on her "Aunt Julia" voice. She thus creates a welcome public persona to give voice to her own private heartache and miserable loneliness.

In June, Maurine went east again, supposedly to present her concept of "The Arizona Strip" as a serial and a novel to Houghton Mifflin. She apparently got no encouragement from Greenslet.[14] She wrote Dean Brimhall from New York City on 24 June 1942, telling him she was staying with Fawn and Bernard Brodie "for a month," trying to rewrite "The Arizona Strip."[15] The Brodies were living in Hanover, New Hampshire, where Bernard was teaching at Dartmouth College and Fawn was pregnant with the first of their four children. Contrary to the impression she gave Brimhall that she was the Brodies' guest, Maurine had her own apartment.

Certainly Fawn's uncle, Dean Brimhall, was a link between Fawn and Maurine, and he would have seen them as compatible in many ways. Although both women saw Mormonism from a historical perspective, the differences between them prevented the development of a lasting friendship. Perhaps the greatest obstacle was Fawn's marriage to a well-educated man with a degree, like her own, from the University of Chicago. Bernard was well launched on his academic career, and they had every reason to anticipate a stable, intellectually stimulating future. Maurine's envy must have been hard to hide, especially since Fawn came from "important" Mormons—the McKays and the Brimhalls. To Maurine, this difference would have been all-important and insurmountable. And almost certainly, Maurine could not have refrained from dumping many of her failed romances—certainly her heartache over Tom Spies—in Fawn's lap. Most women, no matter how sympathetic, would eventually become uncomfortable around Maurine and her unending grief. In 1945, after Fawn's biography of Joseph Smith had resulted in her excommunication, Fawn commented revealingly to Dale Morgan: "I think Juanita suffers, more than anything else, from the isolation of living in St. George. . . . As it is she seems to have only Maurine! And no one is better calculated to make one appreciate the homely Mormon virtues than that gal. I'd prefer the Sunday School superintendent any day."16

But that was three years in the future when Maurine must have worn out her welcome with the Brodies. They maintained surface cordiality, and Maurine for the next few years still ended her letters to Dean Brimhall by telling him to "give my love to Fawn."

The exact date Maurine left New Hampshire is unknown. She went to Chicago so that she could see George off to the Pacific theater of war. In Maurine's lecture, she sometimes told how George showed her a small flask of Dixie sand he was carrying with him, and she would describe him tucking it back into his pocket, squaring his shoulders, and marching off.17 In addition to the worry shared with everybody's family about the chance that their loved one would be killed, Maurine also suffered from the darker worry that George's sensitive spirit would be ravaged by army life. In this premonition, she was correct.

On 30 August 1942 Maurine received a letter from a new friend, Read Bain.18 Another Utahn disillusioned with some of the Church's policies, he was secretary-treasurer and a member of the executive committee of the Sociological Research Association headquartered at Miami University in Oxford, Ohio. He and Maurine had met at some social gathering, but in 1991 she could no longer remember the details. He saw Maurine as someone who could popularize his opinions, and his lengthy letter was to tell her what they were. He had not read *The Giant Joshua* when they first met, a lack for which he apologized. He had now remedied that lack and praised Maurine's writing in glowing terms that must have warmed her heart. He saw her as one with "super-consciousness, this emotionally drenched sensitivity which makes it possible for a person to write a true novel, or poem, or piece of music. And always there is the painful feeling that the symbol, the embodiment of the "hunch," the expression of the impression—is a thousand miles removed from the thing—from the reality which we never experience—except thru a glass darkly." He warmly added that he felt in "tune with her feelings" and, as a result, felt he "had known her all his life." He concluded on a lighter note, by "hoping her tehinder is being kinder."19 He was probably referring to the mysterious automobile accident—date unknown, but probably in September or early October 1942 in Chicago.

The medical mystery is only deepened by a letter among her papers from Philip Lewin, a Chicago doctor, written 7 October 1942, and calling her by her first name: "Before you read this letter, I want you to know that every word was dictated very seriously. The time has passed when we could make fun of a situation such as you find yourself in." He thought she had "a disk syndrome—that is, an intervertebral disk that has slipped out of place and is pressing on one of the spinal nerves." He recommended an extensive course of treatment lasting sixteen days, including an operation. "I consider [that] your back is very highly vulnerable to even the ordinary stresses and strains of life."[20]

Maurine apparently forwarded this letter to an unnamed correspondent in an attempt to attract sympathy. She wrote bitterly at the bottom: "Of course I can't go to see Dr. Love. Two months of constant pain and sleepless nights, and one month of wondering how it will be never to climb the hills again! One month of longing for the comfort of a letter. Isn't it strange? Just a year ago you were down and wanted comfort from me?" (The mention of "two months" also suggests an August date for the accident.)

Spies continued to be featured in the national press. Maurine probably was wounded afresh if she saw "Hunger at Home: Deep South Clinic Symbolizes Battle against Pellagra" in *Newsweek* (16 April 1945), including a photo of "Dr. Tom." The 12 August 1946 issue of *Science* credited him with the discovery of the crucial vitamin, folic acid. The *Science* article April 12 1946 contained this colorful paragraph: "Texas-born Tom is a gregarious, genial sort who can talk his charity patients into doing anything for him, and charm the better-abled into supporting his research. Most of his work is done at the Hillman Hospital in Birmingham, Ala. during an annual eight months' leave of absence from the University of Cincinnati. Unmarried, he refuses to own anything he cannot crowd into a suitcase, lives in hotel rooms to save time, talks little but shop."[21] If Maurine saw this article, it must have confirmed her 1943 view that Tom was a man who could not let himself have a life of his own.

Read Bain wrote late in September, expecting that she was busy on "The Arizona Strip," echoing her hopes for the project, and briskly proposing that she "write several chapters and a general outline as a basis for a dicker, serialize it in a good paying magazine, use that to satisfy the obligation . . . with Houghton Mifflin for a novel, sell it to the movies, and after that be free of Houghton Mifflin or else force them to give a decent contract."[22]

Such a letter must have heartened her. At least some people believed in her. She was trying to do what Bernard DeVoto had done and advised her to do—write a popular light novel to be serialized, which would bring her enough money to live on while she did her serious writing.

A month later, Florence Bain (both Elden Beck and Read Bain's wives were named Florence) even asked Maurine to stand by in case Robert Frost, who had a reputation of being unreliable, didn't show up at the Miami University assembly. Maurine apparently knew Florence well enough to solicit help from her in trying to improve her relationship with Tom, since Florence said, in the same letter, "Perhaps we could have a party and invite

Tom, if we think it politic." Florence had been helping Maurine try to obtain lecture dates and called herself "your Oxford business manager." In the same letter, Florence also gave a good reason why *The Giant Joshua* should be valuable to the Mormon culture for years to come:

> I've been reading your book, and it surprises me how nostalgic [are] the thousand little details you have collected with such painstaking care. There is something in the back country of Utah, by which I mean anywhere away from Salt Lake, Ogden, and Provo, that is only get-at-able by those who were born and bred in it . . . of old pioneer stock, and is so much an unconscious part of us it simply amazes me. I am deeply grateful to you for gathering it up and integrating the pattern before it was too late for me personally. I think all my life I have been, not Conrad [a character in *Lost Horizon*] in search of youth, but Florence in search of her roots, trying to integrate her personality in a series of environments quite far removed from her origins, and a book like yours is an unparalleled aid. That's personal and peculiar to me as an individual. In a larger sense, it serves the same purpose to a complex America, trying to learn to understand itself, getting perspective in a dizzy world.[23]

But most of Maurine's energy seems to have gone into her lectures. It is difficult to decide just how many different lectures dates she had. It appears from the jumbled notes in her papers that she used parts of different lectures, shaping them to her audience, and ad-libbing as necessary. According to Maurine's memory, she lectured for the war effort for four years—in other words, across the entire span of the war throughout the West and in towns and cities as far east as Chicago, generating patriotic commitment and encouraging her listeners to buy war bonds. She was paid expense money and a small stipend. As late as 1970, she continued to adapt this basic talk for presentation to various audiences. In 1976, she wrote a consolidated version, possibly copyrighted. Her cousin, Alta Rae Whipple, worked for a copyright office in New York and may have facilitated the paperwork. Maurine's busiest year for lectures appears to have been 1943.

During the summer of 1943, the *Salt Lake Tribune* reported on a one-day conference of the League of Utah Writers. A photograph shows Maurine in a broad-brimmed hat, a flower pinned to her dress, To the audience of approximately a hundred, Maurine was reported as "making plea for racial tolerance for the equality of peoples, and a more true democracy. 'If men are to be free,' she said, 'they must be free together. The freedom that has been the American dream must be extended to all people if there is to be a lasting peace after this war is won.'"[24]

Maurine felt that she was a gifted and successful lecturer. George M. Miller, one of Utah's state senators, wrote a "To Whom It May Concern" letter of audience reaction, apparently at Maurine's request. He described her address, on "The Quest of the Soul," to about two hundred men at an Exchange Club luncheon in Salt Lake City. The men were so enthusiastic, he said, that "they gave her a standing ovation, so prolonged that she had to respond several times."25

Another rare description of Maurine in action on the lecture platform comes from Elizabeth Dedekind of Chicago, who wrote to Maurine's mother in November 1942 about "the grand job Maurine did speaking to the Women's Club of Evanston: She walked right into their hearts, and received more applause than any guest speaker they have had. She looked too sweet for words in her light colored suit, green blouse and green hat, and her voice carried to every listener."26

One lecture-generated relationship that stuck in Maurine's mind in considerable detail occurred after a Seattle lecture when Clinton Rice and his son introduced themselves. The elder Rice, at age nineteen, had briefly been a Presbyterian missionary in St. George. Rice acknowledged that his missionary efforts "didn't amount to much," but he had retained a fondness for the place and people. He and Maurine launched a correspondence that lasted until 1965 when Rice died.

In her old age, whenever Maurine talked about her lecturing, she acted as if she were still surprised at this season of success and appreciation.

She lived on an emotional roller-coaster, much of it self-generated, during the war years. Her loneliness, physical ailments, and personal misery over Tom almost swamped her. But the success of *Joshua* and her lecturing connected her again with a mighty cause. She responded with genuine emotion to being part of an effort as important as that of the pioneers of Dixie and as patriotic as the construction of Hoover Dam. The evidence that she was successful is important, since some might judge her as having been successful only at writing *The Giant Joshua*. How many women could have gone through the difficult depression and war years alone and created a place for themselves as she did? To be a successful lecturer is not easy, nor is it easy to create recreation and dance classes from scratch. No, whatever Maurine's character flaws, laziness wasn't among them.

DOING HER BIT FOR THE WAR: 1942–43

Notes

[1] Maurine Whipple, Letter to Elden Beck, 27 January 1942; Elden Beck Papers, L. Tom Perry Special Collections, Harold B. Lee Library, Brigham Young University, Provo, Utah (hereafter cited as Beck Collection), with photocopy in Maurine Whipple Collection, Perry Special Collections, and photocopy at Whipple Collection, Dixie College Library, St. George, Utah. Documents in both collections are hereafter cited as BYU, photocopy Dixie College.

[2] Dr. Elmer Belt, urologist and director of the Elmer Belt Clinic, was born 10 April 1893 at Chicago and married Maryruth Smart on 9 June 1918. His entry in *Who's Who* reports an extensive list of awards and honors. Alice Catt Armstrong, ed., *Who's Who in California for 1961* (Los Angeles: Who's Who Historical Society, 1960).

[3] "The Elmer Belt Library," brochure, n.d., Whipple Collection, BYU.

[4] Maurine Whipple, Letter to Elmer Belt, n.d., holograph; BYU.

[5] Loose clipping, unidentified paper, 3 March 1942, BYU. Maurine was living at 4321 Camino Parocela in Palm Springs.

[6] Maurine Whipple, Letter to Elden Beck, 14 March [1942]; BYU, photocopy Dixie College. The letter can be definitely dated to 1942 because it was written while she was in Palm Springs and mentions that her younger brother, George, would be shipped overseas soon.

[7] Flora Truba Lindenberger's parents were Florence M. and Edwin Forest Lindenberger.

[8] L. E. Nelson, University of Redlands, Letter to Maurine Whipple, 17 March 1942; BYU, photocopy Dixie College.

[9] Maurine Whipple, Letter to Dean Brimhall, 3 April 1942, Dean R. Brimhall Papers, Special Collections, Marriott Library, University of Utah, Salt Lake City (hereafter Brimhall Papers); photocopy Dixie College.

[10] *Los Angeles Times*, 24 April 1942, Whipple Scrapbook; BYU, photocopy Dixie College.

[11] Ruth [surname not given], Letter to Maurine Whipple, 4 August 1942; BYU, photocopy Dixie College. The last page is missing; but the husband's first name is Holt.

[12] Maurine probably gained her information about Fife from local people who knew him personally. An interesting historical article on this experience is Helen Gardner, "The Capture of Jack Weston: The Last of the Famous Old Western Outlaws," *Southwest Utah*, Winter 1993, 15–17.

[13] Maurine Whipple, untitled manuscript, ca. 1942, 4 pp. holograph; BYU, photocopy Dixie College.

[14] Later she commented, "No wonder my Strip novel was not accepted" by Houghton Mifflin. Maurine Whipple, draft of letter to Frank Rhoades, n.d.; BYU, photocopy Dixie College.

[15] Maurine Whipple, Letter to Dean Brimhall, 24 June 1942, Brimhall Papers.

[16] Fawn M. Brodie, Letter to Dale L. Morgan, 22 December 1945, quoted in Newell G. Bringhurst, "Juanita Brooks and Fawn Brodie: Sisters in Mormon Dissent," *Dialogue: A Journal of Mormon Thought* 27, no. 2 (Summer 1994): 116–17.

[17] Undated, unpaginated lecture notes; BYU.

[18] Read Bain, born in 1892 in Utah, was eleven years Maurine's senior, a sociologist and college sociology teacher. Maurine's papers include three letters from him, written between 1942 and 1945 on Sociological Research Association letterhead.

[19] Read Bain, Letter to Maurine Whipple, 30 August 1942; BYU, photocopy Dixie College.

[20] Dr. Philip Lewin, Chicago, Letter to Maurine Whipple, 7 October 1942; BYU, photocopy Dixie College.

[21] "Medicine," *Science*, 12 April 1945, 89.

[22] Read Bain, letter to Maurine Whipple, no day, September 1942; BYU, photocopy Dixie College.

[23] Florence Beck, Chicago, Letter to Maurine Whipple, 5 October 1942: Dixie College. Beck's stationery is printed with her name and address, 116 Tallawanda Road, Oxford, Ohio.

[24] "Utah Writers Get Tips on War Markets; League Round-Up Hears Appeal for True Liberty" undated clipping, Whipple Scrapbook; BYU, photocopy Dixie College. Maurine has written "summer of 1943" in the margin.

[25] George M. Miller, "To Whom It May Concern," n.d.; BYU.

[26] Elizabeth Dedekind, Chicago, Letter to Annie Whipple, 17 November 1942; BYU; photocopy Dixie College.

13

ANOTHER LONG SHOT AT LOVE, 1943

In addition to her wartime lecturing and her slow emotional separation from the disastrous love affair with Tom Spies, Maurine tried to write something saleable, though she was frequently interrupted and could not create the environment that had helped draw *The Giant Joshua* out of her.

During this time, she welcomed the lively correspondence with Read Bain and Dean Brimhall, as they made their socialist and humanist arguments. Maurine surely read and weighed the information they sent, but she had a conflicted relationship with their perspective. Their realism—even cynicism—violated her own most deeply held point of view that the "Grand Idea" was silently and secretly at work in life. In a fundamental way, she did not share their dissenting views. Though unorthodox, she was not an apostate like Fawn Brodie, who had rejected her faith tradition. Nor could she adopt the judicious objectivity with which Juanita Brooks balanced her religious commitment. Maurine's goal was celebration, not analysis. She wanted to give her readers the emotional experience of identifying with her beloved, imperfect people and their gallant reaching for the stars, not an intellectual experience in understanding the social and historical forces at work. She lamented about the "hard work" of thinking for oneself, which is why many want strong authority and a clearly marked path to follow. She often mused to me that she thought, given security and a spiritual hope, people would sacrifice a great deal. "Mormonism gave them what they wanted, and because it did, many hugged their spiritual promises and were willing to stick to a difficult land and a demanding culture."

Probably more important than intellectual compatibility, however, was the fact that the emotionally fragile Maurine was flattered and validated by the interest these sophisticated men took in her work, their serious discussions, and their emotional support. She had obviously confided her heartache to Read Bain, who wrote consolingly in early January 1943, about the same time Dr. Kopiloff was advising her not to meddle any more in Tom Spies's life: "Do your Strip act, but don't take off too much. Do a good honest commercial job—one that will make you $25,000 bucks—what with serial, book, and movie." He assured her that, by establishing a cushion of financial comfort, she could then "write your heart out—and into the trilogy. I think you have some kind of hunger of the heart that only creative work can satisfy. You think you want physical love and a child, but these would never completely satisfy you."[1]

Bain's advice was as sound as Brimhall's and John Peale Bishop's—to make her "swell suffering" an artistic asset. Maurine's mind might agree, but her heart and body didn't. Nor did her self-pity, impracticality, moodiness, real and psychosomatic illnesses, demanding neediness, and exaggeration find the same tolerance from long-suffering parents, wives, and patrons as traditionally male creative excesses do—such as binge drinking, sexual profligacy, and spells of absorption. She did work. There is considerable evidence to show that Maurine was working, more or less simultaneously, on "The Arizona Strip," portions of the trilogy, and a long story, "The Time Will Come," but the promise of these works sputtered and faltered short of the finish line.

In early 1943, her authorship of *The Giant Joshua* brought an invitation to review Wallace Stegner's *Mormon Country* (New York, Buell, Sloan and Pearce, 1942.)[2] The book is a collection of essays on the history and culture of Mormonism, including, for example, the ordeal of the handcart pioneers and the distinctive character of Mormon villages with their Lombardy poplars. Maurine praised it: "*Mormon Country* fascinates you to the end and anyone interested in the Western scene will want to finish the book at one sitting." However, she concluded on a negative note: "He wrote up all the scandals like great comets blazing across the sky but he never even saw the daily unfoldment of life, the little stars which lighted the heavens night after night. He says in one place that the Mormons are not a colorful people: perhaps that is because he never really knew them; or, perhaps, as a collection of Mormon Country tales, this book is doomed to leave the reader dissatisfied because, in the author's own words, it is written about a country 'that breeds the Impossibles.'"[3]

Although she considered herself as keen and unsparing an observer as Stegner, she thought of herself as a true native daughter with the right to criticize her own. She also saw herself as giving equal attention to Mormonism's positive aspects, perhaps not realizing the extent to which her negative comments had already marginalized her in the mind of the people she thought she was defending.

Maurine told a reporter in the summer of 1943, "I have just completed the manuscript of a book on Utah for probable publication this fall, and a western fiction serial for the *Saturday Evening Post*."[4] Both statements appear extremely optimistic. "The Arizona Strip," was never finished. Robert Knowles Hurd, a Utahn also trying to break into Hollywood, whom she asked to read it, candidly told her that she "was not writing like the Maurine I know"—that it was "less than yourself"—by which he probably meant that the predictably conventional romance lacked any distinctive feature. It also had organizational problems: she had not "studied the construction of what was accepted." He thought Knopf was justified in rejecting it.[5] Perhaps Maurine agreed with him, laid it aside, and never had the energy or the technical expertise to solve its problems.

The other work, *This Is the Place: Utah,* an appreciative travel book, would not be ready for publication for another two years. It seems unlikely that she had done more than begun to gather and organize material by the summer of 1943. A statement on a page of undated notes seems to describe the scope of this projected book:

> From the building of the Union Pacific [railroad] down to the formal end of polygamy in 1890, Mormon-gentile discord in Utah was at least as violent, physically and emotionally, as reconstruction in the South. It was all-out war, economic at base (which is not generally understood by people who write about it) but heightened by religious bigotry and ecstasy. It is the principal flavor of life in Utah during these years, it would have to be the leading theme of a historical treatment, and it explains a good deal about [the] present shape of Mormonism and of Utah. This sort of thing should not be minimized. Feeling between Mormons and gentiles (today) as between Northerners and more rabid sort of Southerners? "Let her not brush this feeling away." Mormons have an economic strangle-hold on the whole intermountain region. There are gentiles who don't love that. There is financial, economic, and especially social discrimination on both sides, and it gets pretty tense. Is the war-development, especially the industrialization of Utah, going to affect it? Is it, especially, going to impair the cohesion of the Church? Do not minimize these things.[6]

Maurine, who had turned forty in January 1943, still suffered from a variety of physical complaints, including almost continual colds, respiratory complaints, and painful menstrual periods. Responding to her plea, Joseph Walker on 14 April 1943, sent her twenty-five ampules of progesterone.[7]

"SWELL SUFFERING"

In August 1943, Maurine had her new agent, Harold Ober, approach Knopf with her proposal for *This Is the Place: Utah*. Bernard Smith, representing Knopf, offered a contract with a $500 advance, proposing 1 January 1944 as the tentative delivery date for the manuscript—earlier if she could manage, later if need be. The press did not want a "historical and heavily documented work, but something that would be of interest to Utah's present-day residents, both Mormon and non-Mormon." It should be "easily updated so that it could remain in print for many years."[8]

In September 1943, she visited Dinosaur National Monument in Jensen, Utah, on a research expedition.[9] To overcome the restrictions of wartime travel, she appealed to Colonel Converse R. Lewis, stationed at an army air force base at Kearns in the southwest Salt Lake Valley. He graciously provided transportation and an escort, Staff Sergeant Frank Rhoades. Rhoades was assigned to communications, wrote a regular column for the post's *Barracks Bag*, and also wrote feature articles about women in uniform. Maurine had already met Rhoades at an unspecified writers' conference, perhaps the League of Utah Writers meeting in the summer of 1943, and they had struck up a friendship.[10] She admitted to me that, in her love-starved loneliness, she had tried to see Frank as "talented, a profound thinker, and worthy of my love."

In mid-summer, she also participated in the annual midsummer moonlight hike of Mount Timpanogas at the head of Utah Valley, which drew hundreds and, at its peak, perhaps as many as 5,000 participants.[11] The incident appears in *This Is the Place: Utah* (117–20), but for forty-year-old Maurine to undertake a physically strenuous adventure was typical of her, when she was not paralyzed by illness, depression, or romantic obsession. An undated fragment explains her philosophy: "I look around me at the friends I have who are that old, and I discover that the secret of their contentment is that they took their fill of those things while they were young—they held out both hands to life."[12] She also made several attempts to market her experience on the hike as a separate article, and captured part of the hike in an undated and unfinished letter to an unidentified lover, possibly Frank:

> . . . And at last, as the sky grayed and grew luminous in the East, we pulled ourselves over the final ridge. We watched the sun come up. . . . the people around me suddenly ceased to exist. I was alone. I was conscious of being utterly at peace, and yet I felt more alive than at any other time in my life. And I knew then that I had been chasing false gods all my life. For the first time I knew what in the world was wheat for me and what was chaff. We spend all our days running after things, when what really counts is simplicity—the touch of a hand, the love of trees and rocks and everyday living. That morning on Timpanogas the man beside

me took off his cap and we watched the sun baptize the valley and then the aspen and the pines and the glacier and finally us, and he said, "And men build churches in which to worship."

It was a moving thing to say, but there are some moments too deep for words. If you had been there, you would have understood.[13]

There is no indication that Frank went on the hike with her, despite her reference to "two by two," so it seems natural that she would have written to him about it. Frank was married, so she exercised some caution, hoping that Frank would divorce his wife.

Maurine found significant a telling incident early in their relationship. She had been depressed and was crying. To comfort her, he said, "Don't you think you should have married me?"[14] She apparently did not consider the possibility that he may have been joking in an attempt to cheer her up. She took the words literally and personally, then also transmuted them into a romantic scene in her unfinished "The Golden Door," a political novel set during World War II in which she expressed both patriotic enthusiasm and political idealism. The story is highly autobiographical. In fact, Maurine drew on her doomed relationship with Frank with almost reckless abandon. She casts the novel as a romance between Frank, a cynical newspaper reporter, now in the army, from a neglected background, and Callie (or Clara), "a high school teacher of dramatic art in a small Utah town. Held down by a farmer father who never makes much money, by a sickly mother, by brothers and sisters whom she has felt compelled to help educate, she has never had a chance to try her own wings"—by which she means fall in love, marry, and satisfy her hunger for children.[15] Maurine, while borrowing her own autobiography for Callie's background, made Callie into the physical woman Maurine wished to be: younger, five inches taller (Callie was five feet nine to Maurine's five feet four), and a natural redhead (Maurine hennaed hers). She also puts her own wartime lectures into Callie's mouth. Callie's adored younger brother, a dreamy soul, could not face the thought of the draft and commits suicide.

For his part, Frank is "not a bounder," but "merely the product of his times. Love of friends or family, love of country, love of God—to admit these is to admit weakness. So he hides behind cynicism." The love of a good woman will redeem him: "Building a home, raising a family, the simple, decent, ordinary ways of living—these are longings so submerged that he hardly knows they are there himself until Callie brings them to life. Then for a little time he dares to be himself." Frank represents all servicemen, scarred by their immersion in battle: "The war between his two selves will go on as long as he lives," reads Maurine's character sketch of him. "He is just another man in the world of men, sometimes indifferent, sometimes cruel, sometimes fired with a living faith and a God-like devotion.... His problem is that of a million other servicemen: To pick up one's marbles and go on. If in the going on, a man carries with him some reflection of the glory he caught for a moment, there is hope for humanity."[16]

An idealistic U.S. Senator with a vision of a better world, modeled closely on Utah's Elbert D. Thomas,[17] also tries to help the young soldier after Frank explodes in anger about the unfairness of the younger generation having to fight the older generation's battles and the falsity of the American dream.

Maurine was personally acquainted with Thomas and apparently campaigned for him in a minor way—for instance, writing to Utah friends and asking them to vote for him.[18] In their conversations and correspondence he explained a larger historical context to her, which Maurine gratefully accepted and included in her novel. Dialogue between an idealistic senator and the cynical soldier dominates the center of "The Golden Door." Thomas most likely also influenced Maurine's *Utah*.

In 1945, as the war ended, Maurine's papers include a long finished synopsis and two chapters of the novel; but her correspondence contains no encouraging letters from publishers. Perhaps her timing was off. The combat-weary Americans who might have responded earlier to a thrilling appeal to their patriotism may have now wanted to bask in their victory without philosophizing about it. Furthermore, the pacing of the novel was unsatisfactory as action bogged down into talk. The senator delivers lectures, Callie lectures, and even the romantic relationship is mostly talking.

From late September 1943 until probably January 1944, Maurine stayed in St. George, working on *This Is the Place: Utah*. In one of her long, rambling letters to Frank when she still hoped their relationship could lead to marriage, she confided that she was "learning to cook, collecting a trousseau, and in general, acting entirely different—happy, something I haven't much practice feeling." In explaining what had happened with Tom she said: "I could have got over loving him, you see. It was losing faith in him that hurt.... I was a writer who had lost the power to write. Oh there is no agony like it! And you accuse me of being lazy!"[19]

But Frank didn't write back. Almost certainly he was feeling smothered by Maurine's possessiveness and neediness. An undated and unfinished draft of a letter refers vaguely to some "trouble" Frank was having.[20] And as usual, she overreacted and dashed off to Denver in hot pursuit. (The exact dates are uncertain, but she was there by 9 October.[21]) Frank was initially displeased to see her, but she managed to effect a reconciliation, then returned to St. George, basking in his promise that in "two months" they could be married. He never wrote again.

As she had done with earlier relationships that unraveled, she poured out her agony on paper. She graphically described to him the anxiety, the agonizing strain of waiting, the hopeful daily walk to the post office, the depressing return home without a letter, the suspense and fear building, until finally she began to accept that he had lied to her and that their relationship was over. How long this final step took cannot be calculated from the flood of draft letters, nor is it clear whether she ever sent a finished letter. Drearily, this relationship is a rerun of how earlier relationships had ended. As she had done with other men, she begs at least for friendship. Again there was no response.

She obviously confided the smash-up of her brief affair with Frank Rhoades to Read Bain, who wished she would not take the failures of her romances so hard. He comforted her: "Lots of love affairs don't jell, but they are all fun and terribly thrilling." Then he warned her to appreciate her capacity to fall in love. "Every time you do, your capacity for love—and for living and understanding life should be increased."[22]

She could not afford to lose herself in suffering. Knopf's January deadline for *This Is the Place: Utah* was advancing inexorably toward her. In early October, Maurine wrote Dean Brimhall that she had read the book to a group of St. George people consisting of Juanita Brooks, Pearson Corbett, John T. Woodbury, and Jean Hafen, and "they all liked it."[23]

Giving a few insights into her progress is some correspondence with Norman Nevills, a professional Colorado River guide, living in Mexican Hat, San Juan County, Utah. Mexican Hat, twenty-four miles west of Bluff, Utah, is tucked into Utah's southeastern corner, twenty-two miles south of Monument Valley and only forty-four miles from the Natural Bridges National Monument. Norman was helping her with pictures and information about the Colorado River country that lay in Utah. Maurine had particularly wanted to take a boat trip up the Colorado River to see Rainbow Bridge, a free-standing sandstone arch, and photograph it for her book. Norman had apparently set up such an excursion in early October. Maurine had declined that trip but wanted to be included on the next one.

On 21 October 1943, she sent Norman another note from St. George explaining that she had left the Hotel Utah abruptly "that night" because George, who was on a furlough, had been recalled to his unit and she had also received a telegram from "the sergeant" (Frank) telling her that he was being shipped out immediately to New York.

Norman wrote back on 31 October 1943, saying that "December 10 would be perfect for the trip." He had arranged for P. W. Tompkins, a photographer, to provide some visual images and wanted Maurine to be sure that Tompkins received the credit.

Enthusiastically, he wrote: "Regardless of where you've been or what you've seen, the big thrill in scenery is yet to come!" He also passed on a compliment from his wife, Jean, who had heard Maurine lecture and was so enthralled that "the time simply whirled by." He shared Maurine's vision for promoting Utah scenery and summarized: "We need, all over the state, more awareness and publication of what we really have. Utah is in a position to become the 'Playground'—all it needs is the proper handling. We are bound to be the better off all over here for the contacts we make thru an influx of scenic minded travelers. If we can get all the people in the future travel areas to get their minds off the almighty dollar and to concentrate more on really developing each section with an eye to preserving the naturalness—then we'll have something."[24]

Maurine managed to fit in a hurried trip to Rainbow Bridge before the end of 1943, but she remembered it as a strenuous experience that left her with pneumonia. In *This Is the Place, Utah*, she uses two photographs of the bridge.[25]

Year's end found her struggling with illness, her second failed love affair within a year, and a book that had not yet been finished. Worse, on 15 December 1943, her beloved younger brother Ralph, "the sweetest person who ever lived," was killed in a freak accident when a pulley in the lumberyard whipped back, hit him, and broke his neck. He lived long enough to be carried into the house and laid on the kitchen table. Maurine sometimes told this story as if she were there, which seems unlikely; but she certainly told the story in gruesome detail.

Now she was lonelier than ever.

Notes

[1] Read Bain, Oxford, Ohio, Letter to Maurine Whipple, 5 January 1943, Maurine Whipple Collection, L. Tom Perry Special Collections, Harold B. Lee Library, Brigham Young University, Provo, Utah, with photocopy in Maurine Whipple Collection,

Archive, Val A. Browning Library, Dixie College, St. George, Utah. Documents in both collections are hereafter cited as BYU, photocopy Dixie College.

2 Wallace Stegner (1909–93) was a respected novelist, biographer, essayist, short story writer (won three O. Henry prizes) and teacher of writing at the University of Utah, University of Wisconsin, Harvard University, and Stanford University where he founded and, until 1971, directed a writing program that has had a profound effect upon contemporary American fiction.

3 Maurine Whipple, Review, *Saturday Review of Literature*, 2 January 1943, Whipple Scrapbook, BYU.

4 "Utah Writers Get Tips on War Markets; League Round-Up Hears Appeal for True Liberty," n.d., unidentified newspaper, Whipple Scrapbook, BYU. Maurine wrote "summer of 1943" in the margin.

5 Robert Knowles Hurd, Hollywood, California, Letter to Maurine Whipple, 8 February 1945; BYU, photocopy Dixie College.

6 Untitled statement, n.d., ca. 1943; BYU.

7 Joseph Walker, Letter to Maurine Whipple, 14 April 1943; BYU, photocopy Dixie College.

8 Bernard Smith, Letter to Maurine Whipple, 13 August 1943; BYU, photocopy Dixie College.

9 Ernest Unterman, ranger and park director, Letter to J. H. McGibbeny, secretary of the Salt Lake City Chamber of Commerce, 6 September 1943; BYU, photocopy Dixie College, suggested that it would be best if Maurine didn't quote the Seventh-day Adventist George McCreadie Price as saying that "the dinosaurs became extinct because Noah refused them admittance to the ark."

10 Maurine Whipple, Letter to Frank Rhoades, n.d.; BYU, photocopy Dixie College, mentioned that they had met at "the writer's conference" and that she "had gotten a big boost from him."

11 Eugene Roberts organized the first annual Timpanogas/Timpanogos hike. Charles James Hart Sr. directed it from 1929 to 1961.

12 Untitled statement, n.d., holograph; BYU, photocopy Dixie College.

13 Untitled letter draft, no correspondent identified, n.d.; emphasis Maurine's; BYU, photocopy Dixie College.

14 Maurine quotes these words in the draft of a letter to Frank Rhoades, n.d.; BYU, photocopy Dixie College.

15 Maurine Whipple, "The Golden Door," typescript, prologue; BYU, photocopy Dixie College.

16 Maurine Whipple, Character sketch of Frank, n.d.; BYU, photocopy Dixie College.

17 Elbert Duncan Thomas (1883–1953) a Democrat, replaced Reed Smoot, Utah's long-time (1932–51) Republican senator. In Congress, Thomas chaired the Committee on Education and Labor for three sessions, the Committee on Military Affairs, and the Committee on Labor and Public Welfare. He served as high commissioner of U.S. trust territories of the Pacific from 1951 until his death in 1953.

Biographical Dictionary of the United State Congress 1774–1989, Bicentennial Ed. (Washington, D.C.: U.S. Government Printing Office, 1976), 1926–27.

[18] Earl Sylvester, Virgin, Utah, Letter to Maurine Whipple, n.d.; BYU, photocopy Dixie College, comments on Maurine's request for him to support Thomas for reelection.

[19] Maurine Whipple, Letter to Frank Rhoades, n.d., emphasis hers; BYU, photocopy Dixie College.

[20] Maurine Whipple, Letter to Frank Rhoades, n.d. but after November 1943; BYU, photocopy Dixie College.

[21] Maurine Whipple, Telegram to Norman Nevills, 9 October 1943, Norman Nevills Papers, Special Collections, Marriott Library, University of Utah, Salt Lake City, photocopy at Dixie College Archive.

[22] Read Bain, Letter to Maurine Whipple, ca. 1942 or 1943; BYU, photocopy Dixie College.

[23] Maurine Whipple, Letter to Dean Brimhall, 9 October 1944, Dean Brimhall Papers, Special Collections, Marriott Library, University of Utah, Salt Lake City (hereafter Brimhall Papers); photocopy Dixie College Archive.

[24] Norman Nevills, Letter to Maurine Whipple, 31 October 1943, Nevills Papers, Special Collections, Marriott Library, University of Utah, Salt Lake City; photocopy at Dixie College Archive.

[25] Whipple, *This Is the Place: Utah* (New York: Alfred A. Knopf, 1945), 114–15. A color photograph appears facing p. 55, with the courtesy line: "Photograph contributed by Norman Nevills, through the courtesy of P. W. Tompkins, and financed by the citizens of Kanab, the last town on Utah's route to Rainbow Bridge" (55). A black and white photograph is "supplied by Utah State Publicity and Industrial Development Committee" (75). Nevills's name is misspelled as "Nevill" in the text and acknowledgments (114, 219).

14

THIS IS THE PLACE: UTAH

As 1945 opened, Maurine forced herself to work on *This Is the Place: Utah* and retreated from passionate romance into a safer friendship with a tortured poet, Bill Battrick. (See chap. 15.)

In March 1944, Juanita Brooks told Dale Morgan that Ferris Greenslet was interested in her autobiography as a candidate for Houghton Mifflin's "American" series, carrying with it a $2,500 award, with half as an advance on royalties.[1] It is likely that Maurine knew about this offer. In contrast, she had received only $1,000 for *The Giant Joshua*, all advanced from royalties. Always quick to see herself as a victim, she must have bitterly resented Greenslet for turning to someone else for books on southern Utah. Carrying that slight, she continued to try to become the foremost expert on Utah. As was her wont, she wrote to friends whom she thought might be influential in helping her solve problems. Evidently, in April she complained about Knopf, who had committed to publishing a travel book about Utah, to Levi Edgar Young, a General Authority (one of the First Council of the Seventy) and professor of western history at the University of Utah. In late April, Young promised "to write Mr. Knopf and tell him what I think of your JOSHUA. It is a splendid work and will take its place high up in Western literature."[2] It is not clear how this compliment would do more than assure Knopf that Maurine was well-regarded by knowledgeable insiders in her home state.

In addition to stress from her publisher's expectations, Maurine was also feeling pressure from those closer to home with great expectations for *This Is the Place: Utah*. She had persuaded business people throughout Utah to supply her with material and photographs, promising that their cooperation would result in increased business for them. Many of these people had gone to considerable expense and effort to help her and were waiting for the

Maurine about 1944, her "pert" green hat looking considerably bedraggled. Apparently the photo was taken for publicity related to the University of Utah since the unidentified young woman is wearing the sweater of the Spurs, a service sorority. Photo by John Peterson.

book to pay off as advertisement for their area. She was also concerned, rightly so, as it turned out, that Mormon authorities would be angry about some of the things she had included. In her eagerness to research and report every possibility, she had been tactless.

Juanita Brooks wrote Dale Morgan in a huff: "I told her to lay off the subject [the Mountain Meadow Massacre]. She can't quote anything and knows nothing of sources, but she will try to re-tell and will garble everything."[3] Maurine wisely did not mention the Mountain Meadows Massacre.

On 27 July 1944, Maurine wrote a long, chatty letter to Norman Nevills, which was mostly a progress report on *This Is the Place: Utah*. She also complained about a frustrating series of obstacles. For instance, "H. J. Plumhof of the Utah State Publicity Committee had assured her the state would provide "$1500 for kodachromes of Southern Utah scenes," but Maurine would need to lobby the state legislature for the money. In the fall of 1943, Maurine had gone to Salt Lake City and stayed in a hotel at her own expense while she met with the necessary officials.[4] She told Nevills that "when Plumhof read the manuscript, he reacted in a completely unexpected way. A non-Mormon, he is afraid of losing his job if the book made the Church angry." As a result, Plumhof "refused to honor the contract." Regardless of the facts of this tale of paranoia and sectional politics, Maurine was physically and emotionally exhausted. She was also financially depleted and, she told Nevills, had borrowed money from the bank.[5]

The Utah book is 215 pages long, including two double-spread maps, 111 black-and-white photographs, and four colored photographs. There are four additional pages of introduction and four pages of acknowledgements,[6] plus an index to illustrations. It is arranged in four chapters: "Do They Really have Horns?", "Hell of a Place to Lose a Cow," "A Peculiar People," and "The Arsenal of Democracy." Maurine's photo is on the fly leaf. In it, she is wearing the hat with the long pheasant feather she bought for her first visit to Houghton Mifflin in 1938.

The first chapter "Do They Really Have Horns?" embellishes the story Maurine liked to tell about riding up to Salt Lake City to go to college with a "Gentile." She then follows it with an autobiographical summary of her maturation in her dealing with her Mormon upbringing. She confessed the advantages of the Gentiles: better clothes, better manners, more money. "For a God who loved only Mormons," she began to wonder, "He was suspiciously nice to a lot of unchosen people." Then in a passage that is unquestionably among her best writing, she tells of driving down Emigration Canyon with a non-Mormon date after a dance and parking beside the road where they have the first view of the valley: "Staring at the valley below, I suddenly felt myself caught up in a communal memory so much a part of my very blood that I forgot the boy beside me." She imagined she was there with Brigham Young when he first viewed the valley and uttered the words. "This is the place. Drive on."

Alfred A. Knopf had already published ten other "state" books in its Borzoi Books on the American Scene.[7] The series' purpose was to be a reference for visitors to each state. Maurine's book did that, but it also delivered a telling insight into her life and her attitudes—Maurine, the poor, naive, southern Utah daughter of polygamy-raised parents, struggling with her personal dilemma set against a larger world. The writing is reminiscent of the best in *The Giant Joshua*. Many parts sang beautifully the praises of Mormon culture, "Togetherness and greenness and orderliness—these were the warp and wool of Brigham's pattern" (31); but other passages were more critical: "I know. You don't have to be crazy to be a Mormon, but it helps" (24). Maurine never thought of herself as an apostate. She always thought she was trying to help her much-persecuted people be appreciated by a wider world for having "acquired the ability to retain a specific culture without relinquishing allegiance to the larger whole. They have learned the lesson of Diversity within Unity" (15). As a writer, she selected the strategy of presenting "Paradoxical Utah" (170), but unfortunately, it backfired. After acknowledging Utah's clannishness and nepotism, she wrote wryly: "There are Mormons who resent being whitewashed, who prefer the truth . . . but if you convinced them of a fact, they would come back with 'But you wouldn't want the *gentiles* to find that out!'" She thought these duplicitously liberal Mormons should face the fact that "these same gentiles have already heard all about 'that' and worse versions" (173).

Regardless of Maurine's criticism of Mormonism, if anyone understood the power and the nobility of its Grand Idea, Maurine did. "The church has always inspired a remarkable devotion in the hearts of her followers," she wrote. "Wherever you find them, Mormons display a family-like cohesion and loyalty. One Mormon scholar has pointed out that not once did the Prophet Joseph ask for personal allegiance; his counsel to his people was always for them to love the truth, to love the church, rather than any human being who might be at her head. And this spirit prevails with the vast majority of Mormons today" (175).

But loyal and orthodox Mormons, with a hundred years of touchiness behind them, overreacted to uncomplimentary facts and could easily see Maurine as disloyal. Ironically, Maurine genuinely experienced Utah and Mormonism as much the same and angrily resisted when her publishers tried to broaden her focus. She later complained that her book had been "killed by the Mormon Church because the publishers insisted that I include a chapter on the Utah gentiles."[8] She hoped she could be seen as a respected family member pointing out faults that, if worked on, could make an already good thing better. However, even in her old age, she did not understand that a first-time visitor to Utah did not need to be taken straight from the front porch into the family fights in the kitchen.

Chapter 3, "A Peculiar People," was particularly infuriating for her more orthodox LDS readers when they came across statements like: "the church hadn't kept pace with the times," "too much priestly power," "holy jockeying for advantage," "senility bottlenecking progress," "nepotism," "censorship," "political interference," "tithing misuse," "expurgating its history," "word-of-wisdom hypocrisy," "fawning over celebrities," etc. Perhaps her most unpopular passage among Mormon insiders was her criticism of how it spent its money. "Many Mormons feel that the church is losing her spiritual strength and becoming just another high-powered financial institution," she began. The tithes of the faithful are not reserved to help the poor and aged, but to build "an office building with marble-and onyx-walled rooms and lobby flanked by sixteen marble columns costing $3,000 apiece. In 1940 the church spent $2,271,409 for buildings alone." While paying tribute to the "excellence" of work done by seminaries and institutes, Maurine pointed out the price tag: "nearly a million dollars a year" (171).

The Church Security Plan (welfare program), established in the 1930s to take "Mormons off federal relief during the depression," had received much publicity for taking care of its own; but Maurine, without citing Dean Brimhall's research, asserted that the Church was simultaneously "accepting tithing out of federal relief pay checks." She cites a study by Louis Worth, University of Chicago sociologist, proving that "the government had to spend more relief money in Utah in proportion to her population than in any of the other Western states" (172). She accused, "It seems never to have occurred to church leaders that if it is proper for the church to pension them in their old age (most substantially, too) in payment for years of service, perhaps society owes every worn-out working man or woman the same obligation. The Church Security Program cannot take the place of government relief agencies. Mormons will tell you that it provides food but not the self-respect of forty dollars a month" (172).

Even more boldly, she pointed out that Reed Smoot had voted for the Boulder Dam Enabling Act, which specified that the power it generated "might flow into Nevada, Arizona and California, but not into adjacent Utah mines or communities." Why? "The Utah Power and Light Company (owned by Eastern interests, but church-dominated) wanted no competition. Certainly the church put up no battle for the cheap power that would have revolutionized the lives of its common people" (172).

"SWELL SUFFERING"

Perhaps Maurine saw herself as speaking for the marginalized Mormon intellectual community—for the Joseph Walkers, Dean Brimhalls, and Read Bains—when she wrote: "There are two kinds of contemporary Saints. There are the ignorant and lazy, who cling to blind unreasoning obedience, and those others who think for themselves. Today in Utah if you had an omnipotent eye that could penetrate houses of teachers, thinkers, scholars, you would see a medieval gathering. For it is medieval when people must assemble behind locked doors and drawn blinds to speak their minds. Just as surely as the knitting women counted, there is a revolution going on in Mormondom" (174). The fact remains that, however much they might have been pleased to see their opinions being aired, it was Maurine, not they, who was putting her professional neck on the chopping block.

Maurine sent the manuscript off to Bernard Smith at Knopf in July 1944. Next came sixteen months of frustrating delays—many of them caused by Maurine herself, as she fought with editors assigned to the project about their requests to cut material and their insistence that she add more facts that would not be complimentary to the Church.

After finally getting his hands on the finished manuscript, Smith wrote to Maurine, saying that "they were satisfied," that "they were right about the severe cutting and compressing," and that the photographs, most of them by Randall Jones, were "excellent." Smith explained at the end of his letter: "Surely you can understand why we have to be so meticulous."[9] Maurine flared up at the adjective, as if it were an accusation that she had been sloppy. Typically, she overreacted.

Instead of trying to work things out with Bernard Smith, she wrote directly to the company's president, Alfred A. Knopf. After a token apology for "going over Smith's head," she complained that Smith "did not understand the possibility of what could happen to the book, let alone myself, because of the power structure of the state." She felt that her suggestions were "going unheeded" and suspected that Smith "wasn't even reading her letters." Then she outlined five objections to the editing: First, she "felt an obligation to the knowledgeable people of Utah who had helped make sure the captions for the photographs were correct and who felt their suggestions should be used, even if it did make the editor, Mr. Smith, upset to change his final selection." Second, "Mr. Smith had been unfair about the maps not realizing the effort made to produce an up-to-date one." Because he had rejected the first one, she had had influential people from southern Utah pressure the Road Commission to make another at considerable cost, and she said "they better use it or my creditability will be in jeopardy." (She won this fight. The map in the front shows roads throughout the state, in addition to towns, rivers, mountains, and parks.) Third, she felt her wording in several places "was better and more accurate" than the editing. "'Brilliantly quilted into eight miles square' was more accurate than 'eight square miles' and the fact that the Salt Lake valley is laid out in squares does warrant the word 'quilted' to describe the light pattern at night." (Maurine also won that battle. See p. 57.) Fourth, she objected to the way some of the conversations had been punctuated and paragraphed. Fifth, she did not want to cut the paragraph about Joseph Smith, which Bernard Smith had found irrelevant, because "without a Joseph Smith there would not be a Utah as it was."[10]

Maurine and Smith must have reached an acceptable compromise relatively quickly, for in August she left her fight and apparently went to Hollywood again.[11] If she did, she was probably casting about for anything that might make money: selling the movie rights to *The Giant Joshua*, finding a publisher or movie producer for "The Golden Door" or "The Arizona Strip," a position as a scriptwriter, etc. Nothing apparently came of any efforts.

On 9 October, she told Dean Brimhall that "Knopf had been unable to get engravers, printers, and technicians, because of the war," suggesting that she had sent in her revision, probably during September 1944. She had also told Brimhall that she had applied to join the Red Cross and Office of War Information (OWI). Because of her health problems, neither accepted her.

On 31 October 1944, she received a royalty check for $100 from Houghton Mifflin.[12] Maurine was in debt and this sum didn't go very far. Her financial worries no doubt increased the stress that made it difficult for her to work productively.

In 1991 conversations with me, she repeatedly explained why she had put so much effort into the Utah book. She saw it as continuing the work she had commenced with *The Giant Joshua* and was trying to bring into focus with her war-bond lectures. She truly thought "it would last for fifty to a hundred years, with updates made every few years. It would go all over the world, be translated into many languages. Utah would not have a chance like that again and just maybe the Church needed to have a few facts brought into the open."

Elden Beck, whose friendship had been an enduring feature in her life since 1939, was on Guam in the fall of 1944. She sent him a copy of her war-bond lecture. On 1 November 1944, he thanked her, saying he had "sent it the rounds among the men" and a Jewish captain, a physician, had been "particularly impressed." In his opinion she was getting a chance to express her ideals, "the way Clory would have done."[13]

It was an astute compliment. On some level, Clory *was* Maurine—Maurine with the additional traits she longed for: the unshakable dignity, the charm, the winsome femininity that could flirt and tease without being taken advantage of. Those who knew Maurine probably wished she also demonstrated more of Clory's stoicism. But realizing how closely Maurine identified with Clory helps explain why there was no romantic ending with Clory as an adored and cherished wife, despite her merits. Maurine was writing from her heart in portraying that doomed and rebellious gallantry. However, it would not have been Clory's conviction that she should set the Brethren straight with a few home truths.

Maurine was genuinely anxious about the impact of *This Is the Place: Utah* on her reputation. In early November 1944, she telegraphed Bernard Smith, then followed up with a letter asking to have even more input. Her second thoughts at this stage obviously tried his patience, and he wrote back: "I do not want to enter into a transcontinental argument with you." Her book had "taken more time, effort and worry than any other book coming through my office in years." Still, he agreed that he and his co-workers had done the editing "not with an eye to the Utah sale, but to the national and general interest." He just wanted her to say clearly what she wanted.[14] Unfortunately, Maurine's bill of particulars has not survived, except for a comment in another letter from Smith that no photograph of J. Rueben Clark would appear. Neither would Church President's Heber J. Grant "because it would date the book."[15] The book was released, far behind schedule, in November 1945.

In retrospect, *This Is the Place: Utah*, despite Maurine's high hopes, probably had no chance to provide her with a comfortable income. Historian Dale Morgan, a realistic observer, had told Juanita Brooks in the summer of 1943 that the book was a good idea but wouldn't be a "sensational occurrence on the book market. If Maurine must have easy money, she should take to safe cracking."[16] He was right. She had spent months of intensive effort on it but claimed that it never brought in more than six or seven hundred dollars, which didn't even cover her expenses.

In late January 1946, less than three months after its release, Bernard Smith informed her that Knopf had sold a chapter for reprint in *Science Digest* for $50 to be shared equally by Knopf and Maurine. However, sales of the book were "modest and slow," and Knopf was "not contemplating reprinting."[17]

What Maurine lived on during the winter of 1944–45 is not clear. When her six-month royalty check arrived from Houghton Mifflin in late April 1945, it was a paltry $53.47.[18] Her financial situation was desperate. Instead of working, however, she seemed to have spent most of her energy trying to find a new agent. According to her memory in 1991, she asked Bernard DeVoto for advice and he gave her two names, neither of whom became her agent. She had probably wanted to know the secret of his success in writing magazine serials. Under the pseudonym of John August, he had made $20,000 on three separate serials.[19] Her papers contain no letters to or from him, but she liked to tell about how courteous and helpful he was to her, a naive beginner from DeVoto's home state. Maurine found an agent through Hughie Call, the wife of a Montana sheepman. Call had been impressed by the scene in *The Giant Joshua* of Kissy's death, and Houghton Mifflin had published her *The Golden Fleece* (1942), a fictionalized account of her own daughter's death. According to Maurine in 1991, Hughie considered *The Giant Joshua* "an experience matched by none other." Hughie made a trip to Utah expressly to see Maurine, whom she assumed was also a bereaved mother. Maurine and Hughie became friends on the spot and corresponded for a few years. In the spring of 1945, Hughie referred Maurine to her own agent in New York, Maximillian ("Max") Becker of the A.F.G. Literary Agency.

Max accepted Maurine as a client and soon got his first taste of how difficult the relationship would be. Even though, as far as we know, Ferris Greenslet still wanted the sequel to *The Giant Joshua*, Maurine instead tried to interest him in "The Golden Door," which he promptly refused. Maurine wrote Becker a lengthy, outraged letter on 22 May 1945 that is almost hysterical in her frustration and accusations.[20]

Yet it was also typical of Maurine not to succumb to negativism, despite her melodramatic plunges into it, but to shake off defeat. As she often told people, "I could end up laughing at myself, my damned-fool self, and find a way to go on." Unfortunately, her suffering usually did not seem to bring her wisdom, and this emotional resilience came at the cost of reworking her past in such a way that she plunged forward into a future of the same mistakes.

Becker's reply is not among Maurine's papers. If he knew Greenslet personally or had had dealings with Houghton Mifflin, he must have taken Maurine's accusations with a grain of salt. If he was an experienced literary agent, he probably also took overwrought authors in his stride as well.

On 15 May 1945, Maurine had written Norman Nevills telling him: "I am still trying to get out to see you and your San Juan country."[21] Apparently she succeeded. In *This Is the Place: Utah*, she mentioned Harry and Mike Goulding, the husband and wife who ran the trading post in Monument Valley (108–13). She probably planned to write a feature article about them. She could explain such jaunts as both research and public relations, but probably she was also simply restless, fidgety, unable to settle down and work systematically, and she did like to travel and see Utah's back country.

This Is the Place: Utah was finally released on November 22, 1945. At first it received good advertising from the Salt Lake City stores least connected with the Church: J. C. Penney's and Auerbach's. Maurine remembered autographing copies at Penney's. Dale Morgan's influential review in the *Saturday Review of Literature* published that same month praised Maurine's "matchless eye for the sensuous splendor of the red rock country, an impetuous, not to say explosive, interest in people, a shrewd and sometimes summary skepticism." However, he also embarrassed and hurt her by pointing out that she had taken "a number of the *Utah Guide's* best lines and webbed them into her work without benefit of quotation marks, and she has an unexpressed major indebtedness to Nels Anderson's discerning book on Utah's frontier era, *Desert Saints*."22

Juanita Brooks, according to her biography, was "amused" when she read the review, which, in her biographer's words, "bluntly accused Whipple of having plagiarized significant portions" of Morgan's commentary. (*Utah Guide* has no identified author, like other WPA projects, but Dale Morgan had oversight of the project and was widely known as responsible for its final form.) Juanita wrote Morgan that Maurine had visited her after Thanksgiving, angrily defending herself. "I told her I thought she could well let it stand as it was, . . . but she insists that she did not borrow."23

Unsatisfied by Juanita's reaction, Maurine followed up on December 7 with a letter of protest to Morgan. "I am sorry you think I have stooped to plagiarism." She explained that she had consulted more than two hundred books and pamphlets and that "there simply wasn't room" to include so extensive a bibliography in what was "frankly a travel book for tourists." She asserted that she had credited Juanita's work in her text "four or five times" and denied using *Desert Saints* at all except for "read[ing] it some years ago."

In her closing paragraph, she invited him to "point out the paragraphs or sentences in *This Is the Place* that you think need quotation marks" and offered to make corrections in "the next edition."24

Even though she addressed this letter to Morgan, she apparently sent it, not to him, but to Knopf, who promptly forwarded it to Morgan. Affronted by this end-run, which he called "dishonest squash" in a letter to Juanita, Morgan, who was in Arlington, Virginia, responded to Maurine's invitation with a four-page single-spaced letter dated December 15, 1945, terming her letter "disingenuous in some degree and irrelevant in large part" and characterizing his own review as "let[ting] you down easy . . . for you left yourself open for some exceedingly disagreeable comment by any critic ill-disposed toward you or your book." He also observed quite neutrally that he attributed her "misuse of copyrighted sources" to the same methods of composition she had used in *The Giant Joshua*—but with a crucial difference. Drawing on "copyrighted texts" with the same freedom employed in her use of manuscript materials "is not done, for ethical as well as for legal reasons.

I have never criticized the literary methods of *The Giant Joshua*, and I do not now. But I will criticize you or anyone else for non-fiction work which utilizes copyrighted material without credit." He dismissed her defense of the missing bibliography by saying it "was neither expected nor required" and countered that, rather than citing the *Utah Guide* four or five times, she had cited it exactly twice and had mangled at least one of those citations.

Without animus, he added an even-handed acknowledgment: "If you had made a proper gesture of acknowledgment, I should have passed by even the most flagrant of these borrowings, for the *Utah Guide* was conceived and written to be a germinal influence in writing about Utah and the Mormons; moreover, your freedom in writing under a personal byline enabled you in some instances to make improvements on the original which would justify a generous attitude toward your use of the *Guide* text." While dates and statistics are, naturally, impossible to paraphrase, he listed twenty borrowings, none of them properly attributed.[25]

Only in Morgan's concluding paragraphs did he sound a note of strong exasperation. After pointing out that Maurine had drawn so heavily on the *Utah Guide* for some chapters, including its "whole tone and temper, . . . chapter titles and avenues of approach," he concluded, "you could not have written your book without its aid. . . . It does not well become you, then, to ignore the extent of this indebtedness in your acknowledgments and to write me as though the Guide were indistinguishable in your mind from two-hundred odd other books you say you drew upon." He also obviously resented the fact that he had "devoted a number of hours to this letter which might better have gone into productive work of my own." Still, his last sentence is a rebuke wrapped in a high compliment: "You can write, with passion, brains, and skill, and there is no reason why you shouldn't do so independently, without living on the fat of other people's minds."[26]

Obviously, her proper response would have been to admit her guilt, apologize, and promise to mend her ways. Why didn't she? She desperately wanted to be liked, and even valid and not unkind criticism left her smarting with resentment and desolate with what she perceived as rejection. She was so well-intentioned. She had tried so hard to be friends with Morgan. Why didn't he treat her according to those intentions and just *like* her instead of criticizing mistakes she had never intended to make? Surely her three and a half pages of individuals and institutions in the acknowledgments is evidence of her sincerity in trying to give credit where credit was due.

But Morgan was astute when he correctly identified her methods as essentially those of a fictionalist, not a historian, even when her subject was historical. A post-modernist long before her time, Maurine either did not or could not (I suspect the latter) maintain boundaries. She reinvented herself endlessly, according to her audience. Similarly, she did not or could not maintain boundaries that differentiated between her own material and that of other people. Part of the feeling of reality in her fiction resulted from this technique. Boundaries would stymie her kind of genius. Perhaps she did not understand what constituted plagiarism. Even though Morgan's definition is crystal clear and was certainly widely accepted at the time Maurine was writing and she *should* have understood it as he did, she simply didn't "get it." She wrote in the preface: "This book is intended to speak for countless voiceless Utahns through the years. It is my gift to the people of Utah." To have so meticulous a historian as Dale Morgan point out a serious lack of professionalism was crushing.

Writing in late December to Dale Morgan, Juanita Brooks noted that Maurine had gone to Salt Lake City, announcing plans to write her new book: "She severed diplomatic relations with me when your review first came out. . . . She has never been back nor spoken to me since. I don't mind, really. I know that when she needs something that I can help her with she will come, soon enough."[27]

Juanita sounds good-natured, even affectionate in this letter. When I read Peterson's account of the tiff over the review to Maurine in 1991, she had some uncomplimentary adjectives for Juanita: "drab, plodding, secretive, playing both sides of the fence." But as usual after one of these outbursts, Maurine spoke wistfully about Juanita—said she loved her, was grateful for Juanita's frequent kindnesses, and would have liked to have been "best friends." Sitting with Maurine, I felt a pang about might-have-beens. Although the barriers of style and working approach between historian and novelist were very real, if there had been a way for the three—Brooks, Morgan, and Whipple—to enhance each other's strengths instead of exasperating each other into retreating, both the history and the fiction of Utah might have leaped to a new plateau.

But Dale Morgan's review was only part of Maurine's problem. As she feared, the reaction in Utah fulfilled her most paranoid nightmares. The book's poor sales convinced her that J. Reuben Clark had made a personal crusade of discouraging sales in Utah. About three months after *Utah*'s publication, she reported to Dean Brimhall in February 1946: "*Deseret News* gave the Utah book a send-off. . . . But Z.C.M.I. and Deseret Book Store are still selling 'under the counter' both my book and Fawn [Brodie]'s. . . . J. Rueben Clark was so furious because I said free speech was lacking in Utah that he fired the kid who wrote the favorable review in the *Deseret News* and banned the book's sale in Z.C.M.I. and even put pressure on the Tribune." She added that she "liked Fawn's book and thought Fawn had done a magnificent job" but that Fawn was "being boiled in oil and fasted and prayed over."28 Brodie had been summarily excommunicated a few months earlier for her controversial, naturalistic biography about Joseph Smith: *No Man Knows My History* (New York: Alfred A. Knopf, 1945).

Much of what Maurine claims as official but surreptitious suppression of her work cannot be substantiated. In other cases, as the notes show, it can be disproved. Certainly it is possible that access to other records will one day adjust her highly colored picture. However, the national public reaction and the personal letters she received tell a far more positive story.

Harry Hansen, whom she met in New York when *The Giant Joshua* was published, titled his review of *Utah*: "Mormons Are Peculiar: Maurine Whipple Whips Up More about Them and Their Country." He identified some of the peculiarities as stemming from Brigham Young's desire to keep Utah isolated and agricultural, then he recapped some of Maurine's points about the strengths of Mormon society.29

An anonymously authored review from the *Philadelphia Inquirer*, called it "a fascinating history, and what Miss Whipple herself calls a 'peculiar people.' The people, no longer Mormon or gentile, are Americans and perhaps 'even something more . . . For Brigham's vision of Utopia has outgrown the Great Basin. It is world-size.'"30

The *Boston Herald* commented, "Miss Whipple's own mood is one of blitheness and even whimsicality. Thus her volume has a higher entertainment value than its rather dreary prospectus would indicate. This is a book to be read with Wallace Stegner's 'Mormon Country,' not in place of it."31

The *Salt Lake Tribune* review called *This Is the Place: Utah*, "a classic book on Utah. . . . Born in St. George, a Mormon herself, sympathetic to her own people, yet, as an artist, she is able to look at them objectively. . . . She has produced a piece of literature which is alive and glowing, a beautifully written panorama of the state and its people. Humor embroiders the account, old tales are revived—and Miss Whipple discusses with calm logic the many clashes between Utah's Mormons and the encroaching Gentiles."32

The most uncomplimentary review appeared in the *Chicago Sun*: "This sales promotion reaches its climax in Miss Whipple's patriotic pronouncement that Mormons and Gentiles in Utah have forgotten their differences in a blissful wave of win-the-war Americanism. That may be what the American tourist thinks but I doubt if it is true and I question whether it would be desirable if it were. For is it not very wonderfully to Utah's credit that the descendants of the Saints have resisted as much as they have the pattern of 'Americanism' whose focal points are Hollywood, Detroit, Radio City and Washington?"33 This reviewer and Maurine saw "Americanism" differently. To Maurine it carried noble and heroic connotations, to the reviewer overtones of shoddy culture.

The *Ogden Standard-Examiner* review pointed out errors in the captions for the Devil's Slide (44) and Pine River Dam (58), in northern Utah and also identified some of the statements that "rubbed folks the wrong way."[34]

Individuals also responded, many of them warmly positive. A welcome letter came from Elbert D. Thomas, then serving on the Senate's Committee on Military Affairs: "First of all, the book is as it should be—definitely Maurine's Utah. The trouble with most books is that most authors try to write somebody else's book."[35]

Joseph and Tina Walker were giving her book as Christmas presents, and Joe wittily predicted how the book would be accepted in St. George: "It won't be long until they will deny the presence of sandburs, devilgrass, prickly pears and briers there in the early days. Well, life is pretty much a matter of those who build legends and those who demolish them. And without legend builders you and I would live a monotonous life."[36]

Read Bain, to whom Maurine evidently complained at the book's negative reception, fumed angrily: "Probably nothing since Joe's last revelation has done the Church so much good as *Joshua* to present it in a heroic light and to make people feel kindly toward it and proud of it—as a peculiar American element in the Great Epic of Oddities that is the American Ethos. *This Is the Place* will do the same."[37]

St. George friend Anna Carter Cox loyally wrote that she was "thrilled beyond words" with *This Is the Place: Utah*. "Our state is stupid not to give it and you more publicity. This little town should pay you to stay."[38] The Harris sisters, Edith, Lou, and Evelyn, probably felt much the same. The enduring friendship of these women, securely part of the town's "respectable" Mormon culture, meant a lot to Maurine. When I interviewed Anna, then age eighty-two, in the spring of 1991, she described how she and Maurine often went for long walks and talked of many things. She considered herself Maurine's "most intimate" friend, yet Maurine had never confided to Anna the rape in Latuda, her first heartbreak over Hyrum Lee, or any of the other disastrous romances. Maurine's reticence is a measure that she exercised some judgment about what her town would tolerate. But the result, while allowing her a place on the community's margins, left her with crippling loneliness. Anna corroborated: Maurine was "fun to be around. She had a good sense of humor, but there was deep sadness about her."

Elvitta Phillips, then regional editor of the *Spokane Daily Chronicle* and a participant in the Rocky Mountain Writers' Conference (year unknown), wrote to Maurine's publisher: "I loved the Utah book." Furthermore, "the large shipment that came to Spokane had sold out." She remembered how Maurine "lit up" when talking about her work or her Utah at the writers' conference and saw the same "lit-up" quality in the book. She called *The Giant Joshua* "the best historic novel ever written" and said that "if it had not come after *Gone with the Wind* its success would have equaled that historic novel."[39]

The most interesting fan, however, was Wildon Evans, who was serving in the armed forces, and confided to her his feelings about the war. Finding Maurine's book was like a "choral amen," he said. He hoped she would share her war story ("The Golden Door") with him, relying on her description of it as "the best writing" she had done.[40] He was gratifyingly interested in Mormonism, wished he could "get the Tabernacle Choir on the radio," was "re-reading Joshua to prepare for the sequel," and "felt better prepared for [the sequel] this time since I have been to Utah, read your second book, and learned the truth of your 'secret' in your first letter: 'Mormons are no different from anybody else.'" A few months later, he asked again about "The Golden Door," quoting her as saying that it hung in "breathless levitation." He encouraged her to finish it: "If your novel can make us look back and look inward it may yet serve a more admirable purpose."[41] It seemed like the beginning of a promising relationship, but they never met in person. Maurine thought he might have been killed in China, but she didn't know.

Notes

[1] Juanita Brooks, quoted in Dale Morgan, Letter to Fawn Brodie, 10 March 1944, Fawn McKay Brodie Papers, MS 360, Box 7, Special Collections, Marriott Library, University of Utah, Salt Lake City. Juanita did not take up the invitation immediately, although she worked intermittently on her autobiography. When she was already afflicted with Alzheimer's, it was finally published, thanks to the assistance of Trudy McMurrin, an editor at the University of Utah Press. Juanita Brooks, *Quicksand and Cactus: A Memoir of the Southern Utah Frontier* (Salt Lake City: Howe Brothers, 1982).

[2] Levi Edger Young, Letter to Maurine Whipple, 27 April 1945, Maurine Whipple Collection, L. Tom Perry Special Collections, Harold B. Lee Library, Brigham Young University, Provo, Utah, with photocopy in Maurine Whipple Collection, Archive, Val A. Browning Library, Dixie College, St. George, Utah. Documents in both collections hereafter cited as BYU, photocopy Dixie College.

"SWELL SUFFERING"

3 Levi S. Peterson, *Juanita Brooks: Mormon Woman Historian* (Salt Lake City: University of Utah Press, 1988), 145.

4 This trip to Salt Lake City was probably before October 9, because she wrote Dean Brimhall on that date and told him what she had been doing.

5 Maurine Whipple, Letter to Norman Nevills, 14 August 1944, Norman Nevills Papers, Special Collections, Marriott Library, University of Utah, Salt Lake City; photocopy at Dixie College Archive (hereafter Nevills Papers).

6 Even though her affair with Frank Rhoades was long over, she acknowledged his "excellent advice, much of the material for the last chapter, and constant encouragement" (217).

7 The other books in the states series are listed on the first page of the Maurine's book about Utah with volumes for New Hampshire, Vermont, Nevada, Upper Michigan, South Carolina, Connecticut, Georgia, one for Oregon and Washington together, and one for "Our Southwest."

8 Maurine Whipple to Claire M. Smith, Harold Ober Associates, 9 August 1944; BYU. Smith seems to be an associate of her agent Harold Ober. Explaining why sales weren't going well, Maurine carped: "I let Bernard [Smith] have his way often against my better judgment." In fact, the correspondence shows that she made Smith's professional life miserable with her wrangling.

9 Bernard Smith, quoted in Maurine Whipple, Letter to Bernard Smith, 21 July 1944; BYU, photocopy Dixie College. Randall Jones served as the railroad's "special representative" and took slide shows of the park scenery all around the world to promote tourism. He turned sixty-three in 1944 when Maurine was working on the book and died two years later in 1946.

10 Maurine Whipple, Letter to Alfred A. Knopf, n.d.; BYU, photocopy Dixie College.

11 Senator Elbert Thomas, Letter to Maurine Whipple, 22 June 1944, alludes to such a visit—or at least to Maurine's plans for it. BYU, photocopy Dixie College.

12 The accompanying account form specified that it was royalties on 513 copies at the rate of .39875; $204.56 was credited as "trade," with $209.56 listed as "Due March 1, 1945." There were 200 sales of a special edition at .025 giving $5.00 credit in trade and a minus for other income of $100.00 from advance on Italian rights.

13 Elden Beck, Letter to Maurine Whipple, 1 November 1944; BYU, photocopy Dixie College. Maurine had written "Elden while in Guam" on the first page.

14 Bernard Smith, Letters to Maurine Whipple, 9 and 14 November 1944; BYU, photocopy Dixie College.

15 Bernard Smith, Letter to Maurine Whipple, 29 November 1944; BYU, photocopy Dixie College.

16 Dale Morgan, Letter to Juanita Brooks, 31 July 1943, Juanita Brooks Papers, Utah State Historical Society.

17 Bernard Smith, Letter to Maurine Whipple, 25 January 1946; BYU, photocopy Dixie College. "Utah—Foreign Land Gone American," was reprinted in *Science Digest*, February 1946, 27–30.

18 The $53.47 came from a $10.00 payment from copyright use and $43.47 from the sale of 395 books with a Swedish royalty.

19 Wallace Stegner, *The Uneasy Chair: A Biography of Bernard DeVoto* (Layton, Utah: Peregrine Smith Books, 1988), 237.

20 Maurine Whipple, Draft of letter to Max Becker, A.F.G. Agency, New York, n.d.; BYU, photocopy Dixie College.

21 Maurine Whipple, Letter to Norman Nevills, 15 May 1945, Nevills Papers.

22 Dale Morgan, Review, *Saturday Review of Literature*, November 1945, page not identified, Whipple Collection, BYU Library.

23 Quoted in Peterson, *Juanita Brooks*, 169.

24 Maurine Whipple, St. George, holograph letter to Dale Morgan, 7 December 1945; BYU, photocopy Dixie College.

25 Dale Morgan, Arlington, Virginia, Letter to Maurine Whipple, St. George, December 15, 1945, 2–4, typescript; BYU, photocopy Dixie College.

26 Ibid., 4. Charles S. Peterson's article, "Dale Morgan, Writer's Project, and Mormon History as a Regional Study," *Dialogue: A Journal of Mormon Thought* 24, no. 2 (Summer 1991): 47, commented on Morgan's working style, which illustrates why he took the time to refute Maurine's flimsy defense: "In ways Morgan's work was bound by detail. For example, his burning passion for the last fact led him while still at the Records Survey to write literally scores of letters all over the United States sleuthing out the origins and meaning of Tooele County's name."

27 Quoted in Peterson, *Juanita Brooks*, 184–85.

28 Maurine Whipple, Letter to Dean Brimhall, 11 February 1946, Dean R. Brimhall Papers, Special Collections, Marriott Library, University of Utah, Salt Lake City; photocopy at Dixie College Archive.

29 Harry Hansen, "Mormons Are Peculiar: Maurine Whipple Whips Up More about Them and Their Country," undated clipping, *New York World Telegram*; BYU, photocopy Dixie College.

30 Review, *Philadelphia Inquirer*, undated clipping, Whipple Scrapbook; BYU, photocopy Dixie College.

31 Partial clipping without headline, date, or page, *Boston Herald*, Whipple Scrapbook, BYU.

32 Clipping without byline, headline, or page number, *Salt Lake Tribune*, 4 November 1945, Whipple Scrapbook, BYU.

33 James Laughlin, Review, *Chicago Sun*, 16 December 1945, clipping, Whipple Scrapbook; BYU, photocopy Dixie College.

34 Review, *Ogden Standard-Examiner*, 24 October 1945, Whipple Scrapbook, BYU.

35 Elbert D. Thomas, Letter to Maurine Whipple, 18 December 1945; BYU, photocopy Dixie College.

36 Joseph Walker, Letter to Maurine Whipple, 22 December 1945; BYU, photocopy Dixie College.

37 Read Bain, Letter to Maurine Whipple, n.d.; BYU, photocopy Dixie College.

38 Anna Cox, St. George, Utah, Letter to Maurine Whipple, 26 February 1946; BYU, photocopy Dixie College.

[39] Elvitta Phillips, Northwest Editor, *Spokane Daily Chronicle*, Letter to Alfred A. Knopf (forwarded to Maurine Whipple), 27 December 1945, BYU.

[40] Wildon Evans, Hoschton, Ga., Letter to Maurine Whipple, 6 April 1946, Daynes Bldg., 128 S. Main, Salt Lake City; BYU, photocopy Dixie College.

[41] Wildon Evans, Letter to Maurine Whipple, 6 September 1946, BYU. His mother was Marella B. Evans, Hoschton, Georgia.

↣ 15 ↢

TWO SUFFERING SOULS

While Maurine was experiencing professional pressure as she struggled to finish *This Is the Place: Utah*—and to feel finished with it—she revived a correspondence with poet Bill Battrick whom she had met at the Rocky Mountain Writers' Conference in Boulder, Colorado, in 1937 and 1938. In 1938 they had both received fellowship as instructors, which paid them $50 each.

Bill, born in 1906 in Ashtabula, Ohio, was three years Maurine's junior and the only son in a family of four children. Sister Helen, fourteen years Bill's senior, was dean of a girls' school. Mabel, was living in Oxford near their parents, raising a family. The youngest sister, Lucille, lived at home, and Maurine thought she had some mental problems.

Bill graduated from Oberlin College, did graduate work at the University of Colorado, was a high school teacher and superintendent in Ohio, and had first attended the writers' conference in 1935, so he was an old hand by the time Maurine first came in 1937. He began a graduate degree at the University of Colorado beginning in 1937, also teaching half-time in the English Department. On 31 July 1942, he was inducted into the army at age thirty-eight.

From 1942 to 1945 he wrote long, moody letters to Maurine, who must have responded with long, moody letters of her own. He served as radio chief in an infantry unit, was captured by the Germans in 1944, but survived prison camp and returned to the United States in July 1945. He continued his graduate studies, was an editor and technical writer for the Human Resources Research Organization, Fort Knox, Kentucky (1953–71), and also taught English at the University of Louisville, Kentucky. When he retired in 1971, he returned to Boulder, Colorado, where he published about eighty poems in magazines, a poetry collection, and a memoir, *A GI Prisoner in the Third Reich*. Just before his death in 1989, he also finished a novel.[1]

Maurine had already turned to Bill as a confidante and possible romantic interest in the aftermath of her affair with Tom Spies. She eased off when she took up with Frank Rhoades but seriously revived the correspondence in 1944 when the affair with Frank dissolved. Her papers include about twenty-six letters and parts of letters from Bill, most undated. The first seems to have been written on 27 December 1940 and apparently the last was datelined only "Thursday night," probably sometime in 1945. Rather uncharacteristically, there are no draft letters to Bill in Maurine's papers, so her state of mind must be deduced from Bill's references to it in his own letters. Although Maurine almost certainly would have welcomed a romance, Bill never encouraged it, and it remains an almost unique relationship for Maurine with an unmarried man: an epistolary friendship that helped both of them through very trying times.

Bill's first letter had been forwarded to Maurine in St. George from Houghton Mifflin. It sounds like the continuation of a correspondence, so probably there were earlier letters that have not survived. He was visiting his parents in Ohio for Christmas vacation in 1940 and writing as if his poetic impulses needed to find an audience: "I go for a long tramp in the woods and try to think about peace on earth. Instead, I discover that the brambles are the very life of my father's timber, for it is among the thickest stands of blackberry that saplings get their start out of the reach of grazing livestock." He lists Maurine among his "beloved people."[2]

Maurine needed someone, and Bill certainly sounded as if he "spoke her language." Then they discovered they had a similar heartache as both had lost a beloved sibling—Maurine her brother Ralph, and Bill his sister, Helen, whom he claimed had nearly raised him. Besides this, a serviceman needed to receive letters from a girl back home, and Maurine needed to be able to say she had a serviceman boyfriend to write to. They explored the possibility that they might be meant for each other. "Even if you can't be deeply loved at the moment in exactly the way that everyone wants to be loved," mused Bill, "and even if you can't bring yourself to indulge in fleeting amours, however clean and innocent they might prove to be, you can, at least, mean a lot to a number of people, people outside your family."[3]

Later, probably after receiving one of Maurine's long "you see" letters, he wrote: "I've found, in almost 38 years, no answers. . . . I know nothing, I guess, but that there is no substitute for personal strength."[4] For the first time, he confided how Helen's death "left an abyss, somehow; the effect was psychological, beyond analysis. Everything that is I, she helped to create, from my earliest days on. She was one of the few people who really cared what happens to me. I know how you feel,"[5]

In an undated letter, he returned to how they both needed to rebuild. It is an edgy and repetitive letter. His reference to "sex" as their shared but different problem suggests obliquely that Maurine had confided some details of her romantic betrayals. On USO stationary he wrote: "You frightened me, for you and for me. There must be an answer for us. To find it we must relax and not try to find it. I know we must not think so much as we do—not till we get back some of the nervous stamina we've used up." In answer to something Maurine had written about the direction of their relationship, he wrote: "We cannot yet make a home. We could only spoil our own chances. To build a home one must have reserves of calm and quiet strength and certain confidence and courage. We don't have them, yet. . . ." He signed his letter with "all the affection I know how to offer,"[6]

In October 1944, Maurine went to Salt Lake City, with plans to go on east to meet Bill before he went overseas. The Normandy invasion had occurred in June, and the Allied forces were determinedly slogging through France and up the Italian peninsula, closing in on Hitler. Bill's unit was on standby to go to Europe any time after 10 October 1944. Although no letters between July and October have survived in her papers, apparently Bill had agreed to telegraph her the departure time and place as soon as he knew it. She would join him for the farewell. In 1991 she remembered how she waited overnight, nerves taut, at Hotel Utah for his wire. The woman at the check-in desk kept saying no message had come. Maurine's frustration and distress mounted steadily. Finally, the woman apologized—she had missed Maurine's message in the flood of incoming telegrams. It was almost too late. But Maurine said she caught a freight train and went to the meeting point in some eastern city—which one she could not recall. She did not say how much time she and Bill had together or how they spent it. She did remember she had "suppressed her own war fears, tried hard to be positive and encouraging," and talked about getting married upon his return. She apparently followed up immediately after her return to Utah with a letter describing how she had fallen ill as a result of her strenuous efforts but renewing her encouragement and affection.

Bill's next letter said that her illness and heroic efforts made him "feel like an inconsiderate sort of creature," then said, "Your plan for me sounds wonderful, except that I'm not sure I want to get married or sure I'm fitted for it. But that's something I don't need to think about right now, perhaps; I don't know. . . . Thank you for loving me. Perhaps your kindness will someday be the power in me to write some lines of poetry that will move the world to sobs."[7]

She received an undated letter when he reached his assignment overseas. He could not say where he was because of censorship restrictions. The trans-Atlantic voyage "had been good." He'd seen "interesting sights." He wanted to know "how long it took his letters" to reach her and he wanted to "hear about autumn in southern Utah," and how her work "was coming?"[8]

If Maurine had hoped for overflowing love-longings from a responsive heart, she was disappointed. Bill admired Maurine's desire to make a better world and her willingness to struggle against what she perceived as injustices. But he wasn't ready to share her life as her husband.

On 12 January 1945, Maurine received a letter from Lucille Battrick announcing that Bill was missing in action. She had found Maurine's name and address when she had gone through Bill's letters: "Apparently you love him too and we can only wait and hope."[9]

In 1991, Maurine remembered how shattered she was by the news. She started blindly for the Sugarloaf, her favorite place of solace and solitude. On her way, she passed Juanita Brooks's house. Juanita, serving her family supper, happened to look out the window, saw Maurine, and immediately sensed that something was wrong. She came out in the January cold to walk with Maurine for hours. It was an act of kindness and love that Maurine never forgot. She said Juanita told her to never give up hope, to keep saying over and over to herself that he would be all right, that he would come back whole.

Lucille wrote again nine days later: Bill's division, the 106th, had "suffered heavy casualties: 416 dead, 1,246 wounded, and 7,001 were missing—half the division."[10]

In March of 1945 Lucille had some additional news. Bill, as radio chief, "had communicated the last information from his unit. They were "without food or water" and were "destroying" their equipment. Then she expressed her own faith: "Helen had always been able to protect Bill" and she would "have that power in death, too." Then she said she had a comforting picture of children near a cliff with guardian angels protecting them. A steel engraving of this scene, usually hand-tinted, was very popular during the Victorian period. Perhaps Lucille was referring to this image.[11]

Fortunately, their anguish was cut short by the arrival of a short note from Bill written 4 February on a postcard provided by the Germans.[12] He was in a prison camp. Between that point and his release in May, there is only one more short card, reporting that he was all right and begging Maurine to write and "send anything Red Cross will allow," which she told me she did faithfully. She also remembered that Bill's situation was terrible. In the camp, the men were stacked in bunks eleven tiers high and not allowed down even to relieve themselves. Once, on a long, forced winter march without food, Bill, drawing from his rural Ohio upbringing, found frozen turnips in a field, which kept them alive.

TWO SUFFERING SOULS

Bill's situation must have made Maurine doubly frantic, trying to imagine the plight of her brother George in a combat unit on the other side of the world. There are only eight letters from George in Maurine's papers, six of them written between 25 January 1945 and 7 October 1960. The war was winding down in Europe, but heating up in the Pacific. It promised to be a costly campaign against a determined and little understood enemy. George, in one letter to his parents, told of a curious experience that conveys his psychic numbness. "I saw quite a few dead japs yesterday and I didn't mind it at all, they are just like some animals to me. We read a love letter that a jap officer had written to some gal and boy was it mush. I can't understand why it was in English either."[13]

Maurine feared that George would be suffering psychological damage. This was true. He was one of the few survivors in his unit. Later, his commanding officer visited the family to warn them that George might have a hard time readjusting to civilian life. On 10 July 1945, a month before the end of the war with Japan, George, now age thirty, returned home. He had been discharged the previous December.[14] He was almost certainly suffering from post-traumatic stress syndrome, an ailment that was not understood at the time. War veterans suffering from "combat fatigue" or "shell shock" were supposed to just get over it, and most people felt that talking about it did no good.

Maurine often appealed to Charlie to be more understanding and probably inadvertently created family turmoil in her effort to help. Annie's loving but anxious hovering, Maurine said, often annoyed George. George himself continued to suppress his memories and turned to drink, to Maurine's dismay.

According to Mary Phoenix, interviewed in 1993 after Maurine's death, in high school George had gone drinking with some buddies and their car swerved off Black Ridge. Although no one was killed, George had been quite badly hurt, but some of his buddies were injured even more seriously. Mary wondered if this brush with suffering and near-death had had a deeper impact than anyone realized, contributing to George's need to drink.

After a short time in St. George, George and Flora again lived in Palm Springs, California. Here Flora became ill with a baffling malady that Maurine thought was later diagnosed as a strange reaction to an insect bite. Between George's drinking and Flora's illness, the couple could not cope. Flora moved back to her parents' home to recuperate, and the two drifted apart. They had no children and eventually divorced. George's life was a heartbreaking series of misery and failure from that point on, and Maurine periodically devoted much energy and time trying to intervene.

In May 1945, the war ended in Europe; and Bill Battrick, after four months and a week as a prisoner of war, was free. He wrote that he "guessed" he was "anxious to take her up on her offer" to show him around Utah on his upcoming furlough.[15] There is no record of Maurine's response, although it was probably ardent agreement that may have masked secret misgivings. She was still living in her parents' shabby, uncomfortable home. Her own youthful good looks were fading fast—she was now forty-three—and she suffered from a never-ending series of ailments. How could she impress Bill in these circumstances? Yet how could she put him off? He might be her last chance for marriage. Her neediness was exhausting, especially in comparison to the suffering and losses of others caused by the war. She didn't get much sympathy.

She took the bold step of writing to Levi Edgar Young in July, enlisting his help in making a good impression on Bill. Furthermore, she respected Young as a religious leader and thought Bill would need to talk to someone like this to help him assimilate his war experience. From Young's return letter, it appears that Maurine described Bill to him as a person who was feeling lost but was looking for something to believe in. Young responded: "You speak of his being a 'sick spirit.' You also mention that he is a boy with a 'hurt soul.' I love your expressions. It is a day of hurt souls, and how pleasing it is to God for someone to give comfort to such people!"[16]

The United States dropped the atomic bomb on Hiroshima 6 August 1945 and on Nagasaki on 9 August. Japan surrendered on 14 August. Bill arrived in Salt Lake City that same month with enough gas-rationing stamps that he and Maurine could visit some of Utah's scenic locales with friends who had a car. Her papers do not include any descriptions or details of this trip; and in 1991, she could not remember who the friends were. Also, she said the trip did not "amount to much," meaning that it did not turn into the romantic interlude she hoped for. However, their route took them to Kanab where she heard a legend that Mexico's last Aztec ruler, Montezuma, had sent treasure to the area to be hidden from the Spanish. She later researched and wrote a story, which she sent to Stuart Rose at the *Saturday Evening Post* in the spring of 1949. Rose returned it, saying they were interested but that it needed "greater detail." He did, however, suggest a revision.[17] Maurine didn't pick up the project again until later, and no drafts of this early article survive in her papers.

When Bill's furlough ended, he went to Fort Oglethorpe, Georgia, still awaiting discharge. He and Maurine continued their correspondence. During the next months, his surviving letters chart a progressively deepening depression. He admitted his "terrible fear of death," "weaknesses" that he could not control, and his "fear" that he did not "contribute much to the war." He visited his family in Ohio but cut his visit short "to consult with a Doctor friend from the University of Maryland, who helped only temporarily." He saw in the fact that he "had yet to make one friend after forty months in the army" a sign that something was definitely "missing" in his makeup. He was reading Freud and agreed that "sexual repression could be at the root of my problems," but "I am powerless to do anything about it." In one introspective passage, he mused: "I don't know much, except that my whole life as I look back is a tortured mess. I wonder what *life* has taught me, if anything. You say I am fine. How can you tell? It is you who are fine and noble and creative and unselfish. I think I have never known anyone else so much so." Maurine had offered to visit, but he put her off.[18] She maintained to me that Bill was a psychological casualty of the war. "At first, I thought my love and help would bring him around. But he just couldn't shake his depression,"

Despite Bill's disinclination to see her then, Maurine was restless. She visited Read Bain in Oxford, Ohio, in August, and apparently took advantage of the proximity to visit Bill's family. The visit was not a success. Lucille was dirty and "had a crazy look in her eyes." Maurine marveled that this unkempt and disoriented woman could be connected to Bill in any way. Maurine went on to New York City to meet with her agent, Max Becker, hoping that Bill could join her there on leave. He didn't, although she apparently stayed in the city for a month, writing a proposal for Simon and Schuster designed to elicit a contract and an advance for the sequel.

Meanwhile, Maurine's bills were mounting. By mid-October she was staying with T. S. and Gladys Vanderford, Mormon friends in the affluent town of Scarsdale, New York. As late as 1978, Maurine was still on Gladys's Christmas-card list. She received a bitter and self-indulgent letter from Read Bain, forwarded to her in Scarsdale, in which he lamented the negative effects of war and denounced mankind as "the monstrous mess-maker, the abortive offal of creation."[19] Maurine seems to have confided her romantic woes to Bain, for he advised her that the relationship with Bill was "doomed" and she "should make a good clean break to avoid lingering confusion." Maurine was not ready to do that. As much as a year later (the letters are not fully dated), Bain was still encouraging her not to let "that poet get you all balled up—you are a busy woman now with no time for romancing with dubious ducks."[20]

During this same month in the east, she had looked up Faun Schmutz Pickett, a St. George girl who was studying dance at the Martha Graham School. Faun was the daughter of Donald and Amber Schmutz, who had helped Maurine gather information about the Arizona Strip. In *The Giant Joshua*, Maurine listed Amber and her "bucking Lizzie" (Amber's car) in the acknowledgments. Donald later helped her locate the site of "Peter's Leap," a dugway chipped down the Black Hill on the first road into the valley, its deep grooves designed to hold the wheels and prevent the wagons from tipping over. Maurine saw Faun and her roommates as eager young women pursuing their artistic training in the bustle and swirl of the big city—the setting she imagined for her character, Lenzi, who would study singing. She was determined to get the environment right.

When interviewed, Faun remembered that she and her roommates were trying to acquire sophistication and gentility. First, they were flattered that a noted writer was so interested in them but soon became annoyed at the way Maurine imposed on their hospitality. Faun perceived Maurine as socially gauche but said that their associates accepted her as an interesting western eccentric and did not treat her unkindly. She recalled an anecdote. May O'Donald and Sybil Shurr, two well-known teachers of music and dance, invited Faun and Maurine to dinner at five o'clock. Faun said "I did not realize Maurine knew her way around New York so well until at three o'clock we found ourselves in front of the apartment house where we were not due for two more hours. Maurine refused to go any further, so we went to the door, were let in and dinner plans were quickly changed." Faun laughed as she told me how horrified she was when Maurine then kicked off her shoes and relaxed on the couch. She acknowledged that their hostesses were fascinated with Maurine and that Maurine had entertained them with colorful, exaggerated stories of the St. George area. "She was an actress who would try to take any part that would get her what she wanted," summarized Faun. "If that was to be a laid-back, folksy western character then she could be one; or, more rarely, if it was to be a sophisticated, modern woman, she could be that. But her demands became too much for us girls. We probably felt a little insecure in our image."[21]

When Faun and her husband, Evan Pickett, retired and returned to St. George, Faun again befriended Maurine in the rest home. She was one of few who visited Maurine regularly and did many thoughtful things to make her happy. In 1991, one of Faun's visits coincided with mine. Faun reminded Maurine that they had been together on a streetcar on 2 September 1945 when victory in Japan had been announced. A young celebrating serviceman had stepped in front of the car and been killed. They were the only witnesses who stayed to give statements to the police. Maurine marveled that she had forgotten this poignant incident, for it had struck her as "such an irony for a young man to lose his life during the victory celebration."

But back to Bill. Bill arrived on U.S. soil July 9, 1945, but it wasn't until October that he was discharged. He sent Maurine a telegram to meet him at the Pennsylvania Station 14 October 1945.[22] Maurine went with irrepressible hopes, but it was a bust. "The topic of marriage came up," she told me, "and Bill said he could not get married because of his sister, Lucille, since he would not risk fathering a child with her problem." Maurine thought it an unlikely excuse, especially given her advancing age; but she agreed that Lucille had mental problems. She also told me that, in Washington, Bill confided his suspicions that Lucille had poisoned Helen. The meeting was further darkened when Bill introduced her to some other survivors of the prison camp. Their tension was palpable. Bill certainly wasn't going to be her prince charming. Once again, she retreated to St. George, feeling that her hopes for a compatible mate had been betrayed.

In 1991 when Maurine talked to me about Bill, she seemed to be casting about for ways to turn this fizzled relationship into romantic tragedy. To others, as already noted, she sometimes said he committed suicide or even had not survived the war. Although I have not been able to find his death date, he was still alive in Colorado in 1971. He never married.[23]

To at least one correspondent, Maurine confided that "a war injury had castrated him."[24] Again, this seems unlikely. Bill's comments on Freudian sexuality seem to define his problems as exclusively psychological. None of his letters were even mildly encouraging on the topic of marriage.

In 1958, Maurine wrote a page titled "The Left-Overs," which was never published: "What to do with left-over women? Dump us in the garbage too? The thousands of Left-over women? Demanding of society the right to live, as I was silently demanding now? The world is full of left-over women. It is one thing to end in a burst of glory, and then forever after know darkness and peace. It is another thing to live out the long years, dusting a photograph, groping in the night silence for an empty pillow. . . ."[25]

Maurine's papers include what could have been the start of another romance—a letter from Henry Wade Hough of Denver written in September 1945. In 1991, she did not even remember him. In his letter, he described himself as "a writer who had a job editing a trade magazine to support my free lancing." He carried in his wallet a photograph of her "on the Sugarloaf," which he described as "St. Georgian: . . . sweet and unspoiled yet wise enough to know when you're on the edge of a precipice, literally or figuratively." He thought people would see her as "just about any girl in town, not realizing she had been places, known national fame, plumbed the heights and depths of love and the aftermath."[26] He hoped to come to Utah and meet her. Apparently Maurine gave him no encouragement to do so, but it is ironic that she had no memory of this openly appreciative overture. She may have reacted in 1945 the same way she did in 1991 when I read the letter to her. He boasted that he had sold an article to *Liberty* magazine for five hundred dollars "about a ranch I had never visited and some horses I had never seen." Maurine was furious. "How unfair that men reporters who have

"SWELL SUFFERING"

never been here sold stories about my country when I couldn't! I'm glad I never met him!"

Notes

[1] Short biography, William Battrick Collection, Carnegie Branch Library for Local History, Boulder, Colorado, photocopy at Dixie College Archive.

[2] Bill Battrick, Letter to Maurine Whipple, 27 December 1940, Maurine Whipple Collection, L. Tom Perry Special Collections, Harold B. Lee Library, Brigham Young University, Provo, Utah, with photocopy in Maurine Whipple Collection, Archive, Val A. Browning Library, Dixie College, St. George, Utah. Documents in both collections hereafter cited as BYU, photocopy Dixie College.

[3] Bill Battrick, Letter to Maurine Whipple, "Sunday 13," Station Hospital, Fort Jackson, South Carolina; BYU, photocopy Dixie College. He had had the operation May 31 and in June 1940 one of the Sundays fell on the 13th.

[4] Bill Battrick, Letter to Maurine Whipple, n.d., ca. summer or fall 1944; BYU, photocopy Dixie College.

[5] Ibid.

[6] Bill Battrick, Letter to Maurine Whipple, n.d. [ca. May–June 1944]; BYU, photocopy Dixie College.

[7] Bill Battrick, loose pages of letters to Maurine Whipple, n.d. [ca. October/November 1944]; BYU, photocopy Dixie College.

[8] Bill Battrick, Letter to Maurine Whipple, n.d. (ca. November 1944); BYU, photocopy Dixie College.

[9] Lucille Battrick, Williamsfield, Ohio, Letter to Maurine Whipple, St. George, 12 January 1945; BYU, photocopy Dixie College.

[10] Lucille Battrick, Letter to Maurine Whipple, 26 January 1945; BYU, photocopy Dixie College.

[11] Lucille Battrick, Letter to Maurine Whipple, 26 March 1945; BYU, photocopy Dixie College.

[12] Sgt. William Battrick, Gangenennummer 315072, 4 February 1945; BYU, photocopy Dixie College.

[13] George Whipple, Letter to "Mr. and Mrs. Charles Whipple," 4 February 1945; BYU, photocopy Dixie College.

TWO SUFFERING SOULS

14 George Whipple, discharge papers, BYU. George was inducted 25 March 1942, 640th Tank Destroyer Battalion, and discharged 10 July 1945 at Fort Douglas, Utah, grade Tec-5. His specialty was auto mechanics but he had certified as an expert with the .30 carbine. He had received a good conduct medal, the Asiatic-Pacific service medal, and the Philippine Liberation Medal with one bronze star and been demobilized on 15 December 1944.

15 Bill Battrick, Letter to Maurine Whipple, n.d., ca. May 1945; BYU, photocopy Dixie College.

16 Levi Edgar Young, 19 April 1945; BYU, photocopy Dixie College.

17 Maurine Whipple, Letter to Peggy Dowst, Associate Editor, *Saturday Evening Post*, n.d., ca. spring 1949, BYU. This query letter explained how she had written the original article, "Anybody's Gold Mine." She was writing from the Chelsea Hotel in Los Angeles, which dates the letter to the spring of 1949 when Maurine was in California for surgery.

18 Bill Battrick, Letter to Maurine Whipple, n.d.; the envelope had a smudged postmark: only the month, "September," is legible; BYU, photocopy Dixie College.

19 Read Bain, Letter to Maurine Whipple, Oxford, Ohio, 17 October 1945; BYU, photocopy Dixie College.

20 Read Bain, Oxford, Ohio, n.d.; BYU, photocopy Dixie College.

21 Faun Schmutz Pickett, Interviewed April 1993, St. George, Utah, notes in Hale Collection, Dixie College Archive.

22 Bill Battrick, telegram to Maurine Whipple, 13 October 1945; BYU, photocopy Dixie College.

23 William Battrick Collection, Carnegie Branch Library for Local History, Boulder, Colorado, photocopy at Dixie College Archive.

24 Maurine Whipple, Draft of letter to Don Congdon, n.d., ca. 1946; BYU, photocopy Dixie College.

25 Maurine Whipple, "The Left Overs," ca. 1959, ellipses hers; BYU, photocopy Dixie College.

26 Henry Wade Hough, Denver, Colorado, Letter to Maurine Whipple, September 10, 1945; BYU, photocopy Dixie College.

❧ 16 ❧

THE FAILED SEQUEL, 1946–47

It is not clear how much time Maurine spent in New York in the fall of 1945, but it must have been from at least October until late November. Maurine did not feel any particular rapport with her new agent, Max Becker, but she let him handle the negotiations to write the *Joshua* sequel with Simon and Schuster. He managed to arrange advances on the royalties that would give her $150 a month for one year while she wrote the book. The one-year deadline was a surprise condition she had not heard about before; but, as he had requested, she said nothing during the meeting.

In the hall later, she recalled, she told Max she didn't think she could do the book in a year. He shrugged off the exact time-limit as unimportant but then, in the form of a threatening question, asked, "But you will do it?" She was surprised he would even ask. She expected him to know that the only thing that would stop her would be an act of God, such as incapacitating illness. However, if she had looked at her own production record since 1941—as he obviously had—his concern would have seemed more logical.

With a contract in hand, Maurine should have been on the next train west to get to work. Instead, she had to catch up on business affairs, find a place to work, keep an autographing obligation for a week in Salt Lake,[1] and nurse Annie through a gall-bladder attack.

She thus began writing feeling harried by time pressures and dissatisfied with her writing environment. She had been allowed to work on the Utah book in a room in St. George's public library; but in the fall of 1945, the mayor had withdrawn the privilege. It seemed that an unnamed member of the LDS hierarchy was incensed over the Utah book. Not only could she not use the workroom, but the mayor wanted her to leave town.[2] In short, she still had no better place to go than the old north bedroom.

This time, there was no Ferris Greenslet to keep up a steady stream of compliments, incentives, and tactful pressure. The relationship never clicked with Max Becker; and perhaps Maurine, already wounded by negative reactions from her own people about the first two books, feared, on a subconscious level, that the sequel would bring the same punishing reaction. She may also have felt that the sequel was unlikely to produce a sum sufficiently substantial to reward the sustained writing effort that had been required to produce *The Giant Joshua*. Other stresses were the unpleasantness of living at home, worry about brother George's drinking, and the combination of intimacy and distance in her relationship with Bill Battrick that only seemed to underline how lonely she really was.

She had obviously confided her shaky confidence to one of her big-name friends—Harry Hansen of the *New York World Telegram*, who had reviewed both *The Giant Joshua* and *This Is the Place: Utah*. He responded with some excellent advice: "One thing I'd like to see you do: shovel out all these little thoughts of being misunderstood and persecuted, with the dust and trash of 1945. Get them out of your mind, and go full steam ahead." He told her she had more talent than the others but lacked "a tough epidermis. Forget what they say. Sensitivity is a good thing, but keep it in harness and make it serve you."[3] Periodically, Maurine succeeded in taking this advice. For example, in February 1946, she wrote Dean Brimhall that she "didn't give a damn that some relief society gals have made living in St. George hell." She had gone to "Salt Lake City and rented an office on the fourth floor of the Daynes Building" where she planned to write the sequel, tentatively titled "Cleave the Wood."[4] Because of the post-war housing shortage, she was "sharing a room at Hotel Utah with another woman on a floor without housekeeping service but with one meal per day included."[5] In 1991, all she could remember was that she and her unnamed roommate "did not get along very well."

Living in a hotel and renting an office does not seem like a wise financial move, considering that she claimed to have borrowed money at least twice from the St. George bank in 1945. The $150 she received monthly from Simon and Schuster would end after a year, and almost three months had passed. On the plus side, the room was warm, only a block from the city library (then on State Street a few rods down from South Temple), and near supportive friends. Maurine remembers frequently visiting Lillian, doing things together, chatting about ideas, and enjoying Lillian's supportive admiration. She would have also enjoyed the quality and elegance of the grand Victorian-style Hotel Utah.

When I asked about her office, she recalled it as "just a small room. I probably had sent up from St. George the small desk my father had made me." Again, she covered the wall with large papers on which she jotted each character's ideas and key episodes.

Playing much the same role that Joseph Walker had done during the writing of *The Giant Joshua*, Read Bain remained interested and enthusiastic this year. If he were writing the last two volumes of the trilogy, he said, he'd "have the three dramatic events in the first one—the death of Brigham Young and John D. Lee's execution and the manifesto days up to about 1900. Then the last book would be the modern Mormon story, the two wars, the corporation, dollar-dispensation of the ruler J. Reuben Clark, the secularization of the Josephetic myth, and the story of the spiritual struggles now going on, from mysticism to science, from miracles to modern technology and modern mindedness."6 His few surviving letters are light and clever, like Walker's, but more acerbic when it came to the Mormon Church and what he considered its narrow-minded people about whom he lacked Walker's comfortable and affectionate tolerance. Bain probably unconsciously fostered Maurine's own bitterness and paranoia. In psychic pain from her own loneliness, she could easily overreact to the negative voices she heard. She could not take the caustic advice of Bernard DeVoto, who reviewed *The Giant Joshua*: "The Western novelist must tear up his coterie card, immerse himself in the life around him, and write about what he sees in terms of what it seems like to him and not in terms of what the dogmas of his little group or favorite English prof makes it out to be."7

More consolation came from Clayton Rice, the Presbyterian minister who had come up to congratulate Maurine after a war-bond lecture and who, as a young man, had been assigned to work in St. George. At the time he met Maurine, he had been head of the Western Protestant Church League. Now, reassigned to Washington State, he was state president of the Council of Churches and Christian Education, headquartered in Seattle. She must have made him a spiritual and emotional confidante, and he answered her letters consistently, always gently and comfortingly.8

Hughie Call also wrote encouragingly, like Lillian taking the flattering position that she was a fellow writer but not nearly as talented as Maurine. Enthusiastically, she anticipated that "our Maxie will be on the job to see that it [the sequel] gets the publicity it needs and to see that it's pushed to the limit." When Maurine complained that she "trusted no agent," Hughie defended Max: "Honestly I can't agree. Max has always made more money for me than I could possibly have made for myself and he has fought my battles. He really has been a miracle man so far as I'm concerned. I think he's a realist, but I'm a dreamer and I like realists. I need their thinking to balance my half-wit. I would never fight for my rights because I don't even know what they are. I believe you will respect his force and integrity if nothing else after your book comes out."⁹ Maurine may have hinted for an invitation to Hughie's Texas ranch, for Hughie regretfully told her that the ranch situation simply wouldn't allow a visit just then.

Although Maurine continually reinvented and reworked the sequel (including making it a trilogy), her vision for it remained strong: "The dream of brotherhood *is* possible, though only time can tell. Meanwhile, all any member of the human race can do is to seek the Holy Grail amid the dream's debris.—that despite what Thomas Wolfe said, I think you *can* 'go home again'; in fact, you must. For 'going home again' is a prerequisite to going anywhere else! Spiritually at least."[10]

She had managed to make a good start on the sequel during this period—which is not surprising since she had originally conceptualized it as part of *The Giant Joshua*. At this point, she was envisioning a single-volume sequel, not a trilogy, whose chief character would be Jim, Clory's son, who must deal with the bitterness he feels while watching his mother coping so gallantly with her hard life and many misfortunes. He retreats from the village life of the Mormon community to the secular life of an Arizona Strip cowboy but returns to St. George, hoping to make a better life for himself. For this character, Maurine drew on her cousin, Murray Whipple, a cowboy on her Uncle John's ranch who died as a young man when a roping accident jerked off his finger and gangrene set in. Pneumonia finished him first. Also, interestingly enough, Maurine also drew heavily on Charlie, when she constructed a physical description and personality for Jim. Sometimes the borrowing is not even disguised. A photograph of Charlie and two friends sitting at a table puzzling over a skull and bones—a prank they staged when young—has survived; Maurine has written a scene in Chapter 2 in which Jimmy and two friends, Frank and Tony, prominent characters in "Cleave the Wood," carry out the same prank. Maurine admitted to me that she had, indeed, based Jim on her father. Perhaps that was one reason it was so difficult for her to finish the sequel. Subconsciously, she avoided confronting her mixed feelings about her father and knew how hard it would be to withstand Charlie's disapproval. He lived to be ninety-one, and the two of them never had an easy or affectionate relationship.

In the sequel, Jim's anti-religious sentiments remain intact, and Frank Wright, the son of Clory's friend Palmyra in *Joshua*, puts his faith in scientific knowledge. This character may be partially modeled on Joseph Walker.[11]

She added Tony after originally outlining the sequel. He isn't even descended from the original 1861 pioneers. After she had discovered more of herself, she needed this mystical philosopher as a reflection of her own desire to connect all the loose, floating threads and form something she could touch that could be labeled "wisdom."

THE FAILED SEQUEL, 1946-47

The romantic interest in "Cleave the Wood" is represented by Thanksie Hichinoper, whose father is the local Church leader and one of the original St. George pioneers. Jim falls in love with her, then enlists to fight in the Spanish-American war. He is electrocuted while heroically staying at his post to radio his unit's position. This ruins his health. He returns to St. George, marries Thanksie, goes blind, and suffers crippling arthritis. Thanksie, pregnant with Jim's baby, can't stand the thought of being tied to an invalid and flees with a traveling salesman, who abandons her when she is dying after giving birth to the baby. The local bishop, who considers her an apostate, has not helped. Thanksie's father and Jim follow the runaways and bring baby Lenzi home. Although Jim is tortured by memories, which "attack him, flapping into his mind like hideous black bats," he resolves to stay alive, collecting his army pension and providing a stable home until Lenzi is raised. He also wishes to help her escape Mormon indoctrination.

When Lenzi develops an exceptional singing voice, the whole community takes an interest in seeing that she gets the best training available. She subsequently goes to a big eastern city where she becomes a performing success. But she has to choose between marrying her local boyfriend, Briggie, or continuing her career. She first makes a worldly choice but then, at the very pinnacle of her success, realizes that the best place to be is back among her own people as a good man's wife. Maurine later added "Zeb," the infidel, who suggests that he and Lenzi write a book about her life. Another character, "Jack" was Lenzi's former lover, who returns when she is hovering on the brink of fame and fortune, thinking he might profit from the relationship. In another scene, Lenzi confesses her doubts and seeks counsel from a Church leader but is horrified by his self-righteousness.

Lenzi comes back to St. George in time to see her father on his deathbed, sings "Come, Come, Ye Saints" at the funeral, and hopes that Jim finally understood that happiness does not lie in worldly rewards. With new eyes, she sees that her own people, like the battered Joshua trees, continue to thrive by reaching toward heaven and the promised land.[12]

When Max Becker forwarded Maurine's March 1946 check from Simon and Schuster, he said that Donald K. Congdon, her editor at Simon and Schuster, "was asking to see a few chapters," and he "was looking forward to seeing them himself."[13] Although he probably meant this comment to be encouraging, Maurine, already uneasy about the deadline, interpreted it as intolerable pressure. She must have been afraid she deserved criticism, for even before she received his March letter, she had had a Dr. Robert G. Snow tell Max she had been confined to bed with severe tracheitis and bronchitis.[14] In a somewhat melodramatic gesture, she returned the March check with what must have been a highly emotional note. Max promptly sent it back to her on 12 March with apologies "for upsetting" her and the reasonable explanation. "I simply said that Simon and Schuster might ask to see some of the book."[15]

Less temperamental this time, Maurine apparently kept the check.[16] At the end of the month, she asked Max to see about getting *The Giant Joshua* reprinted. She also reported that she was moving out of the hotel into an apartment, even though she was convinced that "local bishops were quietly telling apartment owners not to rent to me," that "the Church was behind the fact that the newspapers had not printed anything about me or my Utah book this year," and that the book was not "being shown in the bookstores anymore."[17]

Maurine's new apartment was near the University of Utah (169 South 13th East); and according to her, the landlady asked her to leave almost immediately. When she refused, the landlady rented the rooms next to her to piano students, who practiced all day. The racket must have reminded her of the ceaseless whine of the saws at her parents' home in St. George; but to do her landlady justice, it was not unreasonable to rent practice rooms during the day when ordinary tenants would be at their jobs. It was Maurine's bad luck that her home also had to be her office. However, in a later letter to Don Congdon, Maurine describes herself during April or May as "putting in a full day's work catching up on necessary research, but I couldn't make Max understand that a book sometimes grows by leaps and bounds when an author has nothing to show except the yeasty gestation that goes on in his mind during hours in newspaper vaults."

The sole surviving letter from her family during this period probably contributed to Maurine's worries. In late February, Florence reported that Annie had cut her hand badly, that Florence had tried "unsuccessfully" to get her to recuperate in the Jolley home, and that "they couldn't even find a hired girl to do some of the housework." For his part, Charlie "was sick with a bad cold," was so angry at the doctor for "charging $200 for his services and prescribing $80 for medicine to take care of the cut hand, he would not go have his operation" (unspecified), but that Maurine shouldn't worry: "that there were enough of them to care for things," and that she should "just concentrate on her book."[18]

Maurine herself was having a year of almost continuous ill health. It is not possible to say how much was psychosomatic and how much real. In addition to the usual round of respiratory ailments, she also continued to suffer from painful menstrual periods. There is no record that Joseph Walker had continued to send her progesterone during 1946–47. She was forty-three and must have been experiencing early menopause; but whatever the cause, her life was largely controlled by the physical reality of difficult menstruation cycles, probably with associated premenstrual syndrome, and the recurring respiratory ailments. The embarrassing urinary incontinence caused by her detached kidney also continued, but she hoped she could finish the book before the operation became unavoidable.

By late August, Maurine had returned to St. George. Maryruth Belt offered Maurine $125 if she would stay for a month in their home with Maryruth's sister, Demi, while they were on a lecture tour. Demi was not an invalid but had a heart condition so she could not be left alone. Maryruth even thought she could help Maurine arrange to do lectures for local clubs after they returned, another possible source of income.[19]

There is no indication that Maurine had confided her urinary or menstrual problems to Max, so he had no way of knowing why she wanted to live closer to this urologist doctor friend. She told me that Max objected so strenuously to her going to California that she declined the Belts' generous offer and tried to tough it out in St. George where her ailing mother worried over her. In December, Elmer Belt sent her tablets of chocolate-coated pyridium, which he said was "an anesthetic substance which worked to numb the bladder and take away the pain."[20]

The next month, the usual respiratory ailments attacked her again. According to her memory in 1991, her St. George physician, Alphonzo McGregor, refused to treat her anymore "because I would not follow his advice to quit work and go to bed." In desperation, she took the bus sixty-five miles to Cedar City to Dr. A. L. Graff, whose children she had tended before starting work on *The Giant Joshua*. She trusted his concern for her—plus his generosity in waiting for his payment. Graff not only treated her but also gave her some money. Then her jinx struck again. The bus broke down on the way home to St. George, and the "miserable, cold delay" aggravated her condition. When Graff's medication failed to cure her, she took an even longer bus ride to Salt Lake City to another doctor who had befriended her and also agreed to "wait for pay." She could not remember whom she saw on this occasion, but she told me she "felt so driven to get back to work that I left Salt Lake City while I was still weak and had another relapse."

Still in shaky health, she apparently went to California where she stayed at a cheap hotel between March and perhaps May 1947. Elmer Belt probably helped her find a specialist who diagnosed a uterine tumor that might be cancerous. She agreed to surgery; but when she woke from the anesthetic, she discovered that the surgeon had performed a hysterectomy. This operation ended her probably unrealistic hopes for a child.[21] She was forty-four. Either she did not try to have the kidney and bladder reparation done at the same time, or the work was unsuccessful, necessitating another surgery later. In 1991 she repeatedly said, "I was so terribly alone and so lonely I hardly cared if I lived or died." She concealed the hysterectomy from her family, claiming that she wanted to protect her mother, who was still not well.

Lonely, broke, a charity case, unable to work, in pain, and terrified that she could not fulfill her contract, she recalls this period as "the low point of my life. Would anyone ever believe all of it?"

Also that spring, Maurine had pinned her hopes, fairly unrealistically, on winning the Guggenheim Award with the finished chapters and synopsis of "The Golden Door." This effort probably took much time away from the sequel. When news came that she did not win, she was very disappointed and wrote to Harry Hansen in quite a state. Although her letter has not survived, his reply indicates that she was sure that the Mormon Church had somehow worked against her behind the scenes. He expressed considerable skepticism about that conspiracy theory but encouraged her warmly: "While your deep emotions hurt you, they also will be your best asset in writing. You are an adorable person, and if you were here I'd tell you so with music."[22]

In late April, she finally sent Max the first chapter of the sequel. It had taken her almost five of the allotted twelve months to produce. She also tried to fend off pressure to finish Chapter 2 by explaining, "I have the second chapter partly finished but . . . after thinking it over, I have decided to collect some more material and rewrite it." She planned to visit the Arizona Strip for more local color.[23]

If what Maurine sent off to Max Becker corresponds to the surviving Chapter 1, "Taproot," it is a substantial piece of work: seventy-two pages long with considerable local color and material recycled from "The Arizona Strip" that establishes Jim as a cowboy. After the long wait, Max's reaction was unreservedly positive. He even thought "it would be better than *Joshua*," that it meant "they would undoubtedly sell both it and *Joshua* to a big movie company."[24]

It is not clear exactly how far Maurine got with the sequel. Her manuscript drafts are all incomplete and in great disorder. The papers include many loose pages without any obvious sequence. Four typed pages, in finished form and the original (most of the others are carbon copies on onion skin), do not fit any of the other finished work and seem to come from a later section of the manuscript. Its existence suggests that there was once a much longer manuscript. She believed that the manuscript was stolen in 1970 when her house was robbed.

High on her litany of laments was this robbery. Anna Cox, whom I interviewed in October 1991, remembered that she and her husband, Loraine, went to the trashed home and tried to help the distraught Maurine gather up the scattered papers and restore order. Both she and her husband remembered that Maurine was sure some books and manuscripts were missing. In fact, according to them, she was more upset about the missing manuscript than anything else. But neither one of them knew just what manuscript she was talking about. Maurine frequently told me in 1991–92 that this theft made it impossible for her to finish the sequel. Somehow this burglary became the explanation for her inability to have finished the sequel more than twenty years earlier.

To make matters even more confusing, Maurine's papers also include another title page headed "*The Giant Joshua* Trilogy," and identifying three parts: (1) "*The Giant Joshua*," (2) "The Candles of the Lord," and (3) "Lenzi." Then there is a title page for "Cleave the Wood" with four parts— "Taproot," "Seeding," "Unfolding" and "Fruition." Because Bill Battrick gave her the suggestion for the title, "Cleave the Wood," this title can be safely dated to after April 1946, when she asked Becker his opinion of "Come Ye Saints" as a possible title.[25] The quotation suggested by Battrick is from a noncanonical scripture: "Raise the stone and thou shalt find me. *Cleave the wood and I am there.*"[26]

Given Maurine's intense but erratic working style, it must have seemed impossible to complete the manuscript in the remaining seven months. It would certainly have required a sustained effort and a detached self-discipline similar to her best efforts when producing *Joshua*. But there were many distractions, besides sickness. One was the possibility of working as a consultant on a movie called *Rainbow over San Juan* being made in Moab. Max flatly opposed the suggestion, since it would distract her once again from the sequel. Maurine reluctantly yielded, explaining to me that she could see how "working on someone else's project while living on Simon and Schuster's money would not be ethical."

Another distraction was working at Zion National Park. She claimed that the job would have provided "a secluded cabin and three meals a day in exchange for a few hours of my time in the evenings" when she would present programs to the tourists.[27] Thus, she could devote most of her time to writing. And in fact, if she did not finish the sequel on time, she would still have an income—at least during the visitors' season. In 1991, she still thought it would have worked, but she said disgustedly, "Max talked me out of it, arguing that the duties would almost certainly be more time-consuming than I thought. But what he was really worried about was that it would reflect badly on him and Don Congdon if I didn't finish the sequel on time." That would have been true, and the fact that she knew it added to her stress. She capitulated to his recommendations resentfully, feeling "that my soul was mortgaged to Eastern powers."

But instead of settling down to her work, she began what seems an obsessive search for a better place to write. It must have seemed to Max that she was making that search a substitute for actually working. She claimed that, before the year's end, she moved six times.[28] From Hotel Utah, she moved to the boarding house near the University of Utah. Driven from it, she claimed, by all-day piano practicing, she moved to Provo in late April or May 1946, with help from friends (no doubt Elden and Florence Beck) and some "gentiles" at Geneva Steel, whom she could no longer remember. She remembered that the house belonged to the War Department and that, because Max did not send the July and August checks until the middle of each month, she couldn't pay on the first and was evicted. She blamed Max personally for this predicament.[29] She then arranged to use an office upstairs over an unidentified store, but that did not last either, because of what she felt again was more prejudice. All of these moves were costly in terms of time, physical effort, and psychic energy.

Probably during this short stay in Provo she tried to help her aunt, Clara McAllister, the first wife of her Uncle Martin McAllister. Clara had been committed to the state insane asylum in Provo and Maurine started to visit her. Maurine did not believe Clara merited institutionalization and said that "the administrator agreed." She said he described Clara as "wonderful for them to have there, that whenever they had trouble with a patient, they asked Clara to come and help quiet her, that she seemed to have a special ability." Maurine said "I wrote letters, trying to find a way to get Clara released, but to no avail."[30]

She also wasted more time trying to fight what she perceived as the Church's persecution of her by spilling out her tales of prejudice to E. R. Rasmussen, who worked for the *Provo Daily Herald*. He suggested she write to Frank Robertson, a novelist, historian, and columnist in Albuquerque, New Mexico, who might be interested in her experiences for his regular Sunday column.[31]

In August 1946, Maurine's short article, "Through the Utah Wonderlands," appeared in *Time* magazine. Her papers do not provide any clues about when she would have written this article. It was not the same article that, in the future, she would try hard to sell to other magazines, but seems to be taken from the same material. Almost certainly, she had done it in the winter or spring of 1946, squeezing out precious time from the sequel schedule. Its publication must have been a boost to her morale, especially given its national publication. It also brought in some money, with which she hoped to pay for the needed kidney operation. It wouldn't have been much, as it was less than one page with no pictures. But Max insisted she keep working and thought she should return to St. George. He wrote another strong letter to this effect and reminded her of her commitment to the book.[32] There is no record of her response, but she still remembered in 1992 how angry the pressure made her. "Once again, I simply could not make an Easterner understand how impossible life in St. George was for me."

Despite her pique, she did move back to St George. She probably thought her mother needed her, and that may have been true. It was late August or early September, blistering hot. Maurine was still in physical pain and agitated by the inexorable deadline which she was even farther from meeting. Four more months had gone by and there is no record that she had even finished Chapter 2. She was still dependent on her parents for working space in the same old north bedroom with the same saws snarling outside the window. The same old marital distress between her parents still poisoned the environment. It could not have been easy for Charlie and Annie, either, to have an adult daughter who was not only single and unemployed but who was writing "those things" that raised community eyebrows.

Maurine described herself to me as "on the verge of mental and physical collapse." She remembered how she took long walks to try for peace. During one of those walks she explored a gully in the red hills above town. There on a small hill she found a shack that she thought some woman had tried to build herself. In reality, it seems to have been on property that either had belonged to Charlie's brother, Eli, or which Charlie subsequently obtained rights to (now 320 North 100 East). When Maurine found the shack, it was dilapidated and filthy, but she seized on the idea of making it habitable. Ironically, although she had been too distracted by physical pain to work on the novel, she threw herself into the physically strenuous effort of creating a home, thus consuming almost the entire month of September. When someone gave her the shell of an old trailer, she positioned it near some cottonwoods by the shack. A friend brought a load of topsoil from Pine Valley, and Maurine planted a small lawn around the trailer, flanking the door with a rosebush and a bush of Clory's bergamot. She furnished the trailer with a table, chair, and cot, but went home to eat most meals and to sleep.

She now thought she had an almost ideal location: her beloved St. George was before her, Sugarloaf rose behind and to the west of her, and solitude and peace were now hers in which to welcome any ghosts from the past. She began work in this new nest, she told me, "by reading over the hundred pages" deciding it was all wrong, and "destroying it." She probably enjoyed my groan.

She wrote a letter of contrived optimism to Max on 3 November 1947, telling him that she didn't like her next few chapters and had destroyed them. Also, she wrote that the work done "was a third of the book but represented half from the standpoint of work involved." She predicted "finishing it by March, if not sooner, if I don't have to worry so much about what my agent and those at the publishing company were saying about me in New York." She predicted somewhat loftily that "it would be a good book, that I have a vision that, while I can't attain it, I can come close." She sent back the last three checks, all uncashed, in a face-saving gesture, with a snippy note that lengthened into accusations and all-too-familiar appeals for understanding.

Max quickly wrote a letter of apology, saying "I just did not understand, especially about the persecution." But he made another blunder when he mentioned the predicament an agent was in who presented a client to a publisher as he had her. He was worried for all, especially for Don Congdon at Simon and Schuster, when she did not seem to be working.[33] Clearly, from Max's perspective, Maurine was the one who didn't understand.

And even before Maurine got this letter of simultaneous reassurance and pressure, she had already taken yet more time away from her book to write a lengthy "you see" letter to Congdon, telling him the story of the failed relationship with Greenslet and Houghton Mifflin and how they had financially exploited her and made life difficult until she could no longer maintain a relationship with them.[34]

Congdon wrote back kindly, saying that "the rumor did not mean a thing" and that his "job was not in jeopardy."[35] Maurine had asked him whether the word "condition," as in "mental condition," was in general use in 1893. He suggested she check William James to see if he used the word in his psychological studies. This little example shows how seriously Maurine tried to keep her characters true to their times.

On 15 January 1947, a routine note from Houghton Mifflin informed her that it had given Ray B. West permission to include pages 529–34, from *The Giant Joshua*, which described Brigham Young's dedication of the St. George Temple, in his forthcoming *Rocky Mountain Reader*. "Enclosed is your half of the twenty-dollar fee."[36]

Maurine still could not let the 1946 matter with Simon and Schuster rest and get on with her writing. A letter from Harry Hansen in December reveals that she sent him a copy of her letter to Max, asking him to help Simon and Schuster understand that none of the "reasons the sequel was not finished was Don's fault." Harry sympathetically agreed that Max was "applying the wrong kind of pressure" and said Max had been "called on the carpet over it and would not do it again." He also complimented her on her epistolary style: "You could write a whole series of letters, just spontaneous work, that could be put in a book."[37]

As December brought winter to St. George, Maurine's short respite was over. It was too cold to continue working in the trailer, and she found her parents' home intolerable. She was in physical pain from her ailments, no doubt exacerbated by psychological stress at missing the deadline.

On 22 December 1946, three weeks after the missed deadline with apparently no additional chapters sent off to Max since April—not even the eighty pages of the new draft—she again wrote a lengthy, confessional letter to Don Congdon: "I can't stick it out here in St. George during the cold weather. By April I'll be able to come back, but if I'm continually ill from working in the cold, I'm not going to be able to get the book out. It looks as if I'm coming down with a relapse of the flu." Then follows again a rambling, piteous explanation of how difficult things were for her including, incidentally, the only mention in her papers of the automobile accident that was causing her kidney problem, but still without details. She told Don she was planning to "find a housekeeping job that would still allow me a few hours in which to write." She also told him that she had written to "a good friend who managed a hotel [Whit Parry, owner of Kanab's Parry Lodge] to inquire about the possibility of giving him publicity in exchange for quarters, but of course the chance for that is slight." The third, she said, was the possibility of getting Max to "sell some of the other things I have written"—she doesn't specify what. She thought she could also write some other short, saleable pieces. "People seem to crave humor these days—as witness, *The Egg and I*.[38] My adventures writing *Joshua* were funny enough, and I've listened to thousands of people roar over them," meaning when she recounted them in a lecture. She enclosed an abbreviation of one of her war-bond lectures.[39]

Few people receiving such naked pleas refused to respond positively. However, in this instance, there is no evidence of Congdon's reaction. Perhaps taking a cold, hard look at Maurine's track record and her obvious physical and emotional instability, he decided that Simon and Schuster should simply cut its losses, merely leaving the door open in case Maurine ever finished the manuscript. In early 1947, he left Simon and Schuster to start his own literary agency. Max, however, did not give up and continued pestering Maurine with reminders about her obligations through the rest of 1946. Maurine appealed to Congdon to rescue her.[40] Again Don did not respond.

Maurine apparently did not begin work on her manuscript again until late January 1947. When the weather permitted, she spent some "glorious days" in her trailer under the Sugarloaf; but instead of spending the energy writing, she revived her project of remodeling the shack. "Even though friends like Katherine Miles Larson and Anna Cox thought I was crazy, they helped me," she said and grudgingly admitted that Charlie also worked on it. Probably he actually did most of the work—an active way of showing his unspoken love and on-going care for her. But instead of giving him credit, Maurine claimed it was a retired school teacher, Merrill Fawson, an easy-going man of her father's generation, as the one who was the most help.

Maurine also spent a great deal of time with Anna during this spring trying to help her with her five children. She wanted to repay Anna for her many kindnesses. Anna's seven-year-old, James Carter ("Jimmy") Cox, was burned severely when the top level of the house caught fire. His father, Loraine, saved his life by catching him up and running through the fire down the stairs. Jimmy was in the hospital for a long time recovering from his burns and needed tutoring for several months. Maurine volunteered to tutor him.[41]

When Redlands University held its sixteenth annual Writers' Week, 20 April 1947, Maurine delivered a lecture on "The Writing of the Historical Novel," repeating it in an afternoon session. Three days later, she taught another seminar, subject unspecified. She kept a newspaper clipping quoting the conference organizers' apologies that so few students had participated (more townspeople had attended) and that the school band made lecturing difficult by "practicing above them."[42] She also apparently attended the 1947 Rocky Mountain Writers' Conference in Boulder, Colorado, where she could earn a little money by teaching classes on novel-writing. No correspondence, however, documents her activities during the spring and summer of 1947.[43]

Despite this record to the contrary, Maurine saw herself as continually working on the sequel. Two more chapters exist in finished form. In Chapter 2 (twenty pages), Jim has left the Arizona Strip, quit his "cowboying" and is in St. George, reestablishing ties with the young people his age. This chapter takes the reader through the town, describing the landmarks, reintroducing characters from *Joshua*, and developing the relationship between Jim and his two friends—Frank Wright, the scientist, and Tony, the philosopher. It also introduces the villain, who is Jim's rival for the love of Thanksie.

Chapter 3 shows Jim in a nostalgic mood, visiting his dead mother's old home. He realizes that he is a "dumb punk" and needs some educating. Maurine's papers also included two other partial chapters. One, presumably designed for the "Seedling" section, is missing the first and twenty-sixth pages. It leaps ahead several years. Jim and Thanksie's daughter, Lenzi, is celebrating her sixth birthday. Thanksie is dead, and Jim is raising Lenzi with the help of his half-sister, Tempie, the daughter of Abijah McIntyre's second wife. In this delightful chapter, Maurine reintroduces characters from the *Giant Joshua*, now a generation older. Lenzi was probably modeled on Maurine's niece, Carol Ann Whipple, born in 1938.

At that point, continuity frays out. It was a project Maurine continued to pick up for the next thirty years. It was proof that she was a writer. It was a comforting mental room into which she could walk and resume the identity of the tale-weaver of St. George's past. It was part of her hopes, her dreams, herself. But it was also a project Maurine continued to put down, lay aside, and override with other projects for the rest of her life.

Notes

1 An undated newspaper advertisement announced that she would be in Penney's Book Department Tuesday to personally autograph the copies purchased of *"This Is the Place: Utah* — a book that everyone will be proud to own." Whipple Scrapbook; Maurine Whipple Collection, L. Tom Perry Special Collections, Harold B. Lee Library, Brigham Young University, Provo, Utah, with photocopy in Maurine Whipple Collection, Archive, Val A. Browning Library, Dixie College, St. George, Utah. Documents in both collections hereafter cited as BYU, photocopy Dixie College.

2 The acknowledgments in *This Is the Place: Utah* thanks "Eric Snow and Vernon Snow, who furnished the workshop."

3 Harry Hansen, *New York World Telegram*, Letter to Maurine Whipple, 4 January 1946; BYU, photocopy Dixie College.

4 Maurine Whipple, Letter to Dean Brimhall, 11 February 1946, Dean R. Brimhall Papers, Special Collections, Marriott Library, University of Utah, Salt Lake City; photocopy Dixie College.

5 Maurine Whipple, Rough draft of letter to Max Becker, November 1946, Dixie College.

6 Read Bain, Letter to Maurine Whipple, 19 February 1946; BYU, photocopy Dixie College.

7 Bernard DeVoto, *Saturday Review of Literature*, 24 April 1937, quoted in Jarvis A. Thurston, "Critic Praises Whipple Book on Polygamy," *Ogden Examiner*, loose clipping, n.d., Dixie College.

8 Reverend Clayton S. Rice, Seattle, Washington, Letter to Maurine Whipple, 20 February 1946; BYU.

9 Hughie Call, Rockdale, Texas, Letter to Maurine Whipple, 25 March 1946; BYU, photocopy Dixie College.

10 Page of incomplete unknown manuscript, Brigham Young University Library, photocopy in Veda Tebbs Hale Collection, Dixie College.

11 Joseph Walker, Letter to Maurine Whipple, 7 July 1943; BYU, photocopy Dixie College.

[12] The manuscripts of the sequel in Maurine's papers at BYU and at Dixie College include: (1) an eleven-page typescript synopsis and a sixty-six-page longer synopsis. The longer one was written first and includes *The Giant Joshua* material. Evidence of the sequence is that the protagonist is named "Chloe," Clory's original name (pages 1–3 are missing) and includes *The Giant Joshua*; (2) "Chapter One," a seventy-two page typescript, includes the quotation, "Cleave the Wood," thus dating it ca. 1945–46; (3) "Chapter Two," 26 pages (page 1 is missing); (4) "Chapter Three," no title, (Jim goes back to his mother's house after deciding to leave the cowboy life.) 20 pages; (5) "Chapter Four, " 75 pages; no title, Jim, Frank, and Tony participate in the St. George young people's society. Thanksie is being wooed by outsider Selwyn Sanderson, a photographer; (6) Another "Chapter One," with first page missing: Lenzi's sixth birthday party with many of the old characters from *Joshua*; (7) "Character Studies of Frank, Jim, Thanksie, Tempie, and Briggie." One loose page reads: "This is the story of one human being's search for faith—for something to believe in. The story begins with Jim MacIntyre, son of Clory MacIntyre, a character in *The Giant Joshua*. Other than this, the book bears no relation to its predecessor."

[13] Maximilian Becker, A.F.G Literary Agency, New York, Letter to Maurine Whipple, 4 March 1946, Whipple Collection, BYU Library. Congdon left Simon and Schuster in January 1947, joining the Harold Matson Company literary agency. He edited *The Thirties: A Time to Remember* (New York: Simon and Schuster, 1932), a compilation of essays about that turbulent decade. In 1962 he edited three books about World War II.

[14] Maurine Whipple, Letter to Max Becker, n.d. [ca. February 1946]; Whipple Collection, BYU; photocopy, Dixie College.

[15] Max Becker, Letter to Maurine Whipple, 12 March 1946; BYU, photocopy Dixie College.

[16] She later described her illness as a "bad cold which laid me up for two weeks" but said she borrowed $200 without mentioning that Max had sent the check back to her again. Maurine Whipple, Letter to Don Congdon, 27 January 1947; BYU, photocopy Dixie College.

[17] Maurine Whipple, draft of letter to Max Becker, 27 March 1946; BYU, photocopy Dixie College.

[18] Florence Jolley, Washington City, Utah, Letter to Maurine Whipple, 22 February 1946; BYU, photocopy Dixie College.

[19] Maryruth Belt, 2201 Fern Dell Place, Los Angeles 28, Calif., Letter to Maurine Whipple, 38 August 1946; BYU.

[20] Elmer Belt, Letter to Maurine Whipple, 12 December 1946; BYU.

[21] This doctor was James C. Doyle, a gynecologist with a prestigious address in Beverly Hills. When some years later, she sent him a copy of her article on the Arizona Strip published in *Collier's* in May 1952 (see chap. 25), he responded with thanks and a copy of his paper, "Unnecessary Ovariectomies," that he had presented at the American Medical Association meeting in Los Angeles in December 1951. This probably left Maurine wondering if she were one of the unnecessary surgeries. Always supersensitive about her health, she started to think so, and the possibility became another source of regret to her. James C. Doyle, MD, F.A.C.S., Gynecology, 9730 Wilshire Boulevard, Beverly Hills, Calif., Letter to Maurine Whipple, (no day) June 1952; BYU.

THE FAILED SEQUEL, 1946-47

22 Harry Hansen, *New York World Telegram*, Letter to Maurine Whipple, 15 May 1946; BYU, photocopy Dixie College.

23 Maurine Whipple, Letter to Maximilian Becker, 18 April 1946; BYU, photocopy Dixie College.

24 Max Becker, Letter to Maurine Whipple, 24 April 1946; BYU, photocopy Dixie College.

25 Maurine Whipple, Letter to Max Becker, 18 April 1946; BYU, photocopy Dixie College. The letter in which Battrick proposed "Cleave the Wood" was typed, and he did not have access to a typewriter until 1946. Since he tells her he was "teaching two sections of Freshman English, a section of fiction, and a section of Poetry: classes begin Monday," this context suggests September 1946 for his undated letter. Bill Battrick, Letter to Maurine Whipple, n.d. [ca. September 1946); BYU, photocopy Dixie College.

26 Bernard S. Grenfell and Arthur S. Hunt, trans. and eds., "Saying no. 30/70," Oxyrhynehus Papyri I, in *The Transcription of Oxyrhynehus* (Oxford, Eng.: Queen's College, October 1907), 654–55. Paragraph 1 is from *Fragment of a Lost Gospel*, the second and third from *New Sayings of Jesus*, and the fourth from the *Logia*. These papyri were discovered around 1900.

27 Maurine Whipple, Letter to Don Congdon, 27 January 1947; BYU, photocopy Dixie College.

28 Ibid.

29 Ibid.

30 Though I didn't often date notes from our discussions, I did this time. It was 4 April 1992.

31 E. R. Rasmussen, *Provo Daily Herald*, Letter to Maurine Whipple, 8 May 1946; BYU, photocopy Dixie College. Frank C. Robertson's column, "The Chopping Block," was a lively commentary on many subjects.

32 Max Becker, Letter to Maurine Whipple, n.d. [ca. August 1946]; BYU.

33 Max Becker, Letter to Maurine Whipple, 8 November 1946; BYU, photocopy Dixie College.

34 Maurine Whipple, Letter to Don Congdon, Simon and Schuster, 14 November 1946; BYU, photocopy Dixie College.

35 Don Congdon, Letter to Maurine Whipple, (no day) November 1946; BYU.

36 Hardwick Moseley, Letter to Maurine Whipple, 15 January 1947, with a copy to Max Becker; BYU, photocopy Dixie College.

37 Harry Hansen, Letter to Maurine Whipple, (no day) December 1946; BYU.

38 *The Egg and I* (1945) by Betty MacDonald was a comical account of "raising chickens and children" on forty-acre run-down farm on the rainy, Olympic Peninsula that was made into a successful *Ma and Pa Kettle* movie.

39 Maurine Whipple, Letter to Don Congder; 22 December 1946; BYU.

40 Maurine Whipple, Letter to Don Congdon, 27 January 1947; BYU, photocopy Dixie College.

41 He earned his master's degree and worked at Dixie State University as the testing director. Camie Carter Higgins, email to Veda Hale, 13 April 2003.

42 Loose undated clipping from unidentified newspaper, no headline; BYU.

"SWELL SUFFERING"

[43] An exception is a request on 21 May 1947 from a Dr. Ralph Richards at the University Club in Salt Lake City thanking Maurine briefly for responding to his request for information about St. George's three early doctors: Israel Ivins, J. T. Affleck, and Silas G. Higgins.

17

UTAH CENTENNIAL, 1947

Whatever work on the sequel Maurine managed to fit in during the spring of 1947 took a decided back seat to the upcoming celebration of the centennial of the Mormon pioneers' entry into the Salt Lake Valley on 24 July 1847. Because Maurine saw herself as a local celebrity and historical expert, a participant in and maker of history, she was determined to find a place for herself in the festivities.

She spent an incalculable amount of time during the summer of 1947 exploring the state's southeastern remoteness with Utah Wonderland Tours run by Stewart Campbell, the same man who had taken her through this scenic country in 1945, when she had been gathering information for her Utah book. Both then and in 1947 she had promised publicity for this new tour business venture. It seems that she mixed the two trips together to write one long article usually referred to as "Utah Wonderland Tour" or "The Celebratory Tour," and a short article, "Through the Utah Wonderlands," printed in *Time* August 1946.[1] Though brief, barely a column long, it must have proven to Campbell that she could give him publicity.

In what may be a draft of a magazine article, "Stewart Campbell," she describes how the tour began with "addle-pated Mormon boys owning a DeSoto Stagecoach and some surplus army sleeping bags." She claims that it was "the first commercial penetration of the Plateau Province," and she may very well be correct. This three-page undated typescript paints a breezy portrait of "Stu," a great-grandson of Brigham Young and Emily Dow Partridge Young, who had earlier been Joseph Smith's plural wife.[2]

Maurine also claimed she was the only woman who made the trip, probably both trips. She was obviously in better health than usual; but, even accounting for her natural hyperbole, it was a tough scramble both times.

"Since there were few if any roads (along one 55-mile stretch we had to build our own road every inch of the way—a road that necessarily crossed a river 65 times), we came close to real danger on several occasions."[3]

To river-runner Norman Nevills on the Colorado, in June 1947 she explained that the tour organizers hoped to "lead a tour per week over the same route." She had accompanied the first group as "a sort of dude-wrangler and yarn-spinner," planning to write up the experience for *Life Magazine*, then America's premier photo-journalism periodical. She claimed the magazine would send along "one of their best photographers." Enthusiastically, she envisioned a feature with several pages of full-color photographs and asked, "Was it possible to see Rainbow Bridge in two days?"[4] A couple of years later, she enthused to the *Saturday Evening Post* about the still-unexploited magazine article possibilities of the Wonderland Tour experience: "Perhaps you know that Utah has 17,000 square miles that are unsurveyed, unexplored and unmapped, supposedly the largest virgin territory left in continental United States and certainly the most inaccessible":

> We built our own roads. We were marooned in one of those catastrophic desert cloud bursts for three days. We heaved boulders for 65 crossings of the Dirty-devil River, and then had to retrace our steps 400 miles. We flew over the goosenecks of the San Juan and crash landed the plane in the funnel of a roaring dust devil. We were lost from the world for ten days during which we couldn't even reach a telephone. But . . . [ellipses hers] we saw 1000 miles of scenery more unbelievable than all the famous red battlements of Southern Utah's National Parks (with which I am not unfamiliar): we interviewed ex-bandits and some not so "ex" (the only surviving member of Butch Cassidy's famous outlaw gang lives out there, still flourishing his artillery); Navajo medicine men; villages so glad to see "outsiders" that the citizenry welcomed us en masse; and finally, "spiritual caretakers," that rare breed of men made of rawhide and bailing wire exclusive to the lost places.
>
> Eventually we "brought 'em back alive"—pictures and research—but it's no exaggeration to say that we, ourselves, almost died doing it. For three years I have felt that the story of the tour, itself, with accompanying photographs, would make one of the most fascinating articles a magazine could publish, since by nature this expedition will always be dependent upon that element of the population willing to risk its neck.[5]

The photographer who made this trip was Loomis Dean.[6] In 1991, she recalled him as "fun and exciting to be with, but frustratingly jaded." By "jaded" she meant that it was terribly hard to arouse his enthusiasm. The magazine promised her a small fee, whether it published her article or not (it didn't) and, despite her lack of official status, gave her a *Life* badge to wear.

To her, it represented belonging, a ticket to big-time magazine writing. She energetically magnified this status symbol, sailing forth in high spirits, demanding and receiving respect and cooperation in most places. For example, she told me about the Nauvoo Caravan, a reenactment by the Sons of Utah Pioneers in automobiles of part of the trek across the plains with plywood cut-outs of oxen and wagons attached to the vehicles.[7] She arranged for "the entire village of Huntsville to stage a one day celebration, including a feast, so the *Life* staff could get good photographs." At this point, Loomis Dean had been joined by a colleague, Grant Allen.

During the 24th of July parade in Salt Lake City in 1947, she arranged for the police to halt Main Street traffic for an hour so Loomis and Allen could get the photographs they needed. Maurine told another interviewer that she acted like a film director, urging the parade participants being photographed to, as she said, "get an expression on their faces that would set them apart," communicate their "loyalty" and their feeling "that showing their history of the Church was great. After I worked with them, a man who had been observing me came up and asked who I was. I told him my name. He commented, 'That is a wonderful thing that you're doing' and introduced himself as George Albert Smith, president of the Church."[8]

The Centennial Tour began at the steps of the capitol. With it, Maurine retraced her steps through many of the sites she had visited for *This Is the Place: Utah*, this time with Loomis Dean, Grant Allen, and perhaps other members of the *Life* team. It was easy to feel the poignancy of Maurine's pride at being one of the *Life* team, flashing her *Life* badge at awestruck locals, and impressing these important journalists with her skill at hunting up interesting people, unusual territory, and newsworthy situations. Obviously, in comparison, the sequel had no charm. Writing would have involved sitting alone, day after day in some dreary room, straining to attune her prose to an elusive historical note on a long piece of fiction that she must have feared would make little money.

Furthermore, it seems likely that she was only too contented to be in male company again. She told me that she found Loomis Dean more attractive than Grant Allen, even though he manifested no romantic interest in her. She admitted "I probably did talk too much about myself"—meaning the tragedies of her life, her exploitation by New York editors and agents, and the LDS Church's sinister campaign against her. She complained to me that Loomis failed to show the proper concern and sympathy. I deduced from what happened later and from Maurine's partly self-pitying, partly self-aware comments, that he wrote her off as a self-absorbed, neurotic woman, foolishly posing as at least a decade younger than her actual age.

"SWELL SUFFERING"

Maurine quartered the state doing research for her second (and last) book, *This Is the Place, Utah!* Here, she cools her feet in the shallow Virgin River. Photo courtesy of Anna Cox.

Loomis, who had probably read *The Giant Joshua*, had reason to respect Maurine's writing ability; and as she remembered it, he suggested she write up their trip through Utah as a text piece for *Life*. She understood that he had authority to give her an expense account and thought he had done so. Therefore, she stayed at Hotel Utah for two weeks after the trip had been completed and wrote a 12,000-word story. Jack Beardwood, chief of *Life's* West Coast office, and Wilson Hicks, assistant managing editor of the same office, were delighted with it, paid her $125, and wrote that, if the story ran, she would get "$20 per day plus expenses from the time you left St. George until your return."[9] They were less delighted when Maurine had the hotel send *Life* her bill for $55.59. She didn't know that the proper procedure would have been for her to pay the bill, then submit it for reimbursement; but she, of course, did not have enough working capital to have paid her own bill. Beardwood seemed most concerned that the misunderstanding would make *Life* personnel less welcome in the future at Hotel Utah.[10]

Before matters were straightened out, Maurine understood that, because of her unprofessional behavior, she was not going to get paid for more writing nor would more expenses be reimbursed. Beardwood did say, when he gave her this bad news, that he had passed on her suggestion about what Maurine called her "Josie" story to the New York office and was "expecting a reply soon."[11] Maurine had met Josie Bassett Morris in 1942 in Vernal and mentioned her briefly in the *This Is the Place: Utah*. Josie was a contemporary of the colorful outlaws who frequented Brown's Hole, a remote area near Vernal, Utah, where Utah, Colorado, and Wyoming meet. Josie was also a self-proclaimed rustler who had homesteaded a ranch in Brown's Hole, lost it when she mortgaged it to help a granddaughter, and then at seventy-eight was determined to get it back. Maurine would naturally admire this self-sufficiency in another lone woman who had had some tough breaks but hadn't given up. The piece she wrote describes Josie's life, emphasizing her "salty, common good sense and resourcefulness" in dealing with men who wanted to take over her land.

Roy Craft, who would turn out to be Maurine's staunchest friend at *Life*, wrote from the Los Angeles office on 18 September, saying "your letters continue to delight us" and adding, "Glad to have Beardwood back in the saddle. Loomis Dean is as screwy as ever." This comment suggests that Maurine had won some confidence back from Beardwood and that she might not have been the only one to have had trouble with Loomis. Roy also told Maurine he had "sent forward a long memo to New York recommending the Josie story." Then he described just the kinds of assignments Maurine would have loved doing—going with Loomis Dean into Joshua tree country with a group of scientists to examine "belly plants" and writing a story about movie star Mary Pickford, her husband, Buddy Rogers, and their two adopted children at Pickfair.[12] It was very easy for Maurine to read herself into these same scenes, a sophisticated, wordsmithing magazine journalist, hobnobbing with celebrities and cultural elites.

Life executives soon gave Maurine the go-ahead for the story on Josie Morris and wrote that they were assigning Grant Allen to the project. Maurine wrote at least one probably lengthy and certainly tactless letter to the New York office explaining that Loomis Dean had a better way with difficult subjects like cowboys and Josie Morris and that Grant probably could not handle the rough going and horseback riding that would be required.[13] She was persuasive, and Loomis was reassigned to her story; but he was not pleased to be jerked off the set of an Ingrid Bergman movie for what he considered to be a minor assignment. Nor, presumably, was Allen pleased to have his skills declared inadequate. Maurine laughed bitterly about this as she told me, "I didn't know that Loomis didn't think the Josie story wouldn't be fun to go on, and didn't know he knew I had requested him. Like a damn fool, I thought I was doing him a favor."

While they were waiting in Salt Lake City in early October for some bad weather to clear, *Life* decided to have Loomis cover the Charles C. Rich family reunion.[14] Maurine told me sadly how she had gone to Salt Lake City early, waiting for Dean to ask her to help on the Rich story. He didn't bother to do so until the night before, giving her no time to do research on the family. Then he treated her with impatience and even rudeness. His behavior at the reunion mystified her—especially why he was not getting the information that was essential for the captions of the pictures. And why was he so angry with her?

She spent Wednesday night, all of Thursday, and most of Friday during the first part of October working on the article, going to bed at 2:00 A.M. and getting up at 5:00 A.M. to skim through the autobiography of the pioneer patriarch. She finished at noon on Friday. Based on her understanding of *Life*'s payment policies, she thought she was making at least $20 a day plus $12 for expenses.[15] She submitted a bill for two days' work. She told me that the story Dean sent back to New York was "in a sloppy condition. You know, he didn't even use my work the way I had put it together. Anyway Robert Girvin criticized the work and Loomis blamed me. So then Loomis was told not to use my work again. Can you imagine how I felt?" But before Loomis had received these instructions, he and Maurine had already left for Vernal.

The trip to Vernal was anything but pleasant. Getting into the back country was an ordeal. According to a spate of letters Maurine wrote in late October and November trying to defend her reputation from charges that she was a sloppy writer and accusing Dean of scapegoating her for matters that were his own fault, she ended up alone in a jeep with a cowboy. When it got stuck, they were there for the night, and she later wrote, "I hadn't closed my eyes the night we spent at Joe's—you knew that—and I had been almost raped, putting the fact baldly. Funny as it seems, that was a terribly upsetting experience."[16]

They finally got to Josie's remote ranch where they took a photograph of her poaching a deer. They also wanted to show Josie rustling a cow—to be paid for by *Life*—but Dean decided to do this on a return trip and sent Maurine home. She was confused. More research was necessary and it would have taken only a few more hours, a few more interviews, and a little research time at the county courthouse.[17]

According to one of the defensive letters—this one to Jack Beardwood and the West Coast *Time-Life* office—the cowboy who had, she said, tried to rape her in the jeep, telephoned her from Vernal saying the *Life* people had been there without her. Was she being double crossed? He was also concerned about what might be written about him and about Josie.[18]

Horrified, she wrote another long letter to Girvin, keeping a copy.[19] She was determined to clear her name, still wanted very much to work for *Life*, but also wanted to protect her Vernal sources. Although there is no indication of how Loomis Dean told the story and Girvin does not seem to have responded directly to her, this treatment does seem unfair, even though her working style and personality undoubtedly made her a difficult journalist partner. Given the attitudes of the time, however, Maurine's dauntless fights to achieve in a man's world are worth cheering.

About this time, she struck up a correspondence with Mary Alves, a secretary in the *Life* East Coast office. They exchanged scenic postcards, and a letter from Mary on 6 October tells Maurine how much she would like to visit the West. She also mentioned that she (Mary) felt that the men in the office treated her shabbily.[20] Maurine apparently hoped Mary would be able to help her, not understanding that a secretary had little, if any, influence. Nothing more came of this relationship.

The 27 October issue of the magazine printed the Rich family reunion story, according to what Maurine told me, "with caption text using my research and my writing, almost verbatim."[21] At this point, Maurine had heard that she had been barred from writing for *Life* because of "sloppy" work on the reunion story. She indignantly wired Loomis Dean, now back in New York, asking, "If my research was good enough to use, why am I cast into outer darkness for supplying it?" She followed up on 20 October with a four-page letter to Dean trying to reverse the unfair decision and also to protect her sources and her work on the Josie Morris story. She had this letter neatly typed and kept a carbon copy. She warned that the letter would be "rather longish" and it was—more than 2,500 words—and the tone ranges from factual to pleading, from outrage to pathos. She laid out the facts from her standpoint and told about how difficult it had been for her, how she had been nearly raped one night, and then asked pointed questions about his motives.[22]

As matters turned out, Loomis half-apologized, telling her in a short letter that he had gone back to Vernal without her because he thought she was "upset" by the near-rape and that she "was ill." Yes, he had taken a few more photographs when they had staged the rustling, but he had never intended not using Maurine's text nor give her credit for it.[23] He followed up with another letter, apparently after she had accepted this apology, by offering a fuller-leafed olive branch: "I'm sorry too, so please try to forgive me." He added astutely, "I'll bet if you put all your letter writing time on writing your book you would have your Hollywood house sooner than you expect."[24]

Furthermore, *Life* bought Josie's story (no information on the amount of money Maurine received) under the title of "Josie, Queen of the Cattle Rustlers," but apparently didn't publish it. Maurine's papers include two manuscript versions, one thirteen pages long, the other twenty-one pages long, accompanied by eight black and white photographs, plus various notes and a few pages that seem to have come from an earlier draft.25

Looking back on this event from the 1990s, Maurine bitterly reflected to me that, even though she was vindicated and had proved she was the wronged party, "I still ended up the loser." It seems that *Life* was no longer interested in working with someone who, though competent as a researcher and writer, brought emotional chaos in her wake. Pathetically, Maurine was the last to realize this situation. In December, she went to Los Angeles, bearing Christmas greenery for her acquaintances at the *Life* office. She hoped that it was only the New York office that found her *persona non grata*, and the image of her trying to ingratiate herself and be "one of the gang" is a painful one. Rather than being included in office parties and holiday visits, she ended up alone in a hotel, ill with a fever of 105, little money, and thinking again of suicide. It was most likely Roy Craft from the *Life* office who paid her hotel bill and got her to the hospital. He had been corresponding personally with Maurine, talking about his own novel in progress. Most certainly he had read *The Giant Joshua* and had been impressed by her skill. In a letter written soon after Christmas 1947, he wrote: "I feel you are included in the hunch I have that 1948 would be a good year."26 Maurine, her memory jogged by this letter, told me that because Roy admired *The Giant Joshua*, he had encouraged her writing, and even took up a collection in the office to get her some money. Despite the well-meaning intentions of these men, they did not understand that what she needed was an emotionally intense but nonromantic relationship that combined cajolery, affection, and firm focus on the writing goal. Even if they had, which of them could or would have offered such a relationship? Writing was solitary work; and Maurine, desperate for an association of friends who "talked her language," had no talent for solitude.

Her correspondence file marked "Roy Craft" contains thirteen letters. After 1948, he was the only person from the Los Angeles *Life* office with whom she had any contact. His last letter to her, written in 1957, is warm: "I'm delighted you're coming down. Gracie [Roy's wife] says to tell you that the spare room (I still laughingly call it the Den! *My* Den!) is vacant."27

The Centennial of the Mormon entrance into Utah was over. So was her hoped-for career as a *Life* writer. She was still broke, still in physical pain, still cripplingly lonely, still rooted in St. George's redrock but essentially homeless. And the sequel was still unfinished.

Notes

[1] The surviving pages having to do with this tour are hard to put together. It appears that the longer version of "Through the Utah Wonderlands" originally was thirty-six pages long, but the surviving version is missing pp. 2–3, 9–11, and 13–20; Maurine Whipple Collection, L. Tom Perry Special Collections, Harold B. Lee Library, Brigham Young University, Provo, Utah, hereafter cited as BYU.

[2] Maurine Whipple, "Stewart Campbell," typescript, 3 pp., quotation from p. 1; photocopy in Maurine Whipple Collection, Archive, Val A. Browning Library, Dixie College, St. George, Utah, hereafter Dixie College.

[3] Maurine Whipple, Letter to *Holiday Magazine*, n.d., Whipple Collection, BYU Library. Apparently *Holiday Magazine* refused the proposal, although there is no rejection letter among her papers.

[4] Maurine Whipple, Letter to Norm Nevills, 18 June 1947, Norman Nevills Collection, Special Collections, Marriott Library, University of Utah, Salt Lake City, photocopy Dixie College.

[5] Maurine Whipple, draft of letter to Miss [Peggy] Dowst, *Saturday Evening Post*, 14 June 1949; BYU, photocopy Dixie College.

[6] In a conversation with me, she was quite sure that it was Loomis Dean who had been the photographer still in Utah (or again) during the October deer hunt. As a prank, "we obtained a stuffed deer in less than tip-top shape, propped it up near the entrance to the tunnel on the road into St. George, hid ourselves, and enjoyed the drivers' reactions."

[7] Cannon D. Jones, *Centennial Caravan Nauvoo, Illinois to Salt Lake Valley, July 14–22, 1947* (Salt Lake City: Sons of Utah Pioneers, 1948).

[8] Maurine Whipple, interviewed by Curtis Taylor, January 1989, transcript, 55–56; Charles Redd Center, Harold B. Lee Library, Brigham Young University; photocopy Dixie College.

[9] Jack B. Beardwood, *Time-Life* Editorial Office, Los Angeles, Calif., Letter to Maurine Whipple, 26 July 1947; BYU, photocopy Dixie College.

[10] Jack Beardwood, Letter to Maurine Whipple, Los Angeles, n.d.; BYU, photocopy Dixie College.

[11] Ibid.

[12] Roy Craft, Letter to Maurine Whipple, 18 September 1947; BYU, photocopy Dixie College. This letter is the first of twenty that have survived from Roy, the last, dated 18 August 1957. Roy became successful as a Hollywood publicist, particularly for Marilyn Monroe.

[13] Maurine Whipple, Letter to "Jack" (presumably Beardwood), *Life* office, ca. late September 1947; BYU. This draft is on a scrap of deteriorating newsprint in Maurine's hand, 3 pp., front and back. It is the only document I have found indicating that *Life* had accepted her "Josie" story. She notes that the distance from St. George to Vernal is 436 miles and that she needed a car—presumably meaning that she needed to rent one.

[14] Charles Coulson Rich, a Mormon apostle and polygamist, was born August 21, 1809, and settled Bear Lake Valley, just across the state line in Idaho.

"SWELL SUFFERING"

[15] Maurine Whipple, Letter to Robert E. Girvin, New York City, July 11, 1948; BYU, photocopy Dixie College. In this lengthy letter, she defends herself, refusing to take the blame for the sloppy work on the Rich reunion story.

[16] Maurine Whipple, Letter to Robert E. Girvin, 11 July '47 [1948]; BYU, photocopy Dixie College.

[17] Ibid.

[18] Maurine Whipple, Letter to Jack Beardwood, 4 November 1947; BYU, photocopy Dixie College.

[19] Maurine Whipple, Letter to Robert E. Girvin, July 11, '47 [1948]; BYU, photocopy Dixie College.

[20] Mary Alves, Letter to Maurine Whipple, 6 October 1947; BYU, photocopy Dixie College.

[21] "Rich Family Reunion," *Life*, 27 October 1947, 59–60, 62. There were no bylines for the photos or captions.

[22] Maurine Whipple, Letter to Loomis Dean, 20 October 1947, 4 pp., typescript; BYU, photocopy Dixie College.

[23] Loomis Dean, Letter to Maurine Whipple, ca. early November 1947; Dixie College.

[24] Loomis Dean, Letter to Maurine Whipple, 8 November 1947; Dixie College.

[25] Maurine Whipple, "The Queen of the Cattle Rustlers," both versions and photographs; BYU. According to Roy Craft, Letter to Maurine Whipple, 24 March 1948, BYU, Maurine received an edited version, which gave her some hope that it would be published.

[26] Roy Craft, *Life*, 9147 Sunset Blvd. Los Angeles 46, Calif., Letter to Maurine Whipple, Saturday, 3 January 1948; BYU, photocopy Dixie College.

[27] Roy Craft, Letter to Maurine Whipple, 18 August 1957; BYU, photocopy Dixie College.

❧ 18 ❦

DETOUR INTO MAGAZINE WRITING, 1948

Maurine dragged herself back from her miserable Christmas in California to find that St. George was a-thrill with news that Kanab Picture Company, the first motion picture company owned and operated by Utahns, was planning to film its first picture, *Wild Horse Range*, in St. George. The story was based on research done by Utahn Henry Heather.[1] When I showed Maurine the clipping I had found in her papers, Maurine sighed, "Yes, I would have liked to be involved. But I wasn't. I don't know what came of it."

"What became of you?" I asked. I knew her sanctuary on the hill was not fit for winter, especially not when she was already ill. "I guess I had another cold, miserable winter in the drafty north bedroom with the three doors," she said. It is not clear what, if anything, Maurine was working on. During late spring and early summer, she seems to have slipped across the line into a minor form of paranoia. She blamed the Mormon Church for squelching sales of *This Is the Place: Utah*. She still felt furious at *Life* for rejecting her writing. She still obsessed over Tom Spies's "betrayal." She still blamed Max Becker, her agent, both for her money problems and for getting her into the high-pressure contract with Simon and Schuster. So instead of working, she launched a quixotic quest for "justice."

Although she had virtually no income during this period, she asked A. Luke Payne, a private investigator from Salt Lake City who had written her his enjoyment of *The Giant Joshua*, to see how bookstores in Salt Lake City were handling *This Is the Place: Utah*. He wrote on 8 June that "Deseret Book did not have a copy," saying they "were sold out but would order [it] for him." In contrast, "ZCMI had about fifty they were selling out for ninety-eight cents each, claiming they were overstocked and the book would not go into a second edition, that contemplated sales had fallen short of expectations." He thought, at that price, that the books "were going fast, people buying multiple copies for presents." He also suspected that "some booksellers were buying them for resale."[2] Whatever the case, the book did not sell up to expectations; and Knopf's accounting letter dated 3 January 1950 showed that bookstores were returning more copies than they were selling.[3] Maurine couldn't do anything about it.

Her second crusade was against *Life* magazine. She didn't want to be like her mother and simply knuckle under to unfair treatment from men. She considered that the New York office owed her $64 for work on a story about the Rich family reunion and for her time and expenses escorting the photographic team for the Centennial Tour through Utah in the fall of 1947. She wanted her "manuscript back," saying she "had a chance to sell it to another magazine."[4] Her efforts bore some fruit, and in July she received a check for sixty-four dollars for the Rich story but nothing for work done on the tour.[5]

Maurine shared news of the Rich payment with Roy Craft, from the *Life* Los Angeles office and he warmly congratulated her for fulfilling her "natural feminine desire to HAVE THE LAST WORD!" Then he reminded her: "You should not let your job of native guide for the beauties of Southern Utah deter you from your basic mission—which is to finish *Cleave the Wood*" (as she was then calling the sequel).[6] He was her main supporter now and consistently encouraged her, writing in November, "Give birth to that book and your troubles are over. I should think you'd be able to lick it this winter." He again encouraged her: "An old trapper in Alaska once told me, you won't get no bear if you don't get some lead in the air."[7] In February 1949, he still sounded hopeful: "The fact that you're in the mood to write and are getting ahead on the book is mighty encouraging."[8]

As for Max Becker, matters were not so easily resolved. Maurine had apparently gotten the idea that, when she had in a fit of scruples refused to take her monthly stipend from Simon and Schuster the previous year, Becker had pocketed it as his commission.[9] She thought she could get rid of him and go with Don Congdon, who was now in his first year with the Harold Matson Company, a literary agency, and whom Maurine felt had been her ally at Simon and Schuster.[10] His response, in early June, was interested but definitely cautious: "I don't think an agent is important to you until you've gotten *Cleave the Wood* finished and delivered to Simon & Schuster."[11]

Another unpleasant complication came up in the early summer of 1948. Maurine had a blow-up with her father, one that still rankled her in 1991. In fact, whenever she was talking about relationships with her family, this upsetting story was one that repeatedly came to her mind. As she usually told the story, she almost killed herself fixing up the trailer studio to make a place of her own, even though it was hardly adequate to her vision of what she deserved. Then she returned from an absence to find her father standing in the doorway of the trailer. He had simply moved in his own books and astronomy equipment without asking her. Maurine exploded in anger and outrage, but he simply laughed at her. Incongruously, one detail stuck in her mind. Wasps were circling about Charlie, who just ignored him, but Maurine became almost frantic about them.[12]

To be fair, Charlie had done much more work on the place than Maurine ever wanted to admit or give him credit for. He must have handled the legal details for getting title to the place, something Maurine likely would not have followed through on systematically. Maurine, who could write so perceptively and sympathetically about Abijah MacIntyre could not analyze, understand and forgive her own father. Often she would discuss what had made him the way he was with considerable insight, but just talking about Charlie would make her so emotionally distraught that she usually lost all perspective.

One of the few times she and Charlie might have been on better terms occurred in the spring of 1949 when she was in California recuperating from an operation. He sent her a light-hearted letter, part of it in rhyme: "We received your shaky letter, and as your Dad I am mighty glad you are feeling better, between you and me I cannot see, with my limited observations, how you can thrive and keep alive with all your operations, But tell the Dock, when you can walk, and feel you can explain, He don't need a knife to save your life, when you have an ache or pain."[13] He also passed on some family details and news about the weather (rainy).

In early 1992, when I read this letter to Maurine and asked her about it, she didn't say much; but that night, unable to sleep, she called her legal guardian, Carol Jensen. Depressed and remorseful, she told Carol that Charlie really was a good man and that she had never treated him well. She was so blue she said she didn't think she could go on living. Concerned, Carol talked to her for over an hour. It seemed as if hearing Charlie's own cheerful, almost playful words to her had broken through the image Maurine had created about him, demanding that she recognize Charlie's own personhood. The next day, I expected her to be in the same mood that Carol had reported. But she had lapsed back into her more comfortable reality: She was a victim, and Charlie was an insensitive, unsupportive ogre who never understood her.

That was the only reality she saw in the fight over the trailer. Outraged at the invasion of what she considered her haven, Maurine snatched at the offer of a friend, Evelyn Harris Ward, by now married to a well-to-do man, to let her stay rent-free at their Saucer-Five Ranch. It was an isolated spot near the village of Central on the road to Enterprise, a place with a bad reputation. The ranch property included the site of the Mountain Meadows Massacre—the September 1847 ambush-slayings of about two hundred California-bound men, women, and children by Mormon settlers and some Paiute Indians.[14] Furthermore, another murder had been committed recently on the ranch property. Maurine had mentioned it in her Utah book: The previous owner, Royal Hunt of St. George, had "surprised a starved waif from a CCC Camp sniffing around some garbage cans. With never a doubt in his naive, generous heart, Royal took the kid ranch-ward to feed him, house him, maybe adopt him. On the way Royal collected a twenty-five-dollar debt. The sight of the greenbacks did it. The kid shot Royal with Royal's own rifle."[15]

Maurine didn't shrink from the ranch's negative ambience. She borrowed a dog and moved out to the ranch, apparently in mid-June.

Her health seems to have continued good. The only specific ailments that can be identified are two minor accidents—a cut knee and a finger on her right hand infected from a porcupine quill. In the fall she mentioned having had only a single case of "something like the flu in six months—a record," and was simply living with "the inconvenience" of recurrent bladder infections.[16] Unnamed neighbors shared garden produce with her, and among her papers is a newsletter from the Center Ward, indicating that she attended church at least once.[17] She also must have arranged to attend a mountain lion hunt with some of the local people. In other words, even thirty miles from nowhere, she still managed to fill her writing hours with distractions. Chief among them was continuing her vendetta by letters against the men who, she thought, had treated her unjustly.

Next, as an indication of just how swamped she had become in paranoia and bitterness, she asked Luke Payne to find Tom Spies. Her letter to Payne has not survived; but from his response, Maurine had evidently presented her treatment by Tom as a breach-of-promise case and felt that he should at least "lend" her money so she could finish "Cleave the Wood." Payne said he was "happy to comply," asking only as his fee "a copy of "Cleave the Wood" when it came out. He reported that Tom was planning to move to Salt Lake City.[18] Maurine wrote, but possibly did not send, her last letter to him. If she did send it, Spies did not respond.[19]

Possibly sensing Maurine's fragile emotional state, Payne went beyond the professional report to add some personal encouragement. Although he expressed concern about Maurine's isolation on the ranch, he thought a "girl who could write *Joshua* could do anything" and that the only thing that could stop her "was lack of faith and confidence in herself and then, of course, finances."[20]

Payne was married, which provided some limitations for the relationship. She must have asked Payne to continue checking on sales of *This Is the Place: Utah*. On 7 August, he reported that ZCMI had, in fact, "already remaindered the rest of its stock." The clerk had told him, "that despite many requests, the publisher did not have any more copies."[21]

In May, before moving to the ranch, Maurine sent off a manuscript to Agnes Ramsey, who had been assigned at Simon and Schuster to handle the sequel. Her cover letter has not survived, and Ramsay's response does not describe the manuscript; but it seems likely it would have been the surviving Chapters 2, 3, and 4—about two hundred pages of the sequel. This deduction is based on Maurine's statement, in the letter to Ramsay, that she destroyed what she had written in Salt Lake City during the winter of 1945–46.

After reading the manuscript, Agnes Ramsay responded with delicacy and tact in June: "We feel here that you have the basis of a fascinating and rewarding book. . . . I have a hunch that a person of your temperament might be thrown off-stride by too much criticism while you are still in the highly creative phase."[22]

Maurine also wrote a lengthy and furious letter firing Max Becker: "Do not for one moment think I am licked! I am a stubborn cuss and I'll never give up while there's a brain to plan and a hand to write! Not agents, creditors nor hell or high water can lick me! That is a promise to the grinning gods. You'll see!"[23]

He responded coolly. He was "unable to see" why she had so many "complaints." He also refused to be sidetracked from the bottom line: "If you want to break our relationship, that is your decision," but "I am still entitled to my full commission." He did not try to change her mind about retaining him as her agent but simply said he would get the "manuscripts together and return them."[24]

Perhaps his firmness called her bluff. She did not terminate their relationship. In late July, she wrote proposing "a monthly letter to be used as a column in some newspaper or magazine." Among the possibilities she mentioned were an article on Josie Morris that would be different from the material submitted to *Life* and another based on the material she had collected when writing "Through the Utah Wonderlands." Becker responded discouragingly, but probably accurately, that "few editors would take on a monthly column." He also thought "the articles were twice too long."[25]

She was somewhat placated when he wrote ten days later saying he would "make some suggestions myself for cuts on the 'Josie' and 'Wonderland' pieces" but "still wanted the long version, since it might interest a movie company." He also said he would check on why "*Holiday* had not made a decision about Maurine's article on the Timpanogas hike."[26] Maurine refused Max's request to shorten the wonderlands piece, telling him that she "still felt it could sell the way it was."[27]

In late August, Becker reported that *Holiday Magazine* had turned down the Timpanogas article, but he had an excellent possibility of marketing four articles of 3,000 words or less on "the four 'spiritual guardians', making each a sort of personality piece about these odd characters." These guardians were not named, but they may have been Zeke Johnson, guardian of Arches National Monument; Randall Jones, guardian of Zion's National Park; Art Greene or perhaps Norman Nevills, guardian of Rainbow Bridge, and Harry Goulding of Monument Valley.[28]

Max was willing, though perhaps not enthusiastic, to work with her shorter pieces. Of course, he wanted her to finish the sequel for "then your financial problems will be lessened."[29] For her part, Maurine was still dividing her energies instead of focusing on "Cleave the Wood."

Also that summer, she sent Bert MacBride, editor of the monthly series "My Most Unforgettable Character" in *Reader's Digest*, a six-page query letter in which she proposed both "Harry Goulding, a Colorful, Monument-Valley-Trading-Post Operator" and his wife "Mike," and also "Old Fats," the Navajo medicine man, as possible subjects. Both ideas were expansions of the material she had collected on her trip with *Life* photographers the fall before.[30]

Max must have expressed some skepticism about the details of the Gouldings' lives and their trading post since the draft of Maurine's response is a self-consciously poetic evocation of the Gouldings in their landscape: "Often when the world is too much with me I like to think of Mike and Harry serene in their tremendous sunny silence, watching the sand boil upward like apricot-colored smoke under the wind, the warm brown shadows creep over the great dunes which lie in every direction like vast plushy breasts, the crimson light fade from the skyline which reminds you of a frieze on the stained-glass window of some earthly cathedral."[31]

The possibility of selling to the *Reader's Digest* had important advantages. In 1948, it was paying $2,000 for an "Unforgettable."[32] Selling it, Maurine thought, would let her finish the sequel. Publishing in the widely read and universally respected *Reader's Digest* would show St. George, especially Charlie Whipple, that she was a success. As a result, she poured unremitting efforts into achieving this goal; and once again, she probably scuttled her own chances by trying too hard and by trying to enmesh MacBride in her personal life. Ultimately, she wearied him by substituting interminable, chatty letters for solid, professional results.

In late September, MacBride confirmed that Goulding would be "a good subject," but he would not make a firm commitment because he "had many western characters at the moment." He suggested not mentioning "occult matters or Harry's ulcers." She needed to clarify "what he was and if and why he had a right to rent Navajo land to the movies. What about the money? Did he pocket it?"[33] Even though he had clearly not accepted the article, Maurine sailed ahead as though he had.[34]

Before she got her $64 from *Life*, she cast around for another rock to throw at them and addressed a lengthy and somewhat exaggerated description of herself as a woman who "came in backwards with a best seller first" to Paul Gallico, president of the Authors' Guild of the Authors' League, an organization formed to win rights for writers: "My publishers advanced me another $100 which I used to find this ranch and buy food," she wrapped up her complaint. ". . . By September I can have the book half done. And then with the aid of another miracle to transport me to a warm place, I can have it all done by Christmas."[35]

Gallico responded sympathetically: "I read your letter in my two capacities, one, a writer who had had his share of luck, and second as the president of the Authors' Guild." (Maurine used both Authors' Guild and Authors' League interchangeably.) He had read and admired *The Giant Joshua* and judged Maurine "worth saving." As president of the Authors' League, he sent her $150 from its fund for needy writers, with the assurance that more could be available as needed, up to a maximum of $500, to be paid back with no interest and no due date when she sold something. Other benefits were membership in the league with her dues prepaid. He also offered to help her find a warm place for the winter. Also important was his sympathy. Even though he expressed some doubt that her editors were mistreating her simply "because she was a woman," he suggested, as a test, that she send in something signed "Maurice" instead of "Maurine."[36] There is no evidence that she ever did.

Maurine's grateful letter of acceptance tried to pull Gallico more tightly into her circle by offering him access to "the exotic American West." Wouldn't he like "to go on a mountain lion hunt?" And "wasn't it time for a contemporary piece on polygamy?" For example, "an eighty-year-old gent lives near me who was waiting for a lass to graduate from the eighth grade so he could make her his sixth wife; When asked how old they had to be, he said, 'Oh we like a gal to reach the age of procurity!'"[37]

Maurine continued her correspondence with Gallico over the summer, writing at least two more witty letters.[38] He responded in the fall that he was asking a friend on the West Coast to help find Maurine "a warm wintering ground" and said the Authors' Guild had "been fighting" for years to get magazines to "pay on acceptance, not on publication." She was trying to bypass Becker, for she asked Gallico's advice on placing articles. He suggested trying the Timpanogas-hike article on "*Saturday Evening Post*, then, if it bounced back, to *True Magazine*." He then asked when she would like the rest of the $500, showing that Maurine had made the earlier $150 and $64 from *Life* last approximately three months.[39]

In mid-July, Maurine received a visit at the ranch from Helen ("Butch") Hoover of Provo. They had met in Salt Lake City during the war and had stayed in touch sporadically afterward. Maurine told me that she "liked Helen," that "no one was as much fun," but she just had "too much to do trying to make a living" and wasn't free to "have fun with Helen." They lost track of each other after 1948. Maurine had invited Helen to the ranch for a visit, and Helen had arrived with a group of friends. Maurine entertained them as best she could, providing them with a place to stay and feeding them watercress from a near-by stream and garden produce given to her by a friend. She apparently asked Helen for return hospitality over the 24th of July weekend in Provo, but Helen regretfully refused.[40]

Maurine's mother also stayed with her, although when or for how long is not clear. None of Maurine's letters comment on her presence, even though Annie would have probably taken over her usual duties of cooking, cleaning, washing, and hovering anxiously over Maurine.

As cold weather closed in, Maurine moved back to St. George where she rented a motel room "with a warm-southern exposure" for $45 a month, hoping she could avoid wintering in California, although unnamed friends (probably Elmer Belt) advised her that, if she worked at his clinic for a month, she would qualify as a California resident and her kidney operation would be "covered by Blue Cross." Considering the years of pain and infections she had already endured, her reluctance to connive to get insurance benefits is admirable.[41]

Her papers reveal another effort to get a man to fight her battles. She wrote Levi Edgar Young of the LDS First Council of the Seventy asking him to pressure *Life* to use more of her Utah pieces. With obvious reluctance and considerable delay, Young did so, letting her know that he had had "a difficult time deciding what to say." He finally wrote, deciding to mention "your qualifications as a writer."[42]

Trespassing on Gallico's advocacy, she pressed him to "get MacBride to take a more careful look at my revisions on the Harry Goulding piece."[43] Like Young, Gallico delayed his response; and when he finally answered, she responded with a gush of relief: "I couldn't bear to lose you. I guess I'm more than a little nuts." In addition to her bottomless need for friendship, Gallico's letter was a relief for a second reason: he assured her that "the rest of the money from the Authors' League Fund would be forthcoming."[44]

He had not responded to her request to put pressure on MacBride, and she may have brought up the question again. He wrote in December

1948, counseling patience and also deflecting her all-too-obvious eagerness to enlist him as her knight to tilt at Bert MacBride's windmill: "If he doesn't buy and doesn't pay off either for the rewrites you have done, that is where we will step in. But I'm sure you've got this one."[45]

It was a reassuring note. Maurine felt confident she would have enough money, between the Authors' League charity and the *Reader's Digest* sale to carry her through the winter. Consequently, "Cleave the Wood" remained on the back burner. Even though she still lacked a firm commitment from *Reader's Digest*, she went to Salt Lake City for more information on the Gouldings from government records (nature unspecified), then badgered friends into driving her to Monument Valley to interview Harry Goulding. The rough country damaged her friends' car, the weather was miserable, and Maurine got sick. She promised these unnamed friends to pay for the repairs when she got paid for the article, but she was once again counting unhatched chickens. Her high hopes glossed over the dark reality that another year had ended with little to show for it.

She promptly made things worse by nagging MacBride about the Goulding feature. He wrote in January 1949, saying it was "in the hands of other people" and he would let her know the results "as soon as possible."[46] Before the end of the month, he sent her a rejection letter: "The opinion of the board had been divided, but the boss had said forget it. . . . Only two anecdotes really stood up." There was "too much unrestrained adulation and not enough action and anecdotes." He sweetened this message with $150.[47] Crushed and angry, Maurine asked twenty-five friends—and even strangers—who knew Goulding to persuade MacBride to accept her piece.

Gallico was cautiously optimistic. The *Reader's Digest* usual figure for a turn-down after requesting rewrites "was three-hundred dollars." He told her to send in copies of the article and all of the correspondence and promised to get more money for her if he could.[48]

Unfortunately, Maurine was too quick to do something on her own and overplayed her hand by asking friends to write to verify what she wrote was indeed true.[49] Among others, she wrote to movie director John Ford of United Artists, who had made movies in Monument Valley.[50] Maurine was certain Ford would validate her article and requested he "write a note to MacBride" to that effect. There is no evidence that he did.

To no one's surprise but Maurine's, her efforts backfired completely. MacBride wrote back an astonished but surprisingly temperate missive on 16 February, after receiving the first "pressure" letter: "No writer in my 17 years experience has ever pulled that sort of pressure on me." Then he patiently spelled out the obvious: "It is not good policy to get outside persons to plead for your manuscript. If a manuscript meets our requirements we *want* it. If not, the testimony of Moses and all the prophets wouldn't influence us."[51] With astonishing generosity, he wrote again the next day: "I am willing to go to bat for you." Even though she had told Paul Gallico she had returned the $150 check, it wasn't true, because MacBride told her she should "hold the check uncashed for a time and I will send the full amount later, if we accept the article."[52]

She responded immediately, trying to smooth things over, thanking MacBride, promising to rewrite, and assuring him that she had only asked people to send in letters "to prove the validity of my facts. You see, a rejection because of poor workmanship is nothing—but a rejection because of questionable research is something I can correct—or try to."[53]

Gallico responded to the copy of her article and the correspondence with MacBride with something like horror. On 19 February, he sent her the final check for $150 from the Author's Guild and some very good advice: "Young lady, haven't you learned yet that one *never* writes letters to editors except to give them information or amuse them?" Then he got down to brass tacks where her article was concerned: "It isn't a good piece or a good unforgettable. Your guy doesn't come to life, the piece doesn't follow a clear, smooth line and just doesn't come off. . . . Stop feeling sorry for yourself, Whipple. It's creeping into your letters and will eventually get into your writing."[54] After lecturing her like a Dutch uncle, he added: "I hope I get your book before I leave for England." He signed his letter with the deliberately homespun, "Yourn, Paul."

MacBride wrote a third letter on 24 February, saying he had "now received four pressure letters" and was "revoking his offer." He claimed he "had never before encountered such tactics on the part of an author of standing."[55] It was a stinging rebuke.

Crushed, Maurine succumbed to the dreaded winter respiratory problems and was bedfast for part of the winter. Furthermore, it was a vicious season, known as the year of the "blue snow" because the first snow layer froze, then was covered with a new snowfall, which in a freakish way had a blue tint. It had started to snow the week before Christmas and kept coming. Roads were often closed; and as a result, mail was erratic. To top things off, the motel owner wanted her to leave because of some kind of gossip and increased the rent $10 a month to force her hand. Maurine agreed to leave by 8 March.

She crept off to California, worked long enough at the clinic to establish residency, and had the kidney and bladder repairs covered by Blue Cross. In one letter, she said that the bladder repair took "three major operations."[56] Unidentified friends underwrote her convalescence in a Palm Springs apartment and she had a final $150 check from the Authors' Guild.

She had also borrowed money from friends the previous year, but they had "had reverses" (or could see that there was no end in sight) and declined to loan her any more money.[57]

Notes

[1] "Utah Motion Picture Company Catches Spirit In 'Wild Horse Range,'" *Washington County News*, 22 January 1948. I could not find a summary of the script nor any evidence that the movie was ever made.

[2] A. Luke Payne, Letter to Maurine Whipple, Salt Lake City, Utah, 8 June 1948; Maurine Whipple Collection, L. Tom Perry Special Collections, Harold B. Lee Library, Brigham Young University, Provo, Utah, with photocopy in Maurine Whipple Collection, Archive, Val A. Browning Library, Dixie College, St. George, Utah. Documents in both collections hereafter cited as BYU, photocopy Dixie College. Payne's fan letter about *The Giant Joshua* was written 3 February 1947; Whipple Collection, BYU; photocopy, Dixie College.

[3] Alfred A. Knopf Company, Letter to Maurine Whipple, 3 January 1950, containing accounting information, BYU, photocopy Dixie College.

[4] Maurine Whipple, Draft of letter, to Mr. Thorndike, n.d.; BYU, photocopy Dixie College.

[5] Robert Girvin, Letter to Maurine Whipple, 17 July 1948; BYU.

[6] Maurine Whipple, Draft letter to Roy Craft, ca. 23 July 1948; Roy Craft, Letter to Maurine Whipple, 4 August 1948; both in BYU, photocopy Dixie College.

[7] Maurine Whipple, Letter to Roy Craft, ca. early November 1948; Craft, letter to Whipple, 21 November 1948; Craft on RKO Radio Pictures letterhead, Letter, ca. early December 1948; all BYU, photocopy Dixie College.

[8] Roy Craft, Letter to Maurine Whipple, 8 February 1949; BYU, photocopy Dixie College.

[9] Maurine Whipple, Letter to Peter Heggie, president of Authors' Guild, ca. 1949; BYU, photocopy Dixie College.

[10] Ibid.

[11] Don Congdon, New York City, Letter to Maurine Whipple, 15 June 1948; BYU, photocopy Dixie College.

12 Maurine usually said that Juanita Brooks was with her and witnessed the quarrel. In 1992, Anna Cox told me that it was she and Katharine Miles Larson instead. According to Anna, she and Katharine were surprised at how angry Maurine became and thought it strange that the wasps did not seem to bother Charlie, who simply ignored them. Anna never did understand why father and daughter could not have shared the place peacefully.

13 Charlie Whipple, Letter to Maurine Whipple, 22 May [1949]; BYU, photocopy Dixie College.

14 An incomplete fragment among Maurine's papers commenting on the massacre says of the people involved: "Good and evil: A people only too human and yet dream-haunted." When I asked her if she felt any identification with John D. Lee, one of my own ancestors, she answered: "I hadn't thought of it like that. I did have a respect for Lee that was hard to express. Maybe it was my feeling that I too would stand being sacrificed to Mormon bigotry, if it meant it would help promote that 'Grand Idea' thing I was such a damn fool about."

15 *This Is the Place, Utah*, 182.

16 Maurine Whipple, draft of letter to Roy Craft, ca. late October or November 1948; BYU, photocopy Dixie College.

17 *Central Ward Newsletter*, n.d., BYU.

18 A. Luke Payne, Letter to Maurine Whipple, 26 June 1948; BYU, photocopy Dixie College.

19 Maurine Whipple, Letter to Tom Spies, n.d. The letter exists as both a holograph and typescript. The fact that the typewritten copy appears to be an original suggests that Maurine never sent it. BYU, photocopy Dixie College.

20 Luke Payne, Letter to Maurine Whipple, 26 June 1948; BYU, photocopy Dixie College.

21 A. Luke Payne, Letter to Maurine Whipple. 7 August 1948; BYU, photocopy Dixie College.

22 Agnes Ramsey, Simon and Schuster, Letter to Maurine Whipple, 25 June 1948; BYU, photocopy Dixie College. This is the last correspondence I found between Maurine and this editor. Sometime in 1950, Simon and Schuster wrote off the investment they had made in Maurine's sequel and sold their option to Jewels Goldner in New York. I have no information about this individual, and Maurine's papers contain no correspondence with him or her.

23 Maurine Whipple, Letter to Max Becker, ca. June 1948, emphasis hers; BYU, photocopy Dixie College.

24 Max Becker, Letter to Maurine Whipple, 28 June 1943; BYU, photocopy Dixie College. He doesn't specify which manuscripts he had in hand. Maurine had sent *Holiday Magazine* one or more articles about Utah, which the magazine politely refused because it had just "scheduled several other pieces about Utah." Since the rejection letter came to her, evidently Becker had not been handling them for her. Al Hine, *Holiday*, Philadelphia, Letter to Maurine Whipple, 17 June 1948; BYU, photocopy Dixie College.

25 Max Becker, Letter to Maurine Whipple, 20 July 1948; BYU, photocopy Dixie College.

26 Max Becker, Letter to Maurine Whipple, 30 July 1948; BYU, photocopy Dixie College.

27 Maurine Whipple, Draft letter to Max Becker, ca. September 1945; BYU, photocopy Dixie College.

28 Maximilian Becker, Letter to Maurine Whipple, 20 August 1948; BYU, photocopy Dixie College.

29 Ibid.

30 Maurine Whipple, rough draft of letter to Bert MacBride, ca. July 1948; BYU, photocopy Dixie College. The Goulding Trading Post is now a museum. At least one documentary, David Bowyer Productions, aired 29 July 1993, KBYU-TV, recorded some of the Gouldings' contributions to the movie industry and their place in the economic and cultural life of the Navajo Nation.

31 Maurine Whipple, draft of letters to Bert MacBride, ca. August 1948 and 31 August 1948; BYU, photocopy Dixie College. She is alluding to William Wordsworth's sonnet, "The World Is Too Much with Us."

32 Paul Gallico, Letter to Maurine Whipple, 8 February 1949; BYU, photocopy Dixie College. Gallico checked on the *Digest*'s prices for Maurine.

33 Bert MacBride, Letter to Maurine Whipple, 22 September 1948; BYU, photocopy Dixie College.

34 Harry Goulding, Letter to Maurine Whipple, 28 December 1948; BYU, photocopy Dixie College.

35 Maurine Whipple, Letter to Paul Gallico, 12 July 1948; BYU, photocopy Dixie College. Gallico (1897–1976), who was fifty-one, had published a best-seller, *The Snow Goose* (1941) and was completing a thriller that was also made into a movie, *The Poseidon Adventure*. He published more than forty books on a wide range of subjects. Although Maurine's letter draft is not dated, she must have written it before 17 July, since Robert Girvin (otherwise unidentified) sent her a check on that date.

36 Paul Gallico, Letter to Maurine Whipple, 23 July 1948; BYU, photocopy Dixie College.

37 Maurine Whipple to Paul Gallico, ca. August 1948; BYU, photocopy Dixie College.

38 Maurine Whipple, Letters to Paul Gallico, n.d., but ca. August–October 1948; BYU, photocopy Dixie College.

39 Paul Gallico, Letter to Maurine Whipple, ca. October 1948; BYU, photocopy Dixie College.

40 "Butch" (Helen Hoover), Letter to Maurine Whipple, 19 July 1948; BYU.

41 Maurine Whipple, draft of letter to Roy Craft, ca. late October or November 1948; Whipple, draft of letter to Paul Gallico, ca. October/November 1948; both in BYU, photocopy Dixie College. Urologist Elmer Belt was probably the "friends" [sic] she was referring to.

42 Levi Edgar Young, Letter to Maurine Whipple, 4 November 1949; BYU, photocopy Dixie College. Young refers to the date of her letter as 1 October.

[43] Maurine Whipple, Draft letter to Paul Gallico, ca. October/November 1948; BYU, photocopy Dixie College. The wording suggests that she had written at least two drafts of the Goulding article.

[44] Paul Gallico, Letter to Maurine Whipple, 15 November 1948; Maurine Whipple, Draft of letter to Paul Gallico, ca. late November or December 1948; both at BYU, photocopy Dixie College.

[45] Paul W. Gallico, Letter to Maurine Whipple, 14 December 1948; BYU, photocopy Dixie College.

[46] Bert MacBride, Letter to Maurine Whipple, early January 1949; BYU, photocopy Dixie College.

[47] Bert MacBride, Letter to Maurine Whipple, 24 January 1949; BYU, photocopy Dixie College.

[48] Paul Gallico, Letter to Maurine Whipple, 8 February 1949; BYU, photocopy Dixie College.

[49] Three of those who did were Mark Anderson, Clayton Rice, and O. C. Christensen. Their letters telling of their attempts are in BYU, photocopy Dixie College.

[50] Maurine Whipple, Letter to John Ford, United Artists, Hollywood, California, 16 February 1949; BYU, photocopy Dixie College.

[51] Bert MacBride, Letter to Maurine Whipple, 16 February 1949; BYU.

[52] Bert MacBride to Maurine Whipple 17 February 1949; BYU, photocopy Dixie College.

[53] Maurine Whipple, Letter to Bert MacBride, ca. February 1948; BYU, photocopy Dixie College.

[54] Paul Gallico, Letter to Maurine Whipple, 19 February 1949; BYU, photocopy Dixie College.

[55] Bert MacBride, Letter to Maurine Whipple, 24 February 1948; BYU, photocopy Dixie College.

[56] Maurine Whipple, Draft letter to unnamed person, ca. November 1949; BYU, photocopy Dixie College.

[57] Ibid.

19

"ANYBODY'S GOLD MINE": 1949

In late spring 1949, Maurine obtained a position as caretaker on the isolated R. W. Von Hake ranch about fifteen miles from Kanab in Johnson Canyon. In 1914, a man named Freddie Crystal had arrived in Johnson Canyon with a newspaper clipping about Mexican petroglyphs. The legend was that Montezuma had sent much of his gold north to save it from the marauding Spaniards, and Crystal thought the petroglyphs indicated that it had been hidden nearby.[1] Six years later, many Kanab citizens spent time living in tents in Johnson Canyon digging for the hidden treasure; but after two years, there was still no sign of it.[2]

Maurine had gathered some information when researching *This Is the Place: Utah* and had drafted an article on the rumored treasure in the summer of 1949. Because Max Becker showed no interest in the article, she sent it directly to the *Saturday Evening Post*, which was, in 1949, a stellar example of a general-interest magazine that claimed Benjamin Franklin as its founder.[3] She told me that the editor, Peggy Dowst, had been interested and asked her to find more information about it. She remembered that she had misplaced the photographs and, when she found them again, realized they were not very good but sent them in anyway with a second draft of the article. Undoubtedly, it was a humbler and wiser Maurine who polished this second draft and tried hard not to get her hopes too high. After all, if the eastern editors thought Harry Goulding was too fantastic, what would they think of a mountain supposedly full of Spanish treasure?

On 14 June, while "Anybody's Gold Mine" was still under consideration, Maurine asked Peggy Dowst about the *Post*'s possible interest in another article she had written based on the Utah Wonderland Tour, which she had already tried on *Life*. "I'd be less than human if I weren't thrilled with the prospect of the 'gold mine' in color," she suggested. "I'm not forgetting Kanab's photogenic lures, but I can only give you my word of honor that there is unstared-at scenery out here that would make Kanab sick with envy."[4] The *Post* bought the treasure story for $750 and sent photographer Pat Coffey[5] to get photographs but passed on other wonderland sites. Most of the money went to settle debts.

When Paul Gallico left his post at the Authors' Guild and went to England in March 1949, Maurine asked Luise Silcox, the guild's secretary-treasurer, to force Max Becker to return her other "manuscripts, particularly her short story, 'The Time Will Come.'" She thought this piece "should be pushed while it could still fit a war-conscious public."[6] There is no record of a response from Silcox, but Becker apparently returned at least this story, for, during the summer of 1949, Maurine sent the story to Betty Coe at *Ladies Home Journal*. At the same time, she queried Coe about the possibilities of a feature on Zaidee Walker Miles, a subscriber to the *Journal* of sixty years.[7] The *Ladies Home Journal* didn't accept either.[8]

Maurine was still at the Von Hake ranch in August when she got a query from Ralph Knight, a *Saturday Evening Post* staff member, asking about a photograph of Maurine kneeling in front of some desert plants in front of the Biology Building at Dixie College in St. George, looking at a snake coiled around her arm with what could be interpreted as affection.[9] Maurine answered on 17 August, giving scientific information about "Willie, the Arizona King Snake,"[10] and mentioning that "Willie the Second, a dead ringer for his namesake," was another king snake who "lives under the kitchen porch" at the ranch.[11]

She tried to get a nibble on a personality profile, "Big Shot in Cow Town." It would be about Whit Parry, owner of Parry Lodge in Kanab and a great booster of the region's movie-making industry. He seems to have been kind to Maurine, possibly arranging her two summer caretaking jobs. In her article about Whit, she told of his early life, his experience finding a way to make his lodge in Kanab successful by selling Hollywood on the idea of making movies in southern Utah, and his subsequent rise to local prominence. But no magazine bought it.[12]

Feeling more optimistic because of selling "Anybody's Gold Mine" to the *Saturday Evening Post*, Maurine tried to smooth things over with Bert MacBride and revive the Goulding article. She did it in the worst possible way, attempting to appeal to his pity by reviewing in exhausting detail the sad circumstances of her life. She lamented about how "ignorant in business matters" she was and begged his forgiveness for doing him "an injustice unwittingly." She implored him for a chance to rewrite the Goulding article,

Maurine poses with a king snake, part of Dixie College's collection, 1949.

using "new information."[13] I found no evidence of an answer. To her credit, she had some of the "hardguttedness" of her characters in *The Giant Joshua*.

When Maurine returned to St. George in the fall of 1949, she rented the one-room office building behind Brigham Young's winter home.[14] It should have been an ideal place to dig into the sequel—compact, private, and very historic. However, she complained of "interruptions" from people wanting a guided tour, the chores of "hauling wood," and the annoyance of making repairs to the "finicky oil heater." She also claimed that sometimes she "could hear a child crying and had seen unexplained figures."[15]

Her article, "Anybody's Gold Mine," appeared in the *Post's* October issue. It was eight pages long, accompanied by a map and a photograph of steps cut in the rock leading to a cave. Best of all, it had little to do with pioneers, polygamy, or the Mormon Church. Maurine had written it with restraint and had worked carefully on her research, laying out Montezuma's history to help make the case that he could have tried to hide his treasure in the north. The tone is light, cheerful, humorous. Mystery man Freddie Crystal, the man who showed up in Kanab in 1914 with his newspaper clipping, rancher Alvin Judd, Lester Little who owned a Kanab motel, and movie stuntman Cowhide Adams come to life, unfolding a mystery for the reader.

Peter Heggie had taken over the Authors' League from Paul Gallico. Maurine now turned to him. He responded to her letter, saying he had "been impressed" with *The Giant Joshua* and was "looking forward with great anticipation and sense of promise toward the completion of the second novel." He enclosed a check for $150 "to handle her immediate pressures" and invited: "Write to me, . . . if it would help to think out your plans."[16]

Although her papers do not include a draft of her answer to him, no doubt she encouraged his belief that she was working on "Cleave the Wood" and, in fact, she probably was. Fae Garda Anderson Picklesimer, a friend who used to play for Maurine's dance classes, told me that she visited Maurine in the Brigham Young office and saw large pieces of paper hung around the room with different characters' names written on them. "Maurine explained to me who each character was and a little about them,"[17] Picklesimer said.

Apparently the money from the league wasn't enough to keep her going, for on 10 May 1950, Maurine also arranged to borrow $50 a month for five months, with the option of arranging for an extension, from Daisy Macfarlane.[18] The reason for the loan was specifically so she could work on the sequel.[19]

Once again, Maurine had undertaken a formal ethical and legal contractual obligation about "Cleave the Wood," but once again, she plunged into what she saw as the quicker and easier money of magazine writing. Three factors were pushing her away from the sequel. First, it seems that, on a deep level, she was frightened at the overwhelming task of trying to produce a book that would inevitably be compared with *The Giant Joshua*. Furthermore, despite *Joshua*'s critical success, it had deepened her alienation from St. George townfolk. Third, she was sure that editors and agents had cheated her out of her rightful earnings, not only on *The Giant Joshua* but also on *This Is the Place: Utah*. If she actually finished "Cleave the Wood," wouldn't Max Becker be the one to profit?

The factors pulling her into magazine writing were strong. It was genuinely possible to make a living during this golden age of magazine popularity in the two decades after World War II. Magazine articles were a wonderful reason to spend time with interesting people who were impressed by her publishing connections. Even though writing articles was time-consuming, they didn't take as long as a book—and Maurine needed quick money. And finally, magazine writing, with its interviewing and travel, relieved her gnawing loneliness.

Maurine was accumulating a file of rejection letters, which any writer must expect; but she had a tendency to take rejection personally. She kept going, however. After the *Saturday Evening Post* said no to her

Timpanogas story, she tried to place it with *Holiday Magazine*, describing it as a new revision, accompanied by new photographs.[20]

After five months had passed, she wrote to *Holiday* editor Al Hines, worried that it had been "six months without hearing anything" and she was apprehensive because she didn't feel very good about the photographs. She promised that she "would do what was needed" to sell the article."[21] Hine refused it, suggesting she try the *Reader's Digest*. Maurine wrote back saying she "laughed out loud" at this suggestion, then told about her run-in with Bert MacBride. She said she would take his advice to try *Coronet*, after "taking the scissors to Harry." She also claimed she was "not beaten."[22] *Holiday* had also rejected the Timp hike story, although Maurine was pleased that Hine "had liked it."[23]

When *Coronet* rejected the "Land of Prayer" article about Harry Goulding in June 1950, the manuscript was delayed in reaching her, and she immediately leaped to a sinister conclusion and sent off an accusatory letter to her local post office.[24] Six months later, the postmaster general's office informed her that another Maurine Whipple, living in Great Barrington, Massachusetts, had probably received the manuscript. This proved to be the case. Maurine kept in touch with this other Maurine for years. Chandler Whipple, husband of the Massachusetts Maurine, was also a writer and a magazine editor.[25]

When a paying customer cancelled at the last minute on one of Art Greene's runs of the Colorado River, he invited Maurine to fill in. She, of course, was interested in publicizing this tourist attraction.[26] Although the trip—at least two days—would have been strenuous, Maurine apparently managed it without much difficulty and sent in an article on the topic to the *Saturday Evening Post*. When the rejection notice came, Maurine responded with a long and carefully crafted letter of appeal to Peggy Dowst (now married and adding the last name "Redmon"). "If I can work uninterruptedly for 6–8 months, finish my book (contracted for by Simon-Schuster who have promised a big sale), I will, as the Irish say 'live to ate the hen that walked over me grave!'" Then she sidled up to the real point of her letter: the hope that the *Post* would reconsider buying the article if she revised it. She concluded: "Forgive me if I seem too presumptuous. It's just that I can't help feeling that if all these people want more western articles, they ought to get 'em. And golly, I ought to write 'em!"[27] The *Post* did not authorize a rewrite.

Becker was still her agent in the spring of 1950 in spite of all her attempts to be rid of him. She wrote a carping (and lengthy) letter to him in March 1950: What had he done with "The Land of Prayer" about Harry Goulding and her "wonderland tour" article? She was fretting because the *Saturday Evening Post* was doing Neil Clark's article on Monument Valley; and if Maurine didn't "beat the *Post*," the Clark story might "kill the chances for mine." Nor was that all: She had "made the sales to *Saturday Evening Post*, *Life* and trade magazines all on my own," and she "had an editor inquiring about 'Josie,' which you [Max] had had for over a year and a half." These complaints were true. She snipped, "If you can't handle magazines, then tell me. You insist on rights in the novel, yet you don't help me make a living while I write it!"[28]

Max answered two weeks later, apologizing for "these misunderstandings. . . . Please believe me," he assured her. "I do have your interests at heart."[29]

The next surviving correspondence with Becker came eight months later. Max reported that he had made a list of fellowships she wanted him to check out, was trying to sell a revision of the Josie story, and was still making the rounds with her Timp hike article, "Lunatics, by One of Them." He claimed he "was getting some nice comments but the market was bad because editors were mostly interested in the Korean situation."[30] MIG-15 jets were attacking United Nations airplanes over North Korea despite the U.N.'s cease-fire resolution. Naval forces had begun evacuating Hungnam. The war could be said to have started this year of 1950 and didn't officially end until three years later, 27 July 1953, with an uneasy truce that has allowed an uncertain peace between the Communist North Korea and the Democratic South Korea since then. It was a time of great tension as a war-weary world held its breath and worried about a nuclear holocaust.

Maurine had basically sold nothing and produced nothing publishable since the Authors' League's $150 check in February 1950, so she must have been ecstatic when Luise M. Silcox, treasurer for the Authors' League fund, wrote on 15 December, enclosing a check for $150. Maurine had sent in a proposed budget; and Luise reported that the committee in charge of allocating funds to needy writers was concerned that she "might be cutting herself too short on food." The league would also pay for her to see a doctor. Furthermore, the state of her clothes "needed consideration." The league even authorized $25 to have her "special desk" (the one Charlie had made for her) shipped to Palm Springs. Then Luise said they wanted her "to approach her work from a new angle" that it could be accomplished only by

> (a) working on a definite budget for six or eight months, and (b) making that budget a livable one, so that at the end of two or three months you could notice a physical improvement so the time wasted on scrimping too much (though there would still be some scrimping) could be put at your desk. Of course, you can't spend every minute there. You will have to have a reasonable amount of time to take care of your health, do your own cooking, etc. But it has got to be routine or you won't be able to concentrate on your work. There has to be one main objective and the

other secondary, and the main objective has to be to *settle down,* and *work* a very close second.[31]

It was excellent advice, just like the excellent advice Maurine had been receiving since Ferris Greenslet first took her in hand. Unfortunately, she was no longer primarily engaged in the positive effort of bringing her characters to life but was enmeshed in an adversarial contest with the publishing world, a world she increasingly saw as hostile to her. Her chief energy was not going into the renewing and replenishing, though difficult, labor of creation, but into the negative struggle to get people to acknowledge her worth as a writer. Ironically, it only made her increasingly incapable of producing work upon which her worth could be acknowledged.

Behind her was a disheartening year of misunderstandings, emotional instability, and impulsive behavior. On the one hand, her determination to take her own fate into her hands and fight for what she wanted is admirable; but in a fight against circumstances when it's usually the circumstances that win, it's easy to discount the courage. And why did Maurine so persistently lose? There is no question that the way she handled relationships often backfired. She never established professional relationships with magazine editors, instead trying to wheedle and coax them into personal relationships that made them uncomfortable.

As for her peers and friends, including her own family, she needed validation so badly that it was difficult to see others close to her receive attention that she was hungry for herself. The only way she could tolerate it was to criticize their efforts, often to their face. She always thought it was "for their own good" and she was doing it because she "cared" for them. Still the way she usually did it meant that she lost good will that could have helped her. Lonely and despairing, she spent too much time shut up in her own head listening to the "what if's" and "if only's" and the "you see's."

Her persistent ill health also hampered her good intentions, and unquestionably the pain distorted her perceptions. It is easy to forget how much energy goes into dealing with physical pain. If we could walk in her misery shoes, likely we would marvel that she accomplished as much as she did.

"SWELL SUFFERING"

Notes

1. Montezuma II (or Moctezuma) was trained as a priest and rose to become leader of the Aztecs in 1502. The Aztecs then controlled most of what is now Mexico and Central America, their capital being the great city of Tenotchitlan (Mexico City). Because Montezuma thought that Cortes and his soldiers were descendants of the god Quetzalcoatl, he allowed them to enter Tenotchitlan unopposed in 1519. He was captured and held hostage by Cortes, then killed, either stabbed by the Spaniards or killed by a blow to the head from his own people. http://www.who2.com/montezumaii.html (accessed November 2003).

2. Ibid.

3. It was a glossy magazine—meaning that it was printed on coated paper that allowed high-quality color photo reproduction in contrast to the "pulps," or magazines printed on newsprint.

4. Maurine Whipple, Letter to Peggy Dowst, 14 June 1949; Maurine Whipple Collection, L. Tom Perry Special Collections, Harold B. Lee Library, Brigham Young University, Provo, Utah, with photocopy in Maurine Whipple Collection, Archive, Val A. Browning Library, Dixie College, St. George, Utah. Documents in both collections hereafter cited as BYU, photocopy Dixie College.

5. I deduce the photographer's name (the captions did not identify him) from a fan letter about the article by someone named "Margaret" (surname not given) who said that Pat Coffey's pictures were "beautiful." Margaret (no surname), Letter to Maurine Whipple, 29 September 1949; BYU.

6. Maurine Whipple, draft of letter to Luise Silcox, March 1949; BYU, photocopy Dixie College.

7. Maurine Whipple, Letter to Betty Coe, *Ladies Home Journal*, 16 November 1949; BYU, photocopy Dixie College.

8. Betty Coe, *Ladies' Home Journal*, Letter to Maurine Whipple, ca. summer 1949; BYU, photocopy Dixie College.

9. Ralph Knight, Letter to Maurine Whipple, ca. August 1949; and Maurine Whipple, Letter to Ralph Knight, 17 August, 1949; both in BYU.

10. Arizona king snakes are nonpoisonous but spectacular—black and yellow and as long as eleven or twelve feet. The one in the photograph with Maurine belonged to the Biology Department at Dixie College.

11. Maurine Whipple, Letter to Ralph Knight, *Saturday Evening Post*, 17 August 1949; ; BYU, photocopy Dixie College. There is no other information about the dog named Hydrogen or whether he is the same dog she had on the Saucer Five Ranch during the summer of 1948.

12. The manuscript itself, if there was one, has not survived, but Maurine outlined it in detail in a letter to *Esquire*, 14 September 1949; BYU, photocopy Dixie College. There is no documentation that Maurine submitted it to other periodicals.

13. Maurine Whipple, Letter to Bert MacBride, 4 August 1949; BYU, photocopy Dixie College.

"ANYBODY'S GOLD MINE": 1949

14 Brigham Young stayed in this comfortable two-story home on the northwest corner of 100 East and 200 North during the winters until his death in 1877, after which the home changed ownership twenty-one times. Brigham Young's descendant, Vera Gates Mitchell, purchased it in 1948. The home may have been rented part of the time but was essentially "left empty and was in a state of disrepair until July 1959." It is now one of the LDS Church's historic sites; and missionary couples conduct guided tours daily of both the house and the office, which has been restored to the 1870s period, complete with a pioneer telegraph line. Elder Harry P. Bluhm, comp., St. George Temple Visitors' Center and Historical Sites Mission, "Resource Material about Brigham Young and his Winter Home," February 1996, 5 pp.

15 Maurine Whipple, Letter to "Dick," ca. winter 1949–50, and to Bob Cahn, 28 January 1952; BYU, photocopy Dixie College.

16 Peter Heggie, Letter to Maurine Whipple, 1 February 1950; BYU, photocopy Dixie College.

17 Fae Garda Anderson Picklesimer, interviewed by Veda Tebbs Hale, 23 April 2003.

18 Daisy was married to Wallace Macfarlane, and they lived at 816 Stratford Ave., South Pasadena, California.

19 Maurine Whipple, Letter "To Whom it May Concern" (Mrs. Wallace ["Daisy"] Macfarlane), 10 May 1950; BYU, photocopy Dixie College.

20 Maurine Whipple, Letter to Al Hine, *Holiday Magazine*, 25 October 1949; BYU, photocopy Dixie College. "Lunatics, by One of Them," ca. 1948, probably revised 1949, exists in four typescript versions, each eleven pages long: (1) "Oberammergau of the Hike," (2) "The Timpanogas Hike," and two different but untitled versions; BYU, photocopy Dixie College.

21 Maurine Whipple, Draft of letter to Al Hine, *Holiday Magazine*, 23 March 1950; BYU, photocopy Dixie College.

22 Maurine Whipple, Letter to Al Hine, 10 June 1950; BYU, photocopy Dixie College.

23 Maurine Whipple, Letter to Al Hine, *Holiday Magazine*, 10 May 1950; BYU, photocopy Dixie College.

24 Maurine Whipple, Letter to David Howard, Authors' League, New York City, 1 October 1950; BYU, photocopy Dixie College.

25 Maurine Whipple from Great Barrington, Mass., to Maurine Whipple, St. George, ca. 1950; BYU.

26 Documentation for this trip is in Maurine's letter a year later to Bob Cahn, 2 July 1951; BYU, photocopy Dixie College.

27 Maurine Whipple, Letter to Peggy Dowst, 22 October 1950; BYU, photocopy Dixie College.

28 Maurine Whipple, Letter to Maximilian Becker, 23 March 1950; BYU, photocopy Dixie College.

29 Max Becker, Letter to Maurine Whipple, 7 April 1950; BYU, photocopy Dixie College.

30 Maximilian Becker, AFG Literary Agency, New York, Letter to Maurine Whipple, 9 December 1950; BYU, photocopy Dixie College.

[31] Luise M. Silcox, Letter to Maurine Whipple, 15 December 1950; BYU, photocopy Dixie College.

⇝ 20 ⇜

FLIRTING WITH *COLLIER'S,* 1951–52

Maurine set off for Palm Springs to spend the winter of 1950–51 with large and hopeful plans to finish the sequel. Even though she had secure financing from the Authors' League for at least three months and a comfortable place to work, she promptly invented another distraction. Some people she had met through her experience with *Life* magazine were now working for the Hollywood office of *Collier's* magazine. She got to know them better and their other associates. She particularly liked Ted Strauss and Robert ("Bob") Cahn.[1]

Although they were impressed with *The Giant Joshua* and willing to treat her as a colleague, nobody was willing to take on the role of mentor, therapist, and deadline enforcer—and especially not lover. So Maurine presented herself as one of the guys, just looking for someone who "spoke her language" and who would help her get the occasional break; but in reality, her emotional neediness made her over-responsive to every suggestion except the most practical one: that she settle down to the hard, lonely task of working on the sequel.

Theodore ("Ted") Strauss was the manager and editor-in-charge of *Collier's* West Coast office, an attractive man eight years Maurine's junior, with two preteen children. When Maurine met him, he was at least separated and may already have been divorced from his alcoholic wife. In 1937, Little, Brown and Company had published his hard-hitting sociological novel, *Night at Hogswallow.* A truck driver working on a road in the Deep South for a tough, kind-hearted Irish contractor knows that a Negro being charged with rape is innocent and tries to protect him from the Ku Klux Klan. The book was a surprisingly strong statement against racial injustice for 1937.

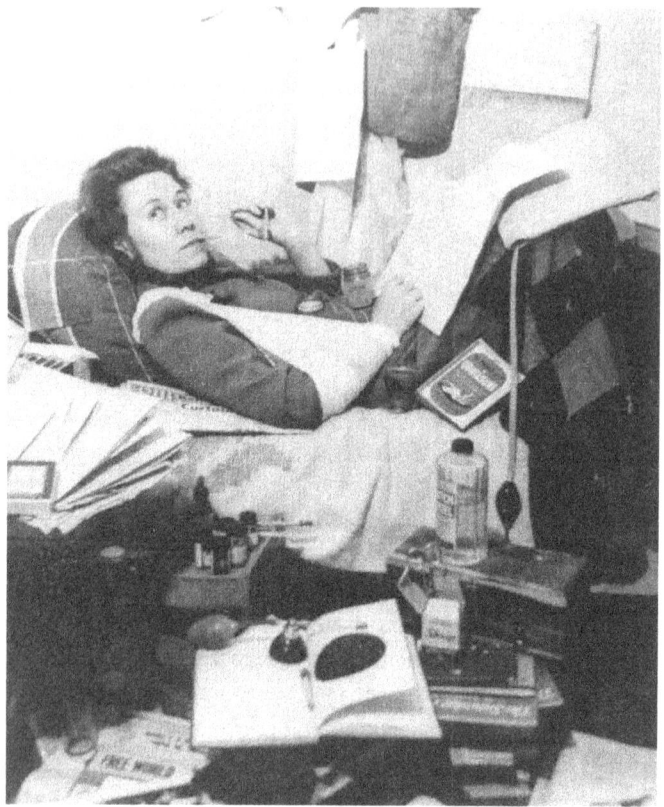

This publicity photo was posed but was not atypical of the clutter with which Maurine surrounded herself when she was working. During this period, she complained of a "paralyzed" arm.

Ted's second book, *Moonrise* (New York: Viking Press, 1948) was cast more as a conventional romance but also had a strong theme of justice.[2]

It is easy to see why Maurine would admire Ted. He believed in the same principles of justice, generosity, honesty, and brotherly love that she did. More to the point, he recognized and appreciated her talent, read and critiqued her work, and must have been attractive to her as a man. Maurine probably felt, too, that he would be of great help in getting her articles accepted by *Collier's*.

She apparently went to Hollywood in December 1950, hoping Ted would have time to work with her on her Arizona Strip manuscript—this time not the novel but a nonfiction article that she hoped to expand into a factual history of the slice of Arizona cut off by the Colorado River and hence reached more easily by Utah roads.[3] Many St. George sheep growers and cattlemen ran their stock there, and she had been fascinated with it for a long time. For most of her life she had been a keen observer of cowboy culture. She spent time at their favorite watering hole, the Big Hand Café, in St. George, which was also the depot for the transcontinental buses in which she often traveled. "Kind, quiet, always a lady" is how long-time waitress Edna Turnbow Harris described Maurine in a telephone interview in 1995. "She was mostly a loner though, not really one to tease or flirt with the cowboys." Nevertheless, Maurine was hearing their conversations, absorbing their idioms and sensing interesting stories in the many snatches of reported "news" that were batted around. All of this experience she had woven into an article. Apparently, Ted gave her instructions on revisions for her article and asked her to do more research. This attention encouraged her to think there was a good possibility for publication.[4] A published article would bring her some money. Several articles a year would be enough to live on. Yes, it meant postponing the sequel, but to write it free of obligation would make it a better book. Of course, everything could be postponed if the relationship with Ted Strauss were to develop in a romantic direction. Part of Maurine must have known that it was unlikely, but another part couldn't help dreaming.

Although her movements and activities are not clearly documented, she traveled into the Strip again, probably in the fall of 1950, with Vern Peterson and Boo Allen, who worked for the U.S. Bureau of Land Management in southern Utah.[5]

However, her hopes for both the article and Ted received enough of a setback later in the fall that she concentrated again on getting settled in Palm Springs. On January 13, 1951, she wrote her mother that she was living "in a nice house with plenty of heat and sunlight" which she could rent through May. Furthermore, she would earn ten dollars a week at Wellwood Murray Memorial Library, "telling or reading stories to the children on Saturday mornings and keep[ing] the books in the afternoons." She said, as if reporting on her writing progress, "I spent Christmas in bed with one of my miserable colds and had been too miserable to do much. I have to make good on the Authors' League loan, or else." Her mother had apparently complained of the cold in the St. George house, for Maurine exasperatedly demanded, "Why can't you get them to build a fire in the dining room?" And why, for that matter, couldn't Annie do it herself? The query reveals Annie's frailty and passivity. But Maurine was not as concerned as usual with events in St. George. Instead, she wrote optimistically about teaming up with a woman writer from New York (unnamed) who also needed to winter in the desert: "We're both going to finish our books, make a lot of dough, and build us a house! Although to tell the truth, for sheer natural beauty I'd rather have a house in St. George than anywhere in the world—but it would have to be steam heated, and that costs too much. Well, enough of houses. I'll never own even a chicken coop."6

There is no objective evidence that she produced either significant new material or made much progress on her revisions of "Cleave the Wood," which was what the sequel was still being called at that time.

At the same time, she negotiated with Luise M. Silcox, treasurer of the Authors' League Fund, for $100 a month in a four-week month and $115 in a five-week month. Luise advised her to get a telephone, and wrote that Maurine could expect "a small check for clothes and shoes soon, plus another when you ran out of vitamins and penicillin." The league would also cover her "$55 premium for California Blue Cross health insurance and be ready to cover emergencies." They worried about her long walks for groceries or to the library. "Isn't there a solution?" Luise asked, and also cautioned about working late night hours. The letter ended, "I really think you are settled for the three months and am very happy about it."7

On February 12, 1951, Ted Strauss wrote, asking her to clear up some small details in her Arizona Strip article.8 For some reason, about this time Maurine apparently got the impression that Ted could arrange for her to be hired as a stringer. A stringer, usually paid a monthly retainer of $150, would do local research as requested for writers. In addition to the status of a position, though a low one, with a national magazine, Maurine also wanted the job because it would give her access to the entertaining, ego-enhancing company of professional people.

Maurine wrote again to Annie in early March, apparently her first letter since January, half-excusing the time lag by saying she had "so darned many letters" to answer "—10 or 12 a batch." Although her job at the library was due to end in May, she said she wanted to "get a good summer set-up here so that I can stay on through next winter." She firmly squelched the possibility of spending the summer in St. George: "This is the place for me, all right. I'm through being sick, which is what I'd be up there. Also there's the question of a place to work up there, even if I did come back next summer. I can't work [at] home. And I do have to put in 8 hours a day on my book. . . . Wish I had a home here, I hate to rent. But this is a good place to work and maybe in time I can pay debts and own a car and a home—anyway, it's nice to dream."9

When she received a whopping $4.48 royalty check for *This Is the Place: Utah* in early March,10 she wrote the next day to Max Becker, again asking him to send back her articles so that she could try to sell them herself. She also tried in the same letter to inveigle a most unprofessional concession out of him. She described herself as having a "desperately bad time" financially, claimed that she had kept herself afloat "only because of the League, friends, the jobs I've managed to get myself, [and] the sales I've made to

LIFE and the POST." She wanted him to forego his commission out of royalties until she got her debts paid.[11]

Even though this proposition was breathtakingly nervy, Becker might very well have decided he had nothing to lose. But Maurine, deep in her self-pitying scenario, then tried two ploys that would have put anybody's back up. First she accused: "It's your responsibility, too, and you've never contributed a thing beyond the initial contract—which I could have gotten on my own. So it does seem to me that if you're going to reap the reward without earning it, you should be willing to make it easier for me to get it written." And then she threatened, "If this proposition is not agreeable, Max, then you may not get the book at all. I've got to pay bills; I've got to live here to keep well, and it's more expensive than elsewhere. Thus, I have no choice. If I can live on definite promises for a while, and stall creditors until I finish—you will have the book. Otherwise, I promise nothing. And frankly, I've gone through so much that I don't care any longer. It's up to you."[12]

Becker apparently wrote back a "nothing doing" letter, which has not survived, reminding Maurine of her contractual engagements. There may have been other exchanges over the summer since, in late August, Maurine turned again to the patient Silcox at the Authors' League Fund, who explained in early September that Maurine "was asking and expecting too much" because "agents were in business to sell, not to finance authors nor to listen to personal problems, etc." But Luise also added, "I think the time is right, because the book, which Max contracted for you with Simon and Schuster, is coming along, so he [Max] needn't worry about that." Maurine would have to handle the cancellation herself. "But you know that Becker and Simon and Schuster have been told that the book is well underway and would be a good one and that Becker would get his 10% commission and then nothing else."[13]

Had she in fact been working on "Cleave the Wood" over the summer, or was the piece of information to Max and Luise part of the necessary presentation of herself as a diligent but struggling author?

Some additional evidence that she was trying to push for her own support is a letter written the day after her "proposition" to Becker—a consciously ingratiating message to Bert MacBride, department editor for "My Most Unforgettable Character" at *Reader's Digest*. He had just airmailed back a rejected (unnamed) manuscript. Alluding to her high-pressure tactics on the Harry Goulding sketch that had backfired so spectacularly two years earlier, she wrote: "What pleased me most was the surmise I got from the gesture: Am I forgiven? Gee, it would make me happy if you weren't mad at me anymore!" She ramblingly explained her situation, repeating points she had made in earlier letters. Apparently, the Authors' Guild didn't see any reason why Maurine couldn't work on a novel and articles simultaneously.

She was unable to place any of her manuscripts. The roller-coaster of hope and discouragement relentlessly consumed much of her time and energy, brought in no income, and distracted her from "Cleave the Wood."

Perhaps realizing the downward spiral of her life and secretly losing confidence in her ability to write saleable work anymore, she applied for a full-time position running a library for Cliff Henderson at the Shadow Mountain Club in Palm Springs.[14] Her application letter, as usual, over-explained. She said that her plays were "all original" and that she helped produce "a children's radio" that "ran several months over KSL in Salt Lake City," arousing interest from "other stations," and which she had "intended to sell . . . commercially."[15] She continued, glamorously but vaguely, creating an image of herself as a brilliant writer plagued by bad luck. She was in Palm Springs, she said, to clear up "a bronchial complaint," wanted to "live in the desert" for her health, and saw the library job as "right up my alley" since it would "give me some hours for writing." She bragged that she could "not only make the library attractive to everybody" but also generate "considerable publicity" for the town. She also hinted that she knew "a money raising scheme which is sure-fire." As personal references, she dropped the names of "Dr. Levi Edgar Young of the LDS Church, and Dr. Clayton S. Rice, a prominent Presbyterian minister who had once lived in St. George."[16]

She did not get the job.

What she did next was unclear. In her letter to Henderson, she had mentioned plans to go to Los Angeles for a week, which means that she was probably still trying to cajole a commitment from Ted Strauss and Robert Cahn for a job connected to *Collier's* and possibly suggesting that she had not yet completely given up on completing her Arizona Strip article.

At this point, it was late April. Maurine had been in the California desert since the previous October with virtually nothing to show for it: little visible work on the sequel, no magazine sales, and not even any new articles. Despite her defiant letter to Annie, she had no option but to return to St. George for the summer. She purchased her first car—an old Ford she nicknamed "Mehitable"—and drove home. How she financed the car, how much it cost, and when she had learned to drive is not known. She probably continued her fantasy of being a *Collier's* stringer, which would certainly be facilitated by a car.

From St. George on 15 June, Maurine sent Ted Strauss a draft of an article about Art Greene, who ran a riverboat on the Colorado River to the Rainbow Bridge. "It isn't a finished essay but merely a sample," she warned. She had left some other articles (unidentified) with him, suggesting that she had made at least one more trip to Los Angeles, probably in April.[17] She warmly invited Ted to visit her in St. George, promising to show him a monster—"a machine in my back yard—for harvesting sugar beet seed. This would make a good article." Her papers contain no response from Ted to this letter or to her next, written only four days later: "I'm like a spider spinning a web—it never spins by degrees; and given web is the best web it can spin at the time."[18] She was talking about her writing, but Ted did not need to be a Freudian to understand that she was also trying to spin a web around him. She had, as usual, disclosed more than she intended to.

Knopf's treasurer informed her that the Department of Commerce regulations required book publishers to "melt obsolete plates—those which, on 1 April 1951, or on the first day of any calendar quarter thereafter, had been in existence for four years without being reprinted." She had the right to purchase the plates for *This Is the Place: Utah* or sign a letter giving permission for the melting. It was probably like getting word that a child was going to be executed, but there was nothing she could do about it.[19]

Meanwhile, she fidgeted and tried to renew interest in her articles. Bob Cahn, in a letter that has not survived, had inquired about the possibility of taking a trip up the Colorado to see Rainbow Bridge. Maurine reported that "it might be hard to arrange, as Art Greene was booked last year in advance." She had gone by slipping into a last-minute cancellation. She must have been wondering why her already written article on the strip, which had been in New York now for almost five months, was not good enough. But she wasn't beaten. She sent "a decent" copy of the Timpanogas hike article, accompanied by some photographs, which she said "should be guarded" because they weren't hers, and enthused about the article possibilities of Rainbow Bridge, which she called "the largest in the world." Then, in a charmingly entertaining passage, she explained her raging enthusiasm for Utah:

> I seem to be a long-winded cuss, but there is so much to see, and so much to tell, and I've waited so long for somebody to appreciate it! You see, Utah has always been a by-passed state—people thought of Utah as a place to rush through to get to the Northwest, or the Southwest. During the war a newly-drafted bunch of Hollywood screen writers were sitting around the last day in the office discussing what should be done to Hitler, and somebody suggested: "Banish the son-of-a-bitch to Utah," and that is how Utah has been regarded up to now. Only lately have eastern editors been aware that something besides polygamy and sand exist out here.

She stated honestly that she would love being "a regular contributor more than anything else in the world" and confessed, "I hate free lancing.

When they do take an article, it's like parting with a drop of salt water and ignoring the whole ocean. . . . I'm fuller of stories than a cactus is of spines."[20] What she said was only too true.

Whichever magazine in New York had been considering the Rainbow Bridge article rejected it, and Maurine shared her disappointment with Bob Cahn, who treated her emotional state with practical professionalism: "Try another magazine." Meanwhile, the Arizona Strip article had been gaining important attention and had been forwarded to the national *Collier's* office. He said he had had lunch with Roy Craft, "who had spoken highly of you." He also mentioned, almost casually, that "Ted couldn't make it to St. George."[21]

In mid-July, Cahn sent a hundred dollars as "expense money to show good faith" and told her that John Florea, a *Collier's* photographer, would be coming to St. George to get photos of the Strip. He didn't say when.[22] Maurine finally had reason for high hopes that this article would be published.

In September, Carma Lee Smithson, a reporter with the *Salt Lake Tribune*, did a lengthy interview with Maurine, illustrated by a photograph of Maurine in shorts and a halter top, straddling a low wire fence around a calf pen. Smithson reported that Maurine was living in the office adjacent to Brigham Young's winter home, that she was "as much 'plain folks' as your next door neighbor," praised "her thick auburn hair laced in a smooth coronet braid," and commented on the "massive writing desk" that "dominates everything" in the office. The desk Charlie made for Maurine could not be described as "massive," so this was another item of furniture, perhaps even the one Brigham had used.

The news peg for the article was obviously the long-awaited sequel, since Smithson reports that the sequel is "scheduled to be completed soon" but that "it was no longer a trilogy." Instead "the last two books have been telescoped into one which will concern the second and third generations of Joshua characters."[23]

This interview is, however, the only indication that Maurine had done more than simply cart the manuscript from St. George to Palm Springs and back again to St. George. The evidence seems to indicate that most of her writing energies were going into the Arizona Strip article.

In one letter to the Hollywood *Collier's* office, Maurine optimistically bubbled over with future plans. She wanted to turn the Strip article into a book "with drawings maybe," stay in St. George for the winter, and "get out the book I've been promising so long"—a much more tentative description than the version she had given Smithson only days earlier. Then she confided: "I had sorta planned on deserting the writing game for social security and running a library for Cliff Henderson at the Shadow Mountain Club. But the Strip has my literary muscles flexed again, I don't want to quit."[24]

FLIRTING WITH *COLLIER'S*, 1951–52

This photograph of Maurine feeding a calf accompanied a newspaper story reporting an optimistic account about Maurine's writing projects, 1952.

As later developments make plain, she was also entertaining tender hopes for her relationship with Ted, interpreting his professional assistance as personal interest. In another letter, apparently about this time, she told him she was sending a package of "arrow heads and pretty rocks" to his son, Eric, also "some old pictures" she thought Eric would like.[25] She told Ted she had read his books and how much she liked them. She called him "a literary natural" and coyly teased, "Sometime I will tell you which book I liked best and why." A separate letter to an apparently rebellious Eric encouraged him "to stay with your father and realize what a great man your father is." This letter is the only evidence that she had spent enough time with Eric to establish a relationship, although her papers contain no correspondence with him.

It also seems likely that, around this time, she dealt her relationship with Ted a fatal blow with one of her lethal "you see" letters, begging for understanding and protection: "I guess I'll just have to endure my maidenly blushes and tell you right out that I came home this last time floating in champagne. I've been tipsy ever since. You see, all my life I've been a looker-on, never a participator." Then she exposed just how much she needed him.

335

"I can't explain it. But Ted, I've never known anybody like you before. It's the truth, you do have a perception, an empathy that's almost psychic.... You see, when you wrote me that marvelous letter last summer, I sort of went into a convulsion of enthusiasm and I couldn't quit writing. With me, a little praise is like a dose of gun powder!" She begged to come to Los Angeles to work on the article. "Being near you would mean everything to me. Before, you offered me two evenings. Believe me, I'd take 'em now! And they'd be gold-plated."[26]

Ted studiously ignored much of her letter, including her plea to encourage her to come to Los Angeles, and instead asked her what had happened with "the business with Warners [Studio] wanting Juanita Brooks to be a consultant on a movie about Mountain Meadow Massacre."[27] Maurine wrote back, begging Ted to help her get the job as consultant on the movie and claiming that she knew as much about the massacre as Juanita did.[28]

A little more insight into this consultant possibility comes from a letter Maurine received the next month from Robert K. Hurd, a movie script evaluator in Los Angeles, whom she had met through Joseph Walker. According to him, Juanita had "given up $40,000 to be a consultant on a movie about the Mountain Meadow Massacre because the church advised it," and he told Maurine to "keep that bit of news just between the two of us."[29]

Maurine was serious about her precarious finances. The long-suffering Authors' Fund had underwritten her for six more months—until the past May, a significant extension from its original plans to finance her for three months during the summer of 1951. She had heard rumors that the Brigham Young Winter Home would be restored and open to the public, meaning that she would have to move.[30] In fact, these plans materialized in 1952.

Although Maurine had, in her letter to Ted, sounded as if she were pinning all of her professional hopes on *Collier's*, job, she was, in fact, simultaneously applying for the directorship of the St. George Library. On November 30, Maurine wrote to Milton Moody, superintendent of Washington County Schools, asking for the job.[31] She began her application letter by claiming that "the quality of the St. George library had deteriorated" in unspecified ways, then asserted, "I believe I have much better qualifications than anyone else in town." When Dr. McGregor's widow, Bertha,[32] seemed to be the front-runner for the job, Maurine, pride piqued and angry, decided to fight. According to what Maurine told me, Bertha McGregor and her supporters inquired about Maurine's employment with the Palm Springs' library and either received a negative report, or interpreted it that way, and circulated it around town. Maurine felt it was unfair and untrue. She wrote the library director in Palm Springs, Dorothy Bear, telling her what was going on and asking for her support.[33] She told me that her friends, Evelyn and Lou Harris, had started a petition on her behalf. She also wrote the St. George library board directly again attacking her rival as incompetent.[34] Naturally, such tactics thoroughly sabotaged her possibilities.

Who knows? The stability of a job that gave her a steady income, visibility, a respected role in the community, and an organizational structure in which she could express her passion for community building—especially her gift for including youngsters—may have been the anchor she needed for a more contented, less fearful life. It might have given her the stability that she had missed by not marrying and might have produced enough contentment to gently release a more measured form of creativity for her writing. But Bertha, then a widow, needed the job and had the local support. Maurine said: "See, that's what I mean. Bertha was from the 'in' group. I just wasn't."

When informed she wouldn't be hired, Maurine compounded the situation by taking the patronizing position that she only wanted the job to help the community by bringing quality to the library. With true insensitivity, she wrote to Bertha McGregor, explaining she had no personal dislike for her, but stating it was "just a fact—the new library director [meaning Bertha herself] wasn't qualified." In my interviews with Maurine she told me this story many times. "If only I had gotten that job, how different my life would have been!"

She must have then gone to California, since she wrote an entertaining report of the return trip when she was stalled in Mesquite by a bus strike for three days. She made arrangements with Oscar Abbott, sheriff in Nevada's Clark County, to drive her home, pumping him en route for new local stories to add to her trove.[35]

The next month, in mid-January, she again wrote to Ted, pleading for "a talk." She again painted a pitiable picture of her finances. The Authors' League had made its last loan to her in December and she could not ask for more "because that would invite investigation and I didn't think they would understand my circumstances." She had sold her car "to pay off the Christmas-trip" and complained bitterly about the discrimination against her in St. George where she had just lost her bid for the library.[36]

She had been offered a six-month—possibly year-long—fellowship at the Huntington Hartford art colony in Pacific Palisades, but did Ted think she should concentrate on her writing instead? Ted did not comment one way or the other. So she tackled Bob Cahn for advice. She saw three options: "1. Borrow $35 from the bank and come to the Hollywood office the first week in February, purpose being to work on my articles. 2. Give the *Collier's* New York office an ultimatum on the Strip article, suggest they use the two-installment deal, or release it so I could sell it to the *Post*. . . . 3. Take the Huntington Hartford fellowship."[37]

If she accepted the fellowship, she had to have enough money to pay some debts. She would also need at least $25 a month spending money, but the terms of the fellowship did not allow outside employment. She would have to work "exclusively" on her stated objective—which would mean the novel—which would mean no more articles. Furthermore, she didn't think she could "flourish" in an artists' colony where "a single girl had to be expert at both liquor and men." She confessed in a moment of self-insight that "a steady diet of lonely writing" was something she just could not do. Then she betrayed the real reason for hesitating about taking the Huntington Hartford Fellowship: "And what I really want is a chance to be a stringer for *Collier's* at $100 to $150 a month. If I can't get that, and if I quit trying to be a contributor, I am afraid I will never get another chance to work with Ted; and I would give up a thousand fellowships to go on working with him. . . . As a pioneer woman, strictly a domesticated female, I'd have excelled; but I just couldn't seem to fit 'today.' Ted gave me an impetus, a boost, that was like a shot of benzedrine. Oh golly, how can I say it? For the first time in years I could put down words without holding my nose. I was happy. And I didn't think I could be happy! I don't want to lose that, Bob."[38]

Every day during January, one can imagine how she felt as she walked to the post office to see if Ted or Bob had written. Her suspense was partially alleviated in February, when the New York *Collier's* office informed her that it would accept the Arizona Strip article and pay her $1,000. She wrote a radiantly happy letter, asking that extra copies of that issue be sent to St. George, Kanab, and Las Vegas where it would be in high demand and also requested many free copies so she could give them to the people who had helped her. She also promptly began planning a visit to the Hollywood office of *Collier's* where Ted would be doing the final edit. Obviously she interpreted the acceptance of this single article as her big break.

On 17 March, she wrote Ted a medical report: She had flu and allergies so miserable that her "eyes were nearly swollen shut." Yet even so, she had heroically "walk[ed] all over town in a bitter wind to talk to the stockmen before they left for the ranges," accumulating more details for the already too-long Arizona Strip article.[39] Even with this break, Maurine admitted to me that everyone advised her to finish the sequel and kept pointing out the conveniences of working at the Huntington Hartford art colony.

The article appeared in *Collier's* 24 May 1952 issue with the title, "America's Tibet: The Arizona Strip." The article played on the area's isolation—how it should have been in Utah, because the Colorado river cut it off from the Arizona government, leaving it virtually lawless. She told of the people, some honest late seekers after the American dream of land of their own and others hiding from the law. She emphasized their courage in sticking with some of the last American land to be claimed, even though it was financially foolish and their neighbors were often not to be trusted.

This success spurred hope for more of the same. In July 1951, Maurine sent Bob Cahn a copy of her "Lunatics, by One of Them." What Bob did with the manuscript is not clear, but her papers include a memo from New York *Collier's* editor, Gordon Manning, to Bob, commenting that Maurine had proposed another idea in her usual "abbreviated" form (apparently Maurine's lengthy letters were an in-joke among *Collier's* editors) but that if Bob "could wade through it," they thought "it would make a good photo story with a short text about the annual hike."[40] The idea went nowhere. Bob must have encouraged her to send it to another editor. She did, but in May of 1952 she got another rejection.[41]

Maurine's moment of basking in the attention roused from the Arizona Strip article didn't last long and it was just another distraction, though a successful one, from "Cleave the Wood." She proposed other feature articles, one about a Kanab rancher being forced off his spread by the drought and another about the town of St. Thomas, covered by the rising waters of Lake Mead but now exposed anew by the intensifying drought. These topics joined other tales she dangled as possibilities: "a haunted hotel (truly!) and a member of Butch Cassidy's gang still alive and ready to 'sing,' and a mine that has had $500,000 sunk in it because a Bishop had a dream of the Three Nephites!"[42]

A small break came. Maurine willingly dashed off to Las Vegas on an assignment from Ted to gather information about an Indian school near the atomic bomb testing grounds. She borrowed a typewriter from a plumbing office on which to write up her research, which did not answer the questions she had been hired to find. Her letters also reveal her plans to teach a "Writers Work Shop at the college at Cedar City the first week in June" and that she suggested timing a river trip for the second week, that Eric [Ted's son] should come, because she "liked looking after kids" and that Eric could stay afterwards for a few days—she would just put him on the bus to Hollywood "because she knew the drivers and they would look out for him."[43] Her coaxing was to no avail. Ted did not come.

The next week, on 24 May 1952, he took a deep breath and gave her some hard and realistic news about her shortcomings as a journalist: "Don't be crushed, and don't be a wilting violet, but do take it seriously. The research you sent in on the kids school at Indian Springs simply wasn't adequate. . . . As a writer you do a magnificent job of filtering through your own sensitive mind and heart long accumulated impressions. However, as a reporter, I suspect that you talk too much, and listen too little." Ted had had to send Bob Cahn to Las Vegas for "the material and quotes" that he had hired Maurine to get. It would be Bob's material, not hers, that would accompany the story, although *Collier's* did send her $150 "for the work" that she put into it. Ted then went to the bother to give her some tips and compliments, saying: "You don't need instruction in how to write, which God knows you do so beautifully, but to insist on [the] discipline that reporting requires."44

Uncharacteristically, she postponed a reply for almost a month, then wrote another of her "you see" letters on 19 June. She begins with determined cheerfulness, expressing her hope that *Collier's* would run her St. Thomas story as a text piece, rather than a photo story. Then she launched into a lengthy explanation, presenting herself as a serious professional, but repeatedly making personal wheedling appeals: "What I do [know about writing], I do almost entirely from instinct. Which means that I have no rules to fall back on. Which means that I cannot be a judge of my own material. . . . I want perfection—and when I can't fulfill what I expect of myself, I'm frantic." She concludes: "I'll need instruction and I'll need help. . . . You see, Ted, it isn't only my respect for your intellect—with you I feel a kinship, a sort of fellow-feeling. I don't think I imagine it. . . . Well, with that rapport, I can write a thousand Strips. All I need is a sense of security—not just physical security."45

How true that last statement was! But what man would take on the responsibility of trying to make such a complicated, needy woman feel secure? Yes, again had a man like Ted taken on her native genius, he might have helped create an American literary landmark, but it was not to be.

A heart-sick Maurine tried to give back the $150 she had received for the unsatisfactory Indian-school work. When Ted would not accept it, she spent it on a handloomed, Navajo-fish-design-embroidered tie for Ted, and a painting for the office by a Navajo artist.46 She also sent Eric Strauss an iron spike from Leeds "where it had helped support the Wells-Fargo bank vault" and a hunk of uranium-bearing carnotite. She renewed her futile invitation for Ted to come to St. George, assured him that she could arrange the river trip with Art Greene with only a few days' notice, told him photographer Pat Coffey had said he "was eager to work" with her again, and listed other possible article topics. Then, fatally, she again slid off professional business into another damning plea for sympathy: "I might as well be even franker, Ted. I'm awfully tired. And sorta low. In all my life I've never needed a break as much as I need it right now. If you could manage the trip soon (oh, I know the difficulties! Damn N.Y.!) it would mean more to me personally than I can possibly tell you. And believe me, I'll come through with the articles."47

To her delight, the New York office accepted her story about St. Thomas's reemergence from Lake Mead. On 11 July, Maurine asked Ted to help with the cutting because she was "flopping in all directions like a chicken with its head off." She said exuberantly, "I'm still having fun."48

She proposed a story about actor Robert Taylor, then in Kanab for the filming of a movie, and "a legend because of his decency and general sweetness."[49] A second possibility was "communist-inspired psychological sabotage going on" at a local metals plant.[50] A third was another movie story, this time about Howard Keel, also then in Kanab.[51]

The return letter from the *Collier's* Hollywood office passed on some compliments for Maurine from Lou Ruppel, a ex-Marine captain with a reputation for toughness, who was then managing editor of the *Chicago Sun-Times*. Maurine must have met him on one of her promotion trips east. She responded with obvious gratitude couched in painfully strained humor: "I envy you knowing Lou Ruppel. Tell him if he'll stay there, I'll come down and go into my Beggar-girl-and-Prince routine."[52]

Maurine's eagerness, combined with her ineptness, make for distressing reading, especially since her relationship with *Collier's*, like her relationship with Ted Strauss, was going nowhere. Ignoring his excellent professional advice to her and the unspoken but equally clear message that only a professional relationship interested him, she approached her fiftieth birthday with another of her desperate "you see" letters, this time writing the tale of her sufferings in third person ("the little girl"). Something had happened that fall: a chance or teasing remark about "a home in Idaho," perhaps Ted confiding his own dream of retiring to Idaho, and Maurine, reading herself into that dream, turned it into a cautious proposal for marriage and headed straight for another broken heart. She had asked for a Christmas present of two hours of Ted's time and construed his response as a promise that she would have those hours. It was 8 January 1953 when she wrote her dreadful, damning missive in the voice of "the little girl."[53] The most significant sentence in the letter is: "It seemed that all her life had been one long rejection and the pattern kept repeating itself." This was exactly what had happened. Perhaps a good angel prevented Maurine from mailing this letter. Perhaps Ted, if he received it, did not read it. One can hope so.

Simultaneously, while Maurine was coaxing *Collier's* and Ted Strauss to pay attention to her and being rejected for two library positions, she had done all the things necessary to apply for the fellowship at the artists' colony in Pacific Palisades near Los Angeles underwritten by the Huntington Hartford Foundation. In 1991, she told me that it had a reputation for "weird people" and that "wild stories" circulated about it, but she was desperate to be settled again and was forced to consider it.

Hartford, heir to the fortune his grandfather had made by establishing the A&P (the Great Atlantic and Pacific Tea Company) found the role of patron of the arts an appealing and socially responsible one. With his nineteen-year-old artist-wife, Marjorie Steele, they began constructing the art colony in Pacific Palisades in 1950.[54]

The main thing Maurine recalled over and over is how she had a bad feeling about going to the place and hesitated, waiting for another option to come along. But when a better situation didn't, she tried to hold out for a twelve-month, rather than a six-month scholarship or grant, as the fellowships were called. Something in the negotiations made her think she had the twelve-month grant. But even then, she delayed her acceptance. She was still rolling out an endless string of article ideas, still hoping for a job offer from *Collier's*, and still trying to pump ardor into her relationship with Ted Strauss. It is obvious that these activities, not the sequel, were siphoning off most of her energy.

She delayed seven months before entering the Huntington Hartford, until February 1953. During those months, she was struggling to find another way to take care of herself financially. It seems obvious, viewed from the outside, that she subconsciously dreaded the task of plunging into serious work on the sequel. The article on the re-emergence of St. Thomas from Lake Mead, which appeared in *Collier's* in the summer of 1952, was not enough to present a viable alternative.

So she went to the Huntington Hartford; but once there, once again set aside "Cleave the Wood" in favor of "The Pickle Is a Dilly," a long-short story about the frivolous responses of the public present at the test of the atomic bomb.[55] Above-ground testing had begun in earnest at the Nevada Test Site in January 1951. Before it stopped in October 1958, 119 bombs had been detonated, their height varying from ground level to 1,500 feet, releasing an estimated 150 million curies of radioactive iodine-131 into the earth's atmosphere. She and Ted had been allowed to witness a test. Although she did not understand the dangers of radiation contamination—few did in the 1950s—the human arrogance and disregard for the golden rule repelled her.

The manuscript of "The Pickle Is a Dilly," unlike many that Maurine began, is finished; but its skeptical attitude countered the aggressive optimism with which the United States had launched itself into the Korean War. She had traded her chance at finishing "Cleave the Wood" for an ahead-of-its-time story no one wanted to publish.[56]

Because she had not accomplished much on her stated purpose, which was the sequel, she was asked to leave the Hartford Foundation after six months. She was hurt and angry and seems to have had no plan after she left. She set out with her luggage and was in desperate straits before her "prince" (*Joshua*) came to the rescue. As she told me the story, a "beautiful, white-haired septuagenarian smiled at me from the porch of an apartment house. I knew I had found refuge. Still obeying my weird compulsion I said

I'd rent an apartment for a hundred dollars a month, even though I didn't know how I'd get the money. The lady let me in and I went straight to bed. An hour later the new landlady came in with a cup of coffee in one hand and *The Giant Joshua* in the other. 'Had I ever heard of the book?'" Her landlady was "Vickie Adolph, once queen of the high-flying trapeze from Barnum and Bailey." According to Maurine, she "lived there for two months, helping Vickie, with the chores." Vickie resourcefully "got herself invited to luncheons, teas, and dinners" among her wealthy acquaintances and came home, her large handbag stocked with pilfered refreshments. Maurine talked of Vickie Adolph as "an angel." But there is no evidence that Maurine kept in touch after their parting, nor could I find any information about Vickie.

The two parted company in May 1953, the first definite date for this period, and Maurine claimed she "was still resolved to finish my book come hell-or-high-water," even though she didn't "feel well enough to find a job." She then went to Dr. Joseph Walker for help, and he let her be his caretaker at a house fifty miles from Banning, California. She had no car or telephone; nor did she settle down, despite her avowed intentions, to work on "Cleave the Wood." Instead, she channeled her energy into writing numerous letters to Huntington Hartford, claiming that she had been economically injured and trying to get a settlement from an insurance company.[57]

Then came another piece of luck—a polygamy story that was the talk of the nation was happening in her own territory: the Arizona Strip. It was the "largest mass arrest of men and women in modern American history," wrote C. R. Waters in the *Mohave Miner* on 30 August 1953. "The entire populace of the small farming community, with the exception of five adults and the children, were charged with conspiracy which includes polygamy."[58] Maurine got involved sometime within the first week after the state of Arizona raided the community on the significant Mormon date of 24 July 1953. By then the polygamous men had been jailed in a facility in Kingman, Arizona. Plans were underway to put the children into foster homes and to "rehabilitate" mothers. Ted asked Maurine to find out what she could and write it up for possible publication. She happily plunged in and ghost-wrote "I Married Five Wives," in the voice of Short Creek fundamentalist Edson Jessup. It was published in the 13 October 1953 issue of *Collier's*.[59] Maurine's papers do not include earlier drafts of this article, but her personal essay, "Story within the Story," makes her role as ghostwriter clear and details the difficulties she had in getting it.[60] The experience drew her back into hoping and angling for more participation in the world of magazine journalism.

With the check from *Collier's* for the Short Creek story, she thought she could afford to have what she called a "complete breakdown" and went

"SWELL SUFFERING"

Maurine Whipple in California about 1954 at the home of Dr. Joseph Walker.

Joseph Walker, a long-time friend of Maurine's and a St. George native, frequently provided medical care and a home when she was in need.

back under Dr. Joseph Walker's umbrella. Naturally, her health problems had not stopped during this period. She complained of heart problems. She also told Maryruth Belt in 1956: "I developed sub-acute meningitis which was at first diagnosed as polio. I had a paralyzed right arm for three years—had to go on public relief."[61]

But now in the fall of 1953 Maurine felt financially stable enough to buy a car—only the second she had ever owned. Unquestionably, not having one had doubled the difficulty for her of doing her Short Creek article, and she must have resolved not to get caught in that situation again.[62]

Although Maurine did not know it, her last chance for the sequel had dissolved, eroded by her happy dreams of magazine journalism.

Notes

[1] Robert Cahn (1917–97) later reported for the *Christian Science Monitor* and won the 1969 Pulitzer Prize for journalism on national matters for his series, "Will Success Spoil the National Parks?"

[2] *Moonrise* was made into a movie in 1948 directed by Frank Borzage and starring Dane Clark, Gail Russell, and Ethel Barrymore, then reprinted in paperback as *Dark Hunger* (New York: Bantam Books, n.d.).

[3] Nellie I. Cox assisted by Helen B. Russell, *Footprints on the Arizona Strip* (Bountiful, Utah: Horizon Publishers, 1973); Nellie I. Cox and Susan Cox, *The Arizona Strip: A Harsh Land and Proud* (Las Vegas, Nev.: Cox Printing, 1982).

[4] She expresses that hope in two letters to Robert Cahn, 15 October 1951 and 6 September 1952; Maurine Whipple Collection, L. Tom Perry Special Collections, Harold B. Lee Library, Brigham Young University, Provo, Utah, with photocopy in Maurine Whipple Collection, Archive, Val A. Browning Library, Dixie College, St. George, Utah. Documents in both collections hereafter cited as BYU, photocopy Dixie College.

[5] Mrs. James Bundy, Mount Trumbull, Arizona, Letter to Maurine Whipple, 15 January 1951; BYU, photocopy Dixie College.

[6] Maurine Whipple, Letter to Annie Whipple, 13 January 1951; BYU, photocopy Dixie College.

[7] Luise M. Silcox, Letter to Maurine Whipple, 24 January 1951; BYU, photocopy Dixie College.

"SWELL SUFFERING"

[8] Ted Strauss, Letter to Maurine Whipple, 12 February 1951; BYU, photocopy Dixie College.

[9] Maurine Whipple, Letter to Annie Whipple, n.d. [ca. March 1951]; BYU, photocopy Dixie College.

[10] Harold Ober Associates, New York, Letter to Maurine Whipple, March 5, 1951; BYU, photocopy Dixie College.

[11] Maurine Whipple, draft of letter to Max Becker, 6 March 1951; BYU, photocopy Dixie College.

[12] Ibid.

[13] Luise M. Silcox, Letter to Maurine Whipple, 4 September 1951; BYU, photocopy Dixie College.

[14] Palm Village was an area north of Highway 111 (the Old MacDonald Ranch).

[15] This letter is the only documentation in her papers of this radio program. The program probably occurred in 1933–34 when she was working for Neighborhood House on Salt Lake City's west side.

[16] Maurine Whipple, Draft of letter to Clifford W. Henderson, Palm Desert Corporation, n.d. [ca. summer 1951], Box 1, Palm Desert, CA, Whipple Collection, BYU. This draft is written in pencil on newsprint.

[17] Robert Cahn, Letter to Maurine Whipple, 3 July 1951, Whipple Collection, BYU.

[18] Maurine Whipple, Letter to Ted Strauss, 19 June 1952; BYU, photocopy Dixie College.

[19] Joseph C. Lesser, Treasurer, Alfred A. Knopf, New York, Letters to Maurine Whipple, 15 June, 18 July, and 7 August 1951, all in Whipple Collection, BYU. The federal regulation, designed to make metals more available during wartime, was National Production Authority, U.S. Department of Commerce order #M-65.

[20] Maurine Whipple, Letter to Robert Cahn, 2 July 1951, Whipple Collection, BYU.

[21] Robert Cahn, Letter to Maurine Whipple, 3 July 1951; BYU, photocopy Dixie College.

[22] Robert Cahn, Letter to Maurine Whipple, 18 July 1951; BYU, photocopy Dixie College.

[23] Carma Lee Smithson, "She Didn't Lose Her Head," *Salt Lake Tribune*, (no day) September 1941, loose clipping; BYU, photocopy Dixie College.

[24] Maurine Whipple, Draft of letter to "Hollywood office," September 16, 1951; BYU, photocopy Dixie College.

[25] Maurine Whipple, draft of letter to Ted Strauss, n.d., possibly fall 1951; BYU, photocopy Dixie College.

[26] Ibid. Apparently the letter Ted wrote "last summer" has been lost.

[27] Ted Strauss, Letter to Maurine Whipple, 30 November 1951; BYU, photocopy Dixie College.

[28] Maurine Whipple, Letter to Ted Strauss, ca. 4 December 1951; BYU, photocopy Dixie College.

29 Robert K. Hurd, Letter to Maurine Whipple, (no day) December 1951; BYU, photocopy Dixie College. Archive. I asked Levi Peterson, Juanita's biographer, about this episode. He suggested that Juanita refused to consult on the proposed movie because the studio wasn't offering enough money. He had no information that the Church had pressured her to say no. However, he also thought that J. Reuben Clark Jr., first counselor in the First Presidency, did some "powerful" asking of Warner Brothers not to do the movie. Conversation with Levi Peterson, Association for Mormon Letters annual meeting, January 25, 1992, Salt Lake City. See also his *Juanita Brooks: Mormon Woman Historian* (Salt Lake City: University of Utah Press, 1988), 215–18. According to D. Michael Quinn, *J. Reuben Clark: The Church Years* (Provo, Utah: Brigham Young University Press, 1983), 170, "President Clark . . . successfully interceded with representatives of the motion picture industry in 1951 to cancel Warner Brothers' intended production of Juanita Brook's The Mountain Meadow Massacre." He cites J. Reuben Clark's Office Diary, January 26, 1942, J. Reuben Clark Papers, L. Tom Perry Special Collections, Lee Library, Brigham Young University.

30 Maurine Whipple, Letter to Milton Moody, Superintendent of Washington County Schools, St. George, 30 November 1951; BYU, photocopy Dixie College.

31 Ibid.

32 Bertha Pendexter Watson McGregor was born 20 July 1886 in Parowan, Utah, to Lorenzo Dow Watson and Sarah Melissa Clark Watson. She married Donald Alpine McGregor 4 June 1909 in Salt Lake City. They had two children. Alma Gertrude Watson, Bertha's sister, was also married to Dr. McGregor. She was the first wife, having married him 21 November 1895. They had seven children. Bertha and Alma were widowed when Dr. McGregor died 11 October 1938. In 1952 Bertha was sixty-six.

33 Maurine Whipple, Draft of letter to Dorothy Bear, Palm Springs Librarian, 9 January 1952; ; BYU, photocopy Dixie College.

34 Maurine Whipple, Draft of letter to Milton Moody, ca. January 1952; BYU, photocopy Dixie College.

35 Maurine Whipple, Letter to Ted Strauss; December 28, 1951; BYU, photocopy Dixie College.

36 Maurine Whipple, Letter to Ted Strauss, 17 January 1952; BYU, photocopy Dixie College.

37 Maurine Whipple, Letter to Bob Cahn, 28 January 1952; BYU, photocopy Dixie College.

38 Ibid.

39 Maurine Whipple, Letter to Ted Strauss, 17 March 1952; BYU, photocopy in Dixie College Archive,

40 Bob Cahn sent Maurine the correspondence in *Collier's* Hollywood office, after *Collier's* closed that office, thus it was found in her papers archived at Brigham Young University.

41 Sey Chassler, Letter to Bob Cahn, 5 May 1952; BYU, photocopy Dixie College: "Here is Whipple's Timpanogas story. We don't want it." Bob forwarded it to Maurine two days later. There is no indication what publication Chassler was with.

42 Maurine Whipple, Letter to "Dearest Kay and Ted and Bob," Friday, 10 P.M., ca. June 1952; BYU, photocopy Dixie College.

43 Maurine Whipple, Letter to Ted Strauss, 8 May 1952; BYU, photocopy Dixie College.

44 Ted Strauss, Letter to Maurine Whipple, 23 May 1952; BYU, photocopy Dixie College.

45 Maurine Whipple, Letter to Ted Strauss, 19 June 1952; BYU, photocopy Dixie College.

46 Maurine Whipple, Letter 18 July 1952; BYU, photocopy Dixie College.

47 Ibid.

48 Maurine Whipple, Letter to Ted Strauss, 11 July 1952; BYU, photocopy Dixie College.

49 Maurine Whipple, Letter to *Collier's*, Hollywood, 18 July 1952; BYU, photocopy Dixie College..

50 I found no further information about this story.

51 Maurine Whipple, Letter to *Collier's* Hollywood office, August 1952; BYU, photocopy Dixie College.

52 Maurine Whipple, Letter to Collier Hollywood office, n.d. The internal evidence would date the letter after 24 May 1952, Whipple Collection, BYU.

53 Maurine Whipple, Letter to Ted Strauss, 8 January 1953; BYU, photocopy Dixie College.

54 Lisa Rebecca Gubernick, *Squandered Fortune: The Life and Times of Huntington Hartford* (New York: G. P. Putnam's Sons, 1991), 84.

55 "The Pickle Is a Dilly," is a short story written in 1952 in three versions, all in the Whipple Collection, BYU Library: (1) 6x8" notebook of research and observations, (2) 4x6" notebook of research and observations, and (3) "The Pickle Is a Dilly," thirty-nine-page final typescript bound in a brown folder. There are also loose pages from other typescript versions in Dixie College Archive.

56 Her papers include a letter from Christopher Publishing House, Letter to Maurine Whipple, 4 June 1954, Whipple Collection, BYU, commenting that the article "was well-written but would not be popular."

57 Maurine Whipple, partial draft of letter, no addressee or date. The page begins: "The next twenty-four months. . . "; BYU, photocopy Dixie College.

58 C. R. Waters, *Mohave Miner*, 30 August 1953.

59 [Maurine Whipple], "I Married Five Wives, A Mormon Fundamentalist Tells His Story" a ghostwritten first-person account by Edson Jessup, 13 October 1953, *Collier's*, five photographs (photographer not identified).

60 "Short Creek Story Within the Story," a fifty-four-page holograph, Dixie College Archive; and a sixteen-page typescript, with the same title, Whipple Collection, BYU. At the Dixie College Archive is a holograph version "Story within the Story," sometimes referred to as "Short Creek, The Story within a Story." 20 pp. Neither version is complete.

61 Maurine Whipple, Letter draft to Maryruth Belt, (no date) 1956, BYU.

62 Lillian [McQuarrie Metcalfe], P.O. Box 2442, Sacramento, Calif. Letter to Maurine Whipple, 6 October 1953; BYU, photocopy Dixie College.

❧ 21 ❧

"GRAND IDEAS": 1954-60

While living at the Walker ranch near Cathedral City, California, Maurine met Dow Hess, an alcoholic doctor who had lost his license to practice medicine.[1] She must have accepted, at this point, that she had no future with Ted Strauss; and desperate for a meaningful relationship, she let herself believe she had enough will-power for herself and Hess. Besides he was a doctor, though a flawed one. With the worst possible chance for success, she tried to recreate her dream of domestic bliss. In doing so, she took on a formidable foe: alcoholism. Besides trying to save her doctor, another motivation for tackling this addiction was her desire to save her younger brother, George, from the same demon. George's high-school yearbook, in Maurine's papers at BYU, shows a teenager who was popular, good looking, musical (he played banjo and guitar), and involved in many school activities. Maurine must have been proud of and happy with George once. It is likely that she never let go of her feeling of responsibility for him, generated during the months she stopped out of school to care for him during a difficult infancy. Certainly she loved him very much.[2] Clearly, even allowing for exaggeration, Maurine had poured time, energy, and money into the attempt to help George. But as she said to me, "He was my brother. What else could I do?" While worried about George and nursing Dow Hess through some of his binges, she decided to become an expert and do an in-depth article about alcoholism. The state of Utah had an active alcoholic rehabilitation program, and the University of Utah sponsored a School of Alcohol Studies. A certificate among her papers attests that she completed the "third annual session" of that school on 19 June 1954.

In 1991, Maurine described Dow Hess as a man who "loved women. You know, that is a disease with some men. My friends could see what he was. I could see what he could be." So she battled on in his behalf, and he drifted in and out of his alcoholic fog, obviously not qualified to practice medicine or be a decent companion to anyone.

While Maurine was attending the University of Utah's course, she spent time with Paul O'Halloran, one of a medical team in Seattle developing a new treatment for alcoholism. "Conditioned Reflex Therapy" was based on the assumption that alcoholism could be cured by making the alcoholic very nauseated every time he took a drink. Maurine believed it. She wanted Ted to let her write an article about it and about the founder of the sanitarium pioneering the treatment, Charles A. Shadel. Either Ted or the New York office declined the story. She decided to go ahead anyway. She persuaded the Shadel sanitarium to admit her as if she were a patient, and let her observe the treatment being offered. Here she found a spirit of cooperation and altruistic thinking that seemed to be calling for someone like her to tell the world about it. Her enthusiasm was boundless. She immediately saw Charles Shadel as someone who was trying to make the grand idea of brotherhood work. She wanted to do Shadel's biography and saw herself as being the first to introduce to a popular audience the best news in the world for alcoholics: a supposedly newly discovered enzyme that would prevent addiction to alcoholism. As Maurine phrased it, "Most people who become alcoholics lacked that enzyme. This world-shaking discovery would change history; for along with a massive educational program where young people would be tested for the enzyme, thus [enabling them] . . . to plan their drinking habits, the enzyme could be made available for those classified as alcoholics now. Soon the world would have a society minus the devastating effects of alcoholism."[3] If she had missed out on the love of Tom Spies because he was too absorbed in bringing the world his vitamin discoveries, wouldn't it be fitting if she helped bring forth an equal or even greater discovery? Then her life of suffering would have meaning. And with that great possibility, choosing to divert her talent, resources, and energy to this great cause seemed the logical thing to do.

Good-bye to the sequel of *The Giant Joshua*.

Although the loss of the sequel is disappointing, Maurine's failure to become a successful and important writer was not because of laziness. When sufficiently inspired, she could concentrate and work long hours. To help with her finances, she arranged with Shadel Sanatorium to be paid a fee for the clients she referred to it. Because she always needed money, she eagerly pursued this option, becoming enmeshed in lives that were usually hopeless. She never seemed to realize that alcoholics, because of their addiction, were seldom truthful and usually skilled at taking advantage of people's good intentions.

Maurine ingeniously tapped a wealthy casino owner in Las Vegas, John DeLuca, for funds by convincing him that the casinos in Las Vegas could use positive publicity by showing they had concern for and a desire to help alcoholics. Just how she knew how to divert charitable money is not known. But she showed DeLuca that he could give money to a non-profit institution, thus making it a tax deduction,[4] who would then give it to her. Her correspondence confirms that such a relationship existed at least for a couple of years with a number of Las Vegas businessmen.[5] She was asking for money to visit research libraries, interview doctors, and "revise a stack of manuscript which seem[s] a mile high!"[6]

One important person she contacted to help her find some money was Norman Cousins. He tried to help and wrote encouragingly: "I still think *The Giant Joshua* is a masterpiece, and I still agree with DeVoto's opinion that the projected trilogy cannot help be as good, if not better than the pioneer version of the whole."[7] However, though he tried to help her by passing her projects before other important people, his efforts did not result in substantive help or sponsorship.

On 6 November 1957, Maurine inquired whether the prestigious Kenyon Fellowships were available for nonfiction as well as fiction. She wanted to submit "one hundred tentative, unpolished, unorganized, eternally-to-be-revised pages" of her work on alcoholism.[8] It was not accepted. She offered the manuscript to Houghton Mifflin in 1957. Houghton Mifflin said "no."[9]

Significantly, as early as the spring of 1955, after Maurine had invested perhaps a year in research about the Shadel treatment, she had access to information that should have cast cold water on her enthusiasm for aversive conditioning and enzyme treatment as a panacea for alcoholism. Evidence was mounting that the treatment did not have permanent effects, nor had anyone discovered the missing enzyme.[10] Because she chose to ignore or downplay the significance of this information, she invested at least parts of four more years in the doomed project.

Another obstacle was Shadel's illness. Maurine tried numerous times to interview him; but, as she told me, "His wife made it impossible. She distrusted me and kept him like a prisoner." This failure was most frustrating. She wanted terribly to give to the world a hero to go with the most magnificent breakthrough to come to humankind. She was hoping to do a full-scale biography, and her papers include seven undated treatments, some of them quite lengthy.[11] Shadel lived until at least May 1960, but Maurine was never allowed to interview him.[12]

Maurine's papers also include a possibly finished manuscript, "The Sanitarium that God Built," consisting of a two-page foreword and a 103-page typescript. The longer typescript describes the facilities, personnel, and methods of the Shadel Sanitarium for the Treatment of Alcoholics in Seattle, Washington.

After Shadel's death in 1960, the new administrators were less willing to be cooperative. Furthermore, the Shadel treatment was being proven as simply wrong, and no missing enzyme caused alcoholism. Maurine's work was useless. But it took her a long time to admit it.

Even after she gave up hope for Dow Hess and the other alcoholics she tried to help, she clung to her cherished hopes for her brother, George. She had convinced him to enter the sanatorium in October 1955, with their father, Charlie, footing most of the bill. To Maurine's dismay and heartbreak, George was not one of the sanatorium's few success stories.

Apparently Dow Hess had by then drifted out of her life, after helping her move from Cathedral City, California, back to Utah in the summer or fall of 1955. Her car was pulling his trailer full of belongings when they had a break-down in Needles, California, She liked to tell the story of how, once again, her one true "prince," *Joshua*, came to the rescue. The garage owner was a fan and fixed the car at a rate she could afford.

Sometime during 1954 or 1955, Maurine, who turned fifty-three in 1955, described her gloomy mood when she contemplated another return to St. George: "I have no reason to expect this homecoming to differ from the others. I'll check in at a hotel for $2.50 a day. I'll eat a 65 cent breakfast and try to 'cadge' dinner. Then because there is no public transportation (and because sad experience has taught me not to expect a lift), I'll walk—5 to 6 miles a day, house-hunting. (Just as I had to walk when I first came up here, sick or not sick.)"[13]

Despite her pessimism, her father came to the rescue. And this time, Maurine accepted his help. Charlie had remodeled the old adobe house at 320 North 100 East into an all-seasons home, and he had retained the near-by trailer, the site of Maurine's earlier nest-building effort, for his own retreat.

Camellia Carter Sullivan Higgins, a niece of Maurine's good friend, Anna Carter Cox, later lived in this house as a bride and described it in her journal: "very nice and it is fixed up quite cute. There was a large bedroom on South side, a remodeled bathroom with a new tub and shower. The kitchen was on the North wall and open to the dining and living area. There was a front lawn, climbing rose bush by the front door, trees, rose bushes, pampas grass bushes, etc."[14] So, thanks to her unappreciated father, Maurine now had a comfortable home. Just what financial arrangement they had, however, is unknown. Likely Maurine intended to pay rent.

In September 1955, Lillian McQuarrie's fourth husband, George Benedict, died. Maurine's letter of condolence revived their flagging correspondence. Lillian was writing again, working on a story about J. W.

McAllister, the music teacher at Dixie College. He was cooperating. He had, in fact, "given her the only copy of his teaching syllabus in existence."[15] If that is the case, it ended up in Maurine's papers now at Brigham Young University. Lillian wanted to come back to St. George to live but felt her son, Lloyd, was better off where they were. She did come for a visit. Lillian's next letter to Maurine, on 18 October 1955, praised Maurine for looking so "sleek and well fed and well dressed—with a house and a car of your own! As we get on, we get on, don't we?"[16]

Maurine took on another cause in 1956 that brought her temporarily into alliance with Juanita Brooks. Vera Black, a plural wife, had not been arrested in the state of Arizona's 1953 raid on Short Creek because she lived on the Utah side of the state line in Hilldale. Although Utah had been content to let Arizona do the litigation (and take the public relations hit) of prosecuting the Short Creek arrestees, Utah was using Vera Black as a test case of whether plural marriage provided evidence of unfit parenthood so that the state could place the children of plural unions in foster care unless they signed an affidavit to renounce teaching and practicing polygamy. When the Utah officials arrived to take the children into custody, Maurine Whipple and Juanita Brooks were both present and unquestionably on Vera Black's side.[17]

At the same time Maurine was focusing on the inviolability of parent-child relationships for polygamists, her mother, who had been in a rest home since at least December of 1953, worsened and died on 24 February 1956. Maurine and Annie had been partners all of Maurine's life in a conspiracy against Charlie, with Maurine being the stronger of the two. She always felt mingled pity and contempt for Annie, loving her gentleness, hating her inability to stand up to Charlie, simultaneously needing Charlie's strength but loathing his insensitivity. Now Charlie was her only parent.

The year 1956 ended with the sad news that *Collier's* was ceasing publication. Bob Cahn told Maurine the news and sent back the correspondence in the magazine's files. He said he didn't know what Ted would do.[18] Now Maurine no longer had any contacts with a national magazine publisher. It must have been a bleak and lonely winter; and apparently at this time, she was brought to such financial straits she applied for and received government relief.[19]

After pulling herself determinedly through this discouraging patch of developments, Maurine spent a couple of years of almost frenzied activity, trying to jump-start her stalled career. She continued trying to find funding or a publisher for the Shadel book, even though the consensus was getting stronger and clearer that aversion therapy and enzymes were not valid. She applied for grants from the Carnegie Foundation and was awarded $200 from its authors' fund.[20] She also collected some money from an insurance claim in early 1958, although she said she could not remember the basis of the claim when I inquired. She asked acquaintances and friends for money, usually presenting her request as a loan, which she intended to repay out of royalties. Sometimes she asked for money as an investment in a worthy cause.

She sent John Crowe Ransom, editor of *The Kenyon Review*, copies of "The Golden Door" and "The Pickle Is a Dilly." He found them old-fashioned but was sufficiently encouraging that she launched a full-scale plea for help in finishing the sequel, which she was now describing as a trilogy:

> Ever since I can remember I've been fascinated by the evolution of the Idea that sustained the Utah pioneers against such odds. The next two books of the trilogy trace this evolution, trace it both in terms of the individual and the whole. The question seems to be: is the idea of brotherly love so naive and impractical that it must be sacrificed if Success is to be achieved? I do not believe such a postulation is inevitable, despite events, despite Church snobbishness. I believe that this present phase is merely part of the larger picture and that a generation or two generations hence the pendulum will slowly swing back to the original Mormon conception for which so many gave their lives. And I also believe (in fact, I know—as many humble people have insisted so long) that my books will help bring about this consummation; will help readjust and clarify Mormon thinking, will help reestablish the Idea. Thus, for ten years I've been trying to get the money to write these sequels.[21]

She chose a new agent, Walter R. Schmidt with the Paul Small Artists Ltd. Inc., in Beverly Hills, and he gave her practical advice about working systematically. If he could place the alcoholism book, even if it wasn't finished, then she could finish it with the advance that would alleviate her immediate financial pressures. Then she could move on to "The Arizona Strip." He thought he could use what she already had written, including the nonfiction articles, to get a contract and another advance for her. She didn't take his advice and their relationship did not last long.

She collected more rejection slips: "No" for "The Pickle Is a Dilly." "No" from the *Saturday Evening Post* to an article about a religious program in Zions National Park. "No" to an article on St. George's Rotarians.

Probably the high point of these years was achieving the dream of a lifetime: buying her own home in August of 1958. Once again, Charlie probably played a major role, and once again she was reluctant to admit it. She gave credit to her cousin, Reed Whipple, a Las Vegas banker, who helped arrange a loan.[22] The home at 410 West 600 North in St. George stood on a two-acre lot (one of which she later sold), surrounded by fruit trees and a row of pomegranate bushes. Charlie again supplying many of the handyman skills to install a furnace, new kitchen, a bathroom, and a storage room. In reminiscing about this happy time, she said she picked out wallpaper, and a neighbor helped her hang it. Someone gave her a newer rug and a couch. Charlie made bookcases for her collection of over two hundred books. Paintings hung on the wall, one by LaVon Gilles, another by her cousin-in-law Holland Crow, and, in later years, a third of a Joshua tree in pastels by Robert L. Shepherd, a local artist. She seldom had local visitors from mainstream St. George society, not only because her sense of "order" did not match the norms of good housekeeping, but because the people who did drop by, like LaVon Gilles and Ernie May, were frequently considered "odd." But she did have a few loyal friends like Katharine Miles Larson and Anna Cox who were locally respected.

She planted a garden and gathered wood to burn in her fireplace. She acquired cats and kept dogs—big ones—because she felt she needed protection, especially from wild teenagers who threw rocks at the house and jeered at her. But much of the time here in her own place she had precious moments of contentment.

Notes

[1] I found no information about Dow Hess; possibly it is not his correct full name.

[2] Maurine Whipple, Letter, addressee unknown at Shadel Sanatorium for Alcoholics, n.d., first page missing; Maurine Whipple Collection, L. Tom Perry Special Collections, Harold B. Lee Library, Brigham Young University, Provo, Utah, hereafter cited as BYU. If there's a photocopy in Maurine Whipple Collection, Archive, Val A. Browning Library, Dixie College, St. George, Utah, the short citation is: BYU, photocopy Dixie College.

[3] Maurine Whipple, loose paper, n.d., BYU.

[4] This information about how she worked out a tax deduction for her supporters in the alcoholic research project comes from an undated (ca. 1956) letter draft to Maryruth Belt, but it did not say who helped her toward these understandings. BYU, photocopy Dixie College.

[5] Maurine Whipple, Letter to Rev. O. T. Phillips, Unity Church, 232 South Eighth Street, Las Vegas, Nevada, 5 February 1959; BYU, photocopy Dixie College.

6 Ibid. She also told him that her next book would be a "historical novel on Las Vegas." Nothing in her papers indicates that she ever did research on this topic, although she was always alert for good stories. Undoubtedly historic Las Vegas, founded by Mormons, caught her interest.

7 Norman Cousins, Letter to Maurine Whipple, no day, April 1959; BYU, photocopy Dixie College.

8 Maurine Whipple, Letter to John Crowe Ransom, 6 November 1957; BYU, photocopy Dixie College.

9 Austin Olney, Letter to Maurine Whipple, 23 September 1957; BYU, photocopy Dixie College. Ferris Greenslet had died in 1956.

10 Clyde Gooderham, executive director of the Utah State Board of Alcoholism, transcription of discussion with Mrs. Frank MacDonald, 2 April 1955; Whipple Collection, BYU.

11 Maurine wrote several versions: (1) A 114-page manuscript, "The House that God Built" ca. 1954–63; (2) 23+ odd pages of typescript, which do not seem to fit anywhere in the 114 pages, yet reference it; (3) A typescript synopsis titled "Synopsis of The House that God Built" 3 pp.; (4) Synopsis and foreword, "The Sanitarium That God Built," 5 pp.; (5) "Foreword," typescript, 2 pp.; (6) untitled typescript, 22 pp.; (6) 103 pp. typescript titled "Mr. Shadel"; and (7) yet another 23 pp. typescript, missing page 4 and all pages after 24.

12 A letter from Maurine's lawyer in Seattle, retained because she thought her work would be stolen, tells her that Mrs. Shadel had instructed him to tell Maurine not to write to them again. John H. Caley, Caley and Armstrong, Attorneys at Law, Seattle, Washington, Letter to Maurine Whipple, 11 May 1960; BYU, photocopy Dixie College.

13 Maurine Whipple, draft letter to Dr. Vincent, Shadel Alcohol Rehabilitation Hospital, n.d. [ca. 1954–55]; BYU, photocopy Dixie College.

14 Camilla Carter Sullivan Higgins, Personal History, n.d., photocopy of typescript in my possession.

15 Lillian McQuarrie, Letter to Maurine Whipple, 22 September 1955; BYU, photocopy Dixie College.

16 Lillian McQuarrie, Letter to Maurine Whipple, 18 October 1955, BYU.

17 Martha Sonntag Bradley, *Kidnapped from That Land: The Government Raids on the Short Creek Polygamists* (Salt Lake City: University of Utah Press, 1993), 174–76.

18 Robert Cahn, Beverly Hills, California Letter to Maurine Whipple, 26 December 1956; BYU, photocopy Dixie College.

19 This detail is in Maurine Whipple, Letter drafts to Norman Cousins, the second dated 5 May 1957; BYU, photocopy Dixie College.

20 Alma A. Mcdonald, assistant Secretary to the Trustees of the Carnegie Fund of the Authors' Club, Letter to Maurine Whipple, March 5, 1958; BYU, photocopy Dixie College.

21 Maurine Whipple, Letter to John Crowe Ransom, 6 November 1957; BYU, photocopy Dixie College.

22 Maurine bought the house on 18 October 1958 from Caddie W. Artlip, assuming the unpaid balance of $1,700.

22

CHARLIE STEEN, 1962–66

Maurine had one more good chance—means, motive, and opportunity—to finish the sequel. It came when she made connections with uranium millionaire Charlie Steen in 1962—in retrospect, a poignant "if only" moment. At the time it seemed like the sunshine at the end of a decade of storms.

Charlie Steen was a geologist with the dream of finding a big uranium deposit on the Colorado Plateau. With the support of a loving wife and their children, he did just that, after much personal struggle and sacrifice. On 6 July 1952, after two years of tramping the desert, Steen hit pay dirt in the Big Indian Wash of Lisbon Valley southeast of Moab, Utah.[1] He had a brief fling as a millionaire before financial problems began in the mid-1960s.

Charlie was Maurine's kind of character; and in the early sixties, before he fell on hard times, she approached him for money to help her finish the sequel. Even at this late date, she still had hopes for the book on alcoholism. His contributions would be tax deductible, if they used the legal maneuvers she had already tried with the Las Vegas casino owners. Maurine also sent along her "ambassador," *The Giant Joshua*, with an exaggerated account of its publishing history. One of the letters tells about the paperback. ". . . just now out. Bancroft Library tells me that Dolphin Books (a subsidiary of Doubleday) emphasize American classics, and that the Dolphin imprint is a testament of permanent value. If this is true, the sequel will be worth the work and the money."[2] The paperback sold for $1.45.

Her approach was not just the good deed he could do by helping a struggling author who needed only a few hundred a month. Didn't it seem reasonable, she argued, that a little bit of that fabulous wealth coming from southern Utah should go to help the world get another good book telling the pioneer success story that would give focus and purpose to post-war America? Wouldn't he, who felt he had been unfairly treated by Mormons, be interested in helping such a cause?[3]

It just so happened that Maurine had found the right approach. Charlie Steen didn't understand the Mormons, couldn't penetrate their lofty citadels, and didn't like it when they made him feel all the ugly connotations of "gentile."[4] He got the idea that Maurine understood. She wrote to Charlie:

> I have perhaps a third of the second book written. (By-the-way, this book is titled "Candles of the Lord," which is the official botanical name of our desert oose [sic]—a plant that glorifies the most barren wastes spring after spring, thus shaming our human pessimism.) But to complete two such books with the necessary research, I would need two years of leisure. And I just haven't had it.
>
> I might add that my current project, a "Western" growing out of a magazine article, THE ARIZONA STRIP, has a TV bid; and if I can finish it, I can thereby make enough money to not only complete the Trilogy, but the treatise on alcoholism as well.[5]

Her description seems to have been mostly wishful thinking, but it does give the date by which she had stopped thinking of the title as "Cleave the Wood," though not her reasons for changing the title. Perhaps the parallelism with the botanical connotations of the Joshua tree appealed to her.

Charlie himself was too busy and involved in multi-million dollar businesses to give much time or thought to Maurine; but luckily, his wife, affectionately called "M. L.," liked the idea of championing a writer who was not appreciated by the Mormon Church. After she read *The Giant Joshua*, she was overwhelmed with awe and saw the sequel as a good cause. So Charlie committed to "loaning" Maurine money to live on while she wrote the sequel. He also bought a large shipment of the paperback edition and kept the inventory. Whenever Maurine needed another box, he sent them to her. Maurine peddled them herself to bookstores, hotels, and motels, and used her contacts at Las Vegas casinos, making a small profit on every book she sold. She said she would use the money to finish the sequel.[6]

She soon found other worthwhile projects she wanted Charlie to help with. Gene Pack, production manager of KUER Radio at the University of Utah, was part of a Salt Lake group of amateur dramatists called the Playmakers. She told Steen: "Gene has offered to work out a stage play of JOSHUA this winter that this group can put on next summer." She foresaw productions in Salt Lake City, St. George, and Park City and optimistically wrote: "I have reason to believe that the New York people will help us to an off-Broadway showing after we prove that the play is worth it. Then the movies will grab it, as they always do any play on a new subject (polygamy should delight them!) and the millennium is here!" Charlie would have none of it. He had agreed only to help her finish the sequel and the book on alcoholism.

But having her daily needs met brought a time of renewal for Maurine and other opportunities kept coming. Pack arranged for Maurine to be one of eight panelists interviewed by Dick Alsop and Pat Thorne for his program called "University Calling You" during the summer of 1963. They discussed subjects such as Utah history, Rainbow Bridge, Indian lore, and "The Pickle Is a Dilly," which someone read on the series "Chapter a Day," beginning 5 August 1963.[7]

In October 1962, Maurine took another trip with Art Greene to Rainbow Bridge, her third.[8] During knee surgery earlier that year, she had charmed her doctors with tales of Rainbow Bridge's wonders. After her recuperation, Dr. Edward F. Addenbrooke paid her expenses for the trip. She made the six-mile hike carrying her own backpack without difficulty. It is documented in an unfinished article and a wonderful photograph of the 1962 group taken by W. L. ("Bud") Rusho. Maurine's article reports that "it rained most the time and spoiled good picture taking,"[9] but recounts how she had found a Navajo, Hoke Denetsosie, and coaxed him to learn and then sing a sacred prayer under the bridge. But the drama she envisioned didn't come off, partly because of the rain, but partly because Hoke, raised by Christian missionaries, only whispered the prayer.

By 22 March 1963, Charlie was obviously putting some limits on his advances to Maurine. On that date, he sent $550 via Ellis Pickett, a St. George lawyer, who supposedly would see the money was used to help with the writing of the sequel.[10]

Steen's support during 1964 remained consistent but cautious and businesslike. Sam Weller of Salt Lake City had offered to retail *The Giant Joshua* "all over the country" through his own booksellers' network, and Charlie approved this proposal in principle on 8 April, pending his review of "Weller's proposal in this regard." Maurine's contact with legendary bookseller Sam Weller was an important one, since he kept *The Giant Joshua* in print, right up to the present. When it turned out that the ambitious plans for a stage version of *Joshua* would require "a loan of $8,000," Charlie made it clear that "he was not interested" and strongly suggested that Maurine "be protected with a contract before Gene Pack went into the dramatization."[11]

A newspaper interview in February 1964 gives detailed information about where Maurine thought she was with the trilogy:

Of the other two books of the trilogy, the second is half finished, and the third is outlined. "The Mormon Story," says Maurine, "offers perfect ground for a series of three books since, in the time stretch from ox to space ship, the Mormons have come full circle. They have given up known comforts for unknown terrors in order to see if human brotherhood could actually work as a way of life. That it did work is a matter of record."

Then the reporter repeated the same description Maurine had used in appealing to Charlie Steen: that the next book would be about the aging pioneer generation, the second generation "who resented the poverty, ostracism and brutishness" that characterized their childhoods, and the third generation, who "achieve material success, but still are left with . . . the paradox of the dream unresolved," feeling "forced to choose between conforming blindly or forsaking the dream altogether." Maurine firmly staked out her own idealistic ground: "I believe that the dream of brotherhood is possible," she told the reporter. "I don't attempt to answer the question of whether there can be a compromise or an alternative in the trilogy."[12]

The reporter asked Maurine what advice she would give an aspiring writer. Maurine replied, with considerable perception: "Writing is a hard job. To write, one must have a queer quirk about him—one must have empathy. One must be two people—one who endures and suffers and one who looks on and mentally says, 'Isn't this wonderful?'" She also told the reporter that she was "finishing a new book, which, although yet unnamed, would be published in the spring." It would be a nonfiction expansion of "America's Tibet."[13]

This second book, which effectively drained her time and attention away from the sequel, was "The Unpromised Land," a travel and description book about southern Utah for tourists that she worked on from 1963 to 1974 and thereafter as health permitted, right up to the end of her life.[14] She apparently planned to recycle some magazine articles as chapters in this book, including "Miracle of the Spillway" and "Peter's Leap," and three short stories: "They Did Go Forth," "A Grain of Mustard Seed," and "The Overcoat" (originally titled, "A Mormon Ghost Story").

Maurine and her recent literary agent, Walter R. Schmidt, had come to a parting of the ways, probably as soon as it became apparent that Maurine would not take his advice and finish the alcoholism book.[15]

M. L. Steen remained loyally supportive until the Steens' financial situation plummeted. In 1966, the loans came to an end. On 27 February 1968, Internal Revenue Service agents locked Charlie Steen's office and confiscated all of his physical assets that they could.[16] He declared bankruptcy.

But until then, Maurine could count on the monthly checks, with only occasional stern reminders that the money was a "loan" and rebukes that she wasn't making the promised progress on the sequel. There was, however, no open breach and apparently none of Maurine's long letters of accusation and complaint. Charlie suffered a head injury on the job in 1971 that hospitalized him, and Maurine visited him in Salt Lake City. M. L. wrote a note, thanking Maurine for her concern for the family.

During this visit, Maurine's home was robbed and vandalized, some of her papers and the sequel manuscript were taken, and the rest were cast about in confusion. If she had made any actual progress on the sequel—and that is far from clear—the robbery put an end to her efforts.

Health problems did not disappear from Maurine's life during this period under Charlie Steen's financial help, but they diminished. Her difficult menopause was finally over. Her sinus infections diminished. After many years of trying numerous painful and ineffectual treatments, such as sniffing saline solution to clear her nasal passages, she was diagnosed in July 1966 at age sixty-three as suffering from allergies that largely disappeared after a series of allergen shots. She was relatively free of sinus and bronchial infections for the rest of her life. When she talked about this breakthrough, it was always with a deep sigh and a comment such as: "Yes, finally, finding some help saved my sanity. But why did it have to come so late? How I did suffer!"

Whether allergies are psychosomatic is, according to one of the doctors who treated her, Dr. Donald A. Dolowitz, hard to say.[17] He hypothesized that, over a long period of continued stress, the body could develop too much histamine, triggering a genuine physical malady. It was his opinion that something like this had happened in Maurine's case. Regardless of the cause, he confirmed that she did suffer physically.

In 1963, she had follow-up therapy on the knee upon which she had had surgery, and it seemed to be successful. During the winter of 1962–63, she started to experience paralysis in her arm—her writing arm. One tentative diagnosis was polio; another was psychosomaticism. The paralysis gradually went away by itself.

For several months in 1966, Maurine was convinced that she was suffering from radiation poisoning due to the atomic bomb testing on the Nevada desert. Certainly she had been exposed, not only for having lived in St. George, now considered "downwind" from the clouds of radioactive dust, but because she also claimed to have been on site for "the last three above-ground tests."[18] However, she told me that she gave up thinking radioactive fallout was a danger because of her friendship with high-ranking

"SWELL SUFFERING"

government officials who were "very nice" to her and whose explanations were "very convincing."

Notes

1 Raye C. Ringholz, "Charles Augustus Steen," http//www.media.utah.edu /UHE/s/steen,charles.html (accessed September 2001).

2 Maurine Whipple, Letter to "Miss Westbrook," 24 March 1962; Maurine Whipple Collection, L. Tom Perry Special Collections, Harold B. Lee Library, Brigham Young University, Provo, Utah, with photocopy in Maurine Whipple Collection, Archive, Val A. Browning Library, Dixie College, St. George, Utah. Documents in both collections hereafter cited as BYU, photocopy Dixie College.

3 Ibid.

4 Charlie Steen, Letter to Maurine Whipple, 13 October 1962, Dixie College Archive; see also Raye C. Ringholz, *Uranium Frenzy: Boom and Bust on the Colorado Plateau* (Santa Fe: University of New Mexico, 1991), 20–36.

5 Maurine Whipple, Letter to Charlie Steen, 29 March 1962; 3 pp., pp. 1, 3 are in the Whipple Collection, BYU; photocopies made in the 1960s of pp. 2–3 are at Dixie College.

6 Charlie Steen, Letter to Maurine Whipple, 13 October 1962; BYU, photocopy Dixie College.

7 "KUER Plans a Variety of Programs for Listeners," *Utah Chronicle*, 26 July 1963, clipping in Whipple Collection, BYU.

8 Maurine had gone on her second Rainbow Bridge trip 25 June 1952, skimming upriver in Art Greene's boat, powered by an airplane motor. They made the round trip in an exhausting twelve-hour day, leaving from Navajo Bridge with Maurine jotting quick impressions in a nickel notebook measuring 2x4 inches. See "Rainbow Bridge," 25 June 1952, holograph notes, notebook; BYU, photocopy Dixie College. *Holiday* and probably several other magazines rejected "Rainbow Gold," an article based on Art Greene's colorful life.

9 Sorting the scattered pages of work dealing with Rainbow Bridge is difficult. What is available simply has "Rainbow Bridge" as perhaps a working title. The various versions are at BYU. On this trip, Maurine and Bud Rusho interviewed Frank Johnson, the proprietor of Lee's Ferry. Transcript at BYU.

10 Charlie Steen, Letter to Maurine Whipple, 20 March 1964; Dixie College Archive.

11 Charlie Steen, Letter to Maurine Whipple, 8 April 1964, Dixie College Archive.

12 Gloria Reible, "Mormon Author Pens about Nevada History," *Las Vegas Sun*, (no day) February 1964, clipping; BYU, photocopy Dixie College.

13 Ibid.

14 This manuscript exists in seven forms: (1) thirty-nine pages of holograph notes; (2) a nine-page typescript outline used in a successful grant application to the Utah Bicentennial Commission for $1,500; (3) a thirty-two-page typescript with centered page numbers, (4) a twenty-two-page typescript titled "The Unpromised Land," 1963, with a second title beneath that, in parentheses, "(Tuenben Noonie Country)," which Maurine crossed out; (5) a nine-page typescript titled "The Unpromised land" and, in parentheses beneath it "('The Substance of Things Hoped for . . . ')" (6) a two-page summary titled "Unpromised Land"; and (7) "Greyhound Tours," a twenty-page prospectus for tours in and around St. George; all at BYU, photocopy Dixie College.

15 Martha Vincent, Letter to Maurine Whipple, (no date) January 1965; BYU, photocopy Dixie College. Martha's surname is on her second letter, written 11 February 1967.

16 Ringholz, *Uranium Frenzy*, 267.

17 Dr. Donald A. Dolowitz, interviewed 11 January 1992, in LaVerkin, Utah, where he had retired. He added that Maurine had visited him there several times and seemed to like him, but "she hadn't been very nice to my wife, so the relationship didn't continue." Dolowitz was in partnership with Dr. Mercer Anderson in Salt Lake City, who also treated Maurine.

18 Maurine Whipple, Letter to Maiben R. Ashby, Justice of the Peace, St. George, 18 December 1965, photocopy of carbon copy; BYU, photocopy Dixie College.

23

EASTER PAGEANT, 1963-75

One of the projects Maurine did while living on Charlie Steen's loans was an Easter pageant. Possibly she couldn't let go of the resentment that she hadn't been allowed to play the role she wanted in Grant Redford's 1937 Easter pageant. (See Chapter 5.) She called it "The Candles of the Lord," the title she had told Steen would be the second volume of *Joshua*. She envisioned it being performed in a natural amphitheater in nearby Snow Canyon.[1]

She must have been working on it during the early 1960s or even during the late 1950s as she struggled to keep the alcoholism project alive, because she had a finished manuscript dated 23 February 1963 and typed in a cursive font that she gave to St. George attorney Ellis Pickett to hold as proof of authorship.[2] Maurine often told me it was "the best thing I ever did." Certainly she wanted it to be.

She talked about how she "poured over books about Christ and all the figures involved in his life." She felt herself "caught up in the drama, especially from Mary Magdalene's perspective." Her mood while writing it, she said, "was much as she had experienced when writing about the St. George pioneers." In the first version, she used the account in the Book of Mormon of Christ's appearance to the people of the Americas and planned to use Indians representing various tribes for this scene. She also prominently featured Mary Magdalene's encounter with the resurrected Jesus at the tomb. One tender scene in the pageant was her "Lament of Mary Magdalene."[3] It is a moving lyric of a woman's need for love, transferred to love for Christ.

She put forth a good effort and produced what could have been an impressive production. Lynn Clark, a photographer in St. George, said she remembered that a touching moment at a presentation that Maurine made for the city council "was the singing of the Lord's Prayer while an Indian girl signed."[4] Lynn and many others who knew of Maurine's vision thought it would be a wonderful production. But getting it produced was a difficult and explosive problem. She told Pickett in early 1963 that she was trying to get the Desert Inn in Las Vegas to sponsor the production.[5] The Desert Inn wasn't interested, but St. George's Chamber of Commerce and city government were intrigued, and planning actually began under their joint sponsorship. Then, the *Washington County News* carried a notice on 14 March 1963 that the pageant had been canceled "because of a combination of circumstances beyond the control of the executive committee," even though "volunteer workers from all parts of Washington County had been working on assignments." The announcement continued:

> Superintendent Maurice Nuttall [was the] . . . executive director who activated organization and administrative personnel. Committee assignments, musical and script rehearsals, casting, directing and costuming and designing were under way.
> Dr. Wm. Purdy and Roene DiFiore were to direct the choral and musical scores, Barbara Watson assistant director in charge of casting, and Mrs. Betty Knight in charge of costume and designing.
> The executive committee regrets that circumstances had developed which in their opinion is sufficient to cancel any further preparation for the production this year. They expressed thanks for the enthusiastic support they had received.[6]

The pageant (or its cancellation) caused a falling out between Maurine and her friend Katharine Miles Larson that was particularly painful. There was some concern that the interpretation of Christ and Mary Magdalene was "anti-Mormon." Maurine had asked Katharine to act as a "censor" but didn't like the results. Mary Phoenix told me, "Maurine was enthused and seemed to have a vision that she just couldn't get the rest of us to see. I think the places where her version of Jesus and Mary Magdalene might have offended people could have been worked out, if she had let someone help. But she took offense too quickly. However, I don't think Eric [Snow] was quite fair. He seemed impatient with everything she tried to do or say. Sure, Maurine could be exasperating and stubborn! But I think some minds were set about her; and no matter what, she couldn't change them."

Two ways in which Maurine exasperated local people, according to Edna Greggerson, who also could have been on her side, is that "Maurine was usually late and never seemed quite ready to give her presentation," and second, she "hounded people to help George—couldn't someone find a job for him? Things like that."[7]

EASTER PAGEANT, 1965–75

Maurine evidently let the pageant languish between 1967 and 1973. Then, as the nation began preparing for its bicentennial in 1976, the federal government appropriated $40,000 for Utah, with the state government providing other funds for local celebrations. Maurine immediately saw "Candles of the Lord" as playing a significant role in St. George's celebration and apparently applied to the State Division of Fine Arts in late 1972. The first surviving correspondence is a letter from its director, Ruth Draper, in February 1973, transferring $400 to Maurine "to assist with the completion of the script." The local funds were disbursed through C. Paul Andersen, president of the Southwestern Utah Arts Council and president of Dixie College.

Maurine, at the five-county committee's invitation, made a presentation about the pageant in August 1974. Even though she exceeded her time limit, the committee accepted it.[8] She also wanted to piggy-back her tourist book, "Unpromised Land," on the bicentennial pageant.

In addition to the $400 for the pageant script, the Utah State Institute of Fine Arts allocated an additional $2,500, apparently for the production. Maurine tried to get this amount increased, but the committee refused, suggesting instead that she get local sponsorship, as Fred Adams had done with his very successful Shakespearean Festival in Cedar City, and also suggesting that she start out "more modestly."[9]

Maurine desperately wanted the pageant to be staged in Snow Canyon's spectacular red-rock natural setting. But there was concern about the acoustics. Dr. Harvey Fletcher, a specialist from BYU, agreed that a "fairly powerful and well planned sound system would be necessary." The best solution was probably to tape the whole production, similar to the Hill Cumorah pageant at Palmyra, New York.[10] When funding dried up, no doubt the costliness of this solution became a heavily negative factor.

Maurine fussed over details and lost more time when she had hip surgery. The weeks dribbled by. The local Arts Council grew restive. Probably in late January or early February 1975, Maurine made another presentation. It went badly, and the committee unanimously recommended canceling the pageant.[11]

Apparently, this turn-down got through to Maurine. She finally took some of the criticisms seriously, worked on revisions, and finished the pageant to her own satisfaction and, she thought, to that of others. She copyrighted the results in August 1975.[12] The only evidence of what happened between February and August is another note from C. Paul Andersen saying that he hadn't been able to reach her by telephone but informing her that she was to work with Robert Shepherd, a local artist, and report progress to the pageant committee the following week. He suggested that Shepherd could attend the meeting instead of Maurine if she were ill. He spelled out the importance of the schedule, tactfully but clearly: "This way we will be informed of any progress which has been made and will be in a position to make recommendations to the Utah Institute of Fine Arts as to disposition of the remaining funds allocated for production of the Pageant. Also, the Board will be in a position to know whether to recommend seeking further funds for the Pageant."[13]

Robert Shepherd was apparently an excellent choice, since he had the knack of working with Maurine. Maurine met enough of the deadline placed upon her that she was sent "$1,700, the amount remaining in the original grant to . . . finalize the script which has so much potential and the Board of the Division of Fine Arts heartily agreed."[14]

Maurine apparently continued working on the script that fall and winter. In early December 1975, she received a letter from Inez S. Cooper, who had reviewed the script with John Lawrence Seymour, who had written the music: "We think you really have the basis for something outstanding."[15]

A clipping from the *St. George Spectrum* in January 1976 also reported that the pageant plans were progressing. Maurine was quoted as saying she "had been working on the pageant for ten years," that "now the Utah Fine Arts Committee would match funds raised locally," and that "several towns and individuals had promised to help meet the expenses." An accompanying photograph showed Maurine with a painted backdrop showing the proposed hilltop site with Christ on the cross.[16]

But it never happened. The reasons are not clear. Perhaps Maurine, for all of her enthusiasm and dreams was simply too old at seventy-three to organize such a huge undertaking, yet she would not step aside for those who had the skills and ability to make it happen. Certainly, her history of disagreements with influential people in St. George would make old combatants reluctant to help her and others hesitant to get involved. Local writer LaVarr G. Webb, who was familiar with the situation, remembered that "the site was also unsuitable." Getting it prepared would have cost an estimated $100,000.[17] This price tag would have been decisive if most of the money had to be raised locally.

After Maurine's death, Carol Jensen donated a copy of "The Candles of the Lord" and permission to use it, to Tuahcan, an outdoor theater at the south end of Snow Canyon, which now owns the rights to the pageant.

The pageant was not the only casualty of Maurine's sesquicentennial hopes. Since 1962, she had been talking grandly about her "Unpromised Land" manuscript, which she had pitched to Charlie Steen as a nonfiction travel, description, and history about the Arizona Strip. When Utah's sesquicentennial plans began to take shape, Maurine saw her book as a natural candidate for southern Utah's celebration of its distinctiveness, and the Fine

Arts Council agreed with her. It could be enlarged to include many interesting places in the area.

In October 1974, Teddy Griffith, director of Special Projects for Utah's American Revolution Bicentennial Commission, announced good news for Maurine. The commission agreed to sponsor "The Unpromised Land" as an official bicentennial project, funded by the St. George bicentennial committee with royalties split 50–50 between it and Maurine.[18] But seven months later, the project was in trouble. In May 1975, Mrs. Griffith sent Maurine a tactful note: "Evidently there is strong concern in Washington County about the progress of 'Unpromised Land.' So much so, in fact, that they want to have a visible 'preview' of the book within one month or they may consider allocating funds elsewhere."[19]

Maurine's papers contain no positive proof that she took this good hint and brought any part of the manuscript to a satisfactory state. However, a completed manuscript titled "The Spillway" may have been part of her attempt to do as she suggested. Her papers also include a rough draft, likely meant for "Unpromised Land," about Dave Flannigan, who lived on Cable Mountain in Zion Canyon. Trying to get home during a snowstorm, he slipped to the verge of a cliff. To save his life, he cut his hands. The blood, freezing on the ice, gave him enough traction to inch his way to safety, possibly on the same principle that makes a tongue stick to a frosty piece of metal.

What exactly happened to derail Maurine's plans for this book is not clear. After her home was vandalized in 1971, she probably had a hard time pulling her work together, perhaps having lost too much of it to reconstruct successfully. In any case, she missed the deadline, and the funding was pulled.

Two years after the bicentennial, however, Maurine gave another of her glowingly enthusiastic interviews that made it sound as if the book was on the verge of coming out: "She says there'll be no rest—no rest until she has captured the hardy pioneer spirit and the essence of the pink afterglow on the red sandstone cliffs after the sun has descended; no rest until these things—and the folklore of Cable Mountain, Peter's Leap, Snow Canyon, Silver Reef, and other historical spots are safely recorded in print, complemented by plenty of color photographs."[20]

As the Easter pageant and Maurine's miracle stories in "The Unpromised Land" show, Maurine felt she had an important religious perspective and wanted to share it. Her papers not infrequently contain explicit, though unconventional, expressions of spirituality. New Age material was becoming popular in the 1970s, and obviously Maurine felt an affinity for some of it. Unfortunately, she let herself become diverted from the significant writing project to which she had made commitments and which could have restored her sagging credibility and wavering self-confidence. She espe-

"SWELL SUFFERING"

cially was attracted to the work of Harold Sherman, a nationally known psychic researcher, author, lecturer, and workshop organizer. She attended one of his workshops June 15–17, 1974, in Dallas, which she very much enjoyed. She wanted to become involved in working with him on publicizing his work, but she had no travel funds and nothing came of this enthusiasm.[21]

Notes

[1] "Candles of the Lord" is an Easter pageant that Maurine reworked between at least 1963 and 1976. At least five versions exist, all with same title, and all in Maurine Whipple Collection, L. Tom Perry Special Collections, Harold B. Lee Library, Brigham Young University, Provo, Utah, with photocopy in Maurine Whipple Collection, Archive, Val A. Browning Library, Dixie College, St. George, Utah. For documents in both collections hereafter, cited as BYU, photocopy Dixie College: (1) numerous loose sheets of holograph notes and manuscript; (2) a thirty-three-page typescript (cursive font) in which only the narrator has a speaking part; (3) thirty-four-page typescript, 1973, with handwritten page numbers (4) forty-four-page typescript, copyright 1976, edited for a nondenominational audience. Its opening and closing scenes feature Native Americans. Maurine had explained to Steen that the title came from the local name for the oose, but it is also a scriptural reference: "The spirit of man is as the candle of the Lord" (Proverbs 20:27).

[2] Maurine Whipple, Letter to Ellis Picket, 23 February 1963; BYU, photocopy Dixie College.

[3] Robert A. Wilkinson, 230 East Shore Drive, Massapequa, New York, Letter to Maurine Whipple, 23 March 1967; BYU, photocopy Dixie College.

[4] Lynn Clark, Interviewed by Veda Hale, 18 September 1992, St. George, Utah.

[5] Eugene Murphy, on letterhead of Wilber Clark's Desert Inn, Las Vegas, Letter to Maurine Whipple, 15 March 1963; BYU, photocopy Dixie College.

[6] "Pageant Cancelled," *Washington County News*, 23 March 1963; unpaginated clipping in Dixie College Archive.

[7] Edna Jenson Greggerson, Interviewed by Veda Hale, 1991. Edna was an English teacher at Dixie College.

[8] Ibid.

[9] Keith M. Engar, Chairman, Utah State Institute of Fine Arts Board of Directors, Letter to Maurine Whipple, 7 December 1974; BYU, photocopy Dixie College.

EASTER PAGEANT, 1963–75

10 Carl I. Nelson, Letter to Mrs. Elizabeth M. Griffith, 8 October 1974; BYU, photocopy Dixie College.

11 C. Paul Andersen, President of Southwestern Utah Arts Council and of Dixie College, Letter to Maurine Whipple, 17 February 1975; BYU, photocopy Dixie College. He sent copies to the other council members: Gerald Olson, Ronald Garner, Guy Hafen, Willard Farr, and Robert Owens.

12 Copyright papers, August 1967, [no agency indicated]; BYU, photocopy Dixie College.

13 Paul Andersen, Letter to Maurine Whipple, 16 May 1975; BYU, photocopy Dixie College. Curiously, in early June, a note from historian Charles S. Peterson at Utah State University mentions that he had heard that her pageant had been completed and hoped "BYU moves ahead quickly with it." Peterson, Letter to Whipple, 5 June 1975; Whipple Collection, BYU. Had Maurine been casting around for another sponsor?

14 Ruth R. Draper, Director, Utah State Division of Fine Arts, Letter to Maurine Whipple, 27 August 1975, and Ruth R. Draper, Letter to Paul Andersen, Dixie College, 6 August 1975; BYU, photocopy Dixie College.

15 Her papers include no evidence that would allow the dating of this event, nor any evidence of further association.

16 (No byline or headline), *St. George Spectrum*, 8 January 1976, unpaginated clipping; BYU, photocopy Dixie College.

17 LaVarr B. Webb, Interviewed 19 March 1992, St. George, Utah. LaVarr Webb had been an investigative reporter for Jack Anderson in Washington, D.C.

18 Mrs. Elizabeth ("Teddy") Griffith, Letter to Maurine Whipple, 8 October 1974; BYU, photocopy Dixie College.

19 Mrs. K. E. ("Teddy") Griffith, Director of Special Projects, Utah American Revolution Bicentennial Commission, Salt Lake City, Letter to Maurine Whipple, 8 May 1975; BYU, photocopy Dixie College.

20 LaVarr G. Webb, "Author of the Giant Joshua in Search of Her Second Novel," *St. George Spectrum*, (no date) February 1978, unpaginated clipping, Whipple Collection, Dixie College. An accompanying photograph shows Maurine standing by a Joshua tree. Webb gave Maurine the original photographs, which are filed with the clipping. He also wrote a shorter version of the same article that appeared in the *Nevadan*, Sunday, 6 March 1977; clipping at Dixie College Archive.

21 Harold Sherman, Letter to Maurine Whipple, (no day) December 1978; Whipple Collection, BYU.

❧ 24 ❧

MAURINE VERSUS ST. GEORGE, 1965-75

A genuine low point in Maurine's life was the sorry record of dissension and mistrust between Maurine and the community of St. George for a decade, beginning in the mid-1960s. Compounding the difficult events associated with the pageant (see Chapter 23), the 1960s and 1970s were poisoned by other controversies and problems with her neighbors. In many ways, Maurine genuinely didn't fit.

An undated letter from Maurine's friend Don Seegmiller, shared his gentle but unvarnished appraisal of St. George people, and Maurine wrote, "I agree" by this paragraph: "What I can think of right now to say about St. George is that it's a desert to the soul and that all the people there are Suaro Cacti. They are made glad there two years out of twenty by a little rainfall and the rest of the time they wrinkle their skins and pull away from each other to conserve their limited spiritual and material resources. The people are not bad. They are pinched; hemmed in by circumstance."[1]

An example of the problems Maurine let get out of hand is a minor automobile accident that led to her belief that the entire power structure of the town was against her. According to Maurine's version, in October 1965 she was pulling onto a busy street at the dangerous intersection of Bluff and Diagonal, still two of St. George's biggest streets; and Edna Rogers, who was driving home from Las Vegas after taking her dog to the vet, hit her. Maurine claimed that Edna, who had a heart condition and should not have been driving anyway, panicked when she saw Maurine's car, grabbed the dog, and fainted, and that her son in the back seat took the wheel. The unsympathetic investigating officers cited Maurine for failure to yield, and matters intensified from there. Maurine alleged that she had been treated roughly, refused to pay the fine, appealed, wrote to influential people, and generally raised hell. On 19 May 1966, she received a two-line letter from the city attorney, John W. Palmer, informing her that he was asking the court to dismiss her case. Apparently she had outlasted the opposition, but she would not let it go. By this time, she was also infuriated by what she considered the city's attempt to cheat her out of part of her intellectual property rights in *The Giant Joshua*.

As Maurine told it, Gene Pack came to St. George in the late spring of early 1965 and spent three months with her, arranging *The Giant Joshua* into thirty-five half-hour dramatized segments. He read this dramatized version over KUER radio five nights a week during August and September. Ellen Winkelmann, the station owner, wanted to tape the reading—which both Gene and Maurine also wanted—and "let" them use the station's equipment for a $75 service fee that Maurine got an unknown friend to pay. But then Mrs. Winkelmann claimed possession of the tapes and sold them to a third party. Maurine fought back for almost two years.[2] The purchaser wanted at least $200 from Maurine, money she didn't have, nor did she agree that Mrs. Winkelmann had the right to sell her work.[3] Maurine rightly felt that the tapes were valuable and were her property. She had been hurt when the city council had refused to accept them as her gift to the city and couldn't understand, if the city refused them, why it didn't give them back to her. Instead it gave them to Mrs. Winkelmann at the local radio station.

Maurine retained Phillip A. Mallinckrodt, a Salt Lake City lawyer specializing in U.S. and foreign patents, trademarks, and copyrights. Maurine had made some derogatory remarks about Mrs. Winkelmann and Winkelmann was in no mood to accommodate Maurine or even save the tapes.[4] Maurine then tried another attorney. She laid out both the accident and the situation involving the tapes in great detail in a lengthy letter on 11 July 1967 to Salt Lake attorney Adam ("Mickey") Duncan.[5] At that point, she was convinced that the treatment she had received after the car accident was only the tip of an iceberg of civic corruption, in which the elites stuck together, making it impossible for ordinary people like herself to get justice. The only way to improve things, she wrote excitedly to Duncan, was "by a public exposure," that "a guilty verdict had made a great change in one man already, that he was so stricken with remorse and desire to make amends it had landed him in the hospital." She claimed that other people helping her were convinced that, if lawyers could follow up the affidavits she had collected with a visit and talk with the mayor, the results would be "explosive." She was anxious to put "the fear of God into the stinkers." She wooed the involvement of Duncan and other attorneys from his firm with promises of guided tours to "the *Joshua* sites, Mountain Meadow Massacre, [and the] pines and brooks and columbines of Pine Valley."

MAURINE VERSUS ST. GEORGE, 1965–75

Later, Maurine claimed that Mrs. Winkelmann burned the tapes. Heartsick, she wrote to Congressman Lawrence J. Burton, asking for the FCC to investigate. He responded sympathetically: "There appears to be nothing that the FCC can do.... I wish there were because I feel outraged that your tapes which were so valuable, should have been destroyed in a pointless act of malice."[6]

Maurine fussed and tried to recruit others to rescue her and also to attack what she saw as other wrongs in the community. Though idealistic, some of her perceptions may have been ill-informed and idiosyncratic. But in any case, her fuming only sapped her energy and kept her from writing anything besides protest letters.[7] One of the people Maurine wrote to was Samuel W. Taylor, a successful Mormon journalist, writer, and historian living in Redwood City, California. She tried to persuade him to write an exposé-type article for *Look* about the prejudice and harassment experienced by intellectuals living in small towns. She thought the article would be stronger if someone else told her side, and Sam agreed to look over her material. "Regarding small Mormon towns, I do know that background, and it is a separate world where you're either in or you're out, and if you're out there's simply no place farther out."[8]

Maurine's files contain no more correspondence with Sam. No doubt Maurine shaded her telling of these events, and no doubt those on the other side would have had their own perspective. Her combative stance and her assumption of deliberate malice and open corruption would not have won her any friends among the people she was treating as opponents. Furthermore, her persistence, while courageous, was also exasperating.

Maurine's quest for justice consumed a great deal of time. But on the brighter side, she went to California in 1966 to discuss a movie option for *The Giant Joshua*, staying with her schoolteacher friend Betty McPherson. When I interviewed Betty, she recalled two pieces of evidence indicating that Maurine was under intense strain. First, she walked in her sleep, something Maurine claimed she had never done before. Second, she asked Betty to accompany her to the visit with the movie representative. The dismayed Betty "could tell almost from the first that Maurine was talking too much" and that "the representative was not impressed."[9]

Camie Higgins, a friendly young woman in St. George who willingly typed for Maurine without charge, remembers some of the criticism during this period. "I always knew Maurine was decent and misunderstood and I tried to set the record straight when I could. But I was young and didn't pay very much attention." She added, "St. George people are basically good people. I'll bet they just didn't know how much Maurine needed help. She was too proud."[10]

In any case, by the end of 1966, the tapes were gone for good. Many people in St. George were angry with her. Maurine was ill, exhausted, and broke. She turned sixty-four that year and thought seriously of moving out of town. The change might have been good, but no friendly refuge offered itself.[11] And still she seemed unable to let go of her vendetta with city hall, which went on for eight or nine more years. Between 1973 and 1975, she tried to interest a number of people besides Sam Taylor in underwriting an autobiographical exposé of the tape incident and the car accident that would also include other incidents of small-town corruption.[12] Several copies of her twenty-three-page letter exist and, valuably, it summarizes from her seventy-year-old perspective a picture of her life for the last few years and what she wanted people to understand about her. Unfortunately, her tone, probably intended to be witty and light, often turns bitter and derogatory, which almost certainly sent up warning flags to the very people she was trying to interest in her plight. Still, the letter presents compelling evidence, not only of episodes that drained Maurine's creative energies, but also of how her typical approach drew upon herself misunderstandings and antagonism.[13]

In 1971 Maurine was assessed $505.48 for curb and gutter improvements with a second assessment of $555.44, and also city taxes of $77.51. She never paid any of these amounts; and according to the city attorney, Ellis Pickett Jr., the son of the attorney she hired in the early 1960s, city officials knew that efforts to collect would be useless and just "let it go."[14] For somebody who felt that the city had continuously mistreated her, it was a minor victory.

MAURINE VERSUS ST. GEORGE, 1965-75

Notes

[1] Don Seegmiller, Letter to Maurine Whipple, n.d. Maurine Whipple Collection, L. Tom Perry Special Collections, Harold B. Lee Library, Brigham Young University, Provo, Utah, with photocopy in Maurine Whipple Collection, Archive, Val A. Browning Library, Dixie College, St. George, Utah. Documents in both collections hereafter cited as BYU, photocopy Dixie College.

[2] Ernest May and H. J. Sanders, "To Whom It May Concern," notarized affidavit, 26 May 1965; BYU, photocopy Dixie College.

[3] W. D. Whipple, "To Whom It May Concern," 22 May 1965; BYU, photocopy Dixie College.

[4] Phillip A. Mallinckrodt, Letter to Maurine Whipple, 13 July 1965; Whipple Collection, BYU Library.

[5] Adam ("Mickey") Duncan, Suite 926 Kennecott Building, Salt Lake City, UT 84111, 9 December 1969; BYU, photocopy Dixie College.

[6] Lawrence J. Burton, Letter to Maurine Whipple, 30 October 1967; BYU, photocopy Dixie College.

[7] Ibid. On 20 September 1967, Maurine filed a "request for record search" to see if Verlene Brinkerhoff Rogers had a valid driver's license at the time of the accident. On the request, she has written, "No license." BYU, photocopy Dixie College.

[8] Samuel W. Taylor, Redwood City, California, Letter to Maurine Whipple, 24 September 1966; BYU, photocopy Dixie College.

[9] Betty Ann McPherson, interviewed September 1993.

[10] Camie Higgins, interviewed 29 October 1992.

[11] Toria (surname not given), Letter to Maurine Whipple, 27 November 1967; BYU, photocopy Dixie College.

[12] One of the people Maurine tried to recruit was Jaren L. Jones, who had retired and was helping to establish the nearby Bloomington as a golf and condominium community. How Maurine met him is not clear; but after writing the letter for him in 1973, she copied it and sent it to other individuals Joseph Rosenblatt, Leonard J. Arrington, Jack Harden, and Howard Folger. Maurine Whipple, Letter to Howard Folger, 15 February 1975, Dixie College Archive. A version of the 1973 letter to Jaren L. Jones is also at Special Collections, College of Southern Utah Library, Cedar City.

[13] Maurine Whipple to Judge Newell Frei, Justice of the Peace, St. George, 9 May 1975; BYU, photocopy Dixie College.

[14] Assessment notices dated (no day) July 1971; BYU; Ellis Pickett Jr., interviewed 1992.

❦ 25 ❦

THE 1970S: FLICKERINGS OF POTENTIAL FLAMES

In the late 1960s and '70s some of Maurine's friends and family were dying, forcing the fact of Maurine's own aging and mortality upon her. In 1967, she wrote a loving and nostalgic letter to Elden Beck, concerned because he "had looked so sick" the last time she had seen him: "Spring in Dixie always reminded me of you: remember the colors? How the hill above Ivins is mauve, while the sand by the highway is orange? . . . So few people have an affinity for all that grows and breathes, as you do. It is a precious gift, and one I'll thank you for giving me all the rest of my life."

She ended by telling him her own feelings about death: "I've had no fear of death at all. I learned then, when I saw him, to laugh at what men call death. . . . So why go back? Instead, why not go *forward?* Tomorrow is a new day; who knows what rapture it will bring? I guess I must have been born with an abiding curiosity, because I just can't wait, even now, to see what happens next!"[1]

Another friend who had been kind and helpful also died during this period: Whit Parry whose lodge in Kanab offered her a refuge, apparently free, at times. She told me that she helped with the work around the place and was Whit's confidante in conflicts with his wife. When he died of cancer, she penned a tribute to him that she sent to the *Salt Lake Tribune*. Her cover letter, which focuses more on herself and which sounds self-serving, may have been the reason the *Tribune* "didn't have a place where it was appropriate." In the tribute, she wrote: "It can truly be said that he didn't deserve what life did to him. But maybe—maybe if he *won*, (I mean, won his integrity out of the battle), life wasn't so hard on him, after all."[2]

In her own family, George had given up any effort to deal with his alcoholism and was sliding slowly into the gutter. There were many times when Maurine hauled him out of a filthy situation, cleaned him up, and probably lectured him so much he drifted off again.

During the 1960s, Charlie was also unwell. In a Mormon version of deathbed repentance, he arranged to have himself rebaptized, canceling out his 1928 excommunication for adultery. (See Chapter 17.) Maurine wrote an eloquent and passionate letter in his defense but also told me, skeptically, that Charlie had not experienced a real change of heart. He was doing it "just in case." Some people in St. George were upset that Maurine wouldn't take full responsibility for his care. According to Mary Phoenix, Maurine replied that this job belonged to Flo Foremaster and Mishie Seegmiller, both of whom had relationships with Charlie that were ambiguous but close.[3] His death came 22 September 1969. He had not left a large estate; but as Alice told me, he asked that Maurine get most of it because "she needed it the most." It was a final generous act on his part for this difficult daughter. Even so, this gesture was marred by Maurine's conviction, apparently groundless, that he had left $4,000 in a joint tenancy bank account in California. Again, she tried to enlist an attorney in solving her problem. There is no evidence of this bank account.[4] Maurine used her inheritance to pay off a loan that Reed Whipple had arranged for her in 1966. Reed's letter acknowledging the payment has a paragraph indicating that the ever-hopeful Maurine had asked him about possible contacts to the eccentric multi-millionaire Howard Hughes, obviously spinning dreams of Hughes as the next rich man who would help her finish some of her writing projects. Reed wrote that he "didn't think it was a good idea" and gave her no leads.[5]

In 1970 Maurine turned sixty-seven. Because she was on welfare, she was annoyed that she had to account for how she used her inheritance—which had been to pay off debts. Confused, she thought the inheritance was why the welfare payments stopped. In fact, she had ignored requests from the Division of Family Services in Washington County about her financial situation, and they had closed the case for lack of response.[6] More time and more letters until she got it straightened out. She had her home and was receiving $90 a month in welfare assistance (raised to $106 in 1972).[7] Thanks to Charlie's legacy, she was briefly out of debt.[8] Because of her health problems, the county's Family Services had found Maurine eligible for assistance with housecleaning during the late 1960s and early 1970s. Pat Learny was the cleaner the county sent in; but when Maurine discovered that Pat could type, housecleaning went by the board. It was Pat who had typed the pageant, or at least some of the versions.[9]

THE 1970S: FLICKERINGS OF POTENTIAL FLAMES

Maurine's feud with the community of St. George had more or less run out of steam; and although her dwindling physical powers meant that the disorder in her life frequently overwhelmed her, she still had flickers of the old brilliance and passion.

In an incomplete letter written in the spring of 1971, she bubbled over with possible projects: being a guide for nearby Bloomington's summer tours; writing "a history of the roads of the region" if the State Road Commission would give her a grant, offering some of her articles to a "new regional magazine, ENCHANTED WILDERNESS,"[10] and writing "some stories on Utah's Dixie."[11] Although she was not mechanically minded, she took a photography class at the college, trying to master the intricacies of the camera. With her "jinx" at work, she loaned her camera to one of the boys in the class, he broke it, and Maurine had to try and get his father to pay the $100 either to fix it or buy a new one.[12] She had wide interests, was almost childlike in her enthusiasm, and met some interesting people. An interview later published in *Dialogue: A Journal of Mormon Thought* gave her an opportunity to simultaneously complain (she should never have stayed in St. George but she couldn't believe that "it could have been as bad as it has been") and glowingly articulate once more about the Mormon ideal. She also unwaveringly affirmed that there were two books to come to complete *The Giant Joshua*.[13]

In retrospect, the sequel was chaining her to the past. She remained stuck between old projects that she couldn't finish and new potential flames that blazed briefly, then flickered out.

As time went on, she added new projects to the list of potential ones: her autobiography-exposé was one; but in her letter to Salt Lake businessman Joseph Rosenblatt,[14] she mentioned three more and tried to persuade him to "loan" her $3,000, also presenting the possibility of making it a tax-deductible contribution through a charitable foundation. For this amount, she dangled the lure of "Unpromised Land" and the last two volumes of the *Joshua* trilogy. With unwonted cynicism, she described the rest of the trilogy as describing how "the Mormon experiment" had "become a money-making financial business, and that's about all," but possibly phrased her description this way thinking that the controversy would appeal to Rosenblatt: "I know that it is a writer's job to picture the truth of his times, shorn of the sophistry so loved by those who never invite their own souls."[15] Rosenblatt was not interested in anything but a peaceful retirement and declined to become involved.[16]

There is some evidence that Maurine wanted to become the *Salt Lake Tribune* correspondent when Vira Henrie Judge Blake retired. The pay was not great—fifty cents a column inch and $5 per photograph—but Vira

Blake often sent a version of the same story to other publications and thought that almost anyone could have made a reasonable supplementary income. Vi was well liked and sincerely interested in other people's accomplishments.[17] When I mentioned that Maurine aspired to her job, it was news to her; and although she was kind, she did not feel that Maurine would have been successful at the job. She recalled: "I went on one story with Maurine—one I'd been assigned by the *Salt Lake Tribune* to cover on the Virgin River Gorge highway construction project. Maurine had gotten the *Arizona Highways* person assigned to take me to the work site to let her come along. She acted as if she were a very important person writing an article for a national magazine, and that whatever I was writing was not very important. I did get a nice spread in the *Tribune* with several pictures. I don't know if Maurine got her article published somewhere nationally or not."[18] There is no evidence that she did. Apparently Maurine was still trying to fill the role of a nationally acclaimed writer who didn't need local jobs. Her papers include at least a few letters to and from *Tribune* editor, Ernie Hoff, but he gave her no encouragement.[19]

    Maurine wrote an article for the *Salt Lake Tribune* on what was called the "Rassy B Corner" (Erastus B. Snow) east of the Tabernacle when the structure was scheduled for demolition. The current owner, Eric Snow, with whom Maurine had been feuding over her pageant, wrote a letter of his own to the *Tribune* claiming that Maurine "has a tendency to write information which isn't correct. She gets carried away to try and make it interesting, when the truth would be much better. Please don't print this material until it has been approved by us."[20] Maurine told me that she had "read every word of it" to Althea Snow Nelsen, Eric's older sister. "She just loved it. After all I made a sort of hero out of her father!" But the *Tribune* chose not to print the article. She condensed it and tried again, writing in her cover letter, "Gosh, Ernie, I hope this gets me more than 25 bucks. I've put in a whole month on the piece, full time. I had to revise it four times to suit Althea! If I could get 50 bucks for each piece, I'd write you a full treatment of Peter's Leap and the Narrows, plus photos."[21] Ernie still didn't accept the article or any of her suggestions.

    Maurine continued her search for money. One of the sources she approached was the Information Service of American Heritage Publishing Company. When she received a courteous turn-down, explaining that the magazine did not give grants, she persisted with a second, cozy, name-dropping letter, leaning on her one success: "I *am* a good writer... and I can even prove this statement, if somebody there takes time to read a book."[22]

    As another funding source, Maurine applied for a grant from the National Park Service. She tried to enlist the services of Utah's Senator Frank E. Moss. The answer from the Park Service was "no" but they suggested she contact the National Endowment for the Humanities.[23] A "no" there, too. Did Utah's Department of Community Affairs have grants? No, but "under the new rural development loan funds would be made available for individual enterprise from the Farmers Home Administration." "Unpromised Land" might qualify.[24] No help here. Could Everett L. Cooley, curator at the Marriott Library for Western Americana, get her a grant? No, he had no grant money.[25] Neither did the Charles L. Redd Center at Brigham Young University.[26]

She appealed to an otherwise unknown acquaintance in California, and her hard-luck story brought a sympathetic response: "They say that into each life some rain must fall, but with you it would seem that Noah's flood is upon you. Enclosed in this letter is not a loan. We hope that you will accept this simply as help from one friend to another."[27] Only the month before, she had renewed a note for $319.56 from Reed Whipple's bank, the First National Bank of Nevada.[28] A few months later, she borrowed an unspecified sum from William E. and Ruth Nielson of LaVerkin, Utah, apparently a short-term loan since she paid back $200 in December (it is not clear whether this is her first payment), leaving a balance of "$260 . . . when you can make it." Two months later, she made two more payments, one of ten dollars, the other of twenty, leaving a balance of $230." Her papers do not include any additional records of payment.[29] She appealed unsuccessfully for fellowships or stipends from the National Foundation on the Arts and Humanities, the National Endowment for the Humanities, the National Endowment for the Arts, and the National Science Foundation. Nothing was forthcoming.

Although she had never paid into Social Security, Maurine was delighted when she found in 1974 that she qualified for $140 a month in supplemental security income.[30] She could almost live on that and welfare. Tension lessened.

A project on which she spent much time and enthusiasm was a proposed real estate promotion by John H. Morgan, which Maurine saw as giving new impetus to her "Unpromised Land" manuscript. Earlier, she had contacted John David Rose, vice president of Terracor and a member of the Utah Travel Council, who was interested in developing the resort community of Bloomington.[31] He expressed interest and "strongly urge[d]" her to combine "well-written and anecdotal history sketches." Her papers do not include any more correspondence from him.

St. George was growing and Maurine wanted to be involved. A racetrack, Dixie Downs, opened in April 1969. A new reservoir was planned near Gunlock, to help meet the demand by neighboring communities for more culinary water. Bloomington Ranches Country Club, the Terracor project, was nearing completion with its eighteen-hole pro golf course, new administration office building, and eight-acre riding club complete with corrals and stalls for fifty horses, double Olympic-size swimming pool, and homes. Residential lots were selling from $3,000 to $13,000. Four Dixie Airline commuter planes were flying between Salt Lake City and St. George, and Interstate-15 was under construction, making St. George more accessible than ever to Wasatch Front residents interested in a sunny getaway.[32]

Maurine watched the changes. She hated it when real estate development threatened to roll over any of the old landmarks. She was concerned about the abandoned cotton mill in nearby Washington and wrote a few letters of inquiry for Brad Eutsler, a rock shop owner who was interested in buying it.[33] Nothing came of these efforts, but it has since been purchased by the Hyrum and Gail Smith family and restored as a historic site. It is now the Star Nursery.

Lynn Empey was still city manager; but after the accusations Maurine had flung around town about his role in the lost tapes, she could count on no support from him. New people, knowing about her only from *The Giant Joshua*, usually started out interested in her and intrigued by her projects but mysteriously disappeared within a few weeks or months.

John Morgan[34] had made his money in oil and ambitiously envisioned building a "Williamsburg-West" in the St. George area. Again Maurine saw the project as a natural tie-in to "Unpromised Land" and was excited by its idealistic content when Morgan talked about helping St. George "fulfill its destiny." When I interviewed him in October 1992, Morgan was complimentary of Maurine's historical knowledge—a point he also made in his letters to her—and noted that she never asked for money. Maurine was easily caught up in Morgan's vision of building "St. George into a great tourist and recreation attraction." He wrote to her that he planned to combine celebrating the completion of the freeway ("it will mean the entrance into Utah from California, Arizona, Nevada, etc.") with announcing the Williamsburg-West Project. He wanted Maurine to ask George Romney, a former U.S. presidential candidate and governor of Michigan, to be the kick-off speaker. (Romney's ancestor, Miles Romney, had worked on the St. George Tabernacle and George Romney was known for espousing the ideal of "voluntary cooperation.") St. George needed a plan for its over-all development, Morgan told Maurine: "Sewer and water and power, etc. But it especially consists of a way by which we can preserve what has taken place in St. George, to really honor those who established it, and to recognize really what has happened there."[35]

Maurine started at the top April 27, 1970, by writing to U.S. President Richard M. Nixon, using Williamsburg-West letterhead and describing the development's patriotic theme. When the project picked up momentum in the fall of 1971, she immediately wrote an admiring letter to George Romney ("I've always admired and loved you for the things you stand for, and . . . I feel that you are my friend") and asking him to hand-deliver a copy of *The Giant Joshua* to Patricia Nixon, the president's wife. Morgan, who saw a copy of the letter, thought it was "great" and that her note to Mrs. Nixon was "just right." He encouraged her to send Mrs. Nixon a copy of the book directly in hopes of engaging the First Lady's interest in the area.

It is not clear if matters developed beyond these initial overtures. Williamsburg-West was never built. Instead, Morgan built the Hilton Hotel and gradually the 950 acres he had bought in the south part of St. George was developed in different ways.

In 1972 there was something else big brewing for sixty-nine-year-old Maurine, but not because of her accomplishments. It was because of the accomplishments of her second cousin, the coloratura singer, Alta Rae Whipple.[36] On 24 January 1972, Alta Rae wrote a long letter to Maurine, asking her to write an introduction for her since she was to sing at the White House for the U.S. President. At first it appeared that Maurine would attend and read the introduction. It never happened, but must have been nice for Maurine to think about. Perhaps the problem was that Alta Rae's White House appearance was suddenly rescheduled earlier than the original date,[37] perhaps one of Maurine's frequent illnesses intervened, or perhaps she simply could not afford the journey, since this event preceded her receipt of social security.

She must have also mused over the fiction/fact irony that, long before Alta Rae was famous, Maurine had written a detailed synopsis for the sequel in which Clory's granddaughter, also a singer, lived a successful and glamorous life, very much like the one Alta Rae now had. This unusual coincidence would have made it difficult for Maurine to write the sequel—assuming she could have still gone ahead with that project—since readers would assume she was simply fictionalizing her cousin's biography. The same thing would have been true, to some extent, in the case of Faun Pickett, another local girl who had gone to New York and had had some degree of success as a dancer. (See Chapter 15.) The fact that Alta Rae wrote kindly letters for the rest of Maurine's life suggests that Maurine had not alienated her and it is interesting that these two cousins who had achieved a measure of national fame felt a close bond.

On 13 July 1972, Camellia ("Camie") Carter Sullivan, president of the camp of Daughters of Utah Pioneers in St. George, organized a reenactment of Erastus Snow's vision of the spillway and coffer dam solution for the Virgin River. About sixty local adults and children in pioneer dress gathered at the spillway site in 110 degree weather. As part of the program,

Maurine read her "Miracle of the Spillway" and Lynn Clark took photographs, followed by a square dance. Camie said that Maurine's story was "very touching and made tears come to many eyes."[38] Lynn also remembered taking photographs at a pond below Washington and of a covered wagon in a field of volcanic rocks. These photos were supposed to accompany stories Maurine had written.[39] The *Spectrum* published an account of the event, including photographs.[40]

Despite such moments of acceptance and contributions to the community, Maurine still sometimes wasted her time and creative energy in complaints and protests. When she was involved in another minor automobile accident and one of the drivers demanded $50 on the spot, she refused, called the police and went to considerable lengths to prove that it wasn't her fault.[41]

She also allowed herself to be diverted from serious writing by attending the trial in Kanab of Kenneth L. Standrod, who was accused of murdering a hitchhiker. Defense attorney Jim Scarth had suggested that Maurine might write a book about it like Truman Capote's *In Cold Blood*. Maurine attended the trial, took many notes, and felt that Standrod had not received a fair trial, but never buckled down to making it a serious writing project. Standrod succeeded in enlisting her sympathy, but she finally told him she was "just too sick and broke" to help him as much as he deserved.[42] He was found guilty of first-degree murder and sent to prison for life.

It is not clear how long the Doubleday paperback edition of *The Giant Joshua* stayed in print nor how long Maurine continued to sell it. Without Charlie Steen to do the bulk ordering for her, she was probably unable to afford the front money. In 1974, she contacted Paul R. Reynolds, a literary agent, to see if he could get *The Giant Joshua* reprinted. He declined.[43] She next contacted Claire M. Smith of Harold Ober Associates, the agency that had represented her for *This Is the Place: Utah*. As usual, she wrote a lengthy, discursive, name-dropping, not-quite-accurate self-introduction, pleading to be understood and taken care of. She claimed that "places like cafes (with gift shops) have been selling all they could get at $4.65 for a 75-cent paperback. For years it was a staple with some of the `Strip' hotels in Las Vegas. I know this, because I used to deliver the books to the STARDUST and the TROPICANA. I also delivered 30 copies to BRENTANO'S in Hollywood. Sam Weller's Zion book store in Salt Lake has been selling the same paperback at $2.95. But everybody has sold out."[44]

Smith responded cautiously, declining to consider involvement with *The Giant Joshua* "unless we also felt there were possibilities for the new book ["Unpromised Land"]. When you feel that is ready to be seen, I would be happy to take a look and let you have my reaction."45 Of course, "Unpromised Land" was never "ready."

In 1976, however, Sam Weller, Salt Lake City's preeminent bookseller, issued a new edition in hardback under his Western Epics imprint. Although he knew he could not quickly recoup his investment, he has continued to keep it in print to this day. Apparently he and Maurine had an informal "understanding," not a formal contract, and he sent Maurine money from time to time when she needed it, whether royalties had accrued or not. He acquired ownership of the copyright, and Maurine consistently assured me that she loved and trusted Sam.46

As part of the general renaissance in Mormon intellectual history, spurred in large part by the college-trained generation after World War II who applied their technical skills to their religious culture, new interest developed in Mormon history (spearheaded by Leonard Arrington) but also including literature. Edward A. Geary of BYU's English Department published an influential article in *BYU Studies* in 1977 looking at Mormon writers of the 1940s like Virginia Sorensen, Blanche Cannon, Ardis Kennelly, and Maurine Whipple, among others.47 He termed them a "Lost Generation," parallel to the expatriate American writers like Gertrude Stein, F. Scott Fitzgerald, and Ernest Hemingway who had found more intellectually congenial homes in Europe a generation earlier between the two World Wars. Unlike most of these authors, Maurine had never really left Utah; so she was readily available when flattering attention and invitations began coming her way.

In 1991, she couldn't remember how she met Carol Lynn and Gerald Pearson, both BYU graduates who were raising their four children in Provo. Carol Lynn was a poet, and her first two books, *Beginnings* and *The Search*, self-published in a handsome edition with exquisite illustrations by Rhodesian artist-sculptor Trevor Southey became unexpected best-sellers.48 They helped launch the renaissance in Mormon literature of the 1970s. Maurine read and admired these poems, and was generous in her praise of them. In appreciation, in June 1973, Carol Lynn sent Maurine her new book, *Daughters of Light* (Provo, Utah: Trilogy Arts, 1973), which had just appeared in May, and which compiled the experiences of early Mormon women with spiritual gifts. "I found doing the research very exciting," wrote Carol Lynn. She also invited Maurine to be their house guest "when you come to Provo this summer." Maurine did, claiming, when I talked with her about these letters in 1991, to have known almost immediately that Gerald was gay but accepting it and befriending the young man who was the "guest in the basement."

When Richard Cracroft and Neal E. Lambert, then two young English professors at BYU, saw the lack of a class in Mormon literature and moved to remedy it, they invited Maurine to come lecture in October 1973. She again stayed with the Pearsons.⁴⁹ Her lecture was a success, and Cracroft thanked her: "My Mormon literature class enjoyed very thoroughly THE GIANT JOSHUA. Despite the fact that you made one of my young gals almost physically ill by this confrontation with the realities of polygamy, she and the rest of the class finally admitted to having enjoyed most thoroughly the experience of your book. A couple of them even wrote papers on the book."⁵⁰

Cracroft and Lambert launched an ambitious project of publishing an anthology that spanned Mormon writing in all genres except scripture from the days of Joseph Smith to the present. In the same letter quoted above, Cracroft asked Maurine's permission to reprint a section from *The Giant Joshua* in their anthology, *A Believing People: The Literature of the Latter-day Saints*.⁵¹

In late 1976, Cracroft sent Maurine a form from the *International Authors and Writers Who's Who*, explaining that it hadn't known how to reach Maurine and had sent her application in care of him, "sure that the literary community would know how to find Maurine." He wrote cheerfully: "I recently bore solemn witness in behalf of the *Giant Joshua* for the *Deseret News*, who promised to do an article on *Joshua*. I am also requiring Joshua for my Mormon Literature class this coming term. If you are going to be coming through Provo any time between January 4 and April 14, please let me know so I can insist on a visit from you to the Department of English and to my Mormon Literature class. We will even stake you to gas money and a luncheon."⁵²

Maurine did not come to Provo that semester. She wrote a long letter explaining that she needed to recuperate from an unspecified "accident" and asking if she could do the lecture in mid-May. Cracroft replied that "our regular school year will be over and a new term just beginning" but promised to "put out feelers among the faculty regarding the possibility of generating such a lecture" and, in any case, warmly invited her to "chat with me and with Eugene England, who is hard at work writing a paper on *Giant Joshua* which will be read at the Association of Mormon Letters meetings next fall. Gene will claim *Joshua* as the best of the Mormon novels, so what else is new?"⁵³

Two years later, Maurine went to Salt Lake City to receive a Merit of Honor Award from the University of Utah's Emeritus Club on May 11, 1978. In 1991, she remembered the event's chairman better than the banquet. He was F. Gerald Irvine, the Gerry Irvine who was enshrined in her memory as the chivalrous escort to the "rotten loggin'" event and who later told her that "had she allowed him to kiss her who knows what would have happened?"⁵⁴

Cracroft was able to arrange a lecture, and other interested parties had also been at work. Youthful and energetic Dennis Rowley, curator of manuscripts for the Lee Library, had been able to win Maurine's consent to deposit her papers there and no doubt sponsored the lecture, "A Writer's Odyssey."55 Preparing her papers to turn them over joined other unfinished projects on Maurine's list for the next five years.

The next month, Maurine asked Cracroft to help her get the local papers to report on the address she had delivered in Provo and also on the symposium where Eugene England had spoken on *The Giant Joshua*. As usual, she tried to engage his sympathy because of her pathetic circumstances: "This town has always been a nightmare to me—so much prejudice. I'm always vulnerable to everybody's ill-will. Some publicity in the papers would help."56

Cracroft was willing to provide articulate and moderate quotations when LaVarr Webb wrote an article for Maurine for a popular regional magazine: "Dr. Cracroft said Miss Whipple is not a Fawn Brodie—not a slayer of faith; however, perhaps she did stray a little further into forbidden areas than did Juanita Brooks. Brooks stayed completely in the faith, while Miss Whipple says, 'I've always tried to be as good a Mormon as I can and still stay true to myself.'"

A newer, less threatened generation was in the ascendancy; and Maurine could have had a place in it that was, for a change, not marginal. But it came possibly a decade too late for her. For example, well-respected historians LeRoy R. and Ann W. Hafen, then living in Murray, Utah, tried to involve her in the State Historical Society's activities. Even though Maurine's historical gifts were not those of the usual historian, she would have been interested, and trips to Salt Lake City were always welcome diversions from the hard and lonely work of writing. But she had no travel funds.57

She also let her disappointments poison relationships that could have been beneficial. Mary Lythgoe Bradford had grown up in the Salt Lake Valley and had written her master's thesis on Virginia Sorensen but then made her adult life in the Washington, D.C., area where she became editor of *Dialogue*. Maurine reacted snippily when Mary gave a paper on Mormon women writers at a professional conference in Salt Lake City. When Mary was at the University of Utah archives after her lecture, someone told her Maurine Whipple was in the stacks. Mary said, "Oh, I'd like to talk to her." The person returned, embarrassed and explained to Mary that Maurine didn't want to see her—she thought *she* should have been invited to give the paper on Mormon women writers.58

Still, no matter how much stress and heartache she experienced, Maurine didn't usually spill out her troubles in face-to-face conversation, saving them for letters. From my own experience, I knew Maurine was usually good company and would exert herself to entertain those who were with her. Despite all of the conflicts with some local people, others were eager to spend time with her, visiting, swapping stories, running errands and doing favors for her. She reciprocated by telling humorous stories and showing the visitor local sites. This was a Maurine who was easy to like.

A typical note of appreciation from one of her visitors was: "I'm glad you enjoyed our day together as much as you did, for I can't tell you what a wonderful day it was for me. It will be a jewel in the crown of memory for both of us, I'm sure."[59]

Notes

[1] Maurine Whipple, Letter to Elden Beck, n.d. 1967, Maurine Whipple Collection, L. Tom Perry Special Collections, Harold B. Lee Library, Brigham Young University, Provo, Utah, with photocopy in Maurine Whipple Collection, Archive, Val A. Browning Library, Dixie College, St. George, Utah. Documents in both collections hereafter cited as BYU, photocopy Dixie Colleg.

[2] Maurine Whipple, Letter to Ernest Linford, 18 August 1967; BYU, photocopy Dixie College.

[3] Mary Phoenix, interviewed 1992. Notes in my possession.

[4] Keith W. Stroud, MSW Field Director, Letter to Maurine Whipple, 13 July 1970; BYU, photocopy Dixie College.

[5] Reed Whipple letter to Maurine Whipple, ca. 1969, BYU.

[6] Stroud to Whipple, 13 July 1970.

[7] Maurine Whipple, Letter to Preston (no surname), 23 March 1972; Maurine Whipple, Letter to Norman Cousins, 15 August 1974; both in BYU, photocopy Dixie College.

[8] On 18 January 1972, she borrowed $100 from Reed Whipple's bank at 5 percent interest. On 29 February 1972, she renewed it for thirty days. Both notes in Whipple Collection, BYU.

[9] Camellia ("Camie") Carter Sullivan Higgins, email to Veda Hale, 26 March 2001.

[10] The editor, Ward Jay Roylance (1920–93) wrote a book with the same title and helped organize the Enchanted Wilderness Association to lead guided tours into southern Utah's canyons.

[11] Loose page from a letter to unidentified addressee, 17 March 1971; BYU, photocopy Dixie College.

[12] Whipple to Preston (no surname), 23 March 1972.

THE 1970S: FLICKERINGS OF POTENTIAL FLAMES

13 Maryruth Bracy and Linda Lambert, "Maurine Whipple's Story of The Giant Joshua," *Dialogue: A Journal of Mormon Thought* 4, nos. 3–4 (Autumn–Winter): 55–61.

14 Joseph Rosenblatt, born 13 January 1903 in Salt Lake City, to Russian Jewish parents, established EIMCO, a mining machinery company. Also a philanthropist, he established the Rosenblatt Prize of $30,000 a year, awarded to an outstanding teacher, plus another $10,000 annual award to a business management teacher. He also donated his home to serve as the residence of the University of Utah president.

15 Maurine Whipple, Letter to Joseph Rosenblatt, 19 June 1973, BYU.

16 Joseph Rosenblatt, The Rosenblatt Investment Fund, Suite 1130 Kennecott Building, 10 East South Temple, Salt Lake City, Utah 84111, Letter to Maurine Whipple, 20 June 1973; BYU, photocopy Dixie College.

17 Vira Henrie Judge Blake, interviewed June 14, 2003, St. George.

18 Ibid.

19 Maurine Whipple, Letter to Ernie Hoff, regional editor, *Salt Lake Tribune*, 8 April 1970; holograph note from Ernie to Maurine on the bottom of her letter; Whipple Collection, Dixie College.

20 Eric Snow, Letter to the *Tribune*, n.d.; Whipple Collection, BYU. How the letter ended up in Maurine's possession is a mystery.

21 Maurine Whipple, Letter to Ernie Hoff, *Salt Lake Tribune*, 7 July 1971, BYU.

22 Barbara F. Connor, Information Services American Heritage Publishing Co., 551 Fifth Avenue, New York 10017, Letter to Maurine Whipple, 23 March 1971; Maurine Whipple, Letter to Barbara F. Connor, 26 March 1971; Dixie College.

23 Raymond L. Freeman, Acting Director, U.S. Department of the Interior National Park Service, Washington, D.C. 20240, Letter to Senator Frank E. Moss, 5 May 1971; BYU, photocopy Dixie College.

24 William G. Bruhn, Letter to Maurine Whipple, 20 October 1972, BYU.

25 Everett L. Cooley, Letters to Maurine Whipple, 26 February 1970, 20 December 1972; BYU, photocopy Dixie College. At least twice, Cooley asked Maurine to contribute her "memorabilia" to the Marriott Library. In his 1972 letter, he also told her he couldn't get her grant money.

26 Maurine Whipple, Letter to Rosenblatt Investment Fund, Suite 1130 Kennecott Building, 10 East South Temple, Salt Lake City, Utah 84111, 19 June 1973; BYU, photocopy Dixie College. Maurine also proposed a "TV series" on the hot-potato topic of the Mountain Meadows Massacre. Politically astute, Arrington told her that his "personal opinion" was that the Church "public relations people here . . . would not look upon such a TV series with favor." Arrington, Letter to Whipple, n.d., BYU.

27 Hon Schneider, El Monte, CA 91733, Letter to Maurine Whipple, 4 April 1974, BYU.

28 L.D. Strate, Loan Officer, Letter to Maurine Whipple, 21 March 1974, BYU.

29 William E. Nielson, LaVerkin, Utah, Letters to Maurine Whipple, 19 December 1975 and 4 February 1976; BYU, photocopy Dixie College.

30 Ralph W. Moon, Branch Manager, Department of Health Education and Welfare Social Security Administration, P.O. Box 769, 689 S. 75 E. Cedar City, Utah

84720, Letter to Maurine Whipple, 24 April 1974, BYU. He also tells her that she is not eligible for any other assistance.

31 Bloomington is a development of Terracor Corporation of Utah (a merger of Johnson Land Company and Ivory-Boyer Realtors in December 1968). [Vi Judge Blake], "Firm Charts Bridge to 'Dixie' Lots," *Salt Lake Tribune*, [no day] June 1969; clipping in Vi's possession.

32 [Vi Judge], "Firm Charts Bridge to 'Dixie' Lots," *Salt Lake Tribune*, [no day] June 1969; clipping in Vi's scrapbook; Vi Judge, "Gov., Mrs. Rampton Tour Dixie, Praise Area Progress," *Salt Lake Tribune*, 17 April 1969, 15.

33 Sam Cline, Cline, Jackson and Jackson, attorneys at law, Milford, Utah, 84751, Letter to Maurine Whipple and photocopy of letter to Brad Eutsler, 26 March 1971; BYU, photocopy Dixie College.

34 John H. Morgan Jr., biography, *Southern Utah Outdoors*, September 2001, 1, no. 6 (September 2001): 21.

35 John H. Morgan Jr., Letters to Maurine Whipple, 16, 18, and 20 September 1971; BYU, photocopy Dixie College.

36 She performed only as "Alta Rae." Coloratura is a kind of music with rapid runs, trills, and ornaments. Maurine's papers included a photocopy of a *New York Times* page, Sunday, November 19, 1972, BYU, photocopy Dixie College. It reports Alta Rae's accomplishments and indicates that she had climbed to the top, just as Maurine envisioned the heroine of her sequel as doing. Alta Rae was born 14 March 1933, and was thirty-nine—thirty years younger than Maurine—when this opportunity came. Alta Rae was the granddaughter of Edgar, the son of Charlie's mother by her first marriage. Edgar dropped his father's name, Peters, and took the Whipple name when Charlie's mother, Caroline, married Eli Whipple. Alta Rae's parents, Jesse Whipple and Phoebe Alta Marshall Whipple, pioneered Logandale, Nevada, near Mesquite. Alta Rae died 6 October 1996 (age sixty-six) of complications of diabetes and is buried in the Logandale Cemetery. She, like Maurine, suffered from many sinus infections, which curtailed her career.

37 Alta Rae Whipple, Letter to Maurine Whipple, 21 January 1972; BYU, photocopy Dixie College.

38 Camie Carter Sullivan Higgins, interviewed June 2001.

39 Lynn Clark, Interviewed 18 September 1992, St. George, Utah.

40 Camellia Carter Sullivan, "Erastus Snow Vision: The Washington Fields Virgin River Dam Re-enactment," *Spectrum*, ca. July 1972, undated clipping; BYU, photocopy Dixie College.

41 Maurine Whipple, carbon copy of letter to Jack C. Mahoney, Dept. Public Safety, 305 State Office Bldg., Salt Lake City, 19 October 1970; BYU, photocopy Dixie College.

42 Maurine Whipple, rough draft of letter to Kenneth Standrod, n.d.; BYU, photocopy Dixie College. Maurine made notes about the case on a yellow pad, found in the desk Charlie built for her. The desk is now in the Dixie College Heritage Room, and the notes are in the Dixie College Archive.

43 Paul R. Reynolds, Inc., Letter to Maurine Whipple, 10 January 1973; BYU, photocopy Dixie College. His letter also refers to her query about some unspecified revi-

sions and republishing her ghost-written article "I Married Five Wives," although *Collier's* probably still held the copyright for a few more years.

44 Claire M. Smith, Harold Ober Associates, 40 East 49th Street, New York 10017, Letter to Maurine Whipple, 9 August 1974, BYU.

45 Claire M. Smith, Harold Ober Associates, Letter to Maurine Whipple, 23 August 1974; BYU, photocopy Dixie College.

46 As Maurine's guardian, Carol Jensen was not initially sure how to handle this informal arrangement. The payments of $200 came quite regularly but with no accounting of the number of books sold. Maurine thought Sam sent money because he liked her, which is partly the case. After some initial conflict, Carol grasped the fact that Sam had been more than fair with Maurine. Even if the arrangement wasn't strictly businesslike, Sam had given Maurine the advantage all these years as her needs dictated. This information comes from my association with Carol Jensen.

47 Edward A. Geary, "Mormondom's 'Lost Generation': The Novelists of the 1940s," *BYU Studies* 18 (Fall 1977): 89–98.

48 Gerald Pearson and Trevor Southey were both gay, and their struggle to honor their fervent Mormonism and their homosexual orientation simultaneously, their eventual divorces, and their continued creative lives became part of the debate about gender that is still on-going within Mormonism. Carol Lynn wrote movingly about their marriage, divorce, and Gerald's death from AIDS, during which she cared for him, in a runaway national best-seller, *Good-bye, I Love You* (New York: Random House, 1986). She successfully continued her career as a Mormon feminist essayist, humorist, poet, and dramatist in California.

49 I deduce this from the fact that Maurine's allergist, D. A. Dolowitz, sent Maurine her allergy medications on 29 October 1973 in care of Trilogy Arts, the Pearsons' publishing company, BYU.

50 Dr. Richard H. Cracroft, BYU English Department, Letter to Maurine Whipple, 14 January 1974; BYU, photocopy Dixie College. He was also writing on behalf of his colleague, Neal E. Lambert.

51 Richard H. Cracroft and Neal E. Lambert, eds., *A Believing People: The Literature of the Latter-day Saints* (Salt Lake City: Bookcraft, 1974). They published an excerpt from *The Giant Joshua* in the Novel section with Nephi Anderson's *Marcus King, Mormon* and Vardis Fisher's *Children of God*.

52 Richard H. Cracroft, Chairman, Department of English, Brigham Young University, Letter to Maurine Whipple, 23 December 1976; BYU, photocopy Dixie College.

53 Richard H. Cracroft, Letter to Maurine Whipple, 20 April 1978; BYU, photocopy Dixie College.

54 F. Gerald Irvine, University of Utah Alumni Association, Letter to Maurine Whipple, 14 April 1978, Dixie College.

55 "Author to Speak on Life as Writer," *Daily Universe*, 18 May 1978, 3; clipping in BYU, photocopy Dixie College.

[56] Maurine Whipple, Letter to Richard H. Cracroft, 10 June 1978. Cracroft gave me this letter on 2 September 1992. He also said he "once interviewed Maurine in about 1978 or so in St. George, but the "*&^%$#@ machine didn't record it."

[57] Ann Hafen, Letter to Maurine Whipple, 15 May 1968; BYU, photocopy Dixie College.

[58] Mary Bradford told me this anecdote in January 1992 at the Association for Mormon Letters annual meeting at Westminster College in Salt Lake City. Obviously, Maurine did not understand the process, common for academic conferences, of submitting paper proposals to a committee who made the decisions about which ones to select.

[59] Inez S. Cooper, Special Collections Room, Library, Southern Utah State College, Cedar City, Utah, Letter to Maurine Whipple, 9 May 1974; BYU, photocopy Dixie College.

⁕ 26 ⁕

A SMALL HOLD ON HOPE

Fan letters still came from readers who had just discovered *The Giant Joshua*. On 4 December 1962, she received an appreciative letter from a small-town reporter, Howard Kibble, in Glen Allen, Alaska. He had just read the novel and found that it whetted his appetite for the sequel. Enthusiastically, he proposed an ambitious slate of possible future topics to write about and volunteered: "All your book needs for an additional send off, as I see it, is a furor of praise and condemnation in the press and periodicals. Such things are often arranged by either publishers or agents as you probably know."[1]

Another reader who was connected with the Shadel Sanatorium's Las Vegas facility, sent Maurine an emotional letter of appreciation:

> I was quite shaken by the last chapter; not only because the book is a tense drama in many ways....
>
> In some respects it was a bitter book, Maurine; but it has magnificence; and it is true... I mean, the insight into human character, is true. ... Such a book should incline a reader toward tolerance of struggling mortals, in general; and I, myself, was more impressed with your observations of human nature, generally,—and your sympathy and forbearance,—than I was with the pitifully un-rewarding life, which had to be endured by Clory.[2]

A woman named W. Phoebe Bailey who had joined the LDS Church in England with her husband, had been so deeply impressed by reading *The Giant Joshua* that she came to visit Maurine in St. George. Maurine must have described her obstacles as a writer during this visit, for Phoebe followed up by letter, suggesting that Maurine rent out her house and move temporarily to Provo. There she could have guest privileges in

Phoebe's home, since Phoebe managed a "halfway house for the mentally ill" and was gone a good deal of the time.³

Maurine didn't pursue this possibility. Perhaps she didn't want to be that close to someone who might see her as "mentally ill." Certainly she couldn't admit that the time for writing the sequel was past.

An earlier letter of counsel—one of the most candid and most stinging—came from Lorna Clayton of Salt Lake City who had enthusiastically thrown herself into promoting the paperback edition of *The Giant Joshua*, helping with the advertising, and encouraging both the radio reading of *Joshua* and the proposed stage version in 1962–63. By the beginning of 1968, Lorna had lost faith, not in Maurine's good intentions, but in her ability to discipline herself to do good work. When Maurine wrote a letter hinting for assistance, Lorna responded, not angrily, but with unsparing candor, telling Maurine that she could not stay with them in Salt Lake City, then adding:

> Your writing is your passport and when you don't get things done everyone loses interest. This sounds like I'm scolding and in a way I am. You have let many opportunities go by ever since I have known you, and no matter what else happens you first must look after your "bread and butter." Procrastination and excuses will not do. It's a big cold world in St. George and in Salt Lake. . . . Don't kid yourself anymore, Maurine, face reality and do something. Don't just wait for that magic someone to subsidize you again. You have been your own worst enemy and you should think it over and try to change the pattern of your own private life in such a way as to bring you success which you should have with your heaven sent ability.⁴

When I cautiously broached the subject with Maurine of why she seemed to have so many repeated problems, she gave this answer: "Because I was trying so hard to force things to happen with my own brand of faith. I just couldn't allow myself to spend time analyzing too much why I had so many problems. That would be giving power to the negatives." This attitude has much to commend it; but at some point for her, the result was not positive energy but denial. And something always came up that deflected her from really coming to grips with the facts. One example was praise from an Ohio family who had been so impressed by *The Giant Joshua* that they had stopped at the information center at the temple to get information about how to contact Maurine. They wanted to know the status of the sequel: "If it can compare at all with `The Giant Joshua' the world shouldn't have to wait any longer. To me, that is the most realistic book I ever read, and so near the truth (probably) that I believed it all. It is a masterpiece."⁵

Another such letter of praise came in late 1976 when her bicentennial hopes had turned to ashes. Brian J. Stowell, a Los Angeles attorney, sent a letter to the *St. George Spectrum*. He and his wife had visited St. George after reading *The Giant Joshua* and felt that the book had helped them appreciate the city and its people. As a result, they lengthened their stay to spend the night in the city rather than driving on. They recommended that "the citizens of St. George take whatever action was possible in order to give the book additional publicity so that other tourists could better appreciate the city."[6] Maurine had tried without success (and not very realistically) for a long time to persuade the city fathers that, if they would only provide a decent living for her, she would write important books and generate revenue in the area because visitors would come to see the places she wrote about.

A California fan wrote ardently: "Having lived in St. George for nigh on twenty years without ever knowing you is a matter of the deepest *annoyance* and shame to me: annoyance because, as I remember, not one of the sonsofbitches ever pointed you out."[7] Maurine answered this letter, seizing the opportunity to pour out her frustrations and depression to a new, enthusiastic admirer. He answered the same day he received it, begging her "not to think it hadn't been worth it" because "it had been and still was." In his opinion "there is nothing at all worthwhile in life, except to escape anonymity . . . and my miraculous friend, you have done that."[8]

As these fan letters continued to come in, warming Maurine's heart in her old age, it was easy for her to postpone dealing with the realities of her problem-filled life. It is also easy to understand why she struggled so hard for recognition and justice instead of shrugging off disappointments and plunging back into her work. No wonder it was so hard for her to know just what she was supposed to be like. No wonder she kept toiling at project after project, trying to rekindle the magic, while simultaneously distracting herself and dissipating her energy. And no wonder that everyone who knew her kept hammering at the one message she could not follow through on: "Maurine, please, please, just finish the sequel!"

Maurine kept a *Spectrum* clipping from 6 April 1977 in which the writer candidly acknowledged, "The woman hasn't always been the most loved person in Utah's Dixie, but she has left an impression on the minds of the people here. . . . She has had a lifetime romance with southern Utah. She nearly eats, drinks, sleeps and breathes her native homeland—the red hills of Brigham Young's Dixie of the desert. She has made the area part of her soul in her search to bring out life in the soul of the land."[9]

Another 1978 article developed this theme: "Miss Whipple's love affair with the red rock country has consumed her entire life. She admits she lives for the country, and she doesn't spare any adjectives in description."[10]

Important people still tried to help her with good advice. Judge F. Henri Henroid, who had been consistently supportive as she fought city hall, was one who did—but only after Maurine asked for it. One letter he wrote had this sound advice: "Please don't undertake 4 or 5 books. Do one at a time,—and the St. George early history ["Unpromised Land"] is a fruitful source for a book, comparable to THE GIANT JOSHUA—and I think, maybe better."[11]

In retrospect, perhaps Maurine's persistent hope, unrealistic through it was, pulled her forward through the late 1960s and 1970s. It is somewhat admirable. She did reach both hands out to life, get them slapped over and over, yet still reached. She did indeed love the earth's beauties, laughter and good times, even though they kept her from accomplishments.

In February 1967 she felt that she was making sufficient progress on some project—or was whistling in the dark loudly enough—that she wrote to an artist friend about book cover possibilities. The friend responded, excited and delighted, but puzzled: "But, which one is it: AA [the Shadel book], Strip ["Unpromised Land"] or, something else entirely new?"[12]

But, as the 1960s ended, nothing had been published nor had her "silver lining" shown up. On 10 October 1969 she was admitted to the hospital in St. George by Dr. M. K. McGregor, with Medicare and Welfare listed as "party responsible."[13] In one letter, she complains that the winter of 1969–70 had been a series of flu, bronchitis, "staph pneumonia," and three relapses.[14]

Maurine may have preferred going to Salt Lake City even for non-specialized medical attention because she had exhausted the patience of St. George nurses. Carol Jensen, then a nurse at the Dixie Regional Medical Center and later Maurine's legal guardian, told me that the nurses were skeptical about the validity of her illnesses when they "saw her coming in with her pretty nightgowns and suitcase full of things like one would take on a vacation." When some nurses didn't want Maurine as a patient, Carol volunteered to trade with them, feeling that she knew how Maurine thought and desiring to do something good for the talented but "downtrodden" woman. She also felt that Maurine's illnesses, however worsened by her emotions and attitude, had a genuine physical basis because Dr. McGregor, Maurine's physician, wasn't the kind who would "let her put anything over on him." Carol would prove to be a true angel for Maurine.

Maurine had never let her health insurance lapse, no matter how destitute she was; and when she became eligible for Medicare, she took advantage of it. In the summer of 1968, she had spent a period of time in a Salt Lake City hospital paid for by Medicare, apparently for arthritis and allergy treatments. She was independent enough to rent an apartment for her recuperation. But the refrigerator leaked freon, making her sicker than she had originally been. Dale Woodward, a psychologist, and his wife, Shirley, had met Maurine in St. George and admired *The Giant Joshua*. She asked them for help, and they took Maurine into their home for two or three weeks. The relationship was warm enough that the Woodwards and their four children once spent three or four days with Maurine in her St. George home, bedding down in the alcove off the living room on cots. Dale Woodward said "her home was white stucco and quite nice. It was tidy enough and Maurine was a good hostess, fixing some meals for us. We took her with us to Pine Valley and stayed overnight. Everywhere we went, Maurine told stories and was good company." He said he was aware she had been having troubles, but "she didn't let them bog her down, nor did she try for charity from us at that time." He thought she was on welfare (she was), but that she was still working hard to try to get something written that could provide a living.[15] His observation provides a balanced view of her life. She could undeniably be good company, enthusiastically sharing her love of the country, and good stories of the oldtimers. Her impulses, too, were in the direction of kindliness, ever anxious to find a way to contribute to someone's happiness, at least for brief periods.

When I interviewed Dr. Westwood in 2001, he reported that Maurine had confided something that she claimed she had never told anyone else or put on paper. This was "that she lived in great fear that she had lost whatever talent she might have had and could never again write anything as good as *The Giant Joshua*." As Westwood, a psychologist, commented, "Such a fear could easily become so terrifying that she could have gone to great lengths to avoid trying."

About this time Maurine become aware that she was eligible for a government program meant for elderly people with no other means of support and no assets except home equity. On 30 January 1969, she signed a public welfare lien agreement on her home which would provide $5,939 in assistance until 1973. This sum paid off debts and gave her some breathing room.

In 1970 and for some time thereafter, she spent a great deal of time helping Morris Shirts, dean of the School of Education at Southern Utah State College, locate "Peter's Leap," a dangerous dugway on the first road that enabled the pioneers to come down into the valley. (Morris was Peter Shirts's grandson.) Though her efforts didn't generate any money, she was delighted when, a couple of years later, Morris Shirts announced that it had become an official historic hike for the Boy Scouts.[16]

In 1969, it had been fifteen years since she had published her last article—the ghost-written account of polygamist Edson Jessop. Someone, she couldn't remember who, "assigned" her to write an article about the fishing at Panguitch Lake in Garfield County; and she talked Brad and Ruth

Eutsler, friends who ran a rock shop, into taking her camping. Maurine wrote the article from the perspective of an uncoordinated woman who had never fished before. It is light-hearted and entertaining writing that flows well and describes the area's scenic appeals. But it appeared as a one-page piece with no photographs in the March 1969 Golden Circle Canyonlands Issue of *Western Gateway* magazine, and probably didn't bring her much money.[17] It was her last publication.

However, she had not, at least in her own mind, given up on the sequel. In her papers are pages torn out of magazines of the time that reminded her of something she wanted to include in the sequel. She would write in the margins the name of a character to whom it would be appropriate.

In fact, Maurine did have in her papers after the theft a typescript of perhaps about two hundred pages, which she could certainly have sent off to a publisher. The right reader/critic/editor may have seen the possibilities in this manuscript and given Maurine enough feed-back and direction to keep her going. It is a mystery to me that she hadn't made use of what she had in a more or less completed form. I surmise that the two hundred pages, or much of it, dated from the late forties. Perhaps her constantly revising, rethinking, researching, and reinventing the sequel/trilogy became so blurred in her mind that she lost track of just what had been done. To the end of her life, the sequel was a perpetual burr under her saddle. She kept telling people she knew she had to finish it. It made her irritable much of the time.

She ended the sixties still in control of her biggest champion, for in 1969 she renewed the copyright on *The Giant Joshua* for another twenty-eight years.

Notes

[1] Howard Kibble, Letter to Maurine Whipple, 4 December 1962; Maurine Whipple Collection, L. Tom Perry Special Collections, Harold B. Lee Library, Brigham Young University, Provo, Utah, with photocopy in Maurine Whipple Collection, Archive, Val A. Browning Library, Dixie College, St. George, Utah. Documents in both collections hereafter cited as BYU, photocopy Dixie College.

[2] Patsie (no surname signed), Letter to Maurine Whipple, n.d.; BYU, photocopy Dixie College.

3 W. Phoebe Bailey, L.P.N. Home Coordinator, Alpine House: A Mental Health Rehabilitation Project, Provo, Utah, Letter to Maurine Whipple, 9 November 1966; BYU, photocopy Dixie College.

4 Lorna Clayton, Letter to Maurine Whipple, 17 January 1968; BYU, photocopy Dixie College.

5 O. L. Roseliun (possibly Roseliuz), Dewey, Ohio, Letter to Maurine Whipple 21 November 1971; BYU, photocopy Dixie College.

6 Brian J. Stowell, Los Angeles, Letter to Maurine Whipple, 1 October 1976; BYU, photocopy Dixie College.

7 Elbert Thomas, 1550 Manhattan Ave., Hermosa Beach, CA 90254, Letter to Maurine Whipple, 30 June 1978; BYU, photocopy Dixie College. I could not determine whether he was a relative of the U.S. Senator Elbert Thomas; however, an Elbert Thomas worked at the Nevada test site, which would have given him a reason for living in St. George; http://web.nmsu.edu/~tomlynch/swlit.whitesands.html (accessed in spring 2001).

8 Elbert Thomas, Letter to Maurine Whipple, 7 September 1978; BYU, photocopy Dixie College. This was apparently the end of their correspondence, and I found no evidence that he published his book.

9 Paul Roberts, St. George *Spectrum* 6 April 1977, Dixie College.

10 LaVarr Webb, "Author of the Giant Joshua in a Search of Her Second Novel," *Mountain West,* February 1978, clipping in Whipple papers, BYU.

11 F. Henri Henroid, Justice Supreme Court, State Capitol, Salt Lake City 84114, Letter to Maurine Whipple, 17 February 1973; BYU, photocopy Dixie College.

12 Martha Vincent, Letter to Maurine Whipple, 11 February 1967; BYU, photocopy Dixie College.

13 Admission papers in Whipple Collection; BYU, photocopy Dixie College.

14 Maurine Whipple, Letter to Toria (no surname given), 21 February 1970; BYU, photocopy Dixie College.

15 Dale Westwood, Interviewed by telephone, July 2001; notes in my possession. Hospital papers in Maurine's collection give her admission date as 11 June 1968.

16 Morris A. Shirts, "Peter's Leap: Road Task Great," 5 July 1973, *Color Country Spectrum*, clipping at BYU.

17 Maurine's papers include four versions with same title "Panguitch: Big Fish Lake" (1) 3 x 6" notebook with research and observations, BYU; (2) seventy-eight-page holograph draft and notes, BYU; (3) nine-page typescript, Dixie College Archives, (4) seven-page (unpaginated) typescript, BYU. All versions have multiple revisions. It appeared in *Western Gateway*, March 1968, 24.

27

AN UNRAVELING LIFE

Maurine turned seventy-seven in 1980. Her life was slipping further out of her control. Whatever one may say about the modern welfare state, the social services safety net had helped give Maurine approximately twelve years of comfort, regular meals, good medical care, and some relief from the worry about financial security that she had resented and fretted about her entire life.

A major project she wanted to see through to fruition was *The Giant Joshua* as a movie. It was a desire that many admirers also shared. One of them was Richard H. Cracroft, who wrote positively in 1978, in response to her request about the film possibilities: "As you well know, I am enthusiastic about the great literary quality of the novel which still stands without threat as the finest Mormon novel to date. The brilliant blend of artistry, Mormon folk ways, Mormon history, and the humanity of the characters makes this a memorable book. . . . I believe wholeheartedly that such a film, were it handled with sensitivity, would be well received by Utah Mormons and others."[1]

Maurine certainly agreed with him. She had envisioned a major motion picture when the book was first published and repeatedly pinned her hopes of financial rescue on seeing it made into the kind of all-star Hollywood blockbuster that *Gone with the Wind* had achieved. Through the years, hope had flared up brightly many times; but now, finally, something real happened. On 30 May 1981, John Earle bought an option on the movie rights for $1,000. Unaccountably, Maurine put the money in the bank and apparently forgot about it.[2] Earle wrote a script based on the novel but apparently got no further. Sterling Van Wagenen,[3] a brother to Lola Van Wagenen, then married to Robert Redford, and Salt Lake City lawyer, John M. Lear, got interested in the project. In about January 1984, Van Wagenen opened negotiations with Earle. It is not clear what happened at this point, but Van Wagenen and Lear formed the Martin Gray Company, specifically to make the movie. Lear was the president. Where the name "Martin Gray" came from is not known, perhaps for the supposed investor.[4] Van Wagenen and Lear apparently bought Earle's option. They did not use his script, but Van Wagenen and his friend, Brian Capener, wrote another script, of which four or five drafts exist.[5] Earle's option expired in early 1984, but he and his associates executed an option extension until 1 May 1984. Then followed a second extension, which was executed until May 18, 1984.[6] The next document available shows that John M. Lear on June 14, 1984, sent Maurine a check for $12,500 "in payment of the one-year option on the rights," along with copies of the signed option agreement and purchase agreement. On 5 June 1985, Lear and his associates renewed a one-year option on *Joshua*, paying $15,000. He said at that time that they were waiting for some expected funds "from our financial partners."[7] The options continued to be renewed. Maurine was kept in a state of anticipation. By 1988, she had received $53,626.11.[8]

In 1988 Van Wagenen came to St. George to start making arrangements to make the movie. For unknown reasons, he did not contact either Maurine or Carol Jensen who, by then, was Maurine's legal guardian. It seems that Robert Redford had long been aware of the book and its great possibilities as an epic, had wanted to direct it, and apparently felt that it needed major financing and presentation as a Hollywood extravaganza to achieve its full success.[9] It was the opinion of Carol and Maurine—and also of Tom Lefler, Van Wagenen's employee—that Redford and Van Wagenen had been on friendly terms to this point, cooperating on various projects for several years. However, when Redford found out about Van Wagnenen's plans to produce *The Giant Joshua*—either because he felt possessive about the project or because he disagreed with the scale which Van Wagenen was envisioning—predicted that the Texas[10] backers would lose their investment because the results would not be commercially viable. The backers withdrew and the project folded, over a hundred thousand dollars in debt.[11]

That collapse must have occurred shortly after the Van Wagenen people were in St. George in 1988 to start arrangements to begin the movie. The project has been in limbo ever since. Sterling Van Wagenen helped organize Leucadia Film Corporation[12] in 1989. In May 1991, he asked Tom Lefler, who worked for him, to have Carol Jensen and Maurine sign a short form of the contract, which he would deposit with the copyrights department of the Library of Congress to show that the Martin Gray Company owned the film rights outright. After crossing out the words "play production" (live dramatization), which had not been in the original contract, Maurine and Carol signed on 12 May 1991. I was present. It was our understanding, after listening to Tom Lefler, that Leucadia could not proceed with the filming until Van Wagenen raised enough money to pay the original Texas investors what they had lost.

However, interviewed in 1995, Van Wagenen was still enthusiastic about the project: "[*The Giant Joshua*] is one of the few things out of Mormon culture that has a story to tell. . . . You have a conflict between faith and spontaneity, between God and life." The reporter added: "It's a story that has resonance for Sterling, but it's also a story he wishes weren't resolved by killing off Clory, the main character."[13]

Maurine remained interested in the movie project; but she no longer wavered between soaring hopes and crushing disappointments. However, I noticed that when Carol and I took her for car rides in 1990–92, she kept a keen eye out for possible shooting locations. And always, she was upset when housing developments crept over the black hill west of town. She just couldn't see how the movie could be made without that landmark. She had strong feelings about keeping the film authentic, and probably anyone who worked with her could quickly tell that she would be an intrusive presence in the project. Possessive authors would be nothing new on a Hollywood lot, so Maurine's sometimes prickly personality cannot account for the fact that *Joshua* failed to make it to the screen while she was alive (and still has not succeeded). Perhaps the problem lies in difficulties about the explosive mix of pioneer polygamy and pioneer religion that would have to be woven into the script.

As Maurine waited for something more positive to happen, old friends continued to die. Her trusted correspondent, Rev. Clayton S. Rice, who had written to her supportively and sympathetically for thirty years— from approximately 1942 to 1973—died 7 November 1973, a few hours after he cast his ballot in a national election, according to a letter from his son.[14] He would have turned eighty-nine at the end of the month. His hobby was hunting and polishing rocks, and he had given Maurine many pieces of jewelry he had made. Maurine gave some to friends but kept the most treasured. She says they were stolen when her home was burglarized in 1971.

Maurine's brother Ray died December 16, 1976. Maurine told me that a wall had been building between them for a long time. "Ray couldn't understand me any better than Papa did," she said, but still, she mourned. She often told me that she felt Ray was the "best one in the family." A few years before his death, an accident with a band saw took off his little finger and ended his banjo-playing, one of the greatest sources of enjoyment in his life. Nor did his death bring Maurine closer to Ray's family. According to Carol Ann, "Aunt Rene decided that she and Mom should move in together. Mother is a very 'on her own' person anyway and would never have been happy moving in with anyone, especially Aunt Rene. My aunt's persistence created a rift between them that never did heal. There was a choice there: either live Aunt Rene's life or her own life. Mother chose her own."[15]

Florence, nine years Maurine's junior, had become ill with cancer and died 14 July 1979 at age sixty-seven. Maurine told me that it didn't seem fair. She had always been the sickly one; now she seemed useless, only a burden. Even though Florence, to keep peace in her own family, had eventually told Maurine to come visit her only when invited and spelled out that those invitations could not be frequent, she was still someone whom Maurine trusted to love her. Maurine's explanation of Ben's distant attitude was: "No man likes to think some woman like me helped him." Ironically, she could not see that neither men nor women like to be reminded so often to be grateful, and Maurine was one to not only remind but even to exaggerate her contribution.

Florence's daughter, Colleen, and Ray's daughter, Carol Ann, were always kind to Maurine and as helpful as they could be, but they did not live nearby and were busy with young families. They cannot be blamed for not doing more. It was a matter of self-preservation.

Only Maurine and George were left, and he was drunk most the time. Still, Maurine clung to him. Edna Greggerson told me in a 1992 interview at her home in St. George a short time before she, too, died of cancer, that when Maurine should have been working on her bicentennial projects, she was often out pleading for someone to help George. Edna knew the worth of *The Giant Joshua*, believed that "The Candles of the Lord" would contribute to the success of the bicentennial celebration, and longed for Maurine to finish "Unpromised Land." When the bicentennial committee asked her to help Maurine, Maurine would not let her. She only wanted Edna and her husband to give George a job. They, like most, knew George was beyond help. But Maurine could not see it. Finally, George died on 13 March 1981 at age sixty-six. Maurine had gone many extra miles for him. As she told me the story, she found him that last time huddled on a pile of rags in the abandoned Liberty Hotel where derelicts hung out. He had pawned all of his clothes, except for what he was actually wearing, for a last bottle. She got him admitted to the hospital and tried to "reach through" to him. But he had given up. Mary Phoenix told me that Maurine arranged for a graveside service,[16] then said she was "just too tired, ill and heart sick to go." "Why wouldn't he fight to live?" she asked Mary more than once.[17]

Maurine's relationship with her loyal friend Lillian apparently had frayed away, too. The last letter from Lillian in Maurine's papers is dated 7 June 1964. Lillian, who was buying a copy of the paperback edition of *Joshua* for a friend, invited Maurine to come for a visit and check out possible outlets for the book. She concluded, "Meanwhile, all is well, really.[18] Lillian died in October 1981 in North Sacramento, California. It is not clear if Maurine even knew about her death.

After decades of suffering spells of ill health, Maurine during the 1970s had continued the pattern.[19] In early December 1973, she wrote to a friend, "When I walked into my house, I tripped, fell, and fractured five ribs! . . . I'm mending beautifully."[20] In the spring of 1974, she returned from a trip to the Canyonlands and spent the next three days in bed, although it's not clear whether she was injured or just tired.[21]

In September 1977, Maurine mentioned to a correspondent that she had been in Salt Lake City for her "very difficult surgery." In the same letter, she mentions having "to borrow so much from Sam [Weller] because of my surgeries." This sounds as if she is referring to more than the hip surgery, which would have been eighteen months earlier, nor does it explain what other surgeries were involved.[22] In December 1978, a correspondent expressed hope "that you are now recovering well from your accident." It is not clear what accident this would have been.[23]

Soon after George's funeral in 1981, she fell again and thereafter was unable to care for herself. She went to Santa Clara, a few miles away, where she lived with Patricia (Patsy) Dorothy Kear Montano, a state-authorized foster parent for youth and adults. Patsy was fun. She apparently took Maurine to see Bryce Chamberlain of Harvest Productions give his acclaimed one-man presentation on Joseph Smith. Maurine, impressed, wrote him what must have been a fan letter, to which she added a lengthy list of her many problems. He responded in January 1982, encouraging her: "You are too noble a person to let the meager trials of life interfere with greatness."[24]

A month before Maurine's eightieth birthday, she was featured in a long article in the *Spectrum*. The reason for the story was that Robert Shepherd, an artist, had donated a painting of Maurine as a local author to the Dixie College Library, and the story ran with a photograph of the painting and the library director, Delmar Gott. Maurine was simultaneously eccentric and charming, telling the reporter, with a straight face, that she was only sixty-seven. She claimed she was working on "a historical fiction about the Mormons settling Utah, entitled *The Impossible Land*," which sounds as if she has confused the sequel with her nonfiction "*Unpromised* Land." She also described a "completed manuscript": "a historical fiction on the Beaver Dam Wash and the towns established there." This sounds as if she had forgotten that "Beaver Dam Wash," which had assured her entry to the 1937 writers' conference, had been lost. She summarized, "A book, if it's a good book—is like a mirror, you get out of it what you put into it."[25]

It is difficult to understand Maurine's living arrangements or what happened next. Apparently she had her debilitating fall in late 1982 or early

1983. Patsy soon moved herself and three young daughters into Maurine's home; and on 20 April 1983, Maurine signed a warranty deed conveying her home to Patsy for ten dollars.[26] The house was reportedly worth between $35,000 and $38,000. Maurine's shaky signature is almost unreadable.

Mary Phoenix, who lived a few blocks away on Diagonal Street remembered, "Patsy was a likable person and Maurine was desperate for a situation that felt like family. She seemed to like the girls, especially the little one, about six. Patsy enjoyed doing crazy things just for the heck of it and Maurine was so desperate for love and care. They sometimes acted like two young girls, doing things like wearing crazy hats and going for long rides."[27] Apparently the state authorities who provided supervision for Patsy as a licensed care giver approved Maurine's arrangement with Patsy.

Patsy probably meant to make her life work caring for old people in exchange for whatever the person still owned. A month after getting possession of Maurine's house, on 24 May 1983 she "subordinated" (the document's word) Maurine's home to the Bank of Iron County to buy a property for $44,887.47 at 66 S. 400 West in LaVerkin, Utah, approximately twenty-five miles from St. George. It was a larger house where she could care for more people.

Maurine's home was rented with most of her possessions in it; when the renters moved out, it was left vacant and was burglarized and vandalized, probably more than once. No one knows what happened to her mother's dishes or other keepsakes. Papers were scattered and left where they were damaged by weather and animals.

Judy Gubler and her husband, Austin Gubler, who lived next door to Patsy's house in LaVerkin, once looked at Maurine's home at 410 North 600 East in St. George when they were house-hunting.[28] She said, her consternation still obvious after the passage of ten years: "Oh it was so terrible what had been allowed to happen to the place. Windows broken, doors kicked in, Maurine's belongings strung all over the house in terrible disarray—books trampled, pages torn out. There were many, many books, a lot of Church books. I was surprised. Then there was something like molasses poured over things. It was a mess. Maurine had a lot of nice things just ruined. It was so sad!"

The home was torn down in approximately 1985 and a new one was constructed on the site. Judy thought Maurine's home had once been nice enough—"small, but the lot was great, a lot of nice trees and plants. Of course, it was all overgrown and neglected when we saw it."

Judy said she understood that "Patsy and her children had lived with Maurine for a while in the St. George house, that the shed, covered with tin, had been fixed up for the girls. That was probably how she got control of the house. She could be fun, could have made Maurine feel she had a family."

In the fall of 1983, a "guardian angel" stepped in. Carol Jean Jensen, a nurse at the Dixie Regional Medical Center who took care of Maurine when others avoided her, volunteered to become her legal guardian. Her appointment was confirmed on 21 September 1983, by the Fifth Judicial District Court in Washington County.

The story of Carol Jean Lamborn Jensen Hallstrom Becker could rival Maurine's for dramatic twists and turns. She was born 22 December 1926 in Salt Lake City, the eldest daughter of Mabel LaVerne Black Lamborn and Willard Owen Lamborn. She married Earl Larsen Jensen on 18 July 1946 in Ogden, Utah, with the marriage later solemnized in the Logan Temple. Before Earl and Carol became involved with Ervil LeBaron's brand of Mormonism, Earl spent two years as a diplomat for the State Department at the American embassy in Tel Aviv, Israel. Carol did much entertaining of local and visiting dignitaries. They left the Middle East in the early 1950s.

According to her family, "She was a seeker of truth during her entire lifetime, inspiring her children and many students with her teaching as well as by example. Carol remained true to her belief in the gospel of Jesus Christ and the principles set forth by the prophet Joseph Smith." Because of her and Earl's "commitment to the gospel," she accompanied him to Colonia LeBaron, in Chihuahua, Mexico, where he became presiding bishop of the Church of the Firstborn, and married five plural wives. Carol was "the closest thing to a doctor" in the colony. Never asking for payment, she served as midwife, delivering many babies and "stitch[ing] up many a wound." As a Sunday School teacher, she instilled a love of Book of Mormon stories in her pupils because of her gift for "storytelling in a meaningful and memorable way. She had a passion for the dramatic arts, especially the works of Shakespeare, and directed many plays, including a play she both wrote, directed and acted (as Portia) entitled 'Shakespeare's Ladies.' She emphasized the importance of reading good literature to her family and instilled a special sensitivity to great music as well. She also gave piano lessons with no compensation to anyone who desired to learn to play."

During the period when Earl had other wives and children, Carol taught school in southern California for several years to help support them. She also cared for her parents during their latter years in Ogden, Utah, and while there obtained a nursing degree from Weber State College.

Under the leadership of Ervil LeBaron, the group eventually became violent.[29] Earl and Carol "escaped" from the group, and Earl died soon thereafter on 6 June 1975. Because Carol was on LeBaron's "hit list" (his disciples murdered another individual on that list—rival polygamous leader Rulon Allred in Murray, Utah), she kept a low profile in St. George. In 1984, she married Floyd Hallstrom. They were divorced but then remarried in 1995. Floyd was killed in an airplane accident a few weeks after their second wedding. The following year, she married William Becker.

When I asked her why she felt motivated to care for Maurine, with all of her own difficulties, Carol explained in her gentle way, "I needed to be involved in something that felt 'Christian,' and Maurine needed a friend, a true friend."

After Carol accepted the guardianship in 1983 for Maurine, the first thing she did, with Maurine's consent, was to call Brigham Young University to come and collect what was left of Maurine's papers. Dennis Rowley, curator of manuscripts, wasted no time. Carol and Maurine signed the transfer papers on 19 September 1983, two days before Carol's appointment became official. Rowley swept through the house putting anything paper into forty-two boxes—everything from pantyhose wrappers to scattered pages from the *Joshua* sequel.

The legal situation for Maurine was a difficult one. If Maurine left the house at LaVerkin, which had been purchased with the money from her St. George house, then she might jeopardize her right to reclaim any of it. So from the summer of 1983 until the fall of 1896, Maurine stayed in a situation that continued to slowly deteriorate while Carol struggled to gain the facts, watched, helped where she could, and tried to take appropriate legal action to safeguard Maurine's investment.

The situation in LaVerkin was far from ideal. My source of information was Judy Gubler, the next-door neighbor. Judy remembers that the community was concerned about conditions there and more than one town council meeting discussed it. She and Austin didn't think Maurine was fed properly. Her hair was often not combed, and her clothes were shabby and old. Judy remembered that Maurine once came to church in an outdated green suit, her hair unkempt. Judy and her husband had looked at this house, too, considering whether to buy it, and had quickly decided against it: "It had been build hodge-podge by a Mr. [Arthur G.] Wilcock. The wiring was a mess, one line, very unsafe." Besides, she said, "Patsy wouldn't answer any questions about price or anything. She would sort of close her eyes when we'd ask about that house and especially about Maurine's home in St. George. How she ever got permission to be a care-giver, I don't know. Requirements to run a home like this said each person needed their own room, so Patsy had hung partitions, using old sheets and such. It was a mess. The bathrooms were inadequate, the kitchen dirty. Patsy had three daughters, one in elementary school, and the two oldest ages about fourteen and fifteen. The oldest one left, couldn't stand it, I guess," noted Judy. "These girls were disrespectful to the old people." The seven-year-old was different: "Maurine was so sweet with her. And the poor little thing needed love."

There were five adults for whom Patsy was responsible in addition to Maurine. A woman named Mary had "brain damage," an "older lady in a wheelchair, and an old man and woman who were married." The fifth one, Elizabeth Schiavo, was a retarded woman who owned a baby grand piano, and would improvise by the hour, particularly the classics. Maurine greatly enjoyed the music and Elizabeth's flowing, creative performance style, including many elaborate flourishes. Maurine was very accepting of people like Elizabeth, perhaps sensing they had some unusual talent that could not find a proper outlet in the world of "normal" people. According to Carol's understanding, Elizabeth's family had placed her in the home, using some of her $50,000 inheritance to assure her care.

Judy's husband, Austin, then in poor health (now deceased), spent a lot of time sitting on a bench in front of the house and frequently visited with Maurine. He reported that sometimes Maurine was "befuddled." But when Austin's older relative, Grant Gubler from St. George, came to visit and also talked with Maurine, he said she was "just as sharp as ever" and would be all right if she only had good care. There were several cats in the house, one of them a white cat with one blue eye and one green eye that belonged to Maurine. Talking to these cats and stroking them "seemed to be one of the bright spots in her life." Judy said Austin and others often expressed regret and sadness that "such a brilliant women as Maurine had been reduced to such circumstances." Then Patsy announced she was married, Judy recalled. "She was showing off this big—I mean, so big—diamond ring. Then they left. I never knew what happened."

Doris Nina George took over as the owner of the house, buying the lot and house from the Bank of Iron County on 11 February 1986, for $45,000. As part of the arrangement, also taken over from Patsy, she assumed a $23,000 promissory note secured by a trust deed on the property, owed to the house's original builders, Arthur G. and Lenna C. Wilcock.

Nina was a former Baptist and a religious zealot. A retired schoolteacher from California, she evidently saw the house as a place for her "ministry," and Patsy definitely needed help in coping. As can be deduced, Patsy resembled Maurine in that she lacked the skills to maintain an even course through the real world. However, one reason Patsy could have had for leaving so quickly was a notice from the Washington County Recorder's office informing her that on "31 January 1969 Maurine had signed a Public Welfare Lien Agreement on her home in the amount of $5,939. This was for assistance until 1973. No other monies had been added since that date. Because of the change of deed, "the lien was due and payable" and ordered Patsy to make arrangements to take care of the obligation within two weeks.³⁰

Furthermore, on 8 July 1982, Maurine (and hence Patsy) received word that, effective 1 August 1982, Maurine's food stamp portion would be reduced. The certification date for food stamps would end March 1983 and the amount allotted was $10.00. This was based on the latest information they had, which was a reported income of $65.³¹ On 18 March 1983 came word from Medicare, Health Care Financing Administration, telling Maurine that the State Public Assistance Agency had stopped paying her medical insurance premiums. If Maurine were well enough to understand that, it would have caused her great concern. Furthermore, in July 1983, the state health department sent Maurine a second notice that she had high blood pressure and reminded her she had still not responded to the first notification.³² Obviously, caring for Maurine was going to become increasingly expensive and challenging, although it is not clear what arrangement Patsy had with the welfare office.

Nina may have been more conscientious about caring physically for her charges, but Maurine was very unhappy with the situation. She told Judy that she "would never have had anything do with someone like Nina, who was about as far from understanding what I was about as anyone could be. Besides she was no fun." Furthermore, Maurine maintained that "the LaVerkin house was haunted." Judy ended her reminiscences with a touching memory: "Once I went to the house in LaVerkin, heard the piano being played and peeked in the window. There was Maurine sitting at this brown baby grand piano. She was playing such sweet music. She looked relaxed, as if the pain was gone, her eyes soft and sweet. I just watched and never did disturb her." Could Judy be remembering correctly? She is positive that it was Maurine at the keyboard, even though Carol is sure that Maurine didn't play the piano and that the piano was Elizabeth's. But was Maurine letting her hands fantasize over the keys? She had had some lessons as a girl and always said she would have traded her talent for writing for a musical talent any day.

Judy also wanted it known how much she loved *The Giant Joshua*. "You know I'm not from here," she told me. "I didn't want to come here to live. We moved because of my husband's health, but I read that book and it made me want to love the place and the people. It really helped me. I've read it three times and it's about time to read it again. You know when I first moved to LaVerkin I went to the Hurricane library to get the book, and an older woman working there said 'Oh, we don't carry anti-Mormon books.' So I had to get it in St. George. I want a copy of my own."³³

Things fell completely apart for Maurine the next year. Nina's religiousness proved to be her weak spot; and when a LaVerkin man named

Wilferd W. Pectol of LaVerkin told Nina "that her name had been given to him in a revelation and that he felt God had a mission and a work for them to perform," she believed him. Wilferd and his wife, Joni M. Pectol, took over the monthly payments to the Wilcockses, and considered that they owned the house. In late May 1987, Nina filed a lawsuit to regain possession.

It had been almost approximately two years of pure misery for Maurine. A fragment found in Maurine's papers could have been written by her during this difficult period; and if she had been younger, very possibly she would have stayed to fight for justice:

> So my newest manuscript is stolen? So I am broke? So the books I would write are vanished like the past? I have learned something. I have launched myself on faith like a springboard into the dark. For now I know that it all scales down to the individual. I can't ask John Doe to do what I won't do! Every time there is a wrong, I have to *speak up*, no matter the cost. Falling down but getting up! Sure there are people who so resist self-knowledge that they must be dragged kicking and screaming into the 20th century! But I don't have to be one of them.[34]

Maurine wrote an unhappy letter to her niece, Carol Ann Anderson, in Canada. She probably thought she had mailed it, but it was found in her desk. Maurine described herself as "vegetating—eating and sleeping but not *working*. I still owe a book to *Simon and Schuster* in New York, but I can't write it here. My little house in St. George is gone. I can't even bear to write about it yet." She expressed her love several times, then resolved, "I'm going to try to leave here before long—but don't know yet where to. I just have to get away. I have to *work*. I'll let you know how it all works out."[35]

She also wrote a desperate nine-page letter on a yellow legal pad, pleading with Carol to get her out of the LaVerkin house. The writing shows great stress and is hard to read, in contrast to her usual rounded, flowing hand. Again, she left it in her desk and never mailed it. In this letter, however, she described intolerable conditions. It was noisy. The only air conditioning was in Nina's rooms. The food did not agree with her finicky colon. It took a long time to fill a bathtub, because the water ran at a trickle and then, likely as not, someone else would take it. She couldn't work. She didn't know how to fight to get her home back or any money, and she didn't understand how she had lost it. Her confusion is as painful as her bereavement.

Worse was to come. The one person in the house whom Maurine enjoyed, Elizabeth Schiavo, was killed in a freak accident during the winter of 1984–85. She had gone out walking and was carrying a giant tumbleweed. Unable to see her, a truck hit and killed her. Nina had to identify the body, and this may have been one reason why she was so adamant that Maurine could not go for walks off the property.

Maurine was sad and very shaken over losing this one friend. Although she had not been able to write anything for a long time, she spoke at Elizabeth's funeral, quoting two poems.[36] It is not clear whether she or someone else was the author. The first one, "Not Understood," ended its seventh verse with:

> Oh! God, that men would see a little clearer
> Or judge less harshly when they cannot see,
> Oh! God, that men would move a little nearer
> To one another. They'd be nearer thee
>   And understood.
>   And understood.

From the markings on the paper, it seems that she had musical accompaniment as she read this one. The second one was titled "To Elizabeth, with Love":

> You were one who held out your arms to life
> And warmed your hands at its rising sun:
> So that when you grew old, and blind,
> The radiance did not forsake you
> But lived on in laughter.
>
> And now, even now my dear, dear friend,
> Now that they say you are dead—
> I perceive your essence still luminous
> In an afterglow
> That shall brighten my heart forever.

Loren Webb, a staff writer for the *Spectrum*, did an article that attempted to sort out the arrangement in LaVerkin involving Maurine. It was too tangled for even the experts. He quoted Maurine as saying she "felt like she was being kept there as a prisoner."[37]

Finally, Carol Jensen, too, had had enough of trying to wade through the tangle. Claim on equity in the house resolved or not, she decided to move Maurine out. Before she could, Maurine ran away, catching a ride with an older couple. Carol says that she went to a halfway house; but according to the *Spectrum* report on the lawsuit, she was back in the house during at least part of the conflict between Nina and the Pectols.

Carol and her husband, Floyd, made arrangements on 14 June 1984 to move Maurine into Meadows Retirement Community at 950 South 400 East in St. George. Floyd paid the expenses until they could sort out Maurine's finances. They also helped her recover as many possessions as possible. Anything of much value was gone. She still had an old green couch and the desk her father had made. Floyd and Carol bought a good bed and made arrangements for Maurine to have her precious white cat with her.

In 1992 I made arrangements to interview Doris Nina George. She was then living on the desert near Colorado City, Arizona, and still saw herself as on a mission from God. I, too, soon decided the situation was far too complicated for easy understanding and left without gathering meaningful facts.

The first Van Wagenen-Lear movie option came through on June 14, 1984—just in the nick of time. It paid for Maurine's stay at the Meadows and financed enough legal investigation to convince Carol that pursuing money from the LaVerkin house would be too time-consuming and expensive. Maurine stayed at the Meadows until 16 May 1989, approximately five years; and during that time, she regained her dignity and much of her ability to enjoy life. Here Maurine had housekeeping help, a nurse if needed,[38] rides to the grocery store and other places, and her beloved cat. Maurine liked living at the Meadows. The management seemed to understand her and catered to her "writing schedule," which was the reason she gave for having her meals brought to her instead of taking them in the dining room with the other residents. Most importantly, she had Carol, a kind and sisterly presence in her life. (Carol was more than twenty years Maurine's junior, but Maurine, always eager to claim a more youthful age, compared her to a sister, not a daughter.) Carol brought Maurine to her home for each holiday celebration, and Maurine rapidly endeared herself to Carol's children and grandchildren.

What Maurine didn't do was write. She still saw herself and talked about herself as creating all the time. "It's in my head," she would say. "Whole pages of conversation are in my head." Then she would admit, "I'm just not up to writing them down anymore," frequently with the implication that she might be tomorrow. In truth, it was too late. Carol provided a stack of yellow legal pads and offered to help in any way she could. But Maurine always had some excuse not to get started. Even if she had had the notes and historical research, now at BYU, it would have been difficult for her to pick up the threads again. But much of the time she was happy. She told an interviewer: "Life interests me terrifically. Just life, just living. Everyday interests me. I've never gotten over that—just liking living, you know, and I have always done things. . . . I am in love with living."[39] One can label such an attitude a blessing, as far as living goes, but for a writer who needs to concentrate on one thing at a time, being fascinated by everything can be a disadvantage.

On 24 March 1989, the rent at the Meadows was raised. The $53,626 from the movie options was nearly gone. Carol took the last of it, bought a funeral plan, and arranged for Maurine to have a private room at the county St. George Care Center. Once again, thanks to Carol's negotiating skills, the management understood that Maurine was "special." Carol arranged her room to be private and as comfortable as possible with a bookcase and the Robert Shepherd painting of the Joshua tree. The green couch and the desk Charlie had built for her were put in storage.

By this time, the eighty-six-year-old Maurine would have been willing to spend much of each day in bed; but Carol knew that activity was important. Almost every day, she got her up and dressed and often took her someplace. Terrill Clove, the assistant director, admired Maurine's writing and took a special interest in her. He occasionally took her home to meet with his family and said "she charmed my children."[40]

Maurine's last publication was a letter to the editor in the *Spectrum*. Unlike her lengthy and indignant letters of the late 1960s, this was a thank you to Glenwood Humphries, a local policeman, who had heard that she wanted some Santa Clara molasses and had gone out of his way to get it for her.[41]

The last articles about Maurine during her lifetime, appeared in the *Spectrum* in the summer of 1989. After a summary of *The Giant Joshua*, it concludes:

> In an interview with Kaylene Preston, co-owner of the R&K Bookstore in the City Center, I learned that sales of the book are steady and fairly brisk.
>
> "People drive in off the freeway and are surprised and delighted to find the book," she said. "The bookstore clerks have told me that many local people buy the book, having lost or given away their original copies. And there's never any hint of the original controversy. All that has faded away."
>
> These sales do not benefit Maurine Whipple financially. When the book went out of print some years ago, the owners of Western Epics, Inc., of Salt Lake City, bought the rights from her. Before she left The Meadows, she said again and again, "I've got to make some money," hinting of a sequel.
>
> Rumors persist that "someone" is going to make a movie of JOSHUA, but so far there has been nothing concrete. It would make a magnificent motion picture, filled as it is with vivid scenes and memorable characters. As a television series it would be a blockbuster.
>
> The winds of change have wrought wonders in St. George and Washington County. What once seemed a hostile environment, today lures tourists and winter residents. But the original Dixie, harsh and dramatic, can never die, thanks to the literary genius of one of Dixie's own—Maurine Whipple.[42]

Maurine and her writings have provoked a wide range of reactions over the years. Some saw as negative the traits that have made it so difficult for her to be accepted by those close to her. Others saw some of those same traits as, perhaps, the reason for her greatness. From my observations, it is the younger generation, those in their thirties, who seem to be drawn to her now, especially men. Perhaps with all the male-directed anger from feminists, they feel understanding from Maurine, who attempted to incorporate understanding of the masculine condition, along with sympathy for the plight of women. For instance, Abijah is depicted as a man torn between his carnal nature, his need to be in control, and his desire to love simply and wholly.

One of those male admirers was Curtis Taylor, writer, editor and publisher, who encouraged the writing of this biography. When he came across and read his father's copy of *The Giant Joshua*, he was so struck by its writing that he, an aspiring writer, arranged to meet Maurine in January 1989. He thought it was significant that he met her the day after the Quail Reservoir broke and washed away most traces of the pioneer spillway that had seemed such a miracle to Maurine. He tape-recorded his impressions and conversations with her during their two-day visit.

He also called her "somewhat innocent" and having within her something "vastly childlike, deeply, anciently childlike. For example, whether people were living or dead, she not only doesn't know, but she doesn't care that much. She speaks of them all in the present tense."

He concluded: "I think in many ways Maurine Whipple was born far beyond most of mankind. She is a lost and chosen soul. I love her, I love her work, but I especially love her. I hope that I can be as honest, as true, as benevolent as she is."[43]

Another young man deeply affected by Maurine's work is Michael Austin, who in 1996 was finishing his Ph.D. in English.[44] He told me that, until he read *The Giant Joshua*, he didn't think there was Mormon literature worthy a serious literary critic's time. Later, the novel came up on the Association for Mormon Letters talk list and spurred an energetic discussion. Michael vigorously defended JOSHUA: "After reading THE GIANT JOSHUA, I felt a great deal of pride and connection to my Mormon heritage. I also felt gratified that someone from my religious tradition could create such a moving portrait of human experience. Had it not been for this book, I would never have begun to explore the possibilities of 'Mormon Literature' and become involved with the AML."[45]

In April 1991, Grant T. Smith, then a doctoral candidate and now teaching at Viterbo College in La Crosse, Wisconsin, read a paper on Maurine's work at the Washington, D.C., Sunstone Symposium: "As a feminist critic, I hope to show how the novel [*The Giant Joshua*] can be read to be in complete harmony with traditional Mormon thought, scripture and practice, and how it does indeed reflect an authentic Mormon doctrine." Smith saw the novel as interpreting the failure of the Zion community because "the members are unable to move beyond a masculine vision of self, nature and community which values aggression more than cooperation, exploitation more than harmony and a competitive economy more than the bishop's storehouse."[46]

One of the steps that Curtis Taylor took as a result of meeting Maurine was to encourage her to go to the temple. He sensed her as so profoundly Mormon that the omission of this rite, the most sacred in Mormon theology, struck him as fundamentally off-balance.[47] While he was encouraging Maurine to take this step, Carol's granddaughter, Tabeetha Moesinger, an outstanding young woman, asked Maurine to go to the temple with her before she left for her cadet's appointment at Annapolis. Richard Wilson, bishop of the ward in whose boundaries the Meadows stood, and Tabeetha seemed to have an intuitive sense about how to communicate with Maurine on a level she could understand and accept.

Tabeetha reported this experience to me in an email on 9 April 2001:

> When it came time to go through the veil, I told her I would go first and wait for her. I went, and I asked the sister temple worker to help push Maurine's wheel chair. When she parted the curtain with one of her hands, she was weeping; she flung her arms open so wide and smiled at me with tears streaming down both sides of her face. She wanted to be hugged and held, and I bent over (almost knelt) and she continued to cling to me and weep for what seemed like a couple of minutes. We stayed in the celestial room for only a few minutes after that.
>
> I will tell you that she seemed to make light of the process taking so long, but I know she was there for the right reasons. I truly believe she had accepted many things in her life for which her family never gave her credit. She had come to terms with her mortality, she felt that life is fragile, and I believe in her heart she wanted to please her parents/grandparents and show them that she had not "strayed too far" from their flock. She truly wanted to belong. I really believe she loved her family, but their rejection and scorn were so painful to her that she built a fortress around herself. This was a defense mechanism, but it resulted in an unconquerable (true to her pioneer spirit & heritage) Mormon Pride. Goodness, she was stubborn!

A particularly significant moment in the temple occurred when Maurine saw the portrait of her grandfather, J. D. T. McAllister, hanging in one of the upstairs rooms. It reduced her to tears again.[48]

Soon after I started meeting with Maurine in 1990, Carol and I thought it would be nice to let her friends know that she was still alive and quite well, so we sent them a copy of the short story "The Christmas Dress," the manuscript of which Carol had found in a box that cats had been using for kitty litter. It had been stored in a back porch cupboard and thus had not been collected when Dennis Rowley gathered the rest of her papers for BYU. At that time, I didn't know Maurine had published it in the 1926 University of Utah literary magazine, then called *The Quill*. She had forgotten about it too. For the next Christmas, 1991, with encouragement from Carol and me, she dictated a letter that told of what had become of the story she had sent out last year: "Two young men, Curtis Taylor and Stan Zenk, said it gave them an idea. They asked all the other Utah writers to give a story or a poem to be compiled in a book called *Christmas for the World*, the profits of which will be contributed to Humanitarian International to help the children of Eastern Europe. I can't tell you how gratifying it is to be a part of an actual doing something with, what I call, 'The Grand Idea.'"[49]

Then she dictated another letter to send to the other authors who contributed stories, thanking them and expressing her gratitude: "My life has been tormented with the deep need to finish the full concept I had for *Joshua*. I tried too hard, driving friends and family away, because they couldn't understand my crazy need. And I just couldn't get it done." This was one of the few times she would admit that she wouldn't finish the trilogy.

She concluded the letter, using words similar to those of a quarter century earlier when she was trying to interest Charlie Steen in her work. Speaking to other writers she said: "For myself I believe the dream of brotherhood is possible. Had I written the sequel I wouldn't have attempted to answer the question of whether there can be a compromise or an alternative. But my characters, the grandchildren of Clory, would have seen all the world had to offer and come back to the ideals their forefathers reached for (yes, even as imperfectly as much of the actual reaching was—and that's what got me in trouble, wasn't it? that I insisted on writing with a pen that told the failings, too?)."[50]

As a final statement goes, this may be one of the best, capturing the essence of who Marine was. She clung to her vision of the Grand Idea throughout her life. It pervades her thinking, like the scent of bergamot that hovered about Clory in *The Giant Joshua*. It dominates and glorifies the groping human endeavors in *The Giant Joshua*. It returns in various guises in much of her unpublished work. It dominates the enthusiasms which swept through her adult life, explaining much its fragmentation. Simultaneously it helps to explain why she wrote so voluminously and compulsively, yet why she so seldom published. This, with her writing talent and her writer's orientation, also explains much of her paradoxical personality. Marred by streaks of vanity, great emotional need, and her vulnerability to exploitation, she often seemed a mystifying and somewhat alien individual to her family and townspeople, yet she could not find a way to function effectively in the larger national writing community, except for short periods of time. And so she struggled to remain in her beloved St. George, returning inevitably, sometimes even unwillingly, to a place that had tried irresistible idealism, her Grand Idea.

On 21 June 1991, novelist Marilyn Brown hosted a jubilee birthday party for *The Giant Joshua* at her home in Hobble Creek Canyon near Springville, Utah. Creative writers from the area came to the picnic and paid their respects to Maurine. On the four-hour drive up from St. George in my car, Carol and I grew tired of trying to convince Maurine it was going to be fun. She had the idea that it would be formal, with a receiving line. "I'll shake their hand, tell them it isn't easy being a writer, and encourage them with some little comment," she kept saying. We kept telling her it would be a picnic. "Well, why in heck did I buy that pretty purple dress then?" she wondered. Carol was always careful to see that Maurine presented herself well in public and had taken Maurine shopping at a point when Curtis Taylor had been talking about a reception.

Aside from her confusion about the picnic/reception, Maurine was delightful company, talking most of the way. I thought she would like a rest before the picnic began at 5:30, but she was too wound up. Curtis Taylor came a little early, and we talked about Sam Weller keeping the book in print. Curtis and Stan then owned Aspen Publishing, and Curtis would have liked to have republished the book himself; but Maurine said, as she had so many times, "Oh, Sam is my best friend. He just loves me. And I just love him. If I had another book, I'd give it to Sam." Sam had been unable to come to the picnic—an old friend whom Maurine did miss.

The party was a big success. About forty people attended, particularly writers and critics like Eugene England, Richard H. Cracroft, Don Marshall, Levi S. Peterson, Bruce W. Jorgensen, and Susan Evans McCloud. Marilyn had purchased an artbook of Western scenery, and all the guests signed it, many adding nice comments about Maurine and her writing. When Marilyn asked Maurine to read a story, she rose to the occasion magnificently, reading without even using her glasses. Marilyn had a sound system, and Carol held the microphone. The story was "They Did Go Forth," based on a folktale of the Three Nephites healing a baby and taking a freshly baked loaf of cornbread in a distinctive napkin to England to the missionary father, who had just prayed for food.[51]

The next morning, Marilyn videotaped Maurine reading a selection from *The Giant Joshua*. When the experience was over, Maurine thought it was "the most wonderful weekend of my life."

Maurine's final illness began in early April 1992 with a draining infection in her right ear. She was fretful and difficult, snapping at me and Carol. We tried to remain patient and loving. When I was alone with her, I happened to mention my Uncle Ray Tebbs reciting Shakespeare's *Hamlet*. I had been surprised and asked how he had come to memorize it. He told me he had had a high school teacher, Wyatt Walker Miles, who had greatly influenced his life. I recognized the name from talks I'd had with Maurine about her girlhood. Maurine's eyes lit up. Wyatt Walker Miles, the handsome older brother of her friend Katharine Miles Larson and nephew of her old friend Dr. Joseph Walker, had been her first infatuation. She wanted to know all I knew about Miles. I told her all my parents and uncle remembered. How handsome and always properly dressed he was. How he had become a doctor, after first teaching high school English in Panguitch, and then he came back to Panguitch to practice medicine. The first baby he had delivered was my brother. He had also saved my life when I was three years old. Maurine thought it meaningful that our lives were connected this way. She became very loving and would not let go of my hand. I needed to leave to attend a family dinner. It was Saturday, 4 April, and I switched on the broadcast of the LDS general conference for her. It was the last time I saw Maurine conscious.

By the next day, she was in a coma and had been transferred to the hospital. Carol thought it might be a reaction to the antibiotics, because something similar had happened before. We took turns sitting with her, talking to her, assuring her of our love.

As I held her hand, I remembered the first time I held it two and a half years earlier. It was a small, delicate hand to have battled so much alone! Her fingers were cold. She was breathing easily, eyes closed. But I knew she was slipping away. I examined her fingernails, making sure they were as neat as possible. Clory on her deathbed had wanted her nails to be clean. So would Maurine.

She died early in the morning on 12 April 1992, Palm Sunday, never having regained consciousness. Metcalf Mortuary, with whom Maurine had her funeral plan, donated her temple clothes. Bishop Wilson, who had facilitated her temple endowment, made the funeral arrangements. We all chuckled at a mistake on the funeral program, giving her birth year as 1906 instead of 1903. That's what Maurine herself would have done.

The funeral on 15 April was not large, attended by Dixie College President Douglas D. Alder, a few other old friends, and hospital staff. Curtis Taylor, Stan Zenk, and Marilyn Brown came from Provo. Curtis, Terrill

Clove, the bishop, and I spoke. Carol read Maurine's "Dream."⁵² Members of the Whipple family offered the prayers and eulogy and were pall bearers. Some expressed regret they couldn't have included Maurine more in their lives. But there was a feeling of understanding and cooperation.

The burial took place in the St. George Cemetery.⁵³ It was a peaceful farewell on a beautiful spring day.

Notes

¹ Richard H. Cracroft, Letter to Maurine Whipple, 4 December 1978. In 1993, Richard gave me Maurine's original letter and a photocopy of his reply. Maurine Whipple Collection, Archive, Val A. Browning Library, Dixie College, St. George, Utah; hereafter cited as Dixie College.

² Carol Jensen told me that she found the documentation of this thousand-dollar option purchase tucked into one of Maurine's books. She was astonished that Maurine had forgotten about it.

³ Sterling Wagenen went to UCF in August 1999 from Brigham Young University where he was an adjunct professor of film and the manager of the university's TV group. He has been in the independent film movement for over twenty years. He is co-founder of the Sundance Film Festival in association with Robert Redford, and the founding executive director of the Sundance Institute. http://www.ldsfilm.com/Leucadia/Leucadia.htm (accessed September 30, 2009).

⁴ The company's office was 19 Exchange Place, Salt Lake City, Utah 84111.

⁵ This information came from Tom Lefler, who was working for Van Wagenen and Brian Capener when I interviewed him on May 15, 1991. Brian Capener was associated with KBYU–TV and KBYU–Radio for several years, but I have no further information about him.

⁶ Carol J. Jensen signed this extension as executrix.

⁷ John M. Lear, president of Martin Gray Company, 19 Exchange Place, Salt Lake City, Utah 84111, Letter to Mrs. Carol Jensen, P.O. Box 323, LaVerkin, Utah 84745. Lear was an attorney.

⁸ The legal papers dealing with the movie rights are in the Whipple Collection, Dixie College.

⁹ Lefler, interview in St. George, May 15, 1991.

10 I assume they were from Texas, from references by Tom Lefler, Carol Jensen, and Maurine.

11 During May 1991 when Tom Lefler was in St. George on an errand for Sterling Van Wagenen to clarify a detail in the movie-rights contract, I was present during the talks. This is my conclusion, after listening to him tell me all he knew about the Whipple movie-rights deal.

12 Leucadia Film, a Utah corporation, was founded in 1989 with a commitment to make quality, feature-length films which could be enjoyed by the whole family. http://www.cinar.com/news-e/0208a99-e.htm (accessed 1998).

13 Daniel P. Sorensen, "My Lunch with Sterling Van Wagenen," *Utah Business*, July/August 1995, 68.

14 Clayton Rice (Rev. Rice's son, Letter to Maurine Whipple, (no day) November, 1973; Maurine Whipple Collection, L. Tom Perry Special Collections, Harold B. Lee Library, Brigham Young University, Provo, Utah (hereafter BYU). Documents in both collections are cited hereafter as BYU, photocopy Dixie College.

15 Carol [Ann Whipple] Anderson, Calgary, Alberta, Letter to Veda Hale, 11 November 2001.

16 George Whipple was born 7 January 1915 and died 13 March 1981, at St. George. The graveside service was held in the St. George City Cemetery, at 2:00 P.M., 18 March 1981, with David Clove, bishop of Seventeenth Ward, presiding. Forty-three people signed the guest book, which is at BYU.

17 Mary Phoenix, interviewed by Veda Hale, n.d.; notes in my possession.

18 Lillian McQuarrie, Letter to Maurine Whipple, 7 June 1964; BYU, photocopy Dixie College.

19 Jack [surname not given], 12742 Highwood St., Los Angeles 90049, Letter to Maurine Whipple, 9 January 1970; BYU, photocopy Dixie College.

20 Maurine Whipple, Letter to friends, Christmas 1973; BYU, photocopy Dixie College.

21 Inez S. Cooper, Special Collections Room, Library, Southern Utah State College, Cedar City, Utah, Letter to Maurine Whipple, 9 May 1974; BYU, photocopy Dixie College.

22 Maurine Whipple, Letter to Carol Lynn and Gerald Pearson, 10 September 1977; BYU, photocopy Dixie College.

23 Cracroft to Whipple, 4 December 1978.

24 S. Bryce Chamberlain, Harvest Productions, 121 West 1400 South, Orem, Utah 84057, Letter to Maurine Whipple, 410 West 600 North. St. George (her home address), 4 January 1981; BYU.

25 Loren Webb, "'The Giant Joshua'—A Legacy that Lives On," *Spectrum*, 20 December 1982, 6.

26 Deed, notarized by Debbie Weyburn, 20 April 1983, Dixie College Archive.

27 Mary Phoenix, Interviewed by Veda Hale, 10 June 1993.

28 Judy Sine Haskell Gubler, now married to Russell Farnsworth, lives in Hurricane, Utah. Interviewed by Veda Hale, 11 August 1991. Judy and I also had numer-

ous conversations. I made notes immediately after these visits but disposed of them after integrating them into the biography.

29 Scott Anderson, *4 O'Clock Murders: The True Story of a Mormon Family's Vengeance* (New York: Dell Publishing, 1993). Ervil LeBaron was apprehended, jailed, and awaiting trial when he died of an apparent heart attack 16 August 1981. He was fifty-six.

30 D. Winter, Investigator for Social Services, Washington Co. Recorder's Office, Letter to Patricia D. K. Montano, P.O. Box 468 LaVerkin, Utah 84745, n.d. (document damaged); BYU, photocopy Dixie College.

31 Letter damaged and first part unreadable, although the date of 8 July 1982 is visible; BYU.

32 Joan Ware, R.N., Director, Cardiovascular Disease/Hypertension Control Program, Bureau of Chronic Disease Control, Division of Community Health Services, Utah State Department of Health, Letter to Maurine Whipple, 13 July 1983; BYU.

33 Ibid.

34 Holograph fragment on lined notebook paper, in pen, Dixie College; emphasis hers. This sheet was found in Maurine's desk, which is now in the Heritage Room of Dixie College Library.

35 Ibid.

36 I deduce this from the fact that Elizabeth was killed in the winter of 1984 and that Maurine left soon after that.

37 Ibid.

38 Maurine's health had improved by 1986 to the point that the referring physician and the home nursing service determined she no longer needed them. Georga Ann Simkins, R.N., Director Nursing Service, Southwest Utah Home Health Agency, 180 North 200 East, #D. St. George, Utah, Letter to Maurine Whipple, 10 November 1986; BYU.

39 Maurine Whipple, Interviewed by Curtis Taylor, January 1989, tape and transcript in Charles L. Redd Center, Lee Library, Brigham Young University.

40 Terrill Clove, Interviewed by Veda Hale, 1992; notes in my possession.

41 Undated clipping from unidentified publication found in Maurine's desk after she died.

42 Jean R. Paulson, "History Lives On in Pages of Book," *Spectrum*, 10 July 1989, 6.

43 Curtis Taylor, tape-recorded recollections of his visit with Maurine Whipple, made January 1989, tape and transcript at the Charles Redd Center for Western History, Lee Library, Brigham Young University.

44 In 2006, he was dean of Graduate Studies, Shepherd University, Shepherdstown, West Virginia, and book review editor for *Dialogue: A Journal of Mormon Thought*.

45 Michael Austin, "Maurine Whipple," 19 November 1996, AML–List, print-out in my possession.

46 Grant T. Smith, paper delivered at the April 1991 Sunstone Symposium, Washington, D.C., photocopy in my possession.

47 Curtis told me that Maurine had told him she had once been asked to go on a mission but that Charlie discouraged it. She never mentioned this to me, to Carol, or to anyone else I have talked to.

48 Tabeetha Moesinger, email to Veda Hale, 9 April 2001.

⁴⁹ Maurine Whipple, Letter to authors, 1991, Dixie College.
⁵⁰ Ibid.
⁵¹ Gene England proposed the possibility of suggesting to *Sunstone* the publication of "A Dress for Christmas," to *Dialogue* "They Did Go Forth," and to the *Ensign* Maurine's poem "To My Child" with a comment on the fiftieth anniversary. He would also revise his article for publication. The *Ensign* declined, but "They Did Go Forth" appeared in *Dialogue* 24, no. 4 (Winter 1991): 165–72, and "A Dress for Christmas or Thou Shalt Love Thy Neighbor" appeared in *Sunstone* October 1991.

⁵² Larry Jolley offered the family prayer before the service began and Steve Jolley dedicated the grave. Yvonne Gentry played the prelude and postlude. Musical numbers were "Look Up to Him," "A Poor Wayfaring Man of Grief," and "How Great Thou Art" sung by Norlene Stephens, Maxine Winmill, and Marie Garrick, accompanied by Relva Winmill. Wayne Jolley gave the opening prayer and Jason Whipple gave the closing prayer. Colleen Haycock read the eulogy. The Twelfth Ward Relief Society provided a nice luncheon after the funeral.

⁵³ The tombstone is engraved with two Joshua trees and reads: "Maurine Whipple, THE GIANT JOSHUA, 1903–1992." The grave is located in the east cemetery block, about 100 feet north of Second South. Due to a miscalculation of space in the family plot, Maurine is buried near but not with other members of her family.

❦ Postscript ❦

Maurine took her last ride in April 1992. She did not want to go, complaining that it was just too hard to get dressed and get down the long hall to the car. But Carol insisted. "Kayenta is beautiful. You'll like seeing this wonderful house."

"But it's going to rain."

"You should enjoy that, Maurine," Carol pressed. "Maybe there will be a rainbow."

By the time we got to Santa Clara, it was a downpour the likes of which none of us—even Maurine—had ever seen. The roads were a running red river under the wheels of Carol's car Maurine was perched forward in the passenger seat, straining to see out. "Oh, turn around," she kept begging. It reminded her of the pioneers' first Christmas and the forty days of rain that washed away a year's work, causing a relocation of Santa Clara. Her vivid imagination put her there in 1861, as though she lived through the drenching and disasters of that earlier downpour.

But it also felt like an adventure. Carol kept reminding Maurine, "You always tell us how you like adventures!"

The car crawled along, water so deep in places it was like going through a pond. Would we get the sparkplugs wet, stalling the car? It *was* an adventure! I felt secure, however, knowing the worst that could happen would be sputtering to a stop and then waiting to be rescued. Even in the storm, the road was far from deserted. It was not cold. Spring, the rain, the grateful earth, no lightning—it was exhilarating.

There was much to talk about. Carol and I had brought Virginia, a new friend with us, a woman with her own unusual life story. Maurine was used to dominating the conversation; but after a few interruptions and after it became apparent that we were going on, she fell silent, listening to our talk.

We crawled along to Kayenta, the new subdivision of picturesque, desert-blended homes seven miles from St. George. Gray sheets of rain obscured the usually impressive red-mountain backdrop. We pulled into the driveway of Cynthia Lurton's home, and she raised the garage door for us.

Maurine cooperated as we helped her walk into the living room and positioned her by the fire before the picture window. Settled, she looked around and uttered one of her characteristic long sighs. It was a beautiful home, decorated with loving care and incorporating Cynthia's special interests and eagle totem. Representations of eagles appeared throughout the house and yard—wood carvings, ceramics, paintings, metal sculptures—that somehow blended so well that the unobservant might miss the emphasis. Interesting. How did she achieve that?

"Children love to go through the house, and count them," said Cynthia. "Gives them something to do."

Maurine understood. I had known she would like Cynthia.

Carol and Virginia plunged into an absorbing conversation with Cynthia. The books on the wall-long shelves were already mutual friends: parapsychology, religion, New Age, alternate healing, the classics.

From time to time, Maurine elbowed her way into the conversation, asserting who she was, what she had done. But her comments were about things too distant in time and sent ripples too weak to lap significantly against new ideas and what money and technology had done.

The downpour continued.

The talk moved gently back and forth from one exotic topic to another. The friendly fire in the elegant fireplace made us all feel secure and comfortable. I was not quite sure what was happening, but it was surely something. We, as a little group, polarized—Maurine and I were quiet, basking in the combination of fire warmth on our skins and the sluicing rain outside the window, the other three still excited to have discovered mutual interests, the house, the pictures, the eagles, the books.

Then, as typical of desert storms, the rain abruptly slowed, then stopped. We two watched a waterfall cascading down the red mountain. Truly, it was glorious—a view of God, raw and definite! Oh, to sit at a window with a view like that! Oh, to have one's physical comforts so artistically met! If Maurine had had these circumstances in her thirties, forties, and fifties, what other creative wonders could have been coaxed out? That's what I was thinking.

Then the view outside became so glorious it demanded attention from all. There was no rainbow from our perspective, but the sun was streaking through, pushing emphatic fingers into the cascading waterfalls and along rock walls. The window, placed to capture the red mountain at its breathtaking best in normal times, was framing a spectacle equaling any grandeur the world could offer. The water was gushing off the rock, not trickles, but energetic waterfalls sluicing the face, the body, the feet of the red mountain, redder even than the Sugarloaf. Scored with such vigorous momentum, it was making a new mountain, washing inches of old dirt down to the desert floor, giving crags and crannies new shadows.

"Can you see the 'Indian' on the wall of the mountain?" Cynthia asked. She explained where to look for the optical illusion. The others could all see it, but neither Maurine nor I had that shift in perception. We stayed quiet.

"I feel I was called here for a purpose," said the hostess. "To be the guardian of these red hills. To see the Indian there and be one with him in this guardianship." She told us that, on the day she arrived, a flying saucer hovered over the hill to the east and stayed there most of the day. She had taken a photograph of it and pointed out where it hung on her wall. We looked at it and wondered. Wasn't it just a cloud?

"And where are your people from?" Did I ask or did Maurine?

"Minnesota. All my people are in Minnesota."

Minnesota? Minnesota! Maurine and I looked at each other. Could someone from Minnesota be the guardian of these red hills? We looked around the elegant house. Does it now take all this and a "foreign" heart for that guardianship? Maurine sighed deeply but was silent.

Not until later did I realize that I had missed something important, missed it as I had missed the Indian on the mountain's face. Cynthia was divorced, severely challenged by rheumatoid arthritis. What else in her life had caused her to make such a sharp break with her past? Suffering? There must have been much. But her spirit was not beaten. She had fought back with everything one could imagine, physical and spiritual, and had come to this land to make a new beginning for herself. She had the same kind of "hard-guttedness" and determination to make the spirit triumph that Maurine celebrated. Suffering, courage, struggle, and a spiritual goal—were these the initiatory criteria that made one a guardian of these southern Utah red mountains?

The perception expanded. The heavy, unusual rain had, indeed, uncovered a new surface for these hills, mountains, deserts. They were never meant to be "claimed" by time or by anyone's blood—Indian or Mormon pioneer.

Maurine and her Grand Idea, I thought. Can your work and mine—can this biography somehow help that Grand Idea of love and brotherhood, like an eagle, fly over this new earth, this new time, over and around new people? I knew we both wanted it to be so.

No, these newcomers could not know what it is like to see the temple and to also see a great-great-grandfather, tools beside him in an unfinished room, taking an afternoon nap in the heat. Or see around the metal ball on the tabernacle steeple a scaffold and the son of the tinsmith showing off with a handstand and knowing he got a scolding from his father, another great-great-grandfather. Or drive by Ancestor Square and remember how, from there, years ago, a little brown-eyed girl, a beauty the Indians admired, had been stolen and then retrieved two days later by a mild, unaggressive but determined father, retrieved and returned to her frantic mother and grandmother, "the two French ladies," my great-great and great-great-great-grandmothers.

Maurine would know only too well what it was like and had her share in helping others know. But the past does not claim the future. Nature reminded us that day. No, the past lives quietly in the future. *The Giant Joshua* and the story of the unusual woman who wrote it will live long after many guardians of the red hills have come and gone, after many other books are written, and after many new faces are washed into the rocks. And Clory will laugh down through the centuries, reminding us how insignificant suffering and disappointment are, when we once become aware of "the Great Smile."

Index

Note: "Maurine Whipple" abbreviated in entries as MW. Page numbers of photographs are in boldface.

A

Abbott, Oscar, 337
Adams, Cowhide, 319
Adams, Fred, 367
Adams, Henry, 110
Addenbrooke, Edward F., 359
Adolph, Vickie, 342–43
Affleck, J. T., 292 note 43
A.F.G. Literary Agency, 253
AIDS, 393 note 48
Albert (name incomplete), 211
Albuquerque, NM, 284
alcoholism, MW researches, 349–52
    manuscript on: "Sanitarium that God Built, The," 351–52, 358
Alder, Douglas D., xi, 421
Alfred A. Knopf Company, 237, 238, 248, 260 note 7, 331
Allen, Boo, 329
Allen, Grant, 297
Allen, Joseph (Mrs.), 220 note 13, 222 note 39
Allred, Rulon, 410
Alsop, Dick, 359
Alves, Mary, 299
Always the Land, 127 note 33
"America's Tibet: The Arizona Strip." *See* Arizona Strip, article.
American Features Writers Syndicate, 219 note 11

American Heritage Publishing Company, 382
American Medical Association, 200, 202, 290 note 21
American Pharmaceutical Manufacturers' Association, 216
Ames, Elizabeth, 140–44, 146–47
Andersen, C. Paul, 367–68
Anderson, Bart, xi
Anderson, Carol Ann Whipple, **138**
    and MW, xii, 137, 155 note 22, 405, 406, 413
    as model for Lenzi MacIntyre, 288
    babyhood, 161
    on Ray Whipple, 27
    on Charlie Whipple, 33 note 9
Anderson, Lavina Fielding, xi
Anderson, Mark, 316 note 49
Anderson, Mercer, 363 note 14
Anderson, Nels, 215, 224 note 72, 254
Anderson, Nephi, 393 note 51
"Anybody's Gold Mine," 273 note 17, 317–19
Apex Mine/Company, 34 notes 18 and 26
Arches National Monument, 308
Arizona Highways (magazine), 382
Arizona Strip, article about ("America's Tibet: The Arizona Strip"), 290 note 21, 328, 330, 332, 334, 337–38, 360
    MW plans to expand, 360
    summary, 338–39

431

Arizona Strip (as region), 21
    MW visits, 178, 212, 282
"Arizona Strip, The" (novel)
    Houghton Mifflin rejects, 233 note 14
    movie rights to, 251
    MW works on, 230, 236, 237, 269, 354
    portions in sequel/trilogy, 278, 282
    summary, 227–28
    TV interest in, 358
Arrington, Leonard J., 291 note 26, 377 note 12, 387
Arrowhead Hotel (St. George), 37
Artlip, Caddie W., 356 note 22
Ascolli, Max, 146, 157 note 56
Ashman, A. J., 58–59, 66
Ashtabula, OH, 263
Asiatic-Pacific service medal, 273 note 14
Aspen Publishing, 420
Association for Mormon Letters, xii, 394 note 58, 417
Atlantic Monthly, 125 note 3, 134
atomic testing, Nevada, 342, 361, 401 note 7
Auerbach's (department store), 253
August, John (pseud.), 253
Austin, Michael, xi, 417, 424 note 44
Authors' Guild, 309, 312, 318
Authors' League, 309–11, 320, 322, 327, 330, 337
Aztecs, 324 note 1

B

Babcock, Maude May, 43, 50 note 23
Backer, Rowena Woodbury, 173 note 15
Bacon, Lucille, **63**
Bailey, Paul Dayton, 181, 189 note 34
Bailey, W. Phoebe, 395–96
Bain, Florence, 230
Bain, Read
    befriends MW, 229, 234 note 18, 235, 250, 269, 277
    corresponds with MW, 236, 241, 269
    on MW's books, 258
Bakersfield, CA, MW in, 39, 118
Bank of Iron County, 411
Banning, CA, 343

Barker, LeBaron ("Lee"), 122, 149–52, 157 note 66, 159, 194
Barker, Leslie, 122, 152
Barnum and Bailey, 343
Barracks Bag, 238
Barron (Associated Press reporter), 122
Barrymore, Ethel, 345 note 2
Battrick, Bill
    biography, 263
    corresponds with MW, 264, 265, 266–69
    in prison camp, 263, 266
    MW's romance with, 245, 263–72, 276
    suggests "Cleave the Wood" as title, 283, 291 note 25
Battrick, Helen, 263, 264, 271
Battrick, Lucille, 263, 266, 269–71
Battrick, Mabel, 263
Bear, Dorothy, 337
Beardsley, Harry M., 126 note 13
Beardwood, Jack, 296–98
Beatty, Jeannie, 29, 112
"Beaver Dam Wash," 64, 206, 210, 407
    at Rocky Mountain Writers' Conference, 1, 103–4
    influences on, 56
    summary, 64
Beaver Mountain, 168
Beaver, UT, 58
Beck, Elden
    biography, 221 note 36
    corresponds with MW, 211, 214, 225–26, 379
    encourages MW, 140, 156 note 36, 201, 284
    response to lecture, 251
Beck, Florence, 201, 284
Becker, Maximillian ("Max")
    activities as agent, 253, 269, 275, 303, 307–8, 314 note 24, 317, 322
    encourages MW, 279–80, 283–85, 286, 308
    Hughie Call defends, 277–78
    MW's relations with, 276, 279–80, 283–84, 285–86, 304, 307–8, 318, 321, 330–31
Becker, William, 410
Beckstrom, Emma Marian Bracken, 132

INDEX

Beckstrom, Peter Ephraim, 132
Bee, Roland, 63
Beehive House, MW lives at, 43, 69, 161
Beginnings, 387
Believing People: The Literature of the Latter-day Saints, A, 388
Bell, Harry Shepard, 56, 70 note 6
Belt, Elmer, 225–26, 233 note 2, 281, 310, 315 note 41
Belt, Maryruth Smart, 225–26, 233 note 2, 345, 355 note 4, 281
Bement, Douglas, 195, 196, 220 note 16
Benedict, George, 126 note 16, 352
Benedict. Lillian. *See* McQuarrie, Lillian.
Bennett, Thelma Maude McQuarrie, 155 note 22
Bennett, William Porter, 155 note 22
Berkeley, School of Public Health, 187 note 8
Bermann, R. A., 156 note 50
bicentennial, and MW's Easter pageant, 367–68
"Big Dog Eats Little Dog," 82
Big Hand Cafe, 181, 189 note 33, 195, 329
Big Indian Wash (Utah), 357
Biography of Parley P. Pratt: The Archer of Paradise, A, 173 note 14
Birmingham, AL, MW in, 191, 203–5
Bishop, John Peale, 1, 97, 103–5, 106 note 1, 123, 144, 180, 236
Black Canyon (Arizona-Nevada Border), 83
Black Hill (near St. George), 269
Black, Parnell, 99 note 19
Black, Vera, 353
Blake, Vira Henrie Judge, xi, 381–82
Bleak, Earl J., 28
Bleak, James Godson, 146
Bleak, Jane Thompson, 109, 132
Bloomington Ranches Country Club, 383
Bloomington, UT, 56, 377 note 12, 392 note 31
blue snow, 312
Blue Cross insurance, 310, 312, 330
Bluff, UT, 241
Bomer, Frances, 204
Bond, J. William, 68–69
Book-of-the-Month-Club Bulletin, 180
Bookseller, 121
Borzage, Frank, 345 note 2

Boston Advertiser, 125 note 3
Boston Conservatory of Music, 12 note 24
Boston Herald, 257
Boston, MA, MW in, 118–19, 192
Boston Public Library, 125 note 3
Boulder Canyon Project Act, 83
Boulder City, NV, MW at, 83–88
Boulder, CO, MW in, 1, 87, 97
Boulder Daily Camera, 104
Boulder Dam. *See* Hoover Dam.
Boulder Dam Enabling Act, 249
Bower, Warren, 190 note 53
Boy Scouts, 399
Bracy, Maryruth, 104, 105
Bradford, Mary Lythgoe, 389, 394 note 58
Brandt and Brandt, 197
Brentano (Las Vegas), 386
Briggie (character in sequel/trilogy), 279, 290 note 12
Brigham Young (movie), 177, 188 note 14
Brigham Young University, xi, 53
Brimhall, Dean R.
    corresponds with MW, 206, 208, 212, 213, 214, 223 note 65, 227, 241, 251, 256, 276
    encourages MW's friendship with Fawn Brodie, 228
    hosts MW, 199, 205
    influences MW, 215, 235, 250
    on LDS Welfare Plan, 249
Brimhall family, MW envies, 228
Brimhall, Lila Eccles, 199, 205, 212
Bristol, NV, 13
Brodie, Bernard, 228
Brodie, Fawn McKay
    and MW, 215, 228, 256–57
    excommunicated, 199, 235, 257
    MW compared to, 389
    on Juanita Brooks, 228
    on MW, 228–29
Brooks, Emily C. B., 34 note 26
Brooks, George Sr., 34 note 26
Brooks, Juanita Leone Leavitt Pulsipher
    and *Giant Joshua* proofs, 178
    and Mountain Meadows Massacre movie, 337, 347 note 29
    and MW, 29, 53–54, 247, 256, 266, 389

433

and *This Is the Place: Utah*, 241, 254
as historian, 35 note 40, 132, 185
as teacher, 29, 53
attitude toward Mormonism, 235
autobiography, 245, 259 note 1
biography, 35 note 40
defends Vera Black, 353
on polygamy, 77–78
portrait of, vii
possibly MW's typist, 212
reaction to ostracism, 185
rumored to be *Giant Joshua* author, xi
WPA, 176
Brooks, Willaneta, 98 note 10
brotherhood/brotherly love. *See* "Grand Idea."
Brown, Loa Moss, xii, 15–16, 33 note 5, 131
Brown, Marilyn, xi, 420–21
Brown's Hole, 297
Bryner, Ruby. *See* Finlayson, Ruby Bryner.
Buchanan, James, 114
Bunkerville, NV, 35 note 40
burglary. *See* Whipple, Maurine, robbed.
Burke (no first name), 83
Burnett, Whit, 103, 104, 106 note 3, 154 note 15
Burraston, Alma Powelson, 39, 47
Burraston, Effie Whipple, 14, 39, 47
Burton, Lawrence J., 375
Butler, Daisy, 228
BYU Studies, 387

C

Cable Mountain (Zion Canyon), 369
Cahn, Robert
    biography, 345 note 1
    corresponds with MW, 327, 331–32, 337, 339
    sends MW her *Collier's* correspondence, 347 note 40, 353
Calgary, Alberta, xii
California Writer's Club, 227
California Writers' Guild, 227
Call, Hughie, 165, 173 note 27, 253, 277
Callie/Clara (character in "The Golden Door"), 239
Callison, Maud Pace, 156 note 41, 200
Callison, Valentine Byrd, 156 note 41
Campbell, Mary Nelson, xi, 30, 35 note 44, 182
Campbell, Stewart, 293
"Candles of the Lord" (Easter pageant), 370 note 1, 406
"Candles of the Lord, The" (novel). *See* sequel/trilogy.
Cannon, Blanche, 387
Capener, Brian, 404, 422 note 5
Capote, Truman, 386
Carnaby, Floyd, 43
Carnaby, Myrtle, 43
Carnegie Branch Library for Local History (Boulder, CO), 107 note 13
Carnegie Foundation, 353
carnotite, 341
Cassidy, Butch, 339
Cathedral City, CA, MW at, 164, 349–52
Cather, Willa, 110, 120
Cedar City Branch Agricultural College. *See* Southern Utah University.
Cedar City, UT, 92–93, 117, 367
"Celebratory Tour, The," 293
Centennial Tour, 295–96, 304, 308
Central, UT, 306
Chamberlain, Bryce, 407
Chamberlain, Neville, 148
"Chapter a Day" (radio program), 359
Charles L. Redd Center (Brigham Young University), 383
Chase, Josiah H. (Mrs.), 176
Chassler, Sey, 347 note 41
Chi Delta Phi, 44, 202
Chicago, IL, MW in, 229
Chicago Sun, 257
Chicago Sun-Times, 341
Chihuahua, Mexico, 409
Children of God, 160, 164, 166, 393 note 51
    compared to *Giant Joshua*, 176, 181
    wins prize, 173 note 25
Chinn (doctor), 195
Chloe (early name for Clory), 126 note 14, 290 note 12
"Chopping Block, The" (column), 291 note 31
Christensen, Flaral Josephine *See* Lee, Flaral Josephine Christensen.

INDEX

Christensen, O. C., 316 note 49
Christian Science Monitor, 345 note 1
"Christmas Dress, The," 44, 50 note 25, 419
Christmas for the World, 419
Church Chronology, 146
Church of the Firstborn, 409
Civilian Conservation Corps, 97, 306
Civil War, 2
Clark, Dane, 345 note 2
Clark, J. Reuben, Jr.
    MW dislikes, 213–14, 252, 256
    MW writes to about Charlie's reinstatement, 61
    on Mountain Meadows Massacre movie, 347 note 29
    requests cancellation of Easter pageant, 97
Clark, Lynn, 365–66, 386
Clark, Neil, 321–22
Clark, Russell, xi, 42, 47
Clark, Walter E., 62, 180
Clayton, Lorna, 396
"Cleave the Wood." *See* sequel/trilogy.
Cloete, Stuart, 110
Cloniger, Charles, 42, 50 note 20
Cloniger, Ralph, 42, 50 note 20
Clory. *See* MacIntyre, Clory.
Clove, David, 423 note 16
Clove, Terrill, 416, 421–22
Coachilla Valley, CA, 164
Coe, Betty, 318
Coffey, Pat, 318, 341
College of Southern Utah. *See* Southern Utah University.
Collier's (magazine), 290 note 21
    ends publication, 353
    Hollywood office closes, 347 note 40
    MW wants job with, 327–45
    publishes MW article, 343, 393 note 43
Colonia Dublan, Mexico, 7
Colonia Juarez, Mexico, 7
Colonia LeBaron, Mexico 409
Colorado City, AZ, 415
Colorado Plateau, 357
Colorado River, 241, 294, 321, 332
Columbia University, 53, 103, 107 note 3, 194, 125 note 3

"Compromise, A," 45
"Confessions of a She–Devil"
    as autobiography, 59–60, 66, 80, 85, 88, 97
    St. George character in, 38–39
    written at writers' conference, 1, 104, 116
Congdon, Donald K., 150, 290 note 13
    contract with, 279
    MW corresponds with, 281, 286, 287, 304
Contemporary Club (Redlands, CA), 227
Cooley, Everett L., 291 note 25, 383
Coolidge, Calvin, 83
Corbett, Pearson, 241
Cornelius Hotel (Virgin, UT), 66
Coronet, 321
Cortes, Hernando, 324 note 1
Cottam, Effie Frie, 221 note 31
Cottam, Walter, 199, 221 note 31
Council of Churches and Christian Education, 277
Cousins, Norman, 351
cowboys, and MW, 21, 181, 329
Cowles, LeRoy, 199
Cox, Anna Carter
    and music, 99 note 26
    friendship with MW, 282–83, 287–88, 352, 355
    husband (Loraine), 15
    on MW, xi, 314 note 12
    on *This Is the Place: Utah*, 258
    photo by, 296
Cox, Elizabeth Ann Stout, 49 note 2
Cox, Isaiah, 49 note 2
Cox, James Carter, 288, 291 note 41
Cox, Loraine, xi, 15–16, 282–83, 288
Cox, Ludie Lytle, xi
Cox, Mary Etta Lee, 49 note 2
Cox, Warren, 37, 49 note 2, 169
    Cracroft, Richard H.
    corresponds with MW, 387–89, 422 note 1
    encouragement, xi
    interviews MW, 394 note 56
    on *Giant Joshua*, 403, 420
Craft, Gracie, 300
Craft, Roy, 297, 300, 301 note 12, 304, 334
Crawford, Fern, and Jasper, xi
Creer, Leland H., 146
Crow, Holland, 355

435

Crystal, Freddie, 317, 319
Cummings, C. R., 99 note 19
Curtis, Elbert R., 214

D

Daily News (New York), 150
Dalby, Fern, 115
Dali, Salvador, 143
Dark Hunger, 345 note 2
Darnell, Linda, 177
Dartmouth College, 228
date ranch, 162, 178, 200, 349. *See also* Walker, Joseph.
Daughters of Light, 387
Daughters of Utah Pioneers, 181, 385
David Bowyer Productions, 315 note 30
Davidson, Edward, 118
da Vinci, Leonardo, 225
Dean, Loomis, 294–95, 297–99, 301 note 6
Declaration of Independence, 119
Dedekind, Elizabeth, 232
de Kruif, Paul, 127 note 33, 191, 193, 219 note 2
    and MW, 206, 211, 281
    and Tom Spies, 201, 202
Delfs, Genevieve, 220 note 13
DeLuca, John, 351
Denetsosie, Hoke (Navajo), 359
de Neuf, Emil ("Buzz"), 78–81
Deseret Book, 256
Deseret News, 256
Desert Inn (Las Vegas), 366
Desert Saints, 254
DeVoto, Avis M., 180
DeVoto, Bernard, 134, 154 note 13, 180
    MW asks advice from, 230, 252
    MW fears comparison with, 163, 188 note 27
    on western writers, 277
    reviews *Giant Joshua*, 180
Dialogue: A Journal of Mormon Thought, 389, 425 note 51
Dictionary of American Biography, 125 note 3
DiFiore, Roene, 366
Dinosaur National Monument, 238

"Divine Artist, The," 45
Division of Family Services, Washington County, 380
Dixie Academy/Junior College, 70 note 1
Dixie Airline, 384
Dixie College, 140, 318, 367
    faculty of, 35 note 40, 353
    Library, 118, 407
Dixie Downs, 383
Dixie High School, 65
Dixie Junior College, 53
Dixie Owl, 29
Dixie Regional Medical Center, 398, 409
Dixie Reviewers (club), 181
Dixie State College/University, vii, 291 note 41
Dodge Pond, 41
Dolowitz, Donald A., xi, 361, 363 note 17, 393 note 49
Dorchester, MA, 127 note 26
Doubleday, Florence, 192–93, 195–96, 198, 220 note 13
Doubleday, Frank N., 192
Doubleday's Dollar Book Club, 227
Dowst, Peggy. *See* Redmon, Peggy Dowst.
Doyle, James C., 290 note 21
Draper, Ruth, 367
Dream Mine, 339
Dreiser, Theodore, 64
"Dress for Christmas, A," 425 note 51
Dunbar (no first name), 211
Duncan, Adam ("Mickey"), 374
Durfey, LaVern, 50 note 22

E

Earle, John, 403
Easter pageant ("The Candles of the Lord")
    at Zion National Park, 93–94, 103
    cancelled, 100 note 51
    summary, 365–66, 367–68
"Easy Chair, The," 154 note 13
Edmunds Act (1882), 8, 11 note 15
Edmunds-Tucker Act (1887), 7, 8, 11 note 15
Egg and I, The, 287, 291 note 38
EIMCO, 291 note 14

INDEX

Electric Theater, 20, 22, 34 note 21, 65–66
El Escalanti (hotel), 92, 93
Ellet, A. E., 99 note 19
Elsinore, UT, 56, 59
Empey, Lynn, 384
Enchanted Wilderness (magazine), 381
Enchanted Wilderness Association, 390 note 10
England, Eugene, 167–68, 185
    attends *Giant Joshua* jubilee picnic, 420
    encouragement of, xi, 425 note 51
    on *The Giant Joshua*, viii, 388–89
    on unfinished trilogy, 197–98
Engle, Paul, 127 note 33
English Review, 106 note 2
Enoch Arden, 58
Ensign, 425 note 51
Enterprise, UT, 306
Escalante, UT, 63
Esquire, 324 note 12
European Passion players, 97
Eutsler, Brad, 384, 399–400
Eutsler, Ruth, 399–400
Evans, Emerson
    and Lillian's daughter, 136, 178
    Lillian McQuarrie's husband, 75, 96–97, 115–17, 126 note 16, 178
    youth, 106 note 3
Evans, Lillian McQuarrie. *See* McQuarrie, Lillian.
Evans, Lloyd, 96–97, 115–17, 126 note 16, 136, 353
Evans, Marella B., 262 note 41
Evans, Wildon, 259
Exchange Club (Salt Lake City), 232

F

Farmers Home Administration, 383
Farnsworth, Judy Sine Haskell Gubler, xi, 408, 410–12, 423 note 28
Farnsworth, Russell, 423 note 28
Fawson, Merrill, 288
FCC (Federal Communications Commission), 375
Federal Education Reclamation Agency, 82–83
Ferber, Edna, 182
Fife, Lewis, 228, 233 note 12
Finlayson, Bliss Lamayne, 70 note 5
Finlayson, Ruby Bryner, 28, 70 note 5
Firestone Company, 84
First National Bank of Nevada, 383
Fisher, Vardis, 160, 173 note 25, 181, 393 note 51. *See* also *Children of God*.
    Ferris Greenslet on, 172 note 4
    MW fears comparison with, 163, 164, 166
Fishing Gazette, 121
Fitzgerald, F. Scott, 387
Flame Within, The, 88, 135
Flannigan, Dave, 369
Fleming, Victor, 11 note 3
Fletcher, Harvey, 367
Florea, John, 334
Folger, Howard, 377 note 12
folic acid, 230
Folsom, Annie Eliza Lutz Lenzi, 37, 49 note 5
Folsom, Hyrum, 37, 49 note 5
Folsom, Nancy Broadbent, 49 note 5
For This My Glory, 181
Ford, Ford Maddox, 103, 105, 106 note 2
Fordham, Alton, 65
Ford, John, 311
Foremaster, Florence ("Flo"), 15, 39, 49 note 13, 380
Fort Bridger, 6
Fort Oglethorpe, CA, 268
Foster, Allen, 6
Foster, Charles Franklin, Sr., 35 note 46
Foster, Julia Putnam, 32, 35 note 46, 40, 45, 228
Foster, Pamelia Asenall D., 35 note 46
Foster, Patience Earl, 6
Freemasons, 111
Freiburg, Germany, 97
Frost, Robert, 230

G

Gallico, Paul, 309–12, 315 note 32, 318, 320
Garfield County, UT, 399
Garland, UT, 92
Garrick, Marie, 425 note 52

437

Geary, Edward A., 387
Geneva Steel, 284
Genie (no surname), 200
Gentry, Yvonne, 425 note 52
George, Doris Nina, 411–14
Georgetown, ID, 62–65, 180
Germ Killers, 219 note 2
GI Prisoner in the Third Reich, A, 263
Giant Joshua, The. *See also* "Grand Idea," Houghton Mifflin, *and* sequel/trilogy.
    alternative conclusions, 171–72
    as possible movie, 175, 194, 212, 225, 251, 282, 375, 403–5, 415–16, 422 note 2
    condensed version, 227
    copyright renewed, 400
    family history in, 2–5, 9–10, 169–70
    family reaction to, 133, 180–81
    fans of, 183, 229, 231, 259, 303, 309, 313 note 2, 320, 342–43, 351, 352, 358, 384, 395–98, 399, 413
    holograph drafts of, xi
    John A. Widtsoe on, 183
    jubilee picnic for, 420
    MW peddles copies, 358
    MW protests editing, 176
    MW reads from, 421
    origins, 109
    plot summary, 138–39, 145, 147, 149, 160–61, 164–66, 167–69, 170–71
    printing history, 196, 281, 357, 359, 365, 386
    quoted in *Reader's Digest*, 221 note 34
    radio drama version, 358–59, 374–76
    reactions to/reviews, 180–87
    royalties, 197, 221 note 25, 245, 251–52, 260 note 12, 261 note 18
    selection anthologized, 388
    stage version, 358, 359
    studied at BYU, 388
    writing/printing schedule, 129, 135, 165–67, 169
Gilles, LaVon, 355
Girvin, Robert, 298–99, 315 note 32
Glen Allen, AK, 395
Glens Falls, NY, 125 note 3
Glenwood, UT, 58
Goddard, Grace, 195, 220 notes 13–14
Goddard, Henry W., 220 note 13
goiter, 32
"Golden Door, The"
    fans encourage, 259
    movie rights to, 251
    MW sends to John Crowe Ransom, 354
    MW submits for Guggenheim, 282
    summary, 239–40
Golden Fleece, The, 173 note 27, 253
gold rush, California, 6
Goldner, Jewels, 314 note 22
Gone with the Wind
    as movie, 403
    Giant Joshua compared to, 2, 259
    success, 11 note 3
Good Soldier, The, 106 note 2
Good–bye, I Love You, 393 note 48
Gott, Delmar, 407
Goulding, Harry, 253, 321. *See also* "Land of Prayer."
    article about rejected, 317
    MW proposes article about 308, 310, 316 note 43
Goulding, Mike, 253, 308
Goulding Trading Post/museum, 315 note 30
Graff, Arnold LaMar, 92–93, 100 note 48, 281
Graff, Delores Jensen, 92–93
"Grain of Mustard Seed, A," 360
"Grand Idea" (brotherhood), 76, 86, 113, 169, 184, 186, 214, 216, 235, 278, 314 note 14, 328, 354, 360, 381, 419–20, 429
Granite High School (Salt Lake City), 106 note 3
Grant, Heber J., 214, 224 note 73, 252
Grant, Jean, 203–5, 207–8, 220 note 13
Grant, Ulysses S., 114
Great Depression, 58, 59, 81, 249
Great Smile, 2, 5, 171–72, 430
Greene, Art, 308, 321, 332–33, 341, 359, 362 note 8
Greenslet, Ella S. Hulst, 118, 121, 125 note 3
Greenslet, Ferris. *See also Giant Joshua and* Houghton Mifflin.
    and Ford Maddox Ford, 105–6
    and Juanita Brooks's autobiography, 245
    after *Giant Joshua*'s publication, 195–96

INDEX

as fisherman, 119, 121
authorizes *Giant Joshua*, 109, 114
biography, 110, 125 note 1
editing on *Giant Joshua*, 175–77
encourages MW, vii, 1, 109–11, 114–15, 118, 120–21, 124, 129, 133–37, 139–41, 145–46, 148–49, 152, 154 note 15, 161–67
financial arrangements with MW, 136, 146–47, 152–53, 160–61, 175
interest in St. George, 144
MW disillusioned with, 151–53, 163
on "Beaver Dam Wash," 109–10, 114
Greenslet, George Bernard, 125 note 3
Greenslet, Josephine Ferris, 125 note 3
Greggerson, Edna, 366, 406
"Greyhound Tours," 363 note 14
Griffith, Teddy, 369
Guam, 251
Gubler, Austin, 408, 410, 411
Gubler, Emil, 66
Gubler, Grant, 411
Gubler, Judy. *See* Farnsworth, Judy Sine Haskell Gubler.
Gubler, Nellie McArthur, 24, 66–67
Guggenheim Fellowship, 166, 282
Gunlock, UT, 383

H

Hafen, Elsie Frei, 53, 211, 223 note 58
Hafen, Jean, 241
Hafen, Keith Leland, 211, 223 note 58
Hafen, Leland, 53, 223 note 58
Hafen, LeRoy R., and Ann, 389
Hale, Brent Jonathan, xii
Hale, Erin Parker, xii
Hale, Glen Tebbs, xii
Hale, Jason Daniel, xii
Hale, Kris Dalton, xii
Hale, Sarah Bradford, xii
Hale, Veda Tebbs, viii x–xi
Hallstrom, Floyd, 410, 414
Hamblin, Jacob, diary, 146
Hamlet, 421

"Handcart Song, The," 10
Hanover, N.H., 228
Hansen, Harry, 257, 276, 286
Harden, Jack, 377 note 12
Harding, Ann, 88, 135
Hardy, Agnes Donald Pymm, 34 note 18
Hardy, A. P., 34 note 17
Hardy, Elizabeth, 34 note 17
Hardy, Isabella M. Grundy, 34 note 18
Hardy, Sherman Capner, 20, 34 note 17
Harold B. Lee Library, xi
Harold Matson Company, 290 note 13, 304
Harold Obert Associates, 386
Harper's Bazaar, 134, 154 note 13
Harper's Poll of the Critics, 185
Harris, Abner B., 24, 34 note 26
Harris, Edith, 34 note 26, 258
Harris, Edna Turnbow, 329
Harris, Evelyn. *See* Ward, Evelyn Harris.
Harris, Goldie, 34 note 26
Harris, Grant B., 34 note 26
Harris, Helene, 34 note 26
Harris, Lou. *See* Smith, Lou Harris Miller.
Harris, May Brooks, 24, 34 note 26
Hart, Charles James, Sr., 243 note 11
Hart, Lucille, 71 note 20
Hartford, Huntington, 343. *See also* Huntington Hartford Foundation.
Hartog, Mrs., 49 note 3
Harvard University, 243 note 2
Harvest Productions, 407
Haun's Mill, in *Giant Joshua*, 145
Haycock, Colleen Jolley, xii, 33 note 9, 112, 161, 199, 406, 425 note 52
Hayward, CA, 161
Heather, Henry, 303
Heber City, UT, MW at, 68–69
Heggie, Peter, 320
"Hell, It's Worth It!" 86–87, 94, 105–6
Hemingway, Ernest, 387
Henderson, Cliff, 332, 334
Henriod, F. Henri, 398
Herald Tribune (New York), 185, 197
Herbert, Elvira ("Vira") Whipple, 11 note 18, 91–92, 100 note 51
Herbert, Ervin L., 11 note 18

Heritage Room, Dixie College Library, 118, 392 note 42
Herrick, J. C., 213
Hess, Dow, 349–52, 355 note 1
Hichinoper, Thanksie (character in sequel/trilogy), 279
Hicks, Wilson, 296
Higgins, Camellia ("Camie") Carter Sullivan, xii, 352, 375, 385–86
Higgins, Margaret, 198, 200, 203, 204, 208
Higgins, Silas G., 292 note 43
Hilda [surname withheld], 16, 59–60
Hill Cumorah Pageant, 367
Hilldale, UT, 353
Hillman Hospital, 191, 198, 202, 230
Hines, Al, 321
History and Crimes of Mormonism, The, 75
Hitler, Adolf, 144, 148
Hobble Creek Canyon, 420
Hoff, Ernie, 382
Holiday Magazine, 301 note 3, 307–8, 314 note 24, 321
Hollywood, CA, MW in, 251, 328
Hoover Dam, 82, 83, 99 note 31, 232
Hoover, Helen ("Butch"), 310
Hoover, Herbert, 83
Horgan, Paul, 127 note 33
Hotel Utah, MW at, 276, 296
Hough, Henry Wade, 271–72
Houghton, Henry, 179
Houghton Mifflin. *See also* Greenslet, Ferris.
    editorial staff, 156 note 51
    fellowship for novel, 110, 112–13, 117, 123, 136, 193
    Joseph Smith biography, 126 note 13
    MW complains about, 197, 206, 210–11, 220 note 16, 226, 245, 286, 374
    publicity for *Giant Joshua*, 192
    rejects Lillian McQuarrie's manuscript, 135, 155 note 18
    rejects MW manuscripts, 206, 253, 351
Houghton, Samuel G., 152, 182
Howard, Sidney/Sydney, 11 note 3, 80, 219 note 2
Howe, Maurice, 215
"How Great Thou Art," 425 note 52

Hub, The, 32, 35 note 46
Hughes, Bernice, 54, 58–60
Hughes, Howard, 380
Humanitarian International, 419
Human Resources Research Organization, 263
Humphries, Glenwood, 416
Hungnam, Korea, 322
Huntington Beach, CA, MW at, 43
Huntington Hartford art colony, 337–38, 341–43
Hunt, Royal, 306
Huntsville, UT, 295
Hurd, Robert Knowles, 237, 337
Hurricane, UT, 50 note 19
Hydrogen (dog), 324 note 11

I

"I, Janet" (movie script), 206
"I Married Five Wives," 343, 393 note 43
ice plant, 14
Imperial Valley (CA), 83
"Impossible [sic] Land, The," 407
Improvement Era, 50 note 25, 183
In Cold Blood, 386
Indians
    in *Giant Joshua*, 132, 178
    in "The Time Will Come," 22 note 57
Indio, CA, MW at, 200
influenza pandemic, 70 note 6
Intermountain Review, 104–5
International Authors and Writers Who's Who, 388
Intimate Disciple: A Portrait of Willard Richards, Apostle to Joseph Smith—Cousin of Brigham Young, 157 note 54
Ipswich Historical Society, 127 note 26
Ipswich, MA, 118–20, 127 note 26
Irvine, F. Gerald ("Gerry"), 46–47, 182, 388
Ivins, Israel, 292 note 43
Ivory–Boyer Realtors, 392 note 31

J

J. C. Penney's, 253–54, 289 note 1
Jack (character in sequel/trilogy), 279
Jacky (dog), **138**

INDEX

Jagger, Dean, 177
Jarvis, Brigham, 20, 132
Jarvis, Mabel, 132
Jefferson Medical College, 173 note 15
Jensen, Carol (Carol Jean Lamborn Jensen Hallstrom Becker)
    and MW papers, ix, 223 note 66
    and "The Candles of the Lord," 368
    as MW's guardian, xi, 404, 410–30
    biography, xii, 409–10
    MW expresses remorse to about Charlie, 305
    nurse at hospital, 398
    on Sam Weller, 393 note 46
Jensen, Earl Larsen, 409
Jensen, Karen, 63
Jensen, Mildred Munk, **63**
Jensen, UT, 238
Jenson, Andrew, 146
Jenson, E. M., 53, 54
Jessop, Edson, 343, 399
John Whipple House (Ipswich), 127 note 26
Johnson, Abraham Owen, 35 note 39, 126 note 8
Johnson Canyon (Utah), 317
Johnson, Frank, 362 note 8
Johnson Land Company, 392 note 31
Johnson, Louisa Elizabeth Bellison, 35 note 39, 126 note 8
Johnson, Zeke, 308
Johnston's Army, 6
Jolley, Ben
    distances self from MW, 199, 406
    injured, 161, 199
    marriage, 69, 112
Jolley, Colleen. *See* Haycock, Colleen Jolley.
Jolley, Florence Whipple, **40**
    childhood/youth, 13–14, 18, 19, 20–22, 24, 39–41
    crippled foot, 26–27, 28, 56
    corresponds with MW, 56, 71 note 18
    death, 406
    distances self from MW, 406
    marriage, 69, 112
    musical ability, 10, 26–27, 28, 34 note 31, 69
    MW assists, 161, 199
    on Great Depression, 67
    popularity, 27–28, 31
Jolley, Charles Larry, xii, 33 note 91, 61, 112, 199, 425 note 52
Jolley, Steve, 425 note 52
Jolley, Wayne, 425 note 52
Jones, Jaren L., 377 note 12
Jones, Holly Miller, 186–87
Jones, Randall, 250, 260 note 9, 308
Jorgensen, Bruce W., xi, 420
Joseph Smith and His Mormon Empire, 126 note 13
Joshua trees, 139–40
"Josie, Queen of the Cattle Rustlers," 299–300, 301 note 13, 322
Judd, Alvin, 319
Judd, Myles, 65, 71 note 21

K

Kanab Picture Company, 303
Kanab, UT, 244 note 25, 268, 287, 317–19, 338, 341
Kayenta, UT, MW in, 427–30
KBYU–Radio/TV, 422 note 3
Kearns, UT, 238
Keel, Howard, 341
Kennecott Copper Company, 224 note 73
Kennelly, Ardis, 387
Kenyon Fellowships, 351
Kenyon Review, 354
Kibble, Howard, 395
Kilsey, Anne D., 99 note 19
Kissy. *See* MacIntyre, Calistra.
Knight, Betty, 366
Knight, Ralph, 318
Knopf, Alfred A., 250–51
Kopiloff, Thomas A., 216–18, 236
Korean War, 322, 342
Kreutzer, Dorothy, 86, 88, 182
Kreutzer, George, 86
Krey, Laura, 110
KUER Radio, 358, 374
Ku Klux Klan, 327

441

L

L. Tom Perry Special Collections, xi
Ladies Home Journal, 318
Lake Mead, 339, 340
Lambert, Linda, 104, 105
Lambert, Neal E., 387–88
Lamborn, Mabel LaVerne Black, 409
Lamborn, Willard Owen, 409
Lamoreaux, Bud, 168
Lamoreaux, La Ree Milne, 168, 174 note 37
"Land of Prayer," 321
Larkin, Montrue, xi
Larson, Andrew Karl, vii, 50 note 19
Larson, Clinton, 185
Larson, Katharine Miles, 35 note 45, 42, 50 note 19, 287, 314 note 12, 355, 366, 421
Las Vegas, NV
    Collier's sells in, 338
    founded by Mormons, 356 note 6
    Jolly family in, xii
    MW and charitable deductions, 351, 357
    MW in, 82
    MW's cousin in, 354
Latuda, UT, 90, 100 note 51, 258
LaVerkin, UT, MW in, 408–14
Lawrence, Ernest, 190 note 52
League of Utah Writers, 208, 222 note 54, 231, 238
Lear, John M., 403–4, 415
Learny, Pat, 380
Leavitt, Dudley Henry, 35 note 40
Leavitt, Mary Hafen, 35 note 40
LeBaron, Ervil, 409, 424 note 29
lecture. *See* Whipple, Maurine, lecture.
Lee, Arthur Edwin, 70 note 6
Lee, Bertha Josephine Anderson, 70 note 6
Lee, Flaral Josephine Christensen, 56–57
Lee, Harold B., 213–14
Lee, Hyrum Levi
    as businessman, 58, 118
    biography, 70 note 6
    MW's romance with, 65, 54–58, 258
Lee, J. Bracken, 58
Lee, John D.
    ancestor of Veda Tebbs Hale, 314 note 14
    and Mountain Meadows, 138, 161, 167

Lee, Lawrence, 134
Lee, Merrill, xi
Lee's Ferry, 362 note 8
Lee's Style Shop, 58
Leeds, UT, 341
Lefler, Tom, 404–5, 422 note 5, 423 notes 10–11
"Left–Overs, The," 271
Legg, Sarah, 7
Leigh, Vivian, 11 note 3
Leighton, Betty, 136–37, 160, 164, 178
Lenzi (character in trilogy). *See* MacIntyre, Lenzi.
Lenzi family, as source for *Giant Joshua*, 133
Leucadia Film Corporation, 404–5, 423 note 12
Leussler, Harrison, 136, 201
Lewin, Philip, 229–30
Lewis, Converse R., 238
Liberty Hotel (St. George), 406
Liberty (magazine), 75, 271
Library of Congress, copyright department, 404
Lieber, Maxim ("Max")
    activities as agent, 150, 211, 225
    biography, 219 note 11
    corresponds with MW, 155 note 24, 155 note 22
    MW complains about, 206
    MW hires/fires, 155 note 24, 180, 195, 210
Life (magazine)
    MW's association with, 294–300, 327
    MW's campaign against, 304, 309–10
    payment from, 310
    rejects article proposal, 317
Little, Brown and Company, 327
Lindenberger, Edwin Forest, 233 note 7
Lindenberger, Florence M., 233 note 7
Lindsay, Rulon Beach, 64
Linscott, Robert
    encourages MW, 137, 161, 176, 179
    on vacation, 178
    publicity for MW, 195, 220 note 17
Lions' Clubs, 92
Lisbon Valley (UT), 357
"Literary Club," 45
Little Kingdom, The, 173 note 27
Little, Lester, 319
Logandale, NV, 392 note 36
Logan Temple, 409

INDEX

Logue, Larry M., 98 note 12
Look (magazine), 213–14, 375
"Look Up to Him," 425 note 52
"Lord Giveth, The," 64
Los Angeles
    Ben and Florence Jolley in, 161
    family visit to (1924), 39
    Lillian McQuarrie in, 135
    MW in, 75, 77, 67, 81, 91–92, 136, 139–40, 198, 200, 273 note 17, 300
    Recreation Department, 82
Los Angeles Star, 75
Los Angeles Times, 227
"Lost Generation," of Mormon writers, 387
Lost Horizon, 231
"Lunatics, by One of Them." *See* Timpanogas.
Lund, Anthon H., 5
Lund, Charles, 150
Lund, NV, 13, 87
Lurton, Cynthia, 427–29
Luzern, Warren County, NY, 6
Lytle, Christena Diana Whitner/Wittner, 6
Lytle family, as source for *Giant Joshua*, 133
Lytle, John, 6

M

Ma and Pa Kettle (movie), 291 note 38
MacBride, Bert, 308–12, 318–19, 321, 331–32
MacDonald, Betty, 291 note 38
MacDowell Art Colony, 166
Macfarlane, Daisy, 320, 325 note 18
Macfarlane, Wallace, 325 note 18
Macferson, Betty, xi
MacGregor, Martha, 150
MacIntyre, characters in *The Giant Joshua* and sequel/trilogy.
    Abijah ("Handsome Mac"), 3, 129, 130, 133, 138, 147, 165, 166, 168, 169, 171, 417
    Bathsheba, 147, 149, 171–72
    Calistra ("Kissy") Agatha, 160, 165
    Clorinda ("Clory") Agatha Lenzi, 2, 44, 113, 129–30, 133, 134, 252–53
    Freeborn, 147, 149, 161, 164
    Jim/Jimmy, 44–45, 113, 115, 166, 168, 215, 278–79, 282, 288, 290 note 12
    Julia, 171
    Lenzi, 44, 113–15, 215, 270, 279, 283, 288
    Templena ("Tempie"), 166, 288
    Thanksie, 288, 290 note 12
    Willie, 166–67
magazines, glossy/pulps, 324 note 3
Magovern (doctor), 150–51
Mallinckrodt, Phillip A., 374
Maltz, Albert, 175, 182–83
Manheim, Ontario, Canada, 154 note 5
Manning, Gordon, 339
Manti Temple, 4, 5, 13, 169–70
Marcellus, Onondago County, NY, 6
Marcus King, Mormon, 393 note 51
Marriott Library, Western Americana (University of Utah), 383
Marshall, Don, 420
Martha Graham School, 269
Martin Gray Company, 404
Massachusetts Book, The, 121
Mathis Market (St. George), 18, 22
Mathis, Wally, 20
Maw, Herbert B., 99 note 19, 182
McAllister, Amy, 5
McAllister, Ann Eliza Wells, 3–4
McAllister, Annie. *See* Whipple, Annie McAllister.
McAllister, Clara, 284
McAllister, Cornelia Agatha Lenzi, **3**
    and sister wives, 59
    as plural wife, 3–5, 127 note 30
    as source for Clory MacIntyre, 3, 5–6, 122, 133
    children, 37
    deafness, 5
    items in room, 5, 130
    locket given to MW, 3
McAllister family, as source for *Giant Joshua*, 133
McAllister, Jane. *See* Moss, Jane McAllister.
McAllister, John Daniel Thomas, **3**
    affluence, 8–9
    as Manti Temple president, 4, 13, 169–70
    as polygamist, 3–4, 59
    as source for Abijah MacIntyre, 133

443

as St. George Stake president, 8–9
as St. George Temple president, 8
death, 4–5, 18
musical ability, 10, 19
personality, 9
portrait in temple, 418
McAllister, Joseph, 10
McAllister, J. W., 353
McAllister, Lucile Young, 51 note 39
McAllister, Martin, 284
McAllister, Matilda Nielson, 5, 59, 170
McAllister, Tempie, 5, 290 note 12
McAllister, Wilford Woodruff Lenzi, 11 note 6, 12 note 23, 48, 51 note 39
McCammon, Agnes, 63, 71 note 16, 180
McCammon, Jess, 63, 180
McCloud, Susan Evans, 420
McFarland/Macfarline (doctor, Salt Lake City), 28, 35 note 36
McGregor (doctor, St. George), 112
McGregor, Alphonzo, 281
McGregor, Bertha Pendexter Watson, 337–38, 347 note 12
McGregor, Donald Alpine, 28, 347 note 32
McGregor, M. K., 398
McKay, David O., 61, 97, 215
McKay family, MW envies, 228
McMurrin, Trudy, 259 note 1
McPherson, Betty, 43, 375
McQuarrie, Agnes Gray, 98 note 4
McQuarrie, Hector, 98 note 4
McQuarrie, Janet Gray, 98 note 4
McQuarrie, Lillian Maude. *See also* Emerson Evans, Lloyd Evans *and* Marian Noelte.
    and George Benedict, 126 note 16, 352–53
    and MW's marriage, 78–79
    and Writers' Round–up, 185–86
    attitude toward Mormonism, 75–76
    death, 406–7
    encourages MW, 74–79, 87, 90, 103, 115–17, 123–24, 133, 135, 161
    hospitality, 94, 97, 179
    in Salt Lake City, 276
    in San Francisco, 75, 126 note 16
    loans MW money, 84
    marriages, 74–75
    MW dislikes her smoking, 76
    MW distances self from, 76–77, 99 note 35, 99 note 35
    polygamy novel, 87, 99 note 35, 155 note 18
    pragmatism, 77, 88–89
    sexual morals, 77–78
    son's birth, 96–97, 115
    writing, 87–88, 99 note 35, 135, 352–53
McQuarrie, Robert Gary, 98 note 4
Meadows Retirement Center, viii, 414–16
Medicare, 398
Meeks, Priddy, 173 note 26, 225
"Meet the Mormons," 214
Mein Kampf, 157 note 61
Men against Death, 219 note 2
Merit of Honor Award, 388
Mesquite, NV, 55, 337, 392 note 36
Metcalf Mortuary, 421
Mexican Hat, San Juan County, UT, 241
Miami University (Oxford, Ohio), 229, 230
Miles, Arthur Fredrick, 35 note 45, 50 note 19
Miles, Ida Walker, 35 note 45
Miles, Katharine. *See* Larson, Katharine Miles.
Miles, Wyatt Walker, 31, 35 note 45, 162, 421
Miles, Zaidee Walker, 50 note 19, 132, 162, 178, 318
Miller, George M., 232
Milne, La Ree. *See* Lamoreaux, La Ree Milne.
"Miracle of the Spillway, The," 170, 174 note 43, 360, 386
Mitchell J. Hamilbing Agency, 206
Mitchell, Margaret, 2. *See also Gone with the Wind.*
Mitchell, Vera Gates, 325 note 14
Moab, UT, 357
Modena, UT, 34 note 31
Moesinger, Tabeetha, 418
Mohave Miner, 343
Monroe Drug Store, 56
Monroe High School, 58–59
Monroe, Marilyn, 301 note 12
Monroe, UT, MW in, 53–59
Montano, Patricia ("Patsy") Dorothy Kear, 407–9, 410–12; and daughters, 408, 410–11
Montezuma/Moctezuma II, 268, 317, 324 note 1
Montpelier (ID) High School, 62–65
Monument Valley, 241, 253, 308, 311, 321
Moody, Margaret, 121, 160

INDEX

Moody, Milton, 337
Moonrise, 328, 345 note 2
Morgan, Dale, 132, 245
    on *This Is the Place: Utah*, 252, 254–55
    working style, 261 note 26
Morgan, John H., 383, 384–85
Mormon Country, 236, 257
"Mormon Ghost Story, A," 360
Mormon literature, interest in (1970s), 387
"Mormon Midwives," 157 note 54
"Mormon Saga," 44, 134, 147, 154 note 15
Mormon Tabernacle Choir, 123
Morrill Act, 11 note 15
Morris, Josie Bassett, 297–98, 307
Moseley, Hardwick, 119, 134, 141
Moss, Frank E., 382
Moss, George McCallister, 39, 49 notes 11–12
Moss, Gilbert, 39, 49 note 12
Moss, Jane McAllister, 12, note 23, 15
    children, 49 note 12
    death, 154 note 3
    disliked *Giant Joshua*, 131
    Florence Whipple Jolley on, 19
    piano, 19
Moss, Thelma Ruston. *See* Villanueva, Thelma Ruston Moss.
Mount Timpanogas. *See* Timpanogas.
Mountain Meadows Massacre, 167, 247
    in *Giant Joshua*, 161
    MW on, 291 note 26, 314 note 14, 337, 374
    proposed movie about, 337
    site, 306
Muddy Mission (NV), 154 note 5
Munk, Lewis, 62–63, 71 note 12
Munk, Mildred. See Jensen, Mildred Munk.
Musser (teacher in St. George), 56
"My Most Unforgettable Character," 308. *See also* Bert MacBride.

N

Nation, 106 note 1
National Endowment for the Arts, 383
National Endowment for the Humanities, 383
National Foundation for Infantile Paralysis, 202
National Foundation on the Arts and Humanities, 383
National Park Service, 382
National Research Council, 202
National Science Foundation, 383
Natural Bridges National Monument, 241
Nauvoo Caravan, 295
Nauvoo, IL, 6
Navajo art, 341
Navajo Bridge, 362 note 8
Navajo Nation, 315 note 30
Nazis, refugees from, 156 note 50
Neighborhood House (Salt Lake City), 73–74, 346 note 15
Nellwyn (no surname), 204
Nelsen, Althea Snow, 382
Nelson, L. E., 201, 226–27
Nevada test site. *See* atomic testing.
Nevills, Jean, 242
Nevills, Norman, 241–42, 244 note 25, 247, 253, 294, 308
New Harmony, UT, 138
Newhouse Hotel (Salt Lake City), 202
Newsweek, 230
New York City
    friends in, 86
    MW in, 121–22, 179, 188 note 24, 192, 194, 205, 269–71, 275
New York Times, 197
New York University, 190 note 53
New York World Telegram, 276
Nicholes, Joseph K., 29–30, 99 note 19, 182
Nielsen, Glen B., xi
Nielson, Mary. *See* Campbell, Mary Nielson.
Nielson, Ruth, 383
Nielson, William E., 20, 383
Night at Hogswallow, 327–28
Nixon, Patricia, 385
Nixon, Richard M., 384
Noah and ark, 243 note 9
Noall, Claire Wilcox, 146, 157 note 54
Noelte, Henry, 74
Noelte, Marian, 74, 96, 117, 178
No Man Knows My History, 257

445

Norris, Frank, 64
Nuttall, Maurice, 366
Nyswander, Dorothy Bird, 176, 187 note 8, 194

O

O'Donald, May, 270
O'Halloran, Paul, 350
O'Hara, Scarlet (in *Gone with the Wind*), 2
Oakason, Jim, 45
Ober, Harold, 238, 260 note 8
"Oberammergau of the Hike." *See* Timpanogas.
Oberlin College, 263
Office of War Information, 251
Ogden Standard-Examiner, 258
oil speculation, 56
Old Fats (Navajo), 308
Omnibook Magazine, 180
Opera House (St. George), 20
Orton, Lollie, 65
Ostenson, Alva, 45
Ostenson, Phillip, 45
"Overcoat, The," 360
Oxford, Ohio, 229, 263

P

Pace, Jane, 98 note 10
Pacific Palisades, CA, 337
Pack, Gene, 174 note 43, 358–59, 374
Palmer, John W., 374
Palm Springs, CA
    George Whipple in, 267
    MW in, 201, 226, 312, 327–32
Palm Village, CA, 346 note 14
Palmyra, NY, 367
Panama Canal, 200
Panguitch Lake, 399
Panguitch, UT, xii, 421
Parade's End, 106 note 2
Paramount Pictures, 106 note 1
Parry Lodge (Kanab, Utah), 287, 318, 379
Parry, Whit, 287, 318, 379

Paul Small Artists Ltd., 354
Payne, A. Luke, 303–4, 306–7
Peabody, George Foster, 141
Pearson, Carol Lynn, 387–88, 393 note 48
Pearson, Gerald, 387–88, 393 note 48
Pectol, Joni M., 413–14
Pectol, Wilferd W., 413–14
pellagra, 191, 230
Perham, George, 44
Peter's Leap, 269–70, 360, 369, 382, 399
Peters, Lyman, 6
Peterson, Charles S., 261 note 26, 371 note 13
Peterson, Levi S., xi, 347 note 29, 420
Peterson, Vern, 329
Philadelphia Inquirer, 257
Philippine Liberation Medal, 273 note 14
Phillips, Elvitta, 258
Phoenix, Mary Morris
    biography, 33 note 6
    on Easter pageant, 366
    on MW, xi, 46
    on Charlie Whipple, 16, 34 note 17, 380
    on George Whipple, 267, 406
    on Patsy Kear, 408
    on Ralph Whipple, 29
Pickett, Ellis, 359, 365
Pickett, Ellis, Jr., 376
Pickett, Evan, 270
Pickett, Faun Schmutz, xi, 269–70, 385
Pickford, Mary, 297
"Pickle Is a Dilly, The," 342, 348 notes 55–56, 354, 359
Picklesimer, Fae Garda Anderson, 320
Pike (of Los Angeles), 67
pine nuts, 21, 135, 216
Pine Valley
    Eli Whipple in, 6–7, 8–9, 100 note 51
    Foster family in, 35 note 46
    MW takes guests to, 374, 399
    stories about, 132
Pioche, NV, 112, 161
Pioneer Stake (Salt Lake City), 214
Playmakers, 358
Plumhof, H. J., 247
Poland Bill, 114
Poland, invaded, 148

INDEX

polygamy. *See also Giant Joshua.*
    contemporary, 309
    in *Giant Joshua*, 2, 3, 8, 166–67
    in Short Creek, 343
    in St. George, 16–17
    laws governing, 11 note 15
    MW on, 7–8
    readers' reactions to, 186
"Poor Wayfaring Man of Grief," 425 note 52
Porter, Katherine Ann, 141
Poseidon Adventure, The, 315 note 32
Poultney River, 6
Power, Tyrone, 177
Pratt, Orson, 157 note 65
Pratt, Orson, Jr., 149, 157 note 65
Preston, Kaylene, 416
Price, George McCreadie, 243 note 9
Prince George Hotel, 179
Prisbey, Arlo, xi, 20, 66, 118
Providence, RI, 127 note 26, 152
Provo Daily Herald, 284
pseudonyms, use of x, 99 note 25
Pulitzer Prize, 11 note 3, 164, 345 note 1
Purdy, William, 366
Pymm, Eva, 20, 21
Pymm, Johnny, 20, 21

Q

Quail Reservoir, 417
"Quest of the Soul, The," 232
Quetzalcoatl, 324 note 1
Quicksand, 103
Quill, The, 419
Quinn, D. Michael, 347 note 29
Quote, 119

R

Rae, Alta. *See* Whipple, Alta Rae.
Rainbow Bridge
    and Art Greene, 332
    and Norman Nevills, 308
    article on, 334, 362 note 8

    discussed on radio program, 359
    MW visits/plans visit, 241–42, 244 note 25, 294, 331, 359, 362 note 8
"Rainbow Gold," 362 note 8
Rainbow over San Juan, 283
Ramsey, Agnes, 307
Rance, Leah Whipple, 7, 14, 39, 65, 118
Ransom, John Crowe, 354
Rasmussen, E. R., 284
"Rassy B. Corner," 382
Rawlins, WY, 75, 88
RCA Photophone, Inc., 79
Reader's Almanac, 127 note 33, 190 note 53, 191, 193
    MW proposes articles to, 308–12, 321
    quotes *Giant Joshua*, 201, 221 note 34
Reading, Lucile Cardon, 12 note 24
Red Cross, 251
Redford, Grant Hubbard, 93–94, 96, 104–5, 365
Redford, Gwen Hubbard, 93–94
Redford, Robert, 403–4, 422 note 3
Redford, Thomas L., 93
Redlands, CA, 226
Redmon, Peggy Dowst, 317, 321
Redwood City, CA, 6, 375
Reeves, Ray, 64
Reporter Magazine, 157 note 56
Reynolds, Paul R., 386, 392 note 43
Rhoades, Frank
    acknowledged in *This Is the Place: Utah*, 260 note 6
    romance with, 238–41, 264
Rice, Clayton S., 277, 316 note 49, 332, 405
Rice, Clinton, 232
Rich, Charles Coulson family, 298–99, 301 note 14, 302 note 15, 304
Richards, Fred Frosty, 69
Richards, Ralph, 292 note 43
Richards, Stephen L., 61
Richardson, Jerry, 89
Richfield, UT, MW at, 68
Riley, Rob (pseud.), x, 47, 91–92, 94–96, 105–6, 108 note 13, 193, 197
Rising Arrow, 173 note 27
Roberts, Eugene, 243 note 11
Robertson, Frank C., 284, 291 note 31

447

Rocky Mountain Reader, 286
Rocky Mountain Writers' Conference
 and Lillian McQuarrie, 87, 97
 MW at, 1, 103–7, 108 note 9, 118, 123–24, 134, 168, 175–76, 182, 258, 263, 288
Rogers, Buddy, 297
Rogers, Edna, 374
Rogers, Verlene Brinkerhoff, 377 note 7
Romney, George, 384–85
Romney, Miles, 384
Romney, Roxy, 181
Roosevelt, Franklin D., 86
Rose, John David, 383
Rosenblatt, Joseph, 291 note 14, 377 note 12, 381
Rosenblatt Prize, 291 note 14
Rose, Stuart, 268
Roundy, Violet, 29
Rowley, Dennis, ix, xi, 388–89, 410, 419
Roylance, Ward Jay, 390 note 10
Ruppel, Lou, 341
Rusho, W. L. ("Bud"), 359, 362 note 8
Russell, Gail, 345 note 2

S

Salinger, J. D., 107 note 3
Saltair, 42
Salt Lake City, UT
 MW in, 199, 222 note 55, 276–81
 Recreation Department, 73
Salt Lake Theater, 42
Salt Lake Tribune
 article on MW, 231, 334
 MW applies for job, 381–82
 reviews *This Is the Place: Utah*, 257
 rejects MW's articles, 379, 382
Samuel Brannan and the Golden Fleece, 173 note 14
Sanderson, Selwyn, 290 note 12
Sand Town (in St. George), 45
"Sanitarium that God Built, The," 351–52. *See also* alcoholism.
Santa Clara Creek, 147
Santa Clara, UT, 16, 59, 407, 416, 427
"Sarah Jane," in MW's wartime lectures, 32

Saratoga, NY, 137, 142
Saturday Evening Post
 MW's articles for, 237, 268, 294, 309, 317–18, 321
 rejects MW articles, 320, 354
Saucer–Five Ranch, 305–6
sawmills, 6, 8
Scarsdale, NY, 123, 269
Scarth, Jim, 386
Schiavo, Elizabeth, 411–14, 424 note 36
Schmidt, Walter R., 354, 360
Schmutz, Amber, 269
Schmutz, Donald, 269
School of Alcohol Studies, University of Utah, 349
Science, 230
Science Digest, 252
Scott, Reva Lucile Holdaway, 161–62, 172 note 14, 173 note 14
Search, The, 387
Seattle, WA, MW in, 93
Seegmiller, Anna Eve Knechtle, 154 note 5
Seegmiller, Artimissia ("Misha/Mishie"), 15–16, 33 note 3, 380
Seegmiller, Charles William, Sr., 33 note 4, 109, 174 note 43
 biography, 154 note 5
 MW interviews, 132
Seegmiller, Donald P., 132–33, 178, 225, 373
Seegmiller, Emma, 33 note 4
Seegmiller, Ida Maria Morris, 33 note 4
Seegmiller, Johann Adam, 154 note 5
Seegmiller, Marianne Forsyth, 154 note 5
Seegmiller, Nita, 65
Seegmiller, Ruby, 98 note 10
sego lilies, in *Giant Joshua*, 160
Selznick, David O., 11 note 3
sequel/trilogy (variously titled "Cleave the Wood," "The Candles of the Lord")
 encouragement for, 131, 253, 338, 396, 398
 forms, 206, 283, 290 note 12
 manuscript stolen (1970), 282
 MW admits inability to finish, 419
 MW blames Tom Spies for inability to write, 197, 199
 MW works on/delays work on, 113, 137, 201, 206, 210, 224 note 72, 236, 275–92, 320, 327, 329–31, 334,

INDEX

339, 304, 342, 343, 350, 375, 381, 400
number of volumes, 109, 283, 354
possible effects, 184–85
reasons for avoiding, 197–98, 320
summary, 184, 278–79, 282, 288, 359–60
titles of, 358–59, 44, 365
Tony (character in), 278, 288, 290 note 12
Sequoia National Park, 39
serials for magazines, 253. *See also* Read Bain.
Shadel, Charles A., 350–51; wife, 351, 356 note 12
Shadel Sanatorium for the Treatment of Alcoholics, 350–52, 395, 398. *See* alcoholism.
Shadow Mountain Club (Palm Springs), 332, 334
Shakespearean Festival (Cedar City), 367
Shepherd, Robert L., 355, 367–68, 407, 416
Sherman, Harold, 370
Shirts, Morris, 399
Shirts, Peter, 399
Shorn Lamb, 173 note 27
Short Creek, AZ, 343, 353
Short Story, 154 note 15
Shurr, Sybil, 270
Silcox, Luise M., 318, 322–23, 330
silk industry, 167
Silver Cord, The, 80
Silver Horn Mine, 13
Silver, Julia May McAllister Nielson, 37, 48, 59
Silver Reef, NV, 369
Simon and Schuster, 150, 269, 275, 279–80, 287, 314 note 22
Sinclair, Marguerite S., 146
Smart, Demi, 281
Smith, Bernard, 238, 250–52, 260 note 8
Smith, Claire M., 260 note 8, 386
Smith, George Albert, 295
Smith, Grant T., 417–18
Smith, Hyrum, and Gail, 384
Smith, Joseph
  dramatic portrayal of, 407
  in *Giant Joshua*, 145
Smith, Joseph F., 16–17
Smith, Lou/Louie Harris Miller, 31, 34 note 26, 181–82, 189 note 37, 258, 337

Smith, Penn, 189 note 37
Smithson, Carma Lee, 334
Smoot, Reed, 18, 243 note 17, 249
Snow Canyon, 367, 368, 369
Snow, Delworth, 50 note 16
Snow, Erastus
  and Eli Whipple, 6
  character in *Giant Joshua*, 145, 149, 164–65, 168–70, 385
Snow, Erastus B., 382
Snow, Eric, 289 note 2, 366, 382
Snow, Glen, 181
Snow Goose, The, 315 note 32
Snow, Jetta ("Jet"), 40, 50 note 16
Snow, Pauline, 40
Snow, Robert G., 279
Snow, Vernon, 289 note 2
Snow, William, 9
Sociological Research Association, 229, 234 note 18
Sons of Utah Pioneers, 295
Sorensen, Virginia, 185, 387, 389
Southern Quarterly, 155 note 15
Southern States Mission, 37
Southern Utah State College/University, 35 note 40, 93, 399
Southey, Trevor, 387, 393 note 48
Southgate, Hallie, 107 note 3
Southwestern Utah Arts Council, 367
Spanish American War, in sequel, 279
Spencer, Nick (pseud.), x, 83–88, 106, 193, 197
Spencer Wire Company, 220 note 13
Spies, Ann, 220 note 13, 222 note 39
Spies, Mary, 202
Spies, Tom Douglas
  as scientist, 127 note 33, 230
  biography, 191–92
  mother, 193
  MW's romance with, 191–225, 264, 303, 306, 350
"Spillway, The"
  in "The Unpromised Land," 369
  reenactment, 385–86
Spokane Daily Chronicle, 258
Spotty (dog), 136
Springville, UT, 420

449

St. George Care and Rehabilitation Center, ix, 50 note 16, 416–21
St. George Library, 337
St. George Spectrum
    MW letter to, 416
    on Easter pageant, 368
    on MW, 397, 407, 416
    on MW's caregivers, 414
    on spillway reenactment, 386
    statistics on plural marriage in, 98 note 12
St. George Tabernacle, 22, 384, 429
St. George Temple, 3
St. George, UT
    as character in *Giant Joshua*, 113, 115
    high school, 22
    intellectual culture, vii
    MW's conflicts with, 373–76, 381
St. Thomas, NV, 339, 340, 342
Standrod, Kenneth L., 386
Stanford University, 243 note 2
Stanley, Reva Holdaway. *See* Scott, Reva.
Stardust (Las Vegas), 386
Star Nursery, 384
Steele, Marjorie, 342
Steen, Charlie, 357–61, 365, 368, 370 note 1, 419
Steen, M. L., 358, 360–61
Stegner, Wallace, 236, 243 note 2, 257
Stein, Gertrude, 387
Stephens, Norlene, 425 note 52
"Stewart Campbell," 293
Stewart, Charlotte S., 73, 82
Stewart Junior High (Salt Lake City), 46
Story Magazine, 103, 107 note 3
"Story of a Man's Life, The," 44, 50 note 26
"Story within the Story," 343
Stowell, Brian J., 397
Strauss, Eric, 335, 341
Strauss, Theodore ("Ted"), 327–30, 332–33, 335–42, 349–50
sugar beets, 331
Sugarloaf, MW's feelings for, 14, 130, **131**, 266, 285
Sulfanilamide, 112
Sullivan, Camellia ("Camie") Carter. *See* Higgins, Camellia ("Camie") Carter Sullivan.
Sullivan, Charles R., 5

Sullivan, Grace McAllister, 5, 12 note 23, 41
Sullivan, Lenzi M., 41
Sundance Film Festival/Institute, 422 note 3
Sunnyside (ranch), 14, 19, 22–23, 87
Sunstone, 50 note 25, 417, 425 note 51
Sweeping Wind: A Memoir, The, 219 note 2
"swell," defined, 107 note 7

T

"Taming of the Virgin River, The," 174 note 43
Tanner, Annie Atkin, 132
Tanner, Vasco, 132
Taylor, Curtis
    attends jubilee picnic, 420
    attends MW's funeral, 421
    encourages biography, xi
    interviews MW, 194, 206–7, 211, 417
    MW's temple endowment, 418
    publishes anthology, 419
Taylor, Robert, 341
Taylor, Samuel W., 375, 376
Tebbs, Daniel, xii
Tebbs, Glen, ix
Tebbs, Karen, xii
Tebbs, Ray, 421
Tel Aviv, Israel, 409
Tennyson, Alfred, 58
Tenotchilan (Mexico City), 324 note 1
Terracor, 383–84, 392 note 31
"They Did Go Forth," 360, 420, 425 note 51
Thi Delta Phi, 202
Thiesen, Earl, 213–14, 216
The Thirties: A Time to Remember, 290 note 13
This Is the Place: Utah
    agent for, 386
    errors in, 258
    fans, 258
    Josie Bassett Morris in, 297–99
    Knopf accepts, 238
    MW blames Church for sales, 281
    MW's evaluation, 251
    MW feels cheated, 320
    MW works on, 237, 240–41, 317, 245–59

INDEX

origin of, 216
printing plates, melted, 331
quotes Joseph Walker, 162
reviews, 252, 254–58
sales, 252, 255–56, 303–4, 330
sites featured in, 295
summary, 247–50
Thomas, Elbert (of St. George), 401 note 7
Thomas, Elbert Duncan, 240, 243 note 17, 258
Thorne, Pat, 359
"Thou Shalt Love Thy Neighbor," 50 note 25
Three Nephites, 339
"Through the Utah Wonderlands," 284, 293, 301 note 1, 307
Time (magazine), 180, 293
"Time Will Come, The," 211, 223 note 57, 236, 284, 318
Timpanogas hike (titled "Lunatics, By One of Them" and "The Timpanogas Hike"), 238–39, 243 note 11, 307, 309, 321, 322, 325 note 20, 331, 339
Tompkins, P. W., 241, 244 note 25
"To My Child," 41, 425 note 51
Transatlantic Review, 106 note 2
Trappe, Jake, 182
Trask, Katrina, 141
Trask, Spencer, 141
trilogy. *See* sequel/trilogy.
Tropicana (Las Vegas), 386
True Magazine, 310
Truman, Ruth Foremaster, 23
Tuahcan, 368
Tucson, AZ, MW in, 225
"Tueben Noonie Country," 363 note 14
Twenty–Fourth of July parade, 295

U

U.S. Bureau of Land Management, 329
U.S. Navy, 201
U.S. State Department, 409
Union Pacific Bus/Railroad, 119
"University Calling You," 359
University Club (University of Utah), 292 note 43
University of Cincinnati, 191, 230

University of Colorado, 263
University of Louisville, 263
University of Redlands, 201, 226–27, 288
University of Utah
    alcoholism research, 349–50
    archives, 389
    Emeritus Club, 388
    honorary degree to Juanita Brooks, 35 note 40
    MW as student at, 37–51, 69, 73, 246
    MW lectures at, 202, 221 note 31
    Physical Education Dept., 50 note 23
    president's home, 291 note 14
    radio station, 358
    Speech Dept., 50 note 23
    Wallace Stegner at, 243 note 2
University of Utah Press, 259 note 1
University of Wisconsin, 243 note 2
University Pen, 44, 50 note 25, 103
"Unnecessary Ovariectomies," 290 note 21
"Unpromised Land, The"
    article, 174 note 43, 363 note 14, 367, 368–69
    book, 360, 381, 383–84, 386–87, 398
Utah Agricultural College. *See* Utah State University.
Utah and the Nation, 146
Utah Beehive Hall of Fame, 35 note 40
Utah Bicentennial Commission, 363 note 14
Utah Department of Community Affairs, 383
Utah Fine Arts Committee, 368
Utah Fine Arts Council, 368–69
Utah Guide, 254–55
Utah Power and Light Company, 249
Utah State Division of Fine Arts, 367, 368
Utah State Historical Society, 146, 389
Utah State Institute of Fine Arts, 367, 368
Utah State Publicity and Industrial Development Committee, 244 note 25, 247
Utah State University, 14, 35 note 40, 93
Utah Travel Council, 383
"Utah Wonderland Tour," 293, 317
Utah's American Revolution Bicentennial Commission, 369
"Utah's Pioneer Women Doctors," 157 note 54

451

V

Val A. Browning Library, vii, xi
Vandegrift, Julia, MW, xii
Vanderford, Gladys, 269
Vanderford, T. S., 123, 269
Van Wagenen, Lola, 403
Van Wagenen, Sterling, 403–5, 415, 422 notes 3 and 5, 423 note 11
Vanity Fair, 106 note 1
Vepricula, The, 168
Vernal, UT, 297, 298
Villanueva, Mitch, 49 note 11
Villanueva, Thelma Ruston Moss, 39, 49 note 11
Virgin Narrows/Gorge, 382
Virgin River, 67, 132, 296
Virgin, UT, 66
Virginia Quarterly Review, 134
vitamin research, 137, 191–92, 193, 196–97
Viterbo College, 417
Von Hake, R. W., 317–18

W

Waddoups, Bernice, 43, 44
Walker, Abigail Middlemass, 132, 173 note 15
Walker, Charles Lowell, 50 note 19, 132, 162, 173 note 15
Walker, Christina ("Tina") Woodbury, 162–64, 169, 173 note 15, 177, 207
Walker, Joseph, **344**
    affection for Mormonism, 277
    biography, 173 note 15
    encourages MW, 162–64, 169, 177, 207, 258, 277
    influence, 250
    introduction to friend, 337
    model for Frank Wright, 278
    nephew, 421
    personality, 162
    provides housing for MW, 162, 200, 342–43, 349. *See also* date ranch.
    treats MW's ailments, 237, 281
Walker, Milton, 65
Ward, Evelyn Harris, xi, 34 note 26, 65–66, 101 note 55, 258, 305, 337

"War from the Standpoint of Your Favorite Old Maid, The," 228
Warner Brothers, 337, 347 note 29
Warren, Robert Penn, 154–55 note 15
Washington Cotton Mill, 384
Washington County News
    letter from Joseph Walker, 178
    on Easter pageant, 366
    on *Giant Joshua*, 181
    on MW, 117, 124, 195
Washington, D.C., MW at, 195, 197, 205, 220 note 15
Washington Normal School, 29
Waters, C. R., 343
Watson, Alma Gertrude, 347 note 32
Watson, Barbara, 366
Watson, Lorenzo Dow, 347 note 32
Watson, Sarah Melissa Clark, 347 note 32
Webb, LaVarr G., 368, 371 note 20, 389
Webb, Loren, 414
Weber State College, 409
Weeks, Stiddy (character in *Giant Joshua*), 173 note 26
Weeks, Ted, 134
Welfare Program (LDS), 214
Weller, Sam, 359, 386–87, 393 note 46, 420
Wells-Fargo bank, 341
Wellwood Murray Memorial Library (Palm Springs), 329
Welty, Eudora, 141
Wesleyan University, 125 note 3
Western Epics, 387, 416
Western Gateway, 400
Western Protestant Church League, 277
Weston, John N. ("Jack"), 228
West, Ray B., 286
Westwood, Dale, xii
Westwood, Shirley, xii
Whipple, Alice Titus
    building new house, 161
    children, 212
    distances self from MW, 405
    encourages MW, xii, 111–12, 118, 137
    on Charlie Whipple's favoritism of MW, 20, 91, 380
    on *Giant Joshua*, 181
Whipple, Alta Rae, 231, 385, 392 note 36

INDEX

Whipple, Annie McAllister, **40**
    and flowers, 22
    and *Giant Joshua*, 147, 181
    and Mormonism, 16
    birth, 8
    corresponds with MW, 55
    death, 353
    depressed, 22–23, 59–60, 329
    marriage, 13–16
    musical ability, 12 note 23, 19
    on movie theater, 22
    on saws, 16
    relation to MW, 67, 111, 168, 221 note 24, 275, 310
    MW on, 18–19
    relation to parents and siblings, 5
Whipple, Caroline Lytle Peters, 6–7, 9, 14, 392 note 36
Whipple, Chandler, 321
Whipple, Charlie, **40**
    and cars, 15–16, **40**, 56
    and Great Depression, 67, 81–82
    and Mormonism, 5, 7, 16, 60
    and MW as schoolteacher, 54, 61–62, 66
    and other women, 15–16, 39
    as businessman, 14–15, 20–22
    as model for Jim MacIntyre, 278
    athleticism, 19
    at Utah Agricultural College, 14
    birth/youth, 8
    death, 380
    excommunication/rebaptism, 61, 71 note 12, 380
    gives Maurine money/help, 46, 51 note 33, 118, 119, 285, 287–88, 305, 352, 354–55, 356 note 22, 380
    intellectual tastes, 20
    makes bookcase, 14
    makes desk for MW, vii, 118, 334, 392 note 42, 415
    marriage, stress in, 12, 32, 111
    MW gives money to, 221 note 24
    MW on, 18–19, 304–5
    on *Giant Joshua*, 147, 180–81
    orders piano for Florence, 34 note 31
    physical description, 13
Whipple/Peters, Edgar, 392 note 36

Whipple, Effie. *See* Burraston, Effie Whipple.
Whipple, Eli, 6–7, 9, 11 note 18, 18, 100 note 51
Whipple, Eli, Jr., 285
Whipple family
    as source for *Giant Joshua*, 133
    poverty, 281
Whipple, Fammie Nelson, 33 note 1, 34 note 26
Whipple, Flora Linderberger, 226
Whipple, Flora Truba, 233 note 7, 267
Whipple, Florence. *See* Jolley, Florence Whipple.
Whipple, George Wayne, **40**
    alcoholism, 22, 27, 112, 267, 276, 349, 352, 380
    biography, 13, 349, 406, 423 note 16
    in U.S. Army, 207, 229, 233 note 6, 241, 267, 273 note 14
    marriage, 226
    MW's protectiveness, 22–23, 366
    on *Giant Joshua*, 181
Whipple, Grace, 13
Whipple, Ida Johnson Beatty, 29, 35 note 39, 112, 126 note 8
Whipple, Jason, 425 note 52
Whipple, Jesse, 392 note 36
Whipple, John (in 1630s), 127 note 26
Whipple, John David, 212
Whipple, John Lytle, 13–14, 19, 34 note 25, 87, 278
Whipple, Leah. *See* Rance, Leah Whipple.
Whipple, Mary Jane Legg, 6–7, 11 note 18, 100 note 51
Whipple, Matthew, 127 note 26
Whipple, Maurine, **40, 328, 335, 344**. *See also titles of works and* McQuarrie, Lillian.
    and cars, 332, 337, 345
    and liberal Mormons, 215
    and Mormonism/Church, 23–24, 53–54, 60–61, 75–76, 85–86, 98 note 10, 99 note 28, 115, 121–25, 167, 213–14, 236, 247–50, 281–82, 284, 303, 369. *See also* "Grand Idea."
    and scriptwriting, 225
    as interviewer. 339–40
    as schoolteacher, 53–71, **63**, 90. *See also individual schools.*
    attachment to St. George/pioneers, viii, 103, 124–25, 131, 397, 420

453

at University of Utah, 37–51, 73
at Yaddo, 141–49, 161
blurs reality/fiction, 24–25, 46–47, 53, 192–94, 213, 217, 228, 255–56, 271, 305, 312, 314 note 12, 369
childhood, 25, **25**
claims attempted rape, 298
claims Declaration of Independence signer as ancestor, 119, 121
conceals age, 90, 116, 295, 407, 415
death and funeral, 421–22, 425 notes 52–53
dislikes parents' house, 21, 44, 111, 130, 147, 148, 168, 285, 303
dramatics, 25, 40, 66, 80
fears losing talent, 399
feels inferior, 26–27, 29–32, 114, 152, 184
harassed by teenagers, 355
health problems, 133
    bladder infections, 225, 306
    car accidents, 373–74, 386
    detached kidney, 200, 229–30, 281
    heart problems, 345
    hysterectomy, 281, 290 note 21
    injury, 74, 212, 225, 360, 407
    insomnia, 169
    menstruation/menopause, 152, 162, 169, 237, 281, 361
    osteopathic problems, 156 note 41
    paralyzed arm, 328, 345, 361
    radiation poisoning, 361
    respiratory ailments/allergies, 41, 136, 152, 162, 198, 220 note 16, 237, 242, 279, 281, 290 note 16, 338, 360–61, 398
    stomach pain, 202
    sub-acute meningitis, 345
    surgeries, 64, 71 note 18, 310, 312, 361, 367, 407
    teeth, 43–44, 55, 152, 162, 178, 187 note 3
    tuberculosis, 81
high school years, 29–31
honesty, 55
incapacity of (1982–92), 407–25, 407
"jinx," 177
job-seeking tactics, 332, 336–37

lacks domestic skills, 18, 49 note 12, 80
lacks writing discipline, 178, 283–84, 295, 300, 308, 311, 323, 338, 386, 396–97, 415
last publications, 400, 416
lectures, for war effort, 200, 225–32, 242, 251
marriage to/divorce from Emil de Neuf, 78–81
money management, 123, 127 note 35, 136, 160, 161, 179, 199, 218, 221 notes 24–25, 247, 276, 290 note 16, 309–11, 312–13, 318, 320, 322, 327, 330, 337, 351, 353, 354, 357–59, 381–84, 390 note 8, 392 note 30, 403
movies as influence on, 21
neediness of, x, 1, 9–10, 105–6, 155 note 22, 197–98, 226, 236, 240, 268, 270, 310–11, 323, 327
on Bernard DeVoto, 188 note 27
on Brigham Young, 121
on Charlie Whipple, 18–19, 33 note 15, 61, 304–5
on Cornelia Lenzi McAllister, 122
on John A. Widtsoe, 184
on Juanita Brooks, 256
on Ralph Whipple, 28–29
on Ray Whipple, 27
on parents' marriage, 14–18, 40, 60, 168
on polygamy, 18, 76–77, 122, 147
on writing, 26, 360
photo collection of, xi
physical appearance, ix, 27, 44
plagiarism, 254–56
poems by, 30, 41, 123, 422, 425 note 51
portrait of, vii
possible LDS mission, 424 note 47
possible role models, 32, 73
rape and abortion, 90–91, 258
receives government relief, 353, 380, 383, 385, 399, 411–12
reviews books, 236
robbed (1971), 3, 283, 361, 369, 408
romances, dysfunctional, vii, 31–32, 38–39, 46–47, 54–58, 61, 83–89, 91–92, 93–94, 115, 191–224, 238–41, 245, 258, 264, 335–41

INDEX

rumors of 1939 abortion, 150
suicidal, 91, 96
senses ghosts, 144, 153, 319, 413
takes photography class, 381
teaches dance/recreation, 29, 59, 67–68, 69, 70 note 8, 80, 82, 84, 88, 92, 98 note 10, 112
temple endowment, 418
trailer at St. George, 285, 287
writing as altered state of consciousness, 109–10, 129
writing methods, 109–10, 112, 130, 133
"you see" letters, 95–96, 97, 150, 197, 208, 218, 240, 264, 286–87, 331–32, 335–36, 341

Whipple, Maurine, of Great Barrington, MA, 321
Whipple, Murray, 278
Whipple, Patience Foster, 6–7
Whipple, Phoebe Alta Marshall, 392 note 36
Whipple, Ralph, **40**
    and Great Depression, 67
    and movie theater, 20
    appendectomy, 38, 64, 81
    birth, 13
    childhood/youth, 14
    death, 126 note 8, 242, 264
    musical ability, 28
    MW gives money to, 221 note 24
    recklessness and drinking, 68, 112
    stammers, 28
    works with Charlie, 28
Whipple, Ray. *See* Charles Ray Whipple.
Whipple, Charles Ray ("Ray"), **40**
    and movie theater, 20
    and theater troupe, 55
    at University of Utah, 55, 68, 73
    birth, 13
    building new house, 161
    childhood, 14
    children, 212
    death, 405
    drinking, 27
    injury, 68
    lumber business, 34 note 23, 111
    musical ability, 28, 58, 111
    MW corresponds with, 65, 71 note 21

    popularity, 27–28
Whipple, Reed, 354, 380
Whipple, Rose Ellen Eleanor, 34 note 25, 87
White, C. A., 58–59
White Pine County, NV, 14
Whittaker, David J., xi
Who, 210
Widtsoe, John A., review of *Giant Joshua*, 147, 183–84, 213–14
Wilcock, Arthur G., 410, 411, 413
Wilcock, Lenna C., 411, 413
Wild Horse Range, 303
Wilford Ward (Salt Lake City), 76
Williamsburg-West Project, 384–85
Willie (king snake), 318, **319**, 324 note 10
Wilson, Richard, 418, 421
Wiltshire Ward (Los Angeles), 76
Winkelmann, Ellen, 374–75
Winmill, Maxine, 425 note 52
Winmill, Relva, 425 note 52
Winsor, Tillie, 15
Wolfe, Thomas, 278
Women's Club of Evanston, IL, 232
Woodbury, Angus M., 221 note 31, 199
Woodbury, Clare Watson, 38–39, 49 note 7, 61, 81, 83
Woodbury, Franklin Jeremiah, 49 note 7
Woodbury, George J., 173 note 15
Woodbury, Grace Atkin, 199, 221 note 31
Woodbury, John T., 241
Woodbury, Lola Andrus, 49 note 7
Woodbury, Melissa Vivian Watson, 49 note 7
Woodbury, Rowena Romney, 173 note 15
Woodruff, Wilford, 5
Woodward, Dale, 399
Woodward, Shirley, 399
Wordsworth, William, 315 note 31
Workman, Carl Fenton, 66, 67
Works Progress Administration, 81, 176, 224 note 72
World War I, 16, 177
World War II. *See also* Maurine Whipple, lecture.
    Ferris Greenslet on, 177
    MW oblivious to, 148, 167
    status, 226, 265, 268
Worth, Louis, 249

455

Wright, David (character in *Giant Joshua*), 160, 168
Wright, Frank (character in sequel/trilogy), 224 note 72, 278, 288, 290 note 12
Wright, Lucy (character in *Giant Joshua*), 165
Wright, Palmyra (character in *Giant Joshua*), 160, 165, 278
Writer's Round Table, 227
Writers for the War Board, 201
Writers' Round-Up, 185
Writers' Week (University of Redlands), 288

Y

Yaddo (artists' colony)
    Greenslet arranges MW's admission, 137–38, 140
    MW at, 141–49, 161
Yellow Jack: A History, 219 note 2
Yellowstone Park, 40
Yosemite National Park, 39
Young, Amelia Folsom, 167
Young, Brigham
    and Utah War, 6
    Beehive House, 43
    descendant, 293
    in *Giant Joshua*, 129, 149, 160–61, 166
    in *This Is the Place: Utah*, 248
    MW considers biography, 202
    praise for MW's portrayal, 167
    Winter Home, MW works at, 319, 325 note 14, 334, 337
Young, David A., 218
Young, Emily Dow Partridge, 293
Young, John R., 6
Young, Levi Edgar
    on *The Giant Joshua*, 185
    MW corresponds with, 245, 268, 310, 332
    scholarly works, 146
Young, Lucy Bigelow, 167
Young Women's Mutual Improvement Association, 73

Z

ZCMI, 256, 307
Zeb (character in "Cleave the Wood"), 279
Zenk, Stan, 419, 420, 421
Zion National Park, 66, 93–94, 283, 308

About the Author

Veda Tebbs Hale grew up in Panguitch, Utah, the descendant of Henrie, Tebbs, Asay, Riding, Prince, Schow, and Lee ancestors who were among the first settlers in southern Utah, including in St. George during the period covered by Maurine Whipple's *The Giant Joshua*. Veda had been deeply moved by her first reading of the St. George saga and returned to it repeatedly.

Veda and her husband, Glen, raised their three sons in Murray, Utah, and then at a cattle ranch in Kamas, Utah. In 1990, they moved to St. George where Glen managed Central Storage, and they owned and operated a mailing service business until 2000.

Surprised to discover that Maurine was still alive, Veda befriended the elderly novelist and Carol Jensen, Maurine's legal guardian, and soon decided to write a full-scale biography. Veda conducted informal interviews with the writer, relatives, and associates, explored deeply in Maurine's papers held at Brigham Young University, and painstakingly reconstructed the national and regional background of Maurine Whipple's life.

Veda, a painter, and Glen spend summers at their dream log cabin on the Tebbs family ranch near Panguitch Lake and market Veda's art in her gallery in downtown Panguitch. Their winters are spent in Pleasant Grove, Utah, near their family. She is the author of a novel, *The Ragged Circle* (Springville, Utah: Salt Press, 2003)."

Also available from
GREG KOFFORD BOOKS

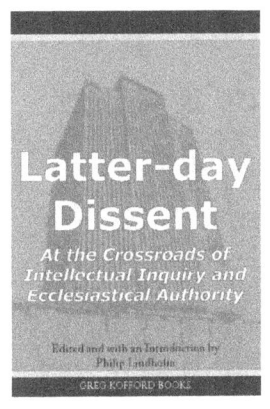

Latter-Day Dissent:
At the Crossroads of Intellectual Inquiry and Ecclesiastical Authority

Philip Lindholm

Paperback, ISBN: 978-1-58958-128-9

This volume collects, for the first time in book form, stories from the "September Six," a group of intellectuals officially excommunicated or disfellowshipped from the LDS Church in September of 1993 on charges of "apostasy" or "conduct unbecoming" Church members. Their experiences are significant and yet are largely unknown outside of scholarly or more liberal Mormon circles, which is surprising given that their story was immediately propelled onto screens and cover pages across the Western world.

Interviews by Dr. Philip Lindholm (Ph.D. Theology, University of Oxford) include those of the "September Six," Lynne Kanavel Whitesides, Paul James Toscano, Maxine Hanks, Lavina Fielding Anderson, and D. Michael Quinn; as well as Janice Merrill Allred, Margaret Merrill Toscano, Thomas W. Murphy, and former employee of the LDS Church's Public Affairs Department, Donald B. Jessee.

Each interview illustrates the tension that often exists between the Church and its intellectual critics, and highlights the difficulty of accommodating congregational diversity while maintaining doctrinal unity—a difficulty hearkening back to the very heart of ancient Christianity.

On the Road with Joseph Smith: An Author's Diary

Richard L. Bushman

Paperback, ISBN 978-1-58958-102-9

After living with Joseph Smith for seven years and delivering the final proofs of his landmark study, *Joseph Smith: Rough Stone Rolling* to Knopf in July 2005, biographer Richard Lyman Bushman went "on the road" for a year, crisscrossing the country from coast to coast, delivering addresses on Joseph Smith and attending book-signings for the new biography.

Bushman confesses to hope and humility as he awaits reviews. He frets at the polarization that dismissed the book as either too hard on Joseph Smith or too easy. He yields to a very human compulsion to check sales figures on Amazon. com, but partway through the process stepped back with the recognition, "The book seems to be cutting its own path now, just as [I] hoped."

For readers coming to grips with the ongoing puzzle of the Prophet and the troublesome dimensions of their own faith, Richard Bushman, openly but not insistently presents himself as a believer. "I believe enough to take Joseph Smith seriously," he says. He draws comfort both from what he calls his "mantra" ("Today I will be a follower of Jesus Christ") and also from ongoing engagement with the intellectual challenges of explaining Joseph Smith.

Praise for *On the Road With Joseph Smith*:

"The diary is possibly unparalleled—an author of a recent book candidly dissecting his experiences with both Mormon and non-Mormon audiences ... certainly deserves wider distribution—in part because it shows a talented historian laying open his vulnerabilities, and also because it shows how much any historian lays on the line when he writes about Joseph Smith."
    -Dennis Lythgoe, *Deseret News*

"By turns humorous and poignant, this behind-the-scenes look at Richard Bushman's public and private ruminations about Joseph Smith reveals a great deal—not only about the inner life of one of our greatest scholars, but about Mormonism at the dawn of the 21st century."
    -Jana Riess, co-author of *Mormonism for Dummies*

Hugh Nibley: A Consecrated Life

Boyd Jay Petersen

Hardcover, ISBN: 978-1-58958-019-0

Winner of the Mormon History Association's Best Biography Award

As one of the LDS Church's most widely recognized scholars, Hugh Nibley is both an icon and an enigma. Through complete access to Nibley's correspondence, journals, notes, and papers, Petersen has painted a portrait that reveals the man behind the legend.

Starting with a foreword written by Zina Nibley Petersen and finishing with appendices that include some of the best of Nibley's personal correspondence, the biography reveals aspects of the tapestry of the life of one who has truly consecrated his life to the service of the Lord.

Praise for *A Consecrated Life*:

"Hugh Nibley is generally touted as one of Mormonism's greatest minds and perhaps its most prolific scholarly apologist. Just as hefty as some of Nibley's largest tomes, this authorized biography is delightfully accessible and full of the scholar's delicious wordplay and wit, not to mention some astonishing war stories and insights into Nibley's phenomenal acquisition of languages. Introduced by a personable foreword from the author's wife (who is Nibley's daughter), the book is written with enthusiasm, respect and insight.... On the whole, Petersen is a careful scholar who provides helpful historical context.... This project is far from hagiography. It fills an important gap in LDS history and will appeal to a wide Mormon audience."
            —Publishers Weekly

"Well written and thoroughly researched, Petersen's biography is a must-have for anyone struggling to reconcile faith and reason."
            —Greg Taggart, Association for Mormon Letters

A Different God?
Mitt Romney the Religious Right and the Mormon Question

Craig L. Foster

Paperback, ISBN: 978-1-58958-117-3

In the contested terrain of American politics, nowhere is the conflict more intense, even brutal, than in the territory of public life also claimed by religion. Mitt Romney's 2007–08 presidential campaign is a textbook example.

Religious historian (and ardent Republican) Craig L. Foster revisits that campaign with an astute focus on the never-quite-contained hostility that Romney triggered among America's religious right. Although few political campaign are known for their kindness, the back-stabbing, mean-spirited attacks, eruptions of irrationalism, and downright lies exploded into one of the meanest chapters of recent American political history.

Foster readjusts rosy views of America as the tolerant, pluralistic society against the context of its lengthy, colorful, and bruising history of religious discrimination and oppression against many religious groups, among them Mormonism. Mormons are now respected and admired--although the image hasn't tilted enough to work for Romney instead of against him. Their turbulent past of suspicion, marginalization, physical violence, and being deprived of voting rights has sometimes made them, in turn, suspicious, hostile, and politically naive. How much of this pattern of mutual name-calling stems from theology and how much from theocratic ideals?

Foster appraises Romney's success and strengths—and also places where he stumbled, analyzing an intriguing pattern of "what-ifs?" of policy, personality, and positioning. But perhaps even more intriguing is the anti-Romney campaign launched by a divided and fragmenting religious right who pulled together in a rare show of unity to chill a Mormon's presidential aspirations. What does Romney's campaign and the resistance of the religious right mean for America in the twenty-first century?

In this meticulously researched, comprehensively documented, and passionately argued analysis of a still-ongoing campaign, Craig Foster poses questions that go beyond both Romney and the religious right to engage the soul of American politics.

"This is My Doctrine": The Development of Mormon Theology

Charles R. Harrell

Hardcover, ISBN: 978-1-58958-103-6

The principal doctrines defining Mormonism today often bear little resemblance to those it started out with in the early 1830s. This book shows that these doctrines did not originate in a vacuum but were rather prompted and informed by the religious culture from which Mormonism arose. Early Mormons, like their early Christian and even earlier Israelite predecessors, brought with them their own varied culturally conditioned theological presuppositions (a process of convergence) and only later acquired a more distinctive theological outlook (a process of differentiation).

In this first-of-its-kind comprehensive treatment of the development of Mormon theology, Charles Harrell traces the history of Latter-day Saint doctrines from the times of the Old Testament to the present. He describes how Mormonism has carried on the tradition of the biblical authors, early Christians, and later Protestants in reinterpreting scripture to accommodate new theological ideas while attempting to uphold the integrity and authority of the scriptures. In the process, he probes three questions: How did Mormon doctrines develop? What are the scriptural underpinnings of these doctrines? And what do critical scholars make of these same scriptures? In this enlightening study, Harrell systematically peels back the doctrinal accretions of time to provide a fresh new look at Mormon theology.

"*This Is My Doctrine*" will provide those already versed in Mormonism's theological tradition with a new and richer perspective of Mormon theology. Those unacquainted with Mormonism will gain an appreciation for how Mormon theology fits into the larger Jewish and Christian theological traditions.

Modern Mormonism: Myths and Realities

Robert L. Millet

Paperback, ISBN: 978-1-58958-127-2

What answer may a Latter-day Saint make to accusations from those of other faiths that "Mormons aren't Christians," or "You think God is a man," and "You worship a different Jesus"? Not only are these charges disconcerting, but the hostility with which they are frequently hurled is equally likely to catch Latter-day Saints off guard.

Now Robert L. Millet, veteran of hundreds of such verbal battles, cogently, helpfully, and scripturally provides important clarifications for Latter-day Saints about eleven of the most frequent myths used to discredit the Church. Along the way, he models how to conduct such a Bible based discussion respectfully, weaving in enlightenment from LDS scriptures and quotations from religious figures in other faiths, ranging from the early church fathers to the archbishop of Canterbury.

Millet enlivens this book with personal experiences as a boy growing up in an area where Mormons were a minuscule and not particularly welcome minority, in one-on-one conversations with men of faith who believed differently, and with his own BYU students who also had lessons to learn about interfaith dialogue. He pleads for greater cooperation in dealing with the genuine moral and social evils afflicting the world, and concludes with his own ardent and reverent testimony of the Savior.

Fire and Sword: A History of the Latter-day Saints in Northern Missouri, 1836-39

Leland Homer Gentry and Todd M. Compton

Hardcover, ISBN: 978-1-58958-103-6

Many Mormon dreams flourished in Missouri. So did many Mormon nightmares.

The Missouri period—especially from the summer of 1838 when Joseph took over vigorous, personal direction of this new Zion until the spring of 1839 when he escaped after five months of imprisonment—represents a moment of intense crisis in Mormon history. Representing the greatest extremes of devotion and violence, commitment and intolerance, physical suffering and terror—mobbings, battles, massacres, and political "knockdowns"—it shadowed the Mormon psyche for a century.

Leland Gentry was the first to step beyond this disturbing period as a one-sided symbol of religious persecution and move toward understanding it with careful documentation and evenhanded analysis. In Fire and Sword, Todd Compton collaborates with Gentry to update this foundational work with four decades of new scholarship, more insightful critical theory, and the wealth of resources that have become electronically available in the last few years.

Compton gives full credit to Leland Gentry's extraordinary achievement, particularly in documenting the existence of Danites and in attempting to tell the Missourians' side of the story; but he also goes far beyond it, gracefully drawing into the dialogue signal interpretations written since Gentry and introducing the raw urgency of personal writings, eyewitness journalists, and bemused politicians seesawing between human compassion and partisan harshness. In the lush Missouri landscape of the Mormon imagination where Adam and Eve had walked out of the garden and where Adam would return to preside over his posterity, the towering religious creativity of Joseph Smith and clash of religious stereotypes created a swift and traumatic frontier drama that changed the Church.

Hearken, O Ye People: The Historical Setting of Joseph Smith's Ohio Revelations

Mark Lyman Staker

Hardcover, ISBN: 978-1-58958-113-5

Awarded 2010 Best Book Award - John Whitmer Historical Association

More of Mormonism's canonized revelations originated in or near Kirtland than any other place. Yet many of the events connected with those revelations and their 1830s historical context have faded over time. Mark Staker reconstructs the cultural experiences by which Kirtland's Latter-day Saints made sense of the revelations Joseph Smith pronounced. This volume rebuilds that exciting decade using clues from numerous archives, privately held records, museum collections, and even the soil where early members planted corn and homes. From this vast array of sources he shapes a detailed narrative of weather, religious backgrounds, dialect differences, race relations, theological discussions, food preparation, frontier violence, astronomical phenomena, and myriad daily customs of nineteenth-century life. The result is a "from the ground up" experience that today's Latter-day Saints can all but walk into and touch.

Praise for *Hearken O Ye People*:

"I am not aware of a more deeply researched and richly contextualized study of any period of Mormon church history than Mark Staker's study of Mormons in Ohio. We learn about everything from the details of Alexander Campbell's views on priesthood authority to the road conditions and weather on the four Lamanite missionaries' journey from New York to Ohio. All the Ohio revelations and even the First Vision are made to pulse with new meaning. This book sets a new standard of in-depth research in Latter-day Saint history."
    -Richard Bushman, author of *Joseph Smith: Rough Stone Rolling*

"To be well-informed, any student of Latter-day Saint history and doctrine must now be acquainted with the remarkable research of Mark Staker on the important history of the church in the Kirtland, Ohio, area."
    -Neal A. Maxwell Institute, Brigham Young University